Lecture Notes in Computer Science　　11068

Commenced Publication in 1973
Founding and Former Series Editors:
Gerhard Goos, Juris Hartmanis, and Jan van Leeuwen

More information about this series at http://www.springer.com/series/7409

Xingming Sun · Zhaoqing Pan
Elisa Bertino (Eds.)

Cloud Computing and Security

4th International Conference, ICCCS 2018
Haikou, China, June 8–10, 2018
Revised Selected Papers, Part VI

 Springer

Editors
Xingming Sun ⓘ
Nanjing University of Information Science
  and Technology
Nanjing
China

Elisa Bertino ⓘ
Department of Computer Science
Purdue University
West Lafayette, IN
USA

Zhaoqing Pan ⓘ
Nanjing University of Information Science
  and Technology
Nanjing
China

ISSN 0302-9743   ISSN 1611-3349 (electronic)
Lecture Notes in Computer Science
ISBN 978-3-030-00020-2   ISBN 978-3-030-00021-9 (eBook)
https://doi.org/10.1007/978-3-030-00021-9

Library of Congress Control Number: 2018952646

LNCS Sublibrary: SL3 – Information Systems and Applications, incl. Internet/Web, and HCI

This Springer imprint is published by the registered company Springer Nature Switzerland AG
The registered company address is: Gewerbestrasse 11, 6330 Cham, Switzerland

Preface

The 4th International Conference on Cloud Computing and Security (ICCCS 2018) was held in Haikou, China, during June 8–10, 2018, and hosted by the School of Computer and Software at the Nanjing University of Information Science and Technology. ICCCS is a leading conference for researchers and engineers to share their latest results of research, development, and applications in the field of cloud computing and information security.

We made use of the excellent Tech Science Press (TSP) submission and reviewing software. ICCCS 2018 received 1743 submissions from 20 countries and regions, including USA, Canada, UK, Italy, Ireland, Japan, Russia, France, Australia, South Korea, South Africa, India, Iraq, Kazakhstan, Indonesia, Vietnam, Ghana, China, Taiwan, and Macao. The submissions covered the areas of cloud computing, cloud security, information hiding, IOT security, multimedia forensics, and encryption, etc. We thank our Technical Program Committee members and external reviewers for their efforts in reviewing papers and providing valuable comments to the authors. From the total of 1743 submissions, and based on at least two reviews per submission, the Program Chairs decided to accept 386 papers, yielding an acceptance rate of 22.15%. The volume of the conference proceedings contains all the regular, poster, and workshop papers.

The conference program was enriched by six keynote presentations, and the keynote speakers were Mauro Barni, University of Siena, Italy; Charles Ling, University of Western Ontario, Canada; Yunbiao Guo, Beijing Institute of Electronics Technology and Application, China; Yunhao Liu, Michigan State University, USA; Nei Kato, Tokyo University, Japan; and Jianfeng Ma, Xidian University, China. We thank them very much for their wonderful talks.

There were 42 workshops organized in conjunction with ICCCS 2018, covering all the hot topics in cloud computing and security. We would like to take this moment to express our sincere appreciation for the contribution of all the workshop chairs and their participants. In addition, we would like to extend our sincere thanks to all authors who submitted papers to ICCCS 2018 and to all PC members. It was a truly great experience to work with such talented and hard-working researchers. We also appreciate the work of the external reviewers, who assisted the PC members in their particular areas of expertise. Moreover, we would like to thank our sponsors: Nanjing University of Information Science and Technology, Springer, Hainan University, IEEE Nanjing Chapter, ACM China, Michigan State University, Taiwan Cheng Kung University, Taiwan Dong Hwa University, Providence University, Nanjing University of Aeronautics and Astronautics, State Key Laboratory of Integrated Services Networks, Tech Science Press, and the National Nature Science Foundation of China. Finally, we would like to thank all attendees for their active participation and the organizing team, who nicely managed this conference. Next year, ICCCS will be renamed as the International Conference on Artificial Intelligence and Security (ICAIS). We look forward to seeing you again at the ICAIS.

July 2018

Xingming Sun
Zhaoqing Pan
Elisa Bertino

Organization

General Chairs

Xingming Sun	Nanjing University of Information Science and Technology, China
Han-Chieh Chao	Taiwan Dong Hwa University, Taiwan, China
Xingang You	China Information Technology Security Evaluation Center, China
Elisa Bertino	Purdue University, USA

Technical Program Committee Chairs

Aniello Castiglione	University of Salerno, Italy
Yunbiao Guo	China Information Technology Security Evaluation Center, China
Zhangjie Fu	Nanjing University of Information Science and Technology, China
Xinpeng Zhang	Fudan University, China
Jian Weng	Jinan University, China
Mengxing Huang	Hainan University, China
Alex Liu	Michigan State University, USA

Workshop Chair

Baowei Wang	Nanjing University of Information Science and Technology, China

Publication Chair

Zhaoqing Pan	Nanjing University of Information Science and Technology, China

Publicity Chair

Chuanyou Ju	Nanjing University of Information Science and Technology, China

Local Arrangement Chair

Jieren Cheng	Hainan University, China

Website Chair

Wei Gu   Nanjing University of Information Science
                                 and Technology, China

Technical Program Committee Members

Saeed Arif   University of Algeria, Algeria
Zhifeng Bao   Royal Melbourne Institute of Technology University,
                                 Australia
Lianhua Chi   IBM Research Center, Australia
Bing Chen   Nanjing University of Aeronautics and Astronautics,
                                 China
Hanhua Chen   Huazhong University of Science and Technology,
                                 China
Jie Chen   East China Normal University, China
Xiaofeng Chen   Xidian University, China
Ilyong Chung   Chosun University, South Korea
Jieren Cheng   Hainan University, China
Kim-Kwang   University of Texas at San Antonio, USA
  Raymond Choo
Chin-chen Chang   Feng Chia University, Taiwan, China
Robert H. Deng   Singapore Management University, Singapore
Jintai Ding   University of Cincinnati, USA
Shaojing Fu   National University of Defense Technology, China
Xinwen Fu   University of Central Florida, USA
Song Guo   Hong Kong Polytechnic University, Hong Kong, China
Ruili Geng   Spectral MD, USA
Russell Higgs   University College Dublin, Ireland
Dinh Thai Hoang   University of Technology Sydney, Australia
Robert Hsu   Chung Hua University, Taiwan, China
Chih-Hsien Hsia   Chinese Culture University, Taiwan, China
Jinguang Han   Nanjing University of Finance & Economics, China
Debiao He   Wuhan University, China
Wien Hong   Nanfang College of Sun Yat-Sen University, China
Qiong Huang   South China Agricultural University, China
Xinyi Huang   Fujian Normal University, China
Yongfeng Huang   Tsinghua University, China
Zhiqiu Huang   Nanjing University of Aeronautics and Astronautics,
                                 China
Mohammad Mehedi Hassan   King Saud University, Saudi Arabia
Farookh Hussain   University of Technology Sydney, Australia
Hai Jin   Huazhong University of Science and Technology,
                                 China
Sam Tak Wu Kwong   City University of Hong Kong, China
Patrick C. K. Hung   University of Ontario Institute of Technology, Canada

Yong Yu	University of Electronic Science and Technology of China, China
Guomin Yang	University of Wollongong, Australia
Wei Qi Yan	Auckland University of Technology, New Zealand
Shaodi You	Australian National University, Australia
Yanchun Zhang	Victoria University, Australia
Mingwu Zhang	Hubei University of Technology, China
Wei Zhang	Nanjing University of Posts and Telecommunications, China
Weiming Zhang	University of Science and Technology of China, China
Yan Zhang	Simula Research Laboratory, Norway
Yao Zhao	Beijing Jiaotong University, China
Linna Zhou	University of International Relations, China

Organization Committee Members

Xianyi Chen	Nanjing University of Information Science and Technology, China
Yadang Chen	Nanjing University of Information Science and Technology, China
Beijing Chen	Nanjing University of Information Science and Technology, China
Chunjie Cao	Hainan University, China
Xianyi Chen	Hainan University, China
Xianmei Chen	Hainan University, China
Fa Fu	Hainan University, China
Xiangdang Huang	Hainan University, China
Zhuhua Hu	Hainan University, China
Jielin Jiang	Nanjing University of Information Science and Technology, China
Zilong Jin	Nanjing University of Information Science and Technology, China
Yan Kong	Nanjing University of Information Science and Technology, China
Jingbing Li	Hainan University, China
Jinlian Peng	Hainan University, China
Zhiguo Qu	Nanjing University of Information Science and Technology, China
Le Sun	Nanjing University of Information Science and Technology, China
Jian Su	Nanjing University of Information Science and Technology, China
Qing Tian	Nanjing University of Information Science and Technology, China
Tao Wen	Hainan University, China
Xianpeng Wang	Hainan University, China

Lizhi Xiong   Nanjing University of Information Science
                             and Technology, China
Chunyang Ye   Hainan University, China
Jiangyuan Yao   Hainan University, China
Leiming Yan   Nanjing University of Information Science
                             and Technology, China
Yu Zhang   Hainan University, China
Zhili Zhou   Nanjing University of Information Science
                             and Technology, China

Contents – Part VI

IOT Security

Multimedia Forensics

IOT Security

Safety Traceability System of Livestock and Poultry Industrial Chain

Xueru Yu[1], Pingzeng Liu[1(✉)], Wanming Ren[2], Chao Zhang[1],
Junmei Wang[1], and Yong Zheng[2]

[1] Shandong Agricultural University, Tai'an 271018, China
lpz8565@126.com
[2] Shandong Provincial Agricultural Information Center, Ji'nan 250013, China

Abstract. In response to the increasing food safety problems of the meat product in the industry chain of livestock and poultry, and the actual demand of enterprises and consumers, combining the development status of the enterprises, considering the safety factors of animal breeding and product processing, this paper designed a food safety traceability system, based on modern internet of things technologies such as RFID, QR code, sensor technology and wireless communication technology, of which the traceability information covers all links of the whole industry chain. Compared with other traceability systems, the system in this paper has improved greatly in terms of its breadth, depth, and accuracy, which is an effective way to solve the food safety problem. The system provides the customers, enterprises, and the government department with multi-channel information traceability service, which has the real significance of the reduction food safety risk and improvement of recall efficiency of defective products.

Keywords: Food safety traceability system · The industrial chain of livestock and poultry · Internet of things · RFID

1 Introduction

With the "mad cow disease", "bird flu", "foot-and-mouth disease" and other zoonotic diseases outbreak, and "Magdala red" duck's egg incident, melamine milk powder incident, clenbuterol event and other food safety problems exposed, quality and safety of livestock and poultry products has attracted the attention of consumers. Food safety traceability is to record and manage the information involved in food production process through modern information science and technology and to integrate the information to form the monitoring of the whole process of the food product, which is an effective way to solve the problem of product quality and safety.

Since traceability system has entered the food industry in the 1980s, Europe, the United States, Japan and other places have been continuously researching and exploring, and agricultural products traceability system and relevant laws and regulations have been established [1]. The traceability system of seafood quality in the US collects information on important links such as fishing products, processing and marketing, and realizes information tracing from fishing to sales, improving seafood

© Springer Nature Switzerland AG 2018
X. Sun et al. (Eds.): ICCCS 2018, LNCS 11068, pp. 3–12, 2018.
https://doi.org/10.1007/978-3-030-00021-9_1

quality and safety management capabilities [2]. After the Cattle Traceability Law was approved by the Diet in June 2003, a cattle traceability system was in operation in Japan since December 2003. This system can trace the cohort and offspring animals of a BSE case within 24 h of its detection [3]. In January 2001, Canada has instituted a national identification program [4], which provided a herd of origin traceback and individual animal identification by ear tags for all beef cattle.

In recent years, specialists and scholars in our country have also carried on a series of exploration to the traceability system of agricultural products [5]. Zhang takes Laiwu black pig as the research object, gathers the data of the whole industry chain through the Internet of things perception, and realizes the information tracking and tracing of the whole industry chain [6]. According to cattle breeding, product processing and other aspects of security elements, Yang constructs the beef varieties, breeding, product processing information database management system through animal identification technology, intelligent data acquisition technology, and network technology, which formed the multi-mode beef product quality safety traceability system [7]. Chen has developed a standard system for broiler production and slaughtering and processing. It has third party certification technology for broiler industry, production monitoring, and product quality traceability platform, taking into account the interests of enterprises, governments and consumers [8]. In general, China has made some achievements in the construction of traceability system in recent years, which effectively improved product quality and safety management ability. However, the traceability systems still have poor information sharing ability and low trace accuracy. In view of the above short-comings and combining the actual demand of livestock and poultry industry chain, a new solution based on the technology of Internet of things is proposed.

2 Status Analysis

Livestock and poultry industry chain include breeding, slaughtering, processing, testing, storage, transportation, sales and other links.

As the upstream link, the breeding section is particularly significant to the whole industrial chain. The breeding section mainly refers to the feeding and breeding of livestock and poultry. At present, it is developing towards large-scale, standardization, and through the unified standard facilities environment, varieties, production scale, feeding manners, nutrition level and immune procedure, which changed the previous disadvantages of random feeding, loose management and low level of epidemic prevention. In this section, the variety information, immune information and culture environment information of livestock and poultry are the decisive factors for the individual quality, and also an important source of information for the tracing process.

The links of slaughtering and processing are usually done by the food processing enterprises. That work is usually done in the form of the production line, which has a high requirement for efficiency. In this section, information such as batch information of livestock and poultry, specifications and types of finished products is the key information for tracing back and the bridge of connecting upstream industry and downstream industry.

The links of detection and storage mainly refer to indicators testing for finished products. After testing and packaging, the accepted products should be moved to the warehouse. The information of inspection results and warehouse environment should be recorded in case of need.

The process of transportation and marketing mainly includes the process of transportation and sales of finished products supplied by the processing enterprise to the sales enterprise. The specification and type information of supply products, transportation vehicles and positioning information are the key to recall the "defective products" when necessary.

In order to achieve the purpose of precise traceability and improve the capability of the system, the key information above need collecting comprehensively and managing validly through PDA, RFID device and information acquisition terminal, which will provide data basis for livestock and poultry industry traceability system. The key information in each link of the industry chain was shown in Fig. 1.

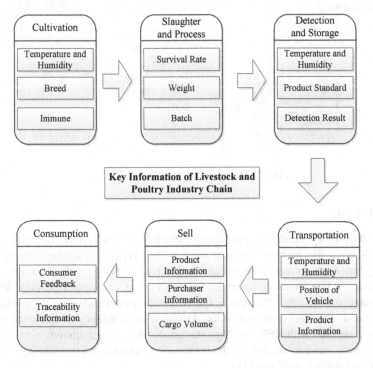

Fig. 1. Key information on livestock and poultry industry chain.

3 Technologies

3.1 RFID

RFID is a non-contact automatic identification technology based on radio frequency signal and spatial coupling transmission characteristics [9], which can get information stored in RFID tags by accessing it. RFID tag has more than 128 bits of storage, and its information storage capacity is almost unlimited in the production field. It makes every item with a unique electronic label. It can be fixed on the individual body by ear-mark, as the "identity card" of the animal and poultry individual in the traceability system [10]. Using the huge storage capacity of RFID label, the information of livestock and poultry breeding and processing can be coded and recorded, so as to achieve the goal of precision tracing. Its operating principle is shown as Fig. 2.

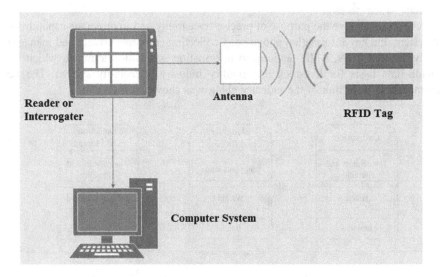

Fig. 2. The operating principle of RFID.

3.2 QR Code

The QR code is a barcode for processing information in a vertical two-dimensional space. QR code has high information storage density, large storage capacity, error checking and error correction, and can set different security levels according to the actual situation. Its vertical direction carries information, can correct printing defect or local damage, restore data information. QR codes are not dependent on the existence of databases and communication networks. Although the efficiency of QR code reading cannot be compared with RFID, its high storage density, a large amount of information and flexible use make it suitable for the information carrier in the traceability system of livestock and poultry products [11].

3.3 Mobile Communication

With the widespread popularization of 4G communication technology and the continuous development of 5G technology, the scope of mobile communication technology can be further expanded. 2G/3G era, through GSM, GPRS, realize the Internet of mobile terminal and server information interaction, rise period of 4G LTE, largely improve the coverage of 3 g and the data transfer rate. However, the rapid development of 5G technology, represented by NB-IOT [12], is developing towards the standardization of Internet of things communication technology. This technique plays a key role in tracking the information collection of the mobile terminal of livestock and poultry products and the information input of the PDA.

3.4 LoRa

As a new low power Wan wireless communication technology, LoRa is a new technology dedicated to radio modulation and demodulation. It combines digital spread-spectrum, digital signal processing, and forward error correction coding technology, with the unprecedented performance. At present, LoRa operates mainly in the global free band, including 433, 868, 915 MHz, etc. LoRa has far distance communication, high anti-interference, and low power consumption. It can greatly reduce the use of SIM card, save communication fees, solve the tedious problems of equipment and communication installation, debugging and maintenance difficulties and so on, and it can be widely used in farms and processing plants.

3.5 Web Service

Web Service is a remote invocation technology across programming languages and across operating system platforms. It is a platform independent, low-coupled Web application. The common format for data in Web services is in XML format, and its advantages are easy to build and easy to analyze, and the format of XML data is both platform-independent and independent. No matter what development language or internal protocol the application uses, it can exchange data with each other as long as it is based on the Web Service specification. Web Service technology enables data exchange between different applications, providing a common mechanism for the business and data flow between the entire traceability system and multiple enterprise management systems.

4 Design

4.1 Outline Design

The food safety traceability system, for livestock and poultry industry chain, covers all aspects of breeding, slaughter, processing, testing, storage, transportation, and sales. Each section needs to establish the corresponding information management subsystem, which should collect and manage the relevant information through PDA, code scanner and IOT information acquisition terminal and other means. And all the data should be uploaded to the central database to achieve the purpose of information sharing in the industrial chain. The function of the traceability system mainly includes information statistics, government supervision, and consumer inquiry.

All enterprises in the industry chain can see the information of their real-time management information, historical data, and part of the supply and demand of the goods of other enterprises and adjust their existing work. The government can use this system to check the key information in livestock and poultry industry, such as immunization, product testing results, warehouse environment and other information, which is conducive to the implementation of government regulation. The consumer can search the product date, place, specification of production and other information by scanning the two-dimensional code pasted on the product. If the product has problems, the system can find the batches and circulation process of the problem products according to the product number, find out the causes of the problems from all relevant information, and recall the products of the same batch, so as to avoid more consumers being harming by the problem products.

4.2   Hardware Design

From above, we can see that besides the management subsystem of every link, livestock, and poultry industry chain traceability system also needs the support of environmental information acquisition of hardware system and the corresponding portable Internet of things hardware terminals.

Environmental Information Acquisition System. The environmental information acquisition system is responsible for collecting environmental information in the process of breeding, processing, storage, and transportation. For the livestock and poultry industry, air temperature, humidity, and ammonia content are the focus of attention.

The system consists of MCU, A/D conversion module, and sensors. We select the MSP430F5438 MCU as the core processing unit, acquires environmental data in real time by the temperature sensor, humidity sensor, ammonia gas sensor and other sensors. After processing of the A/D conversion module, these data can be uploaded to the corresponding management system through the mobile communication network or Ethernet to record the environmental information of livestock breeding, processing, transportation, and storage process, which greatly improve the accuracy of traceability information.

The structure of the environment information collection system is as follows (Fig. 3):

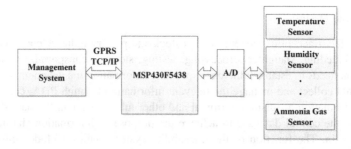

Fig. 3. The environmental information acquisition system based on the internet of things.

Portable Hardware Terminals. The portable Internet of things hardware terminal is used to scan individual animal's RFID tag to get personal identity information, and input data to feeding, immunization, and other data through the touchscreen. Therefore, the terminal needs to have RFID reading and writing function, communication function with the management system, and some terminal needs to have the function of two-dimensional code scanning and printing. The terminal consists of MCU, display screen, RFID reader, code scanner and printer, and the LoRa wireless communication module. We select the MSP430F5438 MCU as the core processor of the terminal, which connected to the display screen, the RFID reader, the code scanner and printer through the serial port respectively. The data, from RFID reader, scanner and display screen, will be uploaded to the management system through LoRa wireless communication module by the MCU (Fig. 4).

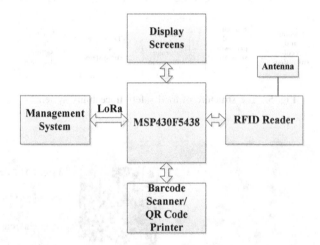

Fig. 4. The portable hardware terminal based on the internet of things.

4.3   System Structure

The system is composed of the integrated management system of traceability information, the management subsystem of each link, and the central database of the industrial chain. The system structure is shown in Fig. 5.

All related enterprises in the industry chain have their own information management subsystem. These systems collect, upload and store the information into the central database. The traceability information management system provides services to consumers, government departments and enterprises through information integration.

4.4   Circulation of Information

The work environment varies between the various links of the industry.

In the breeding link, we can use RFID ear tag or hanging tag as the information carrier. In the links of finished product transportation and selling, we can take the two-dimensional code labels attached to the product package as the information carrier.

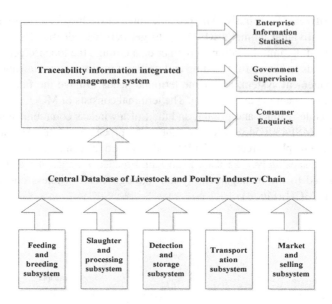

Fig. 5. The structure of food safety traceability system

Fig. 6. The information carrier of industry chain.

In the slaughter and processing link, because of the heavy workload of the production line and complex goods source, the information chain is easy to break. Therefore, in this section, batch management is adopted for the product slaughter and processing. The product manager sets the batch information in the management system and manages the start and end of the batch. In product packaging, the IOT terminal obtains the batch information of the current product from the management system. Then print the two-dimensional code with the corresponding information, attached to the packing box, to realize the flow of information to the other links.

The information carrier in the industry chain is in the form of RFID tag and QR label, as Fig. 6.

5 Conclusion

The food safety traceability system for livestock and poultry industry chain, using new technologies of the internet of things, realized the full coverage of livestock and poultry industry chain information, achieve the purpose of "from farm to table" accurate traceability.

(1) The traceability scope includes breeding, transportation, slaughtering, processing, storage, marketing and other links. The traceable information contains most of the key information of each link,which greatly improved the breadth of the traceability system.
(2) The portable IOT suitable terminal for livestock and poultry industry chain has realized the easy access to information, and the IOT environment information collection system has realized the breeding, processing, storage, transportation and other links of information collection, to ensure the information trace accuracy, integrity, and reliability.
(3) The system has completed the bidirectional traceability of key nodes of the industrial chain, which is of great significance both for the protection of consumers' food safety and the recall of defective products.

With the continuous improvement and perfection of technology, standards and industry system, we still need to strive to overcome core technologies, and formulate a series of corresponding supporting laws and regulations in the industry as soon as possible, and constantly improve and popularize them.

Acknowledgement. This work was supported by the research project "Major Data Application Technology Research and Integration Based on Livestock and Poultry Industry" of Shandong Province Major Agricultural Technological Innovation Project in 2017, and Shan-dong independent innovation and achievements transformation project (2014ZZCX07106).

References

1. Yang, X.T., Qian, J.P., Sun, C.H., et al.: Key technologies for establishment agricultural products and food quality safety traceability systems. Trans. Chin. Soc. Agric. Mach. **45**(11), 212–222 (2014)
2. Takeno, T., Horikawa, M., et al.: Processed food traceability system on seafood supply Chain. J. Jpn. Inf. Cult. Soc. **14** (2007)
3. Yasuda, T., Bowen, R.E.: Chain of custody as an organizing framework in seafood risk reduction. Mar. Pollut. Bull. **53**(10–12), 640 (2006)
4. Stanford, K., Stitt, J., Kellar, J.A., et al.: Traceability in cattle and small ruminants in Canada. Rev. Sci. Tech. **20**(2), 510 (2001)
5. Bai, J.: Study of information management system for food quality and safety traceability. Inf. Sci. **31**(7), 59–63 (2013)
6. Yan, Z., Pingzeng, L., Qun, Y., et al.: Safety traceability platform building for the whole industry chain of Laiwu pig based on IOT. J. Chin. Agric. Mech. **36**(2), 141–144 (2015)
7. Liang, Y., Xiaohua, P., et al.: A development of a beef production traceability system covering rearing to marketing sections. Chin. J. Anim. Vet. Sci. **46**(8), 1383–1389 (2015)

8. Chen, C.X., Zhang, H.F., Jingwei, F.: Traceability platform design of production monitoring and products quality for broilers industry technology system. Trans. Chin. Soc. Agric. Mach. **41**(08), 100–106 (2010)
9. Abad, E., Palacio, F., Nuin, M., et al.: RFID smart tag for traceability and cold chain monitoring of foods: demonstration in an intercontinental fresh fish logistic chain. J. Food Eng. **93**(4), 394–399 (2009)
10. Kelepouris, T., Pramatari, K., Doukidis, G.: RFID-enabled traceability in the food supply chain. Ind. Manag. Data Syst. **107**(2), 183–200 (2013)
11. Tarjan, L., Tegeltija, S., Stankovski, S., et al.: A readability analysis for QR code application in a traceability system. Comput. Electron. Agric. **109**(C), 1–11 (2014)
12. Wang, Y., Lin, X., Adhikary, A., et al.: A primer on 3GPP narrowband internet of things. IEEE Commun. Mag. **55**(3), 117–123 (2017)

Secure Device Pairing via Facial Image Similarity

Zhiping Jiang[1]([✉]), Rui Li[1], Kun Zhao[2], and Shuaiyu Chen[2]

[1] School of Software, Xidian University, Xi'an, China
zpj@xidian.edu.cn
[2] School of Electronic and Information Engineering,
Xi'an Jiaotong University, Xi'an, China

Abstract. In this paper, we propose a secure key pairing system, Face-Match, to enable confidential communication for smartphones. The idea is to leverage a natural human interaction mode: face-to-face interaction. Two users raise up their smartphones to establish a secure channel based on their similar observations via the smartphones' cameras. One user acts as the initiator and uses the front-facing camera to snap his/her face. The other user captures the initiator's face using his/her rear camera. Utilizing the facial appearance as a secret substitution, the initiator delivers a randomly generated key to the other user. Based on this key, two users establish a confidential communication channel between their devices. FaceMatch achieves secure device pairing without the complex operations needed in prior works. We implemented FaceMatch using off-the-shelf iPhones. The experimental results show that FaceMatch can establish a 128-bit encrypted connection in less than 3 s.

Keywords: Facial similarity · Device pairing · Security · ASM

1 Introduction

With the prevalence of mobile computing, secure device pairing becomes the basis of confidential communication. For example, two people are willing to communicate with each other, share information, or perform face-to-face payment via mobile phones. To achieve this goal, establishing keys for the two mobile devices is necessary for supporting confidential communication.

Currently secure device pairing uses password [3], wireless signal [13,25], or action based technologies [12,16,22,23]. The password based technologies [3] require users to negotiate a password or key, and then input it to their devices. The key limitation of this approach is that manually creating and exchanging strong keys is extremely inconvenient for the two users. The security of users is also hard to be guaranteed if some attackers peep or oversee the input. The wireless signal based technology [13,25] uses inherent physical layer information of wireless signals, *e.g.*, the wireless channel properties [25], to generate identical keys. The key limitation of this approach is that mismatch bits often occur

© Springer Nature Switzerland AG 2018
X. Sun et al. (Eds.): ICCCS 2018, LNCS 11068, pp. 13–25, 2018.
https://doi.org/10.1007/978-3-030-00021-9_2

Fig. 1. FaceMatch system illustration. Two users can setup a secure device pairing based on the facial appearance variance.

such that the communication parties have to conduct time-consuming reconciliation, which also risks information leakage. Keys for confidential communications [12,16,22,23] can also be extracted from the similar movements or actions on the devices, *e.g.*, shaking two phones together [16] and slipping fingers (one for each phone) on the touch screen in a ZigZag way [12]. The key limitation of both technologies is that it requires non-trivial, sometimes cumbersome manual operations in initiating or performing the device pairing.

In this paper, we propose a new secure device pairing solution for mobile devices, namely FaceMatch. Our solution is based on the most natural interactive mode: face to face (F2F) interaction. This work leverages the commodity smartphones that are embedded with front and rear cameras. When two users decide to conduct confidential communication, they face to each other and hold up their smartphones. The initiator's face (we call Alice's face in the remaining paper) can be captured by the front camera using her smartphone, and simultaneously the responder (we call Bob in the remaining paper) will also capture the face using his rear camera, as shown in Fig. 1. Based on the face of the Alice, each of the two parties constructs a source, which is highly consistent to that of the other party. A random key is generated by Alice and then securely delivered to Bob. Using this key, they can conduct confidential communication.

To the best of our knowledge, we are the first to leverage facial appearance for secure device pairing over current mobile devices. Using FaceMatch, two users can be naturally authenticated by looking at each other, without performing complicated operations. The FaceMatch system has two key features that make it easy to deploy. First, FaceMatch does not need complex or inconvenient operations, such as putting two smartphones together or inputting passwords.

Second, FaceMatch uses off-the-shelf commercial smartphones that are equipped with front and rear cameras, which have already been a standard configuration for current smartphones.

There are three challenges to realize FaceMatch. First, the human face has distinct features and high correlations among its components. Adversaries can analyze those features and correlations for compromising the delivered key. Second, the images captured by two communicating parties are inconsistent due to the visual parallax. For both parties, we have to convert the captured facial data into a highly consistent feature, which will be used for confidential communication, *e.g.*, key agreement. Third, some key bits may have mismatch due to the inconsistency between the image source of the two sides. Prior works solve this mismatch bit problem by reconciliation which is time-consuming and insecure. We have to pursue a more robust and secure key agreement mechanism.

FaceMatch addresses these challenges with the following techniques. First, to introduce the randomness to facial appearance, we show a white screen with randomly changed luminance on the Alice's smartphone screen. Together with the rapid perspective de-correlation property of human faces, the facial luminance variance can serve as a random source.

Second, we use a set of elaborately designed mechanisms to guarantee the consistency of facial appearance at both sides, including a customized active shape model (ASM) algorithm to provide consistent facial blocks at both sides and a Haar-Like Templates (HLTs) based conversion to convert the appearance into random readings. With these designs, FaceMatch achieves high efficiency and is suitable for mobile platforms.

Based on the above facial appearance conversion mechanism, we use Similarity Preserving Signature (SPS) method to perform key agreement. The details of SPS adoption in FaceMatch is not covered due to the page limit.

2   Randomizing the Facial Appearance Variance

Conducting key agreement between two communicating parties is usually based on a public random source with the property of rapid de-correlation [15]. That means, the random source is publicly accessible, yet able to produce independent outputs for different observers. In particular, only when two or a group of users satisfy certain constraints, such as in close physical proximity [13], their observations on this source is similar. We denote such a random source as PDRS.

In FaceMatch, the facial appearance variance should be such a PDRS. However, human face has distinct features and is not suitable to be directly used as a random source. We generate a PDRS over a user's face via smartphones. We deliberately yield a white screen with randomly changed luminance on the Alice's smartphone. The light casting to the initiator's face will introduce sufficient randomness.

In addition, facial appearance variance has strong perspective selectivity. Human's facial skin is with anisotropic luminance reflection and human face is a 3D surface with distinct concave and convex. They together make the facial appearance highly selective. That is, the observers with small viewing angle differences can perceive highly similar appearance. However, once out of this *coherent perspective range*, the facial perception is quite different. More importantly, what is observed within the range can be hardly estimated if out of the range. This property enables the facial appearance to be perspectively-selective, or *in rapid perspective de-correlation* in cryptographic terms.

3 Capturing the Facial Appearance Variance

To support facial appearance based key agreement, both Alice and Bob should have similar facial appearance images. However, due to difference of viewing angle and distance, the facial appearance captured at both sides is inconsistent.

In this section, dozens of facial anchor nodes are first tracked at both sides. These nodes then serve as a common basis, which permits us to rectify the inconsistent images into a highly similar one.

There are numerous existing solutions to track the facial anchor nodes. However, due to the mobility and real-time constrains, we can hardly find a solution that can be deployed in mobile phone and satisfying the requirements of efficiency and tracking accuracy simultaneously.

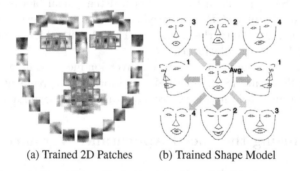

(a) Trained 2D Patches   (b) Trained Shape Model

Fig. 2. (a) shows 67 patch detectors trained from Helen face dataset. The 18 green-squared patches are *near-coplanar* and used for homography estimation. (b) is the extracted facial shape model, which has 4 main parameters, the up/down, left/right, narrow/wide, and left-lean/right-lean. (Color figure online)

Ordinary tracker [7] is apt to drift away. Long-term object trackers, such as TLD [8], can work in real-time but they are not appropriate for multiple feature tracking. Active Appearance Model (AAM) [14] or its variants [2,19] are thought to be an ideal solution. Unfortunately, its tracking accuracy is low. Feature alignment based approaches [9,11] have better accuracy upon large deformations and appearance shifts. Nevertheless, mobile platform cannot afford its computational overhead.

In a typical application scenario of FaceMatch, participants' heads do not exhibit a large pose angle, *i.e.*, most of anchor nodes to be tracked are visible during the whole process. This permits us to adopt an algorithm focusing more on accuracy and efficiency.

3.1 ASM-Based Facial Anchor Node Tracking

To achieve this goal, some facial anchor nodes should be first tracked in images captured by Alice and Bob, respectively. We choose Active Shape Model (ASM) [17], a simple yet efficient approach, as our tracking framework. We customize it for the use in mobile phones and optimize it in terms of tracking accuracy, robustness, and efficiency.

ASM [14] is a global optimization-based approach. It treats the features together as an intact object and then globally optimize the feature localization according their spatial constraints. To realize this idea, ASM relies on two models, namely the *patch* model and *shape* model. A *patch* is a detector trained for a specific feature, while the *shape* model encapsulates the geometric constraints. This intuitive architect makes ASM computational efficient, hence is suitable for mobile platform. However, a drawback of ASM is its unreliability for human face tracking applications [17,21]. The 1-D gradient vector based patch model is unstable for even a small pose variation. We replace the 1-D patch model in original ASM with the following customized correlation-based 2D patch model, which enables accurate and robust tracking for facial anchor nodes on the mobile platform.

Correlation-Based 2D Patch Model. For a given facial feature f_k, we consider the optimal correlation-based patch $\hat{\mathbf{P}}_{f_k}$ is the solution to the following optimization problem:

$$\hat{\mathbf{P}}_{f_k} = \arg\min_{\mathbf{P}} \mathcal{F}(\mathbf{P})$$

$$\mathcal{F}(\mathbf{P}) = \sum_{i=1}^{N}\sum_{x,y} \|\mathbf{R} - \mathbf{P} \cdot \mathbf{T}^i_{(x,y)}\|_F^2$$

$$s.t. \ \arg\max_{\mathbf{T}^i_{(x,y)}} \sum_{i=1}^{N}\sum_{x,y} \mathbf{P} \cdot \mathbf{T}^i_{(x,y)} = \mathbf{T}^i_{f_k} \tag{1}$$

where $\mathbf{R}$ is an ideal response map that has a centered 2D-Gaussian distribution with very small σ, $\mathbf{T}^i_{(x,y)}$ is the small image tile located at (x,y) of the i-th training image, and $\mathbf{T}^i_{f_k}$ is the small tile right-centered at feature f_k in the i-th image. The idea behind Eq. 1 is intuitive: *the optimal patch $\hat{\mathbf{P}}_{f_k}$ should yield the highest response **iff** the test image tile $\mathbf{T}^i_{(x,y)}$ contains the feature f_k.*

Such 2D patch model has an great advantage that, the training for $\hat{\mathbf{P}}_{f_k}$ can be very efficient. Actually, Eq. 1 is in the standard form of linear least square (LLS). The optimal solution can be approximated using stochastic gradient descent approach. The gradient of $\mathcal{F}(\mathbf{P})$ in the i-th step is:

$$\nabla \mathcal{F}(\mathbf{P}) = -2\sum_{x,y}(\mathbf{R} - \mathbf{P}\mathbf{T}^i_{(x,y)})\mathbf{T}^i_{(x,y)} \tag{2}$$

and $\mathbf{P}_{f_k}^{\hat{}}$ can be obtained iteratively as

$$\mathbf{P}_{f_k}^{\hat{i}} = \mathbf{P}_{f_k}^{\hat{}}{}^{i-1} - \alpha \nabla \mathcal{F}(\mathbf{P}) \tag{3}$$

We use 300 annotated images from Helen face dataset [10] to train our correlation-based 2D patch model. Usually tracking more points than required can improve the tracking accuracy and robustness [17], but with a penalty of latency. To balance the latency and accuracy, we carefully set two important parameters, namely, the number of facial anchor nodes N_{ff}, and the side length of 2D patch square L_P. In our currently prototype, $N_{ff} = 67$ and $L_P = 25$. The grey blocks in Fig. 2(a) are the ultimate 2D patches. Note that some patches are partially overlapped to improve the robustness. The *Shape Model* is trained following the standard ASM method. Principle Component Analysis (PCA) is used to capture the shape variations. The four most dominating parameters capture 96% of the shape and pose variations, including the face pose up/down, left/right, lean left/right, and narrow/wide. Figure 2(b) shows the trained shape model and corresponding variations controlled by 4 parameters. Figure 3(a) shows the result of ASM-based facial anchor nodes tracking in an example video.

3.2   Homography-Based Parallax Compensation

Parallax is the visual difference caused by different viewing angles/positions. It should be eliminated at both sides to obtain consistent facial appearance capture. However, the challenge is that, in the FaceMatch scenario, Alice and Bob should never exchange the parallax parameters over insecure channel.

Fortunately, the tracked anchor nodes provide a common basis that may help to eliminate the parallax without communication. The key idea is that, both the communicating parties transform the tracked face, with different sizes, positions, and poses from those of others, into a single rectified form. We use homography estimation to achieve this goal.

Homography estimation is to find the best projective transformation between two coplanar point sets. Let $\mathcal{P}_t^c$ be the coplanar template point set and $\mathcal{P}_i^c$ be the corresponding pixel point set on the i-th image. The optimal result of homography $^{opt}H_i^t$ can be modeled as a transformation:

$$^{opt}H_i^t = \arg \min \|\mathcal{P}_t^c - H_i^t \mathcal{P}_i^c\|_F \tag{4}$$

Theoretically, 3 pairs of points are sufficient to estimate the homography. However, direct estimation may incur large errors because these points are not strictly coplanar. To minimize the error, we use the random sample consensus (RANSAC) technique to approximate the optimal homography $^{opt}H_i^t$. The detected face is then re-projected back into a right upfront face via $inv(^{opt}H_i^t)$. In this way, both Alice and Bob transform the facial area retrieved from different viewing angles into rectified ones. Figure 3(b) shows the *rectified* face images after homography transformation. We can see that the images are stretched and rotated in opposite directions to counteract the parallax.

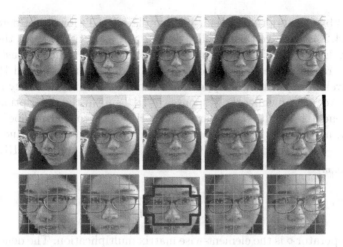

Fig. 3. The first row shows 67 facial anchor nodes tracked by ASM in an example video. The second row shows the homography-based 2D parallax compensation. The third row shows the result of facial area griding upon compensated images. In this example, the griding factor $f_g = 4$. The outlined blocks in the middle figure of the third row is used for secret key agreement.

Note that, the homography-based facial appearance rectification is a 2D approximation to its underlying 3D transformation. Hence its accuracy degrades if increasing the viewing angle. For example, the leftmost and rightmost figures of Fig. 3(b) and (c) show observable mis-alignment. However, in most application scenarios, the viewing angle difference between Alice and Bob are usually within $20°$, in which range the homography-based rectification has small error.

3.3   Griding the Facial Area

Not every part of the facial area is suitable for key agreement, because some area near the margin is not consistent for different viewing angles. We divide the facial area into blocks, and only choose the robust ones. An example of facial area griding is shown in Fig. 3(c). The valid blocks for further computation is out in the middle figure on Fig. 3(c). The grid density is determined by the griding factor f_g, which is the number of blocks between two outer canthuses. f_g usually scales from 3 to 7. For the example shown in Fig. 3(c), $f_g = 4$.

4   Converting the Facial Appearance Variance to Bits

In this step, the rectified face blocks are converted into a description vector which best captures the appearance distinction. The challenge here is, how to balance between the redundancy in the description vector and the computational complexity.

Inspired by the adoption of Haar-like template (HLT) for object detection in CV field [24, 26], we solve this problem from a new aspect. We adopt the similar philosophy. Each HLT is indeed a very weak detector, which is just slightly better than random guessing. However, a group of carefully selected HLTs can collaboratively grasp sufficient appearance details with high accuracy and real-time guarantee. Meanwhile, the responses of HLTs form the description vector.

We extend the traditional binary-valued HLT [24] to real number field. In FaceMatch, a HLT h is a small real-valued square matrix. The value range is defined in $[-1, 1]$. Given the k-th facial area block fb_k and m-th HLT h_m, a response $r_{(k,m)}$ is defined as

$$r_{(k,m)} = \frac{\|fb_k \circ h_m\|_F}{\|fb_k \circ \mathbf{1}\|_F} \tag{5}$$

where the operator $\circ$ is the element-wise matrix multiplication. The denominator $\|fb_k \circ \mathbf{1}\|_F$ is the element-wise sum of fb_k, which is used for normalizing the response value. Based on this definition, each HLT response r becomes a very weak appearance descriptor.

With the above definition, it is easy to convert the facial area. Suppose we have N_T carefully selected HLTs, then for the i-th frame with N_{fg}^i facial blocks, we have a response matrix $R_{N_T \times N_{fg}^i}^i$, where $R_{(m,n)} = r_{(m,n)}$. $\mathcal{R}^i$ is then vectorized into a long vector $\mathbf{VEC}(R^i)$. The elements in $\mathbf{VEC}(R^i)$ is permuted by a public known random order. The permuted vectors are finally combined frame by frame, forming the raw reading stream, denoted as $\mathcal{R}$.

4.1   HLTs Generation and Selection

HLTs-based appearance description derives from a set of carefully selected HLTs. In the follow sections, we use a two-step approach, *Generation and Selection*, to obtain this set. In the first step, as described in Sect. 4.1, we use a cascaded process to generate sufficient HLTs, attempting to cover the template diversity as wide as possible. Apparently, there might result in a very large number of redundant templates. As described in Sect. 4.1, we will adopt several techniques to find a subset of templates which can best capture the intrinsic distribution and is with low redundancy.

Templates Generation. To cover as many diverse templates as possible, we use a *tree-growth* process to generate templates, as illustrated in Fig. 4. All templates are derived from three *Root Templates*, i.e., concentric circles, Gabor filter based stripes [6], and square grids. They each have 10, 60, and 50 variants. Each variant is zoomed-in to three levels, and further splitted into 4, 8, and 16 sub-templates. Ultimately, each sub-template is rotated in 8 directions. A large set of 26880 HLTs are generated, denoted as $\mathbf{T}_{tg}$.

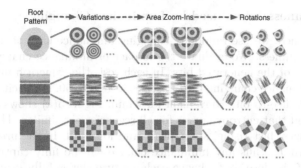

Fig. 4. *Tree-Growth* Templates generation process. The dark green denotes 1 and light green denotes 0. (Color figure online)

Templates Selection. Most of the templates in $\mathbf{T}_{tg}$ should be removed due to the high redundancy. We complete this task by a two-step solution: *coarse-grained template selection*, which removes most of the redundant templates according to their mutual similarity; and *fine-grained templates selection*, which removes the rest redundant templates according to the responses from real-world test videos.

Coarse-Grained Templates Selection: In the first step, we aim to remove the templates that are visually similar. They comprise most of the redundancy. This task can be transformed to an *unsupervised feature selection* problem, whose solution is to identify the most representative features. We use the Laplacian Score (LS) algorithm [5] to perform this task. To apply LS, we first define the *affinity matrix* of these $\mathbf{T}_{tg}$ HLTs templates as $\mathbf{A}_{\mathbf{T}_{tg}}$. For each pair of templates (t_i, t_j) $t_i, t_j \in \mathbf{T}_{tg}$. There is an *affinity score* which measures how these two templates are similar. In FaceMatch, we define the score as $af(t_i, t_j) = \|t_i - t_j\|_F$. We then define the affinity matrix $\mathbf{A}_{\mathbf{T}_{tg}}$, in which each element is an affinity score such that $A_{i,j} = af(t_i, t_j)$, $\forall t_i, t_j \in \mathbf{T}_{tg}$. We denote the selected coarse-grained feature set as $\mathbf{T}_{ac}$, and its size is empirically set to 300 after performing the LS algorithm.

Fine-Grained Templates Selection: We further improve the quality of templates by parsing 50+ test videos using $\mathbf{T}_{ac}$. For the i-th template, the responses across all facial blocks in all frames are organized into a long response vector, denoted as r_i. Similarly, we define the affinity matrix $\mathbf{A}_{\mathbf{T}_{ac}}$ as $a_{i,j} = \frac{r_i \cdot r_j}{\|r_i\| \|r_j\|}, \forall i, j \in [1, \mathbf{N}_{\mathbf{T}_{ac}}]$. LS algorithm is then performed to select the optimal template subset, denoted as $\mathbf{T}_{af}$. The size of $\mathbf{T}_{af}$ is empirically set to 40% of $\mathbf{T}_{ac}$, *i.e.*, $N_{\mathbf{T}_{af}} = 121$.

5   Security Analysis

We implement FaceMatch on the iOS platform using OpenCV library. In this section, we evaluate the security performance of FaceMatch.

5.1   Randomness Introduced by Luminance Changing

As aforementioned, we use randomly changing luminance level of the screen to introduce randomness. We evaluate the impact of luminance changing rate on the randomness of the generated bits. In each test, the camera frame rate f_s is 30, and the luminance changing rate f_r scales from 0 to 50. For each f_r value, we conduct appearance-to-bits conversion for 3 min. Figure 5(a) shows the relative entropy. We find that entropy curves for all scenarios are similar. The trend has generally 3 stages: fast rising, short peak, and long tail. In the first stage, the f_r is lower than f_s, thus any luminance change can be fully captured. In the second stage, f_r is close to f_s, hence each capture slot is fully utilized. In this case, the relative entropy maximized. In the third stage, $f_r > f_s$. Two or more adjacent random luminance values may collide in a same time slot. Therefore, the entropy slowly decreases.

5.2   Randomness of the Converted Bit Stream

Since the key is randomly generated by Alice locally, its randomness is guaranteed. However, FaceMatch uses SPS to deliver the key, If SPS presents certain pattern, the attacker may easily compromise the key. SPS should have be $i.i.d.$ to avoid information leakage. We conduct two tests in two different luminance scenarios to evaluate the SPS value distribution. Figure 5(b) shows the distribution of SPS. We see the SPS values has different distribution for different scenarios. While in the same scenario, The same SPS value retains the highly similar distribution. Therefore, the attacker obtains nothing from the SPS transmitted in the public channel (Fig. 6).

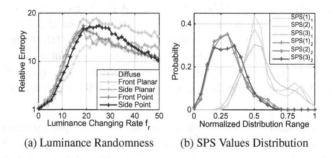

(a) Luminance Randomness   (b) SPS Values Distribution

Fig. 5. (a) Randomness $w.r.t.$ random luminance changing rate f_r. (b) The distribution of SPS values $w.r.t.$ scenario and time.

5.3   Resilience to Shoulder-Surfing Attack

Since FaceMatch is built upon the publicly available facial appearance, "shoulder-surfing" attack is a common attack strategy. We assume that the attacker has the *near-infinite snooping* ability, with which they can place arbitrary number of cameras at any place to snoop the key agreement process. Moreover, the attacker has accurate 3D facial models of the protocol participants, and

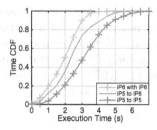
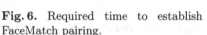
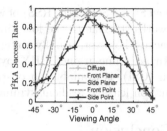

Fig. 6. Required time to establish FaceMatch pairing.

Fig. 7. Shoulder-surfing attack success rate

hence can capture their accurate facial appearance. We also assume the attackers have very powerful computational resource, which supports analyzing the videos in real time. However, we do not assume the attacker has some extremely powerful abilities, such as real-time accurate environmental light reconstruction or high-definition facial appearance reconstruction in real-time. With above assumptions, the attacker's strategy is intuitive: impersonating as the legitimate users by placing multiple cameras within small viewing angles, and then extracting the key via normal key extraction process.

We prototype such a power attacker, Eve. We equip Eve with high performance desktop-level computational power, ERT [9] based facial anchor nodes tracking, and the accurate 3D facial model for each participant. For the 5 typical environmental luminance scenarios, we evaluate the success rate. Figure 7 shows the result. Compared to Bob's result, We find that the attacker does not show obvious advantage over legitimate users, although she is with much more powerful computational resource.

The above result shows that the attacker can compromise the protocol to a certain content. However, in practical scenarios, it is very difficult to conduct such an attack. FaceMatch session can occur at any place in any time. To successfully impersonate as Bob, Eve has to be able to instantly setup a camera upon Alice's request. This action is quite impossible to be conducted without drawing Alice's or Bob's attention. Based on above analysis, we believe attacking FaceMatch requires highly sophisticated setup and rigorous constraints, which leads to negligible probability of successful attacks.

6 Related Work

Schurmann et al. [20] propose an key extraction protocol via ambient acoustic signals. Their work leverages fuzzy-cryptography to "decode" the fingerprint of those signals, and create large amount of keying material. Sethi et al. [22] proposes pairing services that connect two mobile devices by drawing on their touch screens synchronously. Dhwani et al. [18] propose an attack-resilient pairing service based on acoustic near field communication (NFC). There are numerous works trying to extract symmetric keys from Wi-Fi or general wireless signals.

Received Signal Strength (RSS) of wireless signals has been widely used by many prior works [1]. Due to the low dimensionality and noisy natural of RSS, these approaches, however, usually suffer from low efficiency. With the emergence of 802.11n/ac, a fine-grained PHY layer information, namely Channel State Information (CSI), is available on off-the-shelf devices [4]. KEEP [25] presents an information leakage resilient symmetric key verification protocol (LRCV).

7   Conclusion

In this paper, we propose a secure, efficient, and simple device pairing method based on smartphone, named FaceMatch. We present the concrete design of FaceMatch, including the facial appearance consistent capture without communication and Haar-like Templates based appearance variance extraction. We conduct extensive evaluations based on a prototype implementation. The evaluation demonstrates the security, efficiency, and robustness of FaceMatch.

Acknowledgements. This work is supported by the National Postdoctoral Program for Innovative Talent under Grant No. BX20180235, and National Natural Science Foundation of China (NSFC) under Grant No. 61502374 and 61272456. This work is also supported by Fundamental Research Funds for the Central Universities under project No. JB171003.

References

1. Cai, L., Zeng, K., Chen, H., Mohapatra, P.: Good neighbor: ad hoc pairing of nearby wireless devices by multiple antennas. In: Network and Distributed System Security Symposium, NDSS 2011, San Diego, California, U.S. (2011)
2. Cristinacce, D., Cootes, T.F.: Feature detection and tracking with constrained local models. In: British Machine Vision Conference 2006, Edinburgh, UK, pp. 929–938 (2006)
3. Farb, M., Lin, Y.H., Kim, H.J., Mccune, J., Perrig, A.: Safeslinger: easy-to-use and secure public-key exchange. In: ACM International Conference on Mobile Computing and Networking (ACM MobiCom), pp. 417–428 (2013)
4. Halperin, D., Hu, W., Sheth, A., Wetherall, D.: Tool release: gathering 802.11n traces with channel state information. ACM SIGCOMM Comput. Commun. Rev. **41**(1), 53 (2011)
5. He, X., Cai, D., Niyogi, P.: Laplacian score for feature selection. In: International Conference on Neural Information Processing Systems, pp. 507–514 (2005)
6. Jain, A.K., Farrokhnia, F.: Unsupervised texture segmentation using gabor filters. Pattern Recogn. **24**(12), 1167–1186 (1991)
7. Kalal, Z., Mikolajczyk, K., Matas, J.: Forward-backward error: automatic detection of tracking failures. In: International Conference on Pattern Recognition, pp. 2756–2759 (2010)
8. Kalal, Z., Mikolajczyk, K., Matas, J.: Tracking-learning-detection. IEEE Trans. Pattern Anal. Mach. Intell. **34**(7), 1409–1422 (2012)
9. Kazemi, V., Sullivan, J.: One millisecond face alignment with an ensemble of regression trees. In: IEEE Conference on Computer Vision and Pattern Recognition, pp. 1867–1874 (2014)

10. Le, V., Brandt, J., Lin, Z., Bourdev, L., Huang, T.S.: Interactive facial feature localization. In: Fitzgibbon, A., Lazebnik, S., Perona, P., Sato, Y., Schmid, C. (eds.) ECCV 2012, Part III. LNCS, vol. 7574, pp. 679–692. Springer, Heidelberg (2012). https://doi.org/10.1007/978-3-642-33712-3_49

11. Lee, D., Park, H., Chang, D.Y.: Face alignment using cascade Gaussian process regression trees. In: Computer Vision and Pattern Recognition, pp. 4204–4212 (2015)

12. Li, L., Zhao, X., Xue, G.: Near field authentication for smart devices. In: IEEE INFOCOM, pp. 375–379 (2013)

13. Mathur, S., Miller, R., Varshavsky, A., Trappe, W., Mandayam, N.: Proximate: proximity-based secure pairing using ambient wireless signals. In: International Conference on Mobile Systems, Applications, and Services, pp. 211–224 (2011)

14. Matthews, I., Baker, S.: Active appearance models revisited. Int. J. Comput. Vis. 60(2), 135–164 (2004)

15. Maurer, U., Wolf, S.: Information-theoretic key agreement: from weak to strong secrecy for free. In: Preneel, B. (ed.) EUROCRYPT 2000. LNCS, vol. 1807, pp. 351–368. Springer, Heidelberg (2000). https://doi.org/10.1007/3-540-45539-6_24

16. Mayrhofer, R., Gellersen, H.: Shake well before use: authentication based on accelerometer data. In: LaMarca, A., Langheinrich, M., Truong, K.N. (eds.) Pervasive 2007. LNCS, vol. 4480, pp. 144–161. Springer, Heidelberg (2007). https://doi.org/10.1007/978-3-540-72037-9_9

17. Milborrow, S., Nicolls, F.: Locating Facial features with an extended active shape model. In: Forsyth, D., Torr, P., Zisserman, A. (eds.) ECCV 2008, Part IV. LNCS, vol. 5305, pp. 504–513. Springer, Heidelberg (2008). https://doi.org/10.1007/978-3-540-88693-8_37

18. Nandakumar, R., Chintalapudi, K.K., Padmanabhan, V., Venkatesan, R.: Dhwani: secure peer-to-peer acoustic NFC. In: ACM SIGCOMM, pp. 63–74 (2013)

19. Sauer, P., Cootes, T., Taylor, C.: Accurate regression procedures for active appearance models. In: BMVC, vol. 1(6), pp. 681–685 (2011)

20. Schurmann, D., Sigg, S.: Secure communication based on ambient audio. IEEE Trans. Mob. Comput. 12(2), 358–370 (2013)

21. Seshadri, K., Savvides, M.: Robust modified active shape model for automatic facial landmark annotation of frontal faces. In: IEEE International Conference on Biometrics: Theory, Applications, and Systems, pp. 1–8 (2009)

22. Sethi, M., Antikainen, M., Aura, T.: Commitment-based device pairing with synchronized drawing. In: IEEE PerCom 2014 (2014)

23. Sun, Z., Purohit, A., Bose, R., Zhang, P.: Spartacus: spatially-aware interaction for mobile devices through energy-efficient audio sensing. In: Proceeding of the International Conference on Mobile Systems, Applications, and Services, pp. 263–276 (2013)

24. Viola, P., Jones, M.: Rapid object detection using a boosted cascade of simple features. In: IEEE Computer Society Conference on Computer Vision & Pattern Recognition, p. 511 (2001)

25. Xi, W., et al.: Keep: fast secret key extraction protocol for D2D communication. In: IEEE International Symposium of Quality of Service (IWQOS), pp. 350–359 (2014)

26. Zhang, S., Bauckhage, C., Cremers, A.B.: Informed haar-like features improve pedestrian detection. In: Computer Vision and Pattern Recognition, pp. 947–954 (2014)

Security Classification Transmission Method Based on SDN in Industrial Networks

Jianming Zhao[1,2(✉)], Wenli Shang[1,2], Zhoubin Liu[3], and Zixiang Wang[3]

[1] Shenyang Institute of Automation, Chinese Academy of Sciences, Shenyang, China
{zhaojianming, shangwl}@sia.cn
[2] Key Laboratory of Networked Control Systems, Chinese Academy of Sciences, Shenyang, China
[3] State Grid Zhejiang Electric Power Research Institute, Hangzhou, China
{liuzhoubin, wangzixiang}@zj.sgcc.com.cn

Abstract. Software Defined Networking (SDN) is a new type of network architecture, which provides an important way to implement automated network deployment and flexible management. However, security problems in SDN are also inevitable in industrial networks. In the research area of SDN security and traditional network security, feasibility and influence of defense in depth in industrial networks should thus be explored. In this paper, a security classification transmission method based on SDN in industrial networks is proposed, which provides a better security level of transmission paths. In the proposed method, the security classification transmission system is first presented. By designing five service mechanisms, including request, strategy generation, distribution/maintenance, updating/loading and execution, the security classification transmission service model is defined. In an experimental study, the proposed method is shown to be feasible in industrial heterogeneous networks and provide better security paths without affecting availability in the multi-domain and multi-nodes case of industrial networks.

Keywords: SDN · Security classification transmission · Service mechanisms Industrial network

1 Introduction

The combination of internet and industrial control system has been unavoidable. Due to the massive, heterogeneous, and diverse characteristics of industrial field devices, a software defined network (SDN) has attracted attention for industry and academia. SDN uses layered thinking that is currently meeting the requirements of the development architecture and dynamic deployment. It has been considered as a revolutionary technical method by the network domain [1]. However, the new network needs to fully consider the security issues before application deployment [2]. At the same time, the industrial network is increasingly demanding for security. For example, the US Department of Energy (DOE) implemented the SDN-based control system network

© Springer Nature Switzerland AG 2018
X. Sun et al. (Eds.): ICCCS 2018, LNCS 11068, pp. 26–36, 2018.
https://doi.org/10.1007/978-3-030-00021-9_3

security technology project in October 2013, which applied the SDN-based flow controller to its own system. It would achieve a goal of dynamic and security information exchange, and can effectively defend against cyber threats. This function can also maintain the continuous generation of infrastructure.

Over the past years, some SDN-based security transmission methods have been proposed, Adami [3] proposed a security device routing model based on SDN networks. This model combines multiple improved security path selection methods for embedded security devices. It implemented an efficient security device routing strategy, and a network security service scheduling system was constructed based on this method. Shin [4] proposed systems virtualized network security routing, and it completed technology of network security device by using SDN. According to the deployment of different types of network security devices, different routing strategies were adopted. Wang et al. [5] realized detected security classification of the overall strategy. The local detection module was installed in the switch and the global detection module was installed in the controller, the network awareness module and the security path calculation module were added to the Floodlight controller, then they realized the method of authenticating the validity of flow Rules. Binkui et al. [6] studied the security during the development of the new flow table entries. From detection of abnormality to the end of attack defense, the switch could develop security strategies, this would make the switch into the levels of security.

The above studies have effectively solved the aspects of security routing, flow table control management, anomaly detection and security routing linkage. However, some special needs of the Internet of Things in industrial networks, such as the need for multi-service isolation of smart grids and multi-site services isolation for smart oil fields, no method has been proposed for more security strategies in guaranteeing security transmission and validation. Also, industrial networks need to consider heterogeneous nodes [7]. Further, the adaptability of the security mechanism has not been effectively verified. For this reason, this paper proposes a security classification transmission method based on SDN in industrial network, providing a better security level of transmission paths. The simulation of this paper is formed with FloodLight controller and Mininet tools. Experiments are performed from data exchange accuracy, controller algorithm runtime, and packet transmission cost. And the proposed method is feasible under industrial heterogeneous network environments, as well as in multi-domain and multi-nodes by experimental analysis and verification. It provides a better security and ensures that the industrial network is available in real time.

2 Security Classification Transmission System

2.1 SDN Network Architecture

SDN is an innovative architectural network solution. OpenFlow technology is used as the core technology. Through the controller's centralized strategy formulation and switchboard strategy enforcement, the separation between the control plane and the forwarding plane is achieved. It can establish a dynamic strategy enforcement mechanism for the entire network [8]. By comparing with the traditional static route configuration, it transforms into a dynamic transformation software custom strategy form. It separates the control rights and carries out centralized management. The control layer is clearly and correctly abstracted. At the same time, the openness of control rights make transmission paths more intelligent.

2.2 Basic Service Model

In order to ensure the implementation of the security classification strategy for industrial network communication transmission, the method divides the network system into three layers: management layer, data layer, and bottom device layer.

The management layer refers to the control architecture network that composes of control management servers. It is responsible for strategy distribution, strategy formulation, equipment management, the latest version of functional modules, the overall strategy library update, security module library update, QoS support library update, and learning of data layer devices and so on. The general control manager is composed of multiple or one service devices. Multiple service devices need to be processed to save the consistency of the overall library in parallel and synchronization. The control manager should be managed centrally through a unified monitoring interface to providing configuration management. The maintenance of the overall configuration file such as topology visualization, calculation parameter adjustment, and optimization of guarantee parameter adjustment needs the implementation of correct security strategies for each SDN switching device.

The data layer generally refers to the executor that is responsible for the specific packet forwarding of the data layer device. It is responsible for tasks packet forwarding, such as security classification transmission, security algorithm selection, and priority ordering. The security classification transmission of multiple SDN data layer switching equipments is controlled by the flow table of arithmetic expressions, including the message identification code, source node, number of nodes, version number, composition of next hop nodes, and relationship (*/+), forward priority, security priority and other components. The type of security priority is divided into n levels, like level 1 is top secret, level 2 is confidential, level 3 is authentication level, level 4 is user level, etc.

The bottom device layer is the final user equipment. It is generally responsible for the request packet, response packet processing, and application data transmission and reception. It is composed of typical industrial control terminals.

3 Security Classification Transmission Service Design

In order to implement our method, we designed five service mechanisms, including request service, strategy generation service, strategy distribution/maintenance service, strategy updating/loading service, and strategy execution service. The security classification transmission service is described in Fig. 1.

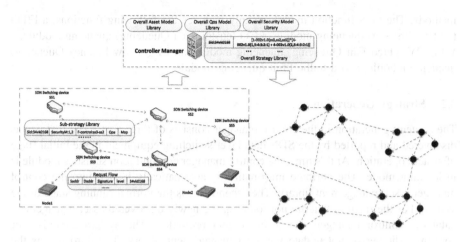

Fig. 1. Security classification transmission service description.

3.1 Request

Control manager sends authentication information, and in the initialization state, SDN data switching device needs requests authentication module to downloading and loading. This can identify the control manager automatically. The request packet structure includes a source identification field, destination identity domain, signature domain, time stamp, action priority, and message identification code.

The control manager allocates the device discovery commands. After receiving the device discovery command, the SDN data layer switching starts the statistics module. This module discovers through a broadcast packet. Table 1 gives an example of devices statistics.

Table 1. An example of device statistics

Switching devices	Statistics
ss1	ss2, ss3
ss2	ss1, ss3, ss4, ss5
ss3	device1, ss1, ss2, ss4
ss4	ss3, ss2, ss5
ss5	device2, device3, ss2, ss4

Each SDN data layer switching devices reports statistical self-learning information, and the control manager automatically adds learning information to its asset management database. It includes asset attribute information, asset network function modules, asset load capacity, asset load status, asset security function module, and asset network connection mapping. The asset management library will fusions the reported information. The asset security function module mainly includes the following functions: RSA, ECC, Hash verification, encrypted Hash verification, AES, DES, and other methods. The QoS function module mainly includes the following functions: a FIFO (first-in, first-out) queueing module, a CQ (customized Queueing) queueing module, a WFQ (Weighted Fair Queueing) queueing module, an LLQ (Low Latency Queueing) queueing module, and a traffic limit queueing module.

3.2 Strategy Generation

The strategy generation in the control manager consists of three parts. The first part is discovered and reported by the SDN data layer switching equipment in the initial stage of system operation. At this time, the control manager configuration statistics module is in learning mode. The attribute information is automatically loaded into the control manager asset management library. The second part is the normal running stage of the system. For the devices that are not found in the newly discovered asset management database, control managers are recorded and prompted. The system administrator confirms whether or not update the asset management library. The third part is the system administrator's manual statistics and update the configuration attributes to the asset management library.

The control manager initializes the status based on the configuration information of the overall network system. It will plan the transfer path automatically by analyzing the address information, configuration attributes, and other related information in the request message, and generate a strategy allocation strategy.

The controller path strategy generally uses Dijkstra algorithm to calculate the shortest path between two nodes [9]. This paper increases the security classification requirements, and provides an improved method for calculating the shortest security path.

The shortest path calculation method is a kind of linear programming and needs calculating a minimum cost flow [10], which can be formalized as an equation.

$$
\begin{aligned}
&\min \sum c_{i,j} \chi_{i,j} \\
&s.t \sum_{j=1}^{n} \chi_{i,j} - \sum_{k=1}^{n} \chi_{k,j}, i = a_i, for\ i = 1, 2, \ldots n' \\
&\chi_{i,j} \geq 0 \quad for\ i, j = 1, 2, \ldots n
\end{aligned}
\tag{1}
$$

where $\chi_{i,j}$ represents the number of nodes in the link from node i to node j, a_i represents the supply amount of node i. If $a_i <= 0$, it represents the demand of this node. In addition, supposing a network can reach equilibrium in $\sum_{i=1}^{n} a_i = 0$, and giving a real number $c_{i,j}$, which is the cost of connecting node i to node j. In the strategy generation phase, this paper designs a path selection algorithm with security classification transmission based on the research of the shortest path computation method. Through calculating, arranging, and security grade transmission path screening in the shortest path sets, the set of paths generated by this method's strategy in those sets are determined. Figure 2 shows the shortest path algorithm with security classification.

3.3 Strategy Distribution/Maintenance

The successful strategy will be generated by the SDN data exchange device node, and different sub-strategies for each SDN data exchange device will be encoded. The sub-

Input : S (start node)

Input : E (end node)

Input : $C_i = N_i$ (security node i), $i = 1, 2, ...n$

Input : $C_{m,n}^i$ = security link level i between node m and node n), $i = 1, 2, ...n$

Output : FR, find one shortest path

foreach C_i **do**

    ⌊ $M_i \leftarrow C_i$;

    $M_i \Leftarrow S$;

    $M_i \Leftarrow E$;

    foreach M_j **do**

        foreach M_l **do**

            if $M_j \neq M_l$ **then**

                $U_{j,l} \Leftarrow$ find_shortest_path(M_j, M_l);

Save $C_{m,n}^i$ in $U_{j,l}$;

while $P_k \neq NULL$ **do**

    $P_k \Leftarrow$ permutation ($M_1, M_2...M_n$);

    $N_u \Leftarrow S, E, P_k$;

    if first $P_k = S$ *then*

        if *last* $P_k = E$ *then*

            foreach $C_{m,n}^i$, (m,n) $\subset P_k$ **do**

                if $C_{m,n}^i \not\subset$ security level *then*

                    continue;

                $Q_t \Leftarrow P_k$;

foreach Q_t **do**

    foreach $U_{j,l}$ **do**

        if $U_{j,l} \subset Q_t$ **then**

            $V_t \Leftarrow U_{j,l}$;

$FR = \min(V_1, V_2....)$;

Fig. 2. Shortest path algorithm with security classification.

strategy includes information such as the execution strategy, function modules, weight priority, and security priority of the SDN data exchange equipment. The overall strategy library will store these. Among them, the main information in the strategy is an arithmetic expression. It consists of message identification code, an execution expression, and strategy expression. The overall structure is as follows:

[Message identification code] [Execution expression] $* / +$ [Strategy expression],

where the Execution expression consists of source node (default is 1), number of nodes (M), version number, and next-hop. the * indicates sequential execution, the + indicates parallel execution and the Strategy expression consists of forwarding priority and security priority.

The format arithmetic expression of a test sample like: [1-002v1.0(ss3,ss2,ss5)] * [4-002v1.0(3,5:4:3:2:1) + 4-002v1.0(2,5:4:3:2:1)]. The "1-002v1.0" represents 1 transmitting end and 2 receiving ends, and arithmetic expressions can be combined, and version is v1.0. The "ss3, ss2, ss5" represents an optimized automatic planning path after taking into account the various attributes of the transmission node. The "*" represents a sequential command relationship and can share an execution expression. The "4-002v1.0" represents that the Qos weighting level is 4 and the function module of the selected queue is 002. The "3,5:4:3:2:1" represents that the final security level is 3 by the automated planning methods in the security classification transmission. The "+" represents performed in parallel relationships.

3.4   Strategy Updating/Loading

The updating module checks whether a local sub-strategy pool already exists according to the strategy arithmetic expression. In the entire industrial system, there is only one control manager or the one control manager is a synchronous and distributed overall strategy library. First, it will detect the existence of a sub-strategy which is been issued based on the numbers. If the numbers is matching, checking whether the assigned sub-strategy is consistent with the content of the local sub-strategy. If it is an exact match, the attributes such as count and time are updated. And if not, the content of the sub-strategy is updated.

When it does not have a function module, the loading module make the SDN data layer switching device to send a loading module request for the control manager, and to load the function module. The request consists of SDN data layer switching device ID, version number, function module identity ID. After the control manager receives the loading request, it start to authenticate and response. When SDN data layer switching devices obtain the updating information, Storing function module contents to sub-loading module library and loading related function modules.

3.5   Strategy Execution

The SDN data layer switching device analyzes the message ID from the contents of the data packets. Then, the arithmetic expression in the sub-strategy database by the message ID are found. The message ID which is matched is selected, and packets are forwarded based on the shortest path calculation in the content of the message ID's sub-policy libraries.

4 Evaluation and Analysis

4.1 Experimental Environment

The simulation of this paper has been formed with FloodLight controller and Mininet tools [11, 12]. We generate mixed traffic by tools of POWERLINK protocol stack software, EtherCat simulation tool, Modbus poll tool [13]. Those traffic corresponds to security policies that is level 1, level 2, level 3. And when testing, the protocol type is determined by the 13th and 14th byte frame type fields. The FloodLight controller can obtain the network topology of the entire network. The function of the security classification route calculation module is implemented through programming, and the calculated shortest security path strategy is delivered to the FloodLight controller through the API interface. The controller delivers those to the relevant OpenFlow switch by flow tables [14].

4.2 Experimental Analysis

In the experimental environment, we set 5 domain controllers, each domain controller randomly simulates 5 to 10 switching device nodes. The scale basically meets the requirements of the industrial field application environment. Experiments were performed from data exchange accuracy, controller algorithm runtime, and packet transmission cost.

Data Exchange Accuracy. Data exchange accuracy represents whether the security classification transmission method can be applied to SDN-based industrial network switching device. Because if Data exchange accuracy is too low, it indicate a high rate of packet loss. In experiment, we control the testing rate at line speed 20% of ten trillion environment, and set 5 kinds of quantity in each domain controller. Each domain controller selects 5, 6, 8, 10 switching nodes for comparison experiment. A host calculates the statistical categorization that packets of receiving, if it is stable below 0.01%, we think that the security classification transmission method is no packet loss. It can be seen from the experimental results that the method designed in this paper can support for mixed traffic access of typical industrial network communication protocols that is selected in experiment. It is also verified that the method of this paper can be applied to industrial heterogeneous network environment.

Controller Algorithm Runtime. Controller algorithm runtime represents the work efficiency, the smaller of this runtime is more effective [15]. We set 5 domain controllers, and each domain controller selects 5 and 10 switching device nodes for comparison experiment. Figure 3 shows the experimental results of the algorithm's runtime. As the number of domains increases and the number of nodes increases, controller algorithm runtime is not a proportionate or exponential increase, and the slope of the line has a decreasing trend. And this runtime meets the industrial network's requirement for time (The normal industrial network time calculation requirement may be less than 100 ms). So in the case of multi domain and multi nodes, it provides better security while ensuring that it is available in time requirement of the industrial control system network (Table 2).

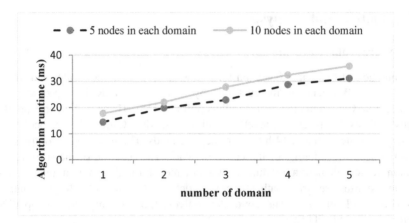

Fig. 3. Controller algorithm runtime testing results.

Table 2. Data exchange accuracy testing result

No.	Testing Rate	Number of Nodes	1st domains	2st domains	3st domains	4st domains	5st domains	Packet loss rate
1	**Line speed 20%**	25	5	5	5	5	5	0.001%
2	**Line speed 20%**	30	6	6	6	6	6	0.002%
3	**Line speed 20%**	40	8	8	8	8	8	0.001%
4	**Line speed 20%**	50	10	10	10	10	10	0.004%

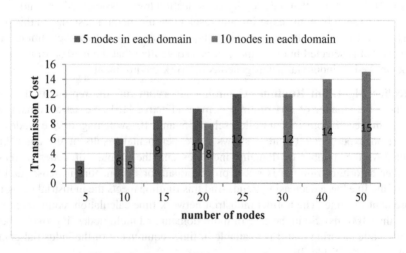

Fig. 4. Packet transmission cost testing results.

Packet Transmission Cost. Packet transmission cost represents the total cost of transferring packets between two nodes. If it is smaller, the routing strategy is superior. We set 5 domain controllers, and each domain controller selects 5 and 10 switching device nodes for comparison experiment. Figure 4 gives the experimental results of the total cost of the data package. From this figure, we can see the characteristics similar to the curve in experiment of controller algorithm runtime. As the number of domains increases and the number of nodes increases, the growth rate of packet transmission cost is reduced. And with the reduced proportion of features, it can show that this paper method can apply to multi-domain multi-node scenarios, and it provides better security transmission paths.

5 Conclusions

This paper proposes a security classification transmission method based on SDN in industrial network, it provides a better security level of transmission paths. we first present the security classification transmission system, and then define the security classification transmission service model, which designs five service mechanisms, including request, strategy generation, distribution/maintenance, updating/loading and execution. The experimental results show that, this proposed method is feasible in industrial heterogeneous networks, and can provides better security without affecting availability in the multi-domain and multi-node case. Due to the development of the Industrial Internet, the next step will further optimize the strategy generation algorithm to reduce the algorithm time and transmission cost. And then industrial network security classification transmission method can be better applied to widely industrial heterogeneous network environments.

Acknowledgments. This work is supported by State Grid Science and Technology Project (Grant No. 52110118001H), the National Natural Science Foundation of China (Grant No. 61501447), the National Natural Science Foundation of China (Grant No. 61773368). The authors are grateful to the anonymous referees for their insightful comments and suggestions.

References

1. Singh, S., Jha, R.K.: A survey on software defined networking: architecture for next generation network. J. Netw. Syst. Manag. **25**, 1–54 (2017)
2. Scott-Hayward, S., O'Callaghan, G., Sezer, S.: SDN Security: A Survey Future Networks and Services, pp. 1–7. IEEE, Trento (2013)
3. Adami, D., Giordano, S., D'Amore, G., et al.: A new SDN traffic control application for security routing in critical infrastructures. In: The 13th International Joint Conference on e-Business and Telecommunications, pp. 129–138. SCITEPRESS-Science and Technology Publications, Lda (2016)
4. Shin, S., Wang, H., Gu, G.: A first step toward network security virtualization: from concept to prototype. IEEE Trans. Inf. Forensics Secur. **10**(10), 2236–2249 (2015)
5. Wang, M., Liu, J., Chen, J., et al.: Perm-guard: authenticating the validity of flow rules in software defined networking. J. Signal Process. Syst. **86**(2–3), 1–17 (2016)

6. Binkui, L., Lei, Z., et al.: Security routing strategy based on switch level division in SDN. Appl. Res. Comput. **34**(2), 522–525 (2017)
7. Henneke, D., Wisniewski, L., Jasperneite, J.: Analysis of realizing a future industrial network by means of Software-Defined Networking (SDN). In: IEEE World Conference on Factory Communication Systems, pp. 1–4. IEEE, Aveiro (2016)
8. Hussein, A., Elhajj, I.H., Chehab, A., Kayssi, A.: SDN security plane: an architecture for resilient security services. In: IEEE International Conference on Cloud Engineering Workshop, pp. 54–59. IEEE, Berlin (2016)
9. Yahya, W., Basuki, A., Jiang, J.R.: The extended dijkstra's-based load balancing for openflow network. Int. J. Electr. Comput. Eng. **5**(2), 289–296 (2015)
10. Singh, V.K., Nimisha, I.K.T.: Applications of maximal network flow problems in transportation and assignment problems. J. Math. Res. **2**(1) (2010)
11. Mininet tools. http://mininet.org/. Accessed 11 Feb 2018
12. Project Floodlight. http://www.projectfloodlight.org/. Accessed 11 Feb 2018
13. Ming, W., Wenli, S., Peng, Z., et al.: Modbus/TCP communication access control method based on function code depth detection. Inf. Control **45**(2), 248–256 (2016)
14. Rotsos, C., Sarrar, N., Uhlig, S., Sherwood, R., Moore, Andrew W.: OFLOPS: an open framework for openflow switch evaluation. In: Taft, N., Ricciato, F. (eds.) PAM 2012. LNCS, vol. 7192, pp. 85–95. Springer, Heidelberg (2012). https://doi.org/10.1007/978-3-642-28537-0_9
15. Gelberger, A., Yemini, N., Ran, G.: Performance analysis of software-defined networking (SDN). In: IEEE International Symposium on Modelling, Analysis & Simulation of Computer and Telecommunication Systems, pp. 389–393. IEEE Computer Society, San Francisco (2013)

Security Solution for Real-Time Data Access in Wireless Sensor Networks

Hanguang Luo[1(✉)], Guangjun Wen[1], and Jian Su[2]

[1] University of Electronic Science and Technology of China, Chengdu, China
luohanguang_uestc@outlook.com
[2] Nanjing University of Information Science and Technology, Nanjing, China

Abstract. Wireless Sensor Networks (WSNs) have rapidly increased to be applicable in many different areas due to their wireless mobile connectivity, large scale deployment and ad hoc network. However, these characteristics make WSNs usually deployed in unattended and hostile field, which may bring some new threats such as information tampering and eavesdropping attacks, etc. User authentication is one of the most important security services that allowed the legitimate user to query and collect the real-time data from a sensor node in WSN. Since the sensor nodes are resource-constrained devices which have limited storage, power and computing resource, the proposed authentication scheme must be low cost and lightweight. Recently, Gope et al. proposed a realistic lightweight authentication for real-time data access in WSN. Unfortunately, through our analysis we identified several flaws exist in their scheme as well as exist in other two-factor schemes. In order to withstand these threats, in this paper, we proposed some solutions to withstand the problems in Gope et al.'s and other schemes. Our solutions provide an important reference for security data access in WSN.

Keywords: Wireless Sensor Network · Authentication · Security
Lightweight

1 Introduction

Recent years, the development of Internet of Things (IoT) has realized the connection between the objects with the Internet, and, the sense, identifying, management and control abilities of IoTs have brought great convenience to people's daily work and live. Wireless Sensor Network as one of the core technologies in IoT supports the sensing capabilities to communicate and interact with its internal states and the external environment. Due to the quickly and easily deployed characteristics of wireless sensors, the WSNs can be used in various application scenarios and environments, such as healthcare monitoring, environment monitoring, traffic monitoring, vehicular tracking, military surveillance and can even be used in smart buildings and homes. Normally, the collected data from wireless sensor nodes are firstly transmitted to the database, and then users obtain the desired data from the corresponding database. However, in some cases, users in WSN need to get the real-time information at a particular moment, such as military surveillance and vehicular tracking or monitoring. In such conditions, users

© Springer Nature Switzerland AG 2018
X. Sun et al. (Eds.): ICCCS 2018, LNCS 11068, pp. 37–48, 2018.
https://doi.org/10.1007/978-3-030-00021-9_4

have to communicate with the wireless sensor nodes directly. Furthermore, in many applications such as target tracking, battlefield surveillance and so on, WSNs often deployed in hostile and unattended environment, so it is of great concern that critical data are well protected from unauthorized access and illegally eavesdropping.

In order to achieve the above security requirements, an efficient mechanism should be employed to the real-time data access in WSN and be depicted in Fig. 1. In this scheme, the legitimately registered user should first communicate and mutual authenticate with the Gateway Node (GWN) or Base Station (BS). After the authentication, the GWN will set a session key for the user and sensor node that the user wishes to communicate with in the following real-time data access process. Of course, the corresponding sensor node should also be mutually authenticated with the GWN. Here the users can login the WSNs ether with mobile terminal or fixed terminal. In this way, not only ensures that none but legitimate user can obtain the critical data, but also guarantees the user that the obtained data is indeed from the legitimate sensor node which she/he wishes to. Meanwhile, resource limitation and the large number of sensor nodes (which may cause a large data access request to the GWN) demand that the proposed security authentication protocol must stay in a low cost and lightweight.

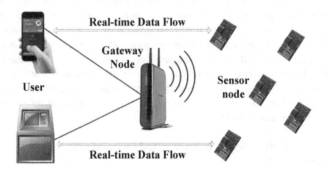

Fig. 1. Real-time data access in WSNs.

In this paper, we use the most recent 2FA (two-factor authentication) protocol of Gope et al.'s [19] as a case of study to show the problems and challenges of designing a lightweight authentication protocol suitable in WSN. By introduce the most recent criteria [24] of 2FA mechanism, we detailedly analyze Gope et al.'s and other 2FA schemes with their drawbacks. Finally, we propose the guides and solutions to design a security data access protocol in WSN. The remainder of this paper is organized as follows. Section 2 discusses the related works. We detailed analyze the problems of Gope et al.'s and 2FA schemes in Sect. 3. In Sect. 4, we give some suggestions and references in designing a security data access protocol in WSN. Finally, we conclude the paper in Sect. 5.

2 Related Work

The remote user authentication has caused widespread concern over last few decades since Lamport firstly presented a password-based scheme in 1981 [1]. In [1], users need to prove their legal identities and pass the authentication only by entering their pre-set passwords correctly. Meanwhile, it claimed that the scheme is secure even if an adversary eavesdrops exist on the communication between a user and remote system. Hereafter, the password-based authentication mechanism [2, 3] rapidly become the most widely used and acceptable identification scheme due to its merit of user-friendly and easy implementation. However, the inherent limitation of these password-only mechanism is that the server has to store a verifier table which contains the passwords (the passwords are probably stored in salted-hash) of all the registered users. Therefore, the hidden secure problem may lead users' passwords to be exposed once the authentication server is compromised or some of the insidious insider has the authority to read the verifier table. In order to deal with this problem, Chang and Wu [4] proposed the first smartcard-based passwords authentication scheme without a sensitive verification table stored on the server in 1991 and is often termed as "two-factor authentication" scheme deployed for various kinds of security-critical applications, such as e-health, e-banking, etc.

To meet the need of accessing the real-time information from the sensor nodes which mentioned before, GWN as the remote third party trust center needs to identity the user and the sensor nodes at the same time in order to avoid illegal access. As a result, several two-factor authentication schemes were proposed for WSN in [5–11]. In these solutions, the smart card and password are utilized by the user to get the access authority to the sensor nodes. In past decade, along with the rapid development of WSN commercialization as well as for the sake of improving WSN security, substantial two-factor authentication protocols have been proposed. Particularly, Wong et al. [12] proposed the first hash-based user authentication scheme with lightweight and less complex in 2007. However, soon after that, some researcher found that it is vulnerable to replay, forgery, and stolen-verifier attacks. Two years later, Das [5] proposed the frequently cited two-factor based scheme which introduced a temporal credential for the authenticated user and only needs hash and XOR computations as well. Unfortunately, this scheme does not provide mutual authentication, key agreement together with some other serious security flaws, such as vulnerable to the denial-of-service attack, node capture attack, etc. Since then, many researchers inspired from this work and proposed several improvements [6–8, 13–15]. Regrettably, each of them more or less has its security problems. So far, over a dozen 2FA schemes have been proposed, among which Turkanovic et al. [16] proposed a lightweight 2FA protocol based on hash function and claimed to be energy efficient and secure. However, Amin and Biswas [17] and Farash et al. [18] respectively showed that the protocol of Turkanovic et al. has several security weaknesses, including offline identity guessing attack, offline password guessing attack, impersonation attack, smart card loss attacks, session key disclosure and proposed the improved schemes. Last year, Gope et al. [19] summarized the various problems existing in the previous schemes and proposed a realistic lightweight real-time application date access anonymous authentication protocol. In this protocol, user can ensure various imperative security properties like user anonymity, untraceability, perfect forward secrecy, etc. However, the proposed scheme also contains some fatal problems and will be illustrated in detail in the Sect. 3.

3　Drawbacks of Gope et al.'s and Two-Factor Schemes

The two-factor schemes used in distributed systems is one of the most convenient and effective authentication mechanism to assure one communicating party of the authenticity of the corresponding party by acquisition of corroborative evidence, and it has been widely deployed for various kinds of daily applications, such as e-banking, e-health and WSN. However, there are severe challenges regarding security [20], privacy [21] and usability [22] in terms of the open and complex characteristics as well as the resource-constrained devices used of distributed systems. As there is no common set of desirable properties for two-factor authentication schemes, to deal with the above problems, several criteria [23, 24] have been proposed to help researchers for the authentication designing in WSN. [24] is one of the most recent and acceptable criterion presented by Wang et al. in 2016 with 12 independent criteria and was briefly depicted as follows: *C1. No password verifier-table:* the server does not have a database to store users' passwords or some derived values of passwords; *C2. Password friendly:* the password is memorable, and can be chosen freely and changed locally by the user; *C3. No password exposure:* the password cannot be derived by the privileged administrator of the server; *C4. No smart card loss attack:* the scheme is free from smart card loss attack, i.e., illegal user cannot easily get or change the password of the lost smart card by using online, offline or hybrid guessing attacks, etc.; *C5. Resistance to known attacks:* the scheme resists various kinds of basic/sophisticated well known attacks, such as replay attack, de-synchronization attack, etc.; *C6. Sound repairability:* the scheme provides smart card revocation with good repairability, i.e., a user can revoke his card without changing her identity; *C7. Provision of key agreement:* the client and the server can establish a common session key for secure data communications during the authentication process; *C8. No clock synchronization:* the scheme is not prone to the problems of clock synchronization and time delay; *C9. Timely typo detection:* the user will be timely notified if she inputs a wrong password by mistake when login; *C10. Mutual authentication:* the user and server can verify the authenticity of each other; *C11. User anonymity:* the scheme can protect user identity and prevent user activities from being traced; *C12. Forward secrecy:* the scheme provides the property of perfect forward secrecy.

　　With the criteria above, the researchers can make their goals clear and definite at the beginning of protocol designing, as well as they can test and verify the protocol when it finished. However, according to our analysis we found that some problems existed in these 2FA criteria, i.e., the contradictions between the functional requirements and the limitation of the secure performance that the 2FA schemes can provide.

　　In order to depict the contradictions between the criteria and 2FA schemes, we take Gope et al.'s recently proposed scheme [19] as the example to analyze the limitations of 2FA scheme. [19] is not only an outstanding but also a representative protocol in 2FA scheme and be briefly divided into following four phases: (i) Registration Phase,

(ii) Authentication and Key Exchange Phase, (iii) Password Renewal Phase and (iv) Dynamic Node Addition Phase. We only focus on the first two phases which we care about, and, the details are depicted as follows. Table 1 gives the notations used in this paper.

Table 1. Notations used in this paper

Symbol	Definition	Symbol	Definition
U	User	PSW_U	Password of the user
GWN	Gateway node	Ts	Time stamp
Sn	Sensor node	K_{ug}	Shared key between U and GWN
ID_U	Identity of the user	K_{em}	Shared emergency key between U and GWN
ID_G	Identity of the gateway node	ω	Secret key of the gateway
AID_U	One-time-alias identity of the user	$h(.)$	One-way hash function
Ts_{ug}	Transaction sequence number	$\|$	Concatenation operation
SID	Shadow identity of user	$\oplus$	Exclusive-OR operation
SK	Session key between Sn and U		

3.1 Review of Gope et al.'s Scheme

Registration Phase

In this phase, a legitimate user U registers or re-registers with the GWN. It needs to execute the following steps:

Step 1. A new user (U) submits his/her identity ID_U to the GWN through a secure channel.

Step 2. After receiving the request from the user, the GWN generates a random number n_g of 128-bit and then computes secret key $K_{ug} = h(ID_U\|n_g) \oplus ID_G$. Subsequently, GWN also generates a set of un-linkable shadow-IDs $SID = \{sid_1, sid_2, \cdots\}$ and emergency keys $K_{em_j} = \{k_{em1}, k_{em2}, \cdots\}$, where $sid_j = h(ID_U\|r_j\|K_{ug})$ and for each $sid_j \in SID$ GWN computes $k_{em_j} = \{ID_U\|sid_j\|r'_j\}$. Here, the parameters r_j and r'_j denote the random numbers of 128-bit. Hereafter, the GWN generates a 64-bit transaction sequence number Ts_{ug}. This sequence number is computed based on the number of requests handled by the GWN, which will be incremented by one after each request (the transaction sequence parameter is m) of any user and the GWN sets $Ts_{ug} = m$, in addition, subsequently, sends it to the user by keeping a copy in its database. The concept of sequence number is mainly used to prevent replay attack, where by checking the Ts_{ug}, the GWN can comprehend who is the user and whether the user request is valid or not. Precisely, if the Ts_{ug} provided by the user does not match the stored value of the GWN's database, the

GW will immediately terminate the connection. In that case, user will be asked to use his/her one of the unused pair of (sid_j, k_{emj}), whereafter, this used pair of (sid_j, k_{emj}) must be deleted from the list of $(SID$ and $K_{em})$ by both the U and GWN.

Step 3. The GWN personalizes a smart card with $\{K_{ug}, (SID, K_{em}), Ts_{ug}, h(.)\}$ and issues it to U through the secure channel. At the same time, the GW uses its ID_G and the secret key ω to encode $\{ID_U, K_{ug}, K_{em}\}$, i.e., $ID_U^{\#} = ID_U \oplus h(ID_G||\omega||Ts_{ug})$, $K_{ug}^{\#} = K_{ug} \oplus h(ID_G||ID_U||\omega)$, $K_{em}^{\#} = K_{em} \oplus h(ID_G||ID_U||\omega)$, and then stores a copy of $ID_U^{\#}, K_{ug}^{\#}, (SID, K_{em}^{\#})$ and Ts_{ug} in its own database for further communication.

Step 4. After receiving the smart card, U chooses a password PSW_U and then computes $K_{ug}^* = K_{ug} \oplus h(h(ID_U) \oplus h(PSW_U))$, $\qquad f_U^* = h(h(K_{ug}) \oplus h(PSW_U) \oplus h(ID_U))$, $SID^* = SID \oplus h(h(ID_U) \oplus h(PSW_U))$, $\quad K_{em}^* = K_{em} \oplus h(h(ID_U) \qquad \oplus h(PSW_U))$. Finally, U replaces K_{ug} with K_{ug}^*, SID with SID^* and K_{em} with K_{em}^* so that the smart card contains $\{K_{ug}^*, f_U^*, (SID^*, K_{em}^*), Ts_{ug}, h(.)\}$.

Anonymous Authentication and Key Exchange Phase
This phase achieves goal of authentication among the user, GW, and the sensor node and consists of the following steps.

Step 1. $M_{A_1} : U \rightarrow GWN : \{AID_U, N_x, Ts_{ug}(if\ req.), Sn_{id}, V_1\}$.
The user who wants to acquire data from a sensor node Sn_{id} at first needs to insert his smart card and enters his ID_U and password PSW_U onto a client. Then, the smart card computes $K_{ug} = K_{ut}^* \oplus h(h(ID_U) \oplus h(PSW_U))$, $f_U = h(h(K_{ug}) \oplus h(PSW_U) \oplus h(ID_U))$, and checks whether $f_U = f_U^*$. If it holds, the smart card verifies the user's identity, otherwise terminates the authentication immediately. After that, the smart card generates a random number N_u and derives the one-time alias identity $AID_U = h(ID_U||K_{ug}||N_u||Ts_{ug})$, $N_x = K_{ug} \oplus N_u$, $V_1 = h(AID_U||K_{ug}||N_x||Sn_{id})$ and sends request message M_{A_1} to GWN. Note that, in case of loss of synchronization, the user needs to choose one of the unused pair of (sid_j, k_{emj}) where $sid_j = sid_j^* \oplus h(ID_U||PSW_U)$, $k_{em} = k_{em}^* \oplus h(ID_U||PSW_U)$ and transmits the sid_j as AID_U, k_{emj} as K_{ug} to the GWN instead. In that case, the user does not need to send Ts_{ug} in M_{A_1}.

Step 2. $M_{A_2} : GWN \rightarrow Sn : \{AID_U, SK', T, V_2\}$.
Upon receiving the request message from user, firstly, the GWN checks whether the transaction sequence number Ts_{ug} is valid or not. If the GWN cannot find the Ts_{ug} in its database, it terminates the authentication process immediately. Otherwise, the GWN uses its ID_G and secret key ω to obtain the ID_U and K_{ug} of the user. Subsequently, the GWN checks whether V_1 is equal to $h(AID_U||K_{ug}||N_x||Sn_{id})$ or not. If so, the GWN verifies the one-time identity AID_U and derives $N_u = K_{ug} \oplus N_x$. Otherwise, the GW terminates the connection. After that, the GWN randomly generates a session key SK and a timestamp T, then computes $SK' = h(K_{gs}) \oplus SK$, $V_2 = h(AID_U|| SK'||T||K_{gs})$, and, sends M_{A_2} to the sensor node Sn_{id}.

Step 3. $M_{A_3} : Sn \rightarrow GWN : \{T', Sn_{id}, V_3\}$.

After receiving the message M_{A_2}, the sensor node first checks the timestamp T and the message V_2. If both of them are valid, the sensor node derives $SK = h(K_{gs}) \oplus SK'$, generates a timestamp T' and computes $V_3 = h(SK||K_{gs}||Sn_{id}||T')$, then sends the response message M_{A_3} to the GWN. Finally, the sensor node updates its shared secret key with $K_{gs_{new}} = K_{gs}$, where $K_{gs_{new}} = h(K_{gs}||Sn_{id})$.

Step 4. $M_{A_4} : GWN \rightarrow U : SK'', V_4, Ts, x (if\ req.)$.

By receiving the response message M_{A_3}, the GWN first checks the timestamp T' and V_3. If valid, the GWN increments the transaction sequence parameter by $m = m + 1$ and computes $Ts = h(K_{ug}||ID_U||N_u) \oplus Ts_{ug_{new}}$, $V_4 = h(SK''||N_u||Ts||K_{ug})$, then sends a response message M_{A_4} to the user. Finally, the GWN updates its database by $K_{ug_{new}} = h(K_g||ID_U||Ts_{ug_{new}})$, $K_{gs_{new}} = h(K_{gs}||Sn_{id})$ and $Ts_{ug_{new}}$.

After receiving the response message M_{A_4}, the user's smart card checks V_4. If valid, the smart card derives $Ts_{ug_{new}} = h(K_{ug}||ID_U||N_u) \oplus Ts$, $K_{ug_{new}} = h(K_g||ID_U||Ts_{ug_{new}})$ and updates $K_{ug} = K_{ug_{new}}$, $Ts_{ug} = TS_{ug_{new}}$. Note that, in case the GWN cannot find any Ts_{ug} in M_{A_1}, the GWN will first validate the AID_U by comparing it with sid_j in its database. If it is found, the GWN will use sid_j and k_{em_j} instead of AID_U and K_{ug} respectively to finish authentication process.

3.2 Problem Statement

According to the Gope et al.'s scheme which used the typical registration and authentication process of 2FA, we can clearly find that some problems exist against the criteria and cannot be well resolved in 2FA mechanism. For example, in criteria [24], criterion C4 and C5 respectively claims that the proposed scheme should be free from smart card loss attack and resist any other well known attacks such as insider attack. On the other hand, the scheme also needs to satisfy the requirement of C9, i.e., the users should be timely notified when they enter wrong passwords. However, in 2FA scheme, if users want to perceive the mistake in password entering process, the validation information about password must be stored in the smart card. Otherwise, an online password authentication process should be taken to confirm its validity. In such case, it must be more time-consuming and complex, and, may not distinguish the password entering mistake from any other mistakes or attacks during the communication. Once the validation message about password is preserved in the smart card like scheme in [19], i.e., $f_U^* = h(h(K_{ug}) \oplus h(PSW_U) \oplus h(ID_U))$, then, even though the password is hidden by the hash function, the insider attack can recover the password easily. Imagine that if the insider of the GWN has the lost/stolen smart card, with Dovel–Yao threat model [25] (the insider can achieve the user ID_U and secret key K_{ug} easily), he can execute the offline password guessing attack using dictionary attack to derive a low-entropy password, i.e., to find the password PSW_U^* which can make $h(h(K_{ug}) \oplus h(PSW_U^*) \oplus h(ID_U)) = f^*$. The same problems also exist in other 2FA schemes. The reason why 2FA scheme cannot satisfy the requirement of the criteria is that, under current technique, the low-entropy and small candidate space of the password make the attackers easy to take offline guessing attack to the password. Hence, password and smart card based 2FA mechanism can hardly satisfy the requirement of remote user authentication.

In addition, Gope et al.'s scheme also has several other problems that make the scheme not really like what they said that it is a realistic authentication scheme for data access in WSN, and the details are illustrated as following:

(1) No measure is taken to resist the de-synchronization attack between GWN and SN. During the authentication and key exchange phase, in Step 3, the SN will update its secret key after transmitting his response message M_{A_3}. Any attacks or loses of message M_{A_3} may cause the GWN and SN de-synchronization, and finally, lead them unable to authenticate each other in next session. Unfortunately, this problem can easily take place spontaneously or implement by the attacker in [19].

(2) The problem with resynchronization mechanism. The proposed scheme used a pair of $\left(sid_j, k_{em_j}\right)$ to resist de-synchronization attack between the user and GWN, however, there is no explicit suggestion for how many pairs there should be. Furthermore, it is easily for an attacker to cause the user and GWN become de-synchronization, such as tampers the transaction sequence number Ts_{ug} in message M_{A_1} by man-in-the-middle attack or simple intercepts response message M_{A_4}. Since each time of desynchronization will consume a pair of $\left(sid_j, k_{em_j}\right)$, the stored pairs of $\left(SID, K_{em}\right)$ will be exhausted soon and unable to be synchronized again. What's more, in the resynchronization process, the GWN must search in the whole data base to find whether a pair of $\left(sid_j, k_{em_j}\right)$ that can make $AID_U = sid_j$ exist. It would be a costly and infeasible method for a large distributed system, even if each user only has several shared pairs of $\left(SID, K_{em}\right)$ with GWN.

(3) Cannot resist clone card attack. During the registration phase in Gope et al.'s scheme, after receiving the smart card from GWN, the user only needs to choose and input a password PSW_U to initialize the smart card. During the authentication phase, the password is only confirmed in the user side, and need not to be verified by the GWN. Imaging that a dishonest legitimate user duplicates a few of smart card before it has been input the password, then he/she can send them to illegal user to log-in the system by entering the different passwords with the same legitimate ID. Although the illegal cloned smart card users may hold the different transaction sequence number Ts_{ug} and K_{ug}, they can still pass the authentication with the resynchronization mechanism by the list of $\left(SID, K_{em}\right)$.

4 Solutions

To solve the problems illustrated above, further security measures should be taken to the real-time data access in WSN. Firstly, in order to meet the low-entropy problem of password which cannot be better resolved in [19] and other 2FA schemes, some extra security factors need to be added to the authentication process. Along with the development of science and technology, both mobile and fixed terminal can be equipped with biometric identification system (the latest generation of iPhone products iPhone-X has both fingerprint and face recognition system). The advantages of using biometric keys are listed as following: (i) It cannot be lost or forgotten; (ii) It is very difficult to copy or share; (iii) It is extremely hard to forge or distribute; (iv) It cannot be guessed easily. Because of these security features, biometric keys can be applied as the third security factor to access the WSN. The reason why we don't design a two-factor scheme which only used smart card and biometrics is that the personal biometrics is unique and immutable. Supposed that, one of the biometrics (e.g., fingerprint, face, irises) key is revealed in an unsecure system, he/she can hardly to use this biometric key as the security information in any other systems.

Secondly, since WSN system is constrained in terms of critical resources of sensor nodes' processing energy and memory, as well as the multi traffic of GWN, special attention should be given to the computation cost of security protocols used in WSN. According to [19], using the modular sensor board MSB-430 with the TI MSP430 micro controller and the temperature and relative humidity sensor Sensirion SHT11, each modular exponential operation in ECC-160 algorithm takes 1.2 Ws energy and 11.69 ms execution time. Here, ECC is the latest and widely used lightweight and less computational complexity public key encryption algorithm. By comparison, symmetric key encryption/decryption (128bit AES-CBC) causes 0.72 Ws energy and 4.62 ms of execution time and hash operation (SHA-256) uses 0.27 Ws energy and 1.06 ms of execution time. The results indicate that the hash function cryptographic primitive is the most lightweight and low cost approach for security protocol in WSN, next is symmetric encryption algorithm and last is public key encryption algorithm.

Accordingly, if there have no constraints of energy and overhead, the best way to deal with the security real-time data access in WSN is to use public key cryptographic primitive, since the public key encryption can better protect the user anonymity and untraceability (also can protect the anonymity and untraceability of the sensor nodes). In public key based scheme, the users can send their IDs to the GWN straight by encrypting them with the public key of GWN. After that, the GWN gets the users' IDs by decrypting the corresponding message with its private key. In this way, no additional measures are needed to update user's secret key k_{ug} and one-time-alias identity AID_U which should be taken to achieve user anonymity and untraceability in non-public key system such as [19]. In other words, the desynchronization problem can also be solved with the public key infrastructure due to no secret information will be updated after each successful session. So, the authentication and key agreement phase will become safer and simpler.

However, if the WSN system is low-cost or resource constrained, hash operation based authentication infrastructure may be a better solution, such as Gope et al.'s scheme [19]. When choosing hash function as the main security operation, further measure should be taken to ensure the security and functionality in data access, such as synchronization mechanism, user and sensor node anonymity and untraceability, resistance to known attack, etc. To achieve anonymity and untraceabilty, effective synchronization mechanism must be employed to make authentication information between user and GWN synchronously (the same goes for sensor node and GWN). We have pointed out the weakness of resynchronization mechanism in Gope et al.'s scheme in previous section. To deal with such problem, the better way for user and GWN keep synchronized is to let

GWN reserve both old and new secret key and one-time-alias identity at the same time, i.e., the GWN stores $\left\{k_{ug}^{old}, AID_U^{old}\right\}_{old}$ and $\left\{k_{ug}, AID_U\right\}$. When come to the next authentication phase, if the matched security information is the old one (i.e. $\left\{k_{ug}^{old}, AID_U^{old}\right\}_{old}$), then GWN replaces $\left\{k_{ug}, AID_U\right\}$ with the updated data $\left\{k_{ug}^{new}, AID_U^{new}\right\}_{new}$ after the successful authentication session, i.e., the GWN reserves $\left\{k_{ug}^{old}, AID_U^{old}\right\}_{old}$ and $\left\{k_{ug}^{new}, AID_U^{new}\right\}_{new}$. Otherwise, if the matched security information is the new record (i.e. $\left\{k_{ug}, AID_U\right\}$), then GWN replaces the $\left\{k_{ug}^{old}, AID_U^{old}\right\}_{old}$ with the updated data $\left\{k_{ug}^{new}, AID_U^{new}\right\}_{new}$. This synchronization mechanism also can be used between GWN and sensor nodes, as well as can be used in other hash function based security data access scheme in WSN.

Finally, in order to resist clone card attack which has been discussed before in Gope et al.'s scheme, we suggest that GWN should keep a verifier-table with users' password and biometric keys together in user registration phase. Of course, the verifier-table will not reserve as plaintext, instead the hashed value can be employed. For example, after registration phase of i-th user, the GWN will reserve a record with $\left\{h\left(ID_U^i \| PSW_U^i \| Bio^i\right)\right\}_{user}^i$ in verifier-table, where Bio^i is the biometric key of i-th user. By this method, on the one hand the GWN cannot obtain the password or biometric key of the user (because the characteristics of biometric key which have been discuss before), on the other hand illegal clone card user will not pass the authentication since biometric key can hardly to be forged in user authentication phase.

5   Conclusion

In this paper, we have first briefly reviewed the recently presented Gope et al.'s scheme and point out some flaws existing in their own and some other two-factor schemes, such as not being able to resist privileged insider attack, clone card attack, etc. In order to withstand such drawbacks, then, we proposed some universal approach to withstand these problems. Through our proposed solutions we can not only solve the problems in Gope et al.'s scheme, but also can provide a reference for future security data access in WSN.

Acknowledgements. This work was supported in part by Sichuan Provincial Science and Technology Planning Program (Technology Supporting Plan) of China under project contracts No. 2016GZ0116 and No. 2016GZ0061, and in part by Guangdong Provincial Science and Technology Planning Program of China under project contract No. 2015B090909004. Moreover, the work was supported in part by The Startup Foundation for Introducing Talent of NUIST under project contract No. 2243141701031.

References

1. Lamport, L.: Password authentication with insecure communication. Commun. ACM **24**(11), 770–772 (1981)
2. Wu, T.D.: The secure remote password protocol. In: NDSS, vol. 98 (1998)
3. Katz, J., Ostrovsky, R., Yung, M.: Efficient and secure authenticated key exchange using weak passwords. J. ACM (JACM) **57**(1), 3 (2009)
4. Chang, C.-C., Wu, T.-C.: Remote password authentication with smart cards. IEE Proc. E (Comput. Digit. Tech.) **138**(3), 165–168 (1991)
5. Das, M.L.: Two-factor user authentication in wireless sensor networks. IEEE Trans. Wirel. Commun. **8**(3), 1086–1090 (2009)
6. Chen, T.-H., Shih, W.-K.: A robust mutual authentication protocol for wireless sensor networks. ETRI J. **32**(5), 704–712 (2010)
7. He, D., et al.: An enhanced two-factor user authentication scheme in wireless sensor networks.". Ad Hoc Sens. Wirel. Netw. **10**(4), 361–371 (2010)
8. Huang, H.-F., Chang, Y.-F., Liu, C.-H.: Enhancement of two-factor user authentication in wireless sensor networks. In: Sixth International Conference on Intelligent Information Hiding and Multimedia Signal Processing (IIH-MSP). IEEE (2010)
9. Vaidya, B., Makrakis, D., Mouftah, H.T.: Improved two-factor user authentication in wireless sensor networks. In: IEEE 6th International Conference on Wireless and Mobile Computing, Networking and Communications (WiMob). IEEE (2010)
10. Yoo, S.G., Park, K.Y., Juho Kim, J.: A security-performance-balanced user authentication scheme for wireless sensor networks. Int. J. Distrib. Sens. Netw. **8**(3) (2012). https://doi.org/10.1155/2012/382810
11. Sun, D.-Z., et al.: On the security and improvement of a two-factor user authentication scheme in wireless sensor networks. Pers. Ubiquitous Comput. **17**(5), 895–905 (2013)
12. Wong, K.H.M., et al.: A dynamic user authentication scheme for wireless sensor networks. In: IEEE International Conference on Sensor Networks, Ubiquitous, and Trustworthy Computing, vol. 1. IEEE (2006)
13. Nyang, D.H., Lee, M.-K.: Improvement of Das's two-factor authentication protocol in wireless sensor networks. IACR Cryptology ePrint Archive 2009:631 (2009)
14. Khan, M.K., Alghathbar, K.: Cryptanalysis and security improvements of 'two-factor user authentication in wireless sensor networks'. Sensors **10**(3), 2450–2459 (2010)
15. Fan, R., et al.: A secure and efficient user authentication protocol for two-tiered wireless sensor networks. In: Second Pacific-Asia Conference on Circuits, Communications and System (PACCS), vol. 1. IEEE (2010)
16. Turkanović, M., Brumen, B., Hölbl, M.: A novel user authentication and key agreement scheme for heterogeneous ad hoc wireless sensor networks, based on the Internet of Things notion. Ad Hoc Netw. **20**, 96–112 (2014)
17. Amin, R., Biswas, G.P.: A secure light weight scheme for user authentication and key agreement in multi-gateway based wireless sensor networks. Ad Hoc Netw. **36**, 58–80 (2016)
18. Farash, M.S., et al.: An efficient user authentication and key agreement scheme for heterogeneous wireless sensor network tailored for the Internet of Things environment. Ad Hoc Netw. **36**, 152–176 (2016)
19. Gope, P., Hwang, T.: A realistic lightweight anonymous authentication protocol for securing real-time application data access in wireless sensor networks. IEEE Trans. Ind. Electron. **63**(11), 7124–7132 (2016)

20. Bond, M., et al.: Chip and Skim: cloning EMV cards with the pre-play attack. In: IEEE Symposium on Security and Privacy (SP). IEEE (2014)
21. Wang, D., Wang, P.: On the anonymity of two-factor authentication schemes for wireless sensor networks: attacks, principle and solutions. Comput. Netw. **73**, 41–57 (2014)
22. Gunson, N., Marshall, D., et al.: User perceptions of security and usability of single-factor and two-factor authentication in automated telephone banking. Comput. Secur. **30**(4), 208–220 (2011)
23. Madhusudhan, R., Mittal, R.C.: Dynamic ID-based remote user password authentication schemes using smart cards: a review. J. Netw. Comput. Appl. **35**(4), 1235–1248 (2012)
24. Wang, D., Wang, P.: Two birds with one stone: two-factor authentication with security beyond conventional bound. IEEE Trans. Dependable Secure Comput. (2016)
25. Dolev, D., Yao, A.: On the security of public key protocols. IEEE Trans. Inf. Theor. **29**(2), 198–208 (1983)

Security Threat and Protection in Industrial Control System

Yixiang Jiang[(✉)] and Chengting Zhang

China Tobacco Zhejiang Industrial Co. Ltd., Ningbo 315000, China
gongkonganquan@163.com, titanbyron@126.com

Abstract. With the deepening integration of informatization and industrialization, the industrial control system is facing more and more serious security threats at the same time of rapid development. At present, the legal norms and national security standards in the field of industrial control system are relatively lacking. And there is no strict market access system. In addition, the state's industrial support for domestic industrial control equipment needs to be strengthened. Especially in terms of system security, data security, application security, and security management system, the research investment needs to be further increased, professional and technical forces need to be cultivated and the research of core technologies need to be focused on. To solve the information security problem of industrial control systems has become one of the key topics that the industry pays close attention to. In this paper, the development history of industrial control system is introduced, the root cause of industrial control system security threats is deeply analyzed, the future security threats of industrial control system is pointed out and the safety precautions of industrial control system is put forward. Based on the analysis of this paper, the personal security awareness of the industrial control system can be raised and the challenges of security threats can be better solved.

Keywords: Industrial control system · Information security · Information security precaution

1 Introduction

Nowadays with the deepening integration of information and industrialization, information technology is increasingly used in industrial control systems. The rise and development of the Internet of Things have brought a boom in the close combination of industrial control systems and the Internet, which have greatly promoted the development of industry. However, at the same time, it inevitably brings about information security risks. Especially in the background that information security is highly valued by the state. The security of some core systems in industrial control system is directly related to the national information security. At present, the legal norms and national security standards in the field of industrial control system are relatively lacking, and there is no strict market access system, in addition, the state's industrial support for domestic industrial control equipment needs to be strengthened. The situation must be completely changed. Otherwise, national security and the well-being of the people will

© Springer Nature Switzerland AG 2018
X. Sun et al. (Eds.): ICCCS 2018, LNCS 11068, pp. 49–58, 2018.
https://doi.org/10.1007/978-3-030-00021-9_5

be shrouded in the shadow of the security risks of the industrial control system. Therefore, it has great significance to analyze the security risks of Industrial control system deeply, strengthen the security of the industrial control system especially that of the core system and protect the security of industrial control systems and the entire country.

2 Development Process of Industrial Control System

The industrial control system in early is a closed independent system, a self-contained system running in the field of industrial control. There is no security threats of external malicious attacks or theft of information because of its closure [1], however, with the rapid development of computer technology, communication technology and control technology, the promotion of informatization, the acceleration of industrialization and the integration of Internet of Things technologies, all of which make the relatively closed industrial control systems open, so that industrial control systems start to develop in the network. As a result, the security issues in industrial control system have become increasingly prominent.

Since 2001, the widespread use of common development standards and Internet technologies have led to a substantial increase in attacks including viruses, Trojan and others for industrial control systems (ICS), resulting in the failure of the overall control system and even malicious security incidents, which has serious consequences to people, equipment and environment. In 2010, Siemens first detected the Stuxnet virus, the Webster virus, which attacked the company's industrial control system. In 2011, Microsoft warned that the newly discovered "Duqu" virus could gather intelligence data from industrial control system manufacturers. In 2012, Two U.S. power plants were attacked by the USB virus and industrial control system at each plant was infected with virus; the worst threat in the industrial system hit in 2017 is crypto-ransomware attack. In addition, security researchers discovered and reported hundreds of new vulnerabilities.

In recent years, there are some security incidents that have occurred in the domestic of power, municipal, and petrochemical industries due to virus intrusion [2], which caused certain economic losses. These security incidents have attracted great attention of the competent authorities and users. The Ministry of Industry and Information Technology has organized relevant units to carry out major security inspections of industrial control systems in the field of electric power, petrochemicals, manufacturing, tobacco, and other industries, timely detecting risks, clearing loopholes, and supervising relevant industry units to carry out rectification. Some key units in the fields of petroleum and petrochemical, water conservancy and electric power, municipal transportation also fully recognize the risks and challenges brought about by information security, they take active actions to strengthen the construction of security guarantees, which greatly enhance the security protection capabilities of industrial control system.

Throughout the world, the potential risks of information security in industrial control systems have seriously affected the national security, which has caused great concern about the security of industrial control information in the world. On September 29,

2011, the Ministry of Industry and Information Technology specially prepared and issued Information on Strengthening Information Security of Industrial Control Systems Management Notice (MIIT [2011] No. 451) "document [3]. In this document, it clearly pointed out that industrial control system information security was faced with a serious situation, the effective strategies of strengthening industrial control system information security management were required, the establishment of industrial control system security was imperative.

3 Security Threats of Industrial Control System

With the increasing demand for integration of management and control, the industrial control system and the traditional management system gradually realize network integration, and the openness of industrial control system is becoming stronger and stronger. The widely used common PC servers, PC terminals, general operating systems and databases are highly integrated with emerging technologies such as embedded technologies and wireless technologies [4], which expand the development space of industrial control systems, but are also more susceptible to attacks from viruses, Trojans, and hackers, resulting in a number of security threats. The root causes of the threats are mainly divided into three aspects: weak network management awareness, misuse of mobile storage media and system loopholes.

3.1 Weak Network Management Awareness

The widely use of Internet in the industrial control system has made an indelible contribution to the progress of society. However, at the same time, the potential threats to industrial control systems are becoming increasingly prominent. On the one hand, the application of the Internet provides an opportunity for hacking. Industrial control systems are exposed to information leakage and information tampering. Hackers can conduct attacks through information collection, network scanning and account cracking. Network spies can invade the internal network or implant viruses to steal confidential information. On the other hand, although national cyber security is receiving more and more attention, the awareness of universal network security is still weak. Corporate information is confronted with the risk of being posted online by the users.

3.2 Misuse of Removable Storage Media

Currently, mobile storage media, as important means to realize information dissemination and exchange, undoubtedly becomes an integral part of our network life. It provides us with convenience but also brings security risks. On the one hand, employees with low security awareness may inadvertently disseminate some important confidential information through storage media while storing information; on the other hand, users' storage devices are easily invaded by viruses, trojans and the like, therefore, internal information may be illegally stolen or tampered with and then disseminated through the Internet by criminals.

3.3 System Loopholes

System loopholes are the design flaws of application software and operating system. System loopholes also exist in industrial control systems and they are important parts of security threats in industrial control systems. Although system loopholes can be repaired later by means of updating system patches, it will take some time from vulnerability discovery to be made up, at the same time, patch updates for each terminal is also a certain degree of difficulty, therefore, the lag of patch updates makes it easy for criminals to take advantage of, it is vulnerable for systems to be infected with malicious attacks and vandalism. Other threats such as computer viruses, internal leaks, external leaks, spy hackers and the like also bring serious challenges to industrial control systems. Take the Stuxnet worm as a representative example, Stuxnet virus transmitted through the U disk and local area network brings a major disaster to the industrial control system. The virus Implements attacks by reprogramming the software, controls the key processes and opens a series of executive procedures, which eventually leads to self-destruction of the entire system, although protection programs, solutions such as system upgrades, virus killing and so on for this security threats are introduced one after another, it does not form a complete set of security management system, it is not enough to meet the security requirements in the field of industrial control. Therefore, industrial control system security is still facing serious challenges urging to be solved.

4   The Future Security Threats of Industrial Control System

4.1   General and Unexpected Malware Infections Are on the Rise

According to statistics, except for a few cases in past industrial control system crime, cybercriminals have not yet developed a simple and reliable solution that can benefit from attacking industrial control systems. They typically use generic malicious code to attack more traditional goals, causing unexpected infections and incidents in industrial networks. This trend will bring more serious security challenges to the industrial environment. Therefore, industrial companies should attach great importance to regularly update the software in industrial systems to keep up with the corporate network.

4.2   Directed Ransomware Attacks Are More Risky and Harder to Protect

Take the WannaCry and ExPetr attacks as examples. The most serious threat to the industrial system in 2017 was crypto-ransomware attacks. The ICS CERT (Industrial Control Systems Network Emergency Response Team) report released by Kaspersky Lab noted that in the first half of the year, experts found 33 malicious software families of encryption ransomware. After analyzing a series of targeted ransomware attacks that have taken place in the past, security experts draw a conclusion that compared with IT systems, operating systems are more vulnerable to attacks because they are generally accessible through the Internet. In addition, the damage caused by malicious software is not only huge but also difficult to protect. Industrial companies demonstrate the difficulty of defending against cyberattacks that operate on technical system infrastructures.

All of these factors have prompted industrial systems to be the target of ransomware attacks. Therefore, industrial companies should attach great importance to such ransomware attacks.

4.3 Industrial Internet Spy Incidents Are on the Rise

The growing threat brought by ransomware attacks on industrial companies has spawned cybercrime in other areas. By stealing data from industrial information systems, targeted attacks are implemented by the attackers.

4.4 Underground Black Market New Activities Provide Attack Services and Intrusion Tools

According to the survey, black market demands for ICS 0Day vulnerabilities have been increasing in recent years, suggesting that targeted attacks may be on the rise and huge gains will drive the growth of the black market. As a result, some new ICS configuration data and credentials of industrial companies are stolen. Also there may be botnets based on industrial node product components. Designing and launching advanced cyberattacks on physical objects and systems requires expertise knowledge about ICS and related industries.

4.5 New Malicious Software and Malicious Tools

In the context of the growing threat from industrial control systems, new malicious software and malicious tools designed to attack industrial networks and assets may emerge. The malicious software has subtle actions, which lurks in IT networks to evade detection and can only be activated in less-secure OT facilities. There may also be ransomware which targets at low-level ICS devices and physical assets (pumps and power switches, etc.). Therefore, industrial control enterprises should pay high attention to the security of the entire industrial network to prevent crime.

4.6 ICS Released by Security Vendors May Be Used by Criminals

Researchers publicly released various attack vectors related to industrial assets and infrastructure, and analyzed the malicious tool sets that they discovered. These efforts have been excellent. However, it also provides criminals with new opportunities. For example, after the CrashOverride/Industroyer toolset was disclosed, hackers launched DOS (denial of service) attacks on power and energy facilities. Criminals also introduced ransomware and even formulated profit plans during the power outage. They can also build operational malicious worms based on programmable logic controller (PLC) worm concepts. There are also criminals who are trying to implement malware using a standard PLC programming language. In addition, they may also improve the concept of this PLC infection. At present, the existing security scheme cannot find these two types of malware.

4.7   Changes Has Happened in National Regulations

In 2018, a number of cyber security regulations related to industrial system will be implemented. For example, companies involved in critical infrastructure and industrial asset facilities may need to conduct more security assessments. It will be bound to raise awareness of protection and security, so that we may discover more new loopholes and expose more threats.

4.8   Industrial Security Insurance Is Getting Hot Day by Day, and Investment Is on the Rise

For industrial enterprises, industrial network risk insurance is becoming an indispensable part of risk management. Network security events, like terrorist events, would not be embodied in insurance contracts in the past. However, the current situation is changing. Network security companies and insurance companies have taken new measures. In 2018, security audit/assessment and event response are all on the rise, which promotes industrial facility managers and operators to raise awareness of network security.

5   Security Precautions in Industrial Control System

The traditional IT security is network security, while industrial control system security includes both network security and security of the underlying physical environment. The industrial control system is directly connected with the production environment and the real physical world. It is the traditional IT embedding in the key infrastructure, integrating the information, communication, sensing, and control to form the CPS (Cyber-Physical Systems) environment [5], once destroyed, it directly inflicts tremendous damage on the actual engineering environment, which causes far greater losses than traditional IT security incidents. The security of industrial control systems needs to handle two types of threats, on one hand, for "unconscious threats", constructing physical environments and alarm systems related to windproof, waterproof, fireproof and lightning protection to avoid natural disasters; On the other hand, for the aging of the instrument itself, using PHM technology to supervise and predict the state of life of the management equipment [6].

A variety of security technologies are required for malicious threat sources. Commonly used industrial control system information protection equipment and technology include industrial firewalls, intrusion detection and prevention, security audit [7]. However, there is still a lack of quantitative evaluation standards for information security protection, and an authoritative assessment, evaluation and verification institution has not yet been set up to effectively assess the vulnerability of industrial control systems and the level of information security. Solving the many security threats for industrial control systems, guarding against all forms of information leakage, preventing the industrial control system from being invaded illegally and taking security precaution measures to provide a more complete and safe environment for the industrial control systems should be the top priority in the field of industrial control.

The security precautions are mainly divided into basic security protection, system security protection, data security protection, application security protection, the improvement of the security management system and the realization of autonomy in industrial control system.

5.1 Basic Security Protection

The basic security protection includes industrial firewalls and intelligent protection devices [8]. It mainly uses network control, application layer control and external device control on industrial control system to prevent system confidential information from being invaded and stolen. Network control is the port management, which will disable TCP, UDP, ICMP and other ports except when necessary. Application layer control is the management of communication tools, such as adding the specified web access address or adding the specified recipient to receive data to effectively prevent the invasion of external viruses and the illegal dissemination of internal information. External device control is the audit and management of external devices. It performs security reviews on removable storage media, hard disks, and peripheral interfaces to prevent Trojan viruses from stealing terminal data through removable storage media.

5.2 System Security Protection

System security protection includes vulnerabilities, configuration defects and unauthorized access to resources and other issues in industrial control system and device-specific operating system, system-level protection is strong and security measures are rich [9]. It mainly Implements uniform management for the distribution of terminals to protect the security of industrial control system. The number of terminals in the industrial control system is very large. It is not enough for security of the entire system to rely solely on the user's personal security awareness. It is also impractical to protect the terminals one by one. System security protection can centrally manage the terminals. It includes account information management, real-time monitoring and automatic updates for anti-virus software, the safe deletion of files, real-time monitoring and automatic updates of system patches. Through the security protection of the entire system, realizing real-time monitoring and upgrade of each terminal to prevent criminals from threatening security of industrial control system using system vulnerabilities.

5.3 Data Security Protection

Data security protection mainly enforces encryption and privilege control to conduct a comprehensive security protection on the internal control system information. It mainly includes data integrity, data confidentiality, backup and recovery, the specific measures should have the ability of detecting system management data, the integrity of the important business data in the transmission and storage process is destroyed, and taking the necessary recovery measures, using encryption or other effective measures to achieve the confidentiality of system management data, authentication information and important business data transmission and storage, the encrypted data, whether accidentally leaked by employee or maliciously stolen by hackers, cannot be accessed once it leaves the security zone of an industrial control system [10]. In addition, providing local data backup and recovery functions, full data backup is performed at least once a day, backup media is stored offsite, providing hardware redundancy of major network devices, communication lines, and data processing systems, which can ensure high availability of system [11]. Data is the core of the entire system. Data security protection prevents hazards of the entire system caused by internal information Leakage. It is the most important part of industrial control system security precautions.

5.4   Application Security Protection

Application security protection mainly includes identity authentication, access control, security audit, remaining information protection, communication integrity, communication confidentiality, non-repudiation, software fault tolerance, and resource control. The specific measures should have the ability of providing a dedicated login control module to perform identity identification and authentication on the logged-in user; using identity authentication, uniqueness checking of the user identity, complexity checking of the user identity authentication information, login failure processing functions, and configuring related parameters according to the security policy [12]. It provides functions of access control, controlling user access to files, database tables, and other objects based on security policies; configuring access control policies by authorized principals, strictly restricting access permissions for default accounts; strictly controlling user's operation on sensitive identification of important information resources based on security policies, providing security audit functions that cover each user, and auditing important security events such as user login, user exit, user addition, and user permission modification in the application system.

5.5   The Improvement of the Security Management System

The semi-closed nature of the industrial control system determines the importance of the management system security to the security of the industrial control system. Under the new situation of growing security problems, our information security standard system of industrial control system still needs to be further perfected, improving the country's capabilities of detection, monitoring and early warning of hidden dangers and risks in information security, performing system security tests, establishing a risk assessment system and focusing on the weak points of the system. The information security standard system in the field of industrial control system should provide clear requirements for the security of industrial control systems in terms of connection, networking, configuration, equipment selection, upgrade, and data emergency management [13]. Higher requirements on the security of industrial control system functions, information and equipment are put forward, at the meantime, it is necessary to consider the issue of integration on functional security and information security [14]. National or authoritative industrial control system information security assessment, evaluation, verification agencies should be established to provide more effective information security rating assessment.

5.6   The Realization of Autonomy in Industrial Control System

Information security has risen to the national strategic issue. In the industrial control system, hardware support is the core chip. At present, China's chip is mainly dependent on imports, and the security of information and data is difficult to guarantee. In addition, according to statistics of national network security inspections in key fields in 2013, the foreign products proportion of key equipment and basic hardware and software in China's important information systems and industrial control systems is also high [15], the security foundation is not strong. According to the statistical situation, the operating systems, databases, servers, and data storage devices in important industrial control systems are all mainly dominated by foreign products. From a category perspective, Supervisory Control And Data Acquisition (SCADA), Distributed Control System (DCS), Process Control System (PCS), and Programmable Logic Controller (PLC) are also based on foreign products. In terms of maintenance of equipment, according to the survey, thousands of industrial control systems are operated and maintained by foreign manufacturers. We do not have the ability to maintain independently, the controllability of system operation is low, and there is a lack of supervision over these products and services, the necessary technical testing measures and security controllable solutions are also not enough, security risk is difficult to control. Therefore, more attention should be paid to speed up the cultivation of professional technical strength and research the core technologies in industrial control system. Realizing the autonomy of core chips and basic software is the cornerstone of the security and prevention in industrial control system, at the same time, it is also the only way to realize the autonomy of China's industrial control system and ensure the information security of the whole country.

6   Conclusion

The security issue of industrial control system is a major strategic issue related to national security. Nowadays, with the deepening integration of informatization and industrialization, the information security situation of China's industrial control systems is becoming more and more serious. It is extremely urgent to strengthen the integration of industrial control system and information security technologies. Especially in terms of system security, data security, application security, and security management system, it is necessary to increase research investment, accelerate the cultivation of professional and technical forces, and focus on the research of core technologies to further improve the information security standard system of China's industrial control system and achieve autonomy in industrial control system, through the active participation in the research work of the international standards for information security in industrial control system, China's standard status in the field of information security of industrial control system can be enhanced, the healthy development of China's industrial control system industry can be better promoted.

References

1. Wang, X., Cui, b., Li, S.: Thoughts and suggestions on information security of industrial control system. Inf. Netw. Secur. (8), 36–37 (2012)
2. Defense against industrial security system security risks, China is in action. Inf. Secur. Commun. Secur. (6), 18–21 (2014)
3. Long, P., Guo, Q., Liu, X.: Information security of industrial control systems. Autom. Instrument. (5), 152–153, +157 (2014)
4. Chen, Z., Zhang, X., Sun, N.: Security threat analysis and protection of industrial control systems. Microprocessors **37**(6), 85–88 (2016)
5. Peng, Y., Jiang, C., Xiang, C.: Modeling and impact evaluation of critical infrastructure information physical attack. J. Tsinghua Univ. (Sci. Technol.) **53**(12), 1653–1663, +1669 (2013)
6. Tao, Y., Li, N., Zeng, G.: Overview of industrial control system security. Comput. Eng. Appl. **52**(13), 8–18 (2016)
7. Qu, H.: A survey of information security research in industrial control systems. Process Autom. Instrument. **38**(7), 4–8 (2017)
8. Wu, J.: Status and solutions of network security in industrial control systems. Petrochem. Autom. **53**(4), 1–5 (2017)
9. Wang, Y., Chen, S., Cheng, N.: Research on information security of industrial control systems. Inf. Netw. Secur. (9), 35–39 (2016)
10. Wang, W., Liu, Y.: The research on analysis of security threats and prevention in industrial control system. Inf. Secur. Commun. Secur. (2), 33–35 (2012)
11. Zhang, M., Zhang, W., Han, G.: Research on information security protection system of industrial control system. Ind. Control Comput. **26**(10), 25–27 (2013)
12. Li, J., Hao, Y., Li, N.: Information security protection in industrial control systems. Electr. Power **48**(10), 139–143 (2015)
13. Xu, L., Xu, J., Tang, G.: The Research on the analysis of network security risk in industrial control system. Electron. Sci. Technol. **2**(6), 679–684 (2015)
14. Zhao, Y., Liu, D.: Analysis on functional security and basic requirements of information security coordination. China Instrument. (12), 48–50 (2015)
15. Yin, L.: China urgently needs to establish an industrial control security system. China Inf. Secur. (4), 54–56 (2016)

Sharing Economy Protocol with Privacy Preservation and Fairness Based on Blockchain

Zhenhua Liu, Yuanyuan Li$^{(\boxtimes)}$, Yaohui Liu, and Dong Yuan

School of Mathematics and Statistics, Xidian University, Xi'an 710071, China
liyuanyuan4621@163.com

Abstract. Blockchain, as the core technology of cryptocurrency, provides a novel idea for the sharing economy. A user pays the agreed money to the property owner without any trust third party in blockchain, which leads to the leakage of privacy due to openness of the blockchain. To alleviate the privacy concern, a protocol is proposed to not only protect privacy through breaking the link between the user and the property owner but also ensure the fairness among parties joined in transaction. In addition, double-spending and double-usage are detected and prevented by applying smart contract in the protocol. Compared with the existing related works, the proposed protocol is secure, effective and practical.

Keywords: Sharing economy · Blockchain · Blind signature
Smart contract

1 Introduction

The emerging blockchain technology plays a special role in the daily life due to its decentralization. The development of the blockchain is divided into three phases: In the blockchain 1.0, the blockchain is only used to build cryptocurrency [1]. In the blockchain 2.0, smart contract combined with cryptocurrency, which has a profound effect on the financial yield. In the blockchain 3.0, the blockchain provides the decentralized solutions for various industries outside financial such as e-voting [2] and medical [3], where the sharing economy that provides great convenience for human emerges in the blockchain 3.0 [4]. For example, the German company (Slock.it) has developed the Ethereum Computer that combines smart objects (such as rooms and bikes) with the blockchain so that these smart objects are rentable without trust.

However, the privacy problem impedes the growth of the sharing economy. In the sharing economy, the renter will be granted access for the smart objects when she/he pays for the property owner. Unpredictably, if the user directly sends their bitcoins to the property owner in plaintext, any malicious users can learn their activities via observing the blockchain and analyzing relevance between the user and the owner, which causes the leakage of privacy.

© Springer Nature Switzerland AG 2018
X. Sun et al. (Eds.): ICCCS 2018, LNCS 11068, pp. 59–69, 2018.
https://doi.org/10.1007/978-3-030-00021-9_6

In order to solve the above problems, many researchers have proposed a series of solutions including anonymous payment and mixing services. Anonymous payment means that anyone cannot learn his real identity when the user performs a transaction in the blockchain. A bitcoin mixing service provides the anonymity by transferring payments from an input set of bitcoin addresses to an output set of bitcoin addresses. In the yield of anonymous payment, Zerocash [5] and Zerocoin [6] provided anonymous payments via the use of zero-knowledge proof, but they are independent with bitcoin. Saxena et al. [7] proposed a scheme that protects user's privacy excellently. Unfortunately, the parties can still violate user's anonymity. In another yield of mixing services, Bonneau et al. [8] constructed Mixcoin that uses a trusted third party to mix bitcoin addresses, but the malicious third party may try to dig out user's privacy and steal bitcoin, where the malicious users can be detected but not prevented. Valenta et al. [9] established Blincoin that improves Mixcoin by preserving user's privacy, but the malicious user cannot still be prevented. Henrik et al. [10] presented CoinParty that is reliable if two thirds of the mixing parties are honest. Maxwell et al. [11] and Ruffing et al. [12] improved the advance works separately via preventing the malicious users. CoinSwap [13] is a fair-exchange mixer that allows two parties to send bitcoin anonymously through an intermediary. CoinSwap cannot provide anonymity against even an honest but curious intermediary.

The proposed protocol mainly focuses on anonymity (i.e., unlinkable transactions). While the blockchain displays the set of payers and payees publicly during an epoch, no one can learn which payer paid which payee. As is described in blindly signed contracts [14], we apply a intermediary (may be malicious) to break the link between all payers and payees.

Our Contributions. We propose a system protocol that can be applied to the sharing economy. The main techniques and contributions are summarized as follows:

- We add an intermediary in the transaction to achieve unlinkable transactions and then ensure anonymity.
- Due to the use of smart contract and blind signature, the fairness among the renter, the property owner and the intermediary is ensured. In addition, double-spending and double-usage are detected and prevented in the proposed protocol.
- We analyze the security and efficiency of the proposed protocol, and give the functionality comparisons with related works.

Organizations. The rest of this paper is organized as follows: Sect. 2 introduces some backgrounds. Section 3 focuses on the system model and secure requirements. Section 4 mainly presents our proposed protocol, analyzes security and efficiency, and gives the comparisons between new protocol and related work in functionality. Finally, the conclusions is shown in Sect. 5.

2 Backgrounds

In this section, some backgrounds of technology are described as follows:

2.1 Blockchain

Blockchain, as the core of cryptocurrency, is considered to be a chained data structure in which data blocks are sequentially connected in a chronological order. Roughly speaking, the blockchain is a system that involves multiple participants who achieve consensus over the dataset. The blockchain system is developed under different trust models with different consensus protocols. There are two main types of trust models: one assumes all participants are equivalent (public blockchain) and another one has participants with different privileges for block construction (private and federated blockchain). Under a given trust model, the system can use sundry consensus protocols including proof-of-work [1], proof-of-stake [15], or BFT [17].

In addition, there are four important features in the blockchain system: (1) decentralization, which means that each participants of the system keeps a complete copy of the blockchain, and the failure of any single node cannot affect the whole blockchain network; (2) public accessibility, that is, all information stored in blockchain is publicly accessible to anyone; (3) immutability, in other words, all information added to the blockchain is not modifiable or removable; (4) anonymity, i.e., any party of the transaction in the blockchain does not breach his identity, which protect privacy of traders.

Blockchain has had a profound impact on IoT [16] life with the development of the society and can also make more goods (e.g. bicycle and tenement) sharing. Blockchain provides a brand-new technical support for the realization of the sharing economy, and it is expected to support multiple sharing economic scenarios such as sharing of transportation, sharing of education, sharing of housing, and sharing of energy. Blockchain is an ideal solution for sharing economy.

2.2 Smart Contract

Smart contract (aka transaction contract) [18] is a protocol that is automatically executed on a computer system when certain conditions are satisfied. Blockchain-based smart contract includes mechanisms of processing and preservation in transaction, as well as a complete state machine for receiving and processing various smart contracts, where processing and preservation in transaction are completed in blockchain. Transactions mainly contain data that needs to be sent, and events are descriptions of these data. After the transaction and event information are included to the smart contract, the state in the contract resource set will be updated, which will trigger the smart contract to perform state machine judgment. If the trigger conditions of one or more instructions in the automatic state machine are satisfied, the state machine will be automatically performed by selecting the instructions in smart contract according to the preset information. Transaction contracts are written as scripts. e.g., the user will pay the owner if some conditions are met. In addition, we can lock a transaction by using the "checklocktimeverify" feature [20] of scripts, so that the funds can be withdrawn if the bitcoin in contract have not been spent within a given locking time t.

2.3 Blind Signature

The proposed protocol will apply Zuo et al.'s [19] blind signature scheme in the standard model to prevent the intermediary from learning information about users. Assuming that the length of message needed to be signed is k, H is hash function, and the scheme consists of three algorithms. The details of the blind signature scheme are described as follows:

- **Setup.** $\mathbb{G}_1$ and $\mathbb{G}_2$ are additive cyclic group and multiplicative cyclic group of order q separately. Let g be the generator of $\mathbb{G}_1$ and $e : \mathbb{G}_1 \times \mathbb{G}_1 \to \mathbb{G}_2$ be a bilinear map. The system selects $k + 2$ numbers $(g_2, u', u_1, \cdots, u_k)$ from $\mathbb{G}_1$. The signer chooses $a \in \mathbb{Z}_q^*$ and computes $pk = g_1 = g^a$, where $(sk = a, pk)$ is the secret and public key pair of singer and $(pk, g_2, u', u_1, \cdots, u_k)$ are the public parameters.
- **Sign.** The user asks signer to sign a blinded serial number m, which requires two rounds of interaction as follows:
  - *Step* 1. The user randomly selects $m \leftarrow \{0, 1\}^k$ and computes $w = u' \cdot \prod_{i \in A} u_i$, where A is the set of index i of $m[i] = 1$, and $m[i]$ is the value of i-th bit in the message m. Finally, the user sends $w' = w \cdot g^k$ to the signer.
  - *Step* 2. After obtaining w', the signer chooses a random number $r \in \mathbb{Z}_q^*$, calculates $\sigma' = (\sigma_1', \sigma_2') = (g_2^a (w')^r, g^r)$ and sends σ' to the user.
  - *Step* 3. After getting σ', the user unblinds σ' to get

$$\sigma = \left(\sigma_1' \cdot (\sigma_2')^{-k}, \sigma_2'\right) = (g_2^a (w')^r \cdot g^{-kr}, g^r) = (g_2 w^r, g^r) = (\sigma_1, \sigma_2)$$

  and sends σ to the owner.
- **Verify.** The verifier checks $e(\sigma_1, g) = e(g_1, g_2) e(w, \sigma_2)$, if the equation holds, returns 1.

3 System Model

We will introduce the system model in this section via two parts including *overview workflow* and *security requirements*.

3.1 Overview Workflow

Assuming that the user would like to rent the bike from the property owner. If the user sends bitcoin directly to the owner in plaintext, any malicious user learn their activities via observing the blockchain and analyzing relevance between the

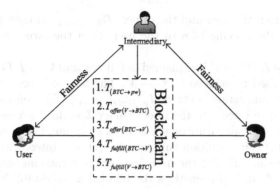

Fig. 1. Overview of the proposed protocol

user and the owner, which causes the leakage of privacy. The solution used to protect privacy between the payer and the payee is to employ an intermediary party $\mathcal{I}$ that breaks the link between them. The owner and the user reach an agreement on renting the bike that the user pays the agreed money (a bicoins) for the owner and the owner grants the power accessed to the specific bike for the user. As is described in Fig. 1, the proposed protocol that is blockchain-based sharing bike involves four parties.

- *Owner.* The property owner rents her/his bikes to the user in exchange for bitcoin. Since the owner is semi-trusted, she/he may attempt to rent the property concurrently to different users for maximizing benefit.
- *User.* The user rents a specific bike from the owner through the blockchain, and she/he also is not fully trusted and may try to minimize costs by double-spending.
- *Intermediary.* The intermediary $\mathcal{I}$ is used to break the link between the owner and the user. $\mathcal{I}$ is semi-trusted since she/he may refuse to provide a valid voucher to the user or redeem the voucher to the owner.
- *Blockchain.* The blockchain is the platform to carry out transaction contracts among the owner, the user and the intermediary. The blockchain is accessible to anyone including malicious users and is maintained by a large number of participants through mining.

We make a little modification to Heilman et al.'s scheme [10] as follows. The user would first send $a + w$ bitcoin to the intermediary $\mathcal{I}$, and then $\mathcal{I}$ would send a bitcoin to the owner, where w bitcoin are reserved by $\mathcal{I}$ as reward. A blind signature scheme [12] is used to prevent $\mathcal{I}$ from learning who the user pays, and bitcoin transaction contract is applied to achieve fair exchange among the user, the owner and the intermediary $\mathcal{I}$. In our protocol, there are two fair exchanges $BTC \rightarrow V$ (implemented via $T_{offer(BTC \rightarrow V)}$ which is created by the user and $T_{fulfill(BTC \rightarrow V)}$ which is created by $\mathcal{I}$) and $V \rightarrow BTC$ (implemented via $T_{offer(V \rightarrow BTC)}$ which is created by $\mathcal{I}$ and $T_{fulfill(V \rightarrow BTC)}$ which is created by the owner). In addition, our protocol also includes a transaction contract

$T_{(BTC \rightarrow pw)}$ between the user and the owner. $T_{(BTC \rightarrow pw)}$ is used to transfer the password about the specific bike to the user when the owner gets the agreed bitcoin.

Fair exchange $BTC \rightarrow V$ is explained as follows, and $V \rightarrow BTC$ is analogous. Locking time is used to achieve $BTC \rightarrow V$. The fair exchange starts when the user generates a transaction contract $T_{offer(BTC \rightarrow V)}$. The contract means that the user offers $a + w$ bitcoin to the intermediary $\mathcal{I}$ under the condition: $\mathcal{I}$ must calculates a valid blind signature on the blinded serial number w' within the time window tw, and if this condition isn't satisfied, $a + w$ bitcoin will be returned to the user. More specifically, the user first selects a random serial number m, blinds it to get w', and then employs the blinded w' to establish a transaction contract $T_{offer(BTC \rightarrow V)}$ with an output of $a + w$ bitcoin that is spendable in a future transaction T_f if one of the following situations occurs:

- T_f is signed by $\mathcal{I}$ and contains a valid blind signature σ' on w' within tw, or
- T_f is signed by the user and the time window tw has expired.

The contract $T_{offer(BTC \rightarrow V)}$ will be accomplished if the intermediary $\mathcal{I}$ posts a transaction $T_{fulfill(BTC \rightarrow V)}$ that contains a valid blind signature to the blockchain. That is to say, the first situation occurs and so the $a + w$ bitcoin in $T_{offer(BTC \rightarrow V)}$ is transferred to $\mathcal{I}$. If $\mathcal{I}$ doesn't accomplish the transaction $T_f = T_{fulfill(BTC \rightarrow V)}$, that is, $\mathcal{I}$ doesn't provide a valid blind signature within locking time tw, then the user signs and submits a transaction to the blockchain that returns $a + w$ bitcoin back to the user, thus satisfying the second situation described above.

3.2   Security Requirements

- *Fair Exchange.* The protocol is a fair exchange [14] between V and BTC, and thus ensures the fairness via the following aspects:
    - The malicious intermediary $\mathcal{I}$ cannot obtain bitcoin from the user unless $\mathcal{I}$ provides a blind signature σ' honestly for the user, and the malicious user cannot refuse to give $a + w$ bitcoin to $\mathcal{I}$ when he/she obtains a valid blind signature σ' from $\mathcal{I}$;
    - The malicious intermediary $\mathcal{I}$ cannot refuse to pay bitcoin for the owner when $\mathcal{I}$ receives a valid voucher from the user, and the malicious owner cannot receive a bitcoin without providing a valid voucher $\mathcal{I}$.
- *Double-Spending.* The user cannot spend the same bitcoin more than once [14].
- *Double-Usage.* The owner cannot rent the specific room to different users [21].
- *Unforgeability.* The user cannot establish a valid voucher V without interacting with $\mathcal{I}$, i.e., the signature is unforgeable [19].
- *Sybil Resistance.* The proposed protocol should be resistant to Sybil that attempt to de-anonymize a target user [14].

4 The New Sharing Economy Protocol

4.1 The Proposed Protocol

As is depicted in Fig. 2, there are two fair exchanges $BTC \rightarrow V$ (implemented via $T_{offer(BTC \rightarrow V)}$ and $T_{fulfill(BTC \rightarrow V)}$ and $V \rightarrow BTC$ (implemented via $T_{offer(V \rightarrow BTC)}$ and $T_{fulfill(V \rightarrow BTC)}$ in our protocol. In addition, our protocol also includes a transaction contract $T_{(BTC \rightarrow pw)}$ between the user and the owner. The process of our protocol are as follows:

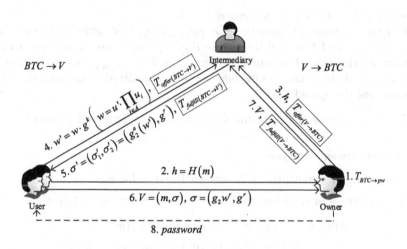

Fig. 2. The interactive process among participants

1. The owner creates a fresh temporary bitcoin address to receive a payment and establishes a transaction contract $T_{(BTC \rightarrow pw)}$.
2. The user selects $m \leftarrow \{0,1\}^k$ randomly and sends $h = H(m)$ to the owner, where k is the length of the message m.
3. The owner sends h to the intermediary $\mathcal{I}$ and asks $\mathcal{I}$ to create a transaction contract $T_{offer(V \rightarrow BTC)}$ offering a bitcoin to the owner under the condition: The owner must provide a valid voucher within locking time t_2.
4. The intermediary $\mathcal{I}$ checks whether h matches any h from prior transaction contracts signed by $\mathcal{I}$. If not, $\mathcal{I}$ creates the requested contract $T_{offer(V \rightarrow BTC)}$ and submits it to the blockchain.
5. The user blinds m to obtain $w' = w \cdot g^k (w = u' \cdot \prod_{i \in A} u_i)$ and waits for $T_{offer(V \rightarrow BTC)}$ to be confirmed. Then the user creates a transaction contract $T_{offer(BTC \rightarrow V)}$ offering $a + w$ bitcoin to $\mathcal{I}$ under the condition: $\mathcal{I}$ must provide a valid blind signature to the user within locking time t_1, where in $T_{offer(BTC \rightarrow V)}$, there are a bitcoin that will be offered to the owner, and w bitcoin are kept by $\mathcal{I}$ as reward for completing its roles.

6. $\mathcal{I}$ must wait for the transaction contract $T_{offer(BTC \to V)}$ to be confirmed to prevent the user from double-spending the bitcoin in $T_{offer(BTC \to V)}$. Then $\mathcal{I}$ establishes a transaction $T_{fulfill(BTC \to V)}$ to accomplish the fair exchange $BTC \to V$ and posts $T_{offer(BTC \to V)}$ to the blockchain, where $T_{fulfill(BTC \to V)}$ includes the blind signature $\sigma' = (\sigma'_1, \sigma'_2) = (g_2^a (w')^r, g^r)$, thus $a + w$ bitcoin of $T_{offer(BTC \to V)}$ are transferred to $\mathcal{I}$.

7. The user learns σ' from $T_{fulfill(BTC \to V)}$ in the blockchain, unblinds σ' to get

$$\sigma = \left(\sigma'_1 \cdot (\sigma'_2)^{-k}, \sigma'_2 \right) = (g_2^a (w')^r \cdot g^{-kr}, g^r) = (g_2 w^r, g^r)$$

and sends $V = (m, \sigma)$ to the owner.

8. The owner creates a transaction $T_{fulfill(V \to BTC)}$ that contains the voucher $V = (m, \sigma)$, and thus the bitcoin in $T_{offer(V \to BTC)}$ are transferred to the owner. At this time, the transaction contract $T_{(BTC \to pw)}$ goes work, that is, the password about the specific bike will be transmitted to the user when the owner gets the agreed bitcoin.

The above process complete the description of the proposed protocol.

4.2   Correctness Analysis

The correctness of signatures are briefly analyzed as follows:

- The correctness of the blind signature σ' on w' is proved as follows:

$$e(\sigma'_1, g) = e(g_2^a (w')^r, g) = e(g_2^a, g) \cdot e((w')^r, g)$$
$$= e(g_2, g^a \cdot) e(w', g^r) = e(g_1, g_2) \cdot e(\sigma'_2, w')$$

- The correctness of the valid signature σ on m is proved as follows:

$$e(\sigma_1, g) = e(g_2^a w^r, g) = e(g_2^a, g) \cdot e(w^r, g)$$
$$= e(g_2, g^a) \cdot e(w, g^r) = e(g_1, g_2) \cdot e(\sigma_2, w)$$

4.3   Security Analysis

- *Fair Exchange.* The proposed protocol can prevent each party from cheating each other.
  - The first fair exchange $BTC \to V$ ensures that the intermediary $\mathcal{I}$ cannot obtain $a + w$ bitcoin in $T_{offer(BTC \to V)}$ without providing a valid voucher V to the user, and the user cannot refuse to pay $\mathcal{I}$ $a + w$ bitcoin after receiving a valid voucher V.
  - The second fair exchange $V \to BTC$ ensures that the property owner cannot get a bitcoin in $T_{offer(V \to BTC)}$ from $\mathcal{I}$ without redeeming V, and $\mathcal{I}$ cannot refuse to redeem $V = (sn, \sigma)$ that issued to the user. The reason is as follows: As is described in the proposed protocol, the intermediary $\mathcal{I}$ commits to redeem the voucher V when $T_{offer(V \to BTC)}$ is posted to the blockchain. In addition, $T_{offer(V \to BTC)}$ is posted to the blockchain before $T_{offer(BTC \to V)}$, which means that the user cannot pay $\mathcal{I}$ $a + w$ bitcoin unless $\mathcal{I}$ has committed to redeem V.

- *Double-Spending.* The intermediary $\mathcal{I}$ will check whether $h = H(m)$ has appeared in the blockchain if the owner sends h to $\mathcal{I}$. If yes, $\mathcal{I}$ will refuse to establish the transaction contract $T_{offer(V \to BTC)}$, which ensures that the valid voucher cannot be double-spent (that is to say, the user cannot spend the same bitcoin more than once).
- *Double-Usage.* At the beginning, since the owner has submitted a transaction contract $T_{(BTC \to pw)}$ to the blockchain, which means that the owner commits to transfer the password to the user when he/she acquires the agreed bitcoin from the user.
- *Unforgeability.* Unforgeability is achieved by the technology of blind signature, which ensures that only the intermediary $\mathcal{I}$ can issue voucher $V = (m, \sigma)$. In addition, unforgeablity of the blind signature scheme is proved to be secure in the standard model, which refers to [18].
- *Sybil Resistance.* The attackers may try to create many Sybil nodes under his control and then deanonymize the target user by forcing the target to mix with Sybil nodes. In order to attack the proposed protocol, m payers and m payees that occupy most of the intermediary $\mathcal{I}$'s resources may be created by the attackers to launch Sybil attack, leaving only a single slot available for the targeted payer and payee. We use transaction fees to raise the costs of Sybil attack by requiring each Sybil node to pay a fee voucher of low value. If $\mathcal{I}$ performs Sybil attack, avoids paying the low value but must pay all five transactions.

4.4   Efficiency Analysis

In the proposed protocol, the blind signature occupies the most of computation costs. Then we analyze the computation costs mainly in the blind signature. We set τ_M, τ_E, τ_B to denote multiplication operating time, exponentiation time and bilinear pairing operating time separately. Since in the process of blinding the message m, the value of i-th bit in m is used to blind the message, then "$<$" means that the computation costs is at most the value of the right side. The costs of each phase in blind signature are as in Table 1:

Table 1. Complexity analysis of the blind signature

Algorithm	Computation costs
Setup	τ_E
Sign	$< (k+1)\tau_M + 4\tau_E$
Verify	$3\tau_B + \tau_E$

4.5   Functionality Comparisons

In the previous work, Xu et al. [21] also put forward an approach for sharing economy that protects privacy by applying a zero-knowledge scheme. The difference with our protocol is that there must exist two proxies in their scheme, which causes greater costs. Our protocol only needs an intermediary to break link so that the costs are reduced. Moreover, the proposed protocol provides fairness among the participants, but Xu et al.'s [21] do not. Finally, our proposed protocol is proved to be secure in the standard model. As is shown in Table 2, "√" means that this scheme achieves the functionality, "×" means that the corresponding functionality isn't achieved in the contrary, and "*" means that this functionality isn't mentioned.

Table 2. Functionality comparisons

Schemes	Others	Fairness	Unforgeablity	Linkability	Double-Spending	Double-Usage
[14]	1	√	random oracle	√	√	*
[21]	2	×	*	√	√	√
Ours	1	√	standard model	√	√	√

5   Conclusions

In this paper, we have presented a practical protocol that can not only protect privacy through breaking the link between the user and the property owner but also ensure the fairness among participants joined in transaction. Meanwhile, the protocol impedes double-usage (a property owner rents his goods to different users) and double-spending (a user spends his bitcoin more than once). Moreover, analysis of security and efficiency explain that the proposed protocol is secure and effective. Finally, functionality comparisons with previous work are also given, then our protocol can achieve much more functionality.

Acknowledgement. This paper is supported by the National Key R&D Program of China under Grant No. 2017YFB0802000, the National Natural Science Foundation of China under Grants No. 61472470 and 61572390, and the Scientific Research Plan Project of Education Department of Shaanxi Province under Grant No. 17JK0362.

References

1. Nakamoto, S.: Bitcoin: a peer-to-peer electronic cash system. Consulted (2008)
2. Zhao, Q., Liu, Y.: E-Voting scheme using secret sharing and k-anonymity. In: Barolli, L., Xhafa, F., Yim, K. (eds.) BWCCA 2016. LNDECT, vol. 2, pp. 893–900. Springer, Cham (2017). https://doi.org/10.1007/978-3-319-49106-6_91
3. Xue, T.F., Fu, Q.C., Wang, C.: Study on medical data sharing model based on blockchain. Acta Autom. Sin. **43**(9), 1555–1562 (2017)
4. Swan, M.: Blockchain: Blueprint for a New Economy. OReilly Media, Inc., Sebastopol (2015)
5. Sasson, E.B., et al.: decentralized anonymous payments from bitcoin. In: IEEE Security and Privacy (SP), pp. 459–474 (2014)
6. Miers, I., Garman, C., Green, M., Rubin, A.D.: Zerocoin: anonymous distributed e-cash from bitcoin. In: IEEE Security and Privacy (SP), pp. 397–411 (2013)

7. Saxena, A., Misra, J., Dhar, A.: Increasing anonymity in bitcoin. In: Böhme, R., Brenner, M., Moore, T., Smith, M. (eds.) FC 2014. LNCS, vol. 8438, pp. 122–139. Springer, Heidelberg (2014). https://doi.org/10.1007/978-3-662-44774-1_9

8. Bonneau, J., et al.: Mixcoin: anonymity for bitcoin with accountable mixes. In: Christin, N., Safavi-Naini, R. (eds.) FC 2014. LNCS, vol. 8437, pp. 486–504. Springer, Heidelberg (2014). https://doi.org/10.1007/978-3-662-45472-5_31

9. Valenta, L., Rowan, B.: Blindcoin: blinded, accountable mixes for bitcoin. In: Brenner, M., Christin, N., Johnson, B., Rohloff, K. (eds.) FC 2015. LNCS, vol. 8976, pp. 112–126. Springer, Heidelberg (2015). https://doi.org/10.1007/978-3-662-48051-9_9

10. Ziegeldorf, J.H., Grossmann, F., Henze, M., Inden, N., Wehrle, K.: Coinparty: secure multi-party mixing of bitcoins. In: Proceedings of the 5th ACM Conference on Data and Application Security and Privacy, pp. 75–86. ACM (2015)

11. Maxwell, G.: Coinjoin: bitcoin privacy for the real world (2013)

12. Ruffing, T., Moreno-Sanchez, P., Kate, A.: CoinShuffle: practical decentralized coin mixing for bitcoin. In: Kutyłowski, M., Vaidya, J. (eds.) ESORICS 2014, Part II. LNCS, vol. 8713, pp. 345–364. Springer, Cham (2014). https://doi.org/10.1007/978-3-319-11212-1_20

13. Maxwell, G.: Coinswap: transaction graph disjoint trustless trading (2013)

14. Heilman, E., Baldimtsi, F., Goldberg, S.: Blindly signed contracts: anonymous on-blockchain and off-blockchain bitcoin transactions. In: Clark, J., Meiklejohn, S., Ryan, P.Y.A., Wallach, D., Brenner, M., Rohloff, K. (eds.) FC 2016. LNCS, vol. 9604, pp. 43–60. Springer, Heidelberg (2016). https://doi.org/10.1007/978-3-662-53357-4_4

15. Kiayias, A., Russell, A., David, B., Oliynykov, R.: Ouroboros: a provably secure proof-of-stake blockchain protocol. In: Katz, J., Shacham, H. (eds.) CRYPTO 2017, Part I. LNCS, vol. 10401, pp. 357–388. Springer, Cham (2017). https://doi.org/10.1007/978-3-319-63688-7_12

16. Novo, O.: Blockchain meets IoT: an architecture for scalable access management in IoT. IEEE Internet of Things J. (IoT) 5(2), 1184–1195 (2018)

17. Vukolić, M.: The quest for scalable blockchain fabric: proof-of-work vs. BFT replication. In: Camenisch, J., Kesdoğan, D. (eds.) iNetSec 2015. LNCS, vol. 9591, pp. 112–125. Springer, Cham (2016). https://doi.org/10.1007/978-3-319-39028-4_9

18. Szabo, N.: Formalizing and securing relationships on public networks. First Monday 2(9) (1997)

19. Zuo, L.M., Zhang, T.T., Chen, Z.S.: A blind scheme based on the standard model. J. Yichun Univ. 39(9), 1–4 (2017)

20. Todd, P.: BIP 65: OP CHECKLOCKTIMEVERIFY. Bitcoin improvement proposal (2014)

21. Xu, L., et al.: Enabling the sharing economy: privacy respecting contract based on public blockchain. In: Proceedings of the ACM Workshop on Blockchain, Cryptocurrencies and Contracts (ASIA CCS 2017), pp. 15–21. ACM (2017)

Smart Transportation Systems for Cities in the Framework of Future Networks

Yanwu Zhang[1], Lei Li[1], Guofu Li[2], Pengjia Zhu[3], Qingyuan Li[1],
Yu Zhang[1], Ning Cao[1,2(✉)], Renhao Jin[4], Gang Tian[5],
and Yanpiao Zhang[6]

[1] School of Information Engineering, Qingdao Binhai University, Qingdao,
China
cn8877503@126.com
[2] School of Computer Science, University College Dublin, Dublin, Ireland
[3] Accenture China, AI Lab, Shanghai, China
[4] School of Information, Beijing Wuzi University, Beijing, China
[5] Shandong University of Science and Technology, Qingdao, Shandong, China
[6] Hebei University of Economics and Business, Shijiazhuang, Hebei, China

Abstract. Smart transportation system is a cross-field research topic involving
a variety of disciplines, in which data plays a central role. Researches that are
driven by data can be traced back to the 1930s, when the British statistician and
biologist Ronald Fisher creates the Iris dataset to study the objective and
automated way to classify iris flower. Early success of data powered research
illustrates the potential value of data in the research topics in either scientific or
social domains. City transportation system is one of the most fundamental
components of the city service. Recent researches show that the quality of the
transportation service largely depends on how well its resources can be managed
and utilized, which in turn relies on how well the data derived from that system
can be collected and processed for the need of the government authority, as well
as any individual citizen. Improvements on the transportation via the smart
transportation system do not only pose an important impact on any individual's
life style, but it is also a great saving of time and energy.

Keywords: Smart transportation system · Wireless networks · Data mining

1 Introduction

Smart transportation system is a cross-field research topic involving a variety of disciplines, in which data plays a central role. Researches that are driven by data can be traced back to the 1930s, when the British statistician and biologist Ronald Fisher creates the Iris dataset to study the objective and automated way to classify iris flower. Early success of data powered research illustrates the potential value of data in the research topics in either scientific or social domains. City transportation system is one of the most fundamental components of the city service. Recent researches show that the quality of the transportation service largely depends on how well its resources can be managed and utilized, which in turn relies on how well the data derived from that

© Springer Nature Switzerland AG 2018
X. Sun et al. (Eds.): ICCCS 2018, LNCS 11068, pp. 70–79, 2018.
https://doi.org/10.1007/978-3-030-00021-9_7

system can be collected and processed for the need of the government authority, as well as any individual citizen [1–3]. Improvements on the transportation via the smart transportation system do not only pose an important impact on any individual's life style, but it is also a great saving of time and energy.

Under this concern, this project targets at the research based on the data that originate from the city transportation system, aiming to provide a theoretical foundation and practical tool-set to improve the management and utilization of the transportation system. To achieve this goal, we divide our research work into two parts: First, we aim to build a data collecting and manipulating system that are specially designed for the transportation system data. Afterwards, researches on the predicative data analysis will be conducted based on the latest trends of deep neural networks and deep reinforcement learning. The output of our learning algorithms will be thoroughly tested on a simulation system.

The purpose of this paper is to provide a theoretical basis and tools for improving traffic management and utilization. The article will begin with the collection and operation of data, predictive data analysis, time series analysis, and application scenario analysis to analyze and demonstrate.

2 Data Collecting and Manipulating Infrastructure

Working on the transportation data is not a trivial thing. Before we can actually start doing the analysis and making any predications, we must consider the infrastructures that we have to build for collecting and manipulating the data. To have a better understanding of the problem, we have identified three major features of the data of the transportation system, which must be concerned for this research project:

2.1 The Volume of the Data Is Vast

Intuitively, the data volume of a system is proportional to the number of objects it contains. As for the transportation system, there are usually tens of millions of people living in large cities of China such as Beijing and Shanghai, and most of them would become the system user on a daily basis. Meanwhile, the number of motor vehicles is also increasing rapidly with the growth of the motor industry of China. For instance, Beijing city has about 5.2 million motor vehicles by the end of 2012. More than just people and motor vehicles, each of the subsystems of the city transportation such as metros, trams, bicycles may introduce potentially large number of objects into transportation system. Each of the devices such as RFID sensors, GPS locators, smart phones that they carry, can become an independent data generator, and keeps producing new data points at each single moment, accumulating into an enormous large data repository to be mined [4, 5]. The volume of the data repository is a key part of the value it, since the pattern within it can be only discovered when data are sufficient.

2.2 The Volume of the Data Is Vast

Transportation system is a great complexity that involves hundreds of different types of the entities. To list just a few, road, rails, trains, trams, buses, cars, bicycles, passengers, pedestrians, these are the typical entity types that can appear in the complex system [2, 6–9]. Each type of the entity may carry its own type of data. Moreover, dealing with the transportation system data also requires the system to be ready to accept the new entity types. For example, the bicycle sharing industry only became a major option as a transportation tool until recently. But its emergent has already given the scope of the road traffic resource a new definition. Before that, we regard the road as the major resource to be scheduled or allocated, when vehicles are considered the consumers. Within a few years, the rapid growth of the sharing economy has made this entire new type of traffic resource a major part of the city transportation system impossible to ignore. Such innovation of the new sub-system is mostly due to modern advancement of the wireless network, and it creates new challenges to the research community of how the data it emits can be used to optimize such a resource [10, 11]. How the location data emitted by each of the available bike can be matched to any potential rider and maximize the bicycle utility, reducing the aimless input is a practical problem which has huge social and economic value behind it.

2.3 The Pattern Is Highly Dynamic

The city transportation is a highly dynamic system. Use patterns in this system are changing rapidly though time [12–14]. The use patterns in the morning time can be totally different from that in the noon or evening time, or even of the same time period between the days. Thanks to the latest advancement of the wireless network technology, we are now able to collect and share these dynamic data from different sources almost simultaneously when they are firstly generated, when the modern online data analysis systems can process them timely. These infrastructures enabled a wide range of valuable applications such as that is only possible when real-time data collection and analysis can be achieved. Services of this kind, such as the real-time rout planning services, opened a whole new type of using experience which may produce a revolutionary impact on the form of the future city transformation, but also put up challenging research problems.

Resolving the issues of data collecting and manipulating is our first step in this project, which builds a corner stone for the rest of the research. The latest achievements of the Big-Data technologies have provided us with several tools to tackle these problems. Our research and development will be based on the bleeding edge of the big-data technologies [26, 28]. More concretely, the Hadoop and its derivatives such as the HBase, Hive database allow us to store huge amount of data in a distributed system with reliability. The Hadoop ecosystem, together with its well-known Map-Reduce architecture, is good at handling large-scale of heterogeneous types of data [19] (Fig. 1).

However, they are known to be weak at providing real-time computing power. At this concern, we consider that Spark system to be an excellent option to compensate for this requirement. Spark provides a distributed memory computing tool [20], which

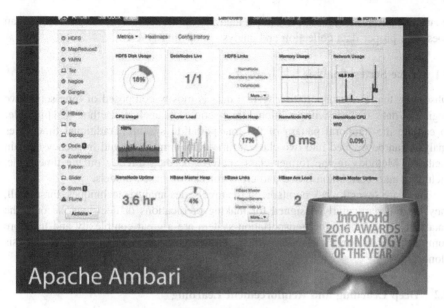

Fig. 1. The Hadoop and its derivatives.

works remarkably well with the Redis distributed memory cache service [22]. These technologies together allow us to scale many of the data analysis algorithms for several orders of magnitude.

3 Predicative Data Analysis

We are living in an ear in which "data is rich but knowledge is poor". Though one would never emphasize too much on the important of the data, but it only presents its value when properly mined. Data mining community commonly classifies the mining methods into explorative methods and predicative methods. Descriptive mining methods characterize the general properties of the data in the dataset, when the predicative methods aim to perform inference on the current data in order to make predictions. For many years, the explorative type of data mining techniques has been the main stream in the transportation data area [15, 16]. Discovering interesting properties of the data and produce comprehensive visual representation to people received most of the attention in the smart transportation area, when the predications or the decision are often left to the humans to make.

Nevertheless, the rapid growth of the AI since the 2010s have suggested that, with proper training, computer programs can out-perform human-level intelligent decisions in various scenarios, especially in the case when the data availability is no longer an issue and real-time response is desired. The overwhelming winnings of AlphaGo over the Go-game world champion Lee Sedol, and more recently Ke Jie, have proved the power of the rational decision that AI systems can make. There is no double that in a smart transportation system, predicative analysis can do a much better job than human does with proper data collection and analysis modeling [17, 18].

3.1   Time Series Analysis

Observing that the transportation system data is mostly composed of time series, we begin our data analysis with traditional time-series data analysis methods [21] in order to capture the temporal pattern of the transportation system. Traditional time-series analysis can be divided into two classes: time-domain methods and frequency-domain methods. Methods in the former class analyze the data directly on the time scale, including auto-correlation based and cross-correlation based models.

There are several weak points lie in the time series analysis techniques. First of all, they are not particularly designed for making predications or decisions; second, the data that derived from the transportation system are a great complexity and far more complicated than pure time-series, which can hardly be handled by time series analysis alone.

3.2   Deep Learning and Reinforcement Learning

Recent research shows the superiority of engaging modern machine learning methodologies, which will be our next and key step for our research on predicative data analysis. Machine learning algorithms are commonly divided into two sub-classes: supervised learning and unsupervised learning. Their learning goal is to either output a class-label (classification), a real-valued number (regression), or find the internal structure of the dataset (representation). In both paradigms, Neural Networks (DNN) are playing a central position in recently years. Deep learning architectures based on DNN enable the learning algorithm to be able to discover the best data representation from a huge repository of raw input. Therefore, deep learning is often classified as a type of "representation learning" or "end-to-end learning". The deep structure and vast amount of the parameters allow the DNNs capable of virtually fitting any distributions or functions [23, 27]. For instance, Recurrent Neural Networks (RNNs), especially with the LSTM (Long Short Term Memory) cells [24], has a way stronger capability than traditional models when handle time series data (Fig. 2).

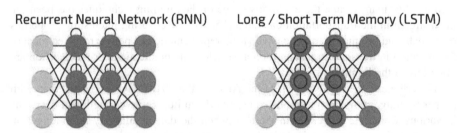

Fig. 2.   RNN and LSTM.

Besides, the Convolutional Neural Networks (CNN) to handle image data or other signal data with local feature. These features of the deep learning make it a perfect choice for handling the vase amount of the heterogeneous types of data from the transportation system (Fig. 3).

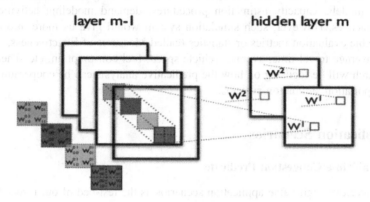

Fig. 3. Convolutional neural network hidden layer

Both supervised learning and unsupervised learning are somewhat similar, in the sense that they both work under a relatively static environment when the entire learning data is present in prior. Comparatively, Reinforcement Learning (RL) is a special type of machine learning paradigm [25], which puts emphasis on the interaction between the agent (system) and the environment, and the correct input-output pairs are never presented, nor sub-optimal actions explicitly corrected. Instead, the goal of the machine learning is to obtain a policy function that maps a state into an action which would give the maximal accumulative reward.

$$V^{\pi}(s) = R(s) + \gamma \sum_{s' \in S} P_{s\pi(s)}(s') V^{\pi}(s'). \tag{1}$$

In addition, RL is particularly well-suited to problems which include a long-term versus short-term reward trade-off. These new settings make the RL a far more an interesting machine learning branch to facilitate the smart transportation system. Due to the obvious advantage of the representation learning by DNNs, recent researches are combing it with the Reinforcement Learning, in which DNNs are used to learn the optimal representation of the state space, resulting into the new class of learning algorithms namely the Deep Reinforcement Learning.

3.3   Evaluation by Simulation

It is common that the evaluation score that generated by the machine learning algorithms on the testing data may not reflect the actual performance in reality. Therefore, predications or strategies derived from the learning algorithms must be thoroughly tested in a simulation environment. Therefore, our final stage is to build a simulation environment to evaluate the wide forms of outputs that our predicative analysis algorithms make. Modern transportation simulation systems would allow us to specify scenarios like highway network configuration and will present the transportation system behaviors in either statistical form or graphical form. On the other hand, researches on the traffic simulation alone will not be capable of solving the problems like optimization models, capacity estimation procedures, demand modeling activities and design practices. However, such simulation system would give us more informative and valuable evaluation metrics or statistics (called Measures of Effectiveness, MOE), such as average travel time, average vehicle speed, fuel consumption, etc. Therefore, our research will be focusing on how the predicative analysis can be cooperating with the transportation simulation systems.

4   Application Scenarios

4.1   Real-Time Congestion Predicate

We consider two high-value application scenarios as the test-bed of our research. The growing number of motor vehicles in big cities of China is a big challenge to their transportation systems. Existing researches or systems for traffic congestion control is either totally passive or on a long-term basis. For instance, we have seen applications that can make real-time rout plan based on the current traffic congestion status, making absolutely no predictions; or we may predicate the traffic congestions status based on the periodical characteristics (i.e., daily or weekly) patterns of the traffic data. However, rare research has been taken on the real-time active congestion predication. Many of the traffic congestion cases are caused by a single local minor event, which quickly spread to a large portion of the entire traffic network, or even across the sub-systems. For example, a slight accident in the high way during the rush hour would very likely to affect the travelling speed over a few miles, or even the passenger number of subway stations. Solving such a problem would ask the system to be able to monitor a wide range of sources of data, detect the slightest abnormal event, and then combine all the pieces of evidence together to make precise and timely judgment.

4.2   Sharing Bicycle Scheduling

The quick expansion of the sharing economy has changed the citizen's daily life in many aspects. It is clear the such a trend will continue for years or decades. However, the mismanagement of the sharing bicycle resource does not only create extra cost to the running company, but also creates social problems. For instance, the flooding deployment of the sharing bike into the central areas of a city has already become an important issue since 2017. Cities like Beijing, Shanghai, or Hangzhou have explicitly banned sharing bicycles in certain areas (Fig. 4).

However, smart transportation system would expect a better solution, in which periodic and real-time operational scheduling are totally controlled by the predicative analysis based on the data that collected from bicycles, riders, and other context like the weather condition or the road conditions. This would require us the push both the data

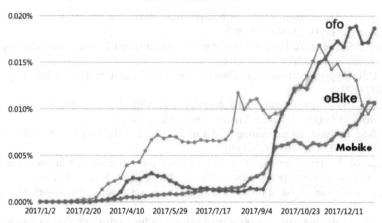

Fig. 4. Shared cycle market weekly active penetration rate trends in 2017

collection and manipulation infrastructure and the predicative analysis to a new frontier that never existed before.

5 Summary

To summarize, ubiquitous sensing and data capture from various components of the transportation system and predicative analysis are key parts of building a smart transportation system, which also make up a major component of this project. This proposed research work will be conducted from two sides. First, we will build an infrastructure for collecting and manipulating the huge volume of the transportation system, which should also address the heterogeneous and dynamic nature of such data; Second, we will proceed with the researches on the analysis on the data based on the classic time-series analysis and modern Deep Learning theories. These researches will be experimented and tested on both the real-time congestion predicate and sharing bicycle operation strategy problems. We have observed that many of the recent achievements of this area are due to the development of the wireless technology. Therefore, we consider the research on the transportation data collection and mining as a coherent part of the entire research project.

Acknowledgement. The work is supported by the National Natural Science Foundation of China under grant No. 61702305, the China Postdoctoral Science Foundation under grant No. 2017M622234, Scientific Research Foundation of Shandong University of Science and Technology for Recruited Talents under the grant No. 2016RCJJ045.

References

1. Zhang, J.P.: Data-Driven intelligent transportation systems: a survey. IEEE Trans. Intell. Transp. Syst. **12**(4), 1624–1639 (2011)
2. Faouzi, N.E.E.: Data fusion in intelligent transportation systems: Progress and challenges – a survey. Inf. Fusion **12**(1), 4–10 (2011)
3. Lee, D.H.: Applying data mining techniques for traffic incident analysis. J. Inst. Eng. **44**(2), 90–102 (2004)
4. Shena, Y.: Investigating commuting flexibility with GPS data and 3D geovisualization: a case study of Beijing, China. J. Transp. Geogr. **32**(7), 1–11 (2013)
5. Liu, B.S.: Research on forecasting model in short term traffic flow based on data mining technology. ISDA **1**, 707–712 (2006)
6. Vanajakshi, L.: Travel time prediction under heterogeneous traffic conditions using global positioning system data from buses. IET Intell. Transp. Syst. **3**(1), 1–9 (2009)
7. Ren, F.: Geovisualization of human hybrid activity-travel patterns. Trans. GIS **11**(5), 721–744 (2007)
8. Ahas, R.: Evaluating passive mobile positioning data for tourism surveys: an estonian case study. Tour. Manag. **29**(3), 469–486 (2008)
9. Lint, J.W.C.V.: A robust and efficient method for fusing heterogeneous data from traffic sensors on freeways. Comput.-Aided Civ. Infrastruct. Eng. **25**(8), 547–629 (2010)
10. Zhang, Y.: Expanding bicycle-sharing systems: lessons learnt from an analysis of usage. PLoS ONE **11**(12), e0168604 (2016)
11. O'Brien, O.: Mining bicycle sharing data for generating insights into sustainable transport systems. J. Transp. Geogr. **34**(219), 262–273 (2014)
12. Ming, S.: On the structure of weekly activity/travel patterns. Transp. Res. Part A: Policy Pract. **37**(10), 823–839 (2003)
13. Kwan, M.P.: GABRIEL: Gis Activity-Based tRavel sImuLator. Activity scheduling in the presence of real-time information. GeoInformatica **10**(4), 469–493 (2006)
14. Ahas, R.: Daily rhythms of suburban commuters' movements in the Tallinn metropolitan area: case study with mobile positioning data. Transp. Res. Part C: Emerg. Technol. **18**(1), 45–54 (2010)
15. Kwan, M.P.: Interactive geovisualization of activity-travel patterns using three-dimensional geographical information systems: a methodological exploration with a large data set. Transp. Res. Part C: Emerg. Technol. **8**(1–6), 185–203 (2000)
16. Wang, Z.C.: Visual traffic jam analysis based on trajectory data. IEEE Trans. Vis. Comput. Graph. **19**(12), 2159–2168 (2013)
17. Moretti, F.: Urban traffic flow forecasting through statistical and neural network bagging ensemble hybrid modeling. Neurocomputing **167**(1), 3–7 (2015)
18. Lippi, M.: Short-Term traffic flow forecasting: an experimental comparison of time-series analysis and supervised learning. IEEE Trans. Intell. Transp. Syst. **14**(2), 871–882 (2013)
19. White, T.: Hadoop: The Definitive Guide, 3rd edn. O'Reilly, Sebastopol (2012)
20. Zaharia, M.: Spark: cluster computing with working sets. Usenix Conf. Hot Top. Cloud Comput. **15**(1), 10–18 (2010)
21. GEP Box.: Time Series Analysis: Forecasting and Control (3rd edn.). J. Time **31**(4), 199–201 (1994)
22. Nelson, J.: Mastering Redis. Packt Publishing, Birmingham (2016)
23. Goodfellow, I.: Aaron Courville. Deep Learning. MIT Press, Cambridge, MA (2016)
24. Hochreiter, S.: Long short-term memory. Neural Comput. **9**(8), 1735–1780 (1997)
25. Richard, S.: Reinforcement Learning: An Introduction. MIT Press, Cambridge, MA (1998)

26. Cheng, J.R.: An abnormal network flow feature sequence prediction approach for DDoS attacks detection in big data environment. CMC Comput. Mater. Continua **55**(1), 95–119 (2018)
27. Yıldızel, S.A.: A study on the estimation of prefabricated glass fiber reinforced concrete panel strength values with an artificial neural network model. CMC: Comput. Mater. Continua **52**(1), 41–52 (2013)
28. CRWu.: Time optimization of multiple knowledge transfers in the big data environment. CMC: Comput. Mater. Continua, **54**(3), 269–285 (2018)

Study on the Internet of Things from Applications to Security Issues

Shuyan Yu[(✉)]

College of Management and Information,
Zhejiang Post and Telecommunication College, Shaoxing 312000, China
shuyanyu1231@qq.com

Abstract. Internet of Things, or IoTs have gained popularity in the recent days for interconnecting the things such as devices, sensors, equipment, software, and information services. Besides, IoT has played a remarkable role in all aspects of daily lives, which covers many fields including healthcare, automobiles, entertainments, industrial appliances, sports, and homes. IOT has also much effect on smart fields, such as smart homes, smart cars, and so on. These smart technologies are not only used at homes but also used in various other sectors such as media, business, agriculture, securities, and transportation. But compared with traditional networks, the sensitive nodes of the IoT are assigned in positions without manual supervision, with the weak capability and limited resources, making the security issues of the IoT quite troublesome, and in addition, the fast development and wider adoption of IoT devices signify the urgency of addressing these security threats before deployment. This paper provides the readers with a basic understanding of IoT, such as its origin, classification, underlying technologies, various applications, and security issues and challenges that IoT is facing with, it also enables the application developers and security researchers to acquire the current development status about the IoT.

Keywords: Internet of Things · Applications · Security issues

1 Introduction

Internet of Things, or IoTs have gained popularity in the recent days for interconnecting the things such as devices, sensors, equipment, software, and information services due to the advancement of technologies like WSN, RFID, and NFC [1]. The IoT enables substantial objects to see, hear, think, and complete jobs by having them communicate and synchronize assignments with each other [2]. The key elements involved in the IoT are identification, sensing, communication, services and semantics [3]: the identification element matches the services with the demand; the sensing element obtains the information from various objects within the network then sends back the sensed data to the cloud or to the database; the communication element interlinks the heterogeneous objects for providing

© Springer Nature Switzerland AG 2018
X. Sun et al. (Eds.): ICCCS 2018, LNCS 11068, pp. 80–89, 2018.
https://doi.org/10.1007/978-3-030-00021-9_8

the specific smart services; the service element can be information aggregation service, ubiquitous service, collaborative service ,and identity-related service; the semantic element is used for extracting the knowledge from multiple machines. IoT also helps transform the objects from being conventional to smart by manipulating its underlying technologies such as omnipresent and pervasive computing, embedded devices, communication technologies, sensor networks, network protocols [2].

The term Internet of Things was first introduced as an idea in 1999 by Ashton [4], which has now evolved into a reality that interconnects real world sensors, electronic devices, and systems to the Internet [5]. The first definition of IoTs was from a *things oriented* perspective, where RFID tags were considered as things, and it was defined as *The worldwide network of interconnected objects uniquely addressable based on standard communication protocols* [6]. The definition of things shown in Fig. 1 in IoT is very wide and includes a variety of physical elements, and this network of a variety of objects can bring ample amount of challenges in developing applications and make existing challenges more difficult to tackle [6].

Fig. 1. IoT definition

In addition, IoT can be classified into three layers [7], namely, application, perception, and network protocol, as shown in Fig. 2. In Fig. 2, the perception layer is similar to physical layer in OSI model which consists of the different types of sensor devices and environmental elements [8]. The perception layer generally copes with the overall device management like identification and collection of specific information by each type of sensor devices, the network layer is mainly responsible for transferring the information from perception layer to the upper layer, and the application layer is responsible for applications management based on the processed information [6].

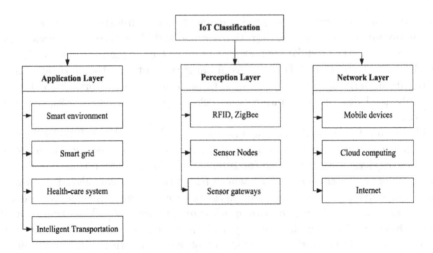

Fig. 2. IoT layers

This paper provides the readers with a basic understanding of IoT, such as its origin, classification, underlying technologies, various applications, and security issues and challenges that IoT is facing with. The organization of the article is as follows. An Introduction is presented in Sect. 1; IoT classification and applications are shown in Sect. 2; IoT security issues and challenges are discussed in Sect. 3; Conclusion is drawn in Sect. 4.

2   IoT Applications

Essentially, IoT is a collection of self-configured electronic and non-electronic devices that have capability to cooperate with each other to control remote devices [9]. Therefore, IOT has much effect on domestic fields, such as smart homes, smart cars, and so on. These smart technologies are not only used at homes but also used in various other sectors such as media, business, agriculture, securities, transportation as in shown in Fig. 3 [9,10].

In business field, IoT has noticeable advancement in manufacturing and service industry such as better services, more production and superior quality. In [2], there are three ways that business can manage IoT using modern techniques: (1) use automated methods for organizing and retaining data based on the content; (2) securely consolidate IoT data regardless of where it came from or where it kept, or where it is kept; (3) offer new ways to access information, be productive and add value. IoT connected devices will have been almost tripled to over 38 billion unites by 2020 [11]. According to Cisco, IoT will consist of 50 billion devices connected to the Internet by 2020 so as to enhance productivity, create new business models, and generate new revenue streams [12]. Vast amount of applications are built by using IoT concepts, and these can be classified into the following domains [13]: telecommunication industry, medical and healthcare

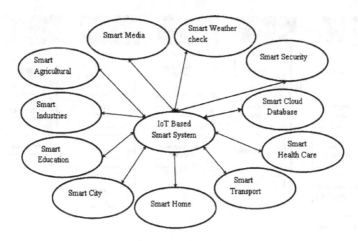

Fig. 3. IoT based smart system

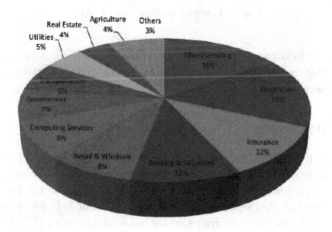

Fig. 4. Market share of main IoT application by 2020

industry, logistics and supply chain management, aerospace and aviation industry, automotive industry, and transportation industry. Figure 4 illustrates the market share of main IoT applications by 2020 [14], and Fig. 5 shows the general applications of IoT [15].

In agriculture, IoT helps the farmer to select the crop depends upon the soil type and weather report, intelligent sensors are also used to monitor weather conditions, and the humidity sensors will send the signal to actuator to control the motor speed to manage the output flow [16].

In [3], IoT is used in medical sector for enhancing the quality of life, patient outcomes, management of real-time diseases and enhancing the user experience. [17] classified the medical applications of IoT into two categories such as services and applications as is shown in Fig. 6. In detail, RFID sensor has the ability to

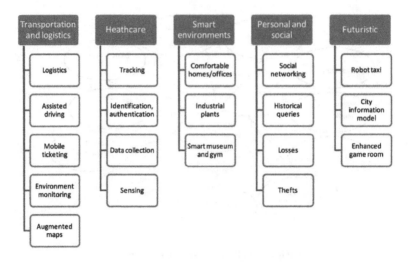

Fig. 5. General applications of IoT

monitor the medical parameters and drug delivery, and it can store the patients medical records in emergency situations such as for diabetes, cancer, and coronary heart diseases [13].

3 Security Issues

Compared with other traditional networks, the sensitive nodes of the IoT are assigned in positions without manual supervision, with the weak capability and limited resources, making the security issues of the IoT quite troublesome, and in addition, the fast development and wider adoption of IoT devices signify the urgency of addressing these security threats before deployment [5]. Thus because of the intrinsic limitation of processing capability and speed, the traditional security counter measures are not applied as it is for IoT based security threats.

The aim of the IoT security is to provide a reliable connection, proper authentication mechanism, and confidentiality about the data to each device connected in the network. The information security regulations commonly suggested are data confidentiality, integrity, and availability. Threats and breach in any of these areas could cause serious damage to the system and have direct impact on the system [18]. According to [18], the three regulations are as follows

(1) Data confidentiality refers to the ability to ensure privacy for the user by providing a secure connection to only the permitted users. The data can be accessed by the permitted user only. Data confidentiality can be achieved by data encryption mechanism where each bit of data is converted into cipher text and followed by two-step verification process, in which two devices allow access only if both the devices pass the authentication test, and a biometric verification in which the person is uniquely identifiable. In IoTs, the devices

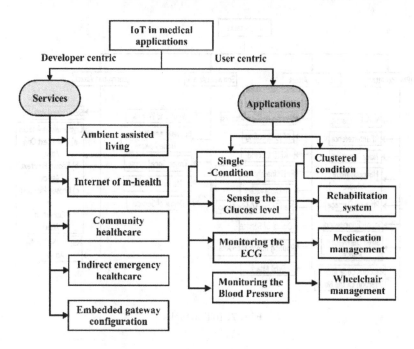

Fig. 6. IoT in medical applications

ensure that sensor network nodes do not connect to neighboring nodes and tags are not transmitted their data to unrecognized reader.

(2) Data Integrity is integrated in the network to secure data from cybercriminals during the communication mechanism, so that data tampering cannot be done without the system catching the threat. The checksum and cyclic redundancy check are error detection methods used to check the data integrity.

(3) The main goal of any IoT security is to provide the data to its users whenever needed. The immediate access of data from the resources by its user not only in normal conditions but also in disastrous conditions should be possible. The firewalls are incorporated into the network to countermeasure the attacks on the services like denial of service attack which can deny the availability of the data to the end user.

Based on the vulnerabilities of IoT, [5] further classifies the attack in four categories, i.e. physical attack, network attack, software attack, and encryption attack as shown in Fig. 7. According to [8], physical attacks are concentrated on hardware devices in the system such as node tampering and node jamming in WSNs [19], RF Interference on RFIDs [20], malicious node injection [21], and sleep deprivation attack and malicious code injection attack [22]; network attacks are focused on the network of IoT system such as traffic analysis attacks [19], RFID spoofing [20], RFID cloning and RFID unauthorized access [23], sinkhole

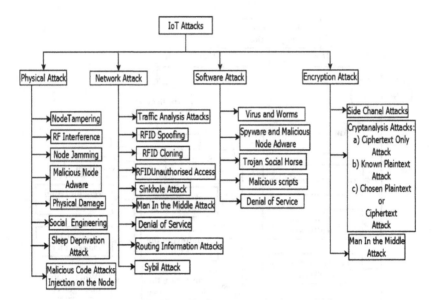

Fig. 7. IoT attacks

attack [24], denial of service [25], and sybil attack [22]; software attacker performs attacks by using virus, worm, spyware to steal data and deny the services; encryption attacks depend on destroying encryption technique and obtain the private key such as side-channel attack [26], cryptanalysis attack [23], and man in the middle attack [22].

Besides, [27] classifies the attacks into attacks against resources, attacks on topology, and attacks on traffic. Attacks against resources typically make legitimate nodes perform unnecessary processing in order to exhaust their resources such as node energy, memory or processing. [27] divides such attacks into direct attack like flooding attack and indirect attack such as version number attack. Attacks on topology are like sinkhole attack, wormhole attack. Attacks on traffic are like sniffing attack, identity attack. IoT security taxonomy is presented in Fig. 8 [7].

According to [28], the security challenges of the IoT are: authentication, access control, trust, and policy enforcement. The authentication ensures the validity of user [29]. The access control algorithm provides new connection when communication quality is ensured already [30]. The trust management system proposed in [31]is used for addressing the key requirements of IoT. In [32], an efficient enforcement security policy is suggested for addressing the security and privacy challenges.

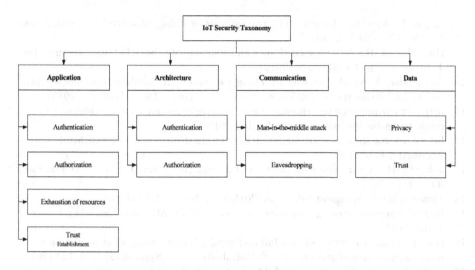

Fig. 8. IoT security taxonomy

4 Conclusion

Compared with traditional networks, the sensitive nodes of the IoT are assigned in positions without supervision, making the security issues of the IoT quite troublesome. In addition, the fast development and wider adoption of IoT devices signify the urgency of addressing these security threats before deployment. This paper provides the readers with a basic understanding of IoT, such as its origin, classification, underlying technologies, various applications, and security issues and challenges that IoT is facing with. It also enables the application developers and security researchers to acquire the current development about the IoT.

References

1. Samani, H., Wahaishi, A.: Privacy in Internet of Things: a model and protection framework. Procedia Comput. Sci. **52**, 606–613 (2015)
2. Shah, S., Yaqoob, I.: A survey: Internet of Things (IoT) technologies, applications and challenges. In: Smart Energy Grid Engineering, vol. 16, pp. 381–385 (2016)
3. Pawar, A.: A survey on IoT applications, security challenges and counter measures. In: 2016 International Conference on Computing. Analytics and Security Trends (CAST), pp. 294–299. College of Engineering Pune, India (2016)
4. Ashton, K.: That 'Internet of Things' thing. RFID J. **2**(5), 97–114 (2009)
5. Deogirikar, J., Vidhate, A.: Security attacks inIoT: a survey. Int. J. I-SMAC **17**, 32–37 (2017)
6. Vashi, S.: Internet of Things (IoT) a vision, architectural elements, and security issues. Int. J. I-SMAC **17**, 492–496 (2017)
7. Alaba, F.: Internet of Things security: a survey. J. Netw. Comput. Appl. **88**, 1–28 (2017)

8. Atzori, L., Iera, A., Morabito, G.: The Internet of Things: a survey. Comput. Netw. **54**(15), 2787–2805 (2010)
9. Dhanalaxmi, B.: A survey on design and analysis of robust IoT architecture. Int. J. Innov. Mech. **15**, 375–378 (2017)
10. Al-Fuqaha, A., et al.: Internet of Things: a survey on enabling technologies, protocols, and applications. IEEE Commun. Surv. Tutor. **17**, 2347–2376 (2015)
11. http://www.juniperresearch.com/press/press-releases/iot-connecteddevices-to-triple-to-38-bn-by-2020. Accessed 1 Jan 2018
12. http://www.cisco.com/c/en/us/solutions/internet-ofthings/overview.html . Accessed 3 Feb 2018
13. Joharan, B.: A fair survey on Internet of Things (IoT). Int. J. Emerg. Trends Eng. **34**, 1–6 (2016)
14. Monaco. http://monacotrades.com/2015/06/. Accessed 4 Feb 2016
15. https://blogs.commons.georgetown.edu/cctp-797-fall2013/archives/838 . Accessed 1 May 2017
16. Rao, P., et al.: Detection of rain fall and wind direction using wireless mobile multi node energy efficient sensor network. Int. J. Appl. Inf. Syst. **3**(12), 102–124 (2012)
17. Islam, S., et al.: The Internet of Things for health care: a comprehensive survey. IEEE Access **3**, 678–708 (2015)
18. Sowmya, S.: Security threats in the application layer in IoT applications. Int. J. I-SMAC **3**(12), 477–480 (2017)
19. Uke, S., Mahajan, A., Thool, R.: UML modeling of physical and data link layer security attacks in WSN. Int. J. Comput. Appl. **70**(11), 22–32 (2013)
20. Li, H., Chen, Y., He, Z.: The survey of RFID attacks and defenses. In: 8th International Conference on IEEE Wireless Communications. Networking and Mobile Computing, Barcelona, Spain, pp. 1–4. World Scientific & Engineering Academy & Society (2012)
21. Kandah, F.: Mitigating colluding injected attack using monitoring verification in mobile ad-hoc networks. Secur. Commun. Netw. **6**(4), 539–547 (2013)
22. Farooq, M., et al.: A critical analysis on the security concerns of Internet of Things (IoT). Int. J. Comput. Appl. **11**(7), 23–35 (2015)
23. Andrea, I., Chrysostomou, C., Hadjichristofi, G.: Internet of Things: security vulnerabilities and challenges. In: Computers & Communication, vol. 2016, pp. 180–187 (2016)
24. Abdullah, M., Rahman, M., Roy, C.: Detecting sinkhole attacks in wireless sensor network using hop count. I. J. Comput. Netw. Inf. Secur. **23**, 50–56 (2015)
25. Abdul, W., Kumar, P.: A survey on attacks, challenges and security mechanism in wireless sensor network. Int. J. Res. Sci. Technol. **1**(8), 189–196 (2015)
26. Zulkifli, M.: Attack on cryptography. Comput. Secur. **12**(5), 33–45 (2008)
27. Arvind K.: Security attacks and secure routing protocols in RPL-based internet of things: survey. In: 2017 International Conference on Emerging Trends and Innovation in ICT (ICEI), pp. 34–39. Pune Institute of Computer Technology, India (2017)
28. Balte, A., Patil, B.: Security issues in Internet of Things (IoT): a survey. Int. J. Adv. Res. Comput. Sci. Softw. Eng. **5**, 450–455 (2015)
29. Kang, N.: Mutual authentication scheme in secure Internet of Things technology for comfortable lifestyle. Sensors **23**, 1–16 (2016)
30. Mahalle, P.N.: Identity establishment and capability based access control (IECAC) scheme for Internet of Things. In: International Symposium on Wireless Personal Multimedia Communications, vol. 2012, pp. 187–191 (2012)

31. Liu, J.: Authentication and access control in the Internet of Things. In: International Conference on Distributed Computing Systems Workshops, vol. 12, no. 7, pp. 588–592 (2012)
32. Neisse R., Steri G., and Baldini G.: Enforcement of security policy rules for the Internet of Things. In: 10th International Conference on Wireless and Mobile Computing, Networking and Communications, USA, pp. 165–172. IEEE (2014)

Survey on IMD and Wearable Devices Security Threats and Protection Methods

Jiaping Yu[1(✉)] and Bingnan Hou[2(✉)]

[1] Chang'an University, Xi'an, China
jiapingy@yahoo.com
[2] National University of Defense Technology, Changsha, China
bingnanhou@163.com

Abstract. In recent years, the developments in electronic science and technology have led to abundant new wearable devices and IMDs, but with the use of those devices increases, the concern about their security also becomes serious. In this paper, we give a survey on the security threat and protection method of IMD and wearable devices and compare those protection methods regarding different factors.

Keywords: Wearable devices · IMD · Survey · Security

1 Introduction

'Wearable Devices' are the devices that consist of smart electronic sensors and microcontrollers that can be worn on the body as implant or accessories. Implantable Medical Devices are the electronic devices that could be implanted in patient's body and support damaged biological structures. Nowadays, the market for IMD and wearable devices has been more than 12 billion dollars. And according to Lamkin [22], the wearable tech market will be worth 34 Billion by 2020. But with the use of those devices increases, the concern about their security also becomes serious. For example, Fitbit, one of the most famous wears the smart band, is used for monitoring user's heart rate and sleep quality. And some wearable devices like Apple Watch can even be used to emailing, texting and banking. So, it is essential to keep those data secure. In this paper, we will mainly analysis two types of security threats: Stealing attack and Disruption attack.

1.1 Data Stealing

Stealing attack may lead to data losses and data leaks. This paper will analyze the data protection against stealing from three aspects:

Stealing via Communication Channel: The communication between wearable devices and the smartphones or computers are likely to be monitored. In practice, Bluetooth sniffing attack [4, 5] and Wi-Fi traffic analysis attack [6] could be considered as this kind of attack.

© Springer Nature Switzerland AG 2018
X. Sun et al. (Eds.): ICCCS 2018, LNCS 11068, pp. 90–101, 2018.
https://doi.org/10.1007/978-3-030-00021-9_9

Stealing via Software. To upgrade the system expediently, most of the wearable devices are open systems and easy to connect with, but this makes it much easier for hardware virus and malicious code to intrude the device system [3].

Stealing via Hardware. When the adversaries take the devices, the design defects of the wearable devices may be used to get the user data from the hardware directly [1, 2]. Reverse engineering is the primary form of this kind of attack.

1.2 Hardware Disruption

Instead of getting user data, hardware attackers mainly focus on destroying the devices directly [7, 8]. In this paper, I will take radio frequency interference and DOS attack as examples because it is a covert way to disable wearable devices. It is a pity that not all the manufacturers applied protection method against those kinds of attacks. In this paper, I will analyze several individual anti-interference antennae and anti-DOS algorithms that could be used in wearable devices [7].

Rest of the paper is organized as follows: Sect. 2 presents the background of this paper. Section 3 describes the specific security threats of the wearable and IMD systems. The protection methods are analyzed in Sect. 4, and the conclusion is drawn in Sect. 6. Section 5 lists the related works.

2 Background

The mechanism of most IMD and wearable devices is getting the user's data through sensors and wireless networks and doing operations on those data such as storing, calculating and transmitting. IMD is a particular type of wearable devices. Instead of wearing, the IMD nodes need to be implanted in the human body for the medical purpose. And as is shown in Fig. 1, the wearable & IMD systems usually consists of three parts:

Part 1: This is the device part, which refers to the wearable devices and IMD nodes or sensors. To the wearable device system, the devices part is usually used to collect user's physical data through the sensors and transmit those data to the second part. And to the IMDs, this part usually refers to the implantable nodes that could be used to collect the patient's physiological data.

Part 2: This is the controller part, which refers to the smartphone that relates to the wearable devices and the programmer that associated with the implanted IMD nodes. Since the smartphone and the programmers have better performance than the first part, they could also be used for some necessary calculation.

Part 3: This is the server part, which refers to the cloud server that accepts, process and stores the data that transmitted from the controller part.

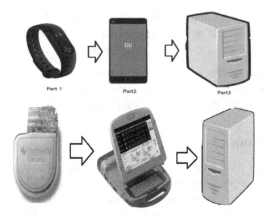

Fig. 1. Structure of wearable and IMD system

3   Security Threats

In this section, we introduce Two types of attacks: Data Stealing and Hardware Disruption.

3.1   Data Stealing

Stealing is the most attacking format in today's world. Most of the scientific researchers aimed at preventing this type of attack. As a stealer, the attacker focuses on stealing the user's data gathered by the wearable devices and IMD. The unauthorized user may try to take the data through hardware, software, or sniff through the communication.

Via Hardware. Since the wearable devices and IMDs are portable, the user's privacy is under threat if the wearable devices are under the adversaries' control.

The wearable devices and IMDs are easy to obtain, so the adversaries may study the hardware structure of the devices and find chances to load the user's data from the hardware memories directly. Take Nike+ Fuel band as an example. According to [1] Fuel band use STM32L151QCH6 as the Central Processing Unit, it is an ultra-low-power platform with a 96-bit unique ID, a preprogrammed bootloader supporting both USB and USART programming, 116 fast input/output pins which are mappable to a 16-interrupt vector table. Figure 2 shows a simplified memory map in STM32. The highlighted part is multiplexed between Flash or System Memory, and its status is depending on the condition of BOOT 0 pin. That means if the adversaries can keep the BOOT 0 pin to a logic 1 state, then they can get access to the system memory and exploit the lack of reading and write protection on the device to get user data. Arias et al. [1] opened the Nike+ fuel band and entered the alternate boot mechanism and gain access to the data in the fuel band. Although the Microprocessor contains the capabilities to lock external reads and writes against the internal flash, the Nike Fuel band did not employ this protection. And although the BOOT0 pin is not externally

Peripheral Initialization	0x400267ff 0x40000000
Option Byte	0x1ff8001f 0x1ff80000
System Memory	0x1ff01fff 0x1ff00000
Data EEPROM	0x08081fff 0x08080000
Flash Memory	0x0803ffff 0x08000000
Flash or System Memory	0x00000000

Fig. 2. Simplified memory map in STM32

provided in Nike Fuel band, the attacker could trace the circuit board to encounter a test point indirectly exposing the BOOT0 pin.

It is the manufacturer's responsibility to keep the device hardware safe, but in reality, things may be different. Ly et al. [2] surveyed the security protection methods of four favorite smart band. Two of them (Nike Fuel band and CODOON Band) use the STM32L series microcontroller without any additional protection. Thus, all the adversaries need to do is to change the microcontroller's BOOT0's logic level to make it boot in DFU mode, then they modify the sensitive data as they want. The third smart band they researched (Huawei Talk band) has unique signatures for each of the firmware, but the bootloader is writeable, and it could be modified without checking the signature so that any firmware could be loaded on the device, and the adversaries can write their firmware with Trojan implanted in it. The last smart band (Xiaomi Miband) use the Dialog DA14580 processor, and the firmware flash was stored in an external SPI flash, making it possible to program using SPI. Like the Nike Fuel band and CODOON band, the adversaries only need to find the SPI line to reprogram it. Besides, Delail et al. [9] stated in his paper that currently, the smart glass does not have a secure user authentication method due to the hardware design.

Since the purpose of the adversaries are stealing the user's data, and the user is not likely to get back their devices if they were stolen. In this condition, user's confidentiality, availability, and privacy are under threats.

Via Software: Software attacks are mainly consisting of malicious code and trojan. Since the wearable devices only have limited capabilities due to the limited power supply, just the lightweight block ciphers could be applied to these devices. And thus, it is much easier for the adversaries to plant malicious codes and trojans in wearable devices. Nohara et al. [3] generated a hardware Trojan aimed at Piccolo, a 64 bit block cipher with 80 bit or 128 bit key. The Trojan will be embedded before the 24th times of round permutation, and only when an intermediate value in the 24th round is all one, the Trojan will be triggered. According to their research, when comparing the power consumption result figure, this Trojan is hard to detect when the trigger is not satisfied, and when the trigger is activated, the Trojan could output the secret key. Therefore, the proposed Trojan generates a severe defect.

Besides the Trojan, the malicious codes and software also pose enormous threats to the data security. And when compared with the hardware trojan, the malicious codes and software are much more flexible.

As is shown in Table 1, Lee et al. [10] stated three types of malware attacks: the first type is called "illegal device pairing attack," first the Hacker installed a cracked app, with this app, the pairing forcibly between the wearable devices and the hacker's smartphone. Then the hacker could get access to the wearable devices because the smartphone and the wearable device will only authenticate each other at the first time when they were connected, after that, the wearable device cannot tell if the user is the authenticated user or not.

Table 1. Attack scenarios, effects, and related weakness

Scenarios	Effects	Weakness
Illegal device pairing attack	The cracked software can access the devices and read the data	Deficient authentication and configurability
Fake wearable gateway attack	Adversaries can change the user's password a sniff the transportation	Deficient authentication and transport encryption
Insecure code-based attack	Adversaries can get access to user's data from the application, and attack query can be sent to a server	Deficient mobile interface and software security

The second type is called "fake wearable gateway attack." With a benign app in a smartphone, the attacker could try to connect to the server with a random id, and if the identifier is valid, then the attack will send a requirement to reset the password. Then, the server will send the authentication message to the original user's gateway, and then the hacker will guess the authentication number based on the discipline that the authentication number may have and connect to the server with the guessed number.

The third attack is called an insecure code-based attack. In this type of attack, the hacker will reverse engineer the app and examine the sensitive codes; then the hacker will send an attack query to the server related to those codes and gain user data from the server.

Via Communication Channel Sniffing. Wireless transmission protocols like Bluetooth, ZigBee, and 802.11 wireless network connection are widely used in wearable devices and IMDs. And the data transmitted through wireless protocol are likely to be interference and sniffed by the adversaries. So, the user data in wearable devices are under threats if without proper protection.

Lotfy et al. [4] examined three wearable devices that cover three types of pairing processes: The first type is called "just works," meaning this process does not require any interactions. The second type is called "numerical comparison" means both central and peripheral devices need to have a user interface for the user to compare the four to six-digit numerical key and ensure they are the same. The Third type is passkey entry. This method requires the central devices has an interface for entering a digit code, the devices will not be successfully paired only if a passkey is entered. According to their research, all of the three kinds of devices' connection packets and subsequent data streams were capturable by the attackers.

Delail et al. [9] stated in his paper that the Google glass's pairing method is based on Bluetooth "Just Work" method, that means the devices will be paired directly if the user accepts the requirement. Although the traffic between the smart glass and other devices could be protected by using AES, which has been proved that could avoid passive eavesdropping, Man in the middle attack could still quickly gain access to the transcription data.

Buttyan et al. [6] hold the view that pure signal processing methods can be used efficiently for performing traffic analysis attacks and identifying the sensor types mounted on the patients. To prove, they use Discrete Fourier Transform and Welch Averaged Periodogram analyzed the spectral domain of the signal that transferred by their simulated system model to identify the most robust frequency components. According to their research, both DFT and WAP could locate the transmission frequency despite the noise.

Besides, what the communication attackers could do is much more than that. According to Nia et al.'s research [5], not only the wearable medical devices but also the human bodies are continuously leaking health information under normal operation. They generated several unique algorithms with individual microphones to sniff Acoustic and Electromagnetic signal from WMD and the human body that may reveal user's privacy like heart rate, breath rate, and even the injected dosage, and thus, show the patient's medical condition.

3.2 Hardware Disruption

Instead of Hardware, Disruption means the attacker aims at disabling the wearable devices. This is a serious threat to most of the IMDs. DoS attack is one of the most representative hardware disruption methods.

Dos Attack means the adversaries keep trying to connect with the target wearable devices and IMDs. This may prevent the authorized connections and even worse, may use up the wearable devices' battery.

Zheng et al. [20] generated an active attacker threat model that the adversaries will not only replay the recorded commands but also create new controls. And Dos Attack is one of the most dangerous attack methods to the IMD nodes due to the limited battery power. Adversaries can launch Dos attack on the IMD by forcing the IMD to communicate with the attacker over wireless communications continually. The IMD only has limited resources regarding computation, communications, memory and battery lifetime. When a programmer attempts to communicate with an IMD, a security module in the IMD has to perform an authentication process. If the request is from an attacker, the authentication will fail, and the attacker cannot have access to the IMD. However, this process consumes the IMD resources, including battery and memory storage. By launching this attack repeatedly, the IMD's battery would be compromised or even be depleted. This, therefore, is a form of a DoS attack peculiar to the IMD.

4   Protection Methods

In this section, we will introduce the protection methods against Stealing and Disruption.

4.1   Stealing Protection

Some protection schemes are aimed at protecting the data from being stolen by the adversaries. In this paper, we will analyze four types of protection method against Data Stealing.

Hardware Structure Strengthen. As we have analyzed in Sect. 3, the hardware defects are quite common in the wearable and IMD devices, and it is not impossible for the adversaries to make use of those defects. The manufactures shall at least apply essential read and write protection on the device to avoid the adversaries from getting user data. Like Arias et al. [1] pointed out that it is necessary for devices with self-contained architecture to secure all update channels and disable all external programmability of the microcontroller and any debug interfaces it may feature. And to avoid adding malicious code and interfaces, the microcontroller must be programmed before being placed on the circuit board.

This type of protection is designed to prevent hardware stealing attack. And it is the easiest and the most direct method to avoid this type of attacks.

Data Encryption and Obfuscation. According to our research, by using appropriate encryption method, the sensitive data could be secured, and malicious access could be denied even the devices are lost. Data encryption is a research hotspot in recent years. Here are some notable results:

Hu et al. [12] generate a one-to-many encryption method based on the fuzzy attribute. The message that produced by this method could be able to read by a group of users that satisfy the control rules in the BAN.

To make wearable devices can perform real-time encryption, with the implementation of AES, Kim et al. [13] propose an encryption module between the application layer and transmission layer, so this module is implementable for all types of wearable devices that encrypt the data before transmitting them.

Data Obfuscation means adding some encoded noise to the data that transmitted in the information channel. It could be considered as a particular type of Data encryption method which could be applicated in Communication Protection. Buttyan et al. [6] think to prevent this kind of attack; traffic patterns must be obfuscated. And they introduced three traffic pattern obfuscation mechanisms: Dummy noise, Dummy source, and Traffic shaping. According to their research, adding dummy noise and using traffic shaping both results in an entropy value close to the theoretical optimum. But according to the resulting spectrum, traffic shaping by introducing carefully chosen inter-transmission delays appears to be the best solution.

Apparently, with an appropriate encryption method, the user data could be adequately protected. But most of the advanced encryption methods need to cooperate with adequate hardware function, high battery capacity, and high cost. Those are the reasons that prevent manufacturers from applying those methods.

Minimize Permission: Though advanced encryption methods could protect the user's data, not all the wearable devices, and IMDs can apply those methods. So, the Permission minimization is a more realistic choice. Permission minimization means to cut off all the dispensable functions of the wearable devices and IMDs and leave most of the calculation to the controller and the cloud server.

Permission minimization is also widely researched. And most manufacturers today choose to use this type of protection method to protect the user's data.

Chen et al. [11] generate a cloud-based medical system. This system could collect the user's body data and transmit them to the nearby cloudlet. Then the adjacent cloudlet will send those data to the remote cloud so that the doctors could access those data. To protect the user's data during the transition to the nearby cloudlet, they use NTRU mechanism to make sure the transmission is safe. Then, to transmit the data from the neighboring cloudlet to the remote cloud server, they use a particular trust model to evaluate the user's trust to decide if they would share the user's data. Next, to protect the privacy of the data in the cloud server, they separate the data and encrypt different types of data in different ways. These methods could strengthen not only the protection of the data but also improve the transmission efficacy. Last but not the least, to protect the whole system, they propose collaborative IDS based on cloudlet mesh.

Zhou et al. [14] proposed a secure and efficient privacy-preserving dynamic medical text mining and image feature extraction scheme PPDM in the cloud-assisted e-healthcare system.

User data will not be stored in the IMD and wearable devices' memory if their permission is minimized. And thus, neither hardware nor software adversaries could obtain the user's data through the wearable device. But the communication between the devices and controller are remained unprotected.

Security Authentication Algorithm and Biometric Authentication: Traditionally, Authentication consists of communication between the wearable devices and the controllers and the critical establishment. It has been proved to be an efficient way to avoid data stealing.

Yohan et al. [15] generated a multi-factor authentication method that could modify its complexity dynamically based on the mobile phone's safety environment. Their mechanism could tight or ease the system's security based on the calculated trust value. And this method could be used continuously to determine if the current user is authorized.

Khan et al. in [16] generated a cloud-based obfuscated authentication service based on the PIN for ATM using wearable devices called Secure-PIN-Authentication-as-a-

Service. Their design does not require any external hardware or any other computation from the external devices.

Liu et al. in [18] generated a WBAN' s hybrid security structure to support communication security in the wireless channel. According to their research, implanted BAN nodes are limited in their power, so the protection should be energy efficient and support reliable operations. Besides, the nodes should be able to detect, collect and transmit the biomedical information to the user.

Biometric means the metric that related to human characteristics. Biometric Authentication could be considered as a particular type of authentication. In recent years, with the development of high-performance sensors, Biometric authentication has been widely used: not only in IMD and Wearable Devices but also in smartphones and computers. Those are matured products in the market. But when it comes to the scientific research field; they are far behind.

Yang et al. in [17] introduced a new user identification system for wearable devices called VibID; it is based on the biological difference between the users. According to their research, the natural variation could review the diversity of user's body, and this kind of variety could be detected as mechanical vibration. And this kind of wave could be used to identify the authorized users. In their design, they use a vibrator motor and three-axis accelerometer to implement the VibID.

Truong et al. in [19] use Elliptic Curve Cryptosystem as security foundation, and instead of using password, they choose the biometrics to enhance security and efficiency of limited-resource devices such as medical devices and wearable devices.

With appropriate authentication method, it is technically impossible for the adversaries to get access to the data that stored in the device memories. But data transportation remains unprotected. And biometric authentication requires additional hardware that could collect the user's metrics, which this is an additional cost to the manufacturer.

Summary: Table 2 summarized the application scenes and characteristics of different protection methods. From the table, we can conclude that Data Encryption and

Table 2. Summary of data-stealing protection method

	Hardware protection	Software protection	Communication protection	Notes
Hardware structure strengthen	Applicable	N/A	N/A	Designed to prevent hardware attack
Data encryption and obfuscation	Applicable	Applicable	Applicable	Adequate hardware function required
Minimize permission	Applicable	Applicable	N/A	Massive data transportation required
Special/biometric authorization	Applicable	Applicable	N/A	Additional hardware and adequate hardware function required

Obfuscation is the most widely used scheme. And three out of four protection method that researched in this paper is not applicable to Communication Protection. But Data encryption requires adequate hardware functions, which may need extra battery capabilities. But the battery in IMDs and Wearable Devices are insufficient, so it is not realistic to apply this type of scheme on limited resources devices.

4.2 Disruption Protection

To avoid Hardware Disruption attack, Biometric Authentication, which we have analyzed before, is an appropriate protection method. Besides the Biometric Authentication, external security proxy device could also be a good choice.

Zheng et al. in [20] summarized the advantages and motivations of external security proxy device. First and foremost, it provides fail-open access to achieve the tradeoff between security and accessibility. Then, the use of an external security proxy requires a little or no modifications to the IMD. Last, but not the least, this design can mitigate battery draining attacks on the IMD because the majority of security operations are delegated to the external proxy device. The battery of the proxy can be quickly changed and replaced.

5 Related Works

Some papers have researched the data-stealing via Software, Kohei et al. [3] investigated the data-stealing via Trojan, and Lee et al. [10] examined data stealing via malicious code and cracked application. Both attack methods are included and summarized as data stealing via software in these papers. Communication channel sniffing is another hot topic, Lofty et al. [4] researched the Bluetooth sniffing, Buttyan et al. [6] analyzed the Traffic Analyze Attack. Readers can find more detailed information from their documents. Cai et al. [23] proposed a new coprocessor architecture that could apply Data Encryption methods more effectively. Cui et al. [24] give a new idea about how to protect sensitive data in mobile devices. Arias et al. [1] tested the hardware security of wearable devices, in their paper, only one specific type of wearable devices are tested. Ly et al. [2] surveyed four important types of wearable devices of their hardware defects, but they did not give out any protection methods. We introduced Arias et al.'s conclusion and explained whether those protection methods apply to the weakness that Ly pointed out. Sun et al. [25] also studied the security and privacy issues in Medical IoT, but their research focused more on the data related requirement about IoT devices. Chang et al. [21] give a comparative survey on critical management in body sensor networks to protect the user security, but they mainly focus on the Data protection. Despite data stealing, we also introduced hardware disruption threats and the protection methods.

6 Conclusion

In this paper, we surveyed the security risks and protection method of IMD and wearable devices. We roughly classify them into two groups: Stealing risks and Protection, Disruption risks and Protection. For each group, we present the related papers and analyze the strengths and deficiencies.

References

1. Arias, O., Wurm, J., Hoang, K., Jin, Y.: Privacy and security in internet of things and wearable devices. IEEE Trans. Multi-Scale Comput. Syst. **1**(2), 99–109 (2015)
2. Ly, K., Jin, Y.: Security studies on wearable fitness trackers. In: 38th Annual International Conference of the IEEE Engineering in Medicine and Biology Society. IEEE (2016)
3. Nohara, K., Nozaki, Y., Yoshikawa, M.: Hardware Trojan for ultra-lightweight block cipher piccolo. In: 4th Global Conference on Consumer Electronics (GCCE), Arigato, pp. 202–203. IEEE (2015)
4. Lotfy, K., Hale, M.L.: Assessing pairing and data exchange mechanism security in the wearable internet of things. In: International Conference on Mobile Services (MS), Hiroshima, pp. 25–32. IEEE (2016)
5. Nia, A.M., Sur-Kolay, S., Raghunathan, A., Jha, N.: Physiological information leakage: a new frontier in health information security. IEEE Trans. Emerg. Top. Comput. **4**(3), 321–334 (2016)
6. Buttyan, L., Holczer, T.: Traffic analysis attacks and countermeasures in wireless body area sensor networks. In: 2012 IEEE International Symposium on World of Wireless, Mobile and Multimedia Networks (WoWMoM), San Francisco, pp. 1–6. IEEE (2012)
7. Ruaro, A., Thaysen, J., Jakobsen, K.B.: Battery coupling impact on the antenna efficiency in a small wearable device. In: Antennas & Propagation Conference (LAPC), Loughborough, pp. 1–4. IEEE (2015)
8. He, L., Yin, W.: Interference evaluation of bluetooth and IEEE 802.11b systems. In: Proceedings of the 4th International Conference on Microwave and Millimeter Wave Technology (ICMMT), pp. 931–934. IEEE (2014)
9. Delail, B.A., Yeun, C.Y.: Recent advances of smart glass application security and privacy. In: 10th International Conference for Internet Technology and Secured Transactions (ICITST), London, pp. 65–69. IEEE (2015)
10. Lee, M., Lee, K., Shim, J., Cho, S., Choi, J.: Security threat on wearable services: empirical study using a commercial smartband. In: IEEE International Conference on Consumer Electronics-Asia (ICCE-Asia), Seoul, pp. 1–5. IEEE (2016)
11. Chen, M., Qian, Y., Chen, J., Hwang, K., Mao, S., Hu, L.: Privacy protection and intrusion avoidance for cloudlet-based medical data sharing. IEEE Trans. Cloud Comput. **1**, 99 (2016)
12. Hu, C., Zhang, N., Li, H., Cheng, X., Liao, X.: Body area network security: a fuzzy attribute based signcryption scheme. IEEE J. Sel. Areas Commun. **31**(9), 37–46 (2013)
13. Kim, J., Lee, B., Yoo, S.K.: Design of real-time encryption module for secure data protection of wearable healthcare devices. In: 35th Annual International Conference of the IEEE Engineering in Medicine and Biology Society (EMBC), Osaka, pp. 2283–2286. IEEE (2013)
14. Zhou, J., Cao, Z., Dong, X., Lin, X.: PPDM: a privacy-preserving protocol for cloud-assisted e-healthcare systems. IEEE J. Sel. Top. Sign. Proces. **9**(7), 1332–1344 (2015)

15. Haar, D.: CaNViS, a cardiac and neurological-based verification system that uses wearable sensors. In: Third International Conference on Digital Information, Networking, and Wireless Communications (DINWC), Moscow, pp. 99–104. IEEE (2015)
16. Khan, R., Hasan, R., Xu, J.: SEPIA: Secure-PIN-authentication-as-a-service for ATM using mobile and wearable devices. In: 2015 3rd IEEE International Conference on Mobile Cloud Computing, Services, and Engineering (MobileCloud), San Francisco, pp. 41–50. IEEE (2015)
17. Yang, L., Wang, W., Zhang, Q.: VibID: user identification through Bio-Vibrometry. In: 15th ACM/IEEE International Conference on Information Processing in Sensor Networks (IPSN), Vienna, pp. 1–12. ACM/IEEE (2016)
18. Liu, J., Kwak, K.S.: Hybrid security mechanisms for wireless body area networks. In: 2010 Second International Conference on Ubiquitous and Future Networks (ICUFN), Jeju Island, pp. 98–103. IEEE (2010)
19. Truong, T., Luong, V., Tran, M., Duong, A.: Secure identity-based authentication scheme suitable for limited-resource devices. In: 12th International Conference on Computational Intelligence and Security (CIS), Wuxi, pp. 271–276. IEEE (2016)
20. Zheng, G., Shankaran, R., Orgun, M.A., Qiao, L., Saleem, K.: Ideas and challenges for securing wireless implantable medical devices: a review. IEEE Sens. J. **17**(3), 562–576 (2017)
21. Chang, S., Jil, S., Shen, J., Liu, D., Tan, H.: A survey on key management for body sensor network. In: 2015 First International Conference on Computational Intelligence Theory, Systems and Applications (CCITSA), pp. 217–221. IEEE (2015)
22. Lamkin, P.: Wearable tech market to be worth $34 billion by 2020. https://www.forbes.com/sites/paullamkin/2016/02/17/wearable-tech-market-to-be-worth-34-billion-by-2020/#13bb51433cb5. Accessed 17 Feb 2016
23. Cai, Z., Wang, Z., Zheng, K., Cao, J.: A distributed TCAM coprocessor architecture for integrated longest prefix matching, policy filtering, and content filtering. IEEE Trans. Comput. **62**(3), 417–427 (2013)
24. Cui, J., Zhang, Y., Cai, Z., Liu, A., Li, Y.: Securing display path for security-sensitive applications on mobile devices. Comput. Mater. Continua **55**(1), 17–35 (2018)
25. Sun, W., Cai, Z., Li, Y., Liu, F., Fang, S., Wang, G.: Security and privacy in the medical internet of things. Secur. Commun. Netw. **2018**, 5978636 (2018). https://doi.org/10.1155/2018/5978636

Temperature and Humidity Monitoring System for Bulk Grain Container Based on LoRa Wireless Technology

Ningli Zhu$^{(\boxtimes)}$, Yuhua Xia, Ying Liu, Chuanzhen Zang,
Hai Deng, and Zhenzhou Ma

Aisino Corporation Inc., Beijing 100195, China
zhuningli@aisino.com

Abstract. This paper introduces the design of key node information collection system for the North-to-South Bulk Grain Container Transportation Project in China. Based on the idea of the Internet of Things (IoT), we combined the current sensing and communication technologies to develop a vehicle-borne information acquisition system and a key node handheld information acquisition system. This project researches on smart front-end products, low-power sensor technology, data acquisition, and wireless communication technology. The whole system combines cloud platform, edge computing, and other technologies to fully utilize the Internet of things resources and artificial intelligence. It demonstrates and certifies the product performance of key node information collection equipment for bulk grain containers. The system adapts to the public railroad and water transport mode while the entire process of food transportation is monitored through intelligent sensor, GPS, LoRa and 3G/4G technologies so that to achieve information traceability in the grain transportation, thus ensuring food quality.

Keywords: IoT · LoRa · Sensor · GPS · 3G · 4G

1 Introduction

Container transport has been increasingly adopted worldwide as a simple, safe, fast and economical multimodal door-to-door transport [1]. In many developed countries, bulk storage and transportation of grain has been fully mechanized and automated. Nowadays, the United States, Canada, and Australia are taking the lead in the transportation technology of grain containers. Owing to the great transportation, the quantity of containerized grain is rapidly increasing in these countries. This promotes a healthy and efficient bulk grain circulation.

By contrast, grain transportation technology of China still requires to be improved to achieve higher volume of grain transportation. In recent years, massive domestic efforts have been made to develop innovative container transportation of bulk grain. Specifically, the development of station facilities, technical equipment, information networks, and business scopes has reached an acceptable scale in a rapid manner [2].

© Springer Nature Switzerland AG 2018
X. Sun et al. (Eds.): ICCCS 2018, LNCS 11068, pp. 102–110, 2018.
https://doi.org/10.1007/978-3-030-00021-9_10

This has provided the foundation of the successful containerized grain transportation in Qingdao, Dalian, Yingkou, Guangdong, etc.

During the long-distance transport, changing in the external environments may affect the quality of bulk grain sealed in the grain containers tank. Currently, the existing information in containers transfer is incomplete. In particular, different modes of transportation in multimodal transportation involve different logistics companies, and the information is sometimes difficult to collect. In addition, the lack of quality and real time location information monitoring of food in transit has given the difficulties in the traceability of grain quality logistics information system. North-to-South Bulk Grain Container Transportation [3] logistically need quality information and traceability platform to achieve traceable, such as the information inside the bulk grain container can be inquired, the trajectory can be traced, the service quality can be traced, It will design for the large planters, warehouse processing companies, logistics companies, vendors and other users. It provides detailed on-the-go food information, which effectively solves the quality of bulk containers in transportation and logistics information traceability problems in the containers transport.

In this paper, we designed several information collection devices for North-to-South Bulk Grain Container Transportation project. Our contributions include system level design for the intelligent sensors, the in-vehicle intelligent gateway, and the key node handheld information acquisition system. In addition, we tested our ideas in the container, indoor, outdoor together with gain warehouse. Furthermore, we demonstrate performance of the temperature and humanity monitoring system based on LoRa wireless technology.

2 System Design

In order to adapt to the special requirements of the "North-to-South Bulk Grain Container Transportation" project, the Aisino Corporation will combine the data collection, storage, and the analysis technologies already accumulated in the field of the IoT to design a set of real-time information for supporting multivariate information transmission for the project. Among them, we will focus on the following four aspects.

We will develop a real-time bulk grain monitoring system based on IoT. The system uses IoT device to record the container identification. At the same time, it utilizes the sensor modules with temperature and humidity in the container to collect grain data in real time, while transmits the data back to the cloud through the wireless network. Based on the cloud open access platform, we will implement an intelligent grain traceability management and big data analysis system.

To implement the above system, we will design and develop IoT sensors that can monitor grain temperature and humidity. This sensor can read information such as temperature and humidity in the environment. The volume is similar to table tennis. The average power consumption of the equipment is small, the average current can reach 1 mA at the lowest, the component protection level is high as IP66, and the supported temperature range is wide, $-35 \sim 100°$.

At the same time, in order to solve the problem of high-intensity isolation and attenuation caused by wireless communication in metal containers used for bulk grain container logistics, we use ultra-high sensitivity, low-power, short-range wireless acquisition technologies such as LoRa to study and implement the reliable wireless communication in high-intensity isolation and attenuation metal environments. Solve the communication difficulties of the information collection terminal for the North-to-South Bulk Grains Transportation System. Finally, we will deploy the system and application to each demonstration area.

The system architecture is illustrated in Fig. 1. The smart sensor obtains the temperature and humidity information in the container through the on-board sensor chips, and transmits them to the gateway with the LoRa [4] network. The gateway integrates 3G/4G communication and the GPS/Beidou [5] positioning module can obtain the sensor information and GPS positioning information of the container together. The gateway combines the sensor and GPS location information, and sends to the server through 3G/4G (or from LoRa to Ocean Communication System). At the same time, the inspectors at various checkpoints can check the pass by containers by handheld readers. The office manager in the backend can track the global status through the management terminal.

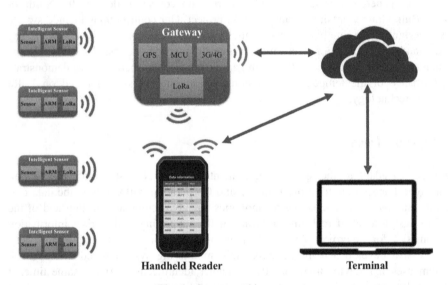

Fig. 1. System architecture.

2.1 Intelligent Sensor

The intelligent sensor includes two parts: hardware and software. The hardware diagram is shown in the Fig. 2. In general, it contains three parts: sensor, MCU and LoRa communication system.

The first part is the sensor. In this design, we use the BME280 [6] for the temperature and humidity information collection. The BME280 is a low power, high accuracy sensor for temperature, humidity and pressure. It is very small with $2.5 \times 2.5 \times 0.93$ mm^3 and 8-pin only. Furthermore, it is very suitable for low power

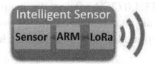

Fig. 2. Intelligent sensor.

application where it only consumes 3.6 μA at 1 Hz sample rate with low noise and high resolution performance. BME280 is widely used in the following applications: temperature changing detection, home automation control, GPS enhancement, weather forecast, and etc.

The second and third parts are the MCU + LoRa communication module CMWX1ZZABZ-091 [7] (Fig. 3). CMWX1ZZABZ-091 is fully integrated. It includes one ultra-low-power STM32L072CZ Series MCUs and a Sigfox compatible SX1276 [8] transceiver. The STM32L072CZ is an ARM$^{(R)}$ Cortex$^{(TM)}$-M0+ [9] core microcontroller, with 192 K bytes of Flash memory for program storing and 20 Kbytes of RAM for application usage. In addition, It supports USB 2.0 FS, 4-channel, 12-bit ADC, 2xDAC, 6-bit timers, LP-UART, I2C and SPI. Where we use the I2C in the STM32L072CZ to connect the BME280 sensor.

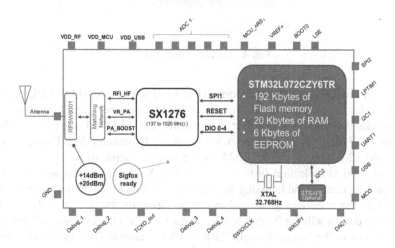

Fig. 3. CMWX1ZZABZ-091.

The LoRa communication system is Sigfox compatible SX1276 transceiver. It supports FSK, GFSK, MSK, GMSK and OOK modulations with selectable +14 dBm or +20 dBm output power. The bitrate can be programmed to 300 kbit/s. Furthermore, it is high sensitive with the receiver down to −137 dBm and with 157 dB link budget. It is also is very low power. For example, the Rx current only 10 mA.

The firmware inside STM32L072CZ triggers the reading operation period in one minute and broadcasts to the air after initialized the system. After it finished the data transfer, it enters into the sleep mode where it consumes less than 1 mA current.

2.2   Intelligent Gateway

The intelligent gateway (Fig. 4) includes more peripherals and more power hungry than the intelligent sensor. It is put in the vehicle where it collects information from multiple intelligent sensors inside the container. The intelligent gateway includes four parts: GPS, MCU, 4G module and LoRa module which as same as the one inside the intelligent sensor. The GPS and 4G module are from U-blox. The GPS module is called MAX-M8Q [10] and the 4G module is called SARA [11].

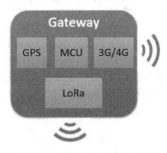

Fig. 4. Intelligent gateway.

The GPS module concurrent supports 3GNSS (GPS, Galileo, GLONASS, BeiDou) which provides the max availability for the usage. On the other side, it supports −167 dBm navigation sensitivity. We use a high-performance ARM$^{(R)}$ Cortex$^{(TM)}$-M3 NXP LPC1768 [12] MCU to control the whole system. It includes 512 KByte on-chip FLASH and 32 KByte on-chips SRAM for the gateway application.

The whole data collection system works as Fig. 5. The intelligent sensors get the reading on temperature and humidity in every minute, sent to the air and enter to sleep mode. While the intelligent gateway is continue receiving the data over the air. If it received any data, it will put it into his receiver queue. When it accumulates 5 min data, it will transmit to the server through 3G/4G with the current GPS localization information. The servers in the cloud received the data and store them into the database server for further process.

2.3   Handheld Reader

The wireless handheld terminal is used for inspection in the middle stage of the transportation. It composes a LoRa module, a SD card storage module, an OLED display module, and a high performance application processor. The system architecture of the handheld terminal is shown in the Fig. 6. The high performance application processor is MSM 8939. It has Octa-core and each core can run up to 1.5 GHz [13]. It

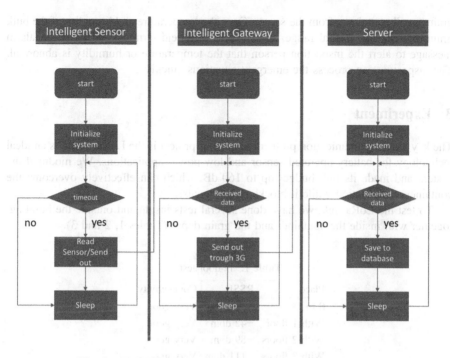

Fig. 5. Work flow of intelligent sensor, gateway and server.

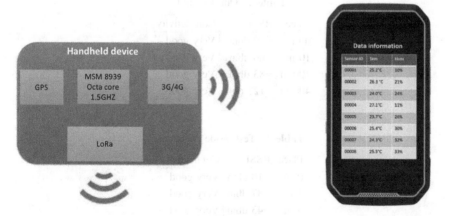

Fig. 6. Handheld terminal

supports widely connectivity such as Wi-Fi 802.11 b/g/n, BT4.0, NFC, GPS/AGPS, BeiDou, RFID HF and etc. Furthermore, it supports Android 5.0 which enables it to run a lot of applications.

From the App software, the supervisor staff can selectively display the temperature and humidity status of the grain of a specific container nearby, and observe the status of grains in all containers from the server. Once the temperature and humidity of the bulk grain exceeds the normal range, the wireless handheld terminal will issue an alarm message to alert the inspection person that the temperature or humidity is abnormal. The inspectors can process the emergent situations quickly.

3   Experiment

The key local communication protocol inside our project is the LoRa. LoRa is an ideal technology for battery-operated sensor and low-power applications. We modified the system and made its link budget up to 160 dB, which can effectively overcome the container's attenuation while it blocks radio signals.

To test the LoRa link, we have done several tests inside and outside the building, together with inside the container and the grain depot (Tables 1, 2 and 3).

Table 1. In-door test.

Place	RSSI	Connectivity
0 m	−10 dbm	Very good
With 1 floor	−42 dbm	Very good
With 2 floors	−89 dbm	Very good
With 3 floors	−111 dbm	Very good

Table 2. Out-door test.

Place	RSSI	Connectivity
0 m	−10 dbm	Very good
10 m	−66 dbm	Very good
100 m	−83 dbm	Very good
400 m	−127 dbm	Very good

Table 3. Test inside container.

Place	RSSI	Connectivity
0 m	−10 dbm	Very good
1 m	−37 dbm	Very good
5 m	−43 dbm	Very good
10 m	−65 dbm	Very good

Our experimental shows that the connectivity is very good under real usage environments: indoor, outdoor and inside containers. The transmitting is very stable in various distance and we got 98% correct packages over 10 min test on every distance in the receiver side. Our experimental results show that this design is suitable for the grain transport project.

To verify the accuracy of humidity and temperature of the sensor, we have done the comparison test with humidity and temperature measurement instrument. The result shows that the accuracy tolerance is less than 3% for humidity and one degree for temperature (Table 4).

Table 4. Field test inside the grain depot.

Place	RSSI	Connectivity	Humidity	Temperature
Close wall	−77 dbm	Very good	34.79%	5.87
In center	−105 dbm	Very good	34.80%	5.88
Inside grain	−121 dbm	Very good	34.82%	5.88

Fig. 7. Photo of the grain depot.

To verify the accuracy of humidity and temperature of the sensor, we have done the comparison test with humidity and temperature measurement instrument inside the grain warehouse (Fig. 7) with three locations (center, close to the wall, inside the grain). The result shows that our intelligent sensor has the accuracy tolerance with less than 3% for humidity and one degree for temperature.

4 Future Work

In the future, we will make the demo system more robust, make the PCB and casing to build industry graded intelligent sensors, gateway and handheld device. Furthermore, we will deploy the whole system and application to each demonstration area.

5 Conclusion

In this paper, we have designed a temperature and humidity monitoring system for North-to-South Bulk Grain Container Transportation project. Our design includes an intelligent temperature and humidity sensor which senses the temperature and humidity information from the container and grain warehouse, an intelligent gateway which help collect sensors' data, position information and sent to the backend via 3G/4G connection, a handheld terminal which facilitates the inspection personnel to view the temperature and humidity information of various containers at any time, and a demo backend system. Our system shows high application value in the North-to-South Bulk Grain Container Transportation Project.

Acknowledgement. This project is supported by the demonstration project of the high efficient quality transportation and information tracing technology of North-to-South Bulk Grain Container Transportation and the Intelligent Sensor project in Aisino Corporation. We thank the Dadushe Grain Depot in Beijing for the help in experiment testing.

References

1. Liao, C.-H., Lu, C.-S., Tseng, P.-H.: Carbon dioxide emissions and inland container transport in Taiwan. J. Transp. Geogr. **19**(4), 722–728 (2011)
2. Li, X.: Development of China's port logistics. In: Liu, B., Lee, S., Wang, L., Xu, Y., Li, X. (eds.) Contemporary Logistics in China. CCERS, pp. 147–169. Springer, Heidelberg (2014). https://doi.org/10.1007/978-3-642-55282-3_8
3. "North Grains Southward Transfer" Makes Great Efforts to Improve Zhejiang Province's Food Security Support Ability, Zhejiang People's Congress (2012)
4. Raza, U., Kulkarni, P., Sooriyabandara, M.: Low power wide area networks: an overview. IEEE Commun. Surv. Tutor. **19**(2), 855–873 (2017)
5. Nadarajah, N., Teunissen, P.J.G., Raziq, N.: Instantaneous BeiDou– GPS attitude determination: a performance analysis. Adv. Space Res. **54**(5), 851–862 (2014)
6. Soy, H., Dilay, Y., Koçer, S.: A LoRa-based Low Power Wide Area Network Application for Agricultural Weather Monitoring
7. Type ABZ. https://wireless.murata.com/eng/products/rf-modules-1/lpwa/type-abz.html. Accessed 20 Feb 2018
8. Nor, R.F.A.M., Zaman, F.H., Mubdi, S.: Smart traffic light for congestion monitoring using LoRaWAN. In: 2017 IEEE 8th Control and System Graduate Research Colloquium (ICSGRC), pp. 132–137. IEEE, August 2017
9. Agrawal, V., et al.: Low power ARM® Cortex™-M0 CPU and SRAM using Deeply Depleted Channel (DDC) transistors with Vdd scaling and body bias. In: 2013 IEEE Custom Integrated Circuits Conference (CICC), pp. 1–4. IEEE, September 2013
10. Ku, J.S., Ho, S., Sarma, S.: Landmark mapping from unbiased observations. In: 2015 IEEE First International Smart Cities Conference (ISC2), pp. 1–6. IEEE, October 2015
11. SARA U2 Series. https://www.u-blox.com/en/product/sara-u2-series. Accessed 20 Feb 2018
12. Kommu, A., Kanchi, R.R.: Design and development of a project-based embedded system laboratory using LPC1768. Am. J. Embed. Syst. Appl. **1**(2), 46–53 (2013)
13. Lamichhane, R.S.: 4G LTE Supported Mobile Phones (2018)

Terrain-Aided Strapdown Inertial Navigation System with Improved ICCP

Qi Wang[1,2(✉)], Chang-song Yang[1,2], and Yu-xiang Wang[1,2]

[1] School of Computer and Software, Nanjing University of Information Science
and Technology, Nanjing 210044, People's Republic of China
wangqiseu@163.com
[2] Jiangsu Engineering Center of Network Monitoring,
Nanjing University of Information Science and Technology,
Nanjing 210044, People's Republic of China

Abstract. Ocean exploration is playing an increasingly significant role in the development of each country because of the huge material resources therein. A terrain-aided strapdown inertial navigation system based on Kalman Filter (KF) is proposed in this paper in order to improve the navigation precision of autonomous underwater vehicles. The characteristics of strapdown inertial integrated navigation system and terrain-aided navigation system are described, and improved ICCP method is applied to the terrain aided navigation system. Simulation experiments of novel integrated navigation system proposed in the paper were carried out comparing to the traditional ICCP method. The simulation experiments suggest that the improved method is able to improve the long-time navigation precision relative to the traditional method.

Keywords: Terrain-aided strapdown inertial navigation system
Autonomous Underwater Vehicle · Strapdown inertial navigation system
Improved ICCP

1 Introduction

Unmanned, untethered and self-propelled Autonomous Underwater Vehicles (AUVs) are capable of a variety of overt and clandestine missions, including oceanographic sampling, bathymetry profiling, underwater system inspection, and military mine counter measure (MCM) operations [1–5]. The developments of wide range AUV put forward new requirements for advanced underwater navigation systems that must be accurate in position information and easy to deploy at sea. Accurate navigation is a crucial aspect of each of these missions mentioned above. The terrain aided navigation system is capable of providing accurate position information if integrated with a SINS to compensate the SINS errors for intermittent reception caused by AUV submergence. In general, terrain-aided SINS integration provides reliable navigation solutions by overcoming shortages of each alone, including the growth of SINS position errors with time. Current integrated navigation systems rely mainly on Kalman filtering to fuse data from GPS and SINS, which have some deficiencies related to observation analysis, immunity to noise, and the stochastic error models of inertial sensors [6–11].

© Springer Nature Switzerland AG 2018
X. Sun et al. (Eds.): ICCCS 2018, LNCS 11068, pp. 111–122, 2018.
https://doi.org/10.1007/978-3-030-00021-9_11

In many of these missions, it is critical that the AUV position be known to a given precision and in real time such that the seafloor can be mapped accurately, and bottom mines acquired with a high degree of confidence despite the fact that the vehicle motion is subject to large wave forces in underwater circumstances. Underwater navigation for AUVs is thus a very challenging research topic. Since AUVs are multi-function platforms, their navigation requirements depend highly on a specific mission and the sensor suite onboard. Strapdown inertial navigation system (SINS) is most used in underwater applications due to its specific advantages of small volume and high precision. Doppler Velocity Sonar (DVS) and the magnetic compass are usually exploited to bound the drift in inertial systems. Even with these aids, the position error of inertial systems drifts off with time because of the scale effects of the velocity sensors. Position fixes are needed to allow the vehicle to stay submerged for a longer time. The wireless signals attenuate greatly in the sea water, and the satellite signals are unavailable in underwater environment. Acoustic positioning is often utilized to provide precision position fixes which also greatly restricts the AUV voyage area within the sonar transponders. A hybrid navigation system based on inertial sensors aided with acoustic velocity sensors was successfully proposed in Refs. [12–17]. Arulampalam et al. and Li [18, 19] proposed integrating DVS signals with the long-baseline system to enhance the position accuracy at deep sea levels. The error sources of the DVS-based navigation system are misalignment noises and scale effects, which directly affects the navigation performance. Fu et al. and Zhou et al. [20, 21] proposed an inertial navigation algorithm assisted by DVS, depth and heading sensors. The inertial navigation aided by the DVS indicates slow drift in estimated position because of the integration of inherent errors from the sensors.

Position fixes derived from terrain profile measurements are obtained to overcome the deficiency of area restriction existing in the underwater acoustic positioning. A novel terrain-aided strapdown inertial navigation system is presented in this paper to make an efficient navigation system which consists of the strapdown inertial navigation system, the terrain-aided navigation system, the DVS and the magnetic compass.

2   Principles of Integrated Navigation System

The block diagram of the integrated navigation system is shown in Fig. 1.

The integrated navigation system consists of SINS, the DVS, the terrain-aided system and the magnetic compass. The DVS and the magnetic compass provide accurate velocity relative to the sea bottom and precision heading of the AUV respectively. The terrain-aided navigation system is able to provide position information intermittently due to the amount of terrain information that can be used in navigation. SINS, composed of three accelerometers measuring specific force and three gyros measuring turning angular rate, is best sensors for pinning and navigation of AUVs due to advantages of low cost and small volume. The SINS calculates position, velocity and attitude using output data from inertial measurement unit (IMU) at a frequency of 100 Hz [22, 23]. Therefore, the integrated navigation system proposed in this paper is able to provide precision navigation information with improved unscented Kalman filter.

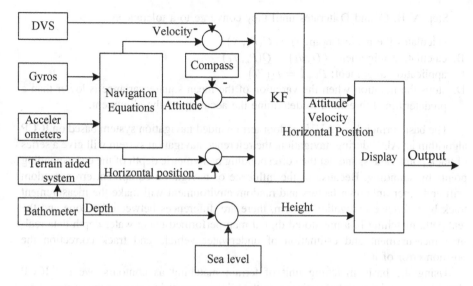

Fig. 1. Block diagram of integrated navigation system

A bathometer is used to measure the underwater geographical features and the related data processing method was applied to position estimation with the digital underwater map stored in a computer. The height is also provided by the bathometer because vertical direction of SINS is not convergent. The velocity from SINS and DVS, the horizontal position from SINS and Terrain aided navigation system are fused with improved unscented Kalman filter. The output information will eventually be used for display and revise the errors of SINS.

3   Improved ICCP Algorithm

ICCP Algorithm (Iterative Closest Contour Point or Iterative Corresponding Contour Point) is a matching method based on the principle of geometry, which was originally applied to the field of image registration. The ICCP algorithm is used to find the global optimal value under the minimum metric sense on the equivalent line, which is the final matching alignment value. It does not need to decide the corresponding points beforehand. The algorithm continuously repeats (initial) motion transformation deter-mines the corresponding relation – the process of motion transformation, and gradually improves the motion estimation.

The basic description of the ICCP algorithm is as follows:

(1)   The set of points set up by the points extracted from the data form (data shape) and the model (shape) model (a supported geometric prototype: point, line or triangle) is given.

(2)   Set the initial value of the iteration and set the initial transformation (including rotation and translation).

Step A, B, C, and D iterates until they converge to a tolerance.

A. calculates the nearest point $Y_k = C(P_k, X)$:
B. calculation alignment: $(T_k, d_k) = Q(P_k, Y_k)$
C. application alignment: $P_{k+1} = T_k(P_k)$
D. stops the iteration when the variation of the mean square variance is lower than a predetermined threshold to determine the accuracy of the alignment.

The basic principle of AUV seafloor terrain aided navigation system based on ICCP algorithm is: AUV during navigation, the reference navigation system will give a series of track point values, and get the corresponding bathymetric depth of the corresponding points by sounding. Because of the influence of navigation equipment error, random drift and other unknown factors and random environment will make the measurement track by reference navigation system, there are differences between the hope and the real path, matching in a pre stored digital map performed using water depth data real-time measurement and estimation of underwater vehicle and track correction the position error of it.

Using the basic matching unit of terrain matching as contours, we use ICCP algorithm to find the global optimum in the minimum metric sense on the contour line, and the global optimal value is the final matching alignment value.

In Fig. 2, the hollow circle represents the measurement position, the solid circle represents the real position, and the real position corresponds to the equivalent line in the measurement point.

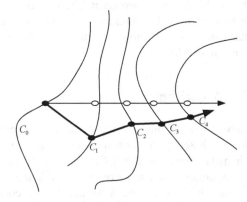

Fig. 2. Nearest point diagram of the measured value corresponding to the equivalent line

The basic flow of terrain matching based on ICCP algorithm is as follows:

(1) the reference navigation system provides location values for carrier track measurement, and sounding provides the depth of the corresponding points, and extracts the corresponding isoline set from the reference digital map.
(2) the initial alignment set is selected, that is, the initial value of the iteration is set.
(3) find the nearest point of the data point corresponding to the equivalent line.

(4) to find the transformation, and to minimize the distance between set $Y = \{y_i\}$ and set $P = \{p_i\}$.
(5) transform the set P to the set TP, that is $P_{k+1} = TP_k$.
(6) setting the terminating condition of the iteration, and the next step is satisfied.
(7) whether the accuracy of the judgment has reached the requirement, and the satisfaction is over, otherwise the match will fail.

4 Error Models

To compare the performance of the KF and EKF, a comparable simulation experiment under the same condition is conducted to determine which algorithm is preferable for improving the AUV navigation accuracy. The linear filter equation for the EKF and nonlinear filter equations for KF are elaborated below.

The linear filter states considered in the EKF are the SINS position, velocity and attitude angles and the gyro and accelerometer constant drift. The state vector of the filter is

$$X_L = \{\, \delta\lambda \quad \delta L \quad \delta V_E \quad \delta V_N \quad \phi_E \quad \phi_N \quad \phi_U \quad \nabla_X \quad \nabla_Y \quad \nabla_Z \quad \varepsilon_X \quad \varepsilon_Y \quad \varepsilon_Z \,\}^T$$

The linear error equation can be expressed in a state-space form as

$$
\begin{aligned}
\dot{\phi} &= -[\omega_{it}^t]\phi - C_b^t \delta\omega_{ib}^b + \delta\omega_{it}^t \\
\delta\dot{V}^t &= f^t\phi - (2\omega_{ie}^t + \omega_{et}^t)\delta V^t + C_b^t \delta f^b + V^t(2\delta\omega_{ie}^t + \delta\omega_{et}^t) \\
\delta\dot{\lambda} &= \frac{\delta V_E}{(R_n+h)\cos L} - \frac{V_E \delta h}{(R_n+h)^2 \cos L} + \frac{V_E \sec L \tan L \delta L}{(R_n+h)} \\
\delta\dot{L} &= \frac{\delta V_N}{R_m+h} - \frac{V_N \delta h}{(R_m+h)^2}
\end{aligned}
\tag{1}
$$

The nonlinear filter states considered in the KF are the SINS position, velocity, quaternion errors and gyro and accelerometer constant drift. The state vector of the filter is

$$X_N = \{\, \delta\lambda \quad \delta L \quad \delta V_E \quad \delta V_N \quad \delta q_0 \quad \delta q_1 \quad \delta q_2 \quad \delta q_3 \quad \nabla_X \quad \nabla_Y \quad \nabla_Z \quad \varepsilon_X \quad \varepsilon_Y \quad \varepsilon_Z \,\}^T$$

The nonlinear error equations can be expressed in a state-space form as [17]

$$\delta\dot{Q}_b^t = \frac{1}{2}\Omega_u(\omega_{ib}^b)\delta Q_b^t - \frac{1}{2}\Omega_d(\omega_{it}^t)\delta Q_b^t + \frac{1}{2}U(Q_b^t)\delta\omega_{ib}^b - \frac{1}{2}Y(Q_b^t)\delta\omega_{it}^t \tag{2}$$

$$\delta\dot{V}^t = \delta C_b^t f^b - (2\omega_{ie}^t + \omega_{et}^t) \times \delta V^t + C_b^t \delta f^b + V^t \times (2\delta\omega_{ie}^t + \delta\omega_{et}^t) \tag{3}$$

where $\Omega_u(\omega) = \begin{bmatrix} 0 & -\omega_x & -\omega_y & -\omega_z \\ \omega_x & 0 & \omega_z & -\omega_y \\ \omega_y & -\omega_z & 0 & \omega_x \\ \omega_z & \omega_y & -\omega_x & 0 \end{bmatrix}$

$\Omega_d(\omega) = \begin{bmatrix} 0 & -\omega_x & -\omega_y & -\omega_z \\ \omega_x & 0 & -\omega_z & \omega_y \\ \omega_y & \omega_z & 0 & -\omega_x \\ \omega_z & -\omega_y & \omega_x & 0 \end{bmatrix}$ $U(Q_b^{n'}) = \begin{bmatrix} -\tilde{q}_1 & -\tilde{q}_2 & -\tilde{q}_3 \\ \tilde{q}_0 & -\tilde{q}_3 & \tilde{q}_2 \\ \tilde{q}_3 & \tilde{q}_0 & -\tilde{q}_1 \\ -\tilde{q}_2 & \tilde{q}_1 & \tilde{q}_0 \end{bmatrix}$

The errors of the gyro and the accelerometer are composed of constant drift and random drift. The constant drift of the gyro and the accelerometer do not change with time.

$$\delta f^b = \begin{bmatrix} \delta f_X \\ \delta f_Y \\ \delta f_Z \end{bmatrix} = \begin{bmatrix} \nabla_X \\ \nabla_Y \\ \nabla_Z \end{bmatrix} + \begin{bmatrix} W_{aX} \\ W_{aY} \\ W_{aZ} \end{bmatrix} = \nabla + W_a \tag{4}$$

$$\delta \omega_{ib}^b = \begin{bmatrix} \delta \omega_X \\ \delta \omega_Y \\ \delta \omega_Z \end{bmatrix} = \begin{bmatrix} \varepsilon_X \\ \varepsilon_Y \\ \varepsilon_Z \end{bmatrix} + \begin{bmatrix} W_{gX} \\ W_{gY} \\ W_{gZ} \end{bmatrix} = \varepsilon + W_g \; \dot{\varepsilon} = [\dot{\varepsilon}_x \quad \dot{\varepsilon}_y \quad \dot{\varepsilon}_z]^T = 0 \tag{5}$$

where W_a and W_g are zero mean Gauss white noises.

Let the real position of the vehicle be $(\lambda_r \quad L_r \quad h_r)$, the position obtained from the Terrain system be $(\lambda_T \quad L_T \quad h_T)$, and the position information obtained from the SINS is

$$\lambda_I = \lambda_r + \delta\lambda, L_I = L_r + \delta L, h_I = h_r + \delta h \tag{6}$$

The position information obtained from the terrain system is

$$\lambda_T = \lambda_r - \frac{N_E}{(R_n + h)\cos L}, L_T = L_r - \frac{N_N}{R_m + h}, h_T = h_r - N_h \tag{7}$$

where N_E, N_N, N_h are the position errors of the terrain system along the east, north and up directions, respectively.

The measurement equation of position is

$$Z_P = \begin{bmatrix} (\lambda_I - \lambda_G)(R_n + h)\cos L \\ (L_I - L_G)(R_m + h) \\ h_I - h_G \end{bmatrix} = \begin{bmatrix} (R_n + h)\cos L\delta\lambda + N_E \\ (R_m + h)\delta L + N_N \\ \delta h + N_h \end{bmatrix} \tag{8}$$

Let the real velocity of the vehicle in a plane be (V_{rE}, V_{rN}), the measured velocity from the DVS be (V_{DE}, V_{DN}), and the velocity of the SINS and the velocity from the DVS are

$$\begin{cases} V_E = V_{rE} + \delta V_E \\ V_N = V_{rN} + \delta V_N \end{cases} \quad \begin{cases} V_{DE} = V_{rE} - M_E \\ V_{DN} = V_{rN} - M_N \end{cases} \tag{9}$$

where M_E, M_N are measurement errors of the DVS along the east and the north directions, respectively.

The measurement equation of velocity is

$$Z_V = \begin{bmatrix} V_E - V_{DE} \\ V_N - V_{DN} \end{bmatrix} = \begin{bmatrix} \delta V_E + M_E \\ \delta V_N + M_N \end{bmatrix} \tag{10}$$

Suppose that the real heading of the vehicle is ϕ_r, the heading from the magnetic compass is ϕ_C, the heading of the SINS and the compass are

$$\phi_I = \phi_r + \delta\phi_I \text{ and } \phi_C = \phi_r - \delta\phi_C \tag{11}$$

The measurement equation of the heading is

$$Z_\phi = \phi_I - \phi_C = \delta\phi_I + \delta\phi_C \tag{12}$$

5   Simulation Experiments

The 3D graph simulation area as shown in Fig. 3, the maximum depth of the seabed 100 m, storage format map for square grid data, the grid spacing of 100 m, the initial longitude (120°, 38°). The course is 45°, the voyage dive depth of 20 m depth, sailing, track the length is 20 points. The reference navigation system uses the SINS/DVL/MCP combination to provide the reference position of the terrain matching system AUV. The simulation experiments of the integrated system are carried out by Matlab/Simulink and VC++ tools. Suppose that the AUV is navigating on a flat plane at a certain depth. The integrated navigation system has initial conditions and model parameters as follows, the initial position error of longitude, latitude and height is $5''$, $5''$, 100 m, the initial velocity of east and north is 10 m/s, 10 m/s, the initial velocity error of east, north and up is 0.1 m/s, 0.1 m/s, 0.1 m/s, the initial attitude angle of heading, pitching and rolling is 45°, 0°, 0°, the initial attitude angle error of heading, pitching and rolling is $10''$, $10''$, $30''$, the constant bias and random drift of 3 accelerometres is100ug, the constant drift and random drift of 3 gyroscopes is 0.1 /h, the swing amplitude of AUV heading, pitching and rolling is14°, 9°, 12°, the swing period of AUV heading, pitching and rolling is 6 s, 8 s, 10 s.

(1) DVL Errors

DVL Velocity Error	0.1 m/s
DVL Coefficient Error	0.01

(2) MCP Errors

MCP Heading Error	0.5°
MCP Pitching Error	0.2°
MCP Rolling Error	0.2°

A general two-dimensional and first order discrete autoregressive equation

$$Z(x_i, y_i) = a_1 z(x_i - \Delta x, y_j) + a_2 z(x_i, y_j - \Delta y) + a_3 z(x_i - \Delta x, y_j - \Delta y) + W(x_i, y_j)$$
(13)

In the same way, the terrain boundary in the X direction and the Y direction can be generated by two one-dimensional random processes, which are as follows:

$$Z(x_i, y_0) = az(x_i - \Delta x, y_0) + W(x_i, y_0)$$
(14)

$$Z(x_0, y_i) = az(x_0, y_j - \Delta y) + W(x_0, y_j)$$
(15)

where $Z(x_i, y_i)$ is (x_i, y_i) the height of the topographic relief, Δx and Δy are sample intervals along the x and y direction. $W(x_i, y_j)$ is the zero mean white noise sequence and covariance is δ_w^2.

It can be assumed that the adjacent terrain sampling points have the same correlation characteristics in the direction and diagonal direction, so that it can be ordered. $a_1 = a_2 = a$, $a_3 = b$. According to the isotropy and stability of the terrain, we know that,

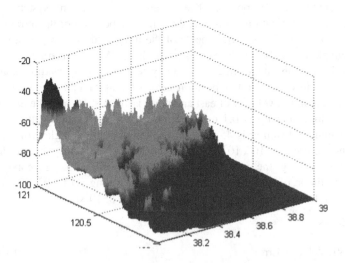

Fig. 3. Undersea terrain diagram

$$\begin{cases} a = \exp\left[-\frac{1}{T_{auc}}\right] \\ b = -a^2 \\ \delta_w^2 = (d_{RMS})^2 \exp\left[-\frac{i+j}{T_{auc}}\right] \end{cases} \quad (16)$$

The correlation function of the above two dimensional random function is

$$R_{ij} = (d_{RMS})^2 \exp\left[-\frac{i+j}{T_{auc}}\right] \quad (17)$$

In this way, the two dimensional random process, whose mean square variance is, attenuates exponentially and the correlation distance is. The following digital maps can be generated by setting the parameters, as shown in Fig. 3.

Figures 4, 5, 6 and 7 above show that latitude and longitude errors of terrain aided navigation system are 80 m (RMS) and 60 m (RMS) respectively, while the longitude error and latitude error of reference navigation system increase with time. In order to investigate the sensitivity of matching algorithm to initial position error, besides other initial location errors, other simulation parameters remain unchanged. The error standard deviation is interval between 100 m, increasing from 100 m to 600 m. Simulation results are shown in Table 1. From the data in the table, we can see that the initial position error has great influence on the ICCP algorithm, and the initial position error is large, and it has little influence on the MAD/ICCP algorithm when the algorithm search box is in the range. Under the condition of abundant information of terrain navigation, MAD coarse matching/ICCP algorithm has higher real-time performance and higher output location accuracy, and the algorithm has higher initial error resistance. It provides reliable location information source for AUV integrated navigation system.

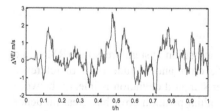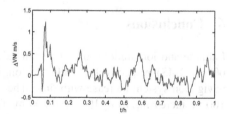

Fig. 4. Variability of velocity along the east and north direction with traditional ICCP

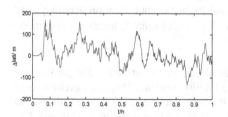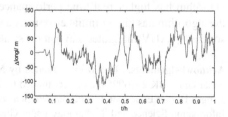

Fig. 5. Variability of position (latitude and longitude) errors with traditional ICCP

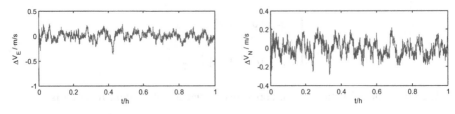

Fig. 6. Variability of velocity along the east and north direction with improved ICCP

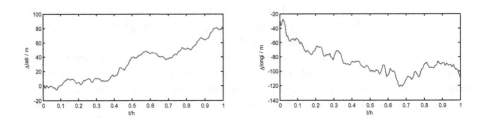

Fig. 7. Variability of position (latitude and longitude) errors with improved ICCP

Table 1. Algorithm error of traditional ICCP and improved ICCP

Initial position error	100 m	200 m	300 m	400 m	500 m	600 m
ICCP algorithm error (RMS)	106.95 m	115.82 m	150.57 m	267.80 m	405.24 m	Unavailable
Improved ICCP algorithm error (RMS)	93.56 m	109.37 m	117.15 m	120.83 m	125.90 m	131.45 m

6   Conclusions

Latitude and longitude errors of terrain aided navigation system are 80 m (RMS) and 60 m (RMS) respectively, while the longitude error and latitude error of reference navigation system increase with time. The error standard deviation is interval between 100 m, increasing from 100 m to 600 m. The initial position error has great influence on the ICCP algorithm, and the initial position error is large, and it has little influence on the MAD/ICCP algorithm when the algorithm search box is in the range. Under the condition of abundant information of terrain navigation, MAD coarse matching/ICCP algorithm has higher real-time performance and higher output location accuracy, and the algorithm has higher initial error resistance. It provides reliable location information source for AUV integrated navigation system.

Acknowledgements. This work is funded by Natural Science Foundation of Jiangsu Province under Grant BK 20160955, a project funded by the Priority Academic Program Development of Jiangsu Higher Education Institutions and Science Research Foundation of Nanjing University of Information Science and Technology under Grant 20110430. Open Foundation of Jiangsu Key

Laboratory of Meteorological Observation and Information Processing (KDXS1304), Open Foundation of Jiangsu Key Laboratory of Ocean Dynamic Remote Sensing and Acoustics (KHYS1405).

References

1. Jalving, B., Gade, K., Hagen, O., et al.: A toolbox of aiding techniques for the HUGIN AUV integrated inertial navigation system. IEEE Proc. Oceans **2**(3), 1146–1153 (2003)
2. Cai, T.: Novel gravity passive navigation system. J. SE Univ. (English Edition) **22**(1), 59–63 (2006)
3. Fu, Z., Wu, X., Wang, Q., Ren, K.: Enabling central keyword-based semantic extension search over encrypted outsourced data. IEEE Trans. Inf. Forensics Secur. **12**(12), 2986–2997 (2017)
4. Chen, B., Qi, X., Sun, X., Shi, Y.: Quaternion pseudo-Zernike moments combining both of RGB information and depth information for color image splicing detection. J. Vis. Commun. Image Represent. **49**, 283–290 (2017)
5. Ren, Y., Shen, J., Liu, D., Wang, J.: Evidential quality preserving of electronic record in cloud storage. J. Internet Technol. **17**(6), 1125–1132 (2016)
6. Nygren, I., Jansson, M.: Terrain navigation using the correlator method. In: Position Location and Navigation Symposium, Monterey, CA, pp. 649–657 (2011)
7. Wang, B., Gu, X., Ma, L., Yan, S.: Temperature error correction based on BP neural network in meteorological WSN. Int. J. Sens. Netw. **23**(4), 265–278 (2017)
8. Sun, Y., Gu, F.: Compressive sensing of piezoelectric sensor response signal for phased array structural health monitoring. Int. J. Sens. Netw. **23**(4), 258–264 (2017)
9. Chen, B., Zhou, C., Jeon, B., Zheng, Y., Wang, J.: Quaternion discrete fractional random transform for color image adaptive watermarking. Multimed. Tools Appl. **77**, 20809–20837 (2017)
10. Fang, W., Wen, X., Xu, J., Zhu, J.: CSDA: a novel cluster-based secure data aggregation scheme for WSNs. Cluster Comput. (2017)
11. Gu, B.: A regularization path algorithm for support vector ordinal regression. Neural Netw. **98**, 114–121 (2017)
12. Gul, F., Fang, J., Gaho, A.: GPS/SINS navigation data fusion using quaternion model and un-scented Kalman filter. In: International Conference on Mechatronics and Automation, Luoyang, China, pp. 1854–1859 (2012)
13. Xie, J., Zhao, R., Xia, Y.: Combined terrain aided navigation based on correlation method and parallel Kalman filters. In: Proceedings of the8th International Conference on Electronic Measurement and Instrument, ICEMI 2007, Xi an, China, pp. 145–150 (2007)
14. Chen, X., Chen, S., Wu, Y.: Coverless information hiding method based on the Chinese character encoding. J. Internet Technol. **18**(2), 313–320 (2017)
15. Tian, Q., Chen, S.: Cross-heterogeneous-database age estimation through correlation representation learning. Neurocomputing **238**, 286–295 (2017)
16. Qu, Z., John, K., Sebastian, R.: Multilevel pattern mining architecture for automatic network monitoring in heterogeneous wireless communication networks. China Commun. **13**(7), 108–116 (2016)
17. Yan, L., Zheng, W.: Learning discriminative sentiment chunk vectors for twitter sentiment. J. Internet Technol. **18**(7), 1605–1613 (2017)

18. Arulampalam, M., Maskell, S., Gordon, N.: A tutorial on particle filters for online nonlinear/non-gaussian bayesian tracking. IEEE Trans. Signal Process. **50**(2), 174–188 (2012)
19. Li, T.: Research on application of nonlinear filtering in navigation system. Institute of Mechatronical Engineering and Automation of National University of Defence Technology, Changsha (2003)
20. Fu, Z., Huang, F., Ren, K., Weng, J., Wang, C.: Privacy-preserving smart semantic search based on conceptual graphs over encrypted outsourced data. IEEE Trans. Inf. Forensics Secur. **12**(8), 1874–1884 (2017)
21. Zhou, Z., Wang, Y., Jonathan, Q., Yang, C., Sun, X.: Effective and efficient global context verification for image copy detection. IEEE Trans. Inf. Forensics Secur. **12**(1), 48–63 (2017)
22. Xia, Z., Wang, X., Zhang, L., Qin, Z., Sun, X., Ren, K.: A privacy-preserving and copy-deterrence content-based image retrieval scheme in cloud computing. IEEE Trans. Inf. Forensics Secur. **11**(11), 2594–2608 (2016)
23. Li, J., Li, X., Yang, B., Sun, X.: Segmentation-based image copy-move forgery detection scheme. IEEE Trans. Inf. Forensics Secur. **10**(3), 507–518 (2015)

The Construction of Solar Greenhouse Control System Based on IoT Data Security

Yan Zhang[✉], Xintong Jiang, Guizeng You, and Pengzeng Liu

Shandong Agricultural University, Tai'an 271018, China
zhangyandxy@sdau.edu.cn

Abstract. Aiming at the relatively low level of solar greenhouse intelligent control in northern China, while considering the data security of the IoT, this paper describes the construction of solar greenhouse control system from four aspects, including hardware design, lower computer program, upper computer program and mobile APP. The control system has been applied in the greenhouse of Lingxian, Dezhou. The use of the system saves the labor force, improves the labor efficiency and farmer's income.

Keywords: IoT data security · Intelligent control · Solar greenhouse

1 Introduction

As a unique greenhouse type in northern China, the solar greenhouse is an important source of winter vegetables, which are planted in the north. Especially in recent years, the technology of facility horticulture has been developing rapidly in China's agriculture, but the level of intelligent control is relatively low and mainly depend on manual controlling, which affects the yield and quality of the facility crops. In order to change this situation, while ensuring the safety of IoT data, this paper describes the construction of solar greenhouse control system based on IoT data security. The system has been applied in the solar greenhouse of Lingxian, Dezhou, which is the main producing area of zucchini. This realizes the increase of production and farmer's income.

2 The Overall Structure of Intelligent Control System for Solar Greenhouse

The intelligent control system of solar greenhouse is divided into two parts: hardware design and software design [2]. As shown in Fig. 1, the whole hardware structure takes the MSP430F5438A as the core, mainly including information collection module, LCD display module, relay module, GPRS module and control module. The software structure mainly includes the lower computer program, the upper computer program, the web program and the mobile phone APP program. The cooperative principle of software and hardware is: the acquisition module acquires the data of air temperature and humidity, soil temperature and humidity, light intensity, and CO_2 concentration by

X. Sun et al. (Eds.): ICCCS 2018, LNCS 11068, pp. 123–132, 2018.
https://doi.org/10.1007/978-3-030-00021-9_12

sensors. According to the collection frequency set by the user and the corresponding transmission protocol, the lower computer program collects data in real time, and transmits the data to the upper computer program through the GPRS module. And then, following the preset database parameters, the upper computer program saves the data to the MySQL database. Using the real-time data and the initial threshold, the APP of the mobile phone determines whether the data of the greenhouse exceeds the limit value. If it exceeds, the upper computer program starts the relay module to open or close the control terminal [3], and then gives the warning (Fig. 2).

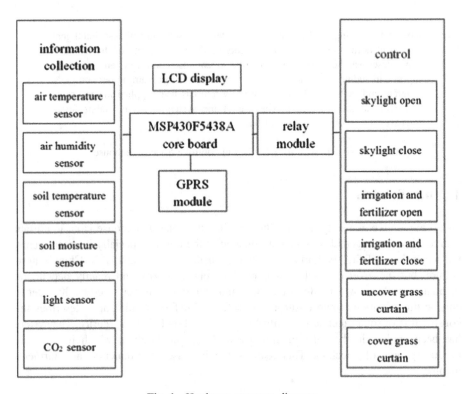

Fig. 1. Hardware structure diagram

3   Realization of Intelligent Control System

3.1   Hardware System Implementation

The lower computer takes MSP430F5438A as the core and integrates a series of powerful peripheral chips such as DS3231 clock chip, two 5 V solid state relays, two TTL-to-485 chips, and universal serial interface (USB) to ensure the low consumption and high reliability of the intelligent terminal. In the sensing terminal design, the SHT11 sensor is selected to measure air temperature and humidity. Its components and processing circuitry are integrated in a miniature circuit board. The working voltage of

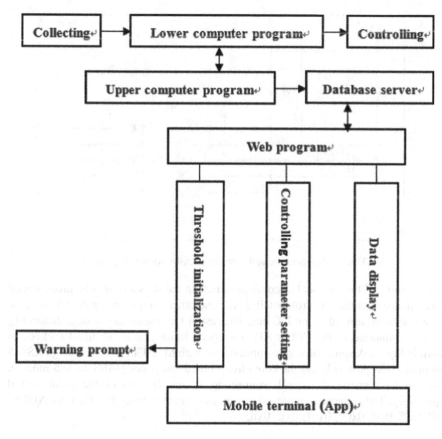

Fig. 2. Software structure diagram

the sensor is 3 V and the output is a fully calibrated two-wire digital signal. Its detail parameters are as follows, the temperature measurement accuracy: ±0.5 °C, the humidity measurement range: 0–100%RH, the humidity measurement accuracy: ±4.5%RH. ARN-GZ light intensity sensor is selected to measure Light intensity. Its parameters are as follows, output signal: 4–20 mA, the measurement range: 0–200Klux, the accuracy: ±3%. The type of soil temperature sensor is TW whose measuring range is – 30 °C–70 °C and the measuring accuracy is ±0.15 °C. The type of soil moisture sensor is FDS-100. The parameters of it are as follows, output signal: 4–20 mA, the measurement range: 0–100%, the accuracy: ±3%. TDR-4 is selected as soil conductivity sensor. The parameters are, output signal: 4–20 mA, the measurement range: 0–100%, the accuracy: ±3%. The NHEY62 of ZhongKeNengHui is selected as carbon dioxide sensor. The output signal of it is 4–20 mA. Its measurement range is 0–2000 ppm, and the accuracy is ±2%.

The output of the temperature and humidity sensor is digital. Its wiring diagram is shown in Fig. 3. SHT11 is connected with the 5 V output pin of MSP430F5438A control center. GND and board are all connected with ground. SHT11 uses a serial

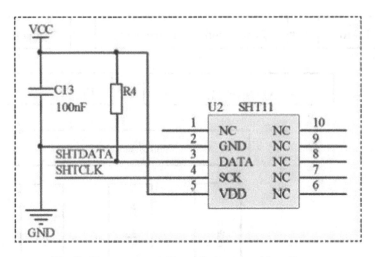

Fig. 3. Temperature and humidity sensor wiring diagram

interface and I2C bus protocol to communicate. But the sensor cannot be programmed in accordance with the I2C protocol, if there is no other component on the I2C bus, the sensor can be connected to the I2C bus. The rest of the sensors are analog sensors [4], which is connected to the CPU's AD conversion input pins by standard sockets, as shown in Fig. 4. Acquisition card communicates with MSP430F5438A through RS485 communication protocol, and the core circuit board integrates UART to 485 module. Data can be transmitted through connecting A and B lines of the serial port 0 respectively. The collection command is a series of instruction codes. They are ADDR, 0x03, 0xff, 0xff, 0x00, 0x01, 0xff, 0xff.

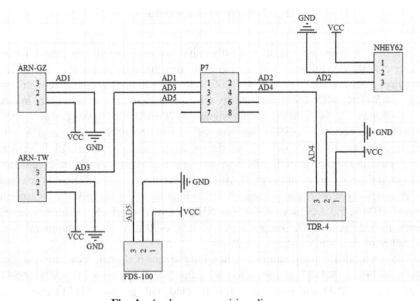

Fig. 4. Analog sensor wiring diagram

The control part controls the relay by signal amplification, which then controls the grass curtain, irrigation and the opening and closing of skylight. The control part is shown in Fig. 5. In order to achieve flexible controlling, the core circuit board has two 5 V relays to control the 12 V on or off and also has the pin of two ports which can be connected with an external 5 V relay. And then the control part can realize 12 V DC controlling 220 V AC through the relay. Taking irrigation as an example, the control principle is as follows: The core processing board comprehensively judges the state of the greenhouse by greenhouse data collected from various sensors and peripheral circuits. According to the soil humidity in greenhouse and pre-designed program, it can control the watering time and watering amount. The P2.6 output pin of the core circuit board can control the contactor through 5 V relay, and finally it achieves automatic or manual irrigation by controlling the pump motor.

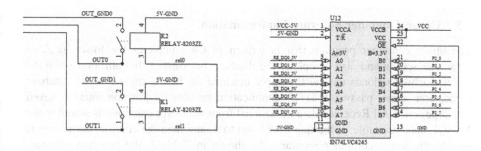

Fig. 5. Control part wiring diagram

3.2 Software Implementation of the Lower Computer

The lower computer software implements terminal data acquisition and information control. The format of the data packets sent by the PC software and the terminal response are shown in Table 1. The header 0xA5 is the beginning of a packet, and 0xAE represents the end of the packet. The data item "check-sum" in the delivery and response formats takes two bytes and the value is the sum from "header" (including "header") to "checksum" (excluding "check-sum"). The "content" item length is variable when the item "set/read-back" is set "read-back", which is the same as the byte length of "packet data" in the delivered data format. And when the item is set "set", the length of "content" is 6 bytes. Through above transmission protocol, the terminal acquires digital information which includes air temperature, air humidity and analog information which includes soil temperature, soil humidity, CO_2 concentration, illumination intensity. The analog information is processing through A/D conversion and filtering. All the collected information is temporarily stored in the array variable, and they are transmitted to the upper computer program through the GPRS module [5] according to the pre-set acquisition frequency. The "instructions" item in the above transmission protocol specifies different control instructions, and then it realizes the opening or closing of terminal equipment.

Table 1. Packet format of PC software sending and terminal response

Send packet format		Terminal reply packet format	
Data	Length (byte)	Data	Length (byte)
packet-header	1	packet-header	1
packet-length	2	packet-length	2
user ID	2	user ID	2
reserved	3	set/read-back	1
instruction	1	reserved	2
packet-data	fixed length	instruction	1
check-sum	2	content	fixed length
packet-tail	1	check-sum	2
		packet-tail	1

3.3   Upper Computer Software Implementation

The upper computer program that is written in C# completes the lower machine parameter setting and also completes the database information Initialization when the lower machine uploads data to the upper machine (including the server IP, database name, user name, password, DTU identification number, acquisition interval, saved data type, etc.); All Received data transmitted from the lower computer is stored in the MySQL database table; If the flag field is set to 1, and then the control instructions is sent to the lower computer program; As shown in Table 2, the program monitors whether the index value collected exceeds the threshold according to the threshold values of different growth period indicators of zucchini. If exceeded, the interface provided by the China SMSC platform will automatically send SMS messages to users. The upper computer software interface is shown in Fig. 6.

Table 2. Different growth cycle thresholds of zucchini

	Germination period	Seedling stage	Early flowering	Fruit period
Air temperature	13–35	10–40	15–30	15–32
Soil Moisture	70%–80%	80%–90%	70%–80%	70%–80%

3.4   Mobile APP Software Implementation

The mobile APP of solar greenhouse control system which is developed by Android studio, Android SDK and other tools realizes the functions of viewing different greenhouse data, viewing the current greenhouse real-time data, viewing a historical record of the data in the form of line chart, capturing image, monitoring real-time monitor video, controlling equipment and feedback, etc. The remote control commands need to be set in the equipment control, and some remote control devices and commands are given in Table 3. There are two ways to achieve solar greenhouse control functions: One is controlling command, and the other is a cell phone text message. Taking controlling of irrigation as an example, the specific realization of the process are

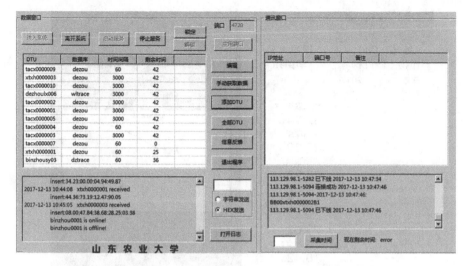

Fig. 6. Upper computer programming window

Table 3. Part remote control instructions

Equipment	Open instruction	Close instruction
Water valve motor	BB00+(11 bit identification code)+AE	BB00+(11 bit identification code)+AF
Fertilizer motor	BB00+(11 bit identification code)+AC	BB00+(11 bit identification code)+AD
Main pipe solenoid valve	BB00+(11 bit identification code)+AA	BB00+(11 bit identification code)+AB
Irrigation and fertilizer (upper and lower limit of watering humidity)	BB01+(11 bit identification code) +#13+(upper limit of water humidity) +:+(lower limit of water humidity)+: +(Maximum watering time)+:$;	
Electric fan	SMS "open"	SMS "close"

as follows: After loading the device control page, the class loading page is called first, and then it uses functions to obtain the current greenhouse number, and stores the number in the variable. The system loads the monitor event which is controlled by the device switch according to the greenhouse number. When the user clicks a command button or enters a watering instruction, the system triggers the corresponding monitoring event and calls the popup window to enter the verification code. After the verification is passed, the system calls class to open a new thread and by using of socket communications, sends instructions to the upper computer program through the TCP/IP protocol. After receiving the operation instruction from the user, the upper

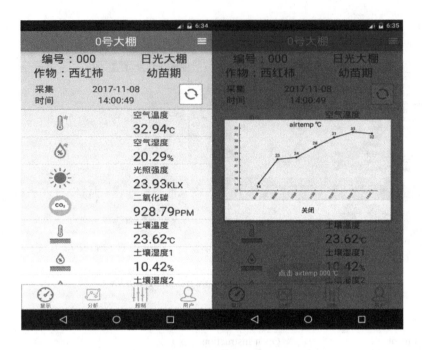

Fig. 7. Mobile app part interface

computer program sends the instruction to the lower computer program located in the greenhouse, and the lower computer makes the greenhouse device respond to the user's instruction. About another controlling method, taking fan controlling as an example, the specific implementation process is as follows: Click the fan switch button, the system will create a Sim object, call the constructor (String message) to enter the operation instruction "open" or "close", and then call the sending message function in the Sim class to send a message to a sim card number which is stored in the Sim class. After receiving the short message, the device responds according to the content of the short message. The mobile phone APP interface is shown in Fig. 7.

4   Realization of IoT Data Security

In order to avoid interference and ensure the accuracy of data received during data transmission of the Internet of Things, CRC32 checksums are added at the sending end and the receiving end. The specific implementation process is: Using a CRC32 "generator polynomial", the sender generates a check code (CRC code) according to the binary code sequence which is transmitted by the sensor, and attaches the original information to form a new binary code sequence. The receiver uses a modulo-two division test to verify the error.

In order to ensure the security of environmental data and control data in IOT database, a trigger is created in the database management system MySQL to implement a daily triggered backup function at 17 o'clock every day. The redundant data is used to protect the environment data and control data security.

5   Conclusion

Currently, the solar greenhouse intelligent control system based on the data security of IOT has been running more than one year in Lingxian, Dezhou. On the one hand, users can use mobile phone to query historical and real-time greenhouse environmental data and watch video of greenhouse. And so, it can provides data support and guide crop production for the daily production of the household. On the other hand, according to the threshold, it realizes the automatic warning of environmental data and realizes the automatic controlling of grasshoppers, skylight and irrigation. Manual controlling can be also achieved through the mobile phone APP. The control method is efficient and flexible. At the same time, it also greatly saves labor and improves production efficiency.

References

1. Zhang, Z., Zou, Z.: Design of solar greenhouse control system based on single-chip microcomputer. Microcomput. Inf. **22**(35), 77–78 (2006)
2. Ma, H., Zhang, C., Zheng, B.: Research on solar greenhouse environment monitoring system based on ZigBee technology. Agric. Mech. Res. **6**, 221–224 (2015)

3. Wang, L., Yang, G., Xu, X.: Study on the fuzzy control system of solar greenhouse temperature and humidity. J. Northeast. Agric. Univ. **36**(5), 625–627 (2005)
4. Wang, S., Feng, Q., Wang, S.: Design and research of the distributed control system of solar temperature room based on wireless RF technology. J. Chin. Agric. Mach. **3**, 72–75 (2006)
5. Wang, J., Liu, Y., Yang, X.: Design of solar greenhouse control system based on mobile phone text. J. Chin. Agric. Mach. **4**, 145–147 (2012)
6. Wang, X., Liu, Z., Li, R.: Design and research on internet of things of sunlight greenhouse. J. Agric. Mech. Res. **8**, 189–192 (2014)
7. Wang, H., Wang, S., Wang, Z., Zhang, L.: The mobile intelligent control system of greenhouse based on IoT and WiFi. J. Agric. Mech. Res. **4**, 187–190 (2014)
8. Guo, X., Zeng, G., Wu, X., Cui, S.: Design of Intelligent Greenhouse Control System Based on AVR Single-chip Microcomputer. J. Tianjin Univ. Sci. Technol. **5**, 65–68 (2012)

The Internet of Things and Big Data in the Submarine Cable Release Process of Finite Element Simulation and Matlab Simulation

Chao Zhang[✉] and Junmei Wang

Department of Mathematics, Shandong Agricultural University, Tai'an 271018, China
zhangch@sdau.edu.cn

Abstract. The cable is a very important tool for information transmission, and the process of laying by ships will be affected by the waves and wind on the sea, in the paper we set up the model of the process, We now by setting the united equipment acquisition cable on each node in the sea water pressure value, according to the motion state on the cable at the same time establish the physical dynamic equation by finite element method (fem) of matlab simulation to determine the movement of the cable to get sea cable in different sea conditions in case of trajectory can provide a scientific reference for laying optical cable and establish the corresponding equations of motion, and simulate the process of laying under different sea conditions in MATLAB.

Keywords: Local cartesian coordinate system · Finite difference
Matlab

1 Introduction

1.1 Background

Driven by the rapid growth of Internet traffic around the world, the global demand for fiber-optic cable is steadily improving, with China being the main driver of the global demand for fiber optic cables. With the gradual improvement of China's optical fiber to household deployment, the household broadband market share is gradually increasing, and the demand growth rate of broadband fiber optic cable in the home will decrease. Corporate broadband is a neglected market compared with home broadband. The era of cloud computing, more and more companies adopt cloud services, corporate clients for business needs of bandwidth, delay, and the service response have higher requirements, especially in areas such as financial, medical, networking, enterprise broadband demand, so more and more enterprises begin to choose to use special line way to get to the Internet, the user viscosity is stronger.

Internet of things and enterprise broadband synergistic drive fiber optic cable demand.

© Springer Nature Switzerland AG 2018
X. Sun et al. (Eds.): ICCCS 2018, LNCS 11068, pp. 133–143, 2018.
https://doi.org/10.1007/978-3-030-00021-9_13

According to the ministry of previously published on comprehensively advancing mobile Internet of things "(NB - IoT) notice of construction and development planning, planning requirements, to the end of 2017, NB - IoT network coverage municipalities directly under the central government, provincial capital cities and other major cities, the base station size to about 400000. By 2020, the nb-iot network will be widely covered nationwide, and the application scenarios of indoor, traffic network and underground pipe network will be fully covered, and the base station will reach 1.5 million. The construction of new base stations will lead to the demand for fiber optic cable connections during the deployment of nb-iot.

And the development of enterprise broadband can further improve the Internet of things network conditions. Due to the business demand, enterprise broadband will have higher requirements for bandwidth, delay and service response, and it will promote the network condition of the Internet of things. In addition, the construction of enterprise broadband can be said to have locked the enterprise customers in the era of the Internet of things in advance, which also has a great effect on the construction of Internet of things. As the Internet of things into each vertical industry, the corresponding vertical industry enterprises and institutions will be one of the main demand of Internet service, both have the same customer group, operators can joint broadband business, provide comprehensive services for the enterprise.

1.2   Technological Development

Currently, the main business line with DDN, optical fiber, SDH, microwave and other means to get to the Internet, in addition to being able to satisfy the business enterprise customer demand for the quality of the network, bandwidth, as well as to the security, stability, etc., can also optimize enterprise dedicated server, VPN, a variety of applications such as video conference. Therefore, the enterprise special line will be the new choice for the future development of the industry.

Sensor technology, microelectronics, communication technologies and internet related software frameworks have made huge progress in recent years. Sensor technology has ignited machine-to-machine-communication.

Embedded microelectronics have led to remarkable levels of automation in production. Wireless and non-wireless communication technology has accelerated data transfer significantly. On the computational side we are witnessing the accelerating dominance of the internet. Innovative software paradigms enable new technologies like in-memory computing, non- SQL database technology, cloud computing and Big Data processing. With significant progress in all technical dimensions, the window for disruptive interconnectivity of machines and humans is now wide open. In industry, Computer Integrated Manufacturing (CIM) and machine-to-machine (M2M) communication with their numerous standards and communication protocols have already changed the shop-floor. CIM and M2M connect machines, mainly as proprietary, closed systems. The Internet of Things (IoT) is much more inclusive than CIM and M2M: everything is connected to everything else (hence also labeled "Internet of Everything") using Internet fabric and protocols. It is the network of uniquely addressable physical assets equipped with sensors which nudge information systems to capture, process, analyze, and exchange data – while including humans as sources, data sinks or something in-between. This convergence of the internet and physical objects is a challenge which creates game-changing opportunities and risks for business development. IoT connects devices, people, places, and even ideas or events. As a final consequence, this disruption is a result of the ability to "make sense" of data, i.e. to leverage the value of data.

The technological advancements and rapid convergence of wireless communication, digital electronics, and micro-electro- mechanical systems (MEMS) technologies have resulted in the emergence of Internet of Things (IoT). According to the Cisco report, 1 the number of objects connected to the Internet has exceeded the number of human beings in the world. These Internet- connected objects, which include PCs, smartphones, tablets, WiFi- enabled sensors, wearable devices, and household appliances, form the IoT as shown in Fig. 1. Reports show that the number of Internet-connected devices is expected to increase twofold from 22.9 billion in 2016 to 50 billion by 2020 as shown in Fig. 2. Most IoT applications do not only focus on monitoring discrete events but also on mining the information collected by IoT objects. Most data collection tools in the IoT environment are sensor-fitted devices that require custom protocols, such as message queuetelemetry transport (MQTT) and data distribution service (DDS). Given that sensors are used in nearly all industries, the IoT is expected to produce a huge amount of data. The data generated from IoT devices can be used in finding potential research trends and investigating the impact of certain events or decisions. These data are processed using various analytic tools [1]. Figure 3 illustrates the process of data collection, monitoring, and data analytics.

Although IoT has created unprecedented opportunities that can help increase revenue, reduce costs, and ameliorate efficiencies, collecting a huge amount of data alone is insufficient. To generate benefits from IoT, enterprises must create a platform where they can collect, manage, and analyze a massive volume of sensor data in a scalable and cost-effective manner [2]. In this context, lever- aging a big data platform that can assist in consuming and read- ing diverse data sources as well as in accelerating the data integration process becomes vital. Data integration and analytics allow organizations to revolutionize their business process. Specifically, these enterprises can use data analytics tools to transform a huge volume of sensor-collected data into valuable insights. Given the overlapping research trends in these areas, this paper focuses on Bashir and Gill [3] propose an IoT big data analytics framework to overcome the challenges of storing and analyzing large amount of data originating from smart buildings. The proposed framework is composed of three components which are big data management, IoT sensors, and data analytics. The analytics are performed in real-time in order to be used in different parts of the smart building to manage the oxygen level, smoke/hazardous gases, and luminosity. The framework is implemented in Cloudera Hadoop distribution where the analytics is performed using PySpark. The results show that the framework can be utilized for IoT-enabled big data ana- lytics. The proposed framework is specifically designed for smart buildings that should be extended to make it generalize so that it can deal with other IoT applications including smart cities and smart airplanes. Lee et al. [4] propose an IoT-based cyber physical system that supports information analysis and knowledge acquisition methods to improve productivity in various industries. This system, which focuses on industrial big data analytics, integrates various data analytics components in the form of reconfigurable and interchange- able modules to meet different business needs. The authors also provide a new context intelligence framework that can help handle industrial informatics based on the sensors, locations, and unstructured data for big data mining. A case study is also performed to illustrate the design of the proposed cyber physical system. Rizwan et al. [5] study the strengths and weaknesses of various traffic management systems. They propose a low cost, real-time traffic management system that deploys IoT devices and sensors to capture real-time traffic information. Specifically, low-cost traffic detection sensors are embedded in the middle of the road for.

1.3   Characteristics of Big Data

From the IoT perspective, Big Data is a subset of the IoT technology where Big Data software addresses data handling and IoT takes responsibility for sensors, devices, data delivery (Dull 2015). Big Data scenarios are usually characterized by the volume, velocity, and variety of data. Additional criteria might be Vs like Validity, Veracity, Value, and Visibility. The basic intention is to collect as many data as possible to detect semantic patterns and correlations in huge data oceans (volume) which fill up continuously or event-driven (velocity) in a structured or unstructured format (variety).

IoT and Big Data are clearly connected intimately as billions of internet-connected "things" generate massive amounts of data (McLellan 2015).

Especially in scenarios with a constant in-flow of data (real-time) it is necessary to efficiently store and analyze data on-line and off-line. This challenge requires new storage concepts, high performance processing approaches etc. The Hadoop ecosystem is at the forefront of the technology.

We now by setting the united equipment acquisition cable on each node in the sea water pressure value, according to the motion state on the cable at the same time establish the physical dynamic equation by finite element method (fem) of matlab simulation to determine the movement of the cable to get sea cable in different sea conditions in case of trajectory can provide a scientific reference for laying optical cable, concrete equipment of the links below.

The pressure sensor connects the information acquisition module, and the information acquisition module converts the current value collected by the pressure sensor into the numerical value. Information acquisition is mainly through signal input processing, signal filtering amplification, A/D conversion processing, photoelectric isolation and other processes, which can complete the collection of pressure information. Information acquisition module will collect information transmission belt information processing module, information processing module based on the data from the received data processing, by good data format prescribed by GPRS wireless communication module is sent to PC, PC for data from the lower machine, select data effectively, and the data stored in the database.

Optical fiber cable is the main transmission tool for various information networks in the information society today. If the "Internet" is called "information highway", then the cable network is the cornerstone of the information highway - the optical cable network is the physical route of the Internet. Once an optical cable is damaged and blocked, the "information superhighway" in that direction will be destroyed. The information transmitted through optical cables, in addition to the usual telephone, telegraph, fax, a large number of transmissions are television signals, bank remittances, stock market quotes and other information can not be interrupted moment. The transmission mode of long-distance communication optical fiber cable has been developed by PDH to SDH. The transmission rate has been developed from the original 140 MB/S to 2.5 GB/S, 4 × 2.5 GB/S, 16 × 2.5 GB/S or even higher, so the installation of the optical cable is A very important task, and laying optical cables on the seabed is a difficult task. It usually requires large-scale vessels to cooperate, and it also adjusts according to different sea and climatic conditions and the conditions of the seabed, thus simulating the movement process of submarine cables. It allows us to know in advance the precise trajectory of the optical fiber's trajectory.

2 Model Establishment

Using the lumped mass method, the cable is divided into N segments, i.e., i = 1, 2, 3... N + 1 nodes, the distance between the nodes is s, the node at the stern is N + 1, and the cable is in the initial state (red line) arrives at a certain moment (black line), during which the boat moves at a fixed speed Vs and the cable is released at a fixed speed Vc, so the total number of nodes has been changing over time. Analysis of the dynamic motion of submarine cables is shown in the figure below:

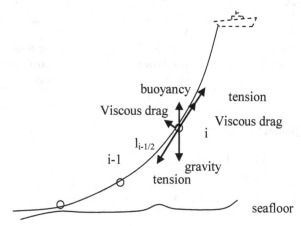

The cable is affected by buoyancy, gravity, tension and resistance during the movement. According to Newton's second law:

$$\mathbf{F}_i = \mathbf{M}_i \ddot{\mathbf{x}}_i = \Delta \mathbf{T}_i + \mathbf{B}_i + \mathbf{G}_i + \mathbf{D}_i$$

Establish a local rectangular coordinate system (o-xyz): the origin is the centerline of the streamer microelement, y is the direction of the ship row, z is the opposite direction of the seafloor, x and y, z constitute the right-handed coordinate system, and the local coordinate system (o-btn) The origin is the towline microelement center of mass, t is the direction of the tangent of the streamer, the direction is the direction of the growth of the cable length, n is the normal direction, and b is orthogonal to the two to form the right-handed coordinate system. The transformation relationship between two coordinate systems is shown in the table.

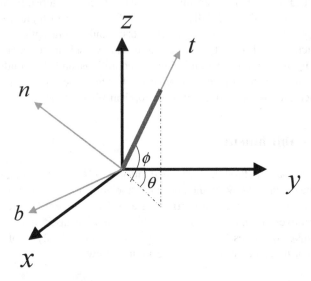

	b	t	n
I	$\cos\theta$	$\sin\theta\cos\phi$	$-\sin\theta\sin\phi$
J	$-\sin\theta$	$\cos\theta\cos\phi$	$-\cos\theta\sin\phi$
K	0	$\sin\phi$	$\cos\phi$

(1) tension (tangential t direction)

$$\Delta \mathbf{T}_i = \mathbf{T}_{i+1/2} - \mathbf{T}_{i-1/2}$$
$$\mathbf{T}_{i+1/2} = E\sigma\varepsilon_{i+1/2} \cdot \tau_{i+1/2}$$
$$\varepsilon_{i+1/2} = \frac{\sqrt{(x_{i+1}-x_i)^2 + (y_{i+1}-y_i)^2 + (z_{i+1}-z_i)^2}}{l} - 1$$
$$\left(\varepsilon_{i+1/2} \geq 0\right)$$

Where τ is the unit tangent vector in the cable length direction, E is the Young's modulus, and l is the cable length between the nodes before stretching.

(2) Buoyancy and gravity (in the opposite direction of Z)

$$\mathbf{B}_i + \mathbf{G}_i = -\rho l_\varepsilon \pi \frac{d_\varepsilon^2}{4}\mathbf{g} + m_i\mathbf{g}$$

(3) Fluid resistance (btn direction)

$$\mathbf{D}_i = (\mathbf{D}_{i+1/2} + \mathbf{D}_{i-1/2})/2$$

$$D_t = -\frac{1}{2}\rho\pi C_t l_\varepsilon d_\varepsilon |V_{rt}|.V_{rt}\mathbf{t}$$

$$D_n = -\frac{1}{2}\rho\pi C_n l_\varepsilon d_\varepsilon \left|\sqrt{V_{rn}^2 + V_{rb}^2}\right| V_{rn}\mathbf{n}$$

$$D_b = -\frac{1}{2}\rho\pi C_n l_\varepsilon d_\varepsilon \left|\sqrt{V_{rn}^2 + V_{rb}^2}\right| V_{rb}\mathbf{b}$$

Cn and Ct are the normal and tangential drag coefficients of the streamers, respectively. U is the speed of the current, which is a function of the sea depth z, expressed as $\mathbf{U} = U_x(z)\mathbf{i} + U_y(z)\mathbf{j} + 0\mathbf{k}$ Vr is the relative speed of the cable speed and the current speed.

3 Numerical Solution of the Model

The discrete solution of the model is solved using the finite difference method. The discrete method is as follows:

$$\ddot{x}_i^j = \frac{1}{\Delta t^2}\left(x_i^{j+1} + x_i^{j-1} - 2x_i^j\right) \quad \dot{x}_i^j = \frac{1}{\Delta t}\left(x_i^j - x_i^{j-1}\right)$$

$$\ddot{y}_i^j = \frac{1}{\Delta t^2}\left(y_i^{j+1} + y_i^{j-1} - 2y_i^j\right) \quad \dot{y}_i^j = \frac{1}{\Delta t}\left(y_i^j - y_i^{j-1}\right)$$

$$\ddot{z}_i^j = \frac{1}{\Delta t^2}\left(z_i^{j+1} + z_i^{j-1} - 2z_i^j\right) \quad \dot{z}_i^j = \frac{1}{\Delta t}\left(z_i^j - z_i^{j-1}\right)$$

Assuming that the tension T is only at time j, without considering the effect of additional mass, the formula is:

$$m_i\ddot{x}_i = T_{i+1/2}\sin\theta_{i+1/2}\cos\phi_{i+1/2} - T_{i-1/2}\sin\theta_{i-1/2}\cos\phi_{i-1/2} + \frac{1}{2}\left(F_{Dx}^{i+1/2} + F_{Dx}^{i-1/2}\right)$$

$$m_i\ddot{y}_i = T_{i+1/2}\cos\theta_{i+1/2}\cos\phi_{i+1/2} - T_{i-1/2}\cos\theta_{i-1/2}\cos\phi_{i-1/2} + \frac{1}{2}\left(F_{Dy}^{i+1/2} + F_{Dy}^{i-1/2}\right)$$

$$m_i\ddot{z}_i = T_{i+1/2}\sin\phi_{i+1/2} - T_{i-1/2}\sin\phi_{i-1/2} + \frac{1}{2}\left(F_{Dz}^{i+1/2} + F_{Dz}^{i-1/2}\right) + \rho l_\varepsilon \sigma_\varepsilon g - m_i g$$

So find the discrete formula at time j + 1:

$$x_i^{j+1} = \frac{\Delta t^2}{m_i}\left[T_{i+1/2}^j \sin\theta_{i+1/2}^j \cos\phi_{i+1/2}^j - T_{i-1/2}^j \sin\theta_{i-1/2}^j \cos\phi_{i-1/2}^j + \frac{1}{2}\left(F_{Dxi+1/2}^j + F_{Dxi-1/2}^j\right)\right] - x_i^{j-1} + 2x_i^j$$

$$y_i^{j+1} = \frac{\Delta t^2}{m_i}\left[T_{i+1/2}^j \cos\theta_{i+1/2}^j \cos\phi_{i+1/2}^j - T_{i-1/2}^j \cos\theta_{i-1/2}^j \cos\phi_{i-1/2}^j + \frac{1}{2}\left(F_{Dyi+1/2}^j + F_{Dyi-1/2}^j\right)\right] - y_i^{j-1} + 2y_i^j$$

$$z_i^{j+1} = \frac{\Delta t^2}{m_i}\left[T_{i+1/2}^j \sin\phi_{i+1/2}^j - T_{i-1/2}^j \sin\phi_{i-1/2}^j + \frac{1}{2}\left(F_{Dzi+1/2}^j + F_{Dzi-1/2}^j\right) + \rho l_\varepsilon \sigma_\varepsilon g - m_i g\right] - z_i^{j-1} + 2z_i^j$$

4   Initial Conditions and Boundary Conditions

Headend (i.e. i = N + 1) boundary conditions:

$$x_{N+1}^j = 0$$
$$y_{N+1}^j = V_s t = V_s(j-1)\Delta t$$
$$z_{N+1}^j = 0$$

Free end (i.e. i = 1) boundary conditions:

$$x_1^j = 0$$
$$y_1^j = 0$$
$$z_1^j = -H$$

Initial conditions: (In the initial state, the cable stays vertically between the bottom and the stern)

$$x_i^1 = 0; \qquad \dot{x}_i^1 = 0$$
$$y_i^1 = 0; \qquad \dot{y}_i^1 = 0$$
$$z_i^1 = -H + (i-1)h; \qquad \dot{z}_i^1 = 0$$

5   Matlab Simulation of the Model

Below we simulate the trajectory of the streamer under different conditions according to the different sea conditions:

The specific physical dynamics explanation is that when the ship is sailing at a constant speed, the streamer is at a constant speed relative to the water surface, so when the bottom cable touches the ground, All should be of a periodic type, so it is only necessary to simulate the impact of the water wave on the Y-axis, that is to say that the water wave function on the Y-axis can be constantly complicated, and on the Z-axis it is only a constant velocity. Therefore, the following explanation will be made for various situations.

Scenario 1 Assume that the impact of the waves is relatively slight, that is, the seawater is only undergoing a slight periodic motion. For the sake of convenience, we assume that in an ideal situation, the waves fluctuate in a cosine fashion. It can be seen Fig. 1.

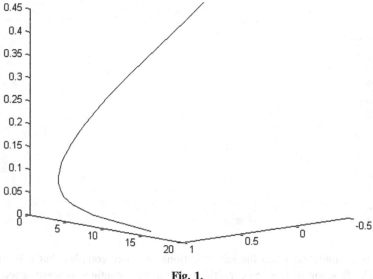

Fig. 1.

Figure 2 shows the simulation of a wave with a large vibration frequency. It can be noted that the vibration at this time is significantly larger than that of Fig. 1, which is in accordance with the actual situation.

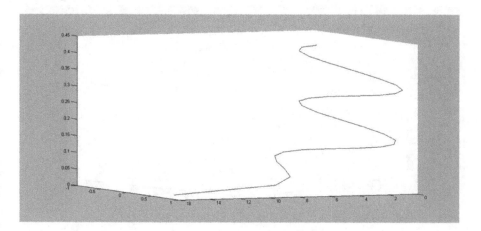

Fig. 2.

$$t = 0 : pi/50 : 2 * pi/3; z = 0.2 * t; x = (\sin(t)).^\wedge(-1);$$
$$y = \cos(8 * t) + \sin(16 * t); plot3(x, y, z'b')$$

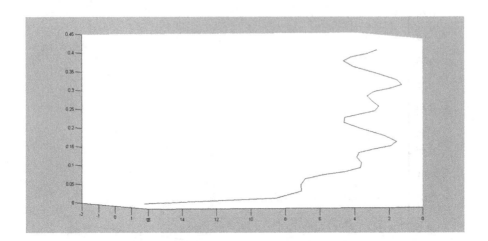

This is a simulation when the sea conditions are more complex, but it is still too simple. The function of real sea conditions should be a continuous wave speed.

Case 3 Simulation of Spatial Curves for Streamers

$$t = 0 : pi/50 : 2 * pi/3; z = 0.2 * t; x = (\sin(t)).^{\wedge}(-1);$$
$$y = (t.^{\wedge}2). * \cos(8 * t) + \sin(16 * t); plot3(x, y, z, 'b')$$

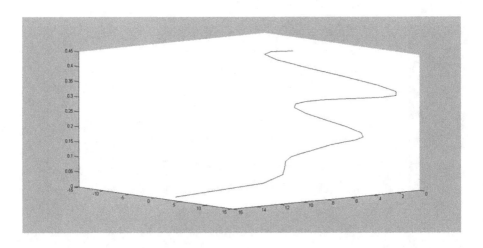

Author's address: Department of Mathematics, School of Information, Shandong Agricultural University, 271018, 15621550101.

References

1. Petrov, V., et al.: When IoT keeps people in the loop: a path towards a new global utility (2017)
2. TR.45.820: Cellular system support for ultra-low complexity and low throughput internet of things (CIoT). Technical report. Release 13, 3GPP (2016)
3. Petrov, V., et al.: Vehicle-based relay assistance for opportunistic crowdsensing over narrowband IoT (NB-IoT). IEEE Internet Things. J. (2017)
4. GPP: Cellular system support for ultra-low complexity and low throughput Internet of Things (CIoT). 3GPP TR 45.820/r13, December 2015
5. GPP: Standardization of NB-IoT completed, June 2016. http://www.3gpp.org/news-events/3gpp-news/1785-nb_iot_complete
6. Pinasco, J.P.: Asymptotic of eigenvalues of the p-Laplace operator and lattice points
7. Drabek, P., Manasevich, R.: On the closed solutions to some nonhomogeneous eigenvalue problems with p-laplacian. Diff. Int. Equtions **12**(6), 773–778 (1999)
8. Courant, R., Hibert, D.: Methods of Mathematical Physics, vol. 1. Interscience Publishers Inc., New York (1953)
9. Falconer, K.: On the minkowski measurability of fractals. Proc. Amer. Math. Soc. **123**(4), 1115–1124 (1995)
10. Fernandez Bonder, J., Pinasco, J.P.: Asymptotic behavior of the eingenvalues of the one dimensional weighted p-laplace operatoer. Arkiv Mat. **41**, 267–280 (2003)
11. Fleckinger, J., Vassiliev, D.: An example of a two-term asympotics for the "Counting Function" of a fractal drum. Trans. A.M.S. **337**(1), 99–116 (1993)
12. Fucik, S., Necas, J., Soucek, J., Soucek, V.: Spectral Annlysis of Nonlinear Operators. Lecture Notes in Mathematics, vol. 346. Springer, New York (1973)
13. Kratzel, E.: Lattice Points. Kluwer Academic Publishers, Berlin (1988). Lapidus, M., Pomerance, C.: The Riemann Zeta-function and the One-dimensional Weyl-Berry Cojecture for Fractal Drums. Proc. London Math. Soc. **66**(3), 41–69 (1993)
14. Sakamura, K.: Challenges in the age of ubiquitous computing: a case study of T-Engine—an open development platform for embedded systems. In: Proceedings of ICSE 2006. Shanghai, China (2006)
15. Dunkels, A., Vasseur, J.P.: IP for smart objects, internet protocol for smart objects (ISO) alliance, White Paper #1 (2009). http://www.ispo-alliance.org
16. Hui, J., Culler, D., Chakrabarti, S.: 6LoWPAN: Incorporating IEEE 802.15.4 into IP architecture–internet protocol for smart objects (IPSO) Alliance, White Paper # 3 (2009). http://www.ispo-alliance.org
17. Toma, I., Simperl, E., Hench, G.: A joint roadmap for semantic technologies and the internet of things. In: Proceedings of the 3rd STI Roadmapping Workshop. Crete, Greece (2009)

The Traceability Information Management Platform of Duck Product Industry Chain

Lining Liu[1], Pingzeng Liu[1(✉)], Wanming Ren[2], Yong Zheng[2], Chao Zhang[1], and Junmei Wang[1]

[1] Shandong Agricultural University, Tai'an 271018, China
lpz8565@126.com
[2] Shandong Provincial Agricultural Information Center, Ji'nan 250013, China

Abstract. In response to various problems existing in the current duck product industry chain. For example, decentralized of the industry chain, lack of data exchange between each link, lack of unified information collection equipment, and so on. An intelligent information management platform for duck product chain was developed, based on the specific needs of each link of the duck and poultry industrial chain. The platform is mainly composed of the information collection equipment and the intelligent management systems. The information acquisition equipment comprehensively uses the current well-perceived and reliable transmission technology of the Internet of Things to achieve the seamless collection of information in each link of the duck product industry chain and the seamless convergence of information in each link. The intelligent management system utilizes big data analysis technology to realize internal automation and digital management. The long-term test of the system shows that the data in each link of the system seamlessly connects. The data collected by the system is accurate and reliable. Its operation is simple and convenient. The system is highly scalable and suitable for use in production.

Keywords: Internet of Things · Traceability platform
Intelligent management systems · Information collection equipment

1 Introduction

In recent years, as people's awareness of dietary safety has increased, people's requirements for food traceability have also increased. So, many food processing companies have begun to trace the source equipment and automated information collection equipment to the processing plant. In this way, information acquisition of the product processing process is achieved to meet the needs of consumers. However, duck product processing companies have many links in their industry chain. And each link is scattered within different companies, and there is a lack of information exchange between companies. This is not conducive to the realization of the product's full industry chain information traceability. With the development of Internet of Things, network communication and big data analysis technology [1–9], people have proposed different solutions to the above problems.

© Springer Nature Switzerland AG 2018
X. Sun et al. (Eds.): ICCCS 2018, LNCS 11068, pp. 144–153, 2018.
https://doi.org/10.1007/978-3-030-00021-9_14

Scholars from various countries have made some studies on the traceability of information in the industry chain. For example, Hu et al. established a vegetable supply chain traceability model based on a language model. It has realized the modeling of product process and quality information in the vegetable supply chain, and provided data and theoretical support for achieving the quality and safety of vegetable products [10]. Abad et al. use RFID technology to achieve real-time traceability of freshwater fish transportation chain information. This system overcomes the shortcomings of traditional tracking tools and enables the accurate positioning and information acquisition of the aquatic product transport process [11]. Zhang et al. took Laiwu black pig as the research object. The system runs through the entire process of the black pig industry in Laiwu through the Internet of Things technology. It achieves information tracking from the entire process of breeding, breeding, slaughter, processing, transportation and sales. The system has improved the traceability of the whole industrial chain of Laiwu black pig products [12].

A comprehensive analysis of the information traceability system of the above industrial chain shows that they have achieved great achievements in their respective research areas. These researches greatly improve the quality and safety control capabilities of related companies. However, there are still some issues that need to be solved and further researched and improved. For example, the existing industrial chain information traceability system has a high production cost and is not suitable for widespread promotion among farmers. The existing livestock and poultry industry information traceability systems are mostly focused on one or two links in the entire industry chain. There is a lack of information traceability systems that apply to the entire industry chain.

2   Requirement Analysis

At present, the domestic duck product industry chain is mainly jointly implemented by several companies. It mainly consists of production, processing, transportation and marketing. Its structure is shown in Fig. 1. There is a lack of a unified data management system among companies, which has a significant impact on the subsequent development of the duck and poultry industry. On the one hand, for business managers, this is not conducive to the data communication and sharing between the various aspects of the duck and poultry industrial chain. If the product information of the previous session is missing, the final quality and safety level of the product will be difficult to determine. For consumers, discrete product traceability information is not conducive to their understanding of product safety and quality information. This will not be conducive to protecting the rights of consumers. For government agencies, this increases the cost of product quality supervision and makes it difficult to achieve information security traceability across the entire industry chain. Now with the actual needs of the industry chain, the specific functions required for the analysis system are as follows.

(1) Data acquisition function
   Because the duck poultry industry chain is actually completed in different companies. There is a lack of unified management standards and information

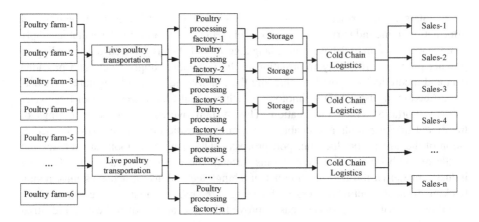

Fig. 1. Structure of the industrial chain

collection equipment among enterprises. Therefore, information collection equipment suitable for different aspects of the duck product industry chain was developed, after fully analyzing the actual needs of different companies. The accurate perception and seamless connection of the information in each link of the industry chain have been realized by the equipment. The internal management model and product processing methods in different companies are fully considered.

(2) The basic information management function

There is a large amount of basic information is included in the traceability information of each processing link. For companies, this information is non-deterministic and easily modified. Therefore, the target system must have excellent integrated data management capabilities. It is easy for the company's administrators to update basic data in a timely manner to ensure data validity.

(3) The data sharing function

Because companies are relatively independent in terms of management and marketing, there is a lack of data interaction among companies. In order to achieve traceability of the product chain of the whole duck c product, the target system must have good data sharing and linking capabilities. Through the seamless integration and accurate interaction of information in each link of the duck product industry chain, it provides complete traceability information for food safety information traceability in the entire industry chain.

(4) The product traceability

The system can realize the traceability information sharing between enterprises and consumers through the collaborative work between the website and the host computer client. Within the enterprise, the management and analysis of product information can be realized through the host computer client and the company's internal website. Consumers can log on to the company's external website by scanning the QR code. And the product processing information is understood by consumers in this way. Through the above methods, the system realizes the protection of the enterprise's information management and consumer rights.

3 Structure

3.1 Architecture

With the development of science and technology, the architecture of the Internet of Things is also developing rapidly [13–20]. It's from the initial three tier structure to the 4 tiers structure, the 5 tiers structure and the domain structure system conceptual model. It has made great progress in data transmission security and speed or structure level division.

The traceability information management platform based on the duck product industry chain aims to achieve the accurate acquisition and information exchange of the traceability information of all links in the whole industry chain. Based on the analysis of production and processing models and information transmission characteristics of each link of the industrial chain, the conceptual model of the domain structure system was selected as the reference model of the system. The overall architecture of the design system is shown in Fig. 2.

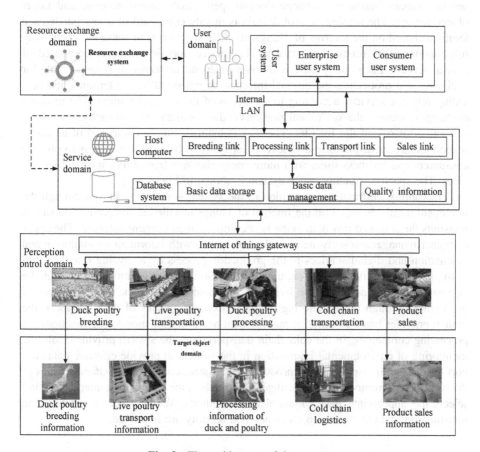

Fig. 2. The architecture of the system

As can be seen from Fig. 2, the system is mainly composed of the user domain, the service domain, the resource exchange domain, the perceptual control domain, and the target object domain. The user domain is the window where the system presents data to consumers and system users. The service domain is the key to data interaction and data analysis. The perceptual control domain is the core of achieving various types of traceability information. The target object domain contains the source of the information that the system wants to sense and control.

3.2   Specific Composition

Using modern Internet of things technology and big data technology, the system has achieved a transformation from traditional management mode to modernization and digital management mode. The system management ensures the information circulation and sharing among all enterprises and realizes the traceability of the quality and safety information of the entire industry chain. The system uses a five-level domain structure system. The structural framework is mainly composed of five parts: user domain, service domain, resource exchange domain, perceptual control domain, and target object domain. The sensing control domain is mainly composed of a few intelligence terminals based on the Internet of Things. Its main function is to sense the traceability information in the production process. The service domain is mainly composed of several servers. Each enterprise has its own independent server. It is responsible for analyzing and processing the original information uploaded by the terminal and providing relevant services according to the needs of the enterprise users. The resource exchange domain is the key to realizing server data exchange within each enterprise. It consists primarily of the Internet. The user domain is mainly composed of an information management platform and several subsystems. Its main function is to provide consumers and business users with more comprehensive traceability information services. The specific structure of the system is shown in Fig. 3.

Traceability information acquisition of the system is mainly achieved through the intelligent terminals based on the Internet of Things installed at the production site. It transmits the acquired raw data to the host computer management software. The upper computer management software provides enterprises with information monitoring and automation and digital services in the production process by analyzing raw data. For example, in the cultivation section, the breeding environment is controlled through the equipment to provide a suitable living environment for the duck. In the process of processing, through the monitoring of the processing process of duck products, the system provides batch automation management and real-time monitoring functions for processing companies. In the cold chain transportation, the system provides real-time monitoring of environmental information in the vehicle to provide effective data support for the safe transportation of products. The system combines the characteristics of the working environment of the intelligent terminals in the enterprise's internal IoT and selects the appropriate data communication methods. While ensuring reliable data transmission, data transmission efficiency and security are improved.

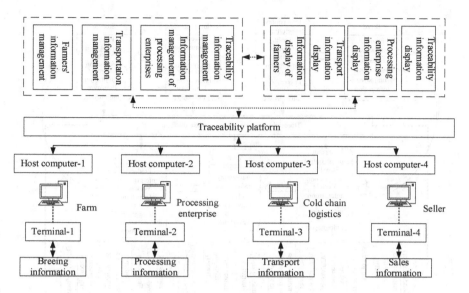

Fig. 3. Specific composition of the system

4 Function

Internet of Things intelligent terminals and upper computer management systems that can be applied to different production and processing links have been developed, based on the actual needs of the duck industry chain. Since different companies have their own characteristics, the intelligent terminals based on the Internet of Things and upper computer management systems applied to different occasions also have their own characteristics. This is mainly reflected in the different types of data obtained by the device and the way the host computer processes the data and presents the data. The specific functions of the system in the duck and poultry industry chain are shown in Fig. 4.

As can be seen from Fig. 4, there is a wide gap between the function of the intelligent terminals based on the Internet of Things in different links. Different upper computers use different algorithms to process different basic data. It uploads the results of data analysis to a unified information management platform. The user provides information services through the platform solution system.

The upper computer management software not only provides basic data information services, but also provides special information service functions according to different users. For example, in the farming process, the host computer management software can analyze whether the current environment needs to be adjusted for livestock and poultry growth based on the environmental information uploaded by the intelligent terminal based on the Internet of Things. For example, the current temperature is suitable, the oxygen content and so on. The upper computer management software shows the results of the analysis by figures and tables in the presentation system. If individual data exceeds the security scope, the upper-level opportunity will send an

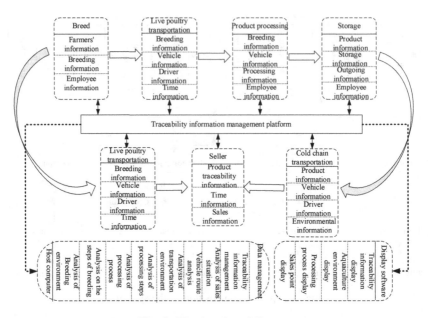

Fig. 4. The function of System

early warning message to the relevant responsible person while controlling the terminal to adjust the environmental control device.

In the transport link, according to the different types of transport products, can be divided into: live poultry transportation and cold chain transportation two. There are two points that need to be noted in live poultry transportation. The first is to ensure the source information of live birds. The other is to ensure the survival rate of ducks during transport, that is, to monitor the internal oxygen content of transport vehicles in real time. The cold chain transportation attaches more importance to the internal temperature, humidity, and other environmental information. The upper computer management software receives the data information of the transport link. It analyzes whether the environment inside the current transporter is suitable for the preservation of the product. If there is an indicator that exceeds the warning value, the superior will send an alert message to the driver to remind the driver to deal with the problem in time.

In the process of processing, due to the significant differences between the processing steps and the processing steps, the operation and function of the intelligent terminals based on the Internet of Things in the processing plants are also slightly different. For example, automatic link management will be used in the higher degree of automation to achieve product batch information management. The manual link will use manual batch management to obtain product source information. In some links, external devices such as scanning guns will be added to achieve accurate product packaging information. In the pounds section through the addition of other automated equipment to achieve automatic access to information and so on. In this process, the host computer management system provides services other than real-time monitoring and traceability analysis of product processing. It will also analyze personnel distribution optimization programs based on past employee distribution and process progress, thereby improving product processing efficiency.

In the sales link, the consumer can enter the product traceability information display page by scanning the two-dimensional code of the product. In this page, the consumer can look at the product quality inspection report of the product's traceability information.

5 Application

At present, the system has passed several experimental tests, and the results show that the system has good stability and reliability. At the same time, considering the operator's demand for time and efficiency, the system is easy to operate, and it has good compatibility and portability. The system realizes information sharing among different enterprises through a unified information management platform, which ensures the integrity and reliability of the traceability information of duck and poultry industry chain. At the same time, the data management service provided by the platform provides help for the optimization of the enterprise's production structure. The system run interface is shown in Fig. 5.

Fig. 5. The interface of System

6 Summary

These questions about the traceability information of duck product industry chain are implemented in this system as follows:

(1) The system has designed and developed the information acquisition terminals based on the Internet of Things. The equipment not only comprehensively

analyzes the actual needs of different companies and different links. At the same time, it also considers the requirements of corporate managers for employee productivity. The system basically uses automatic management to achieve information collection. However, it still retains the ability of employees to manually operate, which provides an effective response to sudden situations.

(2) The terminal equipment of the system has better human-computer interaction function. The system fully considers the situation where people receive various types of mutual information under different production environments. The final sound, SMS, lighting and other methods are used to implement human-computer interaction to ensure that the user can understand the operation of the system in the first place.

(3) The traceability information management platform based on the duck poultry industry chain is an information management platform covering the entire industrial chain. In order to achieve seamless connection and accurate processing of the entire industry chain. The platform integrates product data information from different companies in the industry chain. And it systematically provides the traceability information to consumers to achieve comprehensive, accurate and reliable traceability of duck products. At the same time, the platform provides enterprise managers with a large number of data information service functions, which is conducive to improving the enterprise's information management level.

(4) The system can use the intelligent information acquisition equipment based on the Internet of Things to obtain the traceability information of the product. For example, farming, processing, transportation, warehousing, sales, etc. The system platform uses big data technology to analyze and process the original data. And according to the analysis results for various types of users to provide information services. For example, the platform can provide farmers with scientific environmental regulation information. It provides a scientific personnel distribution plan for processing companies. It also provides consumers with complete traceability information and more.

Acknowledgements. This work was financially supported by the following project:

(1) The research project "Major Data Application Technology Research and Integration Based on Livestock and Poultry Industry" of Shandong Province Major Agricultural Technological Innovation Project in 2017.

(2) Shandong independent innovation and achievements transformation project (2014ZZCX07106).

References

1. Gershenfeld, N., Krikorian, R., Cohen, D.: The Internet of Things. Sci. Am. **291**(4), 76 (2004). https://doi.org/10.1038/scientificamerican1004-76
2. Gluhak, A., Krco, S., Nati, M., et al.: A survey on facilities for experimental internet of things research. IEEE Commun. Mag. **49**(11), 58–67 (2011). https://doi.org/10.1109/MCOM.2011.6069710

3. Atzori, L., Iera, A., Morabito, G.: SIoT: giving a social structure to the Internet of Things. IEEE Commun. Lett. **15**(11), 1193–1195 (2011). https://doi.org/10.1109/LCOMM.2011. 090911.111340
4. Hong, S., Kim, D., Ha, M., et al.: SNAIL: an IP-based wireless sensor network approach to the Internet of Things. IEEE Wirel. Commun. **17**(6), 34–42 (2010). https://doi.org/10.1109/ MWC.2010.5675776
5. Feki, M.A., Kawsar, F., Boussard, M., et al.: The Internet of Things: the next technological revolution. Computer **46**(2), 24–25 (2013)
6. Marx, V.: The big challenges of big data. Nature **498**(7453), 255–260 (2013)
7. Gadouleau, M., Goupil, A.: A matroid framework for noncoherent random network communications. IEEE Trans. Inf. Theor. **57**(2), 1031–1045 (2011). https://doi.org/10.1109/ TIT.2010.2094818
8. Cai, Y., Yu, F.R., Liang, C., et al.: Software-defined device-to-device (D2D) communications in virtual wireless networks with imperfect network state information (NSI). IEEE Trans. Veh. Technol. **65**(9), 7349–7360 (2016). https://doi.org/10.1109/TVT.2015.2483558
9. Hoang, T.D., Le, L.B., Le-Ngoc, T.: Energy-efficient resource allocation for D2D communications in cellular networks. IEEE Trans. Veh. Technol. **65**(9), 6972–6986 (2016). https://doi.org/10.1109/ICC.2015.7248660
10. Hu, J., Zhang, X., Moga, L.M., et al.: Modeling and implementation of the vegetable supply chain traceability system. Food Control **30**(1), 341–353 (2013). https://doi.org/10.1016/j. foodcont.2012.06.037
11. Abad, E., Palacio, F., Nuin, M., et al.: RFID smart tag for traceability and cold chain monitoring of foods: demonstration in an intercontinental fresh fish logistic chain. J. Food Eng. **93**(4), 394–399 (2009). https://doi.org/10.1016/j.jfoodeng.2009.02.004
12. Zhang, Y., Liu, P., Yu, Q., et al.: Safety traceability platform building for the whole industry chain of Laiwu pig based on IOT. J. Chin. Agric. Mech. **36**(2), 141–144 (2015)
13. Yaqoob, I., Ahmed, E., Hashem, I.A.T., et al.: Internet of Things architecture: recent advances, taxonomy, requirements, and open challenges. IEEE Wirel. Commun. **24**(3), 10–16 (2017). https://doi.org/10.1109/MWC.2017.1600421
14. Zhou, W.: Research on architecture of the internet of things. IEEE (2012). https://doi.org/10. 1109/sysose.2012.6333578
15. Weyrich, M., Ebert, C.: Reference architectures for the Internet of Things. IEEE Softw. **33**(1), 112–116 (2015). https://doi.org/10.1109/MS.2016.20
16. Agbinya, J.I.: Framework for wide area networking of inductive internet of things. Electron. Lett. **47**(21), 1199–1201 (2011). https://doi.org/10.1049/el.2011.2757
17. Gohar, M., Ahmed, S.H., Khan, M., et al.: A big data analytics architecture for the internet of small things. IEEE Commun. Mag. **56**(2), 128–133 (2018). https://doi.org/10.1109/MCOM. 2018.1700273
18. Zhang, Y.: Technology framework of the Internet of Things and its application, pp. 4109–4112. IEEE (2011). https://doi.org/10.1109/ICECENG.2011.6057290
19. Sicari, S., Cappiello, C., Pellegrini, F.D., et al.: A security-and quality-aware system architecture for Internet of Things. Inf. Syst. Front. **18**(4), 665–677 (2016). https://doi.org/ 10.1007/s10796-014-9538-x
20. Karakostas, B.: A DNS architecture for the Internet of Things: a case study in transport logistics. Procedia Comput. Sci. **19**, 594–601 (2013). https://doi.org/10.1016/j.procs.2013. 06.079

Topic Model Based Management Frame Authentication Using CSI Information

Zhao Yang[1(✉)], Wei Xi[1], Kun Zhao[1], Xiaohong Wang[1], Colin Allen[2], and Jizhong Zhao[1]

[1] Xi'an Jiaotong University, Xi'an, China
zhaoyang9425@gmail.com, weixi.cs@gmail.com, pandazhao1982@gmail.com,
amanda.wxh@mail.xjtu.edu.cn, jizhongzhao@gmail.com
[2] University of Pittsburgh, Pittsburgh, USA
colin.allen@pitt.edu

Abstract. Traditionally, it is considered that there is no sensitive information in the management frames and only the data frames need encryption protection in the initial 802.11 standard protocol, so no corresponding security mechanism is required in the management frames. But with the popularity of WLAN, the researchers realize that the lack of the management frames security mechanism can lead to many security problems. For example, an attacker can constantly transmit fake management frames to dissociate normal connection between the AP and the legitimate station. Therefore, the management frames security mechanism must be established.

In this paper, we propose a topic model based method to realize the authentication of Wi-Fi management frames using the Channel State Information (CSI). CSI values have a strong correlation with location. That means CSI values between the AP and the legitimate station have significant distinction with the CSI values between the AP and the attacker. We utilize the topic model – an unsupervised machine learning method to extract features automatically from the collected CSI values. Extensive experiments are conducted to analysis the system performance. The experiments prove that topic model can better resist noise interference than the traditional method and achieve average 91% accuracy of the management frame authentication.

Keywords: Management frame authentication · CSI · LDA

1 Introduction

With the continuous evolution of WLAN, people pay more attention to its security. Although wireless security protocols have made great progress in the development of wireless LAN technology, most of the security protocols are only for the security of data frames. For the control frames and management frames, the wireless security protocols in the evolution are still limited. Management frames without substantial security mechanisms can be exploited by attackers. Then

© Springer Nature Switzerland AG 2018
X. Sun et al. (Eds.): ICCCS 2018, LNCS 11068, pp. 154–166, 2018.
https://doi.org/10.1007/978-3-030-00021-9_15

attackers can launch all kinds of attacks on devices in wireless networks, such as frame injection, frame modifications, denial of service attacks [10] can be launched.

With the study and research of CSI, we realize that CSI reflects the communication link properties between the transmitter and receiver, which means that if the relative position between the AP and the station changes, the CSI values between them will also change. Since the position of legitimate station to the AP is different from the position of the attacker to the AP, we can distinguish legitimate station and attacker by analyzing the CSI information.

There are two main problems in reality. First, CSI is too sensitive to the environment changes. A slight change in the environment reacts to the violent jitter on the CSI values, which means that in the condition of the legitimate station and the AP communicate with each other. When there is a person's movement or the mutual movement between the AP and the station, the sharp change of the CSI values is likely to make the legitimate station wrongly recognized. Therefore the process of authentication of legitimate station to be tardy which seriously reduces the performance of the system. Second, transceiver automatically adjusts to transmit and receive power according to channel state. When the channel state is bad, the transmitter will increase transmit power. That means that even if the relative position of transceivers is fixed, CSI values can be rather different because of the change of power.

In view of the above problems, we propose to use LDA – a topic model method to analyze CSI for feature extraction. LDA regards each CSI number as a word and all the words together make up the corpus. LDA can automatically extract topics from the large corpus. Unlike the straight comparison between points in the traditional signal processing, LDA puts every word in a topic. By comparing the similarity between the topics, the similarity between the CSI streams can be judged effectively. So LDA has the ability of strong rejection against noise. Analogous to text processing, when a few wrong words occurs in a text, it does not affect the analysis result of the topic model. So LDA can better solve the problem of management frame authentication in dynamic environment.

Our contributions are summarized as follows:

(1) As far as we know, this paper is the first work to utilize LDA - a topic model method for management frame authentication. We get the topic distribution of a series of documents. Each document is made up of several CSI values. The results show that our method has a rather good system performance.
(2) LDA views each number as a word and finally gathers noise points into a class. So the system can effectively resist the effect of noise.
(3) We do extensive experiments to verify the accuracy of the management frames authentication.

2   Background and Related Work

2.1   Background

CSI. In wireless communication, Channel State Information (CSI) reflects the channel characteristics of a known communication link. This information describes how the signal is affected by the transmitter through the channel to the receiver, such as scattering, fading and attenuation of energy with distance [13,15]. Each frame on the transceiver contains a constant sequence [12] which is named preamble and we note it be **X**. After the frame is transmitted and received by the AP, it will be extract as **Y**, then

$$\mathbf{H} = \frac{\mathbf{Y}}{\mathbf{X}} \tag{1}$$

where **X**, **Y** and **H** are the transmitted vector, received vector and channel matrix respectively. If we do not make a special note, we usually use channel matrix **H** to refer to CSI information.

Management Frame. The function of management frame covers all auxiliary functions of the AP and station except data interaction [17]. For example, when we want to look at all the available networks in the current range, the device doesn't "scan the network", but it will passively monitor the "beacon" management frame broadcast by the Wi-Fi hot spot.

Another kind of management frame is called "probe-request", which represents the accessible distance of the Wi-Fi network. The device transmit this kind of management frame to see whether the network that has been connected around. If the network has been accessed around, the corresponding hot spots will respond with the "probe-response" frame.

The problem with management frame is that they are not encrypted at all [1]. The purpose is to increase the ease of use of WLAN, so that we do not need any key exchange or password confirmation to see the surrounding Wi-Fi network and the hot sport, but this also increases the threat of being attacked.

LDA (Topic Model). Topic model [3], a kind of Latent Dirichlet Allocation topic model, uses the Bag of Word method by transforming text into a word frequency vector. Topic model is an unsupervised machine learning algorithm popular in Chinese natural language processing field in recent years. The topic model can automatically extract topics from large text collections. Compared with the traditional method, its advantage is we can dig out the relationship between the semantic automatically without manual data annotation.

LDA [4], a kind of topic model, is one of the most popular model used in natural language processing in recent years. It is based on probability statistics, assuming that the document is a mixture of different topics in a certain probability distribution. Each topic chooses a word that expresses the meaning of the topic by a certain probability distribution, which can be called a "bag of word". So in general, a document is made up of words that are selected from all the words in a certain probability [16].

2.2 Related Work

Many of the flaws in WLAN are largely related to the lack of necessary security mechanisms for managing frames. The researchers discovered these problems early on and they also mentioned a series of defense methods. Many researches claim to have the ability to detect spoofing attacks based on RSS or Sequence Number [5,8]. Fingerprint based on hardware transceiver profile is thought to be a perfect solution [2], but advanced attacker using arbitrary waveform generator, can still compromise the fingerprint [6]. [7] presents a per-frame authentication scheme to protect 802.11 management frames. With this scheme, every frame received by the wireless client or access point is first authenticated.

WiMAX is an attractive solution to address the infrastructure costs and physical limitations of wired networks. However it is attacked easily because the management frames are not encrypted. Three different authentication mechanisms are proposed to solve the problem in [1]. For the problem of management frame authentication in 802.11w standard, an improved mechanism named Temporary Safe Tunnel (TST) is proposed in [14]. A new attack against management authentication method was mentioned in [11].

During the recent two years, the survey of management frame authentication is going on. Jaspreet Kaur summarized the attack and defense measures of denial of service attacks for the management frames in [10].

3 System Design

In this section, we will introduce the topic model for CSI based method for management frame authentication. First, we will show the overall architecture of the system and then give a detailed introduction to each part.

3.1 System Overview

In this section, we present the design of our management frame authentication scheme. The whole system works in four steps:

(1) CSI Collecting. There is an AP collecting CSI data continually. At the beginning, the server maintains a number of feature information of the legitimate station. The legitimate stations or attackers continuously transmit frames to the AP. The AP calculates the CSI difference between them from the received frames.
(2) Preprocessing. There are three parts included. They are amplitude conversion, filtering and quantization respectively.
(3) Feature Extraction. We use LDA, one of the topic models, for feature extraction. LDA regards each CSI value as a word and several CSI values as a document. All the documents made up the corpus. Using the corpus as input to the topic model, after processing of LDA, we finally obtained the topic distribution of each document and the word distribution of each topic.

(4) Management Frame Authentication. First, the distance matrix is obtained according to the document distribution, then the clustering is realized according to the distance matrix. Finally the management frame authentication is realized according to the clustering results.

3.2   CSI Collecting

For simplicity, let's consider the simplest case. Suppose there is an AP and two transmitters, one of which as a legitimate station and the other as an attacker. The AP continuously receives frames from the transmitters. The legitimate station transmit legitimate management frames, thus the attacker transmit the fake management frames to interrupt the connection between the AP and the legitimate station. The AP extracts the CSI values from the received frames.

It is worth mentioned that the AP maintains a basic CSI database in advance and the CSI values in this database are collected from the legitimate station in a fixed location and from the attackers in many other different locations. The significance of this CSI database is to determine whether the management frames come from the legitimate transmitter in order to compare it with the new CSI values received by the AP.

3.3   Preprocessing

The collected CSI values are a series of complex values. The amplitude of the CSI reflects the attenuation of the channel and the phase reflects the time delay of the channel. However lack of effective way to solve the phase shift problem in the existing commercial equipments, the phase can not provide accurate information. We only take CSI magnitude as the object of study in this paper. The collected CSI values may produce outliers due to unstable device hardware or sudden changes in the environment, so the outliers must be removed in preprocessing phrase.

After the above processing, we get a series of real values. Since LDA views each math number as a word and utilizes word frequency for feature extraction, so the CSI real values as words is not realistic in the topic model. These CSI real values must be mapped to integer range which is called the quantitative process. We leverage standard quantizer to quantize the CSI value v to N enumeration ranks.

$$E(v) = \left\lfloor \frac{v - min(CSI)}{max(CSI) - min(CSI)} \times (N-1) + 1 \right\rfloor \tag{2}$$

where min(CSI), max(CSI) and E(v) are minimum value, maximum value in collected CSI values and new value after quantitation respectively.

3.4   Feature Extraction

The goal of this stage is to extract the hidden structures from the preprocessed CSI signal. We use LDA method for feature extraction. We view the CSI values collected during several times as a document and all the documents are combined to form the corpus. With corpus as input, we set parameters of the LDA algorithm in advance. These parameters consist of super parameter α and β, parameters of the iteration time N and topic number T. With corpus as input, after the operation we will get the document-topic matrix and the topic-word matrix, including document - topic matrix represents each document in the distribution of T on a topic.

The training process of LDA algorithm is:

(1) Random initialization. Each word w in each document in the corpus is randomly assigned to a topic number.
(2) Rescan the corpus, then re-sample its topic according to Gibbs Sampling formula and update it in the corpus.
(3) Repeat the re-sampling process of the corpus mentioned above in (2) until Gibbs Sampling converges.
(4) Calculate the topic-word co-occurrence frequency matrix of the corpus and the matrix is the LDA model.

3.5 Management Frame Authentication

Kullback-Leibler (KL) divergence is a method to describe the difference between two probability distributions. Let $P(\mathbf{V})$ and $P(\mathbf{Y})$ be the two discrete probability distributions of $\mathbf{X}$ values.

$$D(P||Q) = \sum_{x \epsilon \mathbf{X}} \left(P(x) \times log\left(\frac{P(x)}{Q(x)}\right) \right) \tag{3}$$

$$D(Q||P) = \sum_{x \epsilon \mathbf{X}} \left(Q(x) \times log\left(\frac{Q(x)}{P(x)}\right) \right) \tag{4}$$

where D(P||Q), D(Q||P) are the relative entropy of P to Q and the relative entropy of Q to P respectively.

We use KL divergence as a measure of document distance. But in fact KL divergence does not satisfy the concept of distance, because KL divergence is not symmetric, that is D(P||Q) $\neq$ D(Q||P). In this paper, the KL divergence is properly deformed to satisfy the concept of distance. The new KL divergence are defined as:

$$D'(P||Q) = \frac{1}{2}D(P||Q) + \frac{1}{2}D(Q||P) \tag{5}$$

The new KL divergence is used as a measure of the distance between every two documents. Then we can get the distance matrix of documents in the corpus. Then the clustering algorithm is applied. If the CSI values from the new document cluster together with the CSI values from the legitimate station, it is considered that the new document comes from the legitimate station, otherwise it comes from the attacker.

4   Experiment and Evaluation

In this section, we will present the implementation and the performance of the topic model based method for management frames authentication using CSI information. First, we will introduce the establishment of experimental platform. Then we will discuss some of the parameter settings involved in the method. Finally, we will present the experiment result.

4.1   Experiment Setup

We conduct the experiment in an indoor experiment existing other RF noises such as Wi-Fi, RFID and Bluetooth signals. We deploy some mini-computers which are commercial off-the-shelf (COTS) devices equipped Intel 5300 NIC. The Inter 5300 NIC includes 30 subcarriers per frame. We set one as a AP, the others as the stations. The receiver receives frames continually from the stations. We set up each transmitter with one transmitting antenna and three receiving antennas on the receiver end. Their drivers are all modified to enable them to transmit management frames in compliance to IEEE 802.11n standard.

To fully assess the performance of the methods used in this paper, we analyzed and evaluated them in three scenarios mentioned in [9]. The three scenarios are shown in Table 1. The AP is stationary in all three scenarios. Scenario A tests the system performance when both the client and attacker are stationary. Scenario B tests the performance when the condition is the same with scenario A but there are some dynamics caused by crowd flow. Scenario C tests the performance when the client is stationary, while the attacker is moving around.

The frequency of the AP and the client is 800 fps which means the AP can get a $800 \times 30 \times 3$ CSI values stream per second. The client initiates 20 Probe Requests to the AP every 0.3 s, and the AP replies 20 Probe Responses to the client immediately.

Table 1. Test scenarios description

Scenario	Description
A	Both the station and attacker are stationary
B	Same as A, but there is some channel dynamics caused by crowd flow
C	The station is stationary, while the attacker is moving around. There is no crowd flow

4.2   Impacts of Quantization Range

We need to map all the CSI values from real space to the integer space. Here we discuss the impact of quantization range on the system performance. The initial CSI values are between 0 dB and 60 dB. By mapping the initial CSI values to a different integer range, we test the impacts of different integer intervals on the system performance.

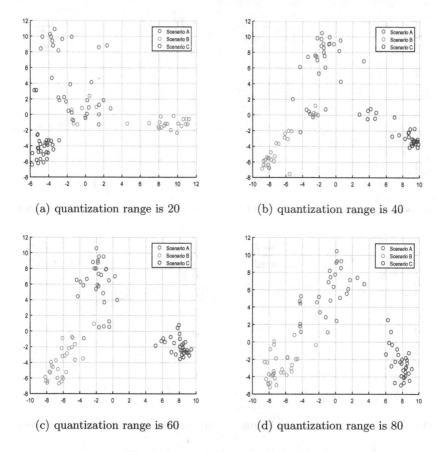

(a) quantization range is 20

(b) quantization range is 40

(c) quantization range is 60

(d) quantization range is 80

Fig. 1. Impact of quantization range

We set the quantization range to be 20, 40, 60, 80 respectively. As is shown in Fig. 1, the red, green and blue circles are documents collected from scenario A, B and C respectively. Each document is made up of several CSI values collected in a period of time. When circles with the same color cluster together and those with different colors disperse, it shows that the system behave good. When the quantization range is too large or too small, the system performance is both bad. However, when the quantization range is near its initial range, intra class is aggregation and inter class is dispersion. So we set the quantization range be 60.

4.3   Impacts of Document Size

We utilize LDA method to extract features of every CSI document. Each document is composed of several frames. Each frame is composed of several CSI values. Here we discuss the impacts of each document size on the system performance.

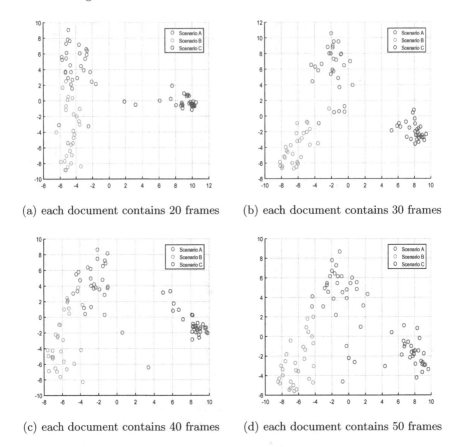

(a) each document contains 20 frames   (b) each document contains 30 frames

(c) each document contains 40 frames   (d) each document contains 50 frames

Fig. 2. Impact of document size

In our experiment, each frame contains 30×3 CSI values. We set each document size is 20, 30, 40, 50 frames respectively. As is shown in Fig. 2, we set the size of each document to be 30. We speculate that it may be because too large text will accumulate errors, while too small text contains less effective information. We will continue to pay attention to this problem in the future.

4.4   Impacts of Topic Numbers

Here we discuss the influence of the number of topics on the system. We set the number of topics to be 20, 40, 60, 80 respectively. As is shown in Fig. 3, we can see that as the topic number increases, clustering effect is better. But larger topic number adds the complexity of the LDA algorithm. So when choosing the value of topic number, we need to ensure that the value of topic number is as small as possible on the basis of ensuring the experimental results.

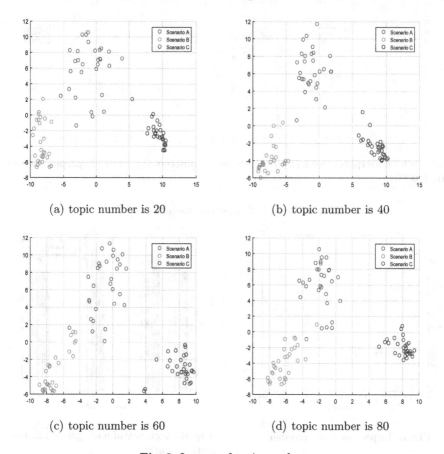

(a) topic number is 20

(b) topic number is 40

(c) topic number is 60

(d) topic number is 80

Fig. 3. Impact of topic number

4.5   Impacts of Hyperparameter α and β

During the model training, it is necessary to select proper parameters by combining the results of the model. In theory, as α gets smaller, it's as much as possible to make a document with only one topic and as β gets smaller, one word is as much as possible belongs to the same topic.

In our experiment, we set each α and β equal. We set their values to be 0.0005, 0.001, 0.01 respectively. As is shown in Fig. 4, we can see that when α and β are too small or too large, the results of clustering both behave worse. This is in accordance with the theoretical analysis. In our experiments, we set α and β to be 0.001.

4.6   Impacts of Iteration Times

Iteration time is a main parameter of LDA algorithm. If the parameter value is too small, the training model underfitting, while if the parameter value is too

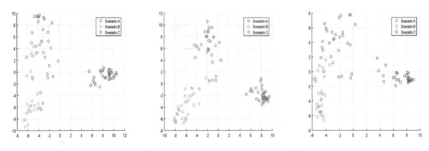

(a) both hyperparameters are 0.0005   (b) both hyperparameters are 0.001   (c) both hyperparameters are 0.01

Fig. 4. Impact of hyperparameter α and β

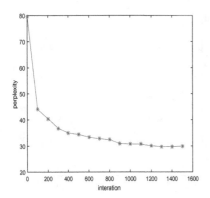

Fig. 5. Impact of topic number

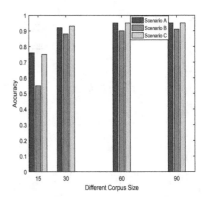

Fig. 6. Accuracy of management frame authentication

large, the training model will overfitting. So a proper parameter of iteration is important for model training. Blei, et al. [4] proposes to utilize perplexity to analyze the impacts of iteration time on the system performance.

As is shown in Fig. 5, when the number of iterations increases, perplexity will gradually decrease and then become stable which means the model is gradually stable.

4.7   The Accuracy of Management Frame Authentication

We evaluate the accuracy of management frame authentication under these three scenarios: scenario A, scenario B and scenario C. As is shown in Fig. 6, we set corpus size to be different values in each scenario. We can see that when the corpus size is above 30, we can achieve high accuracy of system performance. The average accuracy is more than 91% in our experiments.

5   Conclusion

In wireless LANs, data is transmitted through data frames, control frames and management frames. Because of the in-encryption of the management frames, it is easy to be exploited by attackers then attackers can launch various attacks on the network. Based on COTS hardware, we utilize a topic model method to achieve a Wi-Fi Management Frame authentication system. Topic model method views every number as a word. By training corpus consisting of a series of CSI values, we get topic distribution of each "document". Based on the topic distribution, we cluster the documents to achieve the authentication of the management frame. Extensive experiments are conducted to verify the efficiency of the system. These evaluations show excellent authentication ability and strong rejection against attacks.

Acknowledgments. We thank the valuable comments from our reviewers and editors. This work was supported by National Key R&D Program of China 2017YFB1003000, NSFC Grant No. 61751211, 61572396, 61772413, 61672424, and National Social Science Fund of China Grant. 17ZDA028.

References

1. Bakthavathsalu, K., Sampalli, S., Ye, Q.: Management frame attacks in Wimax networks: analysis and prevention. In: Seventh International Conference on Wireless and Optical Communications Networks, pp. 1–7 (2010)
2. Barbeau, M., Hall, J., Kranakis, E.: Detecting impersonation attacks in future wireless and mobile networks. In: Burmester, M., Yasinsac, A. (eds.) MADNES 2005. LNCS, vol. 4074, pp. 80–95. Springer, Heidelberg (2006). https://doi.org/10.1007/11801412_8
3. Blei, D.: Probabilistic topic models. In: ACM SIGKDD International Conference Tutorials, p. 5 (2011)
4. Blei, D.M., Ng, A.Y., Jordan, M.I.: Latent dirichlet allocation. J. Mach. Learn. Res. Arch. **3**, 993–1022 (2003)
5. Chen, Y., Trappe, W., Martin, R.P.: Detecting and localizing wireless spoofing attacks. In: IEEE Communications Society Conference on Sensor, Mesh and Ad Hoc Communications and Networks, pp. 193–202 (2007)
6. Danev, B., Luecken, H., Capkun, S., Defrawy, K.E.: Attacks on physical-layer identification. In: ACM Conference on Wireless Network Security, pp. 89–98 (2010)
7. Ge, W., Li, J., Sampalli, S.: Prevention of management frame attacks on 802.11 WLANs. Int. J. Wirel. Mob. Comput. **3**, 133–144 (2009)
8. Guo, F., Chiueh, T.: Sequence number-based MAC address spoof detection. In: International Workshop on Recent Advances in Intrusion Detection, pp. 309–329 (2005)
9. Jiang, Z., Zhao, J., Li, X.Y., Han, J., Xi, W.: Rejecting the attack: source authentication for wi-fi management frames using csi information. Proc. IEEE Infocom **12**(11), 2544–2552 (2013)
10. Kaur, J.: MAC layer management frame denial of service attacks. In: International Conference on Micro-Electronics and Telecommunication Engineering, pp. 155–160 (2017)

11. Liu, Y., Ning, P.: Enhanced wireless channel authentication using time-synched link signature. In: Proceedings of INFOCOM, pp. 2636–2640. IEEE (2012)
12. Tse, D., Viswanath, P.: Fundamentals of Wireless Communication. Cambridge University Press, Cambridge (2005)
13. Wang, G., Zou, Y., Zhou, Z., Wu, K., Ni, L.M.: We can hear you with Wi-fi!. In: International Conference on Mobile Computing and Networking, pp. 593–604 (2014)
14. Wang, W., Wang, H.: Weakness in 802.11w and an improved mechanism on protection of management frame. In: International Conference on Wireless Communications and Signal Processing, pp. 1–4 (2011)
15. Wang, Y., Wu, K., Ni, L.M.: Wifall: device-free fall detection by wireless networks. IEEE Trans. Mob. Comput. **16**(2), 581–594 (2017)
16. Wei, X., Croft, W.B.: LDA-based document models for ad-hoc retrieval, pp. 178–185 (2006)
17. Yen, C.W., Mao, J.L.: Method of processing management frame and related communication device (2015)

Towards Rule Consistent Updates in Software-Defined Wireless Sensor Networks

Meigen Huang$^{(\boxtimes)}$ and Bin Yu

Zhengzhou Information Science and Technology Institute,
Zhengzhou 450001, China
huang_meigen@163.com, byu2009@163.com

Abstract. The phenomenon of inconsistent network properties such as forwarding loops and packet losses may occur during rule update of software-defined wireless sensor networks. Aiming at this, the idea of scheduling the update order of sensor nodes is adopted to design the rule reverse addition strategy, rule suppression modification strategy and rule obverse deletion strategy. At the same time, parallel execution of sub-updates is supported by dividing the update domain. This method effectively improves the consistency of network update attributes and greatly enhances the update performance. The simulation results based on SDN-WISE show that the proposed strategies could adapt well to the resource-limited wireless sensor networks, and the advantages are especially obvious when the rule dependencies are more complicated.

Keywords: Consistent update · Wireless Sensor Networks (WSN)
Software-Defined Networking (SDN) · Rule · SDN-WISE

1 Introduction

With the rapid development of the Internet of Things (IoT), traditional wireless sensor networks (WSN) [1], which are the key supporting technologies for their perception layer, face increasingly severe challenges in terms of resource interconnection and environmental awareness [2, 3]. A new type of WSN adopting software-defined networking (SDN) concept [4] gradually gained popularity, namely software-defined wireless sensor networks (SDWSN) [5]. In general, the SDWSN follows the separation of control and forwarding. The flow rules are generated by the control plane, and the data plane is only forwarded by matching rules [6]. Flow refers to a series of packets that have some of the same properties.

Due to the dynamic nature of WSN, multi-hop relay communication is also prone to topology changes such as link interruptions. Therefore, the control plane needs to update the data plane rules quickly to ensure the correct forwarding of data packets. However, in the process of rule updating, the network may experience mixed use of new and old rules, which will destroy the consistency of network properties. For example, phenomena such as forwarding loops, routing black holes, and packet loss affecting network performance [7], and even violation of access control policies pose a serious threat to network security [8]. The root cause is the non-atomic nature of the sensor node's rule update. Different sensor nodes cannot complete the rule update

© Springer Nature Switzerland AG 2018
X. Sun et al. (Eds.): ICCCS 2018, LNCS 11068, pp. 167–176, 2018.
https://doi.org/10.1007/978-3-030-00021-9_16

synchronously. Compared to SDN, SDWSN has a greater uncertainty in network delay and a higher possibility of topology change. Therefore, the consistency of rule update is more difficult to guarantee and needs to be solved.

To the best of the author's knowledge, no studies related to the rule updating in SDWSN have been found. However, in SDN, a large number of research results concerning the rule consistent updating have been born. Literature [9] Considering that the network delay is an important factor that destroys the atomicity of the rule update, the authority switch is used to install the rules for the ordinary switch, thereby effectively reducing the time for transmitting rules. However, this way of giving the switch control function violates the idea of control and forwarding separation to some extent. [10] proposes the concept of per-packet (flow) consistency from the perspective of resolving the mixed of old and new rules, that is, each data packet (flow) matches only new or old rules during the entire forwarding process. At the same time, a famous two-phase updating scheme was proposed based on this idea, but this method will double the rules of the switch during the update. Therefore, in order to reduce the switch load, [11] uses the controller to cache the data packets that are difficult to identify the old or new rules to ensure that updates meet the per-packet consistency. However, it introduces a large amount of communication load and cannot be directly applied to WSN. Considering that the per-packet (flow) consistency requirement is too stringent and the implementation cost is high, [7] points out that there are update schemes that do not satisfy the per-packet (flow) consistency but support network properties such as loop-free and no packet loss. Based on this, two loop-free update schemes of reverse update and optimization update are designed by analyzing the rule dependency.

Therefore, this paper adopts the idea of coordinating the update order of the sensor node's rules and designs the consistent update strategies for rules addition, modification, and deletion. First, for the increase of rules applicable to the establishment of a new forwarding link, the rule reverse addition strategy is designed to ensure that the down-stream nodes have completed the rule updating before the current node updates the rule. Secondly, for the case of modifying the forwarding rules of the sensor nodes in the original forwarding link, the rule suppression modification strategy is designed to adjust the sensor node rules to satisfy atomicity by suppressing the data flow transmission. Finally, the rule obverse deletion strategy is designed for the removing of sensor node rules, and the up-stream nodes has completed the rule deletion before the current sensor node deletes the rule. In addition, in order to optimize the network update process and shorten the update time, the entire network update is divided into several sub-updates by the dividing of update domain on the basis of meeting the consistence, and the entire process of rule consistent updating is optimized through parallel scheduling.

The rest of the paper is organized as follows. Section 2 designs the rule consistent update strategies for rule addition, modification and deletion. Section 3 gives a sub-update optimization method that shortens the update time. The experiments and results analysis are given in detail in Sect. 4. Finally, Sect. 5 summarizes this paper.

2   Rule Consistent Update Strategy

Rule updates can be divided into rule addition, rule modification, and rule deletion. The rule addition is usually used to establish a new forwarding path. When the data aggregation node is replaced, a large number of network data collection paths need to be reestablished. The rule modification is usually used to the movement of nodes or load balancing and so on. It is necessary to modify the sensor nodes in a certain range. Rule deletion is usually used to sleep or death of nodes, and it is also used as a pre-operation to rule addition. Therefore, the above three rules update process may have a situation in which the new rule is mixed with the old rule, as shown in Fig. 1.

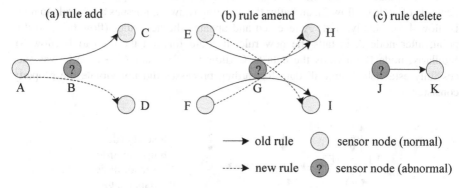

Fig. 1.   The inconsistent update of rule addition, modification and deletion

In Fig. 1(a), if sensor node D is a new node and paths A → B → D need to be re-established, then sensor nodes A, B, and D all need to install corresponding new rules. At this time, if the rule of node B is installed earlier than D, then the packet forwarded by B to D may be discarded by D. In Fig. 1(b), if the network needs to perform forwarding path switching, the traffic of the path E → G → H is switched to E → G → I, and the traffic of the path F → G → I is switched to F → G → H. At this point, regardless of whether the node G first modifies the rule of G → H or G → I, a forwarding error may occur. In Fig. 1(c), if the node K needs to enter the sleep state, both K and J need to delete the flow rule corresponding to the path J → K. However, if the rule deletion operated by K is earlier than J, there may be a case where J forwards data to K and K enters a sleep state. In summary, the foregoing rule update processes may lead to packet forwarding error, thus violating the consistency of network attributes.

In order to update the inconsistency of the above case, three rule update strategies, namely, the rule reverse addition, the rule suppression modification and the rule obverse deletion, are separately designed. By coordinating the updating order of rules among sensor nodes, it is ensured that the entire network update process satisfies the consistency principle.

2.1   Rule Reverse Addition

To make the rule addition process satisfy the attribute consistency, we design the rule reverse addition strategy: before the node adds the new rule, the down-stream nodes corresponding to the rule have already completed the rule addition. In this way, no data forwarded by any node according to the new rule will be discarded by the down-stream node.

Figure 2 shows that the rule reverse addition strategy. After node A generates a data packet, it needs to be transmitted to node C. Therefore, it is necessary to add rules to nodes A, B, and C to connect links A → B → C. According to the rule reverse addition strategy, the update order of sensor nodes rules is as follows. Node A requests the control plane to issue a new rule (flow 1). Then, the control plane first delivers the new rule of node C (flow 2), and after the updating (flow 3), it issues a new rule to node B (flow 4-5). Finally, node A received and updated the new rules (flow 6-7). At this point, after node A installs the new rule, it could forward the data to B (flow 8). Similarly, node B forwards the data to C (flow 9). The path A → B → C was successfully established, and all data forwarding processes did not violate the property consistency.

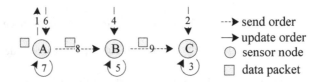

Fig. 2. The rule reverse addition strategy

2.2   Rule Suppression Modification

For the inconsistencies in the rule modification process, the designed rule suppression modification strategy is as follows: before the node modifies the rule, it will not receive the data flow related to the rule to be modified. To ensure that nodes do not receive data flows that affect the consistency of rule modification, suppression rules need to be designed to interrupt the data flow forwarding process of neighboring nodes.

Figure 3 elaborates the rule suppression modification. Node E needs to modify the rule. To ensure that the neighbor nodes D and F do not send data flows related to the rule, node E first sends a release rule to nodes D and F (flow 2) after receiving the rule update instruction (flow 1) and modifying the rule (flow 4) after confirms receipt (flow 3). After the rule is modified, the release rule (flow 5) is sent to nodes D and F, and when confirmation is received (flow 6), the rule modification is completed. Obviously, with the rule suppression modification strategy, the entire rule update process satisfies the atomicity of the update, and the update process will not be interrupted by the data flow, so the update consistency could be satisfied.

The suppression and release rules are essentially flow forwarding rules. The suppression rule is implemented by modifying the "action" field of the original rule, that is, modifying the "forward" action as a "cache" action so that the data flow received by the

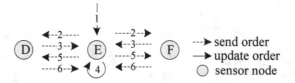

Fig. 3. The rule suppression modification strategy

node is cached first. The release rule is just the opposite, by modifying the "cache" action into a "forward" action and reinserting the original cached data flow into the matching queue. Note that both suppression and release rules are transmitted with the rule modification (flow 1) instruction.

2.3 Rule Obverse Deletion

The rule deletion is simpler, but there is still the risk of data flows being dropped. Therefore, the rule obverse deletion strategy is given: before the node deletes the rule, the up-stream nodes corresponding to the rule have deleted the rule. With this sequence, after any node deletes a rule, it is impossible to receive any data flow associated with it, thus fundamentally avoiding unmatched situations. Figure 4 shows the rule obverse deletion. The path G → H → I is the forwarding link to be deleted. The control plane first issues a rule delete command to node G (flow 1). After the G deletion is completed (flow 2), the control plane deletes the rule of node H (flow 3-4). In the end, control plane deletes the rule of node I (flow 5-6). Obviously, by adopting a rule to delete the policy in a forward direction, all nodes on the link do not experience the case where the data packet is erroneously discarded.

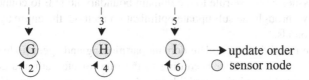

Fig. 4. The rule obverse deletion strategy

3 Sub-update Optimization

Although the above-mentioned rule consistent update strategy could complete the update of all rules in the network, it does not consider the issue of the efficiency of rule updates. The most important reference indicators for updating efficiency are update time and communication overhead. Therefore, under full consideration of the large scale of the network and the complex dependencies of rules, the entire network rule updating is divided into several sub-updates by dividing the network into several update domains. At the same time, the controller coordinates the parallel operations of each sub-update and achieve dual optimization of update time and communication overhead.

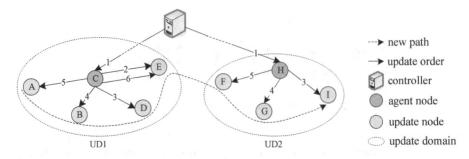

Fig. 5. The sub-update optimization

Figure 5 shows the sub-update optimization. The new path to be created is A → B → D → E → F → G → I. Due to the long path, the rule reverse addition strategy needs at least 7 rounds of updates. Therefore, the controller first divides the node associated with the new path into two update domains, UD1 and UD2. UD1 includes the sub-path A → B → D → E, the selected agent node is C; UD2 includes the sub-path F → G → I, and the agent node is H. At this point, the entire update process is divided into two sub-updates. The sub-updates can be performed in parallel.

Currently, the entire rule update order is as follows. The controller first delivers the rule update command to the agent nodes C and H at the same time. Then, to ensure the isolation between domains, the agent node C first sends a suppression rule to the domain boundary node E to interrupts the data transmission between UD1 and UD2. Then, the agent nodes C and H respectively adopt the rule reverse addition strategy for the rule update in UD1 and UD2, that is, the rule update of nodes E, D, B, A, and I, G, and H are performed in sequence. Finally, after the nodes A and F are updated, the agent node C issues a release rule to the domain boundary node E to connect the entire path. Obviously, through the sub-update optimization method, the entire update process needs only 5 rounds.

It should be noted that the update domain partitioning and agent node selection are all determined by the controller according to the rule update path and could also be directly implemented by existing methods based on clusters or domains. The size of the update domain is related to the size of the network. It also directly impacts the update time and communication cost.

Taking Fig. 5 as an example, if the three sub-updates, i.e., A → B, D → E and F → G → I are created, the entire update process can be completed in only 3 rounds, but at this time, the update domain partitioning and the proxy node selecting will require more communication overhead.

4   Experiments and Results Analysis

This experiment was designed based on SDN-WISE [13] and implemented using the COOJA simulation platform [14]. SDN-WISE is an open source SDWSN architecture based on the OpenFlow protocol. To achieve the consistent update strategies, we added a cache operation in the "action" domain and designed a cache queue in the sensor node. The experimental host uses the ThinkPad T470 laptop (i5 CPU, 4G RAM, and 128G SSD).

In the experimental deployment, a single controller is deployed on the control plane, and the data plane is designed to randomly deploy 50 sensor nodes in the $200 \times 200 \text{ m}^2$ plane area. The node communication radius is set to 50 m, and the node data generation rate is 10 packets per minute. In order to better verify the performance of the rules, the ring, tree, and mesh (acyclic) are separately designed in the experimental topology. Among them, the ring topology update is designed as the reverse of the transmission path, and the tree and mesh topologies are implemented by randomly moving five sensor nodes. The sub-update optimization is achieved by dividing into three update domains.

The experiment is divided into three aspects: update consistency, update time, and communication cost. The update consistency is based on the packet loss ratio in the update process. Finally, considering that [12] is the most authoritative research findings in the field of rule updating, this article chooses to compare with it to better highlight the update strategy performance of this paper. All experiments were performed three times independently and the results were averaged.

4.1 Update Consistency

The packet loss test results are shown in Table 1. Obviously, the consistent updating of rules in this paper can ensure zero packet loss when rules are increased, modified, and deleted in all the topologies. However, [12] lost 34.5% and 16.2% of the data packets in the ring topology under the rule modification and deletion, respectively. The root cause is that [12] is a free-loop bi-directional updating scheme. When the original rule in the network is a ring, no matter where the update starts, the rule loop must be faced, thus failing to satisfy the network property without packet loss.

Table 1. Packet loss rate experiment results.

Scheme	Operation	Ring	Tree	Mesh
This paper	Rule addition	0%	0%	0%
	Rule modification	0%	0%	0%
	Rule deletion	0%	0%	0%
[12]	Rule addition	0%	0%	0%
	Rule modification	34.5%	0%	0%
	Rule deletion	16.2%	0%	0%

4.2 Update Time

The update time refers to the time from moving the sensor node to the network completing the rule consistent update. The shorter the update time, the better the update performance. Figure 6 shows the experiment results of the update time, where the X-axis represents the network topology (including ring, tree and mesh) and the Y-axis represents the required update time.

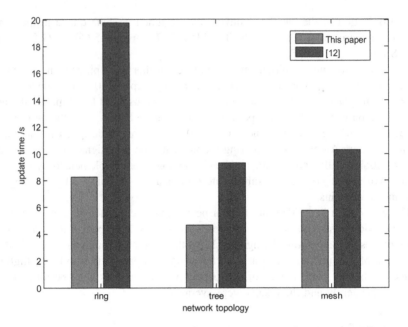

Fig. 6. Update time experiment results

As shown in Fig. 6, it is clear that the update time required to the rule consistent update strategies in this paper is shorter than [12] regardless of the network topology. In the ring topology, the update time in [12] is close to 20 s, but this paper only needs 8.27 s. The root cause is that this paper adopts a sub-update optimization method that divides the update domains, which can greatly shorten the update time.

4.3   Communication Cost

Communication is a relatively expensive part of the rule update process. Especially in WSN, communication overhead is the most energy-consuming event. Therefore, the communication cost during the entire rule update process is counted, and the actual performance of the update strategy could be well evaluated. Figure 7 shows the experimental results of communication cost, where the X-axis is the network topology and the Y-axis is the communication cost, which is characterized by the average number of data sent by the nodes.

As shown in Fig. 7, under the ring topology, the communication cost of update strategy in this paper is slightly higher than [12]. The reason is that the ring transmission distance is long, and the communication cost required to divide the update domain in this paper is large. At the same time, this is also the reason that the communication cost in the ring topology is obviously higher than the other two topologies. In the tree topology and mesh topology, the communication cost of the update strategy in this paper is less than [12] about 30%. Therefore, the communication overhead of the rule consistent update strategy is better than [12].

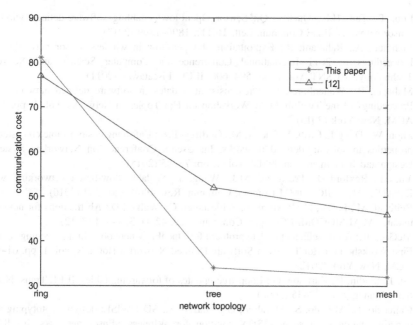

Fig. 7. Communication cost experiment results

5 Conclusion

This paper adopts the idea of coordinating the updating order of sensor nodes and proposes a rule consistent update strategy that includes the rule reverse addition, rule suppression modification, and rule obverse deletion. Subsequently, a sub-update optimization method was designed by dividing the update domains. Finally, based on the open source SDN-WISE architecture, the prototype was implemented. The simulation results show that compared with [12], the proposed strategy can guarantee the rule update of zero packet loss in any topology, and at the same time, it has shorter update time and less communication overhead, and can be well applied to energy-constrained WSN.

References

1. Borges, L.M., Velez, F.J., Lebres, A.S.: Survey on the characterization and classification of wireless sensor network applications. IEEE Commun. Surv. Tutor. **16**(4), 1860–1890 (2014)
2. Huang, M., Yu, B., Li, S.: PUF-assisted group key distribution scheme for software-defined wireless sensor networks. IEEE Commun. Lett. **22**(2), 404–407 (2018)
3. Valdivieso Caraguay, A.L., Benito Peral, A., Barona Lopez, L.I., Garcia Villalba, L.J.: SDN: evolution and opportunities in the development IoT applications. International Journal of Distributed Sensor Networks, **10**(5), (2014). https://doi.org/10.1155/2014/735142
4. McKeown, N.: Software-defined networking. INFOCOM keynote talk. http://infocom2009. ieee-infocom.org/. Accessed 21 Jan 2018

5. Luo, T., Tan, H.P., Quek, T.Q.: Sensor OpenFlow: enabling software-defined wireless sensor networks. IEEE Commun. Lett. **16**(11), 1896–1899 (2012)
6. Mahmud, A., Rahmani, R.: Exploitation of OpenFlow in wireless sensor networks. In: Proceedings of 2011 International Conference on Computer Science and Network Technology, ICCSNT, vol. 1, pp. 594–600. IEEE, Piscataway (2011)
7. Mahajan, R., Wattenhofer, R.: On consistent updates in software defined networks. In: Proceedings of the Twelfth ACM Workshop on Hot Topics in Networks, vol. 1, pp. 1–7. ACM, New York (2013)
8. Zhou, W., Dong J., Croft, J., Caesar, M., Godfrey, P.B.: Enforcing customizable consistency properties in software-defined networks. In: Usenix Conference on Networked Systems Design and Implementation, NSDI, vol. 1, pp. 73–85 (2015)
9. Yu, M., Rexford, J., Freedman, M.J., Wang, J.: Scalable flow-based networking with DIFANE. ACM SIGCOMM Comput. Commun. Rev. **40**(4), 351–362 (2010)
10. Reitblatt, M., Foster, N., Rexford, J., Schlesinger, C., Walker, D.: Abstractions for network update. ACM SIGCOMM Comput. Commun. Rev. **42**(4), 323–334 (2012)
11. McGeer, R.: A safe, efficient update protocol for OpenFlow networks. In: Proceedings of the First Workshop on Hot Topics in Software Defined Networks, HotSDN, vol. 1, pp. 61–66. ACM, New York (2012)
12. Fu, J., Sjodin, P., Karlsson, G.: Loop-free updates of forwarding tables. IEEE Trans. Netw. Serv. Manag. **5**(1), 22–35 (2008)
13. Galluccio, L., Milardo, S., Morabito, G., Palazzo, S.: SDN-WISE: design, prototyping and experimentation of a stateful SDN solution for WIreless SEnsor networks. In: IEEE Conference on Computer Communications, INFOCOM, pp. 513–521. IEEE, Piscataway (2015)
14. Osterlind, F., Dunkels, A., Eriksson, J., Finne, N., Voigt, T.: Cross-level sensor network simulation with COOJA. In: Proceedings of 2006 31st IEEE Conference on Local Computer Networks, pp. 641–648. IEEE, Piscataway (2006)

Towards Secure Device Pairing via Vibration Detection

Zhenge Guo[1]([⊠]), Zhaobin Liu[2]([⊠]), Jizhong Zhao[1]([⊠]), Hui He[1], and Meiya Dong[3]

[1] Xi'an Jiaotong University, Xi'an 710049, China
guozhenge@stu.xjtu.edu.cn, zjz@mail.xjtu.edu.cn, huihe@xjtu.edu.cn
[2] Suzhou Vocational University, Suzhou 215104, China
zbliusz@126.com
[3] Taiyuan University of Technology, Taiyuan 030024, China
dongmeiya@163.com

Abstract. Multi-party applications are becoming popular due to the development of mobile smart devices. In this work, we explore PVKE (Physical Vibration Keyless Entry), a novel pairing mechanism, through which users are able to utilize smart devices to detect a vibration from the smart watch, so as to use information from the vibration to deconstruct security keys. Thus, we perform device pairing without complicated operations. We show that the recognition accuracy of vibration key detection achieves 95% through solid experiments.

Keywords: Device pairing · Vibration detection · Key extraction

1 Introduction

With the recent improvements in modern technology, as well as the popularization of smart phones, smart devices like smart watches and other many multi-party applications have become more popular. In these application, smart devices often need to establish pairing relationships, and transfer data among one another via wireless communication, like Wi-Fi [9] and RFID [6]. As we know, wireless networks are more vulnerable to third party attack, as wireless channels are in a public wireless transport protocol. Hence, it is highly desirable to enforce secure communication channel between the smart devices.

Take automobile door locks system as an example, the Remote Keyless Entry System (RKE) [2] emerged after the Traditional Mechanical Key System. RKS is also know as remote central locking, refers to a lock that uses an electronic remote control as a key which is activated by a handheld device or automatically connect by proximity sensor. It can be used to remote control door lock and unlock requests. The system sends a stream through a specially coded data,

---

Supported by the NSFC program under Grants No. 61672372 and Shaanxi NSF under Grant No. 2017JM6109.

X. Sun et al. (Eds.): ICCCS 2018, LNCS 11068, pp. 177–186, 2018.
https://doi.org/10.1007/978-3-030-00021-9_17

the receiver in car gets the data and decodes with encrypt algorithm. After decrypting the key information, the vehicle performs lock or unlock request.

Hands-free Passive Keyless Entry (PKE) [5] is quickly becoming mainstream in automotive remote keyless entry applications and is a common option on new auto-mobile models. Instead of pressing a transmitter button to unlock or lock a car door, it is possible to gain vehicle access simply having a valid transponder in your possession.

In these applications, smart devices often need to establish pairing relation-ships, and transfer data among one another via wireless communications, like Bluetooth, RFID and Wi-Fi. There are two main problems with those methods: Firstly, information is easily intercepted by third parties. Secondly, information is vulnerable to "man-in-the-middle" attacks.

To solve the above problems, we propose PVKE, a new hands-free passive keyless entry based on physical vibration. This system contains two parts: base station system (bodywork) and transponder (smart wristband/watch). The user generates the key by the vibration of the personal smart device and passes the key to the base station receiving system when touching the door lock. The receiving system opens the device to unlock the door according to the key information. The main contributions of this design are as follows:

Firstly, we design a new intelligent unlocking system PVKE, which transfers the key by physical vibration, and avoiding the lack of interference by third parties in wireless transmission.

Secondly, we study the coding mechanism of key transfer via physical vibra-tion without adding additional equipment. In order to adjust the duration of the vibration of the mechanical motor to key, the encoding is divided into two kinds depending on the coding principle: time dimension based and binary-based.

Thirdly, the feasibility of realizing intelligent unlock by physical vibration transmission key is verified through experiments.

The rest of this paper is organized as follows. Section 2 discusses the related work. In Sect. 3, we describe the overall design of the system, and introduce the details of PVKE on how to detect the vibration in real time and how to extract and negotiate the key. We report the experimental settings and results in Sect. 4. Section 5 concludes the paper.

2   Related Work

How to achieve secure and rapid pairing between devices is a matter of concern for all multi-party applications. We classify the existing approaches as follows:

Wireless Channel-Based Technology. RFID is used for non-contact commu-nication using radio city [16]. NFC (Near Field Communication) [8] is another wireless technology for short-range communication with a maximum communi-cation range of 20CM based on the RFID technology. While Wi-Fi Bluetooth [1], and ZigBee [7] are widely available for longer range communication than NFC, eavesdropping without the knowledge of the user is possible [3] and private com-munication cannot be guaranteed.

Acoustics Based Technology. The authors in [10,11,14,15] generate keys by sound. According to a devices position background sound, it got the key from the frequency domain information and completed the pairing through the changing of FFT (Fast Fourier Transform). Schürmann [12] realizes a safe channel through the sound, Dhwani [13] further uses sound signals to imitate the hardware NFC to reach the goal of communicating in the near field. It uses a microphone and speaker to realize safe communication and the pairing in a near field on the cellphones without the pairing hardware NFC. However, the limitations of the microphone lead to a lot of inconsistent information and low security in the key. In order to improve the security, we need to increase the sampling time, which increases the difficulty of matching.

Light Based Technology. Komine et al. [4] proposed a new communication method using LED lights. This has an advantage in the sense of privacy over the other radio-based wireless communication method. However, it requires a line of sight between communicating devices and one-to-many communication is not possible without an extra apparatus.

3 System Design

3.1 System Overview

Based on the vibration detection [17], PVKE mainly consists of two parts: base station system and transponder system. The base station is used to receive the key and decide whether to open the entrance guard according to the correctness of the password. The transponder is used for generating physical vibration according to the cipher after receiving the instruction from the base station and releasing the key information. The base station part is the main body of the vehicle and continuously sends low frequency messages to activate transponders within the effective communication range. The message is sent in broadcast format in plain code and can be received by all transponders within the signal range. When the transponder enters the communication area and receives the message, it begins to transmit the key in the form of vibration. It is difficult for the base station to decode the sensing data after receiving the vibration information. If the verification is successful, the control instruction executive mechanism opens the door and sends the information to the responder to stop the vibration.

3.2 Key Generation Mechanism

Software/API limitations in smartphones and smartwatch prevent fully exploiting the vibro-motors and accelerometers. It limits the vibration intensity and vibration frequency of the mechanical motor, therefore, we can only adjust the start time and end time of the vibration.

Vibration Detection. Modern accelerometers sense the movement of the seismic mass along 3 orthogonal axes, and report them as an (X, Y, Z) tuple. The gravitational acceleration appears as a constant offset along the axis pointed towards the floor. When using accelerometer to sense data, we ignore the spatial direction of acceleration. The value of the acceleration three directions is computed by vector knowing, and the vector sum is compared with the threshold value to judge whether the vibration has taken place, and then the key is received further. The basic formula is shown in Eq. (1):

$$svm = \sqrt{x^2 + y^2 + z^2} \tag{1}$$

How to set the start and end times of a key word in the transmission process? There are two ways to do this:

The first method: as long as the base station detects the vibration, it is assumed that the key has started to pass. This method is simple and easy to operate. However, in the actual delivery process, the key transfer in this form is easy to generate string code, which leads to the failure of verification. Because the transmission mechanism determines that the intelligent device begins to transfer the key through vibration after receiving the base station activation information. So, under normal circumstances, in order to guarantee the integrity of the transmitted key, the intelligent device must transmit more than one set of keys continuously. If the key is decoded simply by recording continuous vibration data, the wrong string code is easily generated. For example, the responder passes two sets of keys, 213 and 213. Since the base station receives the vibrator from the second encoding in the first group, the key identified by the base station is likely to be 132.

This problem can be solved as follows: Set the threshold value of key transfer interval, the vibration interval of the digital single in the same group of keys is less than that of different groups of keys.

The second method: set a special transmission vibration mode to represent the beginning and the end of the key transmission. Before transferring the key, we set a special vibration to let the base station system know that we will start to transfer the key and to know when we will stop transferring.

Encoding Mechanism. In this paper, in order to adjust the duration of the vibration of the mechanical motor to key, the encoding is divided into two kinds depending on the coding principle: Time Dimension based and Binary-based.

The encoding mechanism based on the time dimension: the number of strings to be transmitted is encoded by the corresponding time length of each digit. For example, the continuous vibration 1 second represents the number 1, the continuous vibration 2 seconds represents the number 2, and so on. Binary-based encoding scheme: sets the password according to binary code. Code each digit in binary.

How to set the number 0 in the key. In wireless signal transmission, color Manchester coding is usually used to transmit data. The data such as continuous 0 or

1 can be identified without clock synchronization signal. However, in the process of passing the key with vibration, if the non-vibration is represented as 0, it is easy to confuse the spatial time without data transfer with the number 0, which leads to the wrong key identification.

In the digital coding process of the vibration key, PVKE use the +1 method to experiment the coding. Use 1 for 0 and 10 for 9. For example, the number 0 is represented by 1 millisecond vibrated time in the encoding process according to the length of time described above. In binary coding, the number 0 is 11, and the number 1 is 12.

4   System Evaluation

Based on the Android Wear intelligent platform, this paper realizes the detection module. Android Wear is the new open intelligence platform that was created by Google to use for smart watches, which allows a third-party to manufacture a wide variety of devices to be compatible in Android Wear. We realize the extraction of acceleration and gyro sensor data through the API that was provided by the Android Wear system, and the adjustment of the sensor sampling frequency as well.

4.1   System Implementation

The experiment used the equipment HUAWEI watch and SAMSUNG X5, their hardware as show in Table 1.

Table 1. Hardware comparison between Galaxy S5 and HUAWEI-WATCH 2

Hardware parameter	Galaxy S5	HUAWEI-WATCH 2
Type	Smart Phone	Smart Watch
RAM	2 GB	768 mb
CPU	Qualcomm Snapdragon 801	Qualcomm Snapdragon Wear 2100
Android version	6.0.1	7.1.1
Sampling frequency	200 Hz	200 Hz

4.2   Experimental Result and Analysis

The Influence of Threshold Value for Vibration Detection Accuracy. In previous sections, we have discussed the relationship between the threshold value and the detection accuracy. PVKE collected 9 number vibration, with each number vibrations 5 times. We use the different threshold to resample in the subsequent vibration detection, finally, due to the different threshold we detect respectively, the result is shown in Figs. 1, 2 and 3. In Fig. 1, we can figure out that when the threshold is 20.05, the deviation is 358.82 ms. Since the threshold is smaller, the motion information the capture is more, making it harder to identify the error. With the increase in threshold to 20.10 in Fig. 2, the deviation is decrease to 112.73 ms. After reaching a certain degree to 20.15 in Fig. 3, however, the deviation is no longer decrease, because most of the vibration information cannot be detection. Considering the recognition accuracy, PVKE choose 20.10 as the threshold value.

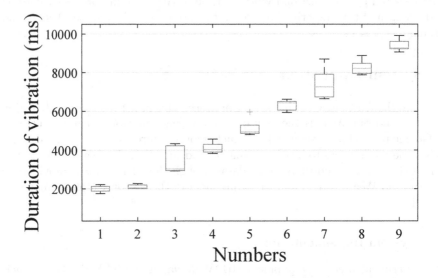

Fig. 1. The duration of vibration with SVM = 0.205

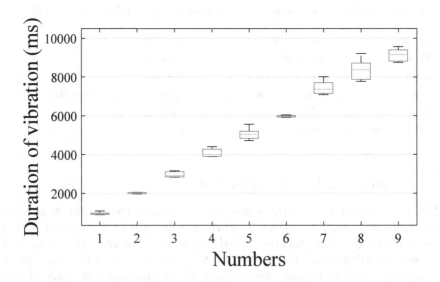

Fig. 2. The duration of vibration with SVM = 0.210

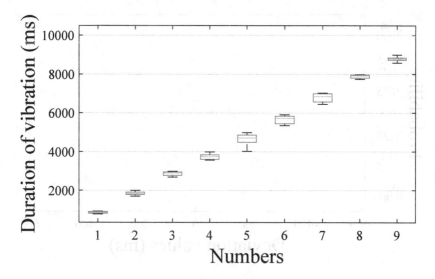

Fig. 3. The duration of vibration with SVM = 0.215

The Influence of Password Length for Vibration Detection Accuracy.
As we all know, the key length determines the security of the key. In vibration-based key transfer systems, will the key recognition rate decrease with the increase of the key length? We test three sets of keys that go up to 2, 3 and 4, respectively. The experimental data are shown in Figs. 4, 5 and 6. It is found from the experiment that the average deviation of identifying vibration cipher

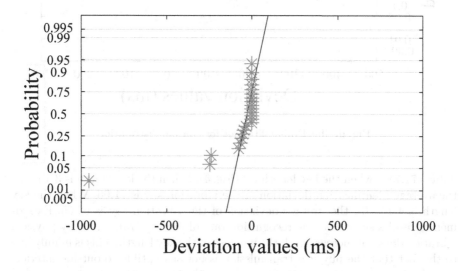

Fig. 4. 2bit Probability plot for Normal distribution

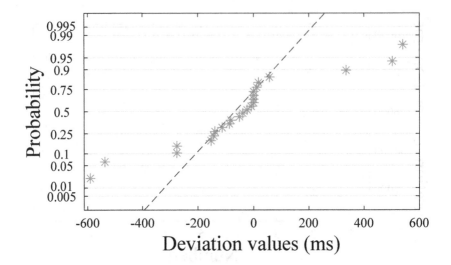

Fig. 5. 3bit Probability plot for Normal distribution

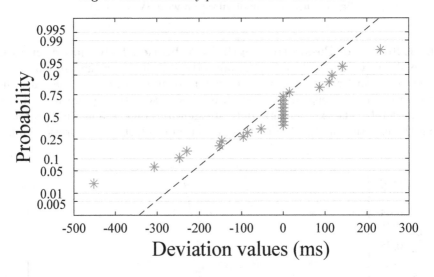

Fig. 6. 4bit Probability plot for Normal distribution

data is 71.7 ms when the key length is 2(Fig. 4), When the key length is 3(Fig. 5), the average identification deviation of the vibration key is 71.06. When the key length is 4(Fig. 6), the average deviation of the vibration key is 62.65. Experimental results show that the recognition rate of the key transferred by physical vibration does not increase with the increase of the key length. This is mainly due to the fact that the physical transmission is not susceptible to outside interference. In the experiment, we also found that in the two-length code, the maximum deviation of 95 data in the vibration key is 250, in the key with length 3, the maximum deviation is 450, and in the key with length 4, the maximum deviation is 350. Therefore, we limit the decoding bias to 450 during the decoding process, which will guarantee a key identification rate of no less than 95%.

5   Conclusion

In this work, we have proposed PVKE, which use a wearable device to generate a vibration password and thus simplify device matching. There are three main contributions: designing the vibration based key transfer method; study the coding mechanism of key transfer via physical vibration without adding additional equipment; completing the vibration key generation method and wireless sensor key generation method. Experiments showed the secure decryption and unlock mechanism without additional device is implemented.

References

1. Haartsen, J.: The bluetooth radio system. IEEE Pers. Commun. **7**(1), 28–36 (2000)
2. Suda, H., Lehmer, M.J.: Remote keyless entry system: U.S. Patent 6,718,240[P] (2004)
3. Weis, S.A., Sarma, S.E., Rivest, R.L., Engels, D.W.: Security and privacy aspects of low-cost radio frequency identification systems. In: Hutter, D., Müller, G., Stephan, W., Ullmann, M. (eds.) Security in Pervasive Computing. LNCS, vol. 2802, pp. 201–212. Springer, Heidelberg (2004). https://doi.org/10.1007/978-3-540-39881-3_18
4. Komine, T., Nakagawa, M.: Fundamental analysis for visible-light communication system using LED lights. IEEE Trans. Consum. Electron. **50**(1), 100–107 (2004)
5. Microchip Technology Inc.: Passive keyless entry (PKE) reference design users manual[Z] (2006)
6. Want, R.: An introduction to RFID technology. IEEE Pervasive Comput. **5**(1), 25–33 (2006)
7. Baronti, P., Pillai, P., Chook, V.W., Chessa, S., Gotta, A., Hu, Y.F.: Wireless sensor networks: a survey on the state of the art and the 802.15.4 and ZigBee standards. Comput. Commun. **30**(7), 1655–1695 (2007)
8. Curran, K., Millar, A., Garvey, C.M.: Near field communication. Int. J. Electr. Comput. Eng. (IJECE) **2**, 371–382 (2012)
9. Wifi (wireless fidelity). http://www.wi-fi.org
10. Nguyen, N., Sigg, S., An, H., Ji, Y.: Using ambient audio in secure mobile phone communication. In: IEEE International Conference on Pervasive Computing and Communications Workshops, pp. 431–434 (2012)
11. Sigg, S.: Adhocpairing: Spontaneous audio based secure device pairing for android mobile devices (2012)
12. Schürmann, D., Sigg, S.: Secure communication based on ambient audio. IEEE Trans. Mob. Comput. **12**(2), 358–370 (2013)
13. Nandakumar, R., Chintalapudi, K.K., Padmanabhan, V., Venkatesan, R.: Dhwani: secure peer-to-peer acoustic NFC. ACM SIGCOMM Comput. Commun. Rev. **43**(4), 63–74 (2013)

14. Miettinen, M., Asokan, N., Nguyen, T.D., Sadeghi, A.R., Sobhani, M.: Context-based zero-interaction pairing and key evolution for advanced personal devices. In: ACM Sigsac Conference on Computer and Communications Security, pp. 880–891 (2014)
15. Zhang, L., et al.: Montage: combine frames with movement continuity for realtime multi-user tracking. IEEE Trans. Mob. Comput. **16**(4), 1019–1031 (2017)
16. Yang, L., Li, Y., Lin, Q., Jia, H., Li, X., Liu, Y.: Tagbeat: sensing mechanical vibration period With COTS RFID systems. IEEE/ACM Trans. Netw. **25**(6), 3823–3835 (2017)
17. Guo, Z., Gao, X., Ma, Q., Zhao, J.: SDP: towards secure device pairing via handshake detection, Tsinghua Science and Technology (2018). https://doi.org/10.26599/TST.2018.9010085

TRFIoT: Trust and Reputation Model for Fog-based IoT

Yasir Hussain[1(✉)] and Zhiqiu Huang[1,2,3]

[1] College of Computer Science and Technology,
Nanjing University of Aeronautics and Astronautics (NUAA),
Nanjing 211106, China
yaxirhuxxain@yahoo.com
[2] Key Laboratory of Safety-Critical Software,
NUAA, Ministry of Industry and Information Technology, Nanjing 211106, China
[3] Collaborative Innovation Center of Novel Software Technology and
Industrialization, Nanjing 210093, China

Abstract. Where IoT and Cloud Computing are revolutionizing today's ecosystem, they also cause alarming security and privacy issues. As a continuum of devices and objects are interconnected with each other in order to share data and information. It is really important to evaluate the trustworthiness of these devices/objects, whether they are trustworthy or malicious. In this work, we propose a novel Trust and Reputation (TR) based model to outsource malicious users in a Fog-based IoT (FIoT). In our model, we used a multi-source trust evaluation by taking into account of the reputation of participating nodes. We use the feedback system to make the trust system reliable and trustworthy. We evaluate our model with simulations and the result shows the effectiveness of TRFIoT.

Keywords: Fog computing · Cloud computing
Internet of Things (IoT) · Trust and Reputation

1 Introduction

IoT and Cloud Computing are one of the cutting edge technologies. According to surveys, trillions of devices will become a part of the internet in near future. According to Cisco [2] "approximately 50 billion things will become a core part of the internet by 2020". Internet of things (IoT) is revolutionizing many fields like smart city, smart farming, traffic management, e-health, industry 4.0, etc. Devices/objects connect with each other to share data and information to help improve the ecosystem. As a lot of devices will connect and disconnect to share data and information or to get services, it is really important to outsource the malicious devices/nodes.

IoT devices highly relay on Clouds [4–7] to take out the computation and data storage due to the resource-constrained nature. In the Cloud-based IoT (CIoT), IoT sensors, devices or objects sense/collect data, whereas cloud carries

© Springer Nature Switzerland AG 2018
X. Sun et al. (Eds.): ICCCS 2018, LNCS 11068, pp. 187–198, 2018.
https://doi.org/10.1007/978-3-030-00021-9_18

the storage and the processing of that data in order to infer useful information. In CIoT, IoT devices outsource the sensed/collected data to the cloud which may cause a large amount of data send to cloud, high network bandwidth usage and delay in system response.

Fog computing [11] is revolutionizing the CIoT by providing the cloud services on the edge of a network. Fog is introduced by Cisco [1]. Fog computing is fairly an expansion of cloud computing on the verge of a network. Fog can be a server, switch, router or any device/object having the capability of storage and processing. FIoT can help overcome many security, privacy, and performance issues that normally resides in a CIoT. Many surveys [4,5,8,9] shows the need and the importance of Fog in IoT. FIoT is a three-layered architecture as shown in Fig. 1. The first layer is the IoT layer where physical object embedded with electronics and sensors to collect data and information. The second layer is the Fog layer, where initial data processing or trust evaluation can be performed before outsourcing the data to the cloud. Finally, the third layer is the cloud layer which helps store or process any extensive computation to infer useful information.

Need of this Work As traditional CIoT provide services in a centralized [12–14] fashion and IoT devices need to outsource sensed and collected data to the cloud due to resource-constrained nature. Which cost high bandwidth usage, delay in response time and no mechanism to identify the malicious nodes before sending data or information to the Cloud. Whereas FIoT provides cloud services on the edge of a network. FIoT can help [8] reduce the amount of data sent to the cloud, conserves network bandwidth and can help improve the response time. FIoT can help outsource malicious nodes at the network edge. Evaluation of a node trustworthiness at the fog layer can provide an aid in FIoT security and privacy issues. As a number of devices will continuously connect and disconnect to share data/information or to get services, trust seems to be a valid approach to evaluate the trustworthiness in a FIoT.

Our Work we propose a Trust and Reputation-based Model to outsourcing malicious nodes in FIoT (TRFIoT). In this work, we use multi-source Trust and Reputation-based evaluation of a node's trustworthiness. Multi-sources are parameterized by weight factors as well as based on their reputation, which helps keep the system reliable, unbiased, and effective. A *"Trust Feed Back"* and *"Periodic Trust Feed Back"* system are used to help keep our model. TRFIoT is evaluated with extensive simulations to help evaluate its effectiveness, reliability, and trustworthiness.

Main Contribution our main contributions are:

- A novel approach for Trust and Reputation-based outsourcing malicious nodes in a FIoT (TRFIoT). The key concept is multi-source trust evaluation.
- To help TRFIoT reliable, effective and unbiased, We propose *"Trust Feed Back"* and *"Periodic Trust Feed Back"* which help the system synced with other nodes.
- A novel approach to help overcome the cold star problem.

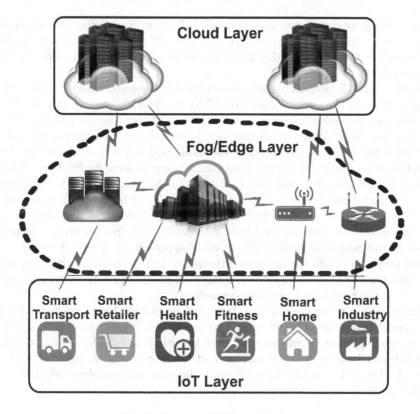

Fig. 1. Fog-based IoT architecture

Paper Outline Rest of the paper is organized as, Sect. 2 covers related work. Section 3 discusses TRFIoT in detail. Then, we continue to Sect. 4, which is about simulation and Results. Finally, Sect. 5 will conclude this work.

2   Related Work

The sole purpose of IoT is to connect "things", regardless of their attributes. As a number of device/objects will continuously connect and disconnect with the system, Trust seems to be a valid approach to outsource untrustworthy/malicious nodes.

Xiao et al. [15] proposed a trust model based on Guarantor and Reputation for social IoT. They used a guarantor based approach, which provides a guarantor based on some agreed commission to provide services and later they use the reputation of such guarantor to evaluate its trustworthiness. Their trust evaluation focuses on two parameters credit and reputation in order to infer the trustworthiness of a node. Kokoris et al. [16] discuss design and implementation of trust and reputation model in social IoT. In their article, they define three types of behavioral maliciousness in social IoT. First is malicious service provision, second malicious recommendations and lastly oscillating behavior. finally, they conclude their paper with simulations which shows feasibility, performance, and scalability of TRM-SIoT.

Fang et al. [17] proposed a beta-based trust and reputation model for evaluation of trustworthiness of a node (BTRES) in a wireless sensor network. They monitor node behavior to infer its trustworthiness. Later they use the trust value to select the relay nodes. By simulations, it shows that BTRES can maximize internal defense for compromised or malicious nodes. Chen et al. [18] in their literature, they proposed a novel trust management system for SOA-based IoT. They consider three types of social relations in their model, first is friendship, second is social contact and third is the community of interest. They also used adaptive filtering technique which adjusts weights automatically. Xiong et al. [19] proposed a reputation based trust mechanism to help alleviate the security issues in the peer-to-peer network. In their approach, they consider only reputable peers and avoid the untrustworthy peers. In the literature [20], proposed a reputation based trust model by computing global trust value to outsource untrustworthy peer in the peer-to-peer network.

In this work, we propose a novel trust and reputation based model for FIoT. Our model takes the previous trust and reputation related work into account and enhancing their capabilities to meet the FIoT architecture requirements. TRFIoT can help in decision making and to improve the security of a FIoT network. TRFIoT can also help alleviate the cold star problem, which is not considered by most of the previous model.

3   Trust and Reputation in FIoT

Trust is a complex concept many authors try to define it. However, it is difficult to summarize trust in a single definition. First, we see some trust definitions to have a better understanding of trust. Gambetta [22] defined trust as *"Trust is the subjective probability by which an individual, A, expects that another individual, B, performs a given action on which its welfare depends".*

Another definition of trust by McKnight et al. [21] *"Trust is the extent to which one party is willing to depend on something or somebody in a given situation with a feeling of relative security, even though negative consequences are possible".*

Whereas Reputation [23] is defined as *"Reputation is what is generally said or believed about a person's or thing's character or standing".*

Trust in IoT can be defined as, *A "Thing" belief in another "Thing's" honesty, reliability, and capabilities based on its experiences".* Whereas Reputation can be defined as, *A "Things belief in another "Thing's" honesty, reliability, and capabilities recommended by other "Things".*

Table 1. TRFIoT system general notations & description

Notations	Description
id	Unique identification number for a node (Cloud,Fog,IoT)
N_{id}	A specific IoT node
F_{id}	A specific Fog node
C_{id}	A specific Cloud node
x	A specific node (IoT,Fog,Cloud)
TV	Trust Value Where TV range between $[0], [1]$
$TV_{N_{id}}$	Trust Value of a specific node in current Fog node
$TV_{N_{id}}^{x}$	Trust Value of a node from an other node
FV	Feedback Value where FV range between $[-1, 1]$
$FV_{N_{id}}^{x}$	Feedback of a node from an other node
RV	Reputation Value where RV range between $[0, 5]$
$RV_{N_{id}}^{x}$	Reputation of a node from an other node
$RD_{N_{id}}$	Reputation Database of a specific IoT node
α, β, γ	The weight factors for TE

4   TRFIoT: Trust and Reputation Model for Fog-Based IoT

In this section, First, we discuss TRFIoT system general abbreviations & notations. Table 1 shows the general terms that will be used to explain the working of TRFIoT model and evaluation process.

This section briefly discusses the system model design of TRFIoT. Figure 2 shows the system model design of TRFIoT. The first layer is the IoT layer in which IoT nodes (sensors, devices, object, things, users, etc.) sense/collect data and information. Every node can be identified by a unique id which will be unique universally like a mac address. Many authentications techniques [24,25] had been proposed by many authors in FIoT. For the sake of simplicity in Trust Evaluation (TE) process, we are assuming a User ID based approach to uniquely identify a user for TE. Then the sensed/collected data and information will be forward to the Fog/Edge layer along with its public key which in this case we assume N_{id} along with its $RD_{N_{id}}$. Here $RD_{N_{id}}$ is the list of node's reputations whom with N_{id} had communicated with. On this layer Fog/Edge nodes which can be any object, thing, router, switch or server having the capabilities of storage and processing will perform the TE.

We used multi-source TE process in which, Fog node will dispatch a query to neighbor nodes for its Trust Value (TV) for its TE. After evaluation of an IoT node $TV_{N_{id}}$, Fog/Edge node will dispatch $FV_{N_{id}}^{F_{id}}$ to reputed Fog/Edge nodes and take appropriate action based on its TV. The process of TE will be discussed in Sect. 4.2 in detail. Finally $TV_{N_{id}}$ along with the sensed/collected data of IoT node will be forward to the Cloud layer. Then cloud can dispatch reward/punishment $(FV_{N_{id}}^{C^{id}})$ for the node N_{id}, Which will help improve the TE process.

4.1 Trust Evaluation Approaches

The process of TE is based on two approaches, first is Reputation-based Approach and second is the Content-based approach.

Reputation-Based Approach. The reputation-based approach is initial TE process which helps the Fog node whether the connecting device is trustworthy. In this process, Fog node evaluates the trust status of a node by collaborating with other nodes and by its own experience. At Fog layer only the N_{id} is used to carry this process. This way our approach keep the evaluation process privacy preserved and trustworthy.

Content-Based Approach. The content-based approach is an extensive TE process. There can be two possible ways to carry this process. First is Local Content-based evaluation and second global Content-based evaluation. In the first approach, a node's content is evaluated at Fog layer to see the relevance and similarity of context/content at a specific location. This approach isolates malicious nodes for any kind of malicious activity in FIoT. In second approach an extensive evaluation of data can be performed by Cloud to check any kind of maliciousness.

4.2 Trust Evaluation Protocol

In the evaluation of trust, it is really hard to trust a single source therefor in TRFIoT we use multi-source trust evaluation process based on reputation. Whenever a node connects to the Fog node for communication, It will share its N_{id} along with $RD_{N_{id}}$. It is to be noted here that $RD_{N_{id}}$ will not affect N_{id} trust evaluation. This $RD_{N_{id}}$ will help the Fog node for TE process for other devices. This approach makes TRFIoT effective and reduces the latency issue. After a connection had been made with an IoT node, Fog node will dispatch a $TV_{N_{id}}$ query to reputed neighbor nodes (Fog/IoT). Here we assume that current Fog node will only share public key of connecting node, which in this case is N_{id}. This approach will help secure the privacy of that node and will help to isolate the Identity-based maliciousness. Then Fog node will check the current Trust status of N_{id} in its own database. If it finds a previous $TV_{N_{id}}$, Then it will compute the trust by the Eq. 1.

$$TV_{D_{id}} = \alpha \times TV_{N_{id}} + \beta \times \sum_{j=1}^{n} \frac{TV_{N_{id}}^{RV^j}}{J} + \gamma \times \sum_{k=1}^{n} \frac{TV_{N_{id}}^{RV^k}}{K} \qquad (1)$$

Here RV^j, RV^k are Reputed IoT and Fog nodes, Whereas J, K are total number of IoT and Fog nodes respectively. The α, β and γ are the weight factors.

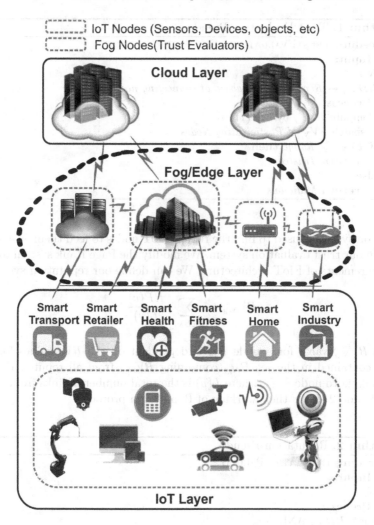

Fig. 2. Trust and reputation based FIoT system model

If there is no $TV_{N_{id}}$ found in current fog node or any neighbor nodes, Then system will assume a default value of 0.5 and put it in monitor to keep track of its behavior. After evaluating the $TV_{N_{id}}$, system will dispatch a $FV_{N_{id}}$ to all the nodes that have participated in TE process. Pseudo 1 shows the working of TRFIoT.

4.3   Reputation Evaluation Protocol

For the reputation evaluation system in TRFIoT, we used a modified version of Page Rank [26] system which is used by Google search for ranking web pages. In our model we assume neighbor Fog nodes to be reputed and trust worthy. The

---

Algorithm 1. Trust Evaluation Pseudo

1: **procedure** TRUSTEVALUATION
        Input:
2:      N_{id}
3:      $RD_{N_{id}} \leftarrow$ *Reputation Database of connecting node*
        Process:
4:      Compute $TV_{N_{id}}$ by Eq. (1)
5:      Dispatch $FV_{N_{id}} \forall$ *Participating Nodes*
6:      **if** $TV_{N_{id}} \geq Range$ **then**
7:          **return** *Trusted*
8:      **else**
9:          **return** *Malicious*

---

reputation system is used to find the reputed IoT nodes to feed them as a second source in our trust evaluation system. We modify the Page Rank system to meet the requirements of FIoT architecture. We can define our reputation system as,

$$RV_{N_{id}} = \sum_{v \in B_{N_{id}}} \frac{RP(v)}{L(v)} \tag{2}$$

The $RV_{N_{id}}$ value for a node N_{id} is dependent on the RV_v values for each node v contained in the set $B_{N_{id}}$ (containing $RV_{N_{id}}$ from all reputed Fog/IoT nodes linking to node N_{id}), where $L(v)$ is the total number of links from the set $B_{N_{id}}$. Pseudo 2 shows their working of Reputation protocol.

Algorithm 2. Reputation Pseudo

1: **procedure** REPUTATIONPSEUDO
        Input:
2:      N_{id}
        Process:
3:      For $\forall RD_{N_{id}}$ AND $RV_{N_{id}}^{F_{id}}$
4:      Compute $RV_{N_{id}}$ by Eq. (2)
5:      **if** $RV_{N_{id}} \geq Range$ **then**
6:          **return** *Reputed*
7:      **else**
8:          **return** *non-Reputed*

4.4   Trust Feedback and Periodic Trust Feedback

After evaluation of trust, TRFIoT will dispatch *Trust Feedback* to all the neighbor fog nodes and reputed IoT nodes which participated in its TE. The feedback value can range between $(-1, 1)$. This approach will let neighbor nodes know if a node is losing or gaining trust.

Whereas *Periodic Trust Feedback* is a time-dependent sync of active nodes that had made communication with the Fog nodes within a specific time period. Fog nodes can sync such nodes trust level with other Fog nodes so that they can keep track of new nodes or old nodes trust status. It can also help in overcoming cold star problem.

5   Simulation and Results

In this section, we will first discuss our simulation setup and will explain each parameter to have a better understanding of TRFIoT. In our simulation, we consider every user as new which will help us overcome cold star problem. We give each new user base trust value as discussed earlier in our Sect. 4.2. In simulation setup, we use $\alpha = 0.7$ which is the weight factor for current Fog node as Direct Trust is more trust worthy as compared to other sources, $\beta = 0.5$ for reputed IoT neighbor nodes and $\gamma = 0.5$ for neighbor Fog nodes. We set $BaseTrust = 0.5$, Which will help out source malicious users and can help monitor them. We use $BaseReputation = 2 - 3$ as reputed for our second source (IoT nodes) in TRFIoT.

5.1   Single-Source Vs Multi Socurce Trust Evaluation

To show why our purposed model is better we compare single source with multi-source trust evaluation. We compute $TV_{N_{id}}$ for every device with single source either it is IoT nodes or Fog nodes. As shown in Figs. 3 and 4, by collaborating with a single source (Devices or Fogs) it gives either height value of trust or low value. And a single source cannot be trusted completely. After computing the single source trust, we apply our proposed multi-source approach. As Fig. 5 shows, it gives more effective, unbiased and reliable Trust evaluation. By comparing the single-source trust evaluation with our multi-source technique we can clearly see that multi-source approach provides more better, unbiased and effective results.

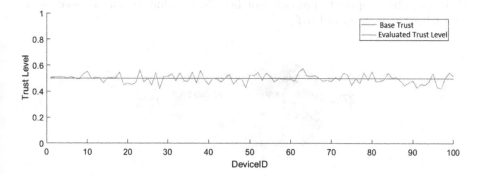

Fig. 3. Single source trust evaluation (IoT nodes)

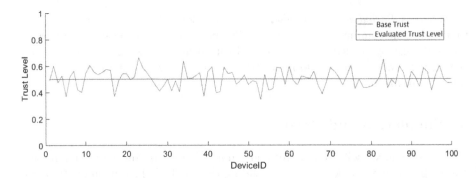

Fig. 4. Single source trust evaluation (Fog nodes)

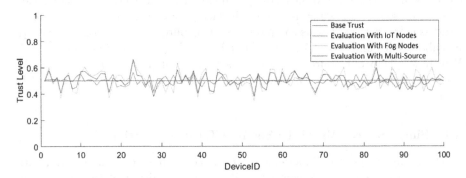

Fig. 5. Comparing multi-source weighted trust level method with single source approach

5.2   Malicious Nodes Outsourcing with TRFIoT

In Fig. 6, We can see that TRFIoT has successfully been able to outsource untrustworthy/malicious nodes from the network. The identified nodes can be put in monitor or Fog/Cloud node can take appropriate action with such kind of nodes. The Proposed approach can help in decision making as well as in improving the security in FIoT.

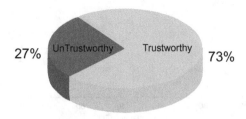

Fig. 6. Outsourced malicious nodes with TRFIoT

6 Conclusion

In this work, we present a novel TRFIoT model to help outsource malicious nodes. In our model, we use multi-source trust evaluation system supported by the reputation of participating nodes. We also define what is Trust and reputation in IoT. A *Trust Feedback & Periodic Trust Feedback* system was used to help alleviate malicious nodes and to make Trust evaluation process effective, unbiased and trustworthy. With simulation, TRFIoT shows that It can help outsource these malicious nodes and can help in decisions making. Our proposed model can be implemented in many FIoT systems and can help overcome many security issues as well as in decision making.

Future Work In this work, We present a novel TRFIoT model to outsource malicious nodes. In future, we want to implement this model, Trust as a Service (TAAS) which can be used in FIoT. In this work we consider Fog nodes to be reputed, Whereas Fog nodes can also be malicious and need to be evaluated.

Acknowledgments. I would like to thank, Professor Zhiqiu Huang and Professor Wang Sen Zhang for their valuable inputs in my research. Without their kind suggestions, it wouldn't have been possible for me to finish this Work.

This work was supported by National Natural Science Foundation of China (Grant nos. 61602262 and 61602237), Jiangsu Natural Science Foundation of China (Grant no. BK20170809), Tech R&D Program of China (2015AA015303).

References

1. Fog Computing. https://www.webopedia.com/TERM/F/Fog-computing.html
2. Fog Computing and the Internet of Things Extend the Cloud to Where the Things Are. https://www.cisco.com/c/dam/en_us/solutions/trends/iot/docs/computing-overview.pdf
3. The NIST Definition of Fog Computing. https://csrc.nist.gov/csrc/media/publications/sp/800-191/draft/documents/sp800-191-draft.pdf
4. Yang, Y., Wu, L., Yin, G., Li, L., Zhao, H.: A survey on security and privacy issues in Internet-of-Things. IEEE Internet Things J. **4662**(c), 1 (2017)
5. Lin, J., Yu, W., Zhang, N., Yang, X., Zhang, H., Zhao, W.: A survey on Internet of Things: architecture, enabling technologies, security and privacy, and applications. IEEE Internet Things J. **4662**(c), 1 (2017)
6. Wang, S., Hu, X., Yu, P.S., Li, Z.: MMRate: inferring multi-aspect diffusion networks with multi-pattern cascades. In: KDD, pp. 1246–1255 (2014)
7. Wang, S., Xie, S., Zhang, X., Li, Z., Yu P.S., Shu, X.: Future influence ranking of scientific literature. In: SDM, pp. 749–757 (2014)
8. Chiang, M., Zhang, T.: Fog and IoT an overview of research opportunities. IEEE Internet Things J. **3**(6), 854–864 (2016)
9. Jalali, F., Khodadustan, S., Gray, C., Hinton, K., Suits, F.: Greening IoT with fog a survey. In: IEEE International Conference Edge Computing, pp. 25–31. IEEE (2017)
10. Wang, S., He, L., Stenneth, L., Yu, P.S., Li, Z., Huang, Z.: Estimating urban traffic congestions with multi-sourced data. In: MDM, pp. 82–91 (2016)

11. Stojmenovic, I., Wen, S.: The fog computing paradigm: scenarios and security issues. In: Federated Conference on Computer Science and Information Systems, Warsaw, pp. 1–8 (2014)
12. Alhamad, M., Dillon, T., Chang, E.: SLA-based trust model for cloud computing. In: 13th International Conference Network-Based Information System, pp. 321–324 (2010)
13. Zissis, D., Lekkas, D.: Addressing cloud computing security issues. In: Future Generation Computer Systems, vol. 28, no. 3, pp. 583–592 (2012)
14. Zhang, Q., Cheng, L., Boutaba, R.: Cloud computing state-of-the-art and research challenges. J. Internet Serv. Appl. 1(1), 7–18 (2010)
15. Xiao, H., Sidhu, N., Christianson, B.: Guarantor and reputation based trust model for social Internet of Things. In: International Wireless Communications and Mobile Computing Conference (IWCMC), Dubrovnik, pp. 600–605 (2015)
16. Kokoris-Kogias, E., Voutyras, O., Varvarigou, T.: TRM-SIoT: a scalable hybrid trust and reputation model for the social Internet of Things. In: IEEE 21st International Conference on Emerging Technologies and Factory Automation (ETFA), Berlin, pp. 1–9 (2016)
17. Fang, W., Zhang, C., Shi, Z., Zhao, Q., Shan, L.: BTRES Beta-based Trust and Reputation Evaluation System for wireless sensor networks. J. Netw. Comput. Appl. 59, 88–94 (2016)
18. Chen, I.R., Guo, J., Bao, F.: Trust management for SOA-based IoT and its application to service composition. IEEE Trans. Serv. Comput. 9(3), 482–495 (2016)
19. Xiong L., Liu L., Society I. C.: Peertrust supporting reputation-based trust for peer-to-peer electronic communities. IEEE Trans. Knowl. Data Eng. 16(7), 843–857 (2004)
20. Kamvar, S.D., Schlosser, M.T., Garcia-Molina, H.: The Eigentrust algorithm for reputation management in P2P networks. In: Proceeding 12th International Conference World Wide Web, no. 03, p. 640 (2003)
21. McKnight, D.H., Chervany, N.L.: The Meanings of Trust. In: Technical Report MISRC Working Paper Series, pp. 96–04. University of Minnesota, Management Information Systems Research Center (1996)
22. Gambetta, D.: Can we trust trust?. In: Trust Making and Breaking Cooperative Relations, pp. 213–238 . Basil Blackwell, Oxford (1990)
23. Audun, J., Roslan, I., Boyd, C.: A survey of trust and reputation systems for online service provision. Decis. Support Syst. 43(2), 618–644 (2007)
24. Hu, P., Ning, H., Qiu, T., Song, H., Wang, Y., Yao, X.: Security and privacy preservation scheme of face identification and resolution model using fog computing in Internet of Things. IEEE Internet Things J. 4, 113 (2017)
25. Ibrahim, M.H.: Octopus an edge-fog mutual authentication scheme. Int. J. Netw. Secur. 18(6), 1089–1101 (2016)
26. Page, L., Brin, S., Motwani, R., Winograd, T.: The PageRank citation ranking bringing order to the web. World Wide Web Internet Web Inf. Syst. 54(199966), 117 (1998)

Vulnerability Analysis and Spoof Scheme on AoA-Based WLAN Location Systems

Gang Hu$^{(\boxtimes)}$ and Lixia Liu

College of Computer, National University of Defense Technology, Changsha, China
{hugang,5460liulixia}@nudt.edu.cn

Abstract. This paper investigates the location security problem of WLAN location systems under multipath communication scenarios. As the location information is critical in some location related applications, it is important to guarantee the user's location security. The scheme that based on the signal's arrival angle is an important kind of the location strategies. The selection of the direct path is critical to the accuracy of the system. We analyse the vulnerability of the angle based system. We show that if the system selects the incorrect direct path, it will potentially lead to a false position. By detailed simulation which based on quasi-mirror reflection model, we demonstrate that the manipulated false direct path can lead to error position effectively.

Keywords: Location security · Direct link · AoA · Spoof attack

1 First Section

Wireless networks are becoming an indispensable infrastructure in modern communication systems. As WiFi is becoming pervasive in indoor WLAN scenarios, security has aroused tremendous interest from both the academic and industry domain [1]. Although there are massive works focusing on the traditional wireless security problems, the indoor location security has received little attention. However, many wireless applications, such as the indoor navigation in supermarkets and patient tracking, need to acquire the device's location information. How to guarantee the security of the location system is important and challenging.

Usually the location techniques are classified into four categories [2]. These are: the RSSI (Received Signal Strength Indication) scheme, the time of flight (ToF) scheme, the angle of arrival (AoA) scheme and fingerprinting based scheme. In this paper we focus on the AoA based network location scheme. More detailed location techniques and their accurate comparison can be found, e.g., in [9].

Although a lot of research works investigate the location accuracy, there are only few works considering the location security problem. Recently, there

Supported by the National Natural Science Foundation of China (No. 61501482, 61572514).

X. Sun et al. (Eds.): ICCCS 2018, LNCS 11068, pp. 199–208, 2018.
https://doi.org/10.1007/978-3-030-00021-9_19

emerged two novel security threats against the WiFi location scheme [3,4]. The two papers illustrate the location spoofing schemes under a singlepath and multipath wireless communication scenario, respectively. Both papers are based on the common assumption that wireless link's signatures can be mimicked by an adversary transmitter [7]. To address this problem more precisely, we need to point out that the location spoofing schemes can be classified into two categories: one is to conceal its real position to the location system; another is to make the system believe it is in another elaborately predesigned position. The latter scheme is more difficult to realize as the attacker needs to acquire the detailed transmission parameters in the disguised position.

We try to answer the follow questions: Are the most advanced angle based location schemes robust under the spoofing attack? What are the prerequisites if the attacker wants to launch such attack? Then, we propose a novel spoof scheme—MIPA (Manipulated direct Path Attack). The contribution of this paper is that it the first research work that aim at the AoA location security, and demonstrate the effectiveness of MIPA scheme. We believe it will have a positive impact on the security design for future location systems.

The organization of the paper is as follows: Sect. 2 introduces the motivation of the research. The network scenario and spoof models are described in Sect. 3. Experimental results and the analysis are addressed in Sect. 4; finally the practical discussion is in Sect. 5.

2   Motivation

As the hacker can use more advanced tools, such as USRP (Universal Software Radio Peripheral) and flexible beamforming antennas, it can spoof the WiFi systems about its real position combining with some reflectors. The open question is whether the existing location systems can still work normally under the location spoof attack in a manipulated multipath communication scenario. This is the direct reason that leads us to analyse the vulnerability of the location systems.

To the best of our knowledge, the most accurate location system until now which uses the commodity hardware is SpotFi [2], which can provide 40 cm accuracy. Except SpotFi, the ArrayTrack [5] and Ubicarse [6] can reach similar accuracy of 30–50 cm. However, the two systems need extra hardware requirements. From the technical perspective, SpotFi and ArrayTrack both use multiple antennas to calculate the AoA of multipath signals. Then, each access point (AP) will determine the direct path from multiple paths. The accuracy is mainly determined by two factors: one is the accuracy of the AoA, another is the selection of the direct path.

The representative location system's strategy [2] is as below: First, each AP collects the CSI (Channel State Information) and RSSI from the transmitter, and sends the information to the server. Second, the server calculates the ToF and AoA of all the propagation paths from the target to each AP. Third, the server determines the direct path to each AP. Finally, the server uses the RSSI and direct path's AoA to locate the target.

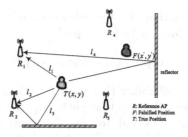

Fig. 1. The illustration of the location principle in a multipath scenario.

Figure 1 shows a location spoofing scenario. The actual position of the user is $T(x, y)$. If AP R_1 and R_2 select l_1 and l_2 as the direct path, the estimation of the position will be correct. But if R_1 and R_2 are spoofed to falsely select l_2 and l_4, the estimated position will be $F(x', y')$. If the position of F is deliberately designed, it can masque another transmitter which is in the position.

The practical multipath scenario will be more complex, as there usually exist multiple subpaths and the angles may not all be predictable. The APs need to measure the characters of each subpath and select one as the direct path. Although the scheme can improve the accuracy of the target, it still faces the severed thread if a certain malicious node wants to spoof it.

3   MIPA Foundation

We consider the WLAN network that has N APs to be centrally managed by a server, and a transmitter. Further there are $L = [1, 2, ..., L]$ multiple links due to several times of reflection. We assume the location system is capable of estimating the AoA for each link [2]. The main idea of MIPA is to use beamforming to deceive the AP, which leads it to believe that the manipulated subcarrier is the direct path subcarrier.

3.1   MIPA Scheme

Even though the location schemes (such as SpotFi) are designed precisely according to the wireless link's essential character, there still exist defects that could be used by adversaries. The main defect of the system is that it only considers the omnidirectional communication between commodity transceivers. But as the adversary is capable of manipulating the wireless link's signature intentionally, the accuracy of the location scheme will be dramatically deteriorated. The adversary can use USRP and a beamforming technique to generate intended links to deceive the system [3, 7].

How to determine the direct path in a multipath environment is complex. Intuitively, each AP can select the lowest ToF path as the direct path, but the practical situation is that the direct path may not exist due to obstacles, this is called NLoS (Non-Line-of-Sight) scenario. If the AP selects the false direct path, it leads to an incorrect position. A latest scheme [2] is proposed to evaluate the probability of being the direct path for all paths:

$$likelihood_k = exp(w_C \overline{C}_k - w_\theta \overline{\sigma}_{\theta_k} - w_\tau \overline{\sigma}_{\tau_k} - w_s \overline{\tau}_k), \tag{1}$$

where $likelihood_k$ is the probability that the kth path is the direct path, $\overline{C}_k$ is the number of points that belong to that path, $\overline{\sigma}_{\theta_k}$ and $\overline{\sigma}_{\tau_k}$ are the population variances of the estimated AoA and ToF for the points to that path, $\overline{\tau}_k$ is the average ToF for the points of the path. Weighting factors of w_C, w_θ, w_τ and w_s are constants to count for different scales of the corresponding terms. Then the highest $likelihood_k$ path is selected at the direct path.

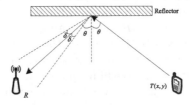

Fig. 2. The one bounce reflection model.

After the above process, all APs can use the RSSI and AoA information to jointly determine the position of the transmitter.

$$P = \min \sum_{i=1}^{N} likelihood_i [(\overline{p}_i - p_i)^2 + (\overline{\theta}_i - \theta_i)^2]. \tag{2}$$

In Eq. (2), θ_i and p_i are AoA and RSSI for the ith AP, $\overline{p}_i$ and $\overline{\theta}$ are the estimated values if the transmitter is in a certain position.

The key idea of MIPA is to create multiple manipulated paths that are directed transmitted in a certain angle. To achieve the goal, it needs the beamforming capability to transmit in an intended angle. Specifically, besides the direction, another method is to add a manipulated delay after the directional

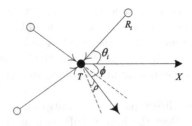

Fig. 3. The calculation of transmitting angle.

signal, just like the method in [3]. According to Eq. (1), $\overline{\tau}_k$ will have a false large value of $(\overline{\tau}_k + \Delta t)$, which decrease the possibility of $likelihood_k$.

In Fig. 2, we model the one bounce reflection model from the reflector. Ideally, if the reflected angle is the same as the incident angle, as shown in the figure as θ, this is called mirror model. More practically, the reflected angle will be a random value within a range of $(\theta \pm \delta)$. If the value of δ is small, we call this quasi-mirror model. If δ is not a fixed value, which means the angle of reflection is unpredictable.

The main objective of MIPA is to manipulate the beamforming angle, as in Fig. 3. The calculation of signal's central angle ϕ is to $max\{min(|\phi - \theta_i|; |360 - \phi + \theta_i|)\}, i \in [1, ...D]$, here D is the set of estimated APs. ρ represent the range of the beam. As the transmitter has intelligent multiple antennas, it can estimated the angle of the AP's signal, such as beacons. The purpose of selecting the angle ϕ is try to avoid the LoS (Line-of-Sight) communication with APs as much as possible.

3.2   Theoretical Analysis of Mirror Reflection

In this section, we will give a theoretical analysis on the foundation of the mirror based scenario.

Definition 1. *Given a real position $T(x, y)$, if the location system estimates the position $F(x', y')$ that satisfies the equation of $|T(x, y) - F(x', y')| > \varepsilon$, where ε is the maximum value for the location error, then we regard the location system is spoofed.*

Theory 1. *There exists at least one position of $F(x', y')$ that satisfies $|T(x, y) - F(x', y')| > \varepsilon$, only if the power and the direction of the signal can be adjusted.*

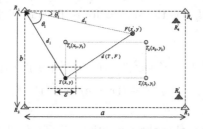

Fig. 4. The mathematical illustration for Theory 1.

Before the formal proof, we first construct the corresponding mathematical scenario in Fig. 4. Usually, we need at least four anchors to locate a transmitter's position without knowing its power level [4]. We assume the rectangular area is divided as squares that have the edge of ε, and the node within the square is regarded at the center. As the practical position of the anchors may not form a strict rectangular, for example, R_3 and R_4 may not be at the expected position, like the position of R_3' and R_4'. Now the problem is to prove if there exists another node, which satisfied the requirement of $d(T, F) > \varepsilon$, meanwhile the position of $F(x', y')$ meets the constraints of Eq. 2. For simplicity, we assume signal's AoA is accurate enough, then the measure error of variation of AoA can be represented by $|\bar{\theta}_i - \theta_i| \approx \sigma$. In fact, it can be realized with enough MIMO antennas in order to make σ small enough, like in [5]. The power level is the remaining main element to be considered. For each AP, we assume the maximum error estimation for the power is α, which leads to $|\bar{p}_i - p_i| < \alpha$.

Proof. We just need to prove that the P_F is existed and satisfies $P_F \leq P_T$, while $\sqrt{(x - x')^2 - (y - y')^2} \geq \varepsilon$. As $P = \min \sum_{i=1}^{4} likelihood_i [(\bar{p}_i - p_i)^2 + \sigma^2]$. Further as $likelihood_i$ can be manipulated, we assume the value of $likelihood_i = likelihood_i'$, then the prove is $\min \sum_{i=1}^{4}[(\bar{p}_i - p_i)^2 + \sigma^2] \geq \min \sum_{i=1}^{4}[(\bar{p}_i' - p_i')^2 + \sigma^2]$, according to the above illustration, it can be simplified as $\min \sum_{i=1}^{4}[((1 \pm \alpha_i)p_i - p_i)^2] \geq \min \sum_{i=1}^{4}[((1 \pm \alpha_i)p_i' - p_i')^2]$, α_i is the ith AP's estimated power error, we assume the variation of the power error will be identical in the same location system, and each AP has the same value, then the equation can be deduced to $\min \sum_{i=1}^{4}[\alpha p_i^2] \geq \min \sum_{i=1}^{4}[\alpha(p_i')^2]$. We assume the position of P_T and P_F is calculated, then we only need to prove $\sum_{i=1}^{4}(p_i^2) \geq \sum_{i=1}^{4}(p_i')^2$, for each AP, the receiving power is calculated as:

$$p_i = p_t G_t G_i \lambda^2 / (4\pi d_i)^n. \tag{3}$$

As p_t is the transmitted signal power, G_i and G_t denote the power gains at the receiver and the transmitter. λ is the wavelength of the transmitted signal, d_i is the distance to the ith AP, n is the environmental attenuation factor, usually we have $n \subseteq [2, 4]$. We assume the values are the same in a fixed indoor environment, then we need to prove: $\sum_{i=1}^{4}(d_i)^{-2n} \geq \sum_{i=1}^{4}(d_i')^{-2n}$, here we have $d_1 = \sqrt{x^2 + (y - b)^2}, d_2 = \sqrt{x^2 + y^2}, d_3 = \sqrt{(x - a)^2 - b^2}, d_4 = \sqrt{(x - a)^2 - (y - b)^2}$, d_i' has the similar form. Because if $j > k$, we got $j^{-1} < k^{-1}$, the prove will be

$$(x^2 + (y - b)^2)^n + (x^2 + y^2)^n + ((x - a)^2 + y^2)^n + ((x - a)^2 + (y - b)^2)^n$$
$$\leq (x'^2 + (y' - b)^2)^n + (x'^2 + y'^2)^n + ((x' - a)^2 + y'^2)^n + ((x' - a)^2 + (y' - b)^2)^n.$$

In Fig. 4, there are another three positions T_1, T_2, T_3 that will have the same value of $\sum_{i=1}^{4}(d_i)^{-2n}$ of T's, as the symmetric geometrical character of rectangular. Within the area of rectangular formed by the four nodes, the value of $\sum_{i=1}^{4}(d_i)^{-2n}$ is smaller than the value of the four nodes. On the contrary, the value of $\sum_{i=1}^{4}(d_i)^{-2n}$ will be larger if the position is farer from the center of the rectangular.

The distance between two nodes is usually a natural number $d \geq 1m$. For $[d_1, d_2, d_3, d_4, d_1', d_2', d_3', d_4'] \subseteq N$. Then we can always find a position that guarantees $\sum_{i=1}^{4}(d_i)^{2n} \leq \sum_{i=1}^{4}(d_i')^{2n}$. Then we have proved $\sum_{i=1}^{4}(d_i)^{-2n} \geq \sum_{i=1}^{4}(d_i')^{-2n}$, the symmetric scenario is proved.

If the four nodes are not formed as a symmetric quadrilateral area, there will be a position $F(x', y')$ that leads to $max|\sum_{i=1}^{4}(d_i')^{-2n}/\sum_{i=1}^{4}(d_i)^{-2n}| = \beta$, according to Eq. 3, if $p_t'G_t' \leq \beta p_t G_t$, it will lead to $min\sum_{i=1}^{4}[\alpha p_i^2] \geq min\sum_{i=1}^{4}[\alpha(p_i')^2]$, which concludes the proof.

4   Simulation of Quasi-Mirror Reflection

In this section, we give a detailed simulation for quasi-mirror reflection. We assume the indoor rectangular area is $50\,m \times 50\,m$. The 4 APs are located at the corner, each has a triangular form. The error distance $\varepsilon = 1\,m$, we set δ as $5°$. According to Eq. (3), we set the parameters except d as a constant. The reflection number is limited to 6 for simplicity and avoids endless reflections. To model a more practical transmission, we set three obstacles and the angle of each signal will be added a random degree between $[-3, 3]$. The estimated position is calculated based on the selected direct path of each AP. The calculated position has the smallest sum of distances to all the APs according to Eq. (2).

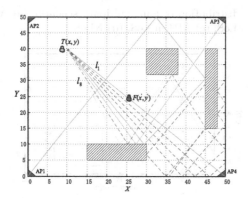

Fig. 5. The illustration of location principle in a multipath scenario.

In Fig. 5, we show a transmitter that sends out a beamforming signal that within a $21°$ arc range. There are eight signals which are named $l_1...l_8$. The signal will not reflect after it gets into the AP area. It is possible that there is more than one signal that reaches a certain AP, like l_1 and l_8 both arrive at AP4, the principle of SpotFi is to select one as the direct path, according to the Eq. (1), l_8 will have a larger ToF and variation of AoA, it is not elected as the direct path.

Figure 6 is the location distribution of four different network scenarios after 100 times simulation. Each circle dot represents an estimated transmitter's position of the network, $T(x, y) = (15, 30)$ is the real position, which is the five-pointed star. When there're 3 LoS APs, the position will be much more accurate,

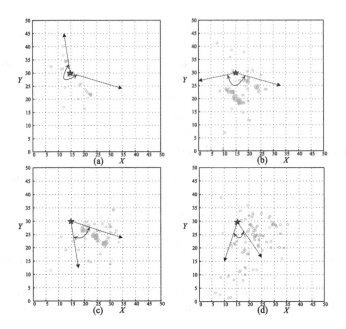

Fig. 6. The Location distribution of four multipath scenario. (a) AP1, AP2, AP4 in LoS, (b) AP1, AP4 in LoS, (c) AP4 in LoS, (d) NLoS.

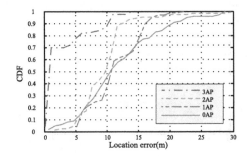

Fig. 7. The CDF of the location error in Fig. 6.

and the variance is much smaller comparing to other scenarios. But the location error will be greatly increased when there are only two APs are LoS. When under no LoS scenario, the estimated position will be more randomly distributed. We can discover that the direct path has an important effect on the distribution of the position, as the position will be more likely at the line of the direct path. The average values and angle range values are listed in Table 1. Practical implementation of the beamforming are two methods: one is to use the beamforming antenna; another is to use a customized reflector to block the transmission direction range while transmitting with an omni-directional antenna.

Table 1. Comparison of Fig. 6

Topology	Start angle (degree)	End angle (degree)	Average error(m)
Fig. 6(a)	−20	−260	2.9226
Fig. 6(b)	−20	−170	9.8605
Fig. 6(c)	−20	−80	11.6888
Fig. 6(d)	−50	−110	12.1731

Figure 7 gives the comparison of the cumulative distribution function (CDF) of Fig. 6. We found that within 3 LoS APs, nearly 70% are within 2 m error, that means the NLoS AP3 has little effect, but the other scenario shows the AP3 has received reflected signals, which increase the error. The NLoS scenarios' CDF is more smooth that the other three, the reason is obvious that the distribution is more random, which leads to much more equal error value.

5 Practical Discussion

Due to the vulnerability of the location system, we propose a novel spoof scheme—MIPA, which can manipulate the link signatures to deceive the location systems. The practical implementation of MIPA is to acquire the beamforming angle that tries to have the maximum number of NLoS links to the APs. It can be done through the measurement of each AP's angle and signals' variance. Another solution is to use another helper node, which does not care about its own position to perform the scan process, then jointly determine the positions of APs. From the system's view, it needs to adjust the location scheme that can distinguish the real and false direct links. The system should design a weight assignment scheme, which gives more weights to the APs that have received real direct links. Also it is better to establish a fingerprint database for the supervised area, this can be helpful when no real direct link can be found. Of course this modification will increase the complexity of the location system. In the next research, we plan to implement the scheme in a practical network system [11–13], which we have realized the key technology of virtual network function.

References

1. Zou, Y.-L., Wang, X.-B., Hanzo, L.: A survey on wireless security: technical challenges, recent advances and future trends. In: Proceedings of IEEE. http://arxiv.org/abs/1505.07919, to be published
2. Kotaru, M., Joshi, K.R., Bharadia, D., Katti, S.: SpotFi: decimeter level localization using WiFi. In: Proceedings of ACM SIGCOMM, pp. 269–282, August 2015
3. Fang, S., Liu, Y., Shen, W., Zhu, H.-J.: Where are you from? Confusing location distinction using virtual multipath Camouflage. In: Proceedings of ACM MobiCom, pp. 225–236, September 2014

4. Wang, T., Yang, Y.-L.: Analysis on perfect location spoofing attacks using beamforming. In: IEEE INFOCOM, pp. 2778–2786 (2013)
5. Xiong, J., Jamieson, K.: ArrayTrack: a fine-grained indoor location system. In: USENIX NSDI, pp. 71–84, April 2013
6. Kumer, S., Gil, S., Katabi, D., Rus, D.: Accurate indoor localization with zero start-up cost. In: Proceedings of ACM MobiCom, pp. 483–494, September 2014
7. Liu, Y., Ning, P.: POSTER: mimicry attacks against wireless link signature. In: Proceedings of ACM CCS, pp. 801–803, October 2011
8. Xiong, J., Jamieson, K.: SecureArray: Improving wifi security with fine-grained physical-layer information. In: Proceedings of ACM MobiCom, pp. 441–452, September 2013
9. Lymberopoulos, D., Liu, J., Yang, X., Choudhury, R.R., Handziski, V., Sen, S.: A realistic evaluation and comparison of indoor location technologies: experiences and lessons learned. In: ACM IPSN, April 2015
10. Kumar, M., Hamed, E., Katabi, D., Li, L.E.: LTE radio analytics made easy and accessible. In: Proceedings of ACM SIGCOMM, pp. 211–222, August 2014
11. Cai, Z., Wang, Z., Zheng, K., Cao, J.: A distributed TCAM coprocessor architecture for integrated longest prefix matching, policy filtering, and content filtering. IEEE Trans. Computers 62(3), 417–427 (2013)
12. Liu, S., Cai, Z., Hong, X., Ming, X.: Towards security-aware virtual network embedding. Comput. Netw. 91, 151–163 (2015)
13. Liu, S., Cai, Z., Xu, H., Xu, M.: Security-aware virtual network embedding. In: Proceedings of ICC (2014)

Water and Fertilizer Integration Intelligent Control System of Tomato Based on Internet of Things

Liyang, Pingzeng Liu$^{(\boxtimes)}$, and Bangguo Li

Shandong Agriculture University, Tai'an 271000, China
lpz8565@126.com

Abstract. The main body of this article shows a system designed to improve the level of greenhouse irrigation and fertilization automation in China, while improving the utilization of water and fertilizer resources. Tomato greenhouse irrigation was used as an example to design an intelligent control system for tomato water and fertilizer integration in the greenhouse. The system is based on the optimal growth conditions of greenhouse tomatoes, combined with the impact of time on greenhouse tomatoes, using NB-IOT technology, information processing technology, information acquisition technology and other networking technology. The system has two sub-modules: tomato water and fertilizer integration intelligent control module and intelligent warning module. The system improves the precision of smart irrigation and fertilization in greenhouse tomatoes. In addition, in order to facilitate the user's real-time supervision of the greenhouse, the system is equipped with a dedicated mobile phone APP. Experiments have shown that the system greenhouse environment information collection and uploading are very stable, and tomato growth environment is controlled reliably. The system satisfies the needs of modern greenhouse planting management, and significantly improves the benefits of tomato production.

Keywords: Integration of water and fertilizer · Intelligent control
Mobile APP · NB-IoT

1 Introduction

China is a large agricultural country, and the greenhouse area has exceeded 2.1 million hectares [1]. However, the irrigation method mainly relies on the experience of vague irrigation, and China's water resources are not abundant, accounting for about 6th in the world [2]. Irrigation methods cause great waste of water resources and fertilizers and have become bottlenecks in agricultural development [3]. With the gradual maturity of the Internet of Things technology, smart greenhouses have been widely developed, and the degree of refinement of greenhouse control has become more and more sophisticated. At the same time, technologies such as water and fertilizer integration and automatic irrigation have achieved considerable development.

The exploration of water and fertilizer integration technology in China began in 1975. It introduced advanced foreign equipment and reached important production

© Springer Nature Switzerland AG 2018
X. Sun et al. (Eds.): ICCCS 2018, LNCS 11068, pp. 209–220, 2018.
https://doi.org/10.1007/978-3-030-00021-9_20

increase and water saving effects through experiments at pilot sites [4, 5]. The integrated smart water and fertilizer control system designed by Guo [6] and others is based on the STM32 micro-controller, which realizes the automatic control of irrigation and fertilization. Cai [7] designed greenhouse intelligent irrigation and fertilizer as an experimental research object. The monitoring system was developed based on the STM32 micro-controller and achieved remote control of the greenhouse through information collection and acquisition, GSM communication technology, etc. The system achieved the purpose of increasing tomato production and reducing irrigation water consumption. Zhong Yongfa [8] designed the automatic control system aimed at grapes. The system consists of computer-controlled terminals, Plc, Ruts, and Dtu. The system implements supervision of environmental information such as soil moisture and soil temperature, and automatic control. With other functions, the economic benefits of crops have been augmented; Zhang Zhuo [9] designed a water and fertilizer integrated automatic irrigation and fertigation system based on the MCU of STC15L2K60S2. The system collected the soil moisture and flow rate of water and fertilizer and sent it to the wireless module NRF905. The upper computer realized real-time data monitoring and the system improved the automation of irrigation and fertilization.

Foreign water and fertilizer integration technology has a long history of development [10]. As early as the end of the 18th century, John Woodward of the United Kingdom planted crops in a well-prepared soil fluid, which was the earliest cultivation of water and fertilizer. In Spain, Italy, France and other countries, the technology of water and fertilizer integration has developed rapidly. From 1981 to 2000, the area of micro-irrigation in the world has increased by 633%, with an average annual increase of 33% to over 3.73 million hectares, and most of them use water and fertilizer integration technologies. Zhang [9] came up with a smart irrigation remote control system based on Internet of Things. The system collects information in real time, real-time on-site monitoring, and development of supporting mobile phone APP, which improves the calculation accuracy of water-saving irrigation; Gao et al. [10]. An intelligent control system was designed based on the wireless sensor network and fuzzy control. The system realized soil information detection, information upload and other functions, and improved the utilization rate of water and fertilizer. The automatic irrigation system based on ZigBee proposed by Zhu et al. [11] saved Water resources and increased economic efficiency.

With the maturity of the Internet of Things technology, people are increasingly demanding the degree of precision in greenhouse control, and the degree of refinement of simple water and fertilizer integration control is far from enough. Most of the water and fertilizer integration control systems lack the judgment on the time point of watering or fertilization when performing irrigation or fertilization operations. Simple automatic control leads to inconstant watering time, insufficient system intelligence, and the system depend on humans a lot. And many greenhouse irrigation or fertilization still use empirical irrigation methods, which results in a huge waste of water and fertilizer resources. Soil information in the greenhouse is difficult to obtain accurately by simple manual collection. This requires an intelligent system to accurately control the greenhouse. After analyzing the process of watering and fertilizing the tomato planting process, it is found that when watering or fertilizing, the length of time has a great influence on it. The tomato planting factors in the greenhouse are integrated, and an intelligent control model for water and fertilizer integration is designed. This model can accurately control the greenhouse. In order to increase the degree of control over the greenhouse, this system also developed a dedicated Android APP which allows users to remotely monitor greenhouses in real time.

2 Requirement Analysis

2.1 Functional Requirement

Real-Time Monitoring. The system needs to monitor the growth of Tomato in the greenhouse in real time, and facilitate the users to adjust the information parameters of the greenhouse environment in time, and improve the stability and reliability of the system.

Intelligent Early Warning. The system tests the environmental information of the greenhouse. When the abnormal information is detected, the system SMS alerts the users.

Remote Intelligent Control. It is convenient for users to manage the greenhouse anytime and anywhere, a special mobile phone APP is developed to realize remote automatic control, remote modification parameters and information production.

2.2 Performance Requirements

Reliability and Stability. In the process of working, the system ensures stable operation, is not easy to fail, has a safe protection mechanism, and reduces the risk to the lowest.

Easy-Using. Most of the users of the system are greenhouse workers, the purpose of this system is to reduce the complexity and to improve the use efficiency.

3 System Design

3.1 System Framework Design

The system framework of this article is based on the concept model of the Internet of Things (IoT), and proposed by the National Information Technology Standardization Technical Committee. The conceptual model of the Internet of Things includes the user domain, service domain, sensing control domain, target object domain, resource exchange domain, and operation and maintenance management domain. Based on this, the time domain is added. The time domain, the sensing control domain and the service domain are the core of the system design. The sensing control domain includes the IoT gateway and the lower machine system. The service domain includes the host machine supporting system. The time domain is used to synchronize system time, allowing the

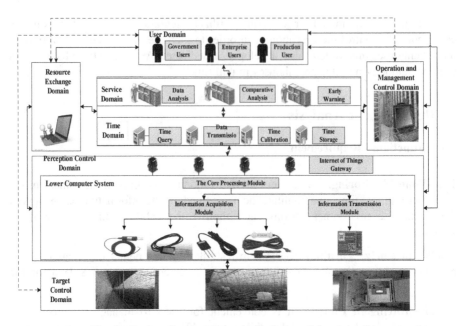

Fig. 1. Design diagram of the whole frame of the system

system to accurately distinguish between day and night, morning and afternoon, to facilitate the system to accurately control the greenhouse, as shown in Fig. 1.

3.2 Lower Machine Design

As shown in Fig. 2, the lower computer is mainly composed of information processing module, information transmission module, information acquisition module and executive agency. The user can through the touch screen to realize the control system in the greenhouse, such as parameter setting, data check, greenhouse control, touch screen through the serial port 3 is connected with a single chip microcomputer, through the relay to control blower, rolling machine and electromagnetic valve.

Information Processing Module. The information processing module is also known as the core microprocessor module is an important part of the whole system, the core of the information processing module for the M430F5438A MCU, M430F5438A MCU with 5 low power modes, strong processing ability and speed advantages, so using it as the main chip of the system is very appropriate, as is shown in Fig. 3.

Information Transmission Module. Due to the limitation of greenhouse's geographical location and working environment, the use of wired transmission is heavy workload and high cost, which is not suitable for an experimental greenhouse environment. The adoption of wireless transmission is more convenient and economical. The comparison of NB-IoT technology and the traditional GPRS technology has better performance. GPRS is the 2G GSM, which will be abolished, with low rate, high delay and low bandwidth utilization. NB-IoT is a low-band LTE, and its signal coverage is

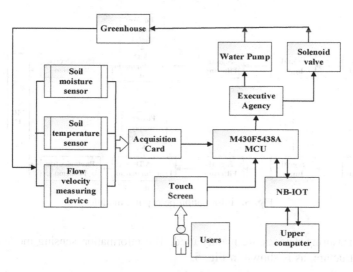

Fig. 2. Design of system lower computer

Fig. 3. Core diagram of information processing module

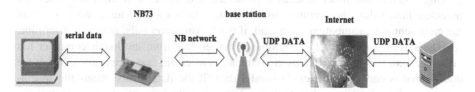

Fig. 4. NB-IoT transmission process

better than that of GSM. It also has various advantages of LTE. This system uses NB-IoT for transmission. The transmission process is shown in Fig. 4.

Information Acquisition Module. The information perception module is responsible for connecting all sensors, collecting the current values of each sensor and converting them into numerical values. Soil humidity sensors, soil temperature sensors and flow

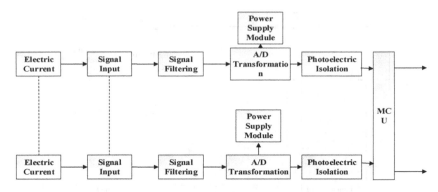

Fig. 5. Information perception module

velocity measuring devices are mainly used. The information sensing module uses a modular structure, as is shown in Fig. 5.

Executive Agency. For the integrated design of water and fertilizer, we need to consider both water and fertilizer. The executive machine connected to the single-chip microcomputer is divided into two parts. The pump control irrigation part and the solenoid valve control the fertilizer part. The system needs to make the two parts separately.

3.3   Upper Computer Design

The upper computer program development environment is MFC. The upper computer mainly sends instructions to the lower computer, receives information from the lower machine, and sends data to the database, which can be remotely controlled by mobile phone or PC login server. As is shown in Fig. 6.

PC through the network initialization (all serial initialization), timer initialization, judging whether the timer reaches a predetermined value, if it does not reach the predetermined value, then return, until the timer reaches a predetermined value, then the crew sent data acquisition command, if the transmission fails, return to determine.

The system automatically determines whether data from the lower computer has been received. If data from the lower computer is received, first, determine whether the data format is correct and exclude invalid data. If the data format meets the specifications, analyze the data packet, finds the data part in the instruction part, and store the data in the database. Then, the system returns to the data receiving judgment, waiting for the new data to continue to determine.

Users can also control the lower machine through the mobile APP, web page or computer program to realize remote parameter modification and remote supervision of the greenhouse.

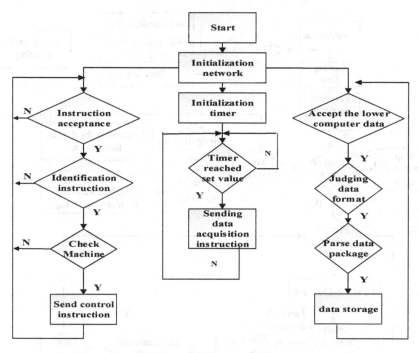

Fig. 6. Upper computer design diagram

4   Model Design

4.1   Integrated Model Design of Water and Fertilizer

For the integrated design of water and fertilizer, full consideration must be given to the actual conditions in the tomato planting process in order to improve the degree of refinement of system control. During the tomato planting process, the user is not in the greenhouse at night, so during the operation of the system, the automatic control function will be disabled. When the system simulates the actual watering of the tomato, assuming that the system time is set in the morning, watering conditions are judged.

When the system is running automatically, in order to increase the reliability and stability of the system, we have added a data check function. This function enables the system to automatically detect greenhouse environmental data. When there is an abnormality in the data, the system performs an SMS alert. The integration of intelligent water control model is shown in Fig. 7.

4.2   Design of Intelligent Early Warning Model

The collected data will be processed inside the MCU. After processing, if the system found that the one or more data is abnormal, the next operation is to send instructions to the host computer. The host computer will send short messages to users via GPRS, so that users can check them in time.

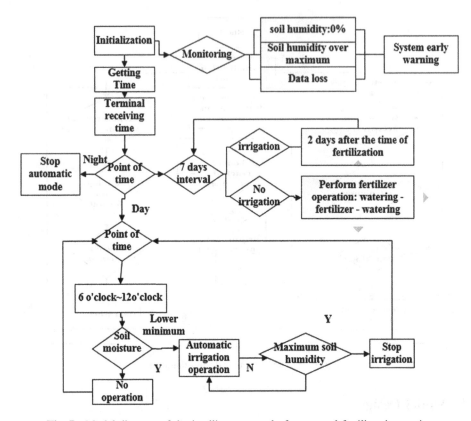

Fig. 7. Model diagram of the intelligent control of water and fertilizer integration

Abnormal values may be caused by the following reasons: the soil humidity sensor is not inserted into the soil, causing the value to be 0 or too low; the sensor fails, causing the value to be too high or too low. The system monitoring and early warning process is shown in Fig. 8.

5   System Implementation

5.1   The Realization of Time Domain

In the process of designing the system, synchronization of system time is critical to achieve accurate system control. In the cultivation of tomato, there are many agricultural operations on the tomato, and it is inseparable from the time limit. The upper computer receives the instruction on time, and after identifying the instruction, the upper computer sends the obtained server time to the lower computer, and the lower computer re-synchronizes the time.

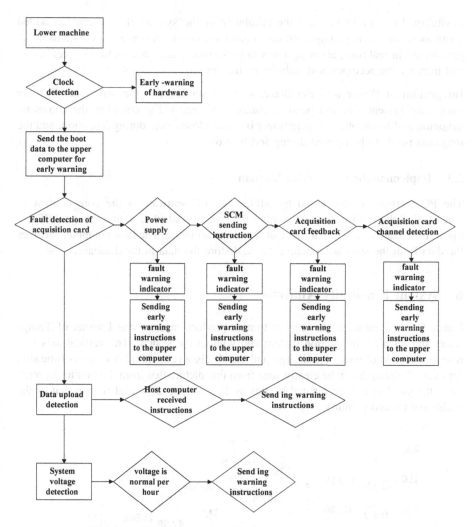

Fig. 8. System monitoring and warning

5.2   Realization of Perception Control Domain

Field Control. In the greenhouse, users can control the greenhouse through the terminal equipment in the greenhouse. Users in the greenhouse can supervise the greenhouse through the LED touchscreen. Users can operate information inquiry, parameter setting and automatic control through the screen.

Remote Control of the Mobile Phone. When users are not in the greenhouse, they cannot directly control the greenhouse through field devices. Users can remotely view information through the mobile phone APP, perform automatic control and remote environment parameter modification and other functions. This method improves system flexibility. In order to increase the reliability of the system, the system has added greenhouse monitoring equipment. Users can view the current crop growth status in the greenhouse in real time, allowing users to make timely adjustments to the greenhouse, and increase the accuracy and stability of the system.

Integration of Water and Fertilizer. In the installation of the water and fertilizer integration system, two independent controls are required to complete the automatic irrigation and fertilization. The fertilizer is in the closed state during irrigation, and the irrigation needs to be opened during fertilization.

5.3   Implementation of Service Domain

The PC software is developed by MFC. The PC software is the core content of constructing the service domain. Neither the remote control of mobile phone APP nor the website can work without the host computer software. The host computer receives the data from the standard machine set, and store the data in the database.

6   System Feasibility Analysis

Figure 9 is a comparison of weekly tomato production using the Internet of Things water and fertilizer integration system and without the system. The vertical axis represents the yield of tomato (unit: kg), and the abscissa is the number of times (one shot for every 7 picks). It can be clearly seen from this picture that from the first to the tenth time, the yield of tomato planted by this system is 13%–20% higher than that of the traditional tomato planting.

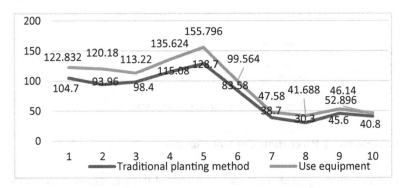

Fig. 9. Comparison chart of cumulative water consumption for tomato irrigation

Figure 10 shows the cumulative water consumption of the ten times tomato irrigation experiments, the ordinate is cubic and the abscissa is watered. From the experimental results, it can be seen that the water consumption of this system is about 16% less than the empirical irrigation water consumption.

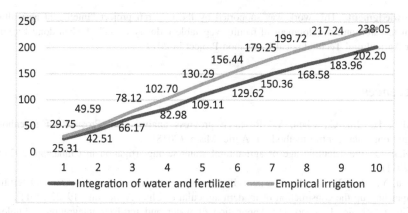

Fig. 10. Comparison chart of cumulative water consumption for tomato irrigation

Therefore, the use of the Internet of things intelligent control system to manage the production of tomato, lead the benefits improved a lot.

7 Summary

7.1 Conclusion

Through the study of greenhouse irrigation and fertilization, the main conclusions are as follows:

(1) This system is based on the basic characteristics of greenhouse tomato irrigation and fertilization, and considers the effect of time on greenhouse tomato irrigation and fertilization, thus designing an intelligent integrated control model for water and fertilizer of greenhouse tomato and an intelligent warning model. The use of NB-IoT technology, information collection technology, and information processing technology and other Internet of Things technologies have enabled the intelligent control of greenhouse tomato irrigation and fertilization, and improved the utilization of water and fertilizer resources.

(2) The system can collect and process current greenhouse information in real time, and then realize real-time information automatic detection of greenhouses and intelligent control of greenhouse water and fertilizer integration. In addition, the user can view the growth status of greenhouse tomato in real time through the mobile phone APP and achieve remote supervision of the greenhouse. In addition, the system has an intelligent warning function, which improves the stability and reliability of the system.

(3) Through experimental verification, this intelligent water and fertilizer control system can increase the yield of tomato and improve the utilization of water and fertilizer resources. Therefore, the system has promotion and application value.

Acknowledgment. This work was supported by the research project "Intelligent agricultural system research and development of facility vegetable industry chain" of Shan-dong Province Major Agricultural Technological Innovation Project in 2017.

References

1. Mao, H., Jin, C., Chen, Y.: Research progress analysis and Prospect of greenhouse environmental control methods. J. Agric. Mach. (2018)
2. Mali: On the scientific age of agricultural water-saving irrigation in China, pp. 202–203 (2011)
3. Wu, Y., Gao, X., Du, S.: Energetically developing the integration of water and fertilizer Speeding up the construction of modern agriculture. Chin. Agric. Inf., 19–22 (2011)
4. Liu, J., Zhang, J., Zhao, H.: Application of water and fertilizer integration technology, existing problems and countermeasures and development prospects. North. Agric. J., 32–33 (2006)
5. Zhao, X., Du, S., Zhong, Y.: The present situation and prospect of the integrated development of water and fertilizer. China Agric. Inf., 14–19 (2015)
6. Guo, Q., Lu, L., Guo, J.: Design of intelligent water and fertilizer integrated control system based on STM32. Ind. Control Comput., 38–39 (2015)
7. Cai, C., Hou, first seal, Zhang, Z.: Greenhouse intelligent irrigation and water and fertilizer integrated monitoring system. Jiangsu Agric. Sci. **45**(10), 164–166 (2017)
8. Zhang, Z.: Water and fertilizer integrated automatic irrigation and fertilization control system. Electronic world (2018)
9. Zhang, Q., Zhang, Y.B., Zhu, H.M.: Intelligent irrigation remote control system based on internet of things. Adv. Mater. Res. **955–959**, 3404–3407 (2014)
10. Gao, L., Zhang, M., Chen, G.: An intelligent irrigation system based on wireless sensor network and fuzzy control. J. Netw. **8**(5), 1080 (2013)
11. Zhu, L., Zhang, Z.Y.: Water-saving intelligence irrigation systems design based on ZigBee technology. Appl. Mech. Mater. **687–691**, 3187–3190 (2014)

Multimedia Forensics

3D Steganalysis Using Laplacian Smoothing at Various Levels

Zhenyu Li[1]⑩, Fenlin Liu[2](✉)⑩, and Adrian G. Bors[1]⑩

[1] Department of Computer Science, University of York, York YO10 5GH, UK
{zl991,adrian.bors}@york.ac.uk
[2] Zhengzhou Science and Technology Institute, Zhengzhou 450000, China
liufenlin@vip.sina.com

Abstract. 3D objects are becoming ubiquitous while being used by many mobile and social network applications. Meanwhile, such objects are also becoming a channel being used for covert communication. Steganalysis aims to identify when information is transferred in such ways. This research study analyses the influence of the 3D object smoothing, which is an essential step before extracting the features used for 3D steganalysis. During the experimental results, the efficiency when employing various degrees of 3D smoothing, is assessed in the context of steganalysis.

Keywords: 3D steganalysis · Laplacian smoothing · Local feature
Information hiding

1 Introduction

3D objects are used in many applications, including graphics, virtual reality, visualization and so on. In order to be used by many applications, 3D objects are increasingly transferred shared between users through clouds or mobile media. When compared to the steganalysis research on other media, such as images [1,15,17,20,30], video [24,29] and audio signals [18,19], the steganalysis for 3D objects is much less developed, resulting in a lower likelihood of identifying the information hidden in 3D objects. Many 3D information hiding algorithms have already been proposed [2,3,5,8,12,16,28]. Nevertheless, secret information transferred through 3D objects could pose a threat to the public security, when used by terrorists or criminals.

So far there are much fewer steganalytic approaches for 3D objects than for images and video signals. The first steganalytic algorithm for 3D meshes was proposed in [26]. This 3D steganalytic algorithm is based on the features of 3D meshes and by using machine learning, for distinguishing stego-objects from cover-objects. During 3D steganalysis, both cover- and stego-objects are smoothed using one Laplacian smoothing iteration. Then, the geometric features such as the vertex location and norm in Cartesian and Laplacian coordinate systems [25], the dihedral angle of edges and face normals, are extracted

© Springer Nature Switzerland AG 2018
X. Sun et al. (Eds.): ICCCS 2018, LNCS 11068, pp. 223–232, 2018.
https://doi.org/10.1007/978-3-030-00021-9_21

from the original mesh and the smoothed one. It calculates the absolute differences between the features from the original mesh and those from the smoothed mesh. The feature vectors used for steganalysis are the four statistical moments of the logarithm of the absolute differences between the object and its smoothed counterpart. Meanwhile, the histograms of the differences between the features corresponding to the original objects and their smoothed counterparts are formed and used for extracting the steganalytic features. Finally, the steganalytic approach uses quadratic discriminate analysis to train the classifiers for separating the stego-objects, produced by several steganographic algorithms from their corresponding cover-objects.

More recently, Yang et al. [27,28] proposed a new steganalytic algorithm, specifically designed for the robust 3D watermarking algorithm, MRS, proposed in [5]. During steganalysis, the number of bins, K, used in the watermarking algorithm is estimated using exhaustive search. For each K, the steganalytic algorithm classifies the bins into two clusters using a standard clustering algorithm fitting the data with a mixture of two Gaussian distributions. The estimate of K corresponds to that which maximizes the Bhattacharyya distance between the two clusters. Then it uses a normality test to decide if the bins of the mesh can be modeled by a single Gaussian, in which case the mesh would not contain any hidden information. Otherwise, the distribution is bimodal and consequently the mesh is watermarked. The limitation of this algorithm is that it is only effective for the information embedded by the MRS algorithm and would not be useful when the mesh is embedded by other information hiding algorithms than MRS.

Li and Bors proposed the 52-dimensional Local Feature Set (LFS52) in [13], which simplified the 208-dimensional feature set YANG208 proposed in [26] and included some new geometric feature for steganalysis, such as the vertex normal, the curvature ratio and the Gaussian curvature. In addition to LFS52, other geometric features extracted from the mesh, such as the edge length and vertex position represented in the spherical coordinate system, form the 76-dimensional feature set for 3D steganalysis in [14]. Kim et al. [9] extended the approach from [13], and proposed to use some additional features such as the edge normal, mean curvature and total curvature as supplement to LFS52 and formed LFS64 for 3D steganalysis.

In this research study we use various levels of high-pass filtering, before extracting various sets of features for image steganalysis. The existing 3D steganalysis framework based on the local feature set is briefly summarized in Sect. 2. The main idea of the proposed method is introduced in Sect. 3. The experimental results and the conclusion are given in Sects. 4 and 5, respectively.

2   3D Steganalysis Framework Based on Local Feature Set

In this section, we provide a brief introduction of the 3D steganalysis framework based on the local feature set, LFS76, proposed in [14], as illustrated in Fig. 1.

The 3D steganalyzer is trained through the following processing stages: preprocessing, feature extraction and supervised learning. During the preprocessing

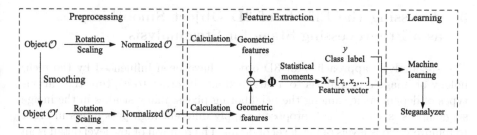

Fig. 1. The 3D steganalysis framework based on learning from statistics of the 3D features and classification by means of machine learning methods.

step, a smoothed version of the given original mesh, $\mathcal{O}'$, is obtained by applying one iteration of Laplacian smoothing on the original mesh, $\mathcal{O}$. Then, the original mesh and its smoothed version are both normalized by using rotation and scaling. The idea of 3D object smoothing was inspired by the calibration technique used in image steganalysis [6,10]. It is based on the assumption that the difference between a mesh and its smoothed version is larger for a stego mesh than for a cover mesh. In most 3D watermarking algorithms, the changes produced to the stego-object can be associated to noise-like changes. Consequently, when smoothing a cover mesh, the resulting modifications will be smaller than those obtained when smoothing its corresponding stego mesh.

During the feature extraction, 19 geometric features, characterizing the local geometry of 3D shapes, are extracted from the original mesh, $\mathcal{O}$, and its smoothed version, $\mathcal{O}'$. These geometric features define the vertex coordinates and norms in the Cartesian and Laplacian coordinate systems, the face normal, the dihedral angle, the vertex normal, the Gaussian curvature, the curvature ratio, the vertex coordinates and edge length in the spherical coordinate system. The differences between the mentioned geometric features from $\mathcal{O}$ and those from $\mathcal{O}'$ are denoted as the vector $\boldsymbol{\Phi} = \{\phi_t | t = 1, 2, .., 19\}$. Afterwards, the first four statistical moments, representing the mean, variance, skewness and kurtosis, of the logarithm of the differences, $\{\lg(\phi_t) | \phi_t \in \boldsymbol{\Phi}\}$, are considered as the steganalytic features, resulting in the 76-dimensional local feature set, LFS76, representing the input into the steganalyzer.

The steganalyzers are trained using the Fisher Linear Discriminant (FLD) ensemble [11] which is broadly used for image steganalysis as well [15,20,21]. The FLD ensemble includes a number of base learners trained uniformly on the randomly selected feature subsets extracted from the whole training data. The FLD ensemble uses the majority voting in order to combine the results of all base learners, achieving a much higher accuracy than any of the individual base learners.

3   Assessing the Effects of 3D Object Smoothing, as a Preprocessing Stage for Steganalysis

The steganalytic approaches for 3D objects have been influenced by the technology of image steganalysis to a large extent. In order to capture the various types of dependencies among the neighboring pixels, many studies in the image steganalysis, such as [7,20], propose to apply different high-pass filters in order to remove various levels of low level of detail. The removal of low level detail is an essential processing stage, which is followed by the robust extraction of steganalytic features. This approach is inspired from image smoothing, commonly used as a pre-processing step for image steganalysis. In the following, we assess the influence, when employing various degrees of smoothing, on the 3D steganalysis.

Let us assume that we have a given mesh $\mathcal{O} = \{V, F, E\}$, containing the vertex set $V = \{v(i)|i = 1, 2, \ldots, |V|\}$, where $|V|$ represents the number of vertices in the object $\mathcal{O}$, its face set F, and its edge set E, respectively. We define the 1-ring neighbourhood $\mathcal{N}(v(i))$ of a vertex $v(i)$ as $\{v(j) \in \mathcal{N}(v(i))|e(i, j) \in E\}$, where $e(i, j)$ is the edge connecting vertices $v(i)$ and $v(j)$.

We consider Laplacian smoothing for the given object $\mathcal{O}$, resulting in its smoothed version $\hat{\mathcal{O}}^{(\lambda,k)}$ after k iterations of smoothing with the scale factor λ. When one iteration of Laplacian smoothing is applied to the 3D object $\mathcal{O}$, it updates the vertex v_i into v_i' in $\hat{\mathcal{O}}$ as follows, [22]:

$$v_i' \leftarrow v_i + \frac{\lambda}{\sum_{v_j \in \mathcal{N}(v_i)} w_{ij}} \sum_{v_j \in \mathcal{N}(v_i)} w_{ij}(v_j - v_i), \tag{1}$$

where λ is the scale factor and w_{ij} are the weights defined as:

$$w_{ij} = \begin{cases} 1 & \text{if } v_j \in \mathcal{N}(v_i) \\ 0 & \text{otherwise.} \end{cases} \tag{2}$$

In Eq. (1) we use a 1-ring neighbourhood for smoothing. So after two iterations of smoothing, the information provided by a 2-ring neighbourhood would be considered for smoothing. It is obvious that a larger number of iterations of the smoothing leads to considering the influence of the vertices from a larger neighbourhood of the given vertex, during the smoothing, resulting in different levels of smoothing as well. However, adjusting the value of λ, we can control the level of the smoothing, without actually enlarging the neighbourhood of the vertex. The influence of choosing different values of λ and numbers of iterations k is investigated in the Sect. 4.

After applying different numbers of iterations of the Laplacian smoothing with various scale factors to the given $\mathcal{O}$, we obtain a set of original and smoothed object pairs $\{< \mathcal{O}, \hat{\mathcal{O}}^{(\lambda,k)} > |\lambda \in \mathbb{R}, k \in \mathbb{N}\}$. The 19 geometric features, $\{\phi_t(i, j)|t = 1, ..., 19\}$, proposed in [14], are extracted from every original and smoothed object pair, $< \mathcal{O}, \hat{\mathcal{O}}^{(\lambda,k)} >$. Then, we follow the same approach as in [14] to form the steganalytic features. Considering the first four statistical moments, representing the mean, variance, skewness and kurtosis, of the logarithm of the statistics, $\{\lg(\phi_t)|\phi_t \in \mathbf{\Phi}\}$, we have the 76-dimensional local feature set for each original and smoothed object pair. Eventually, we combine all the feature sets, obtained from multiple original and smoothed object pairs, into an enlarged feature set to be used for steganalysis.

4 Experimental Results

In the following we provide the results for the proposed 3D steganalytic approach on 354 cover 3D objects from the Princeton Mesh Segmentation project database [4]. This database contains a large variety of shapes, representing the human body under a variety of postures, statues, animals, toys, tools and so on. Some objects used in the experiment are shown in Fig. 2.

Fig. 2. 3D objects used in the steganalytic tests.

We consider identifying the 3D stego-meshes produced by using four different embedding algorithms: the Multi-Layer Steganography (MLS) provided in [3], a blind robust watermarking algorithms based on modifying the Mean of the distribution of the vertices' Radial distances in the Spherical coordinate system, denoted as MRS, from [5], the Steganalysis-Resistant Watermarking (SRW) method proposed in [28] and the Wavelet-based High Capacity (WHC) watermarking method proposed in [23]. When using the MLS method from [3], we set the number of layers to 10, and consider the number of intervals as 10000. For the MRS watermarking methods from [5], we consider $\alpha = 0.04$ for the watermark strength, while fixing the incremental step size to 0.001 and the message payload as 64 bits. During the generation of the stego-meshes using the SRW method from [28], we set the parameter $K = 128$ which determines the number of bins in the histogram of the radial distance coordinates for all vertices. According to [28], the upper bound of the embedding capacity is $\lfloor (K - 2)/2 \rfloor$ bits. The parameter that controls the watermarking robustness of SRW is n_{thr}, which is set at 20. If the smallest number of elements in the bins from the objects is less than 20, we would choose the smallest nonzero number of elements in the bins as n_{thr}. With regards to the parameters involved in WHC, we set the control parameter $\epsilon_{hc} = 100$ and other parameters are all identical to the values from

[23]. The embedded information is a pseudorandom bit stream which simulates the secret messages or watermarks hidden by the steganographier.

The steganalyzers are trained using the FLD ensemble, as in [14]. For each steganalyzer, we split the 354 pairs of cover-mesh and stego-mesh into 260 pairs for training and 94 pairs for testing, repeating independently the experiments for 30 times. The steganalysis results are assessed by calculating the median value of the detection errors which are the sums of false negatives (missed detections) and false positives (false alarms) from all 30 trials. Laplacian smoothing is used as a pre-processing stage on 3D objects, before the feature extraction, as shown in left part of the diagram from Fig. 1. In the following we analyse the effects of various parameters involved in the 3D objects' smoothing.

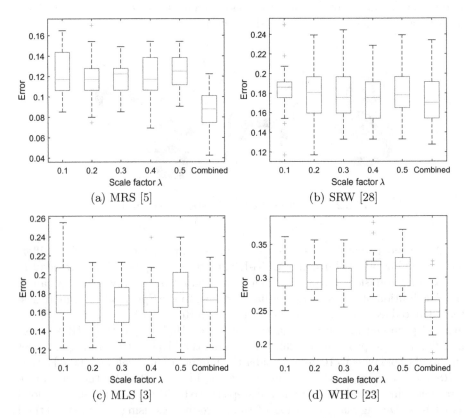

Fig. 3. Box plots showing the confidence intervals for the detection errors for the three 3D information embedding algorithms when the scale factor, λ, varies during the feature extraction when considering the LFS76 feature set. The "Combined" represents the results of the combined feature set with $\lambda \in \{0.1, 0.2, 0.3, 0.4, 0.5\}$.

4.1 Studying the Effect of Smoothing When Varying the Scale Factor λ

In order to investigate the influence of the scale factor, λ, on the efficiency of the steganalytic features, we vary the scale factor $\lambda \in \{0.1, 0.2, 0.3, 0.4, 0.5\}$ which is being used for a single iteration of Laplacian smoothing, according to equation (1), during the preprocessing stage of the extraction of the LFS76 feature set. The LFS76 feature set is extracted from the cover-meshes and the corresponding stego-meshes when embedded with information by four 3D embedding algorithms, MRS [5], SRW [28], MLS [3] and WHC [23]. We also adopt the strategy proposed in this paper by combining the LFS76 feature sets extracted when considering various levels of object smoothing by varying λ.

We use the feature sets obtained as mentioned above to train the steganalyzers for four embedding algorithms respectively. The box plots of the testing results are provided in Fig. 3. It can be observed from Fig. 3, that the steganalysis results do not change much when varying the smoothing scale factor λ, in the case when embedding information into 3D objects by the MRS and SRW algorithms. When the scale factor $\lambda = 0.3$, the steganalysis results for the 3D objects embedded by the MLS and WHC algorithms are slightly better than the results obtained when $\lambda \in \{0.1, 0.2, 0.4, 0.5\}$. Nevertheless, when combining the objects resulting from the smoothing by using all five different scales $\lambda \in \{0.1, 0.2, 0.3, 0.4, 0.5\}$, we achieve a better performance than any of the individual feature sets in the case of MRS and WHC, as it can be observed from the results presented in Fig. 3(a) and (d).

4.2 Varying the Number of Iterations for Laplacian Smoothing

In the following, we evaluate the efficiency of the steganalysis, when varying the number of iterations for the Laplacian smoothing. During the Laplacian smoothing, the scaling factor λ is fixed at 0.3, which provides a stable performance according to the results shown in Fig. 3. We first extract the LFS76 feature set based on the Laplacian smoothing when varying the number of iterations as $k \in \{1, 2, 3, 4, 5\}$. Then, according to the same procedure as that used in the previous section, we combine the 5 feature sets obtained into a whole feature set with the dimensionality of $76 \times 5 = 380$.

The performance of the various feature sets mentioned above are tested by the detecting the embedding changes produced by four embedding algorithms, MRS [5], SRW [28], MLS [3] and WHC [23]. The detection results are provided in Fig. 4. It is shown in Fig. 4(a), (b) and (d) that the combined feature set achieves better performance than any of the individual feature sets (using only a certain number of iterations) in the case of MRS and SRW. However, the combined feature set does not improve the detection accuracy compared to the best individual LFS76 feature set ($k = 1$) when the information are embedded by MLS algorithms, as shown in Fig. 4(c). It also can be seen from Fig. 4(c) that when the number of iterations of the Laplacian smoothing increases, the detection error for the MLS increases as well. This is because by increasing the

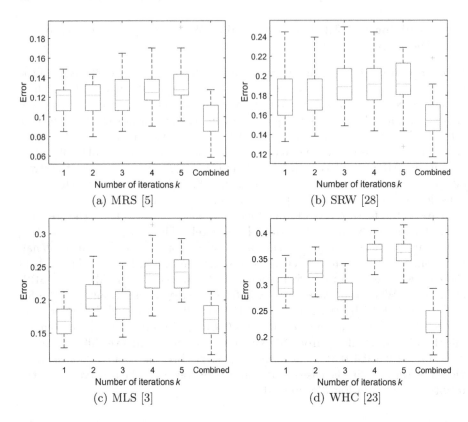

Fig. 4. Box plots showing the confidence intervals for the detection errors for the three 3D information embedding algorithms when the number of iterations of the smoothing, k, varies during the feature extraction. The "Combined" represents the results of the combined feature set with $k \in \{1, 2, 3, 4, 5\}$ iterations.

level of smoothing too much, we may remove essential features produced by the MLS steganographic algorithm or even 3D object features. In such situations, excessive smoothing would affect negatively the 3D steganalysis.

The experimental results provided in Figs. 3 and 4 indicate the effects when varying the smoothing scaling parameter and the number of iterations, respectively. The results when combining feature sets resulting from the application of various parameters have shown improvements in the steganalysis of the changes embedded by MRS [5], SRW [28] and WHC [23]. Meanwhile, no improvements have been observed in the case of the steganalysis on objects with the changes that have been embedded by MLS [3].

5   Conclusion

In order to improve the steganalysis results for the 3D objects, we propose to combine the 3D steganalytic feature sets obtained from 3D objects when considering various degrees of Laplacian smoothing as the input into the steganalyzers. The level of the Laplacian smoothing is controlled by two parameters: the scale factor, λ, and the number of iterations of the smoothing, k. During the experiments undertaken in this research study, we have combined the LFS76 feature sets based on the Laplacian smoothing at various levels. The steganalyzer trained over the combined feature set showed better performance than any of the individual LFS76 feature set, proposed in [14], for the steganalysis of three embedding algorithms. However, the proposed method did not improve the steganalysis results for the MLS embedding algorithm, and we believe this is due to the smoothing parameters which have not been optimally set for the embedding distortion caused by MLS. In future, we will investigate how to find the optimal smoothing parameters.

Acknowledgement. This work was partially supported by National Natural Science Foundation of China (No. 61772549, 61602508, U1736214, 61572052 and U1636219).

References

1. Abdulrahman, H., Chaumont, M., Montesinos, P., Magnier, B.: Color image steganalysis based on steerable Gaussian filters bank. In: Proceedings of the ACM Workshop on Information Hiding and Multimedia Security, pp. 109–114 (2016)
2. Bors, A.G., Luo, M.: Optimized 3D watermarking for minimal surface distortion. IEEE Trans. Image Process. **22**(5), 1822–1835 (2013)
3. Chao, M.W., Lin, C.h., Yu, C.W., Lee, T.Y.: A high capacity 3D steganography algorithm. IEEE Trans. Vis. Comput. Graph. **15**(2), 274–284 (2009)
4. Chen, X., Golovinskiy, A., Funkhouser, T.: A benchmark for 3D mesh segmentation. ACM Trans. Graph. **28**(3), 73:1–73:12 (2009)
5. Cho, J.W., Prost, R., Jung, H.Y.: An oblivious watermarking for 3-D polygonal meshes using distribution of vertex norms. IEEE Trans. Signal Process. **55**(1), 142–155 (2007)
6. Fridrich, J.J., Goljan, M., Hogea, D.: Steganalysis of JPEG images: breaking the F5 algorithm. In: Petitcolas, F.A.P. (ed.) IH 2002. LNCS, vol. 2578, pp. 310–323. Springer, Heidelberg (2003). https://doi.org/10.1007/3-540-36415-3_20
7. Fridrich, J., Kodovský, J.: Rich models for steganalysis of digital images. IEEE Trans. Inf. Forensics Secur. **7**(3), 868–882 (2012)
8. Itier, V., Puech, W.: High capacity data hiding for 3D point clouds based on static arithmetic coding. Multimed. Tools Appl. **76**(24), 26421–26445 (2017)
9. Kim, D., et al.: Improved 3D mesh steganalysis using homogeneous kernel map. In: Kim, K., Joukov, N. (eds.) ICISA 2017. LNEE, vol. 424, pp. 358–365. Springer, Singapore (2017). https://doi.org/10.1007/978-981-10-4154-9_42
10. Kodovsky, J., Fridrich, J.J.: Calibration revisited. In: Proceedings of the ACM Workshop on Multimedia and Security, pp. 63–74 (2009)
11. Kodovský, J., Fridrich, J., Holub, V.: Ensemble classifiers for steganalysis of digital media. IEEE Trans. Inf. Forensics Secur. **7**(2), 432–444 (2012)
12. Li, Z., Beugnon, S., Puech, W., Bors, A.G.: Rethinking the high capacity 3D steganography: increasing its resistance to steganalysis. In: Proceedings of the IEEE International Conference on Image Processing, pp. 510–514 (2017)

13. Li, Z., Bors, A.G.: 3D mesh steganalysis using local shape features. In: Proceedings of the IEEE International Conference on Acoustics, Speech and Signal Processing, pp. 2144–2148 (2016)
14. Li, Z., Bors, A.G.: Steganalysis of 3D objects using statistics of local feature sets. Inf. Sci. **415–416**, 85–99 (2017)
15. Li, Z., Hu, Z., Luo, X., Lu, B.: Embedding change rate estimation based on ensemble learning. In: Proceedings of the ACM Workshop on Information Hiding and Multimedia Security, pp. 77–84 (2013)
16. Luo, M., Bors, A.G.: Surface-preserving robust watermarking of 3-D shapes. IEEE Trans. Image Process. **20**(10), 2813–2826 (2011)
17. Ma, Y., Luo, X., Li, X., Bao, Z., Zhang, Y.: Selection of rich model steganalysis features based on decision rough set α-positive region reduction. IEEE Trans. Circuits Syst. Video Technol. (2018). https://doi.org/10.1109/TCSVT.2018.2799243
18. Ren, Y., Cai, T., Tang, M., Wang, L.: AMR steganalysis based on the probability of same pulse position. IEEE Trans. Inf. Forensics Secur. **10**(9), 1801–1811 (2015)
19. Ren, Y., Yang, J., Wang, J., Wang, L.: AMR steganalysis based on second-order difference of pitch delay. IEEE Trans. Inf. Forensics Secur. **12**(6), 1345–1357 (2017)
20. Song, X., Liu, F., Yang, C., Luo, X., Zhang, Y.: Steganalysis of adaptive JPEG steganography using 2D Gabor filters. In: Proceedings of the ACM Workshop on Information Hiding and Multimedia Security, pp. 15–23 (2015)
21. Tang, W., Li, H., Luo, W., Huang, J.: Adaptive steganalysis based on embedding probabilities of pixels. IEEE Trans. Inf. Forensics Secur. **11**(4), 734–745 (2016)
22. Taubin, G.: A signal processing approach to fair surface design. In: Proceedings of the 22nd Annual Conference on Computer Graphics and Interactive Techniques, pp. 351–358 (1995)
23. Wang, K., Lavoué, G., Denis, F., Baskurt, A.: Hierarchical watermarking of semiregular meshes based on wavelet transform. IEEE Trans. Inf. Forensics Secur. **3**(4), 620–634 (2008)
24. Wang, K., Zhao, H., Wang, H.: Video steganalysis against motion vector-based steganography by adding or subtracting one motion vector value. IEEE Trans. Inf. Forensics Secur. **9**(5), 741–751 (2014)
25. Yang, Y., Ivrissimtzis, I.: Polygonal mesh watermarking using Laplacian coordinates. Comput. Graph. Forum **29**(5), 1585–1593 (2010)
26. Yang, Y., Ivrissimtzis, I.: Mesh discriminative features for 3D steganalysis. ACM Trans. Multimed. Comput. Commun. Appl. **10**(3), 27:1–27:13 (2014)
27. Yang, Y., Pintus, R., Rushmeier, H., Ivrissimtzis, I.: A steganalytic algorithm for 3D polygonal meshes. In: Proceedings of the IEEE International Conference on Image Processing, pp. 4782–4786 (2014)
28. Yang, Y., Pintus, R., Rushmeier, H., Ivrissimtzis, I.: A 3D steganalytic algorithm and steganalysis-resistant watermarking. IEEE Trans. Vis. Comput. Graph. **23**(2), 1002–1013 (2017)
29. Zhang, H., Cao, Y., Zhao, X.: A steganalytic approach to detect motion vector modification using near-perfect estimation for local optimality. IEEE Trans. Inf. Forensics Secur. **12**(2), 465–478 (2017)
30. Zhang, Y., Qin, C., Zhang, W., Liu, F., Luo, X.: On the fault-tolerant performance for a class of robust image steganography. Signal Process. **146**(2), 99–111 (2018)

A Modified U-Net for Brain MR Image Segmentation

Yunjie Chen[✉], Zhihui Cao, Chunzheng Cao, Jianwei Yang,
and Jianwei Zhang

School of Math and Statistics, Nanjing University of Information Science
and Technology, Nanjing 210044, China
priestcyj@nuist.edu.cn

Abstract. Segmenting brain magnetic resonance (MR) images accurately is of great significance to quantitatively analyze brain images. However, many traditional segmentation methods underperforms due to some artifacts in brain imaging such as noise, weak edges and intensity inhomogeneity (also known as bias field). Recent methods based on convolutional neural networks (CNN) suffer from the limited segmentation accuracy for details. To settle these problems and to obtain more accurate results, a modified U-Net model is proposed in this paper. Different sized filters are used in every single conv-layer. The outputs of different filters are concatenated together and then the concatenated feature maps are fed to the next layer. This work makes the network learn features from different scales, be-sides, it also reduce the filter space dimensionality. Both experimental results and statistic results show that our model have higher accuracy and robustness in segmenting brain MR images.

Keywords: Convolutional neural networks · Fully convolutional networks
Magnetic resonance image

1 Introduction

Brain diseases threaten human health seriously all the time, so it is of important sense for us to diagnose brain diseases with brain imaging [1–3]. Among the several brain imaging techniques, brain magnetic resonance imaging (MRI) is easier to be used for diagnosing brain diseases, because the images from MRI have high contrast among different soft tissues and high spatial resolution [4]. Segmenting these brain images to three main tissues: gray matter (GM), white matter (WM) and cerebrospinal fluid (CSF) is fundamental in brain diseases diagnosis, and segmentation methods play an important role in brain MR images analysis. However, most segmentation methods cannot obtain satisfied results when the images have noise, intensity inhomogeneity or weak edges.

In order to obtain satisfied results, a lot of clustering models have been proposed and these models can be classified into two main strategies: the hard clustering scheme and the fuzzy clustering scheme. The conventional hard clustering methods classify each sample of the data set (or each pixel of the image) into each cluster and usually obtain very crisp results. The hard clustering models usually only uses intensity

© Springer Nature Switzerland AG 2018
X. Sun et al. (Eds.): ICCCS 2018, LNCS 11068, pp. 233–242, 2018.
https://doi.org/10.1007/978-3-030-00021-9_22

information without any spatial information, which makes them sensitive to noise, poor contrast, and intensity inhomogeneity. In order to obtain more accurate results, the fuzzy clustering theory [5] has been widely studied and successfully applied in image segmentation [6–10]. The fuzzy c-means (FCM) algorithm [11] is one of the widely used fuzzy methods in image segmentation for its robust characteristics. The spatial information has been utilized to modify the FCM methods to reduce the effect of noise, however, when the image has severe low contrast, the improved methods still hard to find satisfied results [12–15].

In the recent several years, convolutional neural networks (CNN) has outperformed the state of the art in computer vision and pattern recognition tasks, for example, Krizhevsky et al. [16] trained AlexNet and won the ImageNet Large Scale Visual Recognition Competition 2012 (ILSVRC 2012) with a great advantage. Since this breakthrough, even larger and deeper networks have been proposed [17–19].

The typical use of CNN is on classification tasks, where the output of a network is a class label for each image. For the image segmentation tasks, we want to find the label information for each pixels. Hence, Ciresan et al. [20] trained a network (deep neural networks, DNN) to segment images. The DNN classifies each pixel by labeling the neighbor patch in a square window centered on the pixel itself. This work succeeded to apply CNN to image segmentation and won the EM segmentation challenge at ISBR 2012. However, the drawbacks of this strategy is obvious. Firstly, the cost of calculation and the memory is very high, take an image sized by 256×256 for example, we have to classify 65536 patches with the network to obtain a segmented image. Secondly, the patches of adjacent pixels are almost identical, which leads to a lot of calculation redundancy. Thirdly, large scaled patches use more context information while need more pooling layers that reduce the localization accuracy. These shortcomings make the network inefficient.

To obtain a more robust network, Long et al. [21] trained an end-to-end, pixels-to-pixels network called fully convolutional network (FCN). The output of the network is the label for each pixels, and both learning and prediction are performed on whole-image-at-a-time. This method is efficient and need not pre- or post-processing complications. The network transfers some existing classification networks to dense prediction by resetting classification nets as fully convolutional ones. In this model, convolutional layers and pooling layers learn features in the image and up-sampling layers enable pixel-wise prediction, which makes the method can segment images with arbitrary-sized inputs.

Nevertheless, there are some defects of FCN. Firstly, the training is complicated, which need the network be trained for three times (FCN-32s, FCN-16s and FCN-8s) to obtain the final model. Secondly, the network is not sensitive enough to details. Thirdly, the information among pixels is not taken into account, which makes the segmenting lack spatial consistency. What's more, training FCN needs a large amount of training data, but that is unrealistic in medical tasks. Based on FCN, Ronneberger et al. [22] trained a network with U-shaped architecture called U-Net. Compared with FCN, U-Net provides more realistic results with sharper edges, taking shorter time and needs less memory. However, the results of details, such as CSF in brain MR images, are not accurate enough.

Based on the analysis above, it can be found that traditional clustering algorithms cannot segment images with noise and bias field. Although some scholars achieve improvements to some extent with modified models, most improvements are at the expense of increasing parameters and complexity of the model. The U-Net perform well in segmenting images with noise and bias field, while they underperform in details and narrow bands. To address these drawbacks, we propose a Modified U-Net model by using different scaled filters to learn more features and keep more details at the same time. The experiments on clinical brain MR images show that our model can obtain results that are more precise.

2 Backgrounds

The excellent performance of CNN in classification tasks drives scholars to take advantage of it on other computer vision tasks. In image segmentation, patch-wise training is a widely used strategy [20, 23–28], however, the process is complicated and inefficient, which makes it is hard to be used in clinical medicine.

Compared with patch-wise training, FCN is more efficient. Long et al. [21] adapted contemporary classification networks (AlexNet, the VGG Net and GoogLeNet) into fully convolutional networks by replacing dense layers with convolutional layers and adding upsampling (deconvolutional) layers, which enable pixel-wise prediction. FCN performs well in semantic segmentation, but it is not applicable to medical image segmentation because of its complexity in training, easily losing details and the requirement of big training data.

In the light of FCN's drawbacks in medical image segmentation, Ronneberger et al. [22] trained a more elegant network with U-shape. They use small sized filters (3×3) instead of large ones (5×5, 7×7, 11×11) which reduce the parameters of the network a lot. The main modification in this network is that convolutional layers are also used in upsampling part, which allows the network to propagate context information to higher layers. A deconvolutional layer, upsampling at stride 2, follows every two successive convolutional layers in upsampling part. As a result, the upsampling part is symmetric to the contracting part. Then upsampled outputs are concatenated with the feature maps from corresponding low layer, after that, the concatenated results are fed to the next convolutional layer, which makes the network yields results that are more realistic with sharper edges. There are 18 convolutional layers in the network, which makes the network lose details easily.

GoogLeNet is another widely used network, which was proposed in 2014 and won the classification task of ILSVRC2014. An inception module was proposed in the network, where 1×1, 3×3, 5×5 filters and max-pooling are used in the same layer. Multi-scale filters can extract more features from different scales. The 5×5 filters can preserve larger context information and 1×1 filters can reduce the number of depth channels. This work improved the final accuracy to some extent.

Considering the improvement of the inception module in GoogLeNet and the elegant architecture of U-Net, we combine both advantages and use different scaled filters in U-Net without changing the depth of the network.

3   Network Architecture

The modified U-Net architecture is illustrated in Fig. 1. The network consists of two parts: the contracting part and the expansive part. Each part is made up of several blocks (see Fig. 1(b) and (c)) (We show our model with blocks just to illustrate it clearly and briefly). The main modification is in the contracting part, where we use 1×1 and 3×3 filters in the same layer and then concatenate them together as the input of next layer. The outputs of each 2×2 max-pooling layer halves the size of maps, so we double the number of feature channels after each max-pooling layer to preserve information as far as possible. The expansive part is same as U-Net. In final layer, four 1×1 filters are used to map the outputs into a probability matrix, aiming to segment the brain MR images into four classes (WM, GM, CSF and background). Take a pixel for example, numbers in different channels show the probability that the pixel belongs to different classes. Traditional methods underperform when segmenting details, while our strategy is more flexible. The detailed parameters of each layer is reported in Table 1. We do not show the expansive part here because it is same as U-Net.

Considering the difference between segmentation and classification, 5×5 filters have not been utilized in the network. In classification, what we want is the label of the given image, so we can use large scaled filters (5×5, 11×11 or even 13×13) to see more context and get more information. However, when the network has been used for medical image analyze, large scaled filters may lose detail information easily. The 1×1 filters can preserve detail information.

4   Training

The input images and their corresponding segmentation maps are used to train the network with the stochastic gradient descent implementation. The energy function is computed by a pixel-wise soft-max over the final feature map combined with the cross entropy loss function. The soft-max is defined as

$$p_c(I_{ij}) = e^{O_c(I_{ij})} / \sum_{c'}^{C} e^{O_{c'}(I_{ij})} \tag{1}$$

where $p_c(I_{ij})$ is the probability that the pixel I_{ij} belongs to class c, and $O_c(I_i)$ is the activation in feature channel c at position (i,j) in the last layer (the value at (i,j,c) in the probability matrix). The detailed parameters in the network and training process are show in Table 2.

We use cross entropy loss function in the network as the energy function:

$$E = \sum_{I_{ij} \in I} \sum_{c=1}^{C} p'_c(I_{ij}) \log\left(p_c(I_{ij})\right)^{-1} \tag{2}$$

where $p'_c(I_{ij})$ is the true distribution. That means the loss function is computed by adding up pixelwise soft-max over the whole final map with the cross entropy.

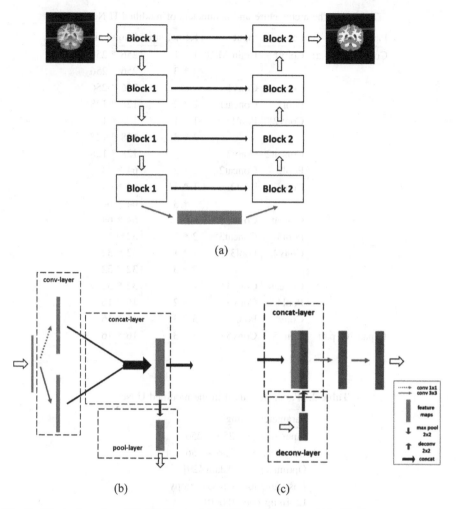

Fig. 1. Illustration of modified U-Net model (a) The architecture of Modified U-Net (b) Block 1 architecture (c) Block 2 architecture and a description of some icons

5 Experiment Results

We experimentally evaluate our model, in this section, with a set of clinical brain MR images, which is generated from Internet Brain Segmentation Repository (IBSR). The experiments are test on Keras and trained on a NVIDIA GeForce GTX 1050Ti GPU (4 GB). Both models are trained with 2000 images for 30 epochs and tested with 200 images. In order to obtain convincing results and show the robustness, we train the models for 10 times and present the average results.

The results on IBSR are shown in Fig. 2. The left column shows the initial images, which have intensity inhomogeneity, low contrast and motion artifact. The second column shows the ground truth. The third column shows the results of U-Net, which

Table 1. The architecture and parameters of modified U-Net

Part	Layer	Input	Kernel size	Output size
Contracting part	Conv1	Brain MRI	1 * 1	256 * 256
			3 * 3	256 * 256
	Concat1	Conv1	-	256 * 256
	Pool1	Concat1	2 * 2	128 * 128
	Conv2	Pool1	1 * 1	128 * 128
			3 * 3	128 * 128
	Concat2	Conv2	-	128 * 128
	Pool2	Concat2	2 * 2	64 * 64
	Conv3	Pool2	1 * 1	64 * 64
			3 * 3	64 * 64
	Concat3	Conv3	-	64 * 64
	Pool3	Concat3	2 * 2	32*32
	Conv4	Pool3	1 * 1	32 * 32
			3 * 3	32 * 32
	Concat4	Conv4	-	32 * 32
	Pool4	Conv4	2 * 2	16 * 16
	Conv5	Pool4	3 * 3	16 * 16
Expansive part	Conv5	Conv5	3 * 3	16 * 16
	...			

Table 2. Parameters used in the modified U-Net

Parameter setting	
Input size	256×256
Output size	$256 \times 256 \times 4$
Optimizer	Adam [29]
Loss function	Cross entropy
Learning rate	0.0001
Batch size	5
Epochs	30

shows that the method is sensitive to low contrast and may lose detail information of tissues with slim structure. The right column shows the results of our method. The results approves the robustness of low contrast, intensity inhomogeneity and preserving of detail information.

In order to quantitatively analyze the results, we use the Jaccard similarity (Js values) [28] as a metric to evaluate the performance. The Js value is a ratio between the intersection and union of two sets S_1 and S_2, which is define as

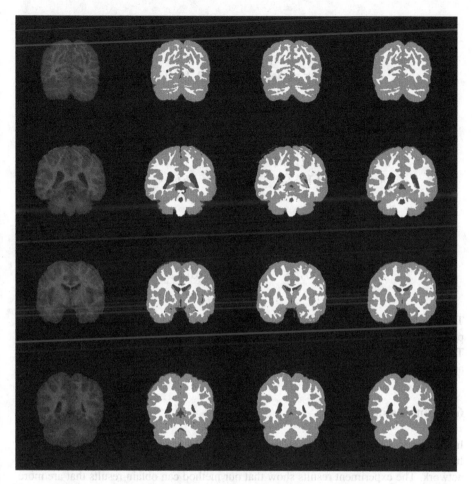

Fig. 2. Segmentation on clinical image. The left column shows the initial images, the second column shows the ground truth, the third column to right column show the results of the U-Net and the modified U-Net, respectively

$$Js(S_1, S_2) = (S_1 \cap S_2)/(S_1 \cup S_2) \tag{3}$$

where S_1 is the segmentation result and S_2 is the groundtruth. A higher Js value means a more accurate segmentation result. We test the two models on 200 clinical brain MR images from IBSR, with both models being trained for 10 times. The average Js values of WM, GM and CSF are shown in Table 3. The proposed model have higher Js value than U-Net, indicating that our model has more accurate segmentation results. The JS values of CSF proved that our method preserved more detail information.

Some other criterions, including Acc, Var, training time and predicting time, are used for the comparison and the results are shown in Table 4. The Acc (accuracy) is defined as $(S_1 \cap S_2)/S_2$ over the whole map. The Var is the variance of Js values.

Table 3. Mean Js values of segmentation results on CSF, GM, WM (%)

	CSF	GM	WM
U-Net [22]	31.79	84.25	83.04
Our method	**39.65**	**87.19**	**86.41**

Table 4. Comparison of accuracy (%) and variances (10^{-4}) of Js values

	Acc	Var(Acc)	Var(CSF)	Var(GM)	Var(WM)
U-Net [22]	89.02	4.42	**91.02**	11.18	23.30
Our method	**91.16**	**2.58**	96.56	**6.68**	**14.80**

Table 5. Training time and predicting time of U-Net and modified U-Net

	Training time(s/epoch)	Running time(s/img)
U-Net	**127.73**	**0.0226**
Our method	177.15	0.0312

The results show that our model have higher Acc and lower Var, proving that the proposed model is more robust. The training time and predicting time are listed in Table 5. Although our model costs longer training time and predicting time, it's acceptable for clinical research.

6 Conclusion

In this paper, a Modified U-Net model for brain MR images segmentation is proposed. In order to preserve more detail information, we utilize different sized filters in the network. The experiment results show that our method can obtain results that are more accurate even when the images have low contrast, intensity inhomogeneity, noise and motion artifact.

Acknowledgement. This work was supported in part by the National Nature Science Foundation of China 61672291.

References

1. Boesen, K., Rehm, K., Schaper, K., et al.: Quantitative comparison of four brain extraction algorithms. Neuroimage **22**(3), 1255–1261 (2004)
2. Le Goualher, G., Argenti, A.M., Duyme, M., et al.: Statistical sulcal shape comparisons: application to the detection of genetic encoding of the central sulcus shape. Neuroimage **11**(5 Pt 1), 564–574 (2000)
3. Logothetis, N.K., Pauls, J., Augath, M., et al.: Neurophysiological investigation of the basis of the fMRI signal. Nature **412**(6843), 150–157 (2001)

4. Wang, L., Shi, F., Yap, P.-T., et al.: Longitudinally guided level sets for consistent tissue segmentation of neonates. Hum. Brain Mapp. **34**(4), 956–972 (2013)
5. Zadeh, L.A.: Fuzzy sets, fuzzy logic, & fuzzy systems. Inf. Control **8**(3), 338–353 (1965)
6. Udupa, J.K., Samarasekera, S.: Fuzzy connectedness and object definition: theory, algorithms, and applications in image segmentation. Graph. Mod. Image Process. **58**(3), 246–261 (1996)
7. Tolias, Y.A., Panas, S.M.: Image segmentation by a fuzzy clustering algorithm using adaptive spatially constrained membership functions. IEEE Trans. Syst. Man Cybern. Part A Syst. Hum. **28**(3), 359–369 (1998)
8. Noordam, J.C.: Geometrically guided fuzzy c-means clustering for multivariate image segmentation. In: International Conference on Pattern Recognition, vol. 1(3), pp. 462–465. IEEE Computer Society, Barcelona (2000)
9. Yang, M.S., Hu, Y.J., Lin, C.R., et al.: Segmentation techniques for tissue differentiation in MRI of Ophthalmology using fuzzy clustering algorithms. Magn. Reson. Imaging **20**(2), 173–179 (2002)
10. Karmakar, G.C., Dooley, L.S.: A generic fuzzy rule based image segmentation algorithm. Pattern Recogn. Lett. **23**(10), 1215–1227 (2002)
11. Dunn, J.C.: A fuzzy relative of the ISODATA process and its use in detecting compact well-separated clusters. J. Cybern. **3**(3), 32–57 (1974)
12. Chen, Y., Zhan, T., Zhang, J., et al.: Multigrid nonlocal gaussian mixture model for segmentation of brain tissues in magnetic resonance images. Biomed. Res. Int. **4**, 1–10 (2016)
13. Chen, Y., Li, J., Zhang, H., et al.: Non-local-based spatially constrained hierarchical fuzzy C-means method for brain magnetic resonance imaging segmentation. IET Image Process. **10**(11), 865–876 (2016)
14. Krinidis, S., Chatzis, V.: A robust fuzzy local information c-means clustering algorithm. IEEE Trans. Image Process. **19**(5), 1328–1337 (2010)
15. Zhang, K., Liu, Q., Song, H., et al.: A variational approach to simultaneous image segmentation and bias correction. IEEE Trans. Cybern. **45**(8), 1426–1437 (2017)
16. Krizhevsky, A., Sutskever, I., Hinton, G.E.: ImageNet classification with deep convolutional neural networks. In: International Conference on Neural Information Processing Systems, pp. 1097–1105. Semantic Scholar, Nevada (2012)
17. Szegedy, C., Liu, W., Jia, Y., et al.: Going deeper with convolutions. In: IEEE Conference on Computer Vision and Pattern Recognition, Boston, pp. 1–9. IEEE Computer Society (2015)
18. Simonyan, K., Zisserman, A.: Very deep convolutional networks for large-scale image recognition. In: International Conference on Learning Representations 2015, San Diego, pp. 1–13 (2015)
19. He, K., Zhang, X., Ren, S., et al.: Deep residual learning for image recognition. In: 2016 IEEE Conference on Computer Vision and Pattern Recognition, Las Vegas, pp. 770–778. IEEE Computer Society (2016)
20. Dan, C.C., Giusti, A., Gambardella, L.M., et al.: Deep neural networks segment neuronal membranes in electron microscopy images. In: Advances in Neural Information Processing Systems, vol. 25, pp. 2852–2860 (2012)
21. Long, J., Shelhamer, E., Darrell, T.: Fully convolutional networks for semantic segmentation. In: 2015 IEEE Conference on Computer Vision and Pattern Recognition, Boston, pp. 3431–3440. IEEE Computer Society (2015)

22. Ronneberger, O., Fischer, P., Brox, T.: U-Net: convolutional networks for biomedical image segmentation. In: Navab, N., Hornegger, J., Wells, W.M., Frangi, A.F. (eds.) MICCAI 2015, Part III. LNCS, vol. 9351, pp. 234–241. Springer, Cham (2015). https://doi.org/10.1007/978-3-319-24574-4_28

23. Farabet, C., Couprie, C., Najman, L., et al.: Learning hierarchical features for scene labeling. IEEE Trans. Pattern Anal. Mach. Intell. **35**(8), 1915–1929 (2013)

24. Ganin, Y., Lempitsky, V.: N^4-Fields: neural network nearest neighbor fields for image transforms. In: Cremers, D., Reid, I., Saito, H., Yang, M.-H. (eds.) ACCV 2014, Part II. LNCS, vol. 9004, pp. 536–551. Springer, Cham (2015). https://doi.org/10.1007/978-3-319-16808-1_36

25. Gupta, S., Girshick, R., Arbeláez, P., Malik, J.: Learning rich features from RGB-D images for object detection and segmentation. In: Fleet, D., Pajdla, T., Schiele, B., Tuytelaars, T. (eds.) ECCV 2014, Part VII. LNCS, vol. 8695, pp. 345–360. Springer, Cham (2014). https://doi.org/10.1007/978-3-319-10584-0_23

26. Hariharan, B., Arbeláez, P., Girshick, R., Malik, J.: Simultaneous detection and segmentation. In: Fleet, D., Pajdla, T., Schiele, B., Tuytelaars, T. (eds.) ECCV 2014, Part VII. LNCS, vol. 8695, pp. 297–312. Springer, Cham (2014). https://doi.org/10.1007/978-3-319-10584-0_20

27. Ning, F., Delhomme, D., Lecun, Y., et al.: Toward automatic phenotyping of developing embryos from videos. IEEE Trans. Image Process. **14**(9), 1360–1371 (2015)

28. Pinheiro, P., Collobert, R.: Recurrent convolutional neural networks for scene labeling. In: International Conference on Machine Learning, Beijing, pp. 82–90 (2014)

29. Kingma, D.P., Ba, J.: Adam: a method for stochastic optimization. In: 3rd International Conference for Learning Representations, San Diego, pp. 1–9. IEEE Computer Society (2015)

A Multichannel Convolutional Neural Network Based Forensics-Aware Scheme for Cyber-Physical-Social Systems

Bin Yang[1](✉), Xianyi Chen[2], and Tao Zhang[1]

[1] Jiangnan University, Wuxi 214122, China
yangbin@jiangnan.edu.cn
[2] Nanjing University of Information Science and Technology,
Nanjing 210044, China

Abstract. Cyber-Physical-Social System (CPSS) involves numerous connected smart things with different technologies and communication standards. While CPSS opens new opportunities in various fields, it introduces new challenges in the field of security. In this paper, we propose a real-time forensics-aware scheme for supporting reliable image forensics investigations in the CPSS environment. The forensic scheme utilizes a multichannel convolutional neural network (MCNN) to automatically learn hierarchical representations from the input images. Most previous works aim at detecting a certain manipulation, which may usually lead to misleading results if irrelevant features and/or classifiers are used. To overcome this limitation, we extract the periodicity property and filtering residual feature from the image blocks. The multichannel feature map is generated by combining the periodic spectrum and the residual map. Micro neural networks module is utilized to abstract the data within the multichannel feature map. The overall framework is capable of detecting different types of image manipulations, including copy-move, removal, splicing and smoothing. Experimental results on several public datasets show that the proposed CNN based scheme outperforms existing state-of-the-art schemes.

Keywords: Image forensic · Cyber-Physical-Social System
Convolutional neural network · Tempering detection

1 Introduction

The CPSS had become an attractive research topic, in which the real entity in physical world becomes virtual entity in cyber world, and both physical and digital entities are enhanced with sensing, processing, and self-adapting capabilities to perform interaction through special addressing scheme. Security has become a crucial challenge due to the development of sophisticated editing software. Even a novice person can tamper the digital contents with an ease. In this work, we concentrate on the field of digital forensic investigation in the CPSS. The means for establishing image authenticity and discovery of tampering are treated by image forensics.

© Springer Nature Switzerland AG 2018
X. Sun et al. (Eds.): ICCCS 2018, LNCS 11068, pp. 243–254, 2018.
https://doi.org/10.1007/978-3-030-00021-9_23

The existing techniques for forgery detection can be classified into two main categories: intrusive and nonintrusive. Intrusive techniques need that some sort of digital signature be embedded in the image at the time of its creation, and so their scope is limited because all digital devices do not have the feature of embedding digital signature at the time of capturing an image. On the other hand, non-intrusive approach needs not any embedded. Recently, deep learning has become popular due to its promising performance in different visual recognition tasks such as object detection and scene classification. There have been a few recent works efforts in detecting tempering by deep learning model [1–3]. However, most of them are based on some certain assumptions or some prior knowledge of the questioned image, which restricts its practical usage. For example, we do not know the manipulation type of a questioned image before further examinations are made. Figure 1 presents two challenge forensic examples. Two different manipulations were performed in different images, respectively.

Fig. 1. Two tempering examples. The first row is an example of clone; the second row is an example of splicing.

In this paper, we propose a universal end-to-end system to expose the tampering based on deep learning. Compared with the current state-of-the-art of image forensic methods, the contribution of our work can be summarized as follows:

- Most existing works aim at detecting a certain operation, which means that their proposed features usually depend on the investigated image operation. This usually leads to misleading results if irrelevant features and/or classifiers are used. Our method is proposed to detect not only pre-operations but also post-operations.

- As the convolutional layers will extract features of an image's content instead of learning filters that identify traces of the tempering. An additional layer is developed and added into the conventional CNN in our modified architecture to increase the performance in forgery detection.
- The proposed scheme uses image blocks to train the CNN instead of whole image, so that it can detect the splicing forgery and locate the forged area, especially in the challenging cases of small size.

The rest of this paper is organized as follows. In Sect. 2, we discuss the related works concerning forgeries detection by using the statistic features. In Sect. 3, we describe how to generate a feature map in frequency-domain. In Sect. 4, the proposed algorithm framework is presented first, then each part of it is described in detail. Section 5 details the experimental results while the conclusion and future work is presented in Sect. 6.

2 Related Work

Pre-operations such as scaling and rotation, and post-operations such as filtering, are usually applied to make the forged regions more consistent with the whole image. We roughly divide the forensic techniques into two class: resampling detection and filtering detection. Popescu and Farid [4] used Expectation-Maximization (EM) algorithm to generate a probability map (p-map) from the residue of a local linear predictor to expose periodicities introduced by interpolation and resampling. However, the EM-based method is susceptible to JPEG attacks. The periodic JPEG blocking artifacts would interfere with the periodic patterns introduced by resampling. Ryu and Lee [5] proposed a technique to detect resampling on JPEG compressed images. They added noise before passing the image through the resampling detector. Yuan [6] proposed a 44-dimensional feature, known as the median filtering forensics (MFF), which extracted five feature subsets based on order statistics and grey levels. The experimental results indicated that the MFF approach can achieve comparable or better performance than SPAM when dealing with low resolution JPEG images. However, MFF approach also suffers performance loss as the JPEG quality factor decreases or as the size of the examined image shrinks. However, most existing methods manually extract reliable features, and then feed them into a classifier like the support vector machine (SVM), which has been trained with lots of labelled images, for detection [7].

Motivated by the rapid developing of machine learning, deep neural networks, such as Deep Belief Network, Deep Auto Encoder and Convolutional Neural Network (CNN), have shown to be capable of extracting complex statistical dependencies from high-dimensional sensory inputs and efficiently learning their hierarchical representations. Machine learning based approaches have been proposed in the passive image forensics. Many filtering detection methods had been proposed to directly detect the filtering features. However, their performance is degraded in when testing on an image that has been JPEG compressed. Kang et al. [8] utilized a feature from the autoregressive (AR) model of median filter residual (MFR), i.e., the difference between an unaltered image and its median filtered version to improve detection performance.

As MFR contains less edge information than the first order difference. Image content can be suppressed which may interfere with median filtering detection. However, it also suffers from performance loss when the resolution of image decreases. Chen et al. [9] made an attempt to adopt a deep learning method by extracting the MFR features from questioned image. The MFR features were then fed into CNN instead of median filtered images itself. Xu et al. [10] proposed a Gaussian low-pass filter bank to obtain a series of frequency residual functions. The filtered image was then identified by the band-width feature SVM.

Although promising results have been reported by investigating various pattern recognition methods for multimodal neuroimage analysis, there are still some limitations in the above feature extraction methods. The ROI-based feature extraction can significantly reduce the feature dimension and provide robust representations, but some minute abnormal changes may be ignored. In addition, the ROIs are generated by prior hypotheses and the abnormal brain regions relevant to AD might not well fit to the predefined ROIs, thus limiting the representation power of extracted features. Liu et al. [11] developed a method to detect the spliced object with artificial blurred boundary based on image edge analysis and blur detection. The blurred edge points were then detected by the well-trained SVM. The experiments showed that the method can detect the splicing with fake blurred boundary. The weakness of [11] is that it cannot be applied to non-filtered images. Hence, it is important to seek a universal feature set that can capture the artifacts left by various operations rather than a specific one that only works for a certain operation. And the traces left in the forgery should be efficiently learned by machine. To accomplish this, we make use of tools from deep learning known as convolutional neural network.

3   The Multichannel Feature Map

Usually, the features learned via deep learning have better. representations of the data than the handcrafted features. Instead of extracting features based on the expert's knowledge about the target domain, deep learning can discover the discriminant representations inherent in data by incorporating the feature extraction into the task learning process. Thus, it can be used by nonexperts for their researches and/or applications, especially in fake image analysis. The structural information of data is an effective way to represent prior knowledge, and has been found to be vital for designing classifiers in real-world problems. Most existing works aim at detecting a certain manipulation, which may usually lead to misleading results if irrelevant features and/or classifiers are used. However, all the operations would inevitably distort some inherent relationships among the adjacent pixels in the image. Furthermore, some common inherent statistics in frequency domain cannot be preserved well. To expose such inherent statistics, a multichannel feature map (MFM), which containing the periodicity property and filtering residual feature, is used as the input of CNN.

3.1 Periodicity Property of Tempering

A signal s(x) is sampled with a step size $\Delta \in R^+$ to produce a discrete data sequence $s_m = s(m\Delta)$. The signal can be reconstructed from its samples:

$$s^{(\varphi)}(x) = \sum_{m=-\infty}^{\infty} s_m \varphi\left(\frac{x}{\Delta} - m\right) \tag{1}$$

where $\varphi(\cdot)$ is the interpolation function. For linear interpolation $\varphi(x) = 1 - |x|$ where $|x| \leq 1$. Mahdian et al. [12] had shown that the interpolation would bring into the signal and their derivatives a specific periodicity. And the periodicity is dependent on the interpolation kernel used. They generalized the method to the kth order derivative as:

$$D^{(k)}s^{(\varphi)}(x) = \sum_{m=-\infty}^{\infty} s_m D^{(k)}\varphi\left(\frac{x}{\Delta} - m\right) \tag{2}$$

where $D^{(k)}$ is an operator of the kth order derivative:

$$D^{(k)}s^{(\varphi)}(x) = \begin{cases} s^{(\varphi)}(x), & k = 0 \\ \frac{\partial^k s^{(\varphi)}(x)}{\partial x^k}, & k > 0 \end{cases} \tag{3}$$

In discrete signals derivative is typically approximated by computing the finite difference between adjacent samples. The variance of $D^{(k)}s^{(\varphi)}(x)$ is periodic over x with period Δ:

$$var\{D^{(k)}s^{(\varphi)}(x)\} = var\{D^{(k)}s^{(\varphi)}(x + \vartheta\Delta)\}, \vartheta \in \mathbb{Z} \tag{4}$$

Then, the 1-D model can be analogously extended to the 2-D case

$$var\{D^{(k)}s^{(\varphi)}(x,y)\} = var\{D^{(k)}s^{(\varphi)}(x + \vartheta\Delta_x, y + \vartheta\Delta_y)\}, \vartheta \in \mathbb{Z} \tag{5}$$

where var$\{\cdot\}$ means variance. In this paper, we will confine to the case of k = 2. The derivative kernel is [1, −2, 1]. The periodicity is dependent on the interpolation kernel used. As the periodic peaks are confirmed in the affine transformed forged region. The periodicity property could be automatically learned by the CNN.

3.2 Filtering Residual Feature Map

Many manipulations may not perform affine transformation. The specific periodic peaks are hard to detect in such case. Therefore, we expend our schema to the additional post-processed manipulations detection (e.g. filtering detection). The filtering process can be defined as:

$$g(i,j) = f(i,j) * F_w(i,j) = \sum_{k=-n}^{n} \sum_{l=-n}^{n} f(i-k, j-l) * G_w(k,l) \tag{6}$$

where $g(i,j)$ and $f(i,j)$ is the filtered and unaltered image, respectively. $F_w(i,j)$ is the filter function with the filter window of $w \times w$.

There are few perceptible differences between the original and the filtered image. The residual feature of filtering can hardly be learned by CNN. Inspired by the prominent results in median filtering residual forensic, we calculate the difference of between original image and its filtered version in frequency-domain. The filtering residual in frequency (FRF) features of an image is defined as:

$$FRF(i,j) = FFT2(f_w(X(i,j))) - FFT2(X(i,j)) \qquad (7)$$

where FFT2 is 2-D Fast Fourier Transform (FFT), f_w is the filtering process with a $w \times w$ filter window. We translate the spectrum and take logarithm transform to the FRF value to improve the identification. The transformation can be expressed as:

$$F' = log(shift(F) + 1) \qquad (8)$$

where F and F' is the original and transformed spectrum, respectively. Then (11) can be written as:

$$FRF = log(shift(FFT2(f_w(I))) + 1) - log(shift(FFT2(I)) + 1) \qquad (9)$$

$X(i,j)$ is filtered by f_u with filter window $u \times u$, the FRF can be presented as:

$$FRF'(i,j) = FFT2(f_w(f_u(I(i,j)))) - FFT2(f_u(I(i,j))) \qquad (10)$$

where $I(i,j)$ is the original unaltered image. The residual between original image and its filtered version can be presented as a band-pass filter signal. The FRF images exhibit distinct patterns which could be learned by CNN.

4 Network Architecture

As the convolutional layers will extract features of an image's content instead of learning manipulations that identify traces of the tempering. In the following, each layer (except the micro neural networks) is denoted by index l. As depicted in Fig. 2, the proposed CNN can be divided into a *f-maps* layer, a micro neural networks module, a convolutional module and a linear classification module (composed of two fully connected layers and a softmax layer).

4.1 Micro Neural Networks

We use a different strategy to skip the feature fusion step. The features are separately characterized in the neural networks. the feature map can be calculated as follows:

$$f_{i,j,m} = \max\left(w_m^T x_{i,j}, 0\right) \qquad (11)$$

where (i, j) is the pixel index in the *f-map*, $x_{i,j}$ stands for the input patch centered at location (i, j), w is the weight and m is used to index the channels of the *f-maps*. Unlike the structure in Network [13], we divide the input feature maps into two f-maps. One *f-*

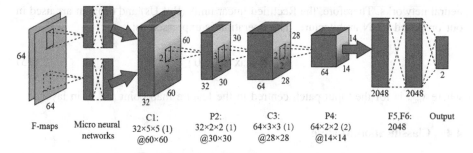

C1:
32×5×5 (1)
@60×60

P2:
32×2×2 (1)
@30×30

C3:
64×3×3 (1)
@28×28

P4:
64×2×2 (2)
@14×14

F5,F6:
2048

Output

F-maps   Micro neural networks

Fig. 2. Architecture of the proposed CNN

map is for periodicity property abstraction, and another is for FRF abstraction. The proposed micro neural network is consisting of two fully connected layers.

4.2 f-map Layer

The traces left by tempering can be investigated after suppressing the interference of irrelevant information (e.g., image edges and textures). The f-map layer is essential in the proposed CNN model. In such layer, the network will take an image block as input, and output the multichannel feature map. There is a trade-off in selecting the image patch size: tampering is more detectable in larger patch sizes because the filter signal is more distinct, but small forged area will not be localized that well. Finally, we choose 64×64 pixels as the size that we can detect reasonably well.

4.3 Convolutional Module

After the micro neural network is two pairs of convolutional (C1 and C3) and pooling layers (P2 and P4) in the proposed CNN. The size of the output (C1) is $64 \times 64 \times 32$, which means the number of feature maps is 32 and the resolution of feature maps is "64×64". The convolution operation can be denoted as:

$$x_j^l = \sum_{i=1}^{n} x_i^{l-1} * k_{ij}^{l-1} + b_j^l \qquad (12)$$

where $*$ denotes convolution, x_j^l is the *j-th* output map in layer l, the convolutional kernel k_{ij}^{l-1} (also called weight) can be updated by training. It connecting the *i-th* output map in layer *l-1* and the *j-th* output map in layer *l*. b_j^l is the trainable bias parameter of the *j-th* output map in layer *l*. After obtaining feature maps using convolution, the pooling layer is used for a down sampling operation. A max pooling layer with filter of size 2×2 is used to decrease the size of feature maps to 30×30 after C1 layer. Let l denotes the index of a max-pooling layer. The layer's output is a set Pl of square maps with size w_l. We get the Pl from Pl-1. The square maps size wl is obtained by $w_l = w_{l-1}$ /k, where k is the size of the square max-pooling kernel. Following the pooling layer (P2) is another pair of convolution and pooling layer with 64 kernels of size 3×3 and a filter of size 2×2. Dropout is a wildly used technique for avoiding overfitting in neural networks. Therefore, the Rectified linear units (ReLUs) and dropout are used in our proposed CNN architecture. The operation is expressed as:

$$f_{m,n} = \max\left(x_{m,n}^l, 0\right) \tag{13}$$

where $x_{m,n}$ is for the input patch centred in the feature map point *(m, n)* in layer *l*.

4.4   Classification Module

After the convolutional module is the classification module. The classification module consists of two fully connected layers and followed by a two-way softmax loss layer. Each fully-connected layer (F5 and F6 in Fig. 2) has 2048 neurons. Dropout is used in both fully-connected layers. The output of the last fully connected layer has two neurons which is fed into softmax. We use back-propagation algorithm to train the proposed CNN. The weights and the bias in the convolutional and fully connected layers are updated adaptively by performing the error propagation procedure as described in [14]. Therefore, we feed back the classification result to guide the feature extraction automatically.

5   Experimental Results

5.1   Experimental Setup

All experiments were performed on a personal computer equipped with one GPU (Nvidia GeForce GTX 1080Ti with 11 GB RAM). To evaluate the performance of the proposed model and compare its performance with other schemes, we tested on a composite image database containing 12120 images. These images are from three image databases: the BOSSbase 1.01, CASIA v2.0, and laboratory database [15, 16]. BOSSbase database contributes 10000 uncompressed images with the size of 512×512. The rest of 3 databases contributes 2120 images with the resolution of 348×256 to 4032×3024. All images were firstly converted into grayscale. Next, we randomly selected 70% images as the training set, while the complement 30% was the testing set. The training and the testing set were generated as follow strategy. As exhibited in Table 1, we applied five types of operations with different factors to every image.

Table 1. Five types of operations

Operation	Factor/Parameter
Scaling	Scaling factor is in the range of {0.5,0.7,0.9,1.1,1.3,1.5}
Rotating	Rotation angle is in the range of {1°,2.5°,5°,15°,30°,45°}
Median filtering	Size of the kernel is {3 × 3, 5 × 5}
Gaussian filtering	Size of the kernel is {3 × 3, 5 × 5}
Average filtering	Size of the kernel is {3 × 3, 5 × 5}

In total we created a training set containing 178164 altered blocks and 8484 unaltered blocks. To measure the detection performance, True Positive Rate (TPR) and False Positive Rate (FPR) were used. Where TP and TN denote as the number of the true detection of forged images and original images, respectively. Denote the FP and FN as the number of the wrong detection of original images and forged images, respectively. Then, the TPR is the fraction of tampered images correctly identified as such, while FPR is the fraction of identifying an original image as a tampered one. They can be represented as:

$$TPR = TP/(TP + FN) \tag{14}$$

$$FPR = FP/(FP + FN) \tag{15}$$

5.2   Experimental Results

Table 2 summarizes the performance of our proposed method for binary classification to detect different image operations. Each operation is named by its first letter and its factor value, for example, S0.5 denotes scaling with factor of 0.5. Detection results demonstrate that the proposed approach is able to handle most common manipulations.

Table 2. TPR (%) of different operations

Operation	S0.5	S0.7	S0.9	S1.1	S1.3	S1.5
TPR	93.23	93.52	92.55	92.09	93.87	94.65
Operation	R1	R2.5	R5	R15	R30	R45
TPR	91.40	93.87	94.52	92.87	93.12	95.32
Operation	M3	M5	G3	G5	A3	A5
TPR	93.09	94.19	94.75	95.74	94.12	94.77

Four methods [1, 3, 7, 10] were implemented and performed on same dataset. SVM models for [3, 7, 10] were performed in MATLAB. The network models used in [1] was also generated for the comparison in Caffe. The comparing results are presented in Table 3. The first and the second row of each method is the TPR and FPR, respectively.

Ryu and Lee [3] exploited the periodic properties of interpolation by the second-derivative of the transformed image in both the row and column directions. They obtained a relative high performance in rotation detection. On the other hand, [7, 10] are proposed for filtering forensic task.

As demonstrated in Table 3, [1] proposed a LSTM network to learn the boundary discrepancy around the manipulated region. They discovered that the boundaries between manipulated and neighboured non-manipulated regions exhibit discriminative features. However, the boundary feature in manipulated region is usually affected by the texture in natural image. Table 3 demonstrates that our method outperforms the state-of-the-art methods.

Table 3. TPR(%) and FPR(%) of different methods.

Method	Scaling	Rotating	Median filtering	Gaussian filtering	Average filtering
Ryu and Lee [3]	80.31	94.45	–	–	–
	15.42	8.87	–	–	–
Liu et al. [7]	–	–	91.41	92.45	90.75
	–	–	9.55	9.82	11.48
Xu et al. [10]	–	–	–	90.64	91.97
	–	–	–	10.42	11.2
Bappy et al. [1]	81.41	82.87	72.11	75.3	72.97
	13.54	15.2	15.56	15.22	14.62
Proposed	93.8	93.84	93.64	95.25	94.44
	8.67	9.03	7.99	7.99	7.93

Figure 3 presents the splicing detection examples in CASIA. As can be seen, the proposed method can perfectly locate the splicing regions. Figure 4. presents the high-resolution example which had performed clone tempering. Note that the smooth operation was performed to blur the boundaries between manipulated and neighboured non-manipulated regions.

Fig. 3. Examples of splicing detection. The detected blocks were marked in green. (Color figure online)

Fig. 4. Examples of clone detection. The detected blocks were marked in green. (Color figure online)

6   Conclusions

In this paper, we focus on the field of digital forensics investigation in the CPSS. A real-time forensics-aware scheme is proposed for supporting reliable image forensics investigations in the CPSS environment. The traces left in the manipulations are automatically learned by the improved neural network. Since the tempering tend conceal to traces left by manipulation. The periodicity property and filtering residual feature are in-depth analysed. The multichannel feature map is generated by combining the periodic spectrum and the residual map. Extensive experimental results demonstrate that our method can efficiently expose the traces of tempering and is robust against JPEG degradation. Future work will be mainly dedicated to increase the universality of our approach by trying filter layers.

Acknowledgments. This work is supported by the Chinese Postdoctoral Science Foundation (NO. 2018M632229).

References

1. Bappy, J.H., Roychowdhury, A.K., Bunk, J., et al.: Exploiting spatial structure for localizing manipulated image regions. In: IEEE International Conference on Computer Vision, pp. 4980–4989. IEEE Computer Society (2017)
2. Bayar, B., Stamm, M.C.: A deep learning approach to universal image manipulation detection using a new convolutional layer. In: ACM Workshop on Information Hiding and Multimedia Security, pp. 5–10. ACM (2016)
3. Ryu, S.J., Lee, H.K.: Estimation of linear transformation by analyzing the periodicity of interpolation. Pattern Recogn. Lett. **36**(3), 89–99 (2014)
4. Popescu, A.C., Farid, H.: Exposing digital forgeries by detecting traces of resampling. IEEE Trans. Signal Process. **53**(5), 758–767 (2005)
5. Kirchner, M.: Fast and reliable resampling detection by spectral analysis of fixed linear predictor residue. In: ACM Workshop on Multimedia and Security, pp. 11–20. ACM (2008)
6. Yuan, H.D.: Blind forensics of median filtering in digital images. IEEE Trans. Inf. Forensics Secur. **6**(4), 1335–1345 (2011)
7. Liu, A., Zhao, Z., Zhang, C., Su, Y.: Smooth filtering identification based on convolutional neural networks. Multimed. Tools Appl. 1–15 (2016)
8. Kang, X., Stamm, M.C., Peng, A., Liu, K.J.R.: Robust median filtering forensics using an autoregressive model. IEEE Trans. Inf. Forensics Secur. **8**(5), 1456–1468 (2013)
9. Chen, J., Kang, X., Liu, Y., Wang, Z.J.: Median filtering forensics based on convolutional neural networks. IEEE Signal Process. Lett. **22**(3), 1849–1853 (2015)
10. Xu, J., Ling, Y., Zheng, X.: Forensic detection of Gaussian low-pass filtering in digital images. In: 2015 8th International Congress on Image and Signal Processing (CISP), pp. 819–823 (2015)
11. Liu, G., Wang, J., Lian, S., Dai, Y.: Detect image splicing with artificial blurred boundary. Math. Comput. Model. **57**(11), 2647–2659 (2013)
12. Mahdian, B., Saic, S.: Blind authentication using periodic properties of interpolation. IEEE Trans. Inf. Forensics Secur. **23**(3), 529–538 (2008)
13. Lin, M., Chen, Q., Yan, S.: Network In Network. Computer Science, Pittsburgh (2013)

14. Haykin, S., Kosko, B.: Gradient Based Learning Applied to Document Recognition. Wiley-IEEE Press, New York (2009)
15. Yang, B., Qiu, X., Hu, W., Guo, H., Song, C.: Exposing copy-move forgery based on improved SIFT descriptor. J. Internet Technol. **18**(2), 417–425 (2017)
16. Yang, B., Sun, X., Cao, E., Hu, W., Chen, X.: Convolutional neural network for smooth filtering detection. IET Image Process. (2018)

A Novel Nonlinear Multi-feature Fusion Algorithm: Multiple Kernel Multiset Integrated Canonical Correlation Analysis

Jing Yang[1(✉)], Liya Fan[1], Quansen Sun[2], and Yuhua Fan[1]

[1] Liaocheng University, Liaocheng 252059, China
yangjing860204@163.com
[2] Nanjing University of Science and Technology, Nanjing 210094, China

Abstract. Multiset integrated canonical correlation analysis (MICCA) can distinctly express the integral correlation among multi-group feature. Thus, MICCA is very powerful for multiple feature extraction. However, it is difficult to capture nonlinear relationships with the linear mapping. In order to overcome this problem, we, in this paper, propose a multi-kernel multiset integrated canonical correlation analysis (MK-MICCA) framework for subspace learning. In the MK-MICCA framework, the input data of each feature are mapped into multiple higher dimensional feature spaces by implicitly nonlinear mappings determined by different kernels. This enables MK-MICCA to uncover a variety of different geometrical structures of the original data in the feature spaces. Extensive experimental results on multiple feature database and ORL database show that MK-MICCA is very effective and obviously outperforms the single-kernel-based MICCA.

Keywords: Canonical correlation analysis · Multiple kernel learning
Multiset integrated canonical correlation analysis · Feature extraction
Feature fusion

1 Introduction

Recently, canonical correlation analysis (CCA) has become one of the important and hot research fields, which has been widely applied to image processing, image analysis, image retrieval [1], pattern recognition [2–4], computer vision [5,6], text analysis and retrieval [7,8] and other fields. CCA is a powerful statistical technique to measure the linear relationship between two multidimensional variables. It finds two linear combinations, one for each multidimensional variable, that are optimal with respect to correlations. Until now, CCA and its variants have received more and more attentions [9–12]. Despite the CCA-based

Supported by National Natural Science Foundation of China (61273251), Natural Science Foundation of Shandong Province (ZR2018BF010, ZR2016AM24) and Research Fund for the Doctoral Program (318051715).

© Springer Nature Switzerland AG 2018
X. Sun et al. (Eds.): ICCCS 2018, LNCS 11068, pp. 255–266, 2018.
https://doi.org/10.1007/978-3-030-00021-9_24

algorithms having many applications, it can cannot analyze linear relationships between more (than two) sets of variables. To remedy this problem, some related extensions, e.g., multiset canonical correlation analysis (MCCA) [13], multiset integrated canonical correlation analysis (MICCA) [14], were proposed and successfully applied into data visualization and pose estimation.

The above-mentioned work on feature extraction is purely based on original high-dimensional data rather than nonlinear multiset features. Generally, these methods are not suitable for nonlinear multiset correlation feature extraction. In order to solve this problem, Rupnik and Shawe-Taylor [15] proposed a kernel MCCA (KMCCA) by using implicitly nonlinear mappings for cross-lingual information retrieval tasks. However, in practice KMCCA must face two problems. One is how to select the types and parameters of the kernels for good performance. Another is that it can only characterize some but not all geometrical structures of the original data. Thus, it is obvious that KMCCA does not sufficiently exploit the geometrical information hidden in each view.

In the past, Refs. [16–19] have shown the necessity to consider multiple kernels rather than a single fixed kernel. Recently, a number of multi-kernel-based [20–22] dimensionality reduction methods have been successfully applied, they have shown that learning performance can be significantly enhanced if multiple kernel functions or kernel matrices are considered. By introducing the multi-kernel-learning, we, in this paper, propose a novel nonlinear dimensionality reduction algorithm, called multi-kernel multiset integrated canonical correlation analysis (MK-MICCA). In order to compare the performance of MK-MICCA, we also propose a single-kernel MICCA.

2   Background and Related Work

2.1   Multiple Kernel Learning Methods

Combination for the multiple kind of characteristics of kernel functions, can gain not only the advantages of multiple kernel functions, but also can get better mapping properties. Multiple kernel learning can serve as a kind of clever ways to interpret study results, allows the application to get a deeper understanding, and can obtain better performance than a single kernel learning. The simplest and most common compositional method for multiple kernel learning is to consider multiple linear combination of the basic kernel function synthesis.

The linear combination methods have two basic categories: unweighted sum and weighted sum. In the unweighted sum case, we can linearly parameterize the combination function:

$$k(x, y) = \sum_{m=1}^{M} k_m(x^m, y^m) \tag{1}$$

where kernel functions $k_m(x^m, y^m)$ take M feature representations of data instances. In the weighted sum case, the combination function is as follows:

$$k(x, y) = \sum_{m=1}^{M} d_m k_m(x^m, y^m) \tag{2}$$

where $d_m \geq 0$ denotes the kernel weights and $\sum_{m=1}^{M} d_m = 1$.

2.2   Multiset Canonical Correlation analysis (MCCA)

Multiset canonical correlation analysis is an important technique which can analyze linear relationships between more (than two) sets of variables. In essence, it is a generalized extension of CCA. At present, MCCA has many different forms [13]. Among them, the following model has been successfully applied to underwater target classification and signal process.

Suppose that m random vectors are $x_i \in R^{p_i}, i = 1, \cdots, m$, the set of projection directions $\{\alpha_i \in R^{p_i}\}_{i=1}^{m}$ is found to maximize the sum of pair-wise correlations between multiset canonical variables. Specifically, the optimization problem of MCCA is as follows:

$$\begin{aligned} \max \rho(\alpha_1, \alpha_2, \cdots, \alpha_m) &= \sum_{i=1}^{m} \sum_{j=1}^{m} \alpha_i^T S_{ij} \alpha_j \\ \text{s.t. } \alpha_i^T S_{ii} \alpha_i &= 1, i = 1, 2, \cdots, m \end{aligned} \tag{3}$$

where S_{ii} is within-set covariance matrix of random variable x_i, and $S_{ij}(i \neq j)$ is between-set covariance matrix between random variables x_i and x_j.

With Lagrangian multiplier method, the solution of MCCA can be equally transformed into a generalized eigenvalue problem (refer [6] for some details).

2.3   Multiset Integrated Canonical Correlation analysis (MICCA)

Multiset integrated canonical correlation analysis (MICCA) is a new correlation analysis which depicts integral relationship among multi-group variables (at least three sets of variables). MICCA is a natural extension for CCA, and it aims at finding a projection matrix for each feature space in multiple different representations of the same patterns such that multiset integrated canonical correlations can be maximized in the transformed representations.

Specifically, given m sets of zero-mean random vectors $x_i \in R^{p_i}, i = 1, \cdots, m$. MICCA computes a set of projection directions $\alpha_1, \alpha_2, \cdots, \alpha_m$, to maximize the generalized correlation among the projected variables $\alpha_1^T x_1, \alpha_2^T x_2, \cdots, \alpha_m^T x_m$, which can be formally written as

$$\rho(\alpha) = \max_{\alpha} \sqrt{1 - \frac{\det(G(\alpha_1^T x_1, \alpha_2^T x_2, \cdots, \alpha_m^T x_m))}{\|\alpha_1^T x_1\| \cdot \|\alpha_2^T x_2\| \cdots \|\alpha_m^T x_m\|}}, \tag{4}$$

where $G(\cdot)$ denotes a Gram matrix, $\det(\cdot)$ represents the determinant of a square matrix, $\|\cdot\|$ is the notation of 2-norm, and $\alpha = (\alpha_1, \alpha_2, \cdots, \alpha_m)^T$. According to [14], if we assume that $k - 1$ sets of multiset integrated canonical vectors $\{\alpha_{i1}\}_{i=1}^m, \{\alpha_{i2}\}_{i=1}^m, \cdots, \{\alpha_{i,k-1}\}_{i=1}^m$, are obtained, then the kth set of $\{\alpha_{ik}\}_{i=1}^m$ can be found by solving the following optimization problem:

$$\min \{\det(S_Y)\}$$
$$\text{s.t.} \begin{cases} \alpha_i^T S_{ii} \alpha_i = 1 \\ \alpha_{ij}^T S_{ii} \alpha_i = 0 (j = 1, 2, \cdots, k - 1) \\ \alpha_i \in R^{p_i} (i = 1, 2, \cdots, m) \end{cases} \tag{5}$$

where S_Y represents the covariance matrix of the projected variables $\alpha_1^T x_1, \alpha_2^T x_2, \cdots, \alpha_m^T x_m$, i.e.,

$$S_Y = \begin{bmatrix} \alpha_1^T S_{11} \alpha_1 & \alpha_1^T S_{12} \alpha_2 & \cdots & \alpha_1^T S_{1m} \alpha_m \\ \alpha_2^T S_{21} \alpha_1 & \alpha_2^T S_{22} \alpha_2 & \cdots & \alpha_2^T S_{2m} \alpha_m \\ \vdots & \vdots & \ddots & \vdots \\ \alpha_m^T S_{m1} \alpha_1 & \alpha_m^T S_{m2} \alpha_2 & \cdots & \alpha_m^T S_{mm} \alpha_m \end{bmatrix} \tag{6}$$

3   Kernel Multiset Integrated Canonical correlation Analysis (KMICCA)

MICCA is a linear technique in subspace learning, it is difficult to capture non-linear relationships with the linear mapping. In order to overcome this problem, we will extend the MICCA algorithm for the nonlinear separated problems by means of the kernel tricks [3,23], called kernel MICCA (KMICCA). Specifically, given m views $\{X^{(i)} \in R^{p_i \times n}\}_{i=1}^m$ from the same n images, where $X^{(i)} = (x_1^{(i)}, x_2^{(i)}, \cdots, x_n^{(i)})$ represents a data matrix of the ith feature representation containing p_i dimensional sample vectors in its column, assume there is a nonlinear mapping for each feature $X^{(i)}$, i.e.,

$$\phi_i : x^{(i)} \longmapsto \phi_i(x^{(i)})$$

which implicitly projects the original data into a higher dimensional feature space $\mathcal{F}_i$. Let $\phi_i(X^{(i)}) = (\phi_i(x_1^{(i)}), \phi_i(x_2^{(i)}), \cdots, \phi_i(x_n^{(i)}))$ denote the transformed data of the original feature $X^{(i)}$. KMICCA aims to compute a set of projection directions $\alpha_1, \alpha_2, \cdots, \alpha_m$, to maximize the multiset integrated canonical correlation among the projected variables $\alpha_1^T \phi_1(X^{(1)}), \alpha_2^T \phi_2(X^{(2)}), \cdots, \alpha_m^T \phi_m(X^{(m)})$. Then the within-set covariance matrix of the ith representation $X^{(i)}$ can be written as $S_{ii}^\phi = \phi_i(X^{(i)})\phi_i(X^{(i)})^T$, the between-set covariance matrix of two different feature sets $X^{(i)}$ and $X^{(j)}$ can be written as $S_{ij}^\phi = \phi_i(X^{(i)})\phi_j(X^{(j)})^T$. Note that we assume that $\{\phi_i(X^{(i)})\}_{i=1}^m$ have been centered. Based on the kernel tricks, the optimization problem in (5) can be written as

$$\min \{\det(S_\phi)\}$$
$$\text{s.t.} \begin{cases} \alpha_i^T S_{ij}^\phi \alpha_i = 1 \\ \alpha_{ij}^T S_{ii}^\phi \alpha_i = 0 (j = 1, 2, \cdots, k - 1) \\ \alpha_i \in R^{p_i} (i = 1, 2, \cdots, m) \end{cases} \tag{7}$$

where $S_\phi = S_\phi^T$. By the theory of reproducing kernel, let $\alpha_i = \phi_i(X^{(i)})\beta_i$ with $\beta_i \in R^n$, the problem in Eq. (7) can be reformulated as

$$\min \{\det(S_\phi)\}$$
$$\text{s.t.} \begin{cases} \beta_i^T K_i^2 \beta_i = 1 \\ \beta_{ij}^T K_i^2 \beta_i = 0 (j = 1, 2, \cdots, k-1) \\ \beta_i \in R^n (i = 1, 2, \cdots, m) \end{cases} \tag{8}$$

where $K_i = \phi_i(X^{(i)})^T \phi_i(X^{(i)})$ is the kernel Gram matrix determined by a certain kernel function. S_ϕ represents the covariance matrix of the projected variables $\alpha_1^T \phi_1(X^{(1)}), \cdots, \alpha_m^T \phi_m(X^{(m)})$, i.e.

$$S_\phi = \begin{bmatrix} \alpha_1^T S_{11}^\phi \alpha_1 & \alpha_1^T S_{12}^\phi \alpha_2 & \cdots & \alpha_1^T S_{1m}^\phi \alpha_m \\ \alpha_2^T S_{21}^\phi \alpha_1 & \alpha_2^T S_{22}^\phi \alpha_2 & \cdots & \alpha_2^T S_{2m}^\phi \alpha_m \\ \vdots & \vdots & \ddots & \vdots \\ \alpha_m^T S_{m1}^\phi \alpha_1 & \alpha_m^T S_{m2}^\phi \alpha_2 & \cdots & \alpha_m^T S_{mm}^\phi \alpha_m \end{bmatrix}$$
$$= \begin{bmatrix} \beta_1^T K_1 K_1 \beta_1 & \beta_1^T K_1 K_2 \beta_2 & \cdots & \beta_1^T K_1 K_m \beta_m \\ \beta_2^T K_2 K_1 \beta_1 & \beta_2^T K_2 K_2 \beta_2 & \cdots & \beta_2^T K_2 K_m \beta_m \\ \vdots & \vdots & \ddots & \vdots \\ \beta_m^T K_m K_1 \beta_1 & \beta_m^T K_m K_2 \beta_2 & \cdots & \beta_m^T K_m K_m \beta_m \end{bmatrix} \tag{9}$$

4 Multi-kernel Multiset Integrated Canonical correlation Analysis (MK-MICCA)

KMICCA only employs a kernel function, in essence it is a single kernel-based subspace learning methods. This makes KMICCA more difficult to discover multiple kinds of geometrical structure information of each original feature in the higher dimensional Hilbert space. On the contrary, MKL [20–22] can significantly improve the learning performance for classification tasks and has the capability of uncovering a variety of different geometrical structures of the original data. Also, MKL can help kernel-based algorithms relax the selection of kernel types and kernel parameters. Motivated by the advantages of MKL, we use the idea of MKL to build a multi-kernel multiset integrated canonical correlation analysis (MK-MICCA), where each feature set of original data are mapped into multiple high dimensional feature spaces.

4.1 Formulation of MK-MICCA Framework

Given m views $\{X^{(i)} \in R^{p_i \times n}\}_{i=1}^m$ from the same n images, where $X^{(i)} = (x_1^{(i)}, x_2^{(i)}, \cdots, x_n^{(i)})$ denotes a data matrix of the ith feature representation and p_i denotes the dimensionality of the samples, assume there are $n_i \geq 2$ nonlinear mappings for each feature $x^{(i)}$, i.e.,

$$\{\phi_j^{(i)} : x^{(i)} \longmapsto \phi_j^{(i)}(x^{(i)})\}_{j=1}^{n_i}$$

which implicitly map the original data into n_i different higher dimensional feature space. Let us denote

$$\phi_i^f(X^{(i)}) = (\phi_i^f(x_1^{(i)}), \phi_i^f(x_2^{(i)}), \cdots, \phi_i^f(x_n^{(i)})) \tag{10}$$

with

$$\phi_i^f(x_j^{(i)}) = f_i(\phi_1^{(i)}(x_j^{(i)}), \phi_2^{(i)}(x_j^{(i)}), \cdots, \phi_{n_i}^{(i)}(x_j^{(i)})) \tag{11}$$

where $f_i(\cdot)$ is an ensemble function of nonlinear mappings, $i = 1, 2, \cdots, m$, $j = 1, 2, \cdots, n$. Let α_i be the projection axis of $\phi_i^f(X^{(i)})$, then the MK-MICCA framework can be defined as

$$\min \{\det(s(\alpha_1^T \phi_1^f(X^{(1)}), \cdots, \alpha_m^T \phi_m^f(X^{(m)})))\}$$
$$\text{s.t.} \begin{cases} \alpha_i^T \phi_i^f(X^{(i)})\phi_i^f(X^{(i)})^T\alpha_i = 1 \\ \alpha_{ij}^T \phi_i^f(X^{(i)})\phi_i^f(X^{(i)})^T\alpha_i = 0 (j = 1, 2, \cdots, k-1) \\ \alpha_i \in R^{p_i} (i = 1, 2, \cdots, m) \end{cases} \tag{12}$$

where $s(\cdot)$ denotes the covariance matrix of $\{\alpha_i^T \phi_i^f(X^{(i)})\}_{i=1}^m$. Note that we assume each $\phi_i^f(X^{(i)})$ has been centered. Using the dual representation theorem, we have $\alpha_i = \phi_i^f(X^{(i)})\beta_i$. Then the optimization problem in Eq. (12) can be reformulated as

$$\min \{\det(s(\beta_1^T[\phi_1^f(X^{(1)})^T\phi_1^f(X^{(1)})], \cdots, \beta_m^T[\phi_m^f(X^{(m)})^T\phi_m^f(X^{(m)})]))\}$$
$$\text{s.t.} \begin{cases} \beta_i^T[\phi_i^f(X^{(i)})^T\phi_i^f(X^{(i)})] \cdot [\phi_i^f(X^{(i)})^T\phi_i^f(X^{(i)})]\beta_i = 1 \\ \beta_{ij}^T[\phi_i^f(X^{(i)})^T\phi_i^f(X^{(i)})] \cdot [\phi_i^f(X^{(i)})^T\phi_i^f(X^{(i)})]\beta_i = 0 \\ (j = 1, 2, \cdots, k-1) \\ \beta_i \in R^n (i = 1, 2, \cdots, m) \end{cases} \tag{13}$$

4.2   Solution of MK-MICCA Framework

To solve the optimization problem in Eq. (13), let $f_i(\phi_1^{(i)}(x_j^{(i)}), \phi_2^{(i)}(x_j^{(i)}), \cdots, \phi_{n_i}^{(i)}(x_j^{(i)})) = (\phi_1^{(i)}(x_j^{(i)})^T, \phi_2^{(i)}(x_j^{(i)})^T, \cdots, \phi_{n_i}^{(i)}(x_j^{(i)})^T)^T$, then we can define $K_k^{(i)} = \phi_k^{(i)}(X^{(i)})^T\phi_k^{(i)}(X^{(i)}) \in R^{n \times n}$ using the kernel trick, where $K_k^{(i)}$ represents the kernel matrix of the kth nonlinear mapping in the ith feature set, and $k = 1, 2, \cdots, n_i$. Then, the optimization problem in Eq. (13) can be formulated equivalently as

$$\min \{\det(S_{\phi^f})\}$$
$$\text{s.t.} \begin{cases} \beta_i^T(\sum_{k=1}^{n_i} K_k^{(i)} \sum_{t=1}^{n_i} K_t^{(i)})\beta_i = 1 \\ \beta_{ij}^T(\sum_{k=1}^{n_i} K_k^{(i)} \sum_{t=1}^{n_i} K_t^{(i)})\beta_i = 0 \\ (j = 1, 2, \cdots, k-1) \\ \beta_i \in R^n (i = 1, 2, \cdots, m) \end{cases} \tag{14}$$

Let

$$K^{(ij)} = \sum_{k=1}^{n_i} K_k^{(i)} \sum_{t=1}^{n_j} K_t^{(j)} = \sum_{k=1}^{n_i} \sum_{t=1}^{n_j} K_k^{(i)} K_t^{(j)}, \tag{15}$$

then the problem in Eq. (13) can be reformulated as

$$\begin{array}{c} \min \{\det (S_{\phi^f})\} \\ \text{s.t.} \ \begin{cases} \beta_i^T K^{(ii)} \beta_i = 1 \\ \beta_{ij}^T K^{(ii)} \beta_i = 0 (j = 1, 2, \cdots, k-1) \\ \beta_i \in R^n (i = 1, 2, \cdots, m) \end{cases} \end{array} \tag{16}$$

where $K^{(ij)} = K^{(ji)T}(i, j = 1, 2, \cdots, m)$ and

$$S_{\phi^f} = \begin{bmatrix} \beta_1^T K^{(11)} \beta_1 & \beta_1^T K^{(12)} \beta_2 & \cdots & \beta_1^T K^{(1m)} \beta_m \\ \beta_2^T K^{(21)} \beta_1 & \beta_2^T K^{(22)} \beta_2 & \cdots & \beta_2^T K^{(2m)} \beta_m \\ \vdots & \vdots & \ddots & \vdots \\ \beta_m^T K^{(m1)} \beta_1 & \beta_m^T K^{(m2)} \beta_2 & \cdots & \beta_m^T K^{(mm)} \beta_m. \end{bmatrix}$$

Obviously, $K^{(ii)}$ is a symmetric and nonnegative definite matrix. Here, we suppose that all $\{K^{(ii)}\}_{i=1}^m$ are positive definite. If $K^{(ii)}$ is not definite in some applications, a small perturbation is added into $K^{(ii)}$ to avoid its singularity according to the perturbation idea in [24]. Then, the Cholesky decomposition $K^{(ii)} = R_i R_i^T$ exists. Let $\eta_i = R_i^T \beta_i$, then the optimization problem in Eq. (16) can be formulated equivalently as

$$\begin{array}{c} \min \{\det (\tilde{S}_{\phi^f})\} \\ \text{s.t.} \ \begin{cases} \eta_i^T \eta_i = 1 \\ \eta_{ij}^T \eta_i = 0 (j = 1, 2, \cdots, k-1) \\ \eta_i \in R^n (i = 1, 2, \cdots, m) \end{cases} \end{array} \tag{17}$$

where

$$\tilde{S}_{\phi^f} = \begin{bmatrix} \eta_1^T \eta_1 & \eta_1^T \Sigma_{12} \eta_2 & \cdots & \beta_1^T \Sigma_{1m} \beta_m \\ \eta_2^T \Sigma_{21} \eta_1 & \eta_2^T \eta_2 & \cdots & \beta_2^T \Sigma_{2m} \beta_m \\ \vdots & \vdots & \ddots & \vdots \\ \eta_m^T \Sigma_{m1} \eta_1 & \eta_m^T \Sigma_{m2} \eta_2 & \cdots & \eta_m^T \eta_m. \end{bmatrix}$$

with $\Sigma_{ij} = R_i^{-1} K^{(ij)} R_j^{-T} (i \neq j)$.

In order to solve the optimization problem in (17), we approximately transform it into the following model without constraints by introducing Lagrange multipliers λ_i and $\xi_{it}(t = 0, 1, \cdots, k-1)$:

$$\max S = \sum_{i=1}^m \sum_{j=1, j \neq i}^m (\eta_i^T \Sigma_{ij} \eta_j)^2 - \sum_{i=1}^m \lambda_i (\eta_i^T \eta_i - 1) - \sum_{i=1}^m \sum_{t=0}^{k-1} \xi_{it} \eta_{it}^T \eta_i, \tag{18}$$

when $t = 0$, we assume that $\xi_{it} = 0$ and η_{it} be a zero vector.

By setting $\partial S/\partial \eta_i = 0$, we get

$$\sum_{j=1,j\neq i}^{m} (\eta_i^T \Sigma_{ij}\eta_j)\Sigma_{ij}\eta_j - \sum_{t=0}^{k-1} \xi_{it}\eta_{it} = \lambda_i\eta_i, i = 1, 2, \cdots, m. \tag{19}$$

Because Eq. (19) with the dynamic complexity is not a normal generalized eigensystem, it is difficult to obtain their analytical solutions. Thus, we give their iterative solutions based on the power-successive over-relaxation (P-SOR) algorithm [25].

It can be clearly seen that if $\eta_{1k}, \eta_{2k}, \cdots, \eta_{mk}$ are the solution vectors of the equation in Eq. (19), then they are the kth set of solutions of the optimization problem in Eq. (18). According to $\eta_{ik} = R_i^T \beta_{ik}$, we use $\beta_{ik} = R_i^{-T}\eta_{ik}$ to get the kth set of projection directions of MK-MICCA.

After obtaining d sets of projection directions $\{\beta_{i1}\}_{i=1}^m, \{\beta_{i2}\}_{i=1}^m, \cdots, \{\beta_{id}\}_{i=1}^m$ from m training sample spaces, let $W_i = (\beta_{i1}, \beta_{i2}, \cdots, \beta_{id}) \in R^{p_i \times d}$. Then, we can perform multiset feature extraction for a given feature vector $x^{(i)}$ by

$$\begin{aligned}
Y^{(i)} &= (\alpha_{i1}^T\phi_i^f(x^{(i)}), \alpha_{i2}^T\phi_i^f(x^{(i)}), \cdots, \alpha_{id}^T\phi_i^f(x^{(i)}))^T \\
&= (\beta_{i1}^T\phi_i^f(X^{(i)})^T\phi_i^f(x^{(i)}), \beta_{i2}^T\phi_i^f(X^{(i)})^T\phi_i^f(x^{(i)}), \cdots, \beta_{id}^T\phi_i^f(X^{(i)})^T\phi_i^f(x^{(i)}))^T \\
&= (\beta_{i1}, \beta_{i2}, \cdots, \beta_{id})^T\phi_i^f(X^{(i)})^T\phi_i^f(x^{(i)}) \\
&= W_i^T \sum_{j=1}^{n_i} \phi_j^{(i)}(X^{(i)})^T\phi_j^{(i)}(x^{(i)}) \\
&= W_i^T \sum_{j=1}^{n_i} K_j^{(i)}(:, x^{(i)})
\end{aligned} \tag{20}$$

where $K_j^{(i)}(:, x^{(i)}) = (k_j^{(i)}(x_1^{(i)}, x^{(i)})), \cdots, k_j^{(i)}(x_n^{(i)}, x^{(i)}))^T$ is an n-dimensional column vector and $k_j^{(i)}(\cdot, \cdot) = \phi_j^{(i)}(\cdot)^T\phi_j^{(i)}(\cdot)$ denoting the jth kernel function in the ith feature.

Alternatively, we adopt the following feature fusion strategy to fuse multiset feature components, i.e.,

$$Y_{fusion} = \sum_{i=1}^{m} Y^{(i)} = \sum_{i=1}^{m} W_i^T x^{(i)}. \tag{21}$$

5   Experiments and Analysis

In this section, in order to evaluate the proposed MK-MICCA in this paper, we systematically compare it with KMICCA on several publicly available data sets.

5.1   Kernel Function Preparation

In our experiments, in order to explain the effective of the proposed methods, we adopt three feature sets in total from the same face images and we use three kinds of kernel functions in our proposed method, as follows:

- Linear kernel: $k(x, y) = x^T y$

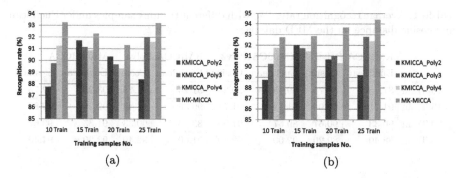

Fig. 1. Comparisons of recognition rates between proposed kernel methods with different distance measure on MFD dataset. (a) Euclidean distance, (b) Cosine distance.

- Gaussian RBF kernel: $k(x, y) = \exp(-\|x - y\|^2/2\sigma^2)$, where σ is set to the average value of all the norm distance $\|x - y\|$ as used in Ref. [26]
- Polynomial kernel: $k(x, y) = (x^T y + 1)^d$, where d is set to $l + 1, l = 1, 2, 3$.

In KMICCA, we use the above three kinds of kernel functions with the same kernel parameters, linear kernel for the first feature set, RBF kernel for the second set, and polynomial kernel for the last.

5.2 Experiments on Multiple Feature Dataset

The multiple feature dataset (MFD) [27] about handwritten numerals in the UCI is adopted for next experiments. MFD includes 10 classes handwritten numerals, i.e., 10 numbers from 0 to 9. Each class has 200 examples. Thus, the sample size is 2000 in total.

In order to verify the effectiveness of calculation, we only use three feature sets, i.e., Fou, Kar and Zer. For each feature set, we choose the first fifty samples of each class in order to form a subset, denoted as subMFD. In the subMFD, we randomly select N samples per class for training, and rest $50 - N$ samples for testing. Ten independent tests are carried out. Euclidean and cosine distance metrics are both adopted as measure criteria and NN classifier is used for final classification. Figure 1 and Table 1 shows the average recognition rates with different training samples.

From Fig. 1, we can see that the proposed MK-MICCA method obviously outperforms KMICCA, no matter how many training samples per class are used. In Table 1, the maximal average recognition rates of MK-MICCA with 25 training samples are, respectively, up to 93.20% and 94.4%, and exceed the corresponding those of KMICCA 4.8% and 5.2%. On the whole, MK-MICCA achieves better recognition rates than KMICCA. These results demonstrate MK-MICCA is a powerful method for nonlinear multi-view learning.

Table 1. Average recognition rates (%) with different training samples under Euclidean and cosine distance on the MFD database

	KMICCA_Poly2		KMICCA_Poly3		KMICCA_Poly4		MK-MICCA	
	Euclidean	Cosine	Euclidean	Cosine	Euclidean	Cosine	Euclidean	Cosine
10 Train	87.75	88.75	89.75	90.25	91.25	91.75	93.25	92.75
15 Train	91.71	92.00	91.14	91.71	90.86	91.43	92.29	92.86
20 Train	90.33	90.67	89.67	91.00	89.33	90.33	91.33	93.67
25 Train	88.40	89.20	92.00	92.80	91.60	92.40	93.20	94.40

5.3   Experiments on the ORL Dataset

The ORL database [28] has 400 images, which consists of 10 images of 40 individuals. All the images were taken against a dark homogeneous background, with slightly varying lighting, facial expressions (open/closed eyes, smiling/nonsmiling), and facial details (glasses/noglasses). The individuals are in up-right, frontal positions with tolerance for some side movement. All the images are grayscale and normalized with a resolution of 112×92. Some images of one person are shown in Fig. 2.

Fig. 2. Images of one person in ORL.

Since orthonormal wavelet transforms can retain the important information of original object images, and the low-frequency sub-images include more shape information in contrast with high-frequency sub-images [2], we make use of wavelet transforms to extract three sets of features from original images. In the following experiments, we perform Coiflets, Daubechies and Symlets orthonormal wavelet transforms to obtain three sets of low-frequency sub-images, respectively. To avoid the singularity of within-set covariance matrices, the K-L transform is used to reduce their dimensions to 150, 150, and 150, respectively. In next experiment, we randomly choose l images (l is 5, 6) of each person for training and the remaining (10-l) for testing. Ten-tests are performed to examine the recognition performances of each algorithm. The average recognition rates corresponding to each method under NN classifier with Euclidean distance and cosine distance are shown in Table 2.

From Table 2, it can be seen that the proposed MK-MICCA method superior to KMICCA, no matter what distance metric is used. Its maximal recognition rate is up to 97.94%, and beyond that of KMICCA 2.85%. This further demonstrates MK-MICCA is a powerful technique for nonlinear feature extraction and classification tasks.

Table 2. Average recognition rates (%) with 5 and 6 training samples under Euclidean and cosine distance on the ORL database

	KMICCA_Poly2		KMICCA_Poly3		KMICCA_Poly4		MK-MICCA	
	5 Train	6 Train	5 Train	6 Train	5 Train	6 Train	5 Train	6 Train
Euclidean	96.28	95.62	95.94	96.25	96.00	95.18	96.50	96.88
Cosine	95.45	96.25	95.50	95.09	96.35	95.63	96.73	97.94

6 Conclusion

In this paper, we propose a multi-kernel learning version of MICCA, called multi-kernel multiset integrated canonical correlation analysis (MK-MICCA). The proposed method not only can uncover a variety of different geometrical structures of the original data, but also can relax the selection of kernel types and kernel parameters. The experiments are conducted on multiple feature database and ORL database, and the experiment results demonstrate that the proposed method MK-MICCA outperforms single-kernel MICCA. As a new nonlinear dimensionality reduction technique, MK-MICCA still has some aspects which deserve further study. In essence, MK-MICCA is an unsupervised subspace learning method. From the viewpoint of classification, the supervised information should be introduced into the proposed algorithm. This is a problem deserving further investigation.

References

1. Hardoon, D.R., Szedmak, S., Shawe-Taylor, J.: Canonical correlation analysis: an overview with application to learning methods. Neural Comput. **16**, 2639–2664 (2004)
2. Sun, Q.-S., Zeng, S.-G., Liu, Y., Heng, P.-A., Xia, D.-S.: A new method of feature fusion and its application in image recognition. Pattern Recognit. **38**, 2437–2448 (2005)
3. Yuan, Y.H., et al.: Multiview correlation feature learning with multiple kernels. In: He, X., et al. (eds.) IScIDE 2015. LNCS, vol. 9243, pp. 518–528. Springer, Cham (2015). https://doi.org/10.1007/978-3-319-23862-3_51
4. Hou, S.-D., Sun, Q.-S., Xia, D.-S.: Supervised locality preserving canonical correlation analysis algorithm. Pattern Recognit. Artif. Intell. **25**(1), 143–149 (2012)
5. Melzer, T., Reiter, M., Bischof, H.: Appearance models based on kernel canonical correlation analysis. Pattern Recognit. **36**, 1961–1971 (2003)
6. Kidron, E., Schechner, Y.Y., Elad, M.: Pixels that Sound. IEEE Proc. Comput. Vis. Pattern Recognit. **1**, 88–95 (2005)
7. Fortuna, B.: Kernel canonical correlation analysis with applications. In: SIKDD 2004 at Multiconference IS 2004, Ljubljana, Slovenia, pp. 12–15, October 2004
8. Shawe-Taylor, J., Cristianini, N.: Kernel Methods for Pattern Analysis. Cambridge Press, Cambridge (2004)
9. Sun, Q.-S., Liu, Z.-D., Heng, P.-A., Xia, D.-S.: A theorem on the generalized canonical projective vectors. Pattern Recognit. **38**, 449–452 (2005)

10. Sun, T., Chen, S., Yang, J., Shi, P.: A novel method of combined feature extraction for recognition. In: Eighth IEEE International Conference on Data Mining, ICDM08, pp. 1043–1048. IEEE (2008)
11. Sun, T., Chen, S.: Locality preserving CCA with applications to data visualization and pose estimation. Image Vis. Comput. **25**, 531–543 (2007)
12. Peng, Y., Zhang, D., Zhang, J.: A new canonical correlation analysis algorithm with local discrimination. Neural Process. Lett. **31**, 1–15 (2010)
13. Kettenring, J.R.: Canonical analysis of several sets of variables. Biometrika **58**(3), 433–451 (1971)
14. Yuan, Y.-H., Sun, Q.-S., Zhou, Q., Xia, D.-S.: A novel multiset integrated canonical correlation analysis framework and its application in feature fusion. Pattern Recognit. **44**, 1031–1040 (2011)
15. Rupnik, J., Shawe-Taylor, J.: Multi-view canonical correlation analysis. In: Proceedings of Conference on Data Mining and Data Warehouses (2010). http://ailab. ijs.si/dunja/SiKDD2010/Papers/RupnikFinal.pdf
16. Sonnenburg, S., Rätsch, G., Schäfer, C., Schölkopf, B.: Large scale multiple kernel learning. J. Mach. Learn. Res. **7**, 1531–1565 (2006)
17. Rakotomamonjy, A., Bach, F., Canu, S., Grandvalet, Y.: More efficiency in multiple kernel learning. In: Proceedings of the 24th International Conference on Machine Learning, pp. 775–782 (2007)
18. Xu, X., Tsang, I.W., Xu, D.: Soft margin multiple kernel learning. IEEE Trans. Neural Netw. Learn. Syst. **24**(5), 749–761 (2013)
19. Zhang, G.Q., Sun, H., Xia, G., Sun, Q.: Multiple kernel sparse representation based orthogonal discriminative projection and its cost-sensitive extension. IEEE Trans. Image Process. **25**(9), 4271–4285 (2016)
20. Kim, S.J., Magnani, A., Boyd, S.: Optimal kernel selection in kernel fisher discriminant analysis. In: Proceedings of the 23rd International Conference on Machine Learning, pp. 465–472 (2006)
21. Yan, F., Kittler, J., Mikolajczyk, K., Tahir, A.: Nonsparse multiple kernel fisher discriminant analysis. J. Mach. Learn. Res. **13**(1), 607–642 (2012)
22. Lin, Y.Y., Liu, T.L., Fuh, C.S.: Multiple kernel learning for dimensionality reduction. IEEE Trans. Pattern Anal. Mach. Intell. **33**(6), 1147–1160 (2011)
23. Gan, H.: Multi-class semi-supervised kernel minimum squared error for face recognition. Opt. Int. J. Light. Electron Opt. **126**(23), 3496–3500 (2015)
24. Sun, Q.-S.: Research on Feature Extraction and Image Recognition Based on Correlation Projection Analysis, Ph.D. Dissertation, Nanjing University of Science and Technology, Nanjing (2006)
25. Sun, J.: An algorithm for the solution of multi-parameter eigenvalue problems (II). J. Comput. Math. **4**, 354–363 (1986)
26. Wang, Z., Chen, S., Sun, T.: MultiK-MHKS: a novel multiple kernel learning algorithm. IEEE Trans. Pattern Anal. Mach. Intell. **30**(2), 348–353 (2008)
27. Jain, A.K., Duin, R.P.W., Mao, J.: Statistical pattern recognition: a review. IEEE Trans. Pattern Anal. Mach. Intell. **22**(1), 4–37 (2000)
28. Li, B., Huo, G.: Face recognition using locality sensitive histograms of oriented gradients. Opt. Int. J. Light. Electron Opt. **127**(6), 3489–3494 (2016)

A Novel Watermark-Based Access Control Model for Digital Imagines

Yan Chen, Wenting Jiang$^{(\boxtimes)}$, and Zhongmiao Kang

Guangdong Power Grid Corporation, Guangzhou 510000, China
jiangwenting@gddd.csg.cn

Abstract. With the development of digital image processing and big data analysis, there exist massive digital images that can be obtained by ordinary online users. However, regarding to the volume of data and the lack of access control embedded within digital images, some images may impose risks of leakage and exposure. Especially, some images need to keep secret totally or at least only can be accessed partially. Those are not be classified and protected with a subtle manner or accessed by fine-grained privileges. In addition, recent most access control strategies separate control lists from accessed objects, so that the execution of access control relies on the networking links to remote servers. Sometimes remote servers may be available, thus the control will be hindered. Moreover, it is not easy to share and distribute a large volume of data together with their access control policies on different servers. In this paper, we propose a novel access control model based on invisible watermarks, where embed access control policies. This model realizes the marriage of accessing objects and access control strategies, and can be delivered together with big data objects such as digital images.

Keywords: Access control · Watermark · Digital imagine
Big data · Tree diagrams networking

1 Introduction

Access control manages the access of objects on computer systems, networks, web servers, and any computing units. The access control system defends against illegal access, and determines the appropriate level of authority for accessors which are identified by the authority system. As a consequence of the popularity of Internet and big data, massive data is distributed over networks and stored in client equipments. Those data downloaded from internet, and shared to public. Moreover, it is envisioned that the speed of data increasing has far exceeded the management workloads including operation rules and system configurations. It is hard to ensure the information breach of sensitive big data during data distribution and publication.

The current access control strategies of digital imagines imposes new challenges in big data era. It mainly confronts two constraints: (1) Access control

© Springer Nature Switzerland AG 2018
X. Sun et al. (Eds.): ICCCS 2018, LNCS 11068, pp. 267–276, 2018.
https://doi.org/10.1007/978-3-030-00021-9_25

strategy targets for entire image area, not partially. However, some images may be required to protected partially. (2) The data can be accessed only when remote servers are available, which relies on the availability of networking links and the workload of policy conformation servers. However, in big data scenarios the accessing workload on servers may lead to large accessing delay. More specifically, current access control mechanism imposes several challenges as follows:

1. The security levels of information and regions within a image are not identical some time, thus the simple access control strategy is not fine-grained and may cause information disclosure for somewhere.
2. Accessing data by relying one remote servers or available networks damages the accessing convenience. In addition, it is difficult to guarantee someone to leak the data to others once after he gains the accessing privilege.

Furthermore, storing access control policies on servers will add the burdens of servers. The servers provide the services of downloading, browsing images, and implementing access control as well. Each time visitors request the view of images, it has to fetch access control policies on serves at first. Moreover, once images have totally downloaded from servers and stored on a client equipment, these images will be out of the control of policy servers.

Base on above observations and analysis, we propose to design a new access control model that has following advantages:

1. Access control strategies do not solely rely on servers. Thus, the burdens of servers can be decreased.
2. Embed access control strategies with accessing objects (e.g., images). Therefore, it can take effect even though servers are not available.
3. Elaborate the differentiation of access control policies for a single image, even to any defined area within an image.
4. The protected data cannot be transmitted to others for accessing even if access privileges are granted.
5. The traceability of data downloading, distribution, and publication can be recorded.

The major contributions of this paper are listed as follows:

1. We propose a watermark-based access control model.
2. Thanks to the advantages of efficiency, convenience, high capacity and easy construction of QR code, we suggest to choose it as a watermark.
3. We present design approaches on keys for different security levels.
4. We propose an architecture of data security in digital imagines.

The rest of the paper is organized as follows. Section 2 surveys related work. Section 3 formulates the research basis and challenges, and Sect. 4 elaborates on the proposed models. Extensive analysis of the proposed scheme is presented in Sect. 5 and we conclude the paper in Sect. 6.

2   Related Work

The topic of watermarks has been explored for decades. Due to powerful softwares and personal computers, there emerges considerable unauthorized copying and distributing of intellectual properties, such as e-books, videos, and digital images. To solve this problem, watermarks are usually used to verify and protect the copyrights [1]. Scientists have already propose kinds of methods to manufacture watermarks aiming at verification and authentication [2,3]. However, there exists rear kinds of watermark to be designed for access control.

The protection of video copyrights is paid considerable attentions. In order to avoid the distribution of films that are pirated by camcorders in movie theaters, DMR schemes are consist of a variety of watermarks [4,5]. For instances, they insert the access control strategy into watermarks to restrict which video players can read the video. However, the video that is recorded by legal video players can still be played and escaped from the accessing control [6]. An alternative pattern of video access control based on contents is proposed [7]. Yet, there are mere access control strategies of digital images, and none of them is based on watermarks.

In recent years, quick response code is popular due to its efficiency and security. It is widely used in mobile phones, e.g., applications of instance messaging, and user login and mobil payment. Many researchers propose to implement various one-time password schemes using smart cards, time-synchronized token or short message service in order to reduce the risk of tampering and maintenance cost. These schemes are impractical owing to the far from ubiquitous hardware devices or the infrastructure requirements. Dramatically, QR code is such an excellent method to realize it [8]. Regarding QR code is a kind of two-dimension matrix code, which has high encryption and decryption speed. It can not only store large information, but also has the error-correction ability [9]. In addition, QR code has high recognition rate, and there are massive algorithm libraries to invoke [10,11]. For these reasons, we choose QR code for the case study of our model.

Fig. 1. Existing traditional access control model.

3   Problem Formulation

3.1   System Model

Figure 1 depicts existing most accessing model. The access control patterns existing in digital images (e.g., geographic image), include publishers, visitors, digital imagines and access control strategy.

All of the existing access control patterns are directed to a whole picture, thus the publisher cannot limit visitors to view only some parts of a picture. Moreover, the digital imagines are classified by different kind of information, such as map, transportation map, city planning diagram, and geologic map. Thus, the visitors cannot view mixed information in a graph.

In addition, access control strategies are stored at servers currently; therefore, access control strategies are not combined with objects to be visited, and the execution of access control cannot complete without servers. Every time when visitors ask servers for some data, the servers need to look up access control strategies. According to the access control policies, the servers decide what data can be provided to visitors.

Most existing access control patterns are aimed at an entire picture, however some parts of the picture cannot be visited by all visitors. Thus, if the attacker attains massive images, it is very likely to gain some information which is not belong to his security level. Meanwhile, because different kinds of information cannot be mixed in a picture, it is not convenient for visitors to look over various categories of information in a picture comparably.

The existing access control patterns rely on servers, and access control policies are stored in servers. Therefore, every time clients want to access the image, they have to link to servers at first to obtain the access control patterns.

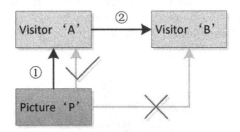

Fig. 2. An attack aims at existing traditional access control patterns that rely on servers.

Figure 2 depicts a possible attack for existing access control model. Given a visitor 'A' with a higher security level, and a visitor 'B' with a lower security level, and a picture 'P' which regulated by the privilege ranges of 'A', but cannot be accessed by 'B'. When the visitor 'A' obtains the picture 'P', she can sends this picture to 'B'; hence the visitor 'B' can fully view this picture. In this situation, visitor 'B' accesses image information out of his privileges.

There is another method to realize access control via servers in local area networks. However, the drawback of this pattern is similar. That is, this method can not support fine-grained access control for a partial image.

4 Proposed Model

Some requirements for the model are listed as follows:

- Digital images can only be viewed via particular client tool such as an image browser that is integrated watermark parser and policies conformation.
- Digital images with watermark can only be downloaded from servers who embeds accessing policy into images by watermarks.
- The format of the watermark usually is aware by corresponding client tools such as browsers.
- The context of the watermark can be recognized by particular client tools such as browsers.
- Accessors should register on servers at first, and they usually login into client tools such as browsers before view images.
- The image browser usually can transparently encrypt images. When visitors do not view the image by designated image browser, the image is encrypted by the browser and stored locally.

4.1 Basic Model

1. Data publishers process data.
    (1) Data publishers formulate access control strategy: <the role of visitors, key, areas can be visited>. For instance, <visitorA, keyA, areaA>.
    (2) Insert access control strategy into QR code.
    (3) Data publishers encrypt sensitive area of digital images.
        - The keys should be classified into different grades based on the roles of visitors. Each role of visitors represents a grade and has got a key.
        - The higher level of key is used to encrypt securer data.
        - The process of encryption:
            • Use the key of highest level first, and decrease in turn.
            • The key of lower level is the child-key of the key of higher level. If the visitor has the key of higher level, he can calculate the key of lower level.
            • childkey = hash(fatherkey)
2. Data publishers put out the data on the internet, and the data can be downloaded and relayed by visitors.
3. Accessors register on servers, and gain the users' ID. The ID defines the role of visitors.
4. Accessors download the data from the servers.
5. Accessors view the digital imagines via particular client tools such image browsers.

(1) Accessors show their ID to log in the picture browser. For instance, visitorA.

(2) The picture browser extracts QR code, gaining access control strategy: <visitorA, keyA, areaA>.
The key which is used to encrypt QR code is stored in the picture browser to ensure that only particular picture browser can read the context of QR code.

(3) Accessors gain the accessible area regarding on the access control strategy. The process of decryption:
   - Gain the key corresponding to the grade of visitor.
   - Decrypt the data of securest level first, and decrease in turn.
   - Calculate child-key: childkey = hash(fatherkey).

6. Accessors close images, and image browsers encrypt data automatically.

4.2   Enhanced Model

Based on the basic model for illustrating our motivation, we add the authentication of data publishers in the enhanced model to ensure the reality and reliability of data. Furthermore, some accessors own the privilege of writing. If the data is published after modified, the name and signature of modifier should be added into watermarks.

1. Data publishers process data.
   (1) Data publishers formulate the access control strategy:<the role of visitors, writing privilege, key, areas can be visited, the name of data publisher, the signature of data publisher>.
   For instance, <visitorA, 0, keyA, area, publisher1, signature1>.
      - Writing privilege is represented by 0 and 1. 1 represents the visitor have writing privilege, and vice versa.
      - Data publishers sign using their private key.
   (2) Insert access control strategy into QR code.
   (3) Data publishers encrypt sensitive area of digital imagines.
      - The keys should be classified into different grades based on the roles of visitors. Each role of visitors represents a grade and has got a key.
      - The higher level of key is used to encrypt securer data.
      - The process of encryption:
         • Use the key of highest level first, and decrease in turn.
         • The key of lower level is the child-key of the key of higher level. If the visitor has the key of higher level, he can calculate the key of lower level.
         • childkey = hash(fatherkey)

2. Data publishers put out the data on the internet, and the data can be downloaded and relayed by accessors.

3. Accessors register on servers, and gain the users' ID. The ID defines the role of accessors.

4. Accessors download the data from servers.
5. Accessors view the digital imagines via particular client tools such as image browsers.
(1) Accessors show their ID to log in image browsers. For instance, visitorA.
(2) The image browser extracts QR code, gaining access control strategy: <visitorA, 0, keyA, area, publisher1, signature1>.
The key which is used to encrypt QR code is stored in the picture browser to ensure that only particular picture browser can read the context of QR code.
(3) The image browser verifies the signature of data publishers using the public keys.
(4) Accessors gain the accessible area regarding on the access control strategy. The process of decryption:
   – Gain the key corresponding to the grade of accessors.
   – Decrypt the data of securest level first, and decrease in turn.
   – Calculate child-key: childkey = hash(fatherkey).
6. Accessors modify pictures.
7. The image browser adds the name and signature of modifiers into QR code.
8. Accessors close the pictures, and the image browser encrypt data automatically.

4.3 Advanced Model

Based on the enhanced model, we classify information in digital images according to the security level of information in the advanced model. Digital images can be classified not only by regions, but also by contexts. In a certain area, the image can be displayed different kinds of information regarding on different accessors. Thanks to this design, access control strategies can be more elaborate, fine-grained, and subtle. It is more convenient for accessors to access various kinds of information in a specific image.

In this model, we take geological digital images as an example, and propose a method for dividing information with access control strategy.

The Method of Dividing Information. If we put access control strategies of each information into watermarks, the data size of watermark will be extremely large. Therefore, we should divide information into several levels and set up an index structure. The divided information levels is corresponding to the roles of accessor.

The structure of information dividing and access control is depicted in Fig. 3.

1. Divide information into different types.
   – Except for the outline of maps in geological digital imagines, there are massive kinds of information. The information can be classified by uses, such as land resource information, traffic information, urban planning information, weather information and so on. Give each piece of information a tab to represent its type.

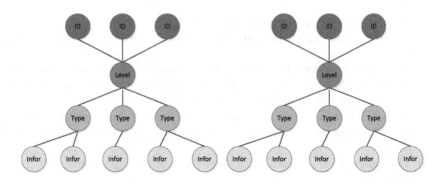

Fig. 3. The structure of access control.

- When the information is added into the images, data publishers should divide information into different types and append tabs to pieces of information.
- A piece of information can belong to different types.
2. Divide information types into different security levels.
   - Divide the types of information in geological digital images into different security levels according to security levels of accessor.
   - Roles of accessors can be classified by occupations, such as the geologist, the urban planner, staff at the meteorology office, undergraduate students, the organizations of oil and gas resources exploitation and utilization, and so on, and giving each role a tab.
   - The security level of some roles are similar, each information level can include some different roles of accessors.
3. Set up tree index structure.
   The context of pictures: A level→some types of information→pieces of information
4. Set up graph access control strategy.
   Access control strategy: A role of accessor → A level → some types of information →pieces of information

Information Index List

1. Set up the list of information and types - CL (Context List).
   - Infori(i=1,2,. . . ,n,n∈N*)
     represents information, Typei(i=1,2,. . . ,n,n∈N*) represents the type of information.
   - Giving the set of information I={Infor1,Infor1, Infor2,. . . ,Infori}, and the set of types T={Type1,Type2,Type3,. . . ,TYPEi}.
   - Put the corresponding relations into Context List.
2. Set up the list of security levels and information types—LL(Level List).

- Leveli(i=1,2,...,n,n∈N*)   represents security levels, Typei(i =1,2,...,n,n∈N*) represents the type of information.
- Giving the set of security levels L={Level1,Level1, Level2,...,Leveli}, and the set of types T={Type1,Type2,Type3,...,TYPEi}.
- Put the corresponding relations into Level List.

5 Security Analysis

The access control strategy in the watermark cannot be modified and extracted arbitrarily, because only the specific image browser possesses the key to decrypt the QR code.

The protected data cannot be modified arbitrarily. We add writing permission into access control strategy, and the image browser can put the names of modifiers into the watermark; thus, images cannot be modified and republished illegally.

Images cannot be viewed illegally regarding on relaying. Our model adds transparent encryption into the image browser, which means when accessors close the picture, the image browser will encrypt it automatically; therefore, accessors of higher level privilege cannot transmit decrypted pictures to accessors of lower level privilege.

This model avoids the information breach according to flexible access control strategies. We elaborate the access control strategies in digital images from aiming at a whole image instead of at sacrificially partial regions and information.

The model can confirm the source of data, owing to the signatures of data publishers are added into the watermark.

We use hash function to set up the relationship between the key of high level and the key of low level. It is impossible to calculate the previous results using the current results. Hence, attackers cannot gain the key of high level by using the key of low level.

6 Conclusion

In this paper, we propose a watermark-based access control model. We integrate access control strategies within watermarks, and embed the watermark into accessing objects such as images. Thus, accessing control can be executed without servers. Moreover, because of fine-grained access control strategies, privilege conformations for accessing data can be more complicated and customized. Especially, even for different areas in a singe image, the privileges can be distinct via this model. In addition, thanks to the signatures of data publishers are added into watermark, the sources of data can be traced. Compared to the existing traditional method that access control strategies are stored on servers, the proposed model makes it possible to let accessors view images without accessing servers, so as to ease the burden of the servers.

Acknowledgement. This work was supported by the science and technology project of Guangdong Power Grid Co., Ltd, (036000KK52170002).

References

1. Wang, Y., Doherty, J.F., Dyck, R.E.V.: A wavelet-based watermarking algorithm for ownership verification of digital images. IEEE Trans. Image Process. **11**(2), 77–88 (2002). https://doi.org/10.1109/83.982816
2. Wong, P.W.: A public key watermark for image verification and authentication. In: Proceedings 1998 International Conference on Image Processing, ICIP98 (Cat. No.98CB36269), vol. 1, pp. 455–459 (1998). https://doi.org/10.1109/ICIP.1998.723526
3. Wolfgang, R.B., Delp, E.J.: A watermark for digital images. In: Proceedings of 3rd IEEE International Conference on Image Processing, vol. 3, pp. 219–222 (1996). https://doi.org/10.1109/ICIP.1996.560423
4. Lin, E.I., Eskicioglu, A.M., Lagendijk, R.L., Delp, E.J.: Advances in digital video content protection. Proc. IEEE **93**(1), 171–183 (2005)
5. Gholve, N., Sutar, S., Dhokey, S., Hande, S.: Cascaded algorithm: DWT-DCT-SVD in watermarking. Digit. Image Process. **3**(13), 814–819 (2011)
6. Pickering, M., Coria, L.E., Nasiopoulos, P.: A novel blind video watermarking scheme for access control using complex wavelets. In: 2007 Digest of Technical Papers International Conference on Consumer Electronics, pp. 1–2 (2007). https://doi.org/10.1109/ICCE.2007.341545
7. Coria, L., Nasiopoulos, P., Ward, R., Pickering, M.: An access control video watermarking method that is robust to geometric distortions. In: 2007 2nd International Conference on Digital Information Management, vol. 1, pp. 460–465 (2007). https://doi.org/10.1109/ICDIM.2007.4444266
8. Liao, K.C., Lee, W.H., Sung, M.H., Lin, T.C.: A one-time password scheme with QR-code based on mobile phone. In: 2009 Fifth International Joint Conference on INC, IMS and IDC, pp. 2069–2071 (2009). https://doi.org/10.1109/NCM.2009.324
9. Kao, Y.W., Luo, G.H., Lin, H.T., Huang, Y.K., Yuan, S.M.: Physical access control based on QR code. In: 2011 International Conference on Cyber-Enabled Distributed Computing and Knowledge Discovery, pp. 285–288 (2011). https://doi.org/10.1109/CyberC.2011.55
10. Liu, Y., Liu, M.: Automatic recognition algorithm of quick response code based on embedded system. In:: Sixth International Conference on Intelligent Systems Design and Applications, vol. 2, pp. 783–788 (2006). https://doi.org/10.1109/ISDA.2006.253712
11. Melgar, M.E.V., Zaghetto, A., Macchiavello, B., Nascimento, A.C.A.: CQR codes: colored quick-response codes. In: 2012 IEEE Second International Conference on Consumer Electronics - Berlin (ICCE-Berlin), pp. 321–325 (2012). https://doi.org/10.1109/ICCE-Berlin.2012.6336526

A Recommender for Personalized Travel Itineraries

Yajie Gu[(✉)], Jing Zhou, Hanwen Feng, Anying Chen, and Shouxun Liu

School of Computer Science,
Communication University of China, Beijing 100024, China
gu_yj@cuc.edu.cn

Abstract. Typically, people would visit travel websites such as tripadvisor.com, mafengwo.cn, or ctrip.com when planning for their next trip. The lowest airfare, the best hotels, and great attractions can be found on these websites based on requirements provided by users. Millions of traveler reviews, photos, and maps, are also available. With all this information, it may still be time-consuming for users to work out a travel plan, which involves section of attractions from a huge candidate list, and more importantly, an itinerary that guides their daily activities. We therefore proposed a recommendation technique that facilitates the creation of personalized travel plans. Using a tag-based mapping algorithm, we create a list of candidate attractions that best match with the user favorite spots. An itinerary containing attractions that are most appealing to users will be derived from the candidate list and we refer to this kind of itinerary as MAI. Meanwhile, by applying K-Means clustering to the list of candidate attractions according to their geographical location, we will be able to produce the shortest itinerary (SI) and the itinerary with the highest performance/price ratio (MEI). A series of experiments have been carried out to help evaluation of our recommendation technique and the results demonstrate that our personalized recommender for travel planning can provide a better and more detailed travel plan that satisfies users with various requirements.

Keywords: Clustering · Similarity · Tag-based recommendation
Travel itinerary planning

1 Introduction

With the rapid development of tourism, various travel websites have emerged, such as tripadvisior.com[1] and ctrip.com[2]. Information on millions of airfares, hotels, and travel reviews can be found on these websites and the volume of such information scales exponentially. So it is time-consuming for one to choose information of interest from these websites when planning for the next trip.

---

[1] http://www.tripadvisor.com.
[2] http://www.ctrip.com.

© Springer Nature Switzerland AG 2018
X. Sun et al. (Eds.): ICCCS 2018, LNCS 11068, pp. 277–288, 2018.
https://doi.org/10.1007/978-3-030-00021-9_26

Meanwhile, personalized recommendation systems have achieved wide adoption in E-commerce, entertainment, content, and etc. They can recommend items according to a user's history behaviors, such as amazon.com. However, it is typically difficult for travel websites to obtain user history records or user travel plan in the past. Furthermore, few can satisfy users by providing an itinerary that is intended to guide their daily activities.

Since it is hard to find out a user's history travel routes, some of the previous studies focused on geotagged photos published online by users and treated these photos as part of the user's travel history. Yu et al. utilized data collected from LBSNs (Location-based Social Networks) and determined users' desirable destinations using collaborative filtering, thus eventually generating travel packages containing multiple points of interest [14]. Cai et al. proposed an itinerary recommender system with semantic trajectory pattern mining from geo-tagged photos, considering spatio-temporal, spatial semantics dimensions, and etc. to customize user requests [1]. Kurashima et al. [5] obtained user preferences and built a user behavior model based on those geotagged photos, and then predicted the sites that they would visit. Vu et al. [13] used P-DBSCAN (Parallel Density-based spatial clustering of applications with noise) to cluster the geotagged photos published on flick.com so as to discover the user's travel model of interest. Lee et al. [6] applied clustering algorithms and association rules , and focused on the relationship between photos and attractions. Kalogerakis et al. [4] assumed the relationship between geotagged photos and user's travel routes, and proposed that time be a reference factor to improve the accuracy of calculating user's history travel route. Shi et al. [11] proposed a personalized recommendation system, based on user's geotagging preferences, that carried out clustering in response to the similarity between user's geotagging.

All the aforementioned studies are based on geotagged photos published online. Hence, itinerary planners would be able to obtain a user's history travel routes by using these photos and then recommend points of interest and routes of interest to users. We propose a recommender that utilizes a tag-based mapping algorithm to create a list of candidate attractions that best match user's preferences and K-Means clustering is applied to help generate the list of candidate attractions according to their geographical location. Finally, we provide travel itineraries of three kinds, MAI (the Most Appealing Itinerary), SI (the Shortest Itinerary), and MEI (the Most Effective Itinerary), from which users are free to select.

The remainder of the paper is organized as follows. In Sect. 2, we examine related techniques, including the tag-based mapping algorithm and K-Means clustering algorithm. This is followed by Sect. 3 in which we propose an itinerary recommender that uses three methods to obtain desirable hotels, points of interest, and route planning, respectively. We carried out a series of experiments on a prototype of the proposed itinerary recommender and reports the experimental results and our analysis in Sect. 4. Section 5 concludes the paper and identifies our future work.

2 Related Work

2.1 Tag-Based Recommendation Algorithms

Tagging is a means in which keywords are used to cluster and organize similar resources. Being increasingly used in various networks, tags are seen as a potential source of user interest, preferences, and user profile construction [2]. Social networks and information-pushing websites prompt users to select the tags that they are interested in right after their registration. In some extent this helps alleviate the cold start problem for recommender systems. Users tag an item when they develop an interest in it. These tags serve as resources for describing such items. Others can also retrieve the item through its tag [8]. By calculating the similarity between user tags, recommender systems can predict the potential rating that a user would give to items, thus eventually being able to recommend the top-N items to her [9]. If we need to calculate the tag similarity between user A and user B, we need to use the cosine similarity equation [9]:

$$Sim(T_{A\to i}, T_{B\to i}) = \frac{T_{A\to i} \cdot T_{B\to i}}{|T_{A\to i}| \cdot |T_{B\to i}|} \tag{1}$$

where $T_{A\to i}$ is the tag vector of the tag i from user A, $T_{B\to i}$ is the tag vector of the tag i from user B. The similarity of a group of users is derived from the similarity of their tags:

$$Sim(A, B) = \frac{1}{2n} \sum_{i=1}^{n} (Sim(T_{A\to i}, T_{B\to i}) + 1) \tag{2}$$

where n indicates that user A and user B have n tags in common. Having calculated the similarity between users, the recommendation system can predict the ratings for items that the users may have never commented on. Suppose the system is going to predict the rating of user A for item X:

$$pre\_score(A, X) = \frac{\sum_{i=1}^{n} Sim(A, B_i) * score(B_i, X)}{\sum_{i=1}^{n} Sim(A, B_i)} \tag{3}$$

where i represent the number of remaining users, B_i is the ith user, and $score(B_i, X)$ denotes the ratings that user B_i gives to item X. In Eq. 3, the ratings of item X by other users, e.g. B_i in this case, is weighted by the similarity between user B_i and user A.

Finally, the recommendation system can select top-N items with the highest ratings and recommend them to user A.

2.2 The K-Means Clustering Algorithm

Clustering is an unsupervised method of classification, aiming to classify similar objects (usually behavior vectors or points in a multi-dimensional space) in the same cluster [3]. The partition-based clustering algorithm and density-based clustering algorithm are the two most popular clustering algorithms [6].

The partition-based clustering algorithm divides a dataset S into user-specified k clusters. The K-means clustering algorithm [7] is the most popular one in the partition-based clustering algorithm because of its simplicity and efficient computation. Meanwhile, K-Means clustering is a common clustering algorithm that uses the error square as a criterion. The sum of square error (SSE) of each data object and the center point of the cluster is typically used to evaluate the performance of the K-means clustering algorithm and it indicates the quality of function fitting. In n-dimensional space, the Euclidean distance equation [12] is adopted to calculate the distance.

The sum of square error is calculated as follows:

$$SSE = \sum_{i=1}^{k} \sum_{X \in C_i} \| X - \bar{X}_l \|^2 \tag{4}$$

where C_i is the ith cluster and $\bar{X}_l$ is the center point of the X_i cluster. Also, $\bar{X}_l$ denotes the mean of all the data objects in the X_i cluster.

In traditional K-Means Clustering Algorithm, the initial number of clusters k is difficult to determine, and different initial cluster center points may lead to completely different results [3]. Hence, we resort to another clustering algorithm that couples the divisive clustering with K-Means clustering [15]. In the first place, we use divisive clustering to obtain k center points and the K-Means clustering is applied. In addition, we use the Manhattan distance equation [12] to calculate the distance between the data objects and the center point.

2.3 Existing Itinerary Planning

Lvxingjia, Tripit[3], Tripcase[4], Roadtroppers [5] and Plnnr are all dedicated to itinerary planning. Among others, Lvxingjia, Tripit and Tripcase are very similar: users only need to forward confirmation emails for their booked hotel, flight, car rental, and restaurants to a specified mailbox and such information will be automatically used for delivering a complete, detailed itinerary for the users. The itinerary is also synchronized to the calendar on user's computer and notifications such as flight alerts are to be sent to the user in due course. Roadtrippers asks users to provide information on the start and end points of their journeys. It shows to users some interesting things along the route, such as good restaurants. The advantage of Roadtrippers is to provide users with niche venues and give them a novel experience. Plnnr is a tool that provides users with personalized travel itineraries free of charge. When generating an itinerary for a user, Plnnr would take into account the user's destination cities, favorite attractions, the time period for travel, and the types of their interested sites. A list of all the hotels near the attractions specified by the user will be recommended to the user for further selection.

---

[3] https://www.tripit.com.

[4] http://travel.tripcase.com.

[5] https://roadtrippers.com.

The itinerary recommender proposed in this paper is similar to Plnnr in that both require users to provide travel information and then work out a day-to-day itinerary. However, we can provide a few candidate hotels that are not only within user's budget but also receive the highest ratings from former visitors. Furthermore, our daily itinerary always treats the hotel as a starting point, thus the first point of interest on daily itineraries always being the closest to the hotel. This reduces the time that users would spend on hotel selection and avoids a roundabout route.

3   An Itinerary Recommender

In this section, we will introduce a recommender system for itinerary planning. With the system, users need to fill out a travel plan questionnaire, giving information on user's name, the destination cities, the time period for travel, the number of visitors, the accommodation budget, and their favorite spots. In response to such information, the itinerary recommender will customize a complete, detailed day-to-day travel itinerary. The overall workflow within the system is illustrated in Fig. 1.

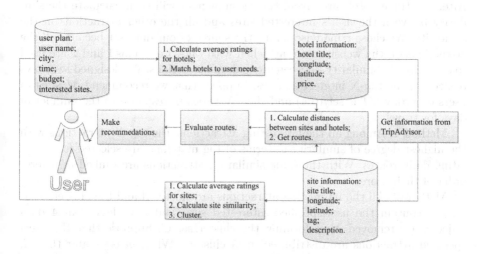

Fig. 1. The workflow in the itinerary recommender

3.1   Selection of Hotels

We compare user's budget on accommodation against the hotel prices available at http://tripadvisor.cn. A set of candidate hotels the price of which is within user's budget are returned.

$$\{H_i | P_i \leq P_b, H_i \in H\} \tag{5}$$

where H_i denotes the ith hotel, P_i is the price of the hotel, P_b is the user's budget, and H is all the hotels we obtain from tripadvisor.cn.

Travel websites adopt one method or another to better interact with users and get their feedback on recommended items. One may use a 5-level rating system in which the ratings, or the scores, range from 1 to 5 with the rating value 5 indicating an excellent hotel. We calculate the average score of each hotel based on the ones given by their former visitors. The top three hotels will be recommended to users (Providing users with three options is intended to leave users with room to select from). The hotels with less than five user ratings are not taken into account when calculating the average score of each hotel:

$$value = \frac{\sum_{i=1}^{5} i * n_i}{\sum_{i=1}^{5} n_i} \tag{6}$$

where i is the level of the user rating and n_i is the total number of users who gave a rating value of i to the hotel.

3.2   Selection of Attractions

After the three hotels are given, the recommender will then calculate the similarity between the user's interested sites and all the other attractions in the same city. We chose tripadvisor.cn as the source of our data set because all the attractions on the website were attached with tags. Equations 1 and 2 are used to calculate the similarity between any pair of attractions. We designed two ways to acquire the top-N interesting sites. Suppose that we recommend M sites to users everyday (M is set to 4) and then N varies in response to the number of days for travel.

Method 1: Among all the interesting attractions, the top N attractions with the highest degree of similarity in terms of tag matching are selected for calculating daily routes. With the same similarity, attractions are ranked in reverse order of their scores.

Method 2: All the interesting attractions are clustered and the clusters that do not contain the user-specified interested sites and have less than 4 data objects, are removed, thus forming the cluster set C. Suppose that the user-specified attractions are distributed in m clusters. When m is greater than d, the following scheme I is selected. Otherwise, scheme II is used instead.

Scheme I: According to the tag similarity, sorting in individual clusters in C is carried out. We set the tag similarity of a cluster is equal to the greatest tag similarity of the data objects in the cluster. We rank clusters in reverse order of their tag similarity. The first d clusters form the candidate list. If clusters share the same tag similarity in common, they will be sorted in terms of the distance between their center point and the specified hotel (See Sect. 3.1).

Scheme II: The distance between the center point and other center points in m clusters is calculated and sorted. Two clusters with the shortest distance are merged. After the merge takes place for $(m - d)$ times, d clusters remain in the final result.

We only get d candidate clusters using Scheme I and Scheme II. The recommender has the user-specified sites join the list of candidate attractions and then sort them in reverse order of the tag similarity, thus acquiring the top M attractions. In the case of sites sharing the same tag similarity, the one with a higher rating is always selected in the first place. Finally, a complete list of candidate attractions is made available for itinerary planning.

3.3   Planning of Trip Itineraries

The recommender has obtained a list of candidate hotels and attractions for itinerary planning. To this end, it divides all attractions into d clusters and there are 4 sites in each group (d represents the number of days for travel). For calculation of the distance between the hotels and sites, the Haversine equation [10] is used.

For the candidate list obtained using Method 1, the recommender picks up the closest site from the hotel. It then selects a site from the remaining sites that is closest to the previous site. The process continues until 4 sites are included on a travel route. The rest of the itinerary is achieved using the same process as described above.

For the candidate list obtained by Method 2, the recommender merely calculates the distance between the hotel and the first site of each cluster[6] from the d clusters. Then only the one from the remaining sites that happens to be the closest site to the first chosen site is picked up. The process continues until all the attractions on the candidate list will be included in the itinerary.

4   Experiments

We anticipated to recommend the itineraries that meet the user's travel needs. A series of experiments were therefore carried out to demonstrate the efficiency of the proposed recommender for itinerary planning.

4.1   Evaluation Metrics

The metrics that were used to evaluate the performance of the proposed recommender include: the tag similarity for the Most Appealing (MAI), the travel distance involved in an itinerary for the Shortest Itinerary (SI), and the efficiency that takes into account the hotel price, tag similarity, and the travel distance for the Most Effective Itinerary (MEI).

Among other, the tag similarity tag_sim_{rou}) for MAI is calculated as follows:

$$tag\_sim_{rou} = \sum_{i=1}^{4d} \sum_{k=1}^{a} simA_k, S_i \qquad (7)$$

---

[6] The first site of each cluster is any site that the user specifies as her favorite site.

where d is the number of travel days, A_k is the kth favorite site of a user, a represents the total number of the user's favorite sites, and S_i denotes the dth site of the candidate attractions. MAI is formed when tag_sim_{rou} reaches its maximum.

The travel distance of an itinerary dis_sum_{rou} for SI can be obtained by using the following equation:

$$dis\_some_{rou} = dis\_ss_{rou} + dis\_hs_{rou} \tag{8}$$

$$dis\_ss_{rou} = \sum_{i=0}^{d-1} \sum_{k=1}^{3} dis(S_{4i+k}, S_{4i+k+1}) \tag{9}$$

$$dis\_hs_{rou} = \sum_{i=0}^{d-1} dis(H, S_{4i+1}) \tag{10}$$

where dis_ss_{rou} represents the distance between a site with its predecessor on the itinerary, dis_hs_{rou} denotes the distance between a hotel and the first site of that day, d is the number of travel days. Moreover, H is the hotel and S_{4*i+1} is the $(4i+1)$th site of the candidate attractions. SI is obtained when dis_sum_{rou} reaches its minimum. dis() in both Eqs. 9 and 10 is calculated using the Haversine equation mentioned in Sect. 3.3.

We use the logarithmic normalization as follows to normalize the indices used in our experiments.

$$x' = \frac{log_{10}x}{log_{10}max} \tag{11}$$

The efficiency $comp_rou$ for MEI can be calculated as follows:

$$comp_{rou} = \frac{(\omega_1 * p_{nor} + \omega_2 * dis\_sum_{nor})}{tag\_sim_{nor}} \tag{12}$$

where p_{nor} is the normalized hotel price, dis_sum_{nor} and tag_sim_{nor} are derived from normalized dis_sum_{rou} and normalized tag_sim_{rou}, respectively, and ω_1 (0.2), ω_2 (0.4), and ω_3 (0.4) are the weights attached to these values. ω_1 is less than the other two weights because, according to Sects. 3.1 and 3.2, the hotel price is already within the user's budget. Hence, the hotel price will contribute less to the efficiency metric than the other two factors. MEI is acquired when $comp_{rou}$ takes its minimum value.

4.2   Experimental Settings and Methodologies

We used a MacBook Pro (Retina, 13-inch, Early 2015) with macOS High Sierra 10.13.1. The CPU is 2.9 GHz Intel Core i5 and the software supporting our experiments includes Python3.5, Node-v-8.4.0, and MongoDB.

We simulated the requirements of users Alva and Bob and filled out a travel questionnaire for them, which is shown in Table 1. Information on 1,006 sites and 3,417 hotels was harvested from tripadvisor.cn and then saved in MongoDb.

Table 1. Travel questionnaire

Name	City	No. of Days	Travel Dates	No. of Persons	Hotel Budget	Favorite Sites
Alva	Beijing	3	03/07-03/10	2	200	Summer Palace
Bob	Beijing	3	03/07-03/10	2	200	Summer Palace
						Lingshui Villag
						The Ming Tombs
						Tanzhe Temple

Given Alva's budget on accommodation, the hotels with less than 5 user ratings are first removed. The ratings of the rest of the hotels, 150 in this case, were calculated and we took the top 3 and included them in the candidate hotel list. The hotels selected are shown in Fig. 2.

In the meantime, we calculated the tag similarity between all the potential sites and Alva's favorites ones. 213 sites matched the tag of "Summer Palace". However, we only considered 12 sites using Method 1 given in Sect. 3.2. These sites are illustrated in Fig. 3.

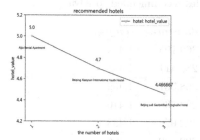

Fig. 2. The list of recommended hotels   **Fig. 3.** The list of recommended sites

We applied both the traditional K-Means clustering and the improved K-Means clustering to the 213 sites. When k is set to 6, we get the best clustering result, which is illustrated by Fig. 4. 6 itineraries in total were then generated for Alva by using Method 1 and Method 2.

Similarly, We calculated and found out 254 sites that matched Bob's favorite sites. Method 1 proceeded the same as in the previous case and we used traditional K-Means clustering ($k = 6$) with Method 2. We provide Bob with 6 itineraries by using both Method 1 and Method 2.

4.3   Experimental Results and Analysis

We evaluated the 6 itineraries provided to Alva and another 6 for Bob in terms of the metrics defined in Sect. 4.1. We compared the MAI, SI and MEI given by

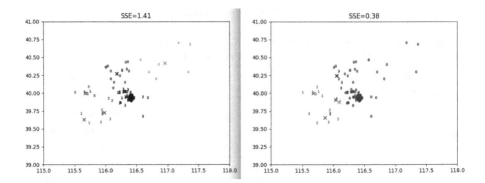

Fig. 4. The clustering result using the traditional K-Means (left) and the improved K-Means (right)

our proposed recommender with a popular itinerary[7] provided by mafengwo.cn for a similar set of favorite sites specified by users. The result is shown in Table 2. Table 3 displays the evaluation of the 6 itineraries for Bob.

Table 2. The evaluation of itineraries recommended to Alva

Hotel	Method	tag_sim_{rou}	dis_sim_{rou}	$comp_{rou}$
Hotel 1	1	8.503	369.795	1.473
Hotel 2	1	8.503	288.411	1.458
Hotel 3	1	8.503	308.567	1.469
Hotel 1	2 (k = 6)	7.948	202.738	1.416
Hotel 2	2 (k = 6)	7.948	190.028	1.433
Hotel 3	2 (k = 6)	8.133	302.832	1.466

For Alva, we work out MAI using Method 1 mentioned in Sect. 3.2, SI using Method 2 ($k = 6$), and MEI using Method 2 $k = 6$).

For Bob, we acquire MAI using Method 1 or Method 2 ($k = 6$), and both SI and MEI using Method 1.

From Table 4, we can tell that the itineraries provided by our recommender are more appealing to users than those from other travel websites. Only the metric of tag_sim_{rou} was used to evaluate all the itineraries mentioned in Table 4 because the popular itinerary does not include recommendations for hotels and therefore we were unable to calculate both dis_sum_{rou} and $comp_{rou}$.

Moreover, we can display SI, MEI and MAI in map and then recommend them to users, as shown in Fig. 5.

---

[7] http://www.mafengwo.cn/mdd/cityroute/10065_5934.html, retrieved at 20:36 on 2018/3/20.

Table 3. The evaluation of itineraries recommended to Bob

Hotel	Method	tag_sim_{rou}	dis_sim_{rou}	$comp_{rou}$
Hotel 1	1	7.593	300.831	1.4728
Hotel 2	1	7.593	184.027	1.414
Hotel 3	1	7.593	203.950	1.432
Hotel 1	2 (k = 6)	7.593	278.579	1.459
Hotel 2	2 (k = 6)	7.593	244.823	1.464
Hotel 3	2 (k = 6)	7.593	266.530	1.479

Table 4. A comparison between itineraries provided by our recommender and a popular itinerary for the same set of favorite sites from mafengwo.cn

Metrics	Popular itinerary	MAI	SI	MEI
tag_sim_{rou}	2.749	8.503	7.948	7.948

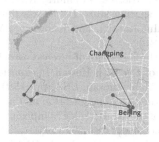

Fig. 5. The recommended SI displayed on map for Alva

5 Conclusions and Future Work

We proposed a recommender for itinerary planning that meets user's requirements by taking into account the user's budget, the number of travel days, and her favorite sites. A tag-based mapping algorithm was used to create a list of candidate attractions that best match with the user's favorite sites. Then the recommender applied an improved K-Means clustering algorithm to help minimize the distance between sites. Eventually the itineraries that would meet different user needs are created and displayed on the map for user selection.

We have performed experiments with a few cities in China, including Beijing, Hangzhou, Wuhan, Suzhou, and Quanzhou, and found out that k (for traditional K-means clustering) should be set to a smaller value (e.g. $k = 3$) while k with a greater value (e.g. $k = 5$ or 6) will always lead to satisfactory clustering that help produce SI. It is also observed that the value of SSE is inversely proportional to the value of k.

In the future, we plan to investigate ways for the recommender to take user's preferences for transportation vehicles as well as weather into consideration to provide more comprehensive, yet flexible itineraries.

References

1. Cai, G., Lee, K., Lee, I.: Itinerary recommender system with semantic trajectory pattern mining from geo-tagged photos. Expert Syst. Appl. **94**, 32–40 (2018)
2. Durao, F., Dolog, P.: A personalized tag-based recommendation in social web systems. In: Proceedings of the Workshop on Adaptation and Personalization for Web 2.0, Trento, Italy, pp. 40–49 (2009)
3. Jain, A., Murty, M., Flynn, P.: Data clustering: a review. ACM Comput. Surv. **31**(3), 264–323 (1999)
4. Kalogerakis, E., Vesselova, O., Hays, J., Efros, A., Hertzmann, A.: Image sequence geolocation with human travel priors. In: Proceedings of the IEEE International Conference on Computer Vision, Tokyo, Japan, pp. 253–260 (2009)
5. Kurashima, T., Iwata, T., Irie, G., Fujimura, K.: Travel route recommendation using geotags in photos sharing sites. In: Proceedings of the 19th ACM International Conference on Information and Knowledge Management, Toronto, ON, Canada, pp. 579–588 (2010)
6. Lee, I., Cai, G., Lee, K.: Mining points-of-interest association rules from geo-tagged photos. In: Proceedings of the 46th Hawaii International Conference on System Sciences, Grand Wailea, Maui, Hawaii, USA, pp. 1580–1588 (2013)
7. MacQueen, J.: Some methods for classification and analysis of multivariate observations. In: Proceedings of the 5th Berkeley Symposium on Mathematical Statistics and Probability, vol. 1, no. 1, pp. 281–297 (1967)
8. Marlow, C., Naaman, M., Boyd, D., Davis, M.: Position paper, tagging, taxonomy, flickr, article, to read. In: Collaborative Web Tagging Workshop at WWW2006, Edinburgh, Scotland (2006)
9. Nakamoto, R., Nakajima, S., Miyazaki, J., Uemura, S.: Tag-based contextual collaborative filtering. IAENG Int. J. Comput. Sci. **34**(2), 214–219 (2007)
10. Robusto, C.: The Cosine-Haversine formula. Am. Math. Mon. **64**(1), 38–40 (1957)
11. Shi, Y., Serdyukov, P., Hanjalic, A., Larson, M.: Personalized landmark recommendation based on geotags from photo sharing sites. In: Proceedings of the 5th International Conference on Weblogs and Social Media, Barcelona, Catalonia, Spain, pp. 622–625 (2011)
12. Singh, A., Yadav, A., Rana, A.: K-means with three different distance metrics. Int. J. Comput. Appl. **67**(10), 13–17 (2013)
13. Vu, H.Q., Li, G., Law, R., Ye, B.H.: Exploring the travel behaviors of inbound tourists to hong kong using geotagged photos. Tour. Manag. **46**, 222–232 (2015)
14. Yu, Z., Xu, H., Yang, Z., Guo, B.: Personalized travel package with multi-point-of interest recommendation based on crowdsourced user footprints. IEEE Trans. Hum. Mach. Syst. **46**, 151–158 (2016)
15. Kaufman, L., Peter, J.R.: Finding Groups in Data: An Introduction to Cluster Analysis. Probability and Statistics, pp. 253–279. Wiley, Hoboken (1990)

A Replay Voice Detection Algorithm Based on Multi-feature Fusion

Lang Lin[✉], Rangding Wang, Diqun Yan, and Can Li

College of Information Science and Engineering of Ningbo University,
Ningbo 315211, China
1300396440@qq.com

Abstract. The popularity and portability of high-fidelity recording devices and playback devices pose severe challenges for speaker recognition systems against replay voice attacks. In this paper, the signal of audio is transformed into the frequency domain through the Fourier trans-form and constant Q transform. Compared with genuine voice, the mean and standard deviation of the replay voice at each frequency bin has changed slightly. And through the coefficient of variation to further analyze the difference between genuine voice and replay voice. A detection algorithm based on fusion feature is proposed. The algorithm uses two kinds of time-frequency transform coefficients and their cepstrum characteristics to train the GMM model and calculate the likelihood ratio score. Finally, the replay voice is detected by the fusion of scores. The experimental results show that the algorithm is about 13% lower than the baseline EER provided by The ASV Spoof 2017.

Keywords: Coefficient of variation · GMM model · Replay voice detection

1 Introduction

In the field of biometrics [1], the voiceprint identification system has been widely used in the fields of life, finance, and justice because of its higher security and more convenient to obtain. While the voiceprint recognition technology continues to evolve, attacks of various spoof voice on the voiceprint system have become increasingly severe. In the past few years, researchers' detection of spoof voice mainly focused on synthesized voice and converted voice [2, 3], and neglected the attack on the voiceprint recognition system by the replay voice to a certain extent. In fact, the replay voice is recorded directly from real voice, it is more threatening than synthetic voice and converted voice. Secondly, the replay voice is more convenient to obtain than other spoof voice. Only one recording device is required to complete playback of the replay voice, and the counterfeiters do not have to have higher professional skills and provide more convenience to the counterfeiters. At the same time, the popularity and portability of high-fidelity devices in recent years has greatly in-creased the threat of replay voice to voiceprint recognition systems.

Earlier studies such as Shang and Stevenson et al. [4] proposed an algorithm for detecting the similarity between the test voice and the legitimate voice on the peak map using the randomness generated by the voice. However, this method can only be

© Springer Nature Switzerland AG 2018
X. Sun et al. (Eds.): ICCCS 2018, LNCS 11068, pp. 289–299, 2018.
https://doi.org/10.1007/978-3-030-00021-9_27

applied to text-related voiceprint authentication systems. Take into account this, Jakub Galka et al. [5] added the position relationship of each frequency point to the peak graph characteristics, further improving the performance of the voiceprint authentication system against replay voice. However, the algorithm is still limited to text-dependent voiceprint systems. Todisco M and Delgado H et al. [6] proposed a Constant Q Cepstral Coefficients (CQCC) feature based on the Constant Q transform in 2016. Although it has a certain effect on the detection of replay voice, the detection accuracy rate still needs to be improved. With the hosting of The ASV spoof 2017 Challenge [7], the detection of replay voice has received extensive attention from researchers. The literature [8] uses several combined features as well as integrated classifier ideas to reduce the equal error rate probability of detection of replay voice by about 10% compared with the baseline provided by the challenge. However, the complexity of the algorithm is extremely high. The literature [9] uses F-ratio method to analyze the difference between genuine and replay voice and proposes the I-MFCC method for replay voice detection. Experiments show that despite the fact that this feature has a certain detection effect, the robustness of the feature is poor.

In this paper, we use the Coefficient of Variation (CV) to analyze the difference between genuine and replay voice in the frequency domain. Experiments have shown that although the playback settings are different. The amplitude of the playback frequency bands will increase or decrease inconsistently. However, its coefficient of variation generally shows a consistent pattern. Fourier transform and constant Q transform are used to perform spectral analysis on speech signals. The coefficient of variation the cepstrum characteristics obtained by the Fourier transform and the constant Q transform are calculated. Then the likelihood ratio scores are calculated by the GMM model. Finally, a multi-feature fusion play-back speech detection algorithm is proposed for the fusion of the four feature score. The experimental results show that the method presented in this paper is about 13% lower than the baseline EER provided by The ASV spoof 2017 Challenge.

2 Prior Work

Figure 1 shows the mathematical model of replay voice. From the mathematical model of it can be seen that the response function of the genuine voice signal is $s_1 = f(x)$, while the response function of the replay voice is $s_2 = f(H(P(J_1(x))))$. Compared to genuine voice, the replay is also affected by factors such as recording devices, playback devices, and environmental noise during recording. Therefore, it will inevitably produce subtle differences between genuine and replay voice.

In order to further explore the subtle differences between genuine voice and replay voice, we perform a short-time Fourier transform (STFT) and a constant Q transform (CQT) on the speech signal to transform the speech from the time domain signal to frequency domain. The short-term Fourier transform essentially uses a windowed method to analyze the spectral properties and thus to understand the sequence characteristics in the time domain. During the entire conversion process, the time-frequency window of the Fourier transform remains unchanged. In an actual scene, it is often desirable to have a good frequency resolution in the low-frequency portion and a good

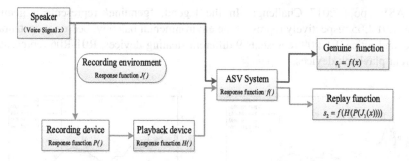

Fig. 1. The mathematical model of payback speech

time resolution in the high-frequency portion. The constant Q transform is essentially a wavelet transform that just overcomes the weaknesses of the Fourier transform. The constant Q transform maintains the constant Q constant so that the window length will change with the frequency, which can have a higher frequency resolution at low frequencies, and good time resolution at high frequencies. Therefore, this paper adopts two kinds of time-frequency transform methods, and then obtain the mean value and standard deviation of the spectrum coefficients obtained by the two time-frequency transforms in frames. The specific solution process is shown in Fig. 2.

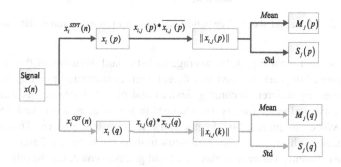

Fig. 2. The process of transformation

First, the speech signal $x(n)$ is preprocessed, and then the signal $x_i(n)$ of each frame is respectively subjected to STFT transformation and CQT transformation to obtain $x_i(p)$ and $x_i(q)$. And for each frequency bin to obtain its amplitude $||x_{i,j}(p)||$ and $||x_{i,j}(q)||$. Finally, the average value $M_j(p)$, $M_j(q)$ and standard deviation $S_j(p)$, $S_j(q)$ of each frequency bin are calculated by frame.

Figure 3(a) and (b) are the mean and standard deviation of the frequency bin under Fourier transform, and Fig. 3(c) and (d) are the mean and standard deviation of frequency bins under constant Q transform. And in order to more intuitively reflect the difference between the mean and standard deviation at each frequency bin, we transform the mean and standard deviation into the logarithmic domain for observation and analysis. The voice samples used in the figure are the DEV data set provided in

The ASV spoof 2017 Challenge. In the legend, 'genuine' represents a genuine voice. E01-E05 respectively represent the environmental balcony, bedroom, restaurant, home, and office. P1-P09 represents 9 different stealing devices. R01-R06 represents 6 different playback devices.

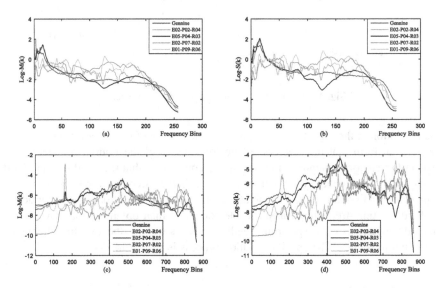

Fig. 3. Mean and standard deviation distribution of genuine and replay voice

As can be seen from Fig. 3, the average and standard deviation of the replay voice at each frequency bins are changed in different degrees compared to the genuine voice. And influenced by different recording devices and playback devices as well as environmental noise and other factors, the changes in the mean and standard deviation of the replay voice' frequency bin do not show a consistent pattern. This is also an important reason why replay voice is difficult to detect. On the one hand, it is difficult to detect the difference between replay voice and genuine voice. On the other hand, due to various factors, different playback settings produce different replay voices.

To unify the measurement of the difference between replay voice and genuine voice, we introduce the coefficient of variation to analyze each frequency bin. The coefficient of variation, also known as the "standard deviation rate," is a statistic that measures the degree of variation in each observation, and is suitable for comparing the degree of dispersion of the two population averages. The coefficients of variation include full-range coefficients, mean difference coefficients, and standard deviation coefficients. Commonly used is the standard deviation coefficient, denoted by CV, which is defined as the ratio of the standard deviation to the mean.

$$CV = \frac{Standard\ \ deviation}{Mean} * 100\% \tag{1}$$

Therefore, The two CV obtained by the Fourier transform and the constant Q transform are defined as CV_{STFT}, CV_{CQT} respectively. The specific solution is as follows

$$CV_{STFT} = \frac{S_j(p)}{M_j(p)} \tag{2}$$

$$CV_{CQT} = \frac{S_j(q)}{M_j(q)} \tag{3}$$

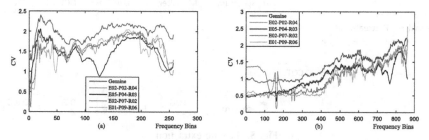

Fig. 4. CV distribution of genuine and replay voice

Figure 4(a) and (b) respectively show the distribution of the coefficient of variation at each frequency point under the Fourier transform and the constant Q transform

As can be seen in (a) and (b) of Fig. 4, the CV of the replay voice produced by different playback settings have varied to varying degrees. But overall, the CV value of each frequency bin is less than the genuine voice. Although in Fig. 4(b) E02-P07-R02 shows the opposite conclusion in the low-frequency region, the mid-high frequency region still satisfies the conclusion reached. Moreover, compared to figure(a), the difference between CV of the replay voice produced by different devices after the CQT transformation is small, and therefore, the robustness is stronger. In addition, we will use CQT and STFT two transformations to extract features of replay voice. The CQT transform makes the feature more robust, and the STFT transform can compensate for the lack of certain playback settings for the CQT transform.

In addition, considering that the cepstrum coefficients have the characteristic of unwrapping, that is, the cepstrum analysis can convert the convolution relationship into an additive relationship, thereby separating the glottal excitation information and the vocal tract response information of the speech signal, and can be more effective extract speech signal features. Therefore, we also use the cepstrum feature obtained by the two transforms for the detection of replay voice.

3   Feature Extraction

According to the analysis in the previous section, the characteristics extracted in this paper are CV_{STFT}, CV_{CQT}, MFCC and CQCC obtained by the Fourier transform and the constant Q transform. The specific extraction flow chart is shown in Fig. 5.

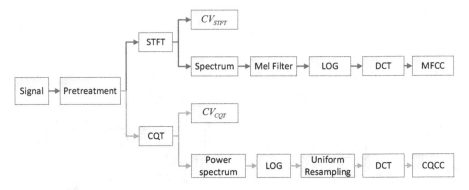

Fig. 5.   Feature extraction

MFCC (Mel-Frequency Cepstral Coefficients) is a cepstrum feature proposed based on human ear characteristics and is widely used in speaker recognition and speech recognition. The extraction process of MFCC is shown in Eqs. 4 and 5, and the specific calculation is as follows:

$$MFCC(p) = \sum_{m}^{M} log[MF(m)]cos[\frac{p(m - \frac{1}{2})\pi}{M}] \tag{4}$$

Where $MF(m)$ represents the Mel spectrum. The formula is as follows:

$$MF(m) = \sum_{k-1}^{K} |X^{DFT}(k)|^2 H_m(k) \tag{5}$$

Where k is the DFT index, $H_m(k)$ is the bandpass filter transfer function, $0 \leq m \leq M$, and M is the number of filters. The p represents the final output dimension after DCT. This article M is 25 and q is 13. In addition, the MFCC and its first-order difference and second-order difference together constitute a 39-dimensional feature.

CQCC (Constant Q Cepstral Coefficients) is a cepstrum feature based on the CQT transform. Since the CQT transform can automatically adjust the window length, it can have a higher frequency resolution and a lower time resolution in the low-frequency portion, a higher temporal resolution and a lower frequency resolution in the high-frequency portion. Therefore, it is widely used in music signal processing.

The extraction process of CQCC is shown in Eq. 6, which is specifically calculated as follows:

$$CQCC(p) = \sum_{l-1}^{L} log|X^{CQ}(l)|^2 cos[\frac{q(l-\frac{1}{2})\pi}{L}]$$ (6)

Where $X^{CQ}(l)$ represents the transformed spectrum of the CQT. The q is the final output dimension. $p = 0, 1 . . . L - 1$, l denotes the resampled frequency bin.

4 Detection Algorithm

In the training phase, the four proposed features are extracted first. A GMM model of genuine voice (recorded as λ_t) and a GMM model of replay voice (recorded as λ_f) are separately trained for each feature. In the test phase, four features are calculated for the likelihood ratio score under the corresponding GMM model. At this point, we will get the score of four characteristics. In order to effectively integrate the scores of the four characteristics, we first normalize the likelihood ratio scores of the four characteristics and then use the average of the required feature score as our last Fusion score. Finally, we determine the final classification by setting a threshold θ. If the likelihood ratio of the test speech is greater than the score, it is determined as a genuine voice; otherwise, it is determined as the replay voice. The likelihood ratio is defined as follows:

$$\sigma = \log\left(\frac{p(X|\lambda_t)}{p(X|\lambda_f)}\right)$$ (7)

The X represents the feature vector. The specific flow chart of the detection algorithm is shown in Fig. 6.

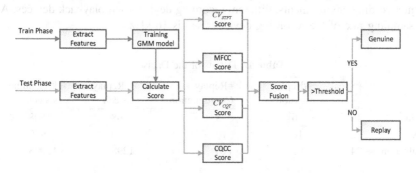

Fig. 6. Detection process of replay voice

The overall judgment result is given in terms of the equal error rate (EER), where EER is calculated as follows:

$$\theta_{eer} = P_{(fa)}(\theta) = P_{(miss)}(\theta) \tag{8}$$

$P_{(fa)}(\theta)$ and $P_{(miss)}(\theta)$ denote the false alarm rate the missed alarm rate at the threshold θ. $P_{(fa)}(\theta)$ and $P_{(miss)}(\theta)$ are functions of θ monotonic decrease and monotonous increase respectively. The false alarm rate $P_{(fa)}(\theta)$ and the false alarm rate $P_{(miss)}(\theta)$ can be adjusted by adjusting the value of the threshold. For the choice of threshold, it can be adjusted according to the actual situation. If in the field of high security, the false alarm rate can be minimized by adjusting the threshold to improve the security. If used in areas of low security such as attendance, the threshold can be appropriately lowered to increase the missed rate to allow for ease of use.

5   Experimental Simulation and Analysis

5.1   Database

In order to illustrate the effectiveness and applicability of this algorithm, this paper uses the data set provided by The ASV spoof 2017 Challenge. The ASV spoof 2017 Challenge was presented at a special meeting on automatic speaker recognition held in 2013 [10] and 2015. The organizers of the conference were the Finnish University of Eastern Finland and the Edinburgh University in the United Kingdom. The theme of this challenge is the replay voice attack detection.

The entire dataset of The ASV spoof 2017 Challenge is divided into three subsets, namely training set, development set, and evaluation set. The dataset corpus uses the most commonly used phrase in the RedDots corpus [11]. Table 1 lists the number of speakers in the three subsets, the number of phrases, the number of playback settings, and the number of genuine and replay voices. For playback settings, it includes different recording environments, different recording devices, and playback devices. And the sampling rate of the recording devices used is 16 kHz.

Table 1. Details of the Dataset

	#Speak	#Replay session	#Replay Configuration	# Replay speech	# Genuine speech
Train	10	6	3	1508	1508
Dev	8	10	10	760	950
Evaluation	24	161	110	1298	12008

5.2   Experimental Results and Analysis

Test Results with Different Characteristics. We use the characteristics of CV_{STFT}, CV_{CQT}, $MFCC$, $CQCC$ and $I - MFCC$ proposed in literature [9] as the basic features of this paper. In addition, in order to improve the robustness of cepstrum features, we use Cepstral Mean and Variance Normalization (CMVN) to remove channel mismatch and additive noise interference. In this paper, the CMVN method is used for the MFCC feature and the CQCC feature. The resulting features are denoted as $MFCC_{CMVN}$ and $CQCC_{CMVN}$. Finally, the above-mentioned seven characteristics are respectively trained in two training sets: Train set, Train set + Dev set, and the evaluation data set is used as a test set for testing. The results of the detection are shown in Table 2.

Table 2. Detection results under different features

Features	Train set	Train set + Dev set
	EER%	EER%
CV_{STFT}	27.91	27.88
CV_{CQT}	36.25	35.74
$MFCC$	38.64	25.54
$CQCC$	28.65	24.55
$I - MFCC$	36.30	33.46
$MFCC_{CMVN}$	24.92	22.64
$CQCC_{CMVN}$	19.69	14.84

As can be seen from Table 2, for the five basic features, the Train set + Dev set shows better performance than using a separate Train data set. The best performance among them is the baseline feature CQCC proposed by ASV spoof 2017, followed by our proposed CV_{STFT} features and MFCC features. However, the I-MFCC feature detection performance proposed in literature 6 is not good. In addition, two cepstrum features MFCC and CQCC show excellent detection performance after CMVN processing, especially the EER probability of $CQCC_{CMVN}$ features compared with CQCC features is reduced by about 10%.

Score Fusion of Different Characteristics. From the analysis in previous section, we can see that $CQCC_{CMVN}$ and $MFCC_{CMVN}$ exhibit good performance in the detection performance of replay voice, and then the characteristics of CV proposed in this paper also perform well. Therefore, in order to further reduce the EER, we fused the likelihood score by combining these four features to further improve the detection performance. Combination of feature scores we first chose the simplest equal weight addition method. That is, the likelihood ratio scores of various features are added directly, without adding weight coefficients. The test results are shown in Table 3. It can be seen that the fusion feature used by the best detection result is the result of the fusion of three features $MFCC_{CMVN}$, $CQCC_{CMVN}$, and CV_{STFT}. The detection EER on the Train set + Dev set data set is 11.74%, which is about 13% lower than the baseline EER proposed by the ASV Spoof 2017. When the four features are fused together, the detection performance decreases. Explain that the fusion of CV_{CQT} features reduces our detection rate. This also corresponds exactly to the analysis of our CQT coefficient of variation in the second quarter. From Fig. 4(b) of the second section, we can see that CV_{CQT} will mutate in some playback settings, which interferes with our detection of replay voice.

Table 3. Detection results under unweighted feature

Features	Train set EER%	Train set + Dev set EER%
$MFCC_{CMVN} + CV_{STFT}$	21.74	19.58
$CQCC_{CMVN} + CV_{CQT}$	23.64	17.79
$MFCC_{CMVN} + CQCC_{CMVN}$	16.14	12.14
$MFCC_{CMVN} + CQCC_{CMVN} + CV_{STFT}$	15.40	**11.74**
$MFCC_{CMVN} + CQCC_{CMVN} + CV_{CQT}$	19.21	13.88
$MFCC_{CMVN} + CQCC_{CMVN} + CV_{STFT} + CV_{CQT}$	19.11	13.83

Finally, the detection performance of the replay voice on the database provided by ASV Spoof 2017 reduced the baseline EER proposed by the competition from 24.55% to 11.74%. Compared to other 48 team methods in the competition ASV spoof 2017 Challenge [12], our algorithm is second only to the deep learning method used by the first team.

6 Conclusion

In this paper, a detailed analysis of genuine and replay voice is performed through the coefficient of variation. And through the fusion of three features, the performance of replay voice detection has been greatly improved. Out of the test results provided by 48 competition teams, it ranked second. Then, as a manual feature of the conventional method, compared to the machine learning feature used in the first place, there is a greater improvement in replay voice detection. Subsequent efforts will focus on machine learning methods to study replay voice detection. In addition, since the recording devices and playback devices in the real-life scene emerge in endlessly, the application scenarios of the voiceprint recognition system are not the same. Therefore, the follow-up work will also focus on the impact of the device and the recording environment on replay voice detection.

Acknowledgments. This work is supported by the National Natural Science Foundation of China (Grant No. U1736215, 61672302), Zhejiang Natural Science Foundation (Grant No. LZ15 F020002, LY17F020010), Ningbo Natural Science Foundation (Grant No. 2017A610123), Ningbo University Fund (Grant No. XKXL1509, XKXL1503).

References

1. Zhu, D., Ma, B., Li, H.: Speaker verification with feature-space MAPLR parameters. IEEE Trans. Audio Speech Lang. Process. **19**(3), 505–515 (2010)
2. Wu, Z., Kinnunen, T., Evans, N., et al.: ASV spoof 2015: The first automatic speaker verification spoofing and countermeasures challenge. In: 16th Annual Conference of the International Speech Communication Association, INTERSPEECH 2015, vol. 11, pp. 588–604. INTERSPEECH, Dresden (2015)

3. Alegre, F., Janicki, A., Evans, N.: Re-assessing the threat of replay spoofing attacks against automatic speaker verification. biometrics special interest group. In: Proceedings of the 2014 Biometrics Special Interest Group, pp. 1–6. IEEE, Piscataway (2014)

4. Shang, W., Stevensin, M.: A playback attack detector for speaker verification systems. In: International Symposium on Communications Control and Signal Processing, ISCCSP 2008, pp. 1144–1149. IEEE, Piscataway (2008)

5. Jakub, G., Marcin, G., Rafal, S.: Playback attack detection for text-dependent speaker verification over telephone channels. Speech Commun. **67**, 143–153 (2015)

6. Todisco, M., Delgado, H., Evans, N.: A new feature for automatic speaker verification anti-spoofing: constant Q cepstral coefficients. In: Odyssey 2016-The Speaker and Language Recognition Workshop, pp. 283–290. IEEE, Piscataway (2016)

7. Wu, Z., Yamagishi, J., Kinnunen, T., et al.: ASV spoof: the automatic speaker verification spoofing and countermeasures challenge. IEEE J. Sel. Top. Signal Process. **11**, 588–604 (2017)

8. Ji, Z., Li, Z.Y., Li, P., et al.: Ensemble learning for countermeasure of audio replay spoofing attack in ASVspoof2017. In: INTERSPEECH 2017, pp. 87–91. INTERSPEECH, Stockholm (2017)

9. Lantian, L., Yixiang, C., Dong, W.: A study on replay attack and anti-spoofing for automatic speaker verification. In: INTERSPEECH 2017, pp. 92–96. INTERSPEECH, Stockholm (2017)

10. Evans, N.W.D., Kinnunen, T., Yamagishi, J.: Spoofing and countermeasures for automatic speaker verification. In: Proceedings of the 2013 Conference of the International Speech Communication Association, INTERSPEECH 2013, pp. 925–929. INTERSPEECH, Lyon (2013)

11. Lee, K.A., Larcher, A., Wang, G., et al.: The reddots data collection for speaker recognition. In: 16th Annual Conference of the International Speech Communication Association, INTERSPEECH 2015, pp. 2996–3000. INTERSPEECH, Dresden (2015)

12. Kinnunen, T., Sahidullah, M., Delgado, H., et al.: The ASV spoof 2017 challenge: assessing the limits of replay spoofing attack detection. In: INTERSPEECH 2017, pp. 1–6. INTERSPEECH, Stockholm (2017)

A Robust Recoverable Algorithm Used for Digital Speech Forensics Based on DCT

Zhenghui Liu[1], Yanli Li[1], Fang Sun[1], Junjie He[1], Chuanda Qi[1],
and Da Luo[2($\boxtimes$)]

[1] College of Computer and Information Technology,
Xinyang Normal University, Xinyang 464000, China
[2] School of Computer Science and Network Security,
Dongguan University of Technology, Dongguan 523000, China
luoda@dgut.edu.cn

Abstract. Recoverable speech forensics algorithm not only can locate the attacked frames, but can reconstruct the attacked signals. Meanwhile, the method can provide useful information for the prediction of attacker and attacker's intent. We proposed a robust recoverable algorithm used for digital speech forensics in this paper. We analyze and conclude that large amplitude DCT coefficients play a more significant role for speech reconstruction. Inspired by this, we regard the large amplitude coefficients as compressed signal, used for the reconstruction of attacked frames. For embedding, we scramble samples of each frame, and embed frame number and compressed signal into less amplitude DCT coefficients of scrambled signal by substitution. Frame number is used for tamper location of watermarked speech, and compressed signal is used for the reconstruction of attacked signals. Experimental results demonstrate that the algorithm is inaudible and robustness to signal processing operations, has ability of tamper recovery and improves the security of watermarking system.

Keywords: Watermarking · Speech forensics · Speech compression

1 Introduction

So far, many audio watermarking methods have been developed [1], including time domain methods and transform domain methods. The time domain methods include time aligned methods [2] and echo-based methods [3]. The transform domain methods include spread spectrum methods [4], quantization index modulation methods [5], patchwork methods [6, 7]. Transform domain methods are generally more robust because they can take advantage of signal characteristics and auditory properties [8]. So, most robust audio watermarking schemes for copyright protection are based on transform domain [9, 10].

For digital speech, as a carrier to transmit information, the semantic should be intact and authentic. If audiences regard the semantic of attacked speech as authentic and act according to the wrong instructions, it can cause serious consequences. So, apart from copyright protection, speech forensics is indispensable, which is one of the applications of digital audio watermarking [11].

© Springer Nature Switzerland AG 2018
X. Sun et al. (Eds.): ICCCS 2018, LNCS 11068, pp. 300–311, 2018.
https://doi.org/10.1007/978-3-030-00021-9_28

There have been some schemes for speech forensics [12, 13]. In [12], as to compressed speech by using codebook-excite linear prediction, authors proposed the scheme used for compressed speech forensics, and embedded watermark into the least significant bits [14]. Least significant bits are fragile, and will be changed after signal processing operations. For the scheme, it will regard common signal processing operation as hostile attack. So, the scheme is unsuitable for the speech subjected to signal processing. In [13], authors proposed audio amplitude cooccurrence vector features used for verifying whether audio signal is subjected to post process. The features can exploit cooccurrence patterns of audio signals, and have the ability of distinguish between the original audio and the postprocessed audio with an average accuracy of above 95%.

The semantic of hostile attacked speech is different to the original one. For the speech, expressing emergency tasks and important directives, the greatest wish of audience maybe to acquire the semantic of the original signal. In this case, reconstructing the attacked speech is the users to pray. There have been a considerable amount of recovery schemes for digital images [15–17]. While, there are comparatively few recovery schemes for digital speech [18].

Considering the background and motivation above, we proposed a robust recoverable algorithm used for digital speech forensics. By the statistical distribution rule of Discrete Cosine Transform (DCT) coefficients, we analyze and conclude that large amplitude coefficients play a more significant role for speech reconstruction. Inspired by this, we give the digital speech signal compression method, and get the conclusion that original speech can be reconstructed by using the compressed signal, under the condition of keep semantic. We scramble samples of each frame, and substitute the less amplitude DCT coefficients to embed frame number and compressed signal into host speech. Use frame number to locate the attacked frame. And then extract compressed signal and reconstruct the attacked frame to perform tamper recovery. Theoretical analysis and experimental results demonstrate that the proposed scheme is inaudible and robustness to signal processing operations, and can recover the attacked signals.

2 Speech Compression Based on DCT

2.1 Distribution of Discrete Cosine Transform Coefficients

Select one speech signal randomly, and we perform DCT on the signal. Figure 1 gives the DCT coefficients. It can be seen that the amplitudes of low-band DCT coefficients is great than high-band coefficient, and the energy is mainly distributed in the low frequency domain (results shown in Fig. 1 also validate the conclusion). It means that low-band coefficients, or large amplitude coefficients play a more significant role than small amplitude coefficients for speech reconstruction.

We select 500 speech signals recorded in four different environments, including quiet room, seminar, park and railway station. The length of each signal is about 10 s, and sampled at 8 kHz. In Fig. 2, we show the statistical result of the number of DCT coefficients taking different values, for the 500 speech signals. And the horizontal coordinate is the DCT coefficients value, and the vertical coordinate represents the

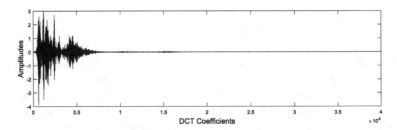

Fig. 1. DCT coefficients of one speech signal

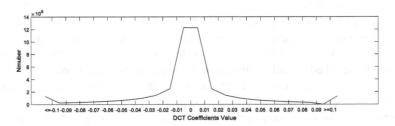

Fig. 2. The number of DCT coefficients for different value

number of DCT coefficients. Figure 2 indicates that most of the DCT coefficients are close to 0, except for the coefficients greater than 0.1 and less than −0.1.

Inspired by the results shown in Figs. 1 and 2, we analyze and obtain the conclusion. (1) The amplitudes of low-band DCT coefficients are great than high-band coefficients, and the energy is mainly distributed in the low frequency domain. And for speech reconstruction by inverse DCT, large amplitude coefficients play a more significant role than small amplitude coefficients. (2) Even if we set the small coefficients (greater than −0.1 and less than 0.1) to 0, we can obtain the signal having the same semantic to original one by inverse DCT.

From the distribution of DCT coefficients shown in Fig. 2, we can see that the number of larger amplitude coefficients is about 4% of the total coefficients. Simultaneously, based on the conclusion obtained by Fig. 1 that large amplitude coefficients are almost all the low-band DCT coefficients, we record the 4% low-band DCT coefficients as the compressed signal in this paper.

2.2 Speech Compression and Reconstruction

2.2.1 Speech Compression

We denote $A = \{a(l), 1 \leq l \leq L\}$ as the L length speech signal, and $a(l)$ represents the l-th sample.

(1) We cut A into P frames. Denote N as the length of each frame and A_i as the i-th frame.

(2) Perform DCT on A_i, for the large amplitudes are almost all low-band DCT coefficients, we select the 4% low-band DCT coefficients and denote as $C_i = \{c_l, 1 \leq l \leq N/25\}$.

(3) Narrowing the amplitudes of $C_i = \{c_l, 1 \leq l \leq N/25\}$, by using Eq. (1).

$$\bar{c}_l = c_l/MC_i \tag{1}$$

where $MC_i = \max\{|c_l|, 1 \leq l \leq N/25\}$, and $|c_l|$ represents the amplitude of c_l. We denote the $\bar{C}_i = \{\bar{c}_l, 1 \leq l \leq N/25\}$ as the compressed signal.

2.2.2 Speech Reconstruction

We can reconstruct A_i under the condition of keeping semantic by using the compressed signal $\bar{C}_i$.

(1) Except for the 4% low-band DCT coefficients, we set other coefficients to 0, to construct N length DCT coefficients.

(2) Perform inverse DCT on the N length constructed DCT coefficients. Then we normalize the signal, and can obtain the reconstructed signal.

We take the speech signal shown in Fig. 3 as an example. Cut the signal into 3 frames, each frame is 1000 length. Figure 4 shows DCT coefficients of the 3 frames. By using the above compression and reconstruction method, we can get the compressed signal (large amplitudes coefficients) of the 3 frames, shown in Fig. 5. Based on the compressed signal, we construct N length DCT coefficients of each frame, and perform inverse DCT on the coefficients to reconstruct the signal approximatively, shown in Fig. 6.

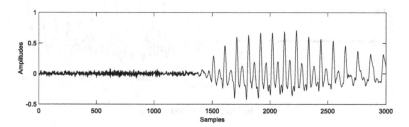

Fig. 3. 3000 length speech signal

For speech signals, they have mute parts and non-silence parts generally. The non-silence parts play an important role for semantics expression, while the mute parts have no semantics. By comparing with the waveform of speech signal (shown in Fig. 3) and the reconstructed one (shown in Fig. 6), we can conclude that the reconstruction method can recover the non-silence parts of speech signal approximately, and the reconstructed mute parts are obviously different to the original ones. For mute parts have no semantics, the reconstructed mute parts can be considered as acceptable for semantics expression.

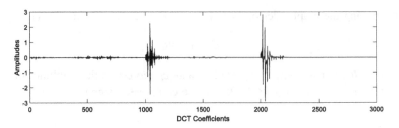

Fig. 4. DCT coefficients of the 3 frames

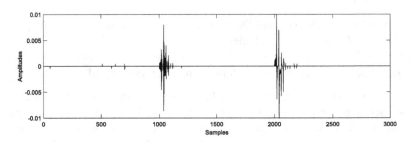

Fig. 5. Constructed DCT coefficients based on compressed signal

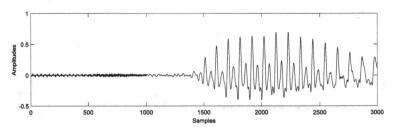

Fig. 6. Reconstructed signal

3   The Scheme

3.1   Preprocessing

Step 1: Divide the signal $A = \{a_l | 1 \leq l \leq L\}$ into divide the signal into N-sample frames. $A_i = \{a_{i,j} | 1 \leq j \leq N\}$ represents the i-th frame, $1 \leq i \leq P$, and $P = L/N$.
Step 2: We compress A_i with the method in Sect. 2.2, and obtain the compressed signal $\bar{C}_i$.

The compressed signal should not be embedded into the current frame, because the reconstruction will fail in the case that the current frame itself is malicious attacked. In order to reconstruct A_i, the compressed signal $\bar{C}_i$ should be embedded into other frame except for A_i. In this paper, we adopt the method in [18] to scramble the compressed signal $\bar{C}_i$, and denote the i-th compressed signal after being scrambled as SC_i, $1 \leq i \leq P$. The initial value of Logistic chaotic mapping k_0 and the parameter μ are regarded as the key.

Step 3: We map frame number i to $F_i = (i/(10)^{n_1})^{|n|}$. In this paper, we define $Y^{|n|}$ as the Eq. (2), and $P < 10^{n_1}$.

$$Y^{|n|} = \underbrace{Y \cup Y \cup \cdots \cup Y}_{n} \tag{2}$$

Step 4: Denote $W_i = (SC_i)^{|n_1|}$, $F_i \cup W_i$ as watermark embedded into A_i.

3.2 Embedding

Step 1: We scramble the sample of A_i by using the method [18], and then perform DCT on the scrambled signal. Denote the DCT coefficients as $C_i = \{c_1, c_2, \cdots, c_N\}$.

Step 2: We use F_i to substitute the n coefficient $c_1, c_2, \ldots, c_n$, and use W_i to substitute the $3N/25$ coefficients, amplitudes less than 0.1.

Step 3: Perform inverse DCT on the DCT coefficients after being substituted, and anti-scrambling on the signal obtained to generate the watermarked signal.

By using the method, we can embed F_i and W_i into A_i, $1 \leq i \leq N$.

3.3 Forensics and Tamper Recovery

Suppose $A' = \{a'_l | 1 \leq l \leq L\}$ represents the watermarked signal. The steps of forensics and tamper recovery are described in following.

Step 1: Cut A' into N length frames, and denote the i-th frame as A'_i, $1 \leq i \leq L/N$.

Step 2: We scramble the samples of the signal A'_i, and perform DCT on the scrambled signal. Denote the DCT coefficients as $C'_i = \{c'_1, c'_2, \cdots, c'_N\}$.

Step 3: Extract frame number from the first n DCT coefficients, $c'_1, c'_2, \cdots, c'_n$. By using Eq. (3), we calculate $F1_i = f\left(c'_1, c'_2, \cdots, c'_{n/2}\right)$. Similarly, we can get $F2_i = f\left(c'_{n/2+1}, c'_{n/2+2}, \cdots, c'_n\right)$.

$$f\left(c'_1, c'_2, \cdots, c'_{n/2}\right) = \sum_{l=1}^{n/2} \left\lfloor (100 \times c'_l) + \frac{1}{2} \right\rfloor / n/2 \tag{3}$$

If $F1_i = F2_i$, it indicates that the signal A'_i is authentic. Otherwise, it indicates that the i-th frame has been tampered, and the tamper location and tamper recovery steps are described in following.

Step 4: Tamper location and tamper recovery. Suppose the 1st to i-1th frame are all intact, and the next N samples cannot pass the authentication.

(1) Search the next N samples that can be authenticated, and denote the frame as $A'_{i'}$. We can extract frame number from $A'_{i'}$ ($F1_{i'} = F2_{i'}$), and denote the frame number as i'.

(2) We regard the frame between i-1th to i' th as the attacked signal.

(3) Based on the scrambling method, suppose the compressed signal used for reconstructing one attacked frame is embedded into the $\bar{i}$-th frame $A'_{\bar{i}}$. We scramble the sample of $A'_{\bar{i}}$, and perform DCT. Then, by using the principle of the minority subordinating to the majority, we extract compressed signal from the $3N/25$ coefficients, amplitudes less than 0.1. Then we can reconstruct the attacked frame using the method in Sect. 2.2.

4 Performance Analysis and Experimental Results

In this section, the comprehensive performance of the scheme is analyzed and tested, including inaudibility, security, robustness, tamper location and tamper recovery. We select 500 speech signals recorded in four different environments as the test signal, denoted by T1, T2, T3 and T4. They represent the signals recorded in quiet room, seminar, park and railway station, respectively. The signals are sampled at 8 kHz, WAVE format 16-bit quantified mono signals. The parameters are set as follows, $L = 80000$, $P = 80$, $N = 1000$, $n = 5$, $n_1 = 3$, $n_2 = 3$, $k_0 = 0.82$, $\mu = 3.9875$.

4.1 Inaudibility

Inaudibility means that watermark embedding is inaudible, and reflects the change degree of original speech after watermarking. We use signal to noise ratio (SNR) and subjective difference grades (SDG) to test the inaudibility of the scheme proposed. The definition of SNR is in [19], and the meaning of the scores of SDG is in the references [18].

The mean values of SNR and SDG of the four types watermarked speech signal are listed in Table 1. SDG values are acquired from 30 listeners. The test results listed in Table 1 indicate that the scheme proposed is inaudibility.

Table 1. The SDG and SNR values of watermarked signals

Speech type	SDG	SNR(dB)
T1	−0.78	26.64
T2	−0.72	26.73
T3	−0.66	27.41
T4	−0.53	28.26

4.2 Robustness

For the convenience of storage and playing, and many other reasons, speech signal may be subjected to some signal processing operations. If watermark embedding is fragile, it will extract false watermark, and regard common signal processing operation as hostile attack. Thereby the authentication schemes should be robust against signal processing operations. We use bit error rate (BER) [20] to test the robustness of the proposed scheme. BER is defined by Eq. (4), and less BER value implies stronger robustness to signal processing operations.

$$BER = \frac{W_e}{W_t} \tag{4}$$

where W_e represents the number of watermark erroneously extracted, and W_t represents the number of watermark embedded.

We list the average BER value of the 800 test signals, after being subjected to different signal processing operations, containing MP3 compression, re-sampling and low pass filtering. And compare the results with the schemes proposed in [21, 22], which are shown in Table 2. The results shown in Table 2 indicate that the scheme proposed has the ability to tolerate common signal processing operations.

Table 2. BER values after being subjected to common signal processing

Signal processing		BER		
		Ref. [21]	Ref. [22]	Proposed
MP3 compression	64 kbps	0.0748	0.0919	0.0612
	96 kbps	0.0516	0.0697	0.0452
	128 kbps	0.0482	0.0465	0.0364
Low pass filtering	6 kHz	0.0685	0.0662	0.0209
Gauss noise	30 dB	0.0553	0.0684	0.0436
Echo	40% and 100 ms delay	0.0470	0.0446	0.0335

4.3 Tamper Location and Tamper Recovery

We select one speech from the 800 test signals, and show the signal in Fig. 7. Authors in [23] say that all attack channels can be viewed as deletion, insertion and substitution channel for watermarking. We perform the 3 types attack on the signal shown in Fig. 7, and then give the tamper location and tamper recovery results.

Because of space cause, we only give the detailed steps, tamper location and tamper recovery results of deletion attack. For other attacks, the tamper recovery results are similar.

(1) Delete 8000 samples from the watermarked speech shown in Fig. 7, and show the attacked signal in Fig. 8.
(2) Cut the attacked signal into N length frames, and scramble the first frame. Then we perform DCT on first frame, and extract frame number $F1_1$ and $F2_1$.

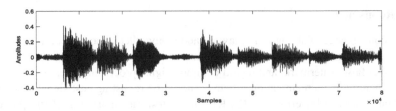

Fig. 7. Watermarked speech

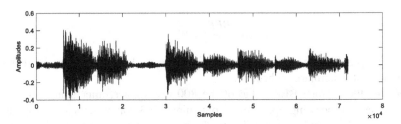

Fig. 8. Watermarked speech of 8000 samples deleted

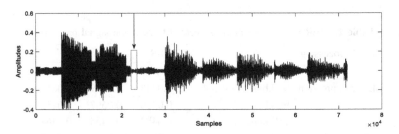

Fig. 9. Finding the N successive samples that cannot pass authentication

If $F1_1 = F2_1$, we regard the first frame is intact, and record $F1_1$(or $F2_1$) as the frame of the first frame. By using the method, we can verify the authenticity of next frames, until finding the N successive samples that cannot pass authentication. The result is shown in Fig. 9.

(3) Move and verify the next N successive samples, until that the N samples can pass the authentication. We show the result in Fig. 10, and reconstruct the frame number.

(4) The difference between the two reconstructed frame numbers is the frame attacked, as the tamper location result shown in Fig. 11, in which $TL = 1$ represents the frame is attacked, and $TL = 0$ represents the frame is intact.

Based on scrambling method, we find and extract the compressed signal of attacked frames, 23rd to 30-th frame, from 76th, 69th, 21st, 45th, 13th, 31th, 61th and 65th frame.

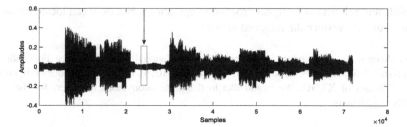

Fig. 10. Finding next N successive samples can pass the authentication

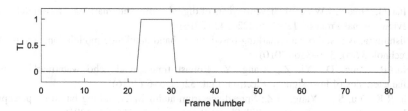

Fig. 11. Tamper location result

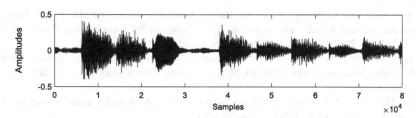

Fig. 12. Tamper recovery result of deletion attack

(5) By using the reconstruction method, we reconstruct the attacked frames based on the compressed signal to perform tamper recovery, and show the result in Fig. 12.

From the tamper recovery results above, we get the conclusion that scheme proposed can locate the attacked frames precisely, and has a good ability of tamper recovery.

5 Conclusion

In this paper, by using the proposed speech compression method, we obtained the compressed speech, used for the reconstruction of attacked frames. We embedded frame number and compressed signal into host speech, by the substitution of less amplitude DCT coefficients. Using frame number to locate the attacked frame, after that we extracted compressed signal and reconstructed the attacked frame to perform tamper recovery. Simulation results demonstrate that the proposed recoverable algorithm is inaudible and robustness to signal processing operations. Not only can locate the attack frames, but can recover the attacked signals.

Acknowledgments. This paper is supported by the National Natural Science Foundation of China (Grant No. 61502409, 61602318, 61602318, 61631016), and Nanhu Scholars Program for Young Scholars of XYNU. We would like to thank the anonymous reviewers for their constructive suggestions.

References

1. Hua, G., Huang, J.W., et al.: Twenty years of digital audio watermarking—a comprehensive review. Signal Process. **128**(11), 222–242 (2016)
2. Nishimura, A.: Audio watermarking based on subband amplitude modulation. Acoust. Sci. Technol. **32**(5), 328–336 (2010)
3. Hu, P., Peng, D., Yi, Z., Xiang, Y.: Robust time-spread echo watermarking using characteristics of host signals. Electron. Lett. **52**(1), 5–6 (2016)
4. Li, R.K., Yu, S.Z., Yang, H.Z.: Spread spectrum audio watermarking based on perceptual characteristic aware extraction. IET Signal Process. **10**(3), 266–273 (2016)
5. Chen, B., Wornell, G.W.: Quantization index modulation: a class of provably good methods for digital watermarking and information embedding. IEEE Trans. Inf. Theory **47**(4), 1423–1443 (2001)
6. Natgunanathan, I., Xiang, Y., et al.: Robust patchwork-based embedding and decoding scheme for digital audio watermarking. IEEE Trans. Audio Speech Lang. Process. **20**(8), 2232–2239 (2012). IEEE Signal Processing Society
7. Xiang, Y., Natgunanathan, I., et al.: Patchwork-based audio watermarking method robust to de-synchronization attacks. IEEE/ACM Trans. Audio Speech Lang. Process. **22**(9), 1413–1423 (2014)
8. Hu, H.T., Hsu, L.Y.: Robust, transparent and high-capacity audio watermarking in DCT domain. Signal Process. **109**(3), 226–235 (2015)
9. Kang, X., Yang, R., Huang, J.: Geometric invariant audio watermarking based on an LCM feature. IEEE Trans. Multimed. **13**(2), 181–190 (2011)
10. Erfani, Y., Pichevar, R., Rouat, J.: Audio watermarking using spikegram and a two-dictionary approach. IEEE Trans. Inf. Forensics Secur. **12**(4), 840–852 (2017)
11. Liu, Z.H., Wang, H.X.: A novel speech content authentication algorithm based on Bessel-Fourier moments. Digit. Signal Process. **24**(1), 197–208 (2014)
12. Chen, O.T.C., Chia, H.L.: Content-dependent watermarking scheme in compressed speech with identifying manner and location of attacks. IEEE Trans. Audio Speech Lang. Process. **15**(5), 1605–1616 (2007)
13. Luo, D., Sun, M.M., Huang, J.W.: Audio postprocessing detection based on amplitude cooccurrence vector feature. IEEE Signal Process. Lett. **23**(5), 688–692 (2016)
14. Xia, Z., Wang, X., Sun, X., Liu, Q., Xiong, N.: Steganalysis of LSB matching using differences between nonadjacent pixels. Multimed. Tools Appl. **75**(4), 1947–1962 (2016)
15. Chamlawi, R., Khan, A., Usman, I.: Authentication and recovery of images using multiple watermarks. Comput. Electr. Eng. **36**(3), 578–584 (2010)
16. Li, C.L., Wang, Y.H., Ma, B., Zhang, Z.X.: Tamper detection and self-recovery of biometric images using salient region-based authentication watermarking scheme. Comput. Stand. Interfaces **34**(4), 367–379 (2012)

17. Roldan, L.R., Hernandez, M.C., Miyatake, M.N., Meana, H.P., Kurkoski, B.: Watermarking-based image authentication with recovery capability using halftoning technique. Signal Process. Image Commun. **28**(1), 69–83 (2013)
18. Liu, Z.H., Zhang, F., Wang, J., Wang, H.X., Huang, J.W.: Authentication and recovery algorithm for speech signal based on digital watermarking. Signal Process. **123**(1), 157–166 (2016)
19. Hu, H.T., Chang, J.R., Lin, S.J.: Synchronous blind audio watermarking via shape configuration of sorted LWT coefficient magnitudes. Signal Process. **147**(1), 190–202 (2018)
20. Hu, H.T., Hsu, L.Y., Chou, H.H.: Perceptual-based DWPT-DCT framework for selective blind audio watermarking. Signal Process. **105**(12), 316–327 (2014)
21. Liu, Z.H., Luo, D., Huang, J.W., Wang, J., Qi, C.D.: Tamper recovery algorithm for digital speech signal based on DWT and DCT. Multimed. Tools Appl. **76**(10), 12481–12504 (2017)
22. Ali, A.H.: An imperceptible and robust audio watermarking algorithm. EURASIP J. Audio Speech Music Process. **37**(1), 1–12 (2014)
23. Wang, Y., Wu, S.Q., Huang, J.W.: Audio watermarking scheme robust against desynchronization based on the dyadic wavelet transform. J. Adv. Signal Process. **13**(1), 1–17 (2010)

A Steganographic Method Based on High Bit Rates Speech Codec of G.723.1

Fufang Li[1], Binbin Li[1], Lingxi Peng[2], Wenbin Chen[1],
Ligang Zheng[1(✉)], and Kefu Xu[3(✉)]

[1] School of Computer Science and Educational Software,
Guangzhou University, Guangzhou 510006, Guangdong, China
lffgz@163.com, zlg@gzhu.edu.cn
[2] School of Mechanical and Electric Engineering, Guangzhou University,
Guangzhou 510006, Guangdong, China
[3] Cyberspace Institute of Advanced Technology, Guangzhou University,
Guangzhou 510006, Guangdong, China
64637717@qq.com

Abstract. With compressed speech codecs having been widely used as the key technology for VoIP and mobile communications, steganography based on compressed speech streams has been flourishing in recent years. In this paper, based on the codec's characteristic features, we present a steganographic method using the excitation pulse positions of the high bit rate speech codec of ITU-T G.723.1. In the proposed method, the codes of excitation pulse-positions in the speech codec (i.e., codebook positions) are finely modulated according to the secret information that is being hidden. Sensitive data may thus be transmitted in secret without affecting the transmission quality of the normal speech data. Using the algorithm developed in this work and with the all-odd/even characteristics of pulse code positions being utilized, steganography experiments at high bit rates (6.3 Kbit/s) ware conducted on four kinds of voices: male or female voices speaking Mandarin or English. By using the proposed approach, an embedding rate of 2.6% and secret information transfer rate of 166 bits/s resulted in <5.0% degradations of the Perceptual Evaluation of Speech Quality (PESQ) score. And when the data hiding capacity reached 8.8% and the rate of secret information transfer came to 566 bits/s, the PESQ score was still reduced by <12.1%. The experiments show that our algorithm performs a higher degree of secrecy and steganographic efficacy compared with existing similar algorithms.

Keywords: G.723.1 compressed speech codec · Steganography
Codebook · Pulse code positions

1 Related Work

Steganography entails the embedding of secret information in digitalized carriers to conceal both its transmission behavior and contents, thus ensuring its secrecy and security during transmission; this has become an important technical tool for secure secret information transfers [1–3]. VoIP-based low bit-rate codec voice services have

© Springer Nature Switzerland AG 2018
X. Sun et al. (Eds.): ICCCS 2018, LNCS 11068, pp. 312–322, 2018.
https://doi.org/10.1007/978-3-030-00021-9_29

developed rapidly with the widespread popularization and application of Internet technology. Therefore, studies on steganographic techniques based on low bit-rate VoIP are highly significant in theory and in practice [4]. VoIP-based steganographic techniques had been developed rapidly between the multitudes of steganographic methods using streaming media as carriers. This is because the secret information embedded within VoIP communications are highly dynamic, which renders these steganographic methods robust against attacker's tampering. Furthermore, VoIP speech codecs can provide excellent imperceptibility and hiding capacity [5]. VoIP-based steganographic schemes usually employ one of the two following approaches [6]: network protocol-based steganography, and speech stream-based steganography. The parameters' redundancy of the G.723.1 speech codec at bit rates of 5.3 kb/s and 6.3 kb/s were analyzed in References [7, 8]. Paper [9] proposed a G.723.1-based steganographic method, where steganography was performed using the least significant bit (LSB) of noise frames. Reference [10] proposed a novel QIM steganography based on the replacement of quantization index set in linear predictive coding (LPC). Their steganography is conducted by treating each quantization index set as a point in quantization index space. Their algorithm had significantly improved the embedding efficiency. In [11], Huang et al. put forward a new steganography algorithm by embedding data while pitch period prediction is conducted during low bit-rate speech encoding. Their approach has great compatibility and can achieve high quality of speech and prevent detection of steganalysis without causing further delay by data embedding and extraction. By revealing that the inactive frames of VoIP streams are more suitable for data embedding than the active frames of the streams, paper [12] presented a novel high-capacity steganography algorithm for embedding data in the inactive frames of low bit-rate audio streams. Their algorithm had achieved perfect imperceptibility and high data embedding rate up to 101 bits/frame, which the data embedding capacity is very much larger than most of existing algorithms. In [13], Chunhui et al. proposed a highly imperceptible, high-capacity steganographic algorithm based on the noise coding frames of the G.723.1 codec. Reference [14] developed an Internet low bit rate Codec (iLBC)-based steganographic approach by using the compression domains of dynamic codebook quantization, which has a hiding capacity of 450 bps when iLBC operates at a carrier rate of 13.3 Kbps; this method also has excellent imperceptibility. Reference [15] proposed a steganographic method using the LSB of G.729a speech frames, which can be used for hiding data, in combination with matrix encoding. It was experimentally demonstrated that this algorithm has considerable hiding capacities, embedding rate, and imperceptibility. Reference [16] proposed a steganographic method based on dynamic codebook grouping that exploits the dynamic generation of codebooks in low bit rate speech codecs, and they used iLBC as an example to design a steganographic method based on dynamic codebook segmentation. Lin [17] bring forward an imperceptible information hiding approach on 5.3 kbit/s codec of G.723.1. To increase the data embedding capacity, they also propose a voice-activity detection method that uses the residual signal energy of the speech signal. Paper [18] studied invisible data hiding method for embedding data in encoded bits of the ACELP parameters for G.723.1 speech codec. This method can achieve an inaudible distortion in the occult-speech quality. Based on multiple vector quantization characteristics of the Line Spectrum Pair (LSP) of the speech codec, Peng [19] proposed a steganography scheme for ITU-T G.723.1 codec by using a 3D-sudoku matrix to enlarge capacity and improve quality of speech. Theoretical analysis and experimental results show their scheme has large hidden capacity while has little impact on the quality of speech.

In summary, steganography researchers have paid significant attention to G.723.1 speech codec-based steganographic methods, and obtained notable achievements in this regard. However, the aforementioned steganographic methods have their own specific strengths and weaknesses. The focus of this work is a steganographic method based on the excitation pulse positions of the high-bit rate MP-MLQ speech coding algorithm in the G.723.1 standard (this method is also applicable for the low-bit rate ACELP algorithm). In this method, the secret transmission of sensitive information is achieved by finely modulating excitation pulse positions. It was experimentally demonstrated that the use of this algorithm with an embedding rate of 3.1% and secret information transfer rate of 166 bits/s resulted in <5% degradations (i.e., reductions) in Perceptual Evaluation of Speech Quality (PESQ) scores, which indicates a high degree of imperceptibility. When the data hiding capacity was 16.146%, i.e., a secret information transfer rate of 1033 bit/s, the reduction in PESQ score was still less than 12%; hence, our method still retains a high degree of imperceptibility and steganographic efficacy under these conditions.

2 Brief Description of the G.723.1 Codec

The G.723.1 speech coding standard is a low bit rate coding scheme that was formulated by the International Telecommunication Union (ITU) for visual telephony. This speech coding scheme is a part of the overall ITU-T H.324 family of standards, and it is able to compress speech or the audio signal components of multimedia devices at a very low bit rate. The excitation signals corresponding to the high (6.3 kbit/s) and low (5.3 kbit/s) bit rates of this standard are Multipulse LPC with Maximum Likelihood Quantization (MP-MLQ) and Algebraic Code-Excited Linear Prediction (ACELP), respectively [9]. The G.723.1 standard recommends speech coding using the Code-Excited Linear Prediction (CELP) and MP-MLQ algorithms to minimize a perceptually weighted error signal. The analogue input signal is first passed through a telephone bandwidth filter, followed by sampling at 8 kHz and conversion into 16-bit linear PCM for input to the encoder, which operates with a frame length of 30 ms (240 sampling points at 8 kHz); this 16-bit linear PCM signal would be restored to its original data format after being decoded. An analysis is then performed on the delayed speech to extract its CELP parameters (LSP parameters, codebook indices, and gains), followed by the transmission of these parameter codes. In the decoder, these parameters are used to reconstruct the excitation signal and synthesis filter; the excitation signals are then passed through the synthesis filter to reconstruct the speech signal [20].

The codebook search of the G.723.1 speech codec is implemented as follows: a closed-loop pitch analysis is performed in a small range around the open-loop pitch estimate using the impulse response, h(n), and target signal, t(n), to compute the pitch period and estimated gain. A fifth order long-term predictor is used in the G.723.1 encoder, and gain is estimated via vector quantization. The pitch periods of even subframes (0 and 2) are coded using 7 bits, while the pitch periods of odd subframes (1 and 3) are coded differentially using 2 bits. An adaptive codebook is then used to calculate the long-term contribution, P(n), using the long-term predictor, which is then subtracted from the target signal, t(n), to obtain the residual signal, r(n). Finally, h(n) and r(n) are used to search for non-periodic impulse components of the excitation signal; MP-MLQ is used for the high bit rate (6.3 kbit/s) and ACELP is used for the low bit rate [21]. The allocation of the 192 encoding bits in the G.723.1 standard during high bit rate (6.3 Kbit/s) operation is shown in Table 1.

Table 1. Allocation of the 192 bits in high bit rate (6.3 Kbit/s) operation

Codec parameter	Subframe 1	Subframe 2	Subframe 3	Subframe 4	Total of each subframe
Control bit					2
LPC indices					24
Adaptive codebook lags	7	2	7	2	18
All gains combined	12	12	12	12	48
Parity bit	1	1	1	1	4
Reserved bit					1
*Pulse positions of the first 4 bits combined					13
Pulse positions	16	14	16	14	60
Pulse signs	6	5	6	5	22
Total	192				

*Pulse positions of the first 4 bits of each subframe are combined to form a 13-bit index.

3 Steganographic Method Based on High Bit Rates Speech Codec of G.723.1

3.1 Information Embedding and Extraction Approach Based on High Bit Rates Speech Codec of G.723.1

The embedding and extraction of secret information based on the excitation pulse positions of the G.723.1 speech codec is illustrated in Fig. 1.

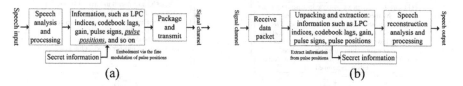

(a)   (b)

Fig. 1. Methods for the embedding and extraction of secret information

As is shown in Fig. 1(a), the method for embedding secret information is presented as follows: Firstly, speech analysis and processing is performed, followed by the calculation of LPC indices, adaptive codebook lags, the combinatorial codes of all gains, pulse signs, and pulse positions. Secondly, the pulse positions are then finely modulated according to the secret information. Finally, the digitized parameter data is packaged for transmission via ordinary communication channels. The extraction of secret information is illustrated by Fig. 1(b). After the data packets have been received from a communication channel, they are unpacked to extract all of the relevant parameters. The secret information hidden in the excitation pulse positions is then extracted according to its embedding rules, before the data is passed on to the decoder for speech reconstruction.

3.2   Steganographic Algorithm Based on the Excitation Pulse Positions of High Bit Rate Speech Codec of G.723.1

The high bit rate MP-MLQ algorithm specified by G.723.1 standard uses adaptive codebook searches. The MP-MLQ codec performs vector quantization through multipulse maximum likelihood estimation, and each subframe has four positions that generate excitation pulses. In high bit rate MP-MLQ codec, even and odd subframes have 6 and 5 non-zero excitation pulses respectively, and the positions of all non-zero pulses are either all odd or all even. Therefore, there are fewer than 30 pulse positions in each subframe. The algorithm of performing steganography based on the high bit rate MP-MLQ codec of G.723.1 is described as below.

As mentioned previously, the bitstream of the secret information being embedded has the form of St = [St(0), St(1), St(2), St(i), … St(L − 1)] and has a length of L, the sensitive secret information embedding sub-algorithm is as shown in Fig. 2(a). Given that the length of the embedded secret information is L, and the secret information bitstream that is being extracted is St = [St(0), St(1), St(2), St(i), … St(L − 1)], the information extraction sub-algorithm is as shown in Fig. 2(b).

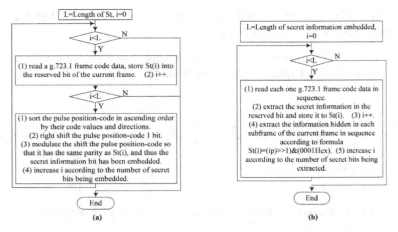

(a)   (b)

Fig. 2. Two sub-algorithms of the proposed steganographic algorithm: (a): the information embedding sub-algorithm; (b): the information extraction sub-algorithm.

4 Experimental Results and Analysis

4.1 Design of Experimental Scheme

To examine the steganographic efficacy of our algorithm, we examined the change in objective speech quality scores (i.e., PESQ score) in different types of voices, before and after the embedding of secret information, at different levels of hiding capacity (i.e., hiding rate). In the experiments, we used edited clips by ourselves of Chinese and foreign male and female voices that were sampled at 8 kHz to perform the PESQ tests. For these four kinds of voices, we created 40 edited clips of each voice and perform 200 time of tests; we then recorded the average PESQ score of these 200 time of tests of each kinds of voice. To provide an intuitive representation of the steganographic efficacy of our algorithm, the degradation percentage (i.e., reduction percentage) of the PESQ scores were also listed, in addition the raw PESQ scores obtained in each test. The effectiveness of our algorithm was then examined in further detail by performing comparative experiments with other similar algorithms. The results of this experiment indicate that our algorithm is an improvement over similar algorithms in terms of hiding capacity and imperceptibility. A detailed description of the aforementioned experiments and their results is provided in the followings.

4.2 Steganography Experiment and the Results

4.2.1 Selection of a Data Hiding Scheme for the Proposed Algorithm

In addition to the concealment of 1 bit of information in the reserved bit, there four kinds of conditions of information hiding schemes for the proposed algorithm: (1) If 5 bits of information are hidden in each frame (i.e., 1 bit of data is hidden in each subframe), there are then 6 usable positions in the 1st and 3rd subframes, and 5 usable positions in the 2nd and 4th subframes. Based on tests, we found that *the last pulse of each subframe is the optimal position in terms of steganographic efficacy.* (2) If 8 bits of information are being hidden in each frame (i.e., 2 bits of data are hidden in each subframe), there are then 150 different pulse position combinations that can be used to hide data according to the parity of the frame. A foreign male voice was used to screen the best combination from the combinations which yield the best steganographic efficacy and each average score was obtained from 200 repetitions of this test. The averaged PESQ scores of each combinations are shown in Table 2. *As is shown in Table 2, the last two pulses in each subframe are the optimal positions for hiding data which is indicated by the bolded entries in Table 2.* (3) If 16 bits of information are being hidden in each frame (i.e., 4 bits of data are hidden in each subframe), there are 60 possible pulse position combinations that may be used to hide data. Again, the foreign male voice was used to screen for the optimal combinations, and the average scores were obtained from 200 repetitions of this test. The average PESQ scores of each combinations are shown in Table 3. *Here, it is shown that the combinations using the 1st, 2nd, 5th, and 6th pulses of the 1st and 3rd subframes or the last four pulses of the 2nd and 4th subframes (bolded entries in the table) yield the best steganographic efficacy* (please refer to the bolded entries in Table 3). (4) If 23 bits of information are being hidden in each frame, i.e. 22 bits of information must be hidden in the subframes

Table 2. The average PESQ scores of the 150 possible scenarios when 9 bits of data are being hidden in each frame

#Col a	*Col b	^Pesq score	#Col a	*Col b	&Pesq score	#Col a	*Col b	&Pesq score	#Col a	*Col b	&Pesq score	#Col a	*Col b	&Pesq score
12	12	3.0559	13	23	3.0400	12	13	3.0360	12	15	3.1137	12	25	3.1033
23	12	3.0612	14	23	3.0437	23	13	3.0222	23	15	3.1027	23	25	3.0938
23	12	3.0652	15	23	3.0710	34	13	3.0403	34	15	3.1023	34	25	3.1016
45	12	3.1009	16	23	3.1598	45	13	3.0634	45	15	3.1348	45	25	3.1320
56	12	3.1962	24	23	3.0239	56	13	3.1678	56	15	3.2382	56	25	3.2284
12	23	3.0611	25	23	3.0303	13	13	3.0156	13	15	3.0928	13	25	3.0801
23	23	3.0465	26	23	3.1087	14	13	3.0175	14	15	3.0923	14	25	3.0753
34	23	3.0626	35	23	3.0444	15	13	3.0380	15	15	3.1034	15	25	3.0860
45	23	3.0902	36	23	3.1283	16	13	3.1245	16	15	3.1992	16	25	3.1825
56	23	3.1918	46	23	3.1386	24	13	2.9789	24	15	3.0711	24	25	3.0755
12	34	3.0829	13	34	3.0490	25	13	3.0141	25	15	3.0677	25	25	3.0638
23	34	3.0551	14	34	3.0522	26	13	3.0962	26	15	3.1645	26	25	3.1515
34	34	3.0720	15	34	3.0650	35	13	3.0219	35	15	3.0934	35	25	3.0834
45	34	3.0793	16	34	3.1450	36	13	3.0975	36	15	3.1790	36	25	3.1607
56	34	3.1993	24	34	3.0351	46	13	3.0952	46	15	3.1800	46	25	3.1708
12	45	3.1750	25	34	3.0343	12	14	3.0498	12	24	3.0246	12	35	3.1008
23	45	3.1513	26	34	3.1208	23	14	3.0319	23	24	3.0288	23	35	3.0841
34	45	3.1486	35	34	3.0413	34	14	3.0449	34	24	3.0335	34	35	3.1109
45	45	3.1787	36	34	3.1399	45	14	3.0618	45	24	3.0534	45	35	3.1261
56	**45**	**3.2949**	46	34	3.1336	56	14	3.1492	56	24	3.1547	56	35	3.2476
13	12	3.0461	13	45	3.1111	13	14	3.0310	13	24	3.0225	13	35	3.0798
14	12	3.0505	14	45	3.1303	14	14	3.0229	14	24	3.0247	14	35	3.0843
15	12	3.0766	15	45	3.1303	15	14	3.0459	15	24	3.0340	15	35	3.1040
16	12	3.1545	16	45	3.2507	16	14	3.1327	16	24	3.1323	16	35	3.2048
24	12	3.0214	24	45	3.1096	24	14	3.0151	24	24	3.0011	24	35	3.0574
25	12	3.0560	25	45	3.1086	25	14	3.0097	25	24	3.0057	25	35	3.0520
26	12	3.1194	26	45	3.2130	26	14	3.0888	26	24	3.0727	26	35	3.1585
35	12	3.0586	35	45	3.1122	35	14	3.0246	35	24	3.0149	35	35	3.0720
36	12	3.1337	36	45	3.2103	36	14	3.1003	36	24	3.0914	36	35	3.1759
46	12	3.1459	46	45	3.2218	46	14	3.1026	46	24	3.0991	46	35	3.1818

Note: #Col a represents "Combination of pulses in the 1st and 3rd subframes."
*Col b represents "Combination of pulses in the 2nd and 4th subframes."
^Pesq score represents "Average PESQ score."
All the '12, …, 35' entries in the table indicate the pulses selected in each subframe, for instance: '12' represents the 1st and 2nd pulses while '35' represents the 3rd and 5th pulses.

while 1 bit is hidden in the reserved bit of the codebook bits. Steganography using this scheme results in an excessive reduction in average PESQ scores, and therefore a significant change in speech quality. Hence, *this scheme is unsuitable for steganography*.

4.2.2 Results of the Steganographic Experiment of the Proposed Algorithm

Based on the experimental scheme described in Sub-Sect. 4.1, objective speech quality tests of PESQ score were carried out by using edited clips of four types of voices sampled at 8 kHz. The average PESQ scores of these voices (that do not contain any

Table 3. The average PESQ scores of the 60 possible scenarios when 17 bits of data are being hidden in each frame

#Col c	*Col d	^Pesq score	#Col a	*Col b	^Pesq score	#Col a	*Col b	^Pesq score	#Col a	*Col b	^Pesq score	#Col a	*Col b	^Pesq score
1234	1234	2.9577	1345	1234	2.9278	1234	1245	2.9737	1234	1235	2.9852	1234	1345	3.0018
2345	1234	2.9032	1456	1234	2.9379	2345	1245	2.9189	2345	1235	2.9259	2345	1345	2.9316
3456	1234	2.9079	2456	1234	2.9098	3456	1245	2.9176	3456	1235	2.9135	3456	1345	2.9252
1234	2345	3.0206	1235	1234	2.9400	1235	1245	2.9700	1345	1235	2.9380	1345	1345	2.9565
2345	2345	2.9601	2346	1234	2.8918	1236	1245	2.9567	1456	1235	2.9391	1456	1345	2.9667
3456	2345	2.9421	1236	1234	2.9468	2346	1245	2.8929	2456	1235	2.9023	2456	1345	2.9030
1245	1234	2.9623	1345	2345	2.9761	1345	1245	2.9276	1235	1235	2.9394	1235	1345	2.9766
1256	1234	2.9791	1456	2345	2.9874	1456	1245	2.9365	1236	1235	2.9751	2346	1345	2.9812
2356	1234	2.8937	2456	2345	2.9335	2456	1245	2.8834	2346	1235	2.9092	1236	1345	2.9204
1245	2345	3.0232	1235	2345	3.0009	1245	1245	2.9682	1245	1235	2.9800	1245	1345	2.9924
1256	**2345**	**3.0258**	1236	2345	2.9980	1256	1245	2.9876	1256	1235	2.9768	1256	1345	3.0085
2356	2345	2.9432	2346	2345	2.9515	2356	1245	2.9111	2356	1235	2.9189	2356	1345	2.9318

Note: #Col c represents "Combination of pulses in the 1st and 3rd subframes"
*Col d represents "Combination of pulses in the 2nd and 4th subframes"
^Pesq score represents "Average PESQ score". And All the '1234, ..., 2356' entries in the table indicate the pulses selected in each subframe,
for instance: '1234' represents the 1st, 2nd, 3rd and 4th pulses.

hidden data) were slightly lower than the standard PESQ score of the 6.3 kb/s G.723.1 speech codec (which is 3.98). To facilitate an intuitive and convenient observation of steganographic efficacy, the results of experiments are represented as percentage reductions in PESQ scores (or degradation percentage). The degradation percentages in average PESQ scores before and after steganography was performed by using the presented algorithm are shown in Table 4, while Table 5 illustrates how PESQ scores are affected by hiding capacity and embedding rate.

Table 4. The degradation in average PESQ scores before and after steganography was performed by using the proposed algorithm

	China-male	China-female	Foreign-male	Foreign-female
No data hidden	3.503025	3.356881	3.653155	3.243805
5 bits of data are hidden in each frame (including 1-bit in the reserved bit)	3.312811 94.57%	3.181987 94.79%	3.479995 95.26%	3.101402 95.61%
9 bits of data are hidden in each frame (including 1-bit in the reserved bit)	3.206319 91.53%	3.070203 91.46%	3.345924 91.59%	3.011224 92.83%
17 bits of data are hidden in each frame (including 1-bit in the reserved bit)	3.070051 87.64%	2.944992 87.73%	3.212219 87.93%	2.872065 88.54%

Table 5. The hiding capacity and embedding rate of secret information by using the proposed algorithm

Hiding capacity per frame	Hiding capacity per second	Embedding rate	Average PESQ scores	Degradation percentage in average PESQ scores
5 bits	166 bits/s	2.59%	3.269049	4.95%
9 bits	300 bits/s	4.69%	3.158418	8.16%
17 bits	566 bits/s	8.84%	3.024832	12.05%

As is shown in Tables 4 and 5, the PESQ score of the speech carrier decreases with increasing hiding capacity and embedding rate when steganography was performed by using the proposed information hiding algorithm based on the pulse positions of the high bit rate G.723.1 codec. From Table 5, we can see that the degradation in PESQ score was less than 5% when the embedding rate was 2.59% and the hiding capacity was 166 bits/s. Nonetheless, the degradation in PESQ score was less than 12.1% even when the embedding rate increases to 8.8% and the hiding capacity increases to 566 bits/s, which indicate the proposed algorithm has an excellent level of secrecy, imperceptibility and rubustness.

4.3 Comparative Experiment Between the Algorithm Developed in This Work and Similar Algorithms

To examine the steganographic efficacy of our algorithm in further depth, we compared our algorithm with the method detailed in Reference [8], which is the most similar steganographic method in the current literature to our method. The algorithm in Reference [8] also performs steganography using the high bit rate G.723.1 codec. This experiment was also conducted using the scheme described in Sect. 4.1; the Reference [8] algorithm was used at its maximum hiding capacity (16 bits or 533 bits/s), while our algorithm was used with a hiding capacity of 17 bits, i.e., 566 bits/s. The PESQ scores before and after steganography were examined by using edited clips of the four aforementioned voices, and the results of this experiment are shown in Table 6. Table 6 shows the results of the comparative experiment in terms of reductions in PESQ scores when steganography was performed using our algorithm and the algorithm described in Reference [8].

Table 6. Results of the comparative experiment between algorithm 3_1 and a similar algorithm

Voice type	PESQ score without data hidden	Our algorithm		Algorithm in Reference [8]	
		PESQ score	Degradation percentage	PESQ score	Degradation percentage
China-male	3.503025	3.070051	12.36%	3.042377	13.15%
China-female	3.356881	2.944992	12.27%	2.905045	13.46%
Foreign-male	3.653155	3.212219	12.07%	3.151577	13.73%
Foreign-female	3.243805	2.872065	11.46%	2.801350	13.64%

As is shown in Table 6, the percentage reduction in PESQ scores was lower when our steganographic was used, as compared to the algorithm described in Reference [8], while a slightly higher hiding capacity being used with the former than the latter. It is thus shown that our algorithm has a greater degree of secrecy, imperceptibility and robustness, or in other words, higher levels of steganographic efficacy.

5 Conclusion and Outlook

In this paper, we have developed a steganographic method based on the fixed codebook pulse positions of the G.723.1 speech codec. It was experimentally demonstrated that the steganographic method developed in this work has high levels of imperceptibility at high hiding capacities. By exploiting the fully odd or even characteristic of the high bit rate G.723.1 codec's pulses, we were able to achieve a data hiding capacity of 8.8% (i.e., the transmission of 566 bits of secret information per second) with <12.1% reductions in PESQ scores, thus retaining a high level of speech quality. The comparative experiment also demonstrated that our algorithm has a higher level of overall efficacy than similar algorithms in the literature. In the future, we will focus on studies of applications for the steganographic method developed in this work. In addition, we will investigate the possibility of performing steganography based on other speech codec parameters, so as to discover more effective approaches for steganography based on compressed speech codecs.

Acknowledgment. We would like to thank the anonymous referees for their careful readings of the manuscripts and many useful suggestions. This work has been co-financed by: Natural Science Foundation of China under Grant No. 61472092, U183610049; Guangdong Provincial Science and Technology Plan Fund with grant No. 2013B010401037; GuangZhou Municipal High College Science Research Fund under grant No. 1201421317; State Scholarship Fund by China Scholarship Council under Grant No. [2013]3018-201308440096; and Yuexiu District Science and Technology Plan Fund of GuangZhou City with grant No. 2013-GX-005. We also discussed the work with the classmates and colleagues of School of Computer Science & Educational Software of GuangZhou University, thanks for their self-giving helps.

References

1. Liu, L., Li, M., Li, Q., Liang, Y.: Perceptually transparent information hiding in G.729 bitstream. In: Proceedings of 2008 4th International Conference on Intelligent Information Hiding and Multimedia Signal Proceeding, IIH-MSP 2008, Harbin, pp. 406–409. IEEE Press (2008)
2. Wang, C.-D., Ma, D.F.: Information hiding based on real-time voice in DCT domain. Comput. Eng. Des. **33**(2), 474–478+555 (2012). in Chinese
3. Gu, C., Cao, X.L.: Research on information hiding technolgy. In: Proceedings of the 2nd International Conference on Consumer Electronics, Communications and Networks, CECNet 2012, Yichang, pp. 2035–2037. IEEE Press (2012)
4. Wei, Z., et al.: An ovel steganography approach for voice over IP. J. Ambient Intell. Humaniz. Comput. **5**(4), 601–610 (2014)

5. Mazurczyk, W.: VOIP steganography and its detection: a survey. ACM Comput. Surv. 2(46), 20 (2013)
6. Fraczek, W., Mazurczyk, W., Szczypiorskik, K.: Hiding information in a stream control transmission protocol. Comput. Commun. 2(35), 159–169 (2012)
7. Xu, T.T., Yang, Z.: Simple and effective speech steganography in G.723.1 low-rate codes. In: 2009 International Conference on Wireless Communications and Signal Processing, WCSP 2009, Nanjing, pp. 1–4. IEEE Press (2009)
8. Yang, J., Bai, S., Zhu, G.B., Liu, J.: Information hiding algorithm of G.723.1 high-rate speech flow. Comput. Eng. 37(22), 114–115+118 (2011). (in Chinese)
9. ITU. Dual Rate Speech Coder for Multimedia Communications Transmitting at 5.3 and 6.3 kbps. ITU-T Recommendation G.723.1, http://www.itu.int/rec/T-REC-G.723.1/recommendation.asp?lang=en&parent=T-REC-G.723.1-200605-I (2006)
10. Liu, P., Li, S., Wang, H.: Steganography in vector quantization process of linear predictive coding for low-bit-rate speech codec. Multimedia Syst. 23(4), 485–497 (2017)
11. Huang, Y., Liu, C., Tang, S., Bai, S.: Steganography integration into a low-bit rate speech codec. IEEE Trans. Inf. Forensics Secur. 7(6), 1865–1875 (2012)
12. Huang, Y.F., Tang, S., Yuan, J.: Steganography in inactive frames of VoIP streams encoded by source codec. IEEE Trans. Inform. Forensics Secur. 6(2), 296–306 (2011)
13. Chunhui, W., Yongfeng, H., Weihua, W., Beixing, D.: A large-capability self-adaptive steganography algorithm based on G.723.1. J. Wuhan Univ. Technol. (Inf. Manage. Eng.) 32(4), 522–525 (2010). (in Chinese)
14. Yang, W.-X., Sun, D.-H., Huang, Y.-F.: Steganographic method in Self-adaptive codebooks of speech codec. Comput. Eng. Des. 34(8), 2656–2661 (2013). (in Chinese)
15. Guo, S.T., Tian, H.: An information hiding method based on G.729a speech. J. Huaqiao Univ (Nat. Sci.) 3(35), 277–282 (2014). (in Chinese)
16. Yang, W.-X., Yu, H., Hu, P.: Research on steganographic method integrated in the compressed speech codec. Acta Electron. Sin. 07(42), 1305–1310 (2014). (in Chinese)
17. Lin, R.S.:. An imperceptible information hiding in encoded bits of speech signal. In: Proceedings - 2015 International Conference on Intelligent Information Hiding and Multimedia Signal Processing, IIH-MSP 2015, pp. 37–40 (2015)
18. Lin, R.S.: Imperceptible data hiding in the encoded bits of ACELP codebook. In: Ubi-Media 2017 - Proceedings of the 10th International Conference on Ubi-Media Computing and Workshops with the 4th International Workshop on Advanced E-Learning and the 1st International Workshop on Multimedia and IoT: Networks, Systems and Applications, Ubi-Media 2017, pp. 201–225 (2017)
19. Peng, X., Huang, Y., Li, F.: A steganography scheme in a low-bit rate speech codec based on 3D-sudoku matrix. In: Proceedings of 2016 8th IEEE International Conference on Communication Software and Networks, ICCSN 2016, pp. 13–18 (2016)
20. Li, C., Shen, B.: Analysis and optimization of ITU-T G.723.1 speech coder. Electron. Meas. Technol. 30(9), 104–106+139 (2007). (in Chinese)
21. Yang, S.T., Zhou, J.-L., Yu, S.-S.: Clustering optimization strategy for G.723.1 speech coder and its application. J. Commun. 22(2), 113–117 (2001). (in Chinese)

A Variable-Angle-Distance Quantum Evolutionary Algorithm for 2D HP Model

Yu Zheng[(⊠)], Zhenrong Zhang, Wei Fang, and Wenjie Liu

School of Computer & Software, Jiangsu Engineering Center of Network Monitoring, Nanjing University of Information Science and Technology, Nanjing 210044, Jiangsu, China
yzheng@nuist.edu.cn

Abstract. The computational simulations under the two dimensional hydrophobic-polar (2D-HP) model from protein's amino is a fundamental and challenging problems in computational biology. In this paper, we propose an improved quantum-inspired evolutionary algorithm based on variable angle-distance rotation strategy (QEA-VAR) for this NP-hard combinatorial protein folding problems. The QEA-VAR method is based on the concept and principles of quantum computing, such as quantum bits, quantum rotation gates and superposition of states. Comparing to the previously well-known evolutionary algorithm for the protein folding problem, QEA-VAR can find optimal or near-optimal energy structure from the benchmark sequences with a small simulating samples. Moreover, the proposed method's global convergence is faster than the other evolutionary algorithms. The application studies have demonstrated the superior performance and feasibility of the proposed algorithm for the protein folding problem.

Keywords: Quantum-inspired evolutionary algorithm
Quantum angle-distance rotation · (2D-HP) hydrophobic-polar
Protein folding

1 Introduction

Protein structure prediction (PSP) from its primary sequence is a challenging task in computational biology [1]. Protein folding, the problem of protein structure prediction, is one of the core issues in the field of bioinformatics. The problem of protein folding is to study how the natural structure of a protein is formed, that is, how a polypeptide chain with a certain amino acid sequence gradually forms the unique spatial structure of a protein. At present, many "conformational diseases" or "folding diseases" are caused by abnormal aggregation of proteins caused by molecular aggregation or even precipitation, such as: Alzheimer's disease (protein conformational changes), cystic fibrosis (protein cannot fold), familial high Cholesterol (protein miss-folding), familial amyloidosis (protein deposits), etc. Therefore, the need to understand the mechanism of protein folding has become more urgent.

© Springer Nature Switzerland AG 2018
X. Sun et al. (Eds.): ICCCS 2018, LNCS 11068, pp. 323–333, 2018.
https://doi.org/10.1007/978-3-030-00021-9_30

With the deepening of protein folding research, the biological function of proteins depends largely on the spatial folding structure of proteins, so understanding the spatial structure of proteins is of great significance in the biological field. Through experimental means, the composition of the protein chain can be measured, but it is very difficult to observe the spatial structure of the protein. Studies have shown that the use of theoretical calculations to predict protein structure is a feasible method based on the amino acid sequence and energy model of the protein. At present, this method has become an important tool in protein engineering.

Because the real protein folding problem is too complexity, the theoretical community has proposed some simplified models. Among them, the most widely studied is the HP grid model proposed by Dill et al. [2]. This model divides twenty amino acids into two classes: hydrophobic amino acids (H) and hydrophilic amino acids (P). Each amino acid monomer can be seen as a small ball, H as a black ball and P as a white ball. In this way, an amino acid sequence can be viewed as a chain of black and white spheres with a distance of 1 from the center of the sphere. The HP grid model puts the amino acid chains on two-dimensional or three-dimensional unit grids without overlapping, requiring that each ball must be placed on one grid point, and two adjacent balls on the chain are placed on the grid point plane or space. The rear position is still adjacent.

Although the HP grid model is a simplified model, the solution to the protein folding problem of this model is still difficult. This problem has been proved to be a NP-complete problem [3–5], so it is impossible to solve using a deterministic algorithm. The number of optimization heuristics applied to the HP model is extensive with a significant number of the contributions made in recent years [7]. In the past decade, some scholars have tried to use some evolutionary algorithms to solve the HP model to find the lowest energy configuration, such as: genetic algorithm (GA) [6], differential algorithm (DE), particle swarm optimization (PSO) [11], and so on. Most of these algorithms use a certain scale of HP grid point coordinates as the problem solution, and they are evolved through iterative methods to try to obtain the optimal coordinate solution (i.e., the lowest energy configuration). However, these algorithms all have certain defects. Among them, the genetic algorithm can't obtain the optimal solution as the scale increases (for example, the number of amino acids is 50, 60, 64, and 85, the lowest energy configuration cannot be found), and the convergence speed is slow; the difference algorithm performs better than the genetic algorithm, and the lowest energy configuration can be found for the published examples. However, the convergence speed needs to be improved. The PSO algorithm has a good improvement in the convergence speed, but there are defects that are easily trapped in the local optimum.

The rest of the paper is organized as follows. Section 2 introduces the protein folding problem related to the new algorithm. In Sect. 3, the quantum-inspired evolutionary based on variable angle-distance algorithm (QEA-VAR) is described in detail. The experimental results and performance analysis are given in Sect. 4. Finally, a conclusion and the future work are provided in Sect. 5.

2 Protein Two-Dimensional HP Grid Model

In the HP model, proteins are thought to consist of two types of residues: hydrophobic (H) residues and hydrophilic or polar (P) residues. Each amino acid can be thought of as a node. A protein is considered a sequence of these two types of nodes, such as *HHHPHPPPPPH*, which are located in regular lattice models forming self-avoided paths. Given a pair of residues, they are considered neighbors if they are adjacent either in the chain (connected neighbors) or in the lattice but not connected in the chain (topological neighbors). A legitimate protein chain space configuration must satisfy the following three conditions:

(1) Any node (H or P) must be placed on an integer point coordinate in two dimensions;
(2) Adjacent nodes in the chain sequence are still adjacent in the placed space (distance is 1);
(3) At most one node can be placed on any grid point in two-dimensional coordinates.

The energy function of the HP model is as follows:

$$E = \sum_{\substack{i,j=1 \\ i<j-1}}^{n} \sigma_{ij} \tag{2-1}$$

Where n is the chain length.

If i, j are black balls and their center distance is 1, $\sigma_{ij} = -1$; in other cases, $\sigma_{ij} = 0$.

Function 2-1 measures the interaction between topological neighbor residues is defined as $E_{HH} = -1$ and $E_{HP} = E_{PP} = 0$. The HP problem consists of finding the solution that minimizes the total energy.

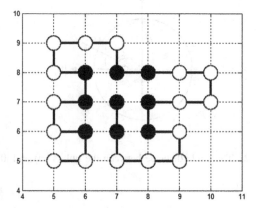

Fig. 1. An example of legal conformations of proteins containing 25 sites.

Figure 1 shows the graphical representation of a possible configuration for sequence *PPHPPHHPPPPPHHPPPPPHHPPPPPHH*. Here, the black ball represents hydrophobic (H) residues and the white ball represents polar (P) residues. If the black balls are not adjacent in sequence but spatially adjacent, the energy between the two black balls is recorded as −1. So the energy that the HP model associates with this configuration is −8.

3   QEA-VAR for HP Grid Model

In 1996, Narayanan and Moore proposed the first quantum-inspired genetic algorithm inspired by the quantum superposition mechanism, which is considered to be the prototype of QEA [12, 13]. However, evolutionary operators still use traditional crossover and mutation operations. Until 2000, Ha and Kim proposed a novel quantum heuristic genetic algorithm (QGA) [12]. Since the algorithm first uses quantum chromosomes to represent individuals and introduces quantum revolving doors as evolution operators, it is considered to be the first truly quantum evolutionary algorithm. After 2 years, the QGA was improved and the algorithm name was corrected by QEA. In order to solve the problem of numerical optimization and multi-objective optimization, Han and Kim et al. proposed a two-stage QEA algorithm and a multi-objective quantum evolution algorithm MQEA in 2004 and 2006, respectively. In addition, in order to speed up the convergence rate while avoiding premature convergence, Xing et al. proposed a new improved quantum genetic algorithm (NIQGA) [14] that uses a dynamic step-size strategy to adjust the rotation angle of the quantum gate and achieved good results. In 2010, we proposed a quantum-inspired evolutionary algorithm based on variable angle-distance rotation strategy (QEA-VAR) [15].

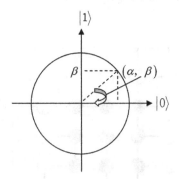

Fig. 2. The angle distance between the qubits $|\varphi\rangle$ and $|0\rangle$.

3.1 A Subsection Sample

Definition 1. The rotation angle distance $\Delta\theta$ between two qubits $(|\varphi\rangle, |\varphi'\rangle)$ describes the deflection angle of the qubit from $|\varphi\rangle$ to $|\varphi'\rangle$ and can be expressed as: $\Delta\theta_{|\varphi\rangle,|\varphi'\rangle} = \arctan(\beta'/\alpha') - \arctan(\beta/\alpha)$.

Obviously, the angle distance is a vector (including deflection amplitude and deflection direction), such as the angle distance between the qubits $|\varphi\rangle$ and $|0\rangle$ is $\Delta\theta_{|\varphi\rangle} = -\arctan(\alpha/\beta)$ (Fig. 2).

3.2 QEA-VAR Flow for HP Grid Model

The QEA-VAR algorithm flow is similar to the general quantum evolution algorithm framework, but the tedious look-up table mechanism is abandoned on the selection of the rotation angle, and the angle of rotation is used to adjust the rotation angle. The rotation angle θ_i is calculated according to the following formula:

$$\theta_i = \frac{1}{k}\Delta\theta_{|\varphi\rangle_i,*} \tag{3-1}$$

Where, k selects the random constant of the normal distribution between [2, 8]; $\Delta\theta_{|\varphi\rangle_i,*}$ denotes the angular distance between the i-th qubit $|\varphi\rangle_i$ and the ground state $|0\rangle$ or $|1\rangle$ in the quantum chromosome. Defined by the angular distance, it can be calculated by the following formula:

$$\Delta\theta_{|\varphi\rangle_i,*} = \begin{cases} \Delta\theta_{|\varphi\rangle_i,|0\rangle} = -ac\,\tan\frac{\beta_i}{\alpha_i} & (f(b) \geq f(x)) \wedge (b_i = 0) \wedge (x_i = 1) \\ \Delta\theta_{|\varphi\rangle_i,|1\rangle} = \frac{\pi}{2} - ac\,\tan\frac{\beta_i}{\alpha_i} & (f(b) \geq f(x)) \wedge (b_i = 1) \wedge (x_i = 0) \\ 0 & \text{otherwise} \end{cases} \tag{3-2}$$

Where α_i and β_i are the probability of $|\varphi\rangle_i$; x_i is the measured value of $|\varphi\rangle_i$ (0 or 1); b_i is the current optimal binary solution b with the i-th bit value (0 or 1).

In the Table 1, we will briefly define some notations which will be used in the algorithm flow.

Table 1. Summary of Notations.

Symbol	Definition
t	Variable that represent generation
$Q(t)$	The quantum population
moveDirect(t)	Direction solution population
bestSolFar	The best solution at present

The basic flow of the QEA-VAR algorithm for solving HP model protein prediction problems is as follows:

Procedure QEA-VAR
begin
    t ← 0
    initialize Q(t)
    make moveDirect (t) by P(t)
    do while(moveDirect (t) is illegal)
      Repair(t)
    end do
    evaluate moveDirect (t)
    save the best solution to bestSoFar
    do while (not termination-condition) do
      begin
        t ← t + 1
        make moveDirect (t) by observing Q(t - 1) states
        do while(moveDirect (t) is illegal)
            Repair(t)
        end do
        evaluate moveDirect (t)
        update Q(t) with quantum gates using the variable-angle-distance strategy
        save the best solution to bestSoFar
      end
    end do
end

In this algorithm, the quantum population is initialized so that the probability of 0 or 1 when measuring qubits is 1/2. And the qubits in the quantum population are measured to generate 0 or 1. If the binary bits is 00, the corresponding direction value is 1, indicating that the direction is upward; if it is 01, the corresponding direction value is i, indicating that the direction is right; if it is 10, the corresponding direction value is − 1, indicating that the direction is downward; if it is 11, the corresponding direction value is −i, indicating that the direction is to the left. According to this rule, it generates a solution population. Is there a loop according to the direction solution? If a loop occurs, the sum of the direction values of some points is 0, indicating that the configuration is invalid and needs to be repaired. The repair method is to make the conflict point try other directions that have not been tried. If it is still in conflict with the previous point and then select another direction, if all the directions have been tried and have not been repaired, then it will regress to the previous point. The previous point is repaired according to this method until a valid configuration is formed.

The traction condition is that if the optimal individual is not changed for 10 generations or every 30 generations, then all configurations are towed. The purpose of traction is to bend the directly connected portion of the configuration, increasing the number of unconnected but adjacent H pairs on the chain. To a certain extent, it is beneficial to jump out of the local optimum.

4 The Experiment Result and Performance Analysis

This section gives some simulation-based experiments and analysis of the results and performance of the QEA-VAR. All experiments are simulated on the MATLAB R2014a.

In order to illustrate the high efficiency of this algorithm, two types of algorithms (differential algorithm and particle swarm algorithm) with better performance are selected to conduct comparative experiments. The population size selected for this algorithm is 30 (difference algorithm and particle swarm algorithm is selected as 100), and the number of amino acids is chosen as 20, 24, 25, 36, 48, 50, 60, 64, 85. The largest evolutionary generation is determined according to the scale (20, 24, 25, 36 is 500 generations; 48, 50, 60, 64, and 85 are 800 generations). During the testing process, the three algorithms were executed 25 times. The statistics of the average minimum energy values of each generation were used to obtain the evolution comparison results of the three algorithms, as shown in the Fig. 3 and the test sequences as shown as Table 2.

In the Fig. 3, the black line is the difference algorithm, the green line is the particle swarm algorithm, and the blue line is the QEA-VAR proposed in the present invention. It is easy to see that the QEA-VAR finds public minimum energy faster than the other two algorithms. Although, the Particle swarm algorithm(PSO) achieves a lower average energy than some quantum evolution algorithms at some stages and the descending speed is faster, the convergence rate is not as stable as the QEA-VAR,, especially in the later period, the average minimum energy is lower than the QEA-VAR in the later period, on the whole, the performance of the PSO algorithm is lower than the QEA-VAR. Although the difference algorithm finally finds the public minimum energy value, it can be seen from the Fig. 3 that the running speed and the convergence speed are the lowest. In summary, the QEA-VAR has the best overall performance among the three algorithms.

Table 3 further illustrates the effect of the three algorithms in finding the lowest energy for different protein sequences. The published minimum value that achieved in [8–10] shows that in the case of protein structure prediction. The second column in the table is the size of the protein sequence, the third column is the published minimum value, and the third, fourth, and fifth are the corresponding minimum values of the three methods, where the Avg. column shows the average minimum energy value after 25 executions. Parentheses indicate the number of times the lowest value was found in 25 runs.

Table 3 shows that when the protein sequence is 60, 64, and 85, the lowest energy average is higher than the particle swarm algorithm, that is, the number of times to find the disclosed minimum value is higher. Therefore, as can be seen from Table 3 and Fig. 3, the QEA-VAR method outperforms the other two algorithms in terms of efficiency.

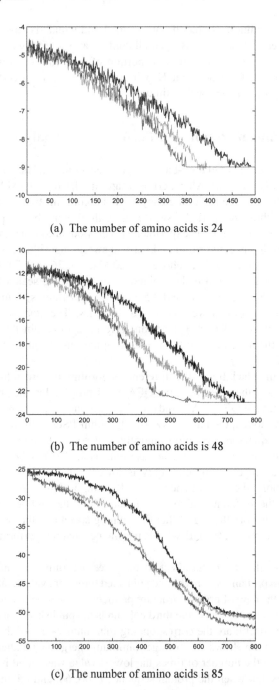

(a) The number of amino acids is 24

(b) The number of amino acids is 48

(c) The number of amino acids is 85

Fig. 3. The average minimum energy value, the evolution comparison results of the three algorithms.

Table 2. Test sequences.

No.	Length	Sequence
1	20	$(HP)_2PH(HP)_2(PH)_2HP(PH)_2$
2	24	$H_2P_2(HP_2)_6H_2$
3	25	$P_2HP_2(H_2P_4)_3H_2$
4	36	$P(P_2H_2)_2P_5H_5(H_2P_2)_2P_2H(HP_2)_2$
5	48	$P_2H(P_2H_2)_2\ P_5H_{10}P_6(H_2P_2)_2HP_2H_5$
6	50	$H_2(PH)_3PH_4PH(P_3H)_2P_4(HP_3)_2HPH_4(PH)_3PH_2$
7	60	$P(PH_3)_2H_5P_3H_{10}PHP_3H_{12}P_4H_6PH_2PHP$
8	64	$H_{12}(PH)_2((P_2H_2)_2P_2H)_3(PH)_2H_{11}$
9	85	$H_4P_4H_{12}P_6(H_{12}P_3)_3HP_2(H_2P_2)_2HPH$

Table 3. Test sequences.

Seq No	Size	E*	DE	PSO		Our Approach	
				Max	Avg	Max	Avg
S1	20	9	9	9	9.00	9 (25)	9.00
S2	24	9	9	9	9.00	9 (25)	9.00
S3	25	8	8	8	8.00	8 (25)	8.00
S4	36	14	14	14	14.00	14 (25)	14.00
S5	48	23	23	23	23.00	23 (25)	23.00
S6	50	21	21	21	21.00	21 (25)	21.00
S7	60	36	35	36	35.12	36 (20)	35.80
S8	64	42	42	42	41.23	42 (20)	41.75
S9	85	53	52	53	51.9	53 (20)	52.14

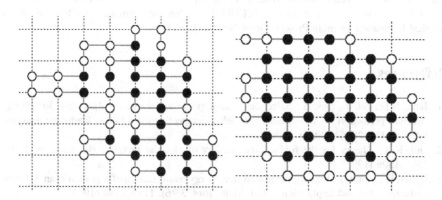

Fig. 4. Best solutions of the HP model for sequence 50 (Left) and for sequence 60 (Right). The optimal energy values are -21 and -36 for the functional and HP model, respectively.

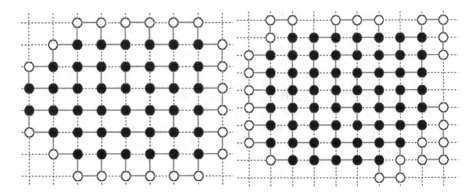

Fig. 5. Best solutions of the HP model for sequence 64 (Left) and for sequence 85 (Right). The optimal energy values are −42 and −53 for the functional and HP model, respectively.

Figures 4 and 5 show optimal configurations of the HP model for sequence 50,60,64 and 85, respectively.

5 Conclusion

In this paper, the QEA-VAR algorithm is proposed for the protein folding problems. By comparison with other three algorithms, the proposed algorithm enables to effectively for searching the lowest energy and takes less time. These characteristics fully reflect the advantages of strong searching ability, difficulty in falling into local optimum, and high efficiency.

Acknowledgments. This work is supported by Natural Science Foundation of Jiangsu Province(Grant No. BK20171458), the   Six Talent Peaks Project of Jiangsu Province (Grant No. 2015-XXRJ-013), Jiangsu Province College Students Practical Innovation Training Project (Grant No.201810300085).

References

1. Jana, N.D., Sil, J., Das, S.: Selection of appropriate metaheuristic algorithms for protein structure prediction in AB off-lattice model: a perspective from fitness landscape analysis. Inf. Sci. **391**, 28–64 (2017)
2. Dill, K.A.: Theory for the folding and stability of globular proteins. Biochemistry **24**(6), 1501–1509 (1985)
3. Unger, R., Moult, J.: Finding the lowest free energy conformation of a protein is an NP-hard problem: proof and implications. Bull. Math. Biol. **55**(6), 1183–1198 (1993)
4. Crescenzi, P., Goldman, D., Papadimitriou, C., Piccolboni, A., Yannakakis, M.: On the complexity of protein folding. J. Comput. Biol. **5**(3), 423–465 (1998)
5. Berger, B., Leighton, T.: Protein folding in the hydrophobic–hydrophilic (HP) model is NP-complete. J. Comput. Biol. **5**(1), 30–39 (1998)

6. Unger, R., Moult, J.: Genetic algorithms for protein folding simulations. J. Mol. Biol. **231**, 75–81 (1993)
7. Santana, R., Larrañaga, P., Lozano, J.A.: Protein folding in simplified models with estimation of distribution algorithms. IEEE Trans. Evol. Comput. **12**(4), 418–438 (2008)
8. Santana, R., Larrañaga, P., Lozano, J.A.: Combining variable neighborhood search and estimation of distribution algorithms in the protein side chain placement problem. J. Heuristics **14**(5), 519–547 (2007)
9. Schug, A., Wenzel, W.: An evolutionary strategy for all-atom folding on the 60-amino-acid bacterial ribosomal protein L20. Biophys. J. **90**(12), 4273–4280 (2006)
10. Pedersen, J.T., Moult, J.: Protein folding simulation with genetic algorithms and a detailed molecular description. J. Mol. Biol. **269**(2), 240–259 (1997)
11. Clerc, M., Kennedy, J.: The particle swarm: explosion, stability, and convergence in a multi-dimensional complex space. IEEE Trans. Evol. Comput. **6**(1), 58–73 (2002)
12. Han, K.H., Kim, J.H.: Genetic quantum algorithm and its application to combinatorial optimization problem. IEEE Trans. Evol. Comput. **6**(6), 580–593 (2002)
13. Han, K.H., Kim, J.H.: Quantum-inspired evolutionary algorithms with a new termination criterion, $H_\varepsilon$gate, and two-phase scheme. IEEE Trans. Evol. Comput. **8**(2), 156–169 (2004)
14. Xing, H., Pan, W., Zou, X.: A novel improved quantum genetic algorithm for combinatorial optimization problems. Acta Electron. Sin. **35**(10), 1999–2002 (2007)
15. Liu, W., Ma, T., Yan, Q., Zheng, Y.: Improvement on NIQGA and novel quantum-inspired evolutionary algorithm based on variable angle-distance. J. Southeast Univ. (Nat. Sci. Ed.) **41**(3), 487–491 (2011)

A Word Embeddings Training Method Based on Modified Skip-Gram and Align

Chang-shuai Xing[(✉)], Gang Zhou, Ji-Cang Lu, and Feng-juan Zhang

State Key Laboratory of Mathematical Engineering and Advanced Computer,
Zhengzhou 450001, China
xcsshr@qq.com

Abstract. To solve the problems that there is no sufficient annotated data in low-resource languages and it is hard to mine the deep semantic correspondence between languages via existing bilingual word embedding learning methods, this paper presents an effective text processing method based on transfer learning and bilingual word embedding model CWDR-BiGRU (Cross-context window of dynamic ratio bidirectional Gated Recurrent Unit) which contains an enhanced Skip-gram called cross-context window of dynamic ratio and encoder-decoder. The method can process low-resource language text effectively only using sentence-aligned corpus of bilingual resource languages and annotated data of high-resource language. The experimental results of semantic reasoning and word embedding visualization show that CWDR-BiGRU can effectively train bilingual word embeddings. In the task of Chinese-Tibetan cross-lingual document classification, the accuracy of transfer learning method based on CWDR-BiGRU is higher than the conventional method by 13.5%, and higher than the existing Bilingual Autoencoder, BilBOWA, BiCCV and BiSkip by 7.4%, 5.8%, 3.1% and 1.6% respectively, indicating CWDR-BiGRU which has reduced the difficulty of acquiring corpora for bilingual word embeddings can accurately excavate the deep alignment relationship and semantic properties.

Keywords: Bilingual word embeddings · Transfer learning · Low-resource language · Cross-context window of dynamic ratio

1 Introduction

In general, when we process different language tasks, we need to redesign models for different language features, with poor generalization ability. Moreover, for low-resource languages, there are few linguistic researches, and it requires high expert knowledge to annotate, especially for different tasks. Therefore, annotated data of low-resource language has been in shortage for a long time and it is difficult to carry out processing models design for low-resource language features, leading to low accuracy of related task learning algorithms.

Cross-lingual knowledge transfer can migrate high-resource languages' knowledge to low-resource languages. The premise of this thought is to acquire the similarities between the two languages. However, the existing bilingual word embedding learning methods have the following three shortcomings: (1) the methods have not take into

© Springer Nature Switzerland AG 2018
X. Sun et al. (Eds.): ICCCS 2018, LNCS 11068, pp. 334–346, 2018.
https://doi.org/10.1007/978-3-030-00021-9_31

account the monolingual and cross-lingual limitations. (2) the methods used expensive word-aligned corpus. (3) single alignment method is relatively simple and has not considered context fully.

The contribution of this paper is to improve the bilingual embedding learning model with better alignment called CWDR-BiGRU especially for low-resource languages. The model is based on Skip-gram language model [1] which is simple and efficient. Inspired by the recent research on neural machine translation, we propose a BiGRU encoder-decoder based on attention mechanism, taking context into account to enhance the alignment of bilingual words and completing bilingual word embeddings updating.

2 Preliminary

Bilingual Word Embedding Training Model
The existing bilingual word embedding training methods can be divided into three categories: monolingual mapping, cross-lingual training and joint training. The general bilingual word embedding training algorithm is as follows:

Algorithm 1: The general bilingual word embedding training algorithm
  1. initialization: $W = W^0$, $V = V^0$
  2. optimization objective function: (W^*, V^*)
$= arg\ min(\alpha(W) + \beta(V) + \gamma(W, V))$

Where, W^0, V^0 represent the monolingual embeddings in two vector space respectively, and W^*, V^* represent the bilingual embeddings in the same vector space respectively. α, β and γ are parameters for monolingual and cross-lingual loss functions. The general model structure is shown in Fig. 1.

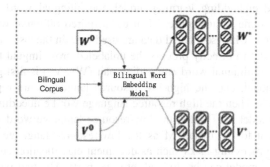

Fig. 1. The general bilingual word embedding training model

Monolingual mapping refers to training monolingual embeddings in a large number of monolingual corpora, and then learning the mapping relationship between different language word embeddings. Mikolov et al. [1] used this idea to learn bilingual word embeddings. But due to the lack of word-aligned resources and the existence of a large number of Out-Of-Vocabulary (OOV) words, it is difficult to establish the correct mapping relationship, resulting in a just effect.

Cross-lingual training means using parallel corpus to train word embeddings by optimizing the vector space constraints of different languages. That is, in Algorithm 1, let $\alpha = \beta = 0$ and only cross-lingual restriction (W, V) is considered. Hermann and Blunsom et al. [2] used sentence-aligned parallel corpus, and converted each pair of aligned sentences into two fixed-length vectors to minimize the Euclidean distance of the two vectors. Although it performs well in bilingual tasks (such as cross-lingual text classification), ignoring the restrictions of the monolingual embeddings may harm the internal distribution structure of monolingual embeddings.

Joint training refers to using parallel corpus to train word embeddings jointly optimizing the monolingual and cross-lingual loss functions. That is, in Algorithm 1, we set $\alpha = \beta = 1$, taking into account both monolingual and cross-lingual loss $(W), (V), (W, V)$. Zou et al. [3] adopted this idea and formally proposed the concept of bilingual word embedding. In the study, bilingual word embeddings were trained by constructing a neural network language model by defining a semantic similarity matrix and a bilingual loss function, achieving high accuracy in machine translation. Based on the fact that there are fewer corporas for word alignment and relatively large numbers of parallel corporas. This method is currently the most popular, but there is still room for improvement, such as a more rigorous loss function.

The summarization among the three method is showing in Table 1.

3   Framework

3.1   Basic Ideas

The core idea of cross-lingual text processing method based on bilingual word vectors with enhanced alignment and transfer learning in this paper is as follows. Firstly, using the bilingual word embedding learning model, the bilingual word embeddings are represented in the same vector space. Then the acquired bilingual word embeddings and a large number of Chinese labeled data are used to train the task model. Finally we use the trained model to directly process the unlabeled cross-lingual text.

Specifically, the bilingual word embedding pair (W*, V*) is first generated by the CWDR-BiGRU model, and the high-low resource languages are represented in the same vector space S. Then the high resource language word embedding W* is used as input to train the model M. Finally, the low-resource language word vector V* in the same space is input to the model M as the low-resource language text features to complete the text processing tasks such as document classification etc.

CWDR-BiGRU model can be divided into two parts. The first part is pre-training bilingual word embedding. We use cross-context window of dynamic ratio to align words quickly, taking into account the monolingual and cross-lingual constraints. The second part is to strengthen the training of bilingual word embeddings. The pre-trained word embeddings are used as input, and we use the Bi-GRU encoder-decoder based on

Table 1. Summarization among the three methods

Objective function	Training method	Parallel corpus category
monolingual objective function	Mikolov et al. (2013)	Word-aligned corpus
	Faruqui and Dyer et al. (2014)	Word-aligned corpus
	Xing et al. (2015) [4]	Word-aligned corpus
	Vulić and Korhonen et al. (2016) [5]	Document-aligned corpus
Cross-lingual objective function	Hermann and Blunsom et al. (2014)	Sentence-aligned corpus
	Lauly et al. (2014) [6]	Sentence-aligned corpus
	Luong et al. (2015) [7]	Sentence-aligned corpus
Joint objective function	Klementiev et al. (2012)	Word-aligned corpus
	Zou et al. (2013)	Word-aligned corpus
	Gouws and Søgaard et al. (2015) [8]	Word-aligned corpus
	Vyas and Carpuat et al. (2016) [9]	Word-aligned corpus
	Gouws et al. (2015)	Sentence-aligned corpus
	Coulmance et al. (2015) [10]	Sentence-aligned corpus
	Vulić et al. (2016) [11]	Document-aligned corpus

attention mechanism to update them, enhancing their alignment with contextual semantic information.

3.2   Cross-Context Window of Dynamic Ratio

Training bilingual word embeddings can be seen as aligning words. Existing methods or open source tools for aligning include Giza++ [12] or self-defined word alignment models, which are computationally complex and less robust.

In 2013, Mikolov et al. proposed the CBOW and Skip-gram models whose goal is to learn available word embeddings efficiently and characterize the co-occurrence relationship between the target words and the context via a window.

For the entire corpus, the model's objective function is as follows:

$$\sum_{(w,c)\in\mathbb{D}} P(c|w) = \sum_{(w,c)\in\mathbb{D}} \sum_{w_i\in c} logP(w_i|w) \tag{1}$$

Where,

$$P(w_i|w) = \frac{\exp\left(e_{w_i}^T \cdot e_w\right)}{\sum_{w' \in \mathbb{V}} \exp\left(e_{w'}^T \cdot e_w\right)} \tag{2}$$

The disadvantage of Skip-gram is that it is difficult to process two languages directly. This paper extends the processing scope of Skip-gram by designing a cross-context window of dynamic ratio so that it can process two languages at the same time. Bilingual word embeddings are pre-trained by parallel corpus.

Cross-context window of dynamic ratio refers mixing sentences of two languages fully into a new sentence according to the ratio of the source and target language sentences' length. The words from source language and target language are alternately inserted into cross-context sentence (initial value is empty), keeping the word order in their original sentences. The length of a sentence is defined as the number of segmented words, and the length of a pair of parallel sentences (S_1, S_2) is denoted by M_1 and M_2, respectively. Assuming $M_1 \geq M_2$, the specific process is as follows:

(1) Define a cross-context sentence set S', $S' = \{\}$;
(2) Calculate the length ratio of each pair of parallel sentences dynamically: $R = \{R_1, R_2, \ldots\}$, where $R_i = (M_{1i}/M_{2i})$ is the length ratio of $S_i = (S_1, S_2)$;
(3) For each pair of parallel sentences, we replace R source language words by one target language word, and substitutes only one at a time. Then we add the cross-context sentence to S'. In this process, M_2 substitutions are made for each pair of parallel sentences. Conversely, we use R source language words replace one target language word. In this process, M_2 substitutions are also made for each pair of parallel sentences. We do this until all the parallel sentences added to S'.

As the following example shows:

$S_1 : a_1 a_2 a_3 a_4 a_5 a_6$.
$S_2 : b_1 b_2 b_3$.

It is easy to see that the length M_1 of S_1 is 6 and the length M_2 of S_2 is 3, so the length ratio R is 2. According to cross-context window of dynamic ratio in this paper, we consider that "$a_1 a_2$" corresponds to "b_1", "$a_3 a_4$" corresponds to "b_2", and "$a_5 a_6$" corresponds to "b_3". First, we use the words in S_2 to replace the words in S_1, and we can get the following three sentences by changing only one pair of corresponding words at one time $b_1 a_3 a_4 a_5 a_6$, "$a_1 a_2 b_2 a_5 a_6$" and "$a_1 a_2 a_3 a_4 b_3$". Then we use the words in S_1 to replace the corresponding words in S_2 to get the following three sentences "$a_1 a_2 b_2 b_3$", "$b_1 a_3 a_4 b_3$" and "$b_1 b_2 a_5 a_6$". Parallel sentences of other length can be mixed in the similar manner.

In order to facilitate the calculation, we assume that the two parallel sentences of source language and target language are S_1 and S_2, where $w_i^{(1)} \in S_1$, $w_j^{(2)} \in S_2$, and $w_i^{(1)}$ aligns with $w_j^{(2)}$ with a certain probability. In order to construct a simpler model, we use the uniform distribution hypothesis and obtain that the context window of $w_i^{(1)}$

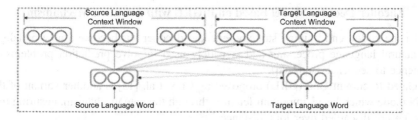

Fig. 2. Cross-context window of dynamic ratio

in the target language is S_2 as the same that the context window of $w_j^{(2)}$ in the source language is S_1. The method is shown in Fig. 2.

Based on cross-context window of dynamic ratio, our objective function includes two parts for pre-training. One is the internal objective function of one language, which is consistent with the objective function of Skip-gram. The other is the cross-lingual objective function, which uses a cross-context window of dynamic ratio with self-defined loss function. For the cross-lingual objective function, it can make sure that the source and target language have the same context with cross-context window of dynamic ratio. In other words, the bilingual word embeddings trained by this method are close to each other in the vector space.

Supposing the parallel corpus of sentences $\mathbb{D}_1$ and $\mathbb{D}_2$ in the active language and the target language contains N pairs of parallel sentences, for any $k \in [1, N]$, the source language sentence $S_k^{(1)} \in \mathbb{D}_1$, the target language sentence $S_k^{(2)} \in \mathbb{D}_2$, both $S_k^{(1)} \parallel S_k^{(2)}$, that is, the sentences in two languages are aligned. Supposing that the target words are $w^{(1)}$ and $w^{(2)}$, respectively), the objective functions of the same language are:

$$L_{11} = \sum\nolimits_{\left(w^{(1)}, S^{(1)}\right)} P\left(S^{(1)} | w^{(1)}\right) = \sum\nolimits_{S_k^{(1)} \in \mathbb{D}_1} \sum\nolimits_{w_i^{(1)} \in S_k^{(1)}} P\left(w_i^{(1)} | w^{(1)}\right) \quad (3)$$

$$L_{22} = \sum\nolimits_{\left(w^{(2)}, S^{(2)}\right)} P\left(S^{(2)} | w^{(2)}\right) = \sum\nolimits_{S_k^{(2)} \in \mathbb{D}_2} \sum\nolimits_{w_j^{(2)} \in S_k^{(2)}} P\left(w_j^{(2)} | w^{(2)}\right) \quad (4)$$

Using a dynamic cross-over window, the cross-language objective functions are:

$$L_{12} = \sum\nolimits_{\left(w^{(1)} \in S^{(1)}, S^{(2)} \parallel S^{(1)}\right)} P\left(S^{(2)} | w^{(1)}\right) = \sum\nolimits_{S_k^{(2)} \in \mathbb{D}_2} \sum\nolimits_{w_j^{(2)} \in S_k^{(2)}} P\left(w_j^{(2)} | w^{(1)}\right) \quad (5)$$

$$L_{21} = \sum\nolimits_{\left(w^{(2)} \in S^{(2)}, S^{(1)} \parallel S^{(2)}\right)} P\left(S^{(1)} | w^{(2)}\right) = \sum\nolimits_{S_k^{(1)} \in \mathbb{D}_1} \sum\nolimits_{w_i^{(1)} \in S_k^{(1)}} P\left(w_i^{(1)} | w^{(2)}\right) \quad (6)$$

In the above formulas, $P(w_i | w) = \dfrac{\exp\left(V_{w_i}^T \cdot V_w\right)}{\sum_{w' \in V} \exp\left(V_{w'}^T \cdot V_w\right)}$, the total goal is to maximize the formula (3)–(6) and the sum.

3.3   Encoder-Decoder Model Based on BiGRU with Attention Mechanism

Under the end-to-end training strategy, encoder-decoder has become a new paradigm for natural language processing and is widely used to solve prediction problems of sequence to sequence (seq2seq).

Gated Recurrent Unit (GRU) proposed by Cho et al. [13] is another variant of the RNN mode which keeps important features through the gate mechanism, ensuring that they are not discarded over long distance.

Instead of using the fixed-length vector of the entire source language sentence, attention mechanism dynamically generates contextual vector of the source language word for each target language word. Attention mechanism can be regarded as a context-based semantic alignment to maximize word alignment probability between the source language and the target language. Therefore, BiGRU encoder-decoder based on attention mechanism is adopted to enhance the alignment effect. Based on the above semantic model through dynamic adjustment, we can further mine the deep alignment between words. The model structure is shown in Fig. 3. The model objective function is:

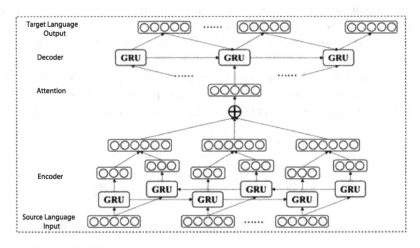

Fig. 3. Bi-GRU encoder-decoder architecture based on attention mechanism

$$\sum_{k=1}^{N} \log P_\theta(S_k^{(2)} | S_k^{(1)}) \tag{7}$$

Where θ is the model parameter, and the bilingual word embedding with enhanced alignment can be obtained after training.

4 Experiment

In order to verify the effectiveness of CWDR-BiGRU model, three experiments including semantic reasoning, visualization and document classification are carried out on Chinese-Tibetan language texts. The comparison models include the Bilingual Autoencoder model proposed by Lauly et al. (short for BA model), the BilBOWA model proposed by Gouws et al. and BiSkip model proposed by Luong et al. and BiCCA model proposed by Faruqui et al.

4.1 Datasets and Experimental Settings

The parallel corpus of Chinese-Tibetan sentences used in this experiment is selected from the People's Daily of Chinese version and the Tibetan version from 2015 to 2016. The content includes five fields such as politics, economy, religion, society and entertainment with 100,000 parallel sentences. Bilingual word embeddings derived from our CWDR-BiGRU model are qualitatively and experimentally analyzed in semantic reasoning and visualization.

In addition, we train document classification model with labeled Chinese documents. This part experimental training data is the Chinese version of People's Daily from 2015 to 2016. There are 5 categories including politics, economy, religion, society and entertainment, with 1200 articles in each category, totaling 6,000. There are a small number of labeled Tibetan documents from the Tibetan version People's Daily of the same category and period, with 200 for each category, totaling 1000 for comparative experiments. We select 500 articles of the Chinese version and Tibetan version People's Daily of the same period as the test data, respectively.

Data preprocessing includes data cleaning and word segmentation. We use the word segmentation tools provided by jieba and Tibetan information processing technology platforms to segment Chinese and Tibetan texts. The bilingual word embedding dimension is set to 100, and the cross-window size is dynamically adjusted with the length of parallel sentences. We use negative sampling for optimization and the experimental framework is tensorflow.

4.2 Semantic Reasoning and Visualization

The Chinese-Tibetan bilingual word embeddings trained by our CWDR-BiGRU model can be found in the vector space as follows:

$$V(\text{"中国"})-V(\text{"ཟེ་ཅིང་"})\approx V(\text{"法国"})-V(\text{"པ་རི་"})$$

Among them, "ཟེ་ཅིང་" and "པ་རི་" are the Tibetan words of "北京" and "巴黎" respectively. It can be seen that the semantic reasoning feature also exists in the vector space of bilingual word embeddings, as shown in Fig. 4. In the figure, "ཏུང་ཅིང་", "ཟེར་ལིང་", "ལོན་ཊོན", "རོམ" and "མོ་སི་ཁོ་" are the Tibetan translation of "东京", "柏林", "伦敦", "罗马" and "莫斯科" respectively.

This paper adopts a non-linear dimensionality reduction algorithm t-SNE [14]. Based on the bilingual word embeddings obtained from the training, we select some

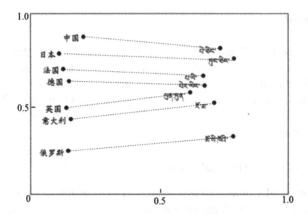

Fig. 4. Chinese-Tibetan linear semantic reasoning visualization

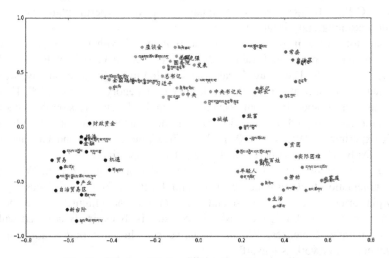

Fig. 5. Chinese -Tibetan bilingual vector visualization

terms of Chinese-Tibetan economic and political aspects. The visualization results are shown in Fig. 5.

Figure 5 shows that Chinese-Tibetan words with similar semantic distances are similar in space. For example, "贫困", and "དབུལ་ཕོངས", "总书记" and "སྤྱི་ཁྱབ་དྲུང་ཆེ". In monolingual, the words distance between Chinese words "贸易", "产业" 与 "金融" have similar meanings. Similar to the Tibetan word "དངུལ་རྩ" (金融), "ནོར་སྲིད་མ་དངུལ" (财政资金) 和 "དཔལ་འབྱོར" (经济) have similar meanings of the word distance is also similar. This phenomenon further proves that the model proposed in this paper can learn the vector representation of bilingual words while maintaining the distribution within the monolingual vector, and the result is better.

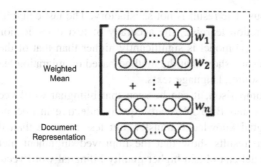

Fig. 6. Document representation based on average word vector

4.3 Validation

Traditional document classification models are derived from the training of a single language text, it is difficult to use directly for other language documents classification tasks. Klementiev et al. [15] first used bilingual word vectors to classify cross-language documents and used them to test bilingual word vector effects. This paper uses the model to verify the bilingual word vector effect. The model is shown in Fig. 6.

In this experiment, two sets of control experiments were designed. (1) Bilingual word vector generation model, Bilingual Autoencoder (abbreviated BA) proposed by Lauly et al., BilBOWA model proposed by Gouws et al., Luong BiSkip model proposed by Faruqui et al. And BiCCA model proposed by Faruqui et al. (2) comparison of document classification methods, (1) a large number of Chinese texts (6000) are used to train document classification models; (2) a few labeled Tibetan texts (1000) are used to train document classification models; and (3) the model obtained in (1) is used to process Tibetan directly. The above models were tested on Chinese and Tibetan texts (500 for each), and the experimental results are shown in Table 2.

Table 2. Experimental results

Chinese (marked)	Tibetan (a small amount of labeled)	Model	Transfer learning
87.3%	69.4%	BA	75.5%
		BilBOWA	77.1%
		BiSkip	81.3%
		BiCCV	79.8%
		CWDR-BiGRU	**82.9%**

Longitudinally, it can be seen from Table 2 that the first column shows that the accuracy of using Chinese model for Chinese classification is 87.3%. Assuming that there are 6000 datasets of labeled Tibetan language training, the classification results of Tibetan text should be close to 87.3%. The second column shows that using the model in (2), the accuracy rate of Tibetan text classification is only 69.4%, which is limited by the number of corpus. The result is not satisfactory. The last column shows that using the method of migration learning, the accuracy of text classification of Tibetan language directly using ① model is significantly higher than that of the second column. The experimental results show that the method based on migration learning is effective to deal with low-resource language texts.

In horizontal comparison, it can be seen that bilingual word vectors obtained by models such as BA and BilBOWA are equally effective in document classification based on cross-lingual knowledge transfer, but less accurate than the model in this paper. Experimental results show that the improved alignment method used in the CWDR-BiGRU model can obtain higher quality bilingual word vectors, which makes the vector distribution in the same vector space more realistic and improves the document classification accuracy based on cross-language knowledge transfer.

Further,   we   used   the   parallel   sentences   to "我在内地读书期间不同民族同学很多的认识了"   and   "ངས་ ནང་མར་ སློབ་སྦྱོང་བྱེད་པར་ རིང་ལ་ མི་རིགས་ མི་འདྲ་བའི་ སློབ་གྲོགས་ མང་པོ་ཞིག་ ངོ་ཤེས་བྱུང་" In addition, As an example, compare the pre-align and enhance alignment effects, as shown in Fig. 7. The upper part of the figure is pre-aligned. It can be seen that the pre-alignment using the dynamic cross-over method is a one-to-one replacement due to the same number of words in the two sentences after the word segmentation, and fast word alignment can be achieved. In fact, part of the word order has been changed when Chinese is translated into Tibetan parallel sentences, and pre-alignment alone can not effectively handle such situations. The attention-based encoder-decoder can solve the above problem through semantic alignment. As shown in the lower part of Fig. 7, after the semantic alignment is enhanced, the error problem corresponding to word order in pre-aligned is better corrected and the contextual information characterization is more accurate.

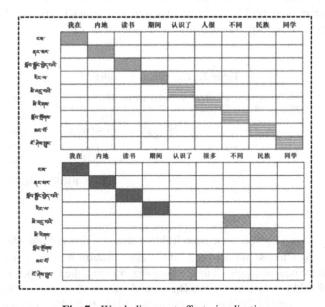

Fig. 7. Word alignment effect visualization

5 Summary

This paper presents a cross-language text processing method based on bilingual word vector learning model CWDR-BiGRU. Firstly, the Skip-gram model is improved by dynamic cross-over method to achieve word pre-training and word pre-training. Secondly, a bi-directional GRU coding-decoder based on attention mechanism is used to enhance word alignment through contextual semantic information, update pre-training results and obtain bilinguals Word vector. Compared with other models, CWDR-BiGRU learns the bilingual word vectors by means of enhanced alignment. It can directly train bilingual corpus at the sentence level, reducing the difficulty of corpus acquisition and mining deep-seated multi-lingual semantic correspondence. The results show that the CWDR-BiGRU model can effectively train bilingual word vectors. On the basis of this, using the migration learning theory without applying any Tibetan marked data will apply to The Chinese document classification model is directly used to process Tibetan texts. At the same time, the veracity of bivariate vector classification using CWDR-BiGRU model is 7.4%, 5.8%, 3.1% and 1.6% higher than the existing Bilingual Autoencoder, BilBOWA, BiCCV and BiSkip models, respectively.

References

1. Mikolov, T., Le, Q.V., Sutskever, I.: Exploiting similarities among languages for machine translation. Computer Science (2013)
2. Hermann, K.M., Blunsom, P.: Multilingual models for compositional distributed semantics. arXiv:1404.4641 (2014)
3. Zou, W.Y., Socher, R., Cer, D.M.: Bilingual word embedding for phrase-based machine translation. In: Empirical Methods in Natural Language Processing, pp. 1393–1398 (2013)
4. Xing, C., Wang, D., Liu, C.: Normalized word embedding and orthogonal transform for bilingual word translation. In: Conference of the North American Chapter of the Association for Computational Linguistics: Human Language Technologies, pp. 1006–1011 (2015)
5. Vulić, I., Moens, M.F.: Bilingual word embeddings from non-parallel document-aligned data applied to bilingual lexicon induction. In: Meeting of the Association for Computational Linguistics and the, International Joint Conference on Natural Language Processing, pp. 719–725(2015)
6. Chandar, A.P.S., Lauly, S., Larochelle, H.: An autoencoder approach to learning bilingual word representations, pp. 1853–1861 (2014)
7. Luong, T., Pham, H., Manning, C.D.: Bilingual word representations with monolingual quality in mind. In: The Workshop on Vector Space Modeling for Natural Language Processing, pp. 151–159 (2015)
8. Gouws, S., Søgaard, A.: Simple task-specific bilingual word embeddings. In: Conference of the North American Chapter of the Association for Computational Linguistics: Human Language Technologies, pp. 1386–1390 (2016)
9. Vyas, Y., Carpuat, M.: Sparse bilingual word representations for cross-lingual lexical entailment. In: Conference of the North American Chapter of the Association for Computational Linguistics: Human Language Technologies, pp. 1187–1197 (2016)
10. Coulmance, J., Marty, J.M., Wenzek, G.: Trans-gram, fast cross-lingual word-embeddings (2016)

11. Vulić, I., Moens, M.F.: Bilingual distributed word representations from document-aligned comparable data. Computer Science, pp. 748–756 (2015)
12. Mikolov, T., Chen, K., Corrado, G.: Efficient estimation of word representations in vector space. Computer Science (2013)
13. Cho, K., Merrienboer, B.V., Gulcehre, C.: Learning phrase representations using RNN encoder-decoder for statistical machine translation. Computer Science (2014)
14. Maaten, L.V.D., Hinton, G.: Visualizing data using t-SNE. J. Mach. Learn. Res. 9(2605), 2579–2605 (2008)
15. Bhattarai, B., Klementiev, A., Titov, I.: Inducing crosslingual distributed representations of words. J. Comput. Syst. Sci. 55(1), 36–43 (2012)

AAC Audio Compression Detection Based on QMDCT Coefficient

Qijuan Huang$^{(\boxtimes)}$, Rangding Wang, Diqun Yan, and Jian Zhang

College of Information Science and Engineering,
Ningbo University, Ningbo 315211, China
1796814970@qq.com

Abstract. Audio compression history detection is a significant part of audio forensics, which is important to detect whether audio has been tampered or forged. When the structure of AAC audio frame is destroyed, its spectral coefficient distribution is similar to that of audio after the first compression. An algorithm of AAC audio compression detection was presented by using the statistical characteristics of QMDCT coefficients before and after removal of sampling points as the discriminative feature. Experimental results demonstrate that the proposed method can distinguish the single, double compressed AAC audios effectively, and from the low-bit-rate transcoding to high-bit-rate, the average classification accuracy achieves 99.84%, the same-bit-rate compression detection accuracy achieves 98.60%. In addition, the results of comparison experiments show that our algorithm outperforms the state-of-the-art algorithm.

Keywords: AAC audio · Double compression · QMDCT coefficients
Remove the sampling point

1 Introduction

Digital audio forensics is an important part of digital multimedia forensics technology, and audio compression history detection is one of the hot issues in audio forensics technology. Currently on the market of multimedia equipment, the audio files are stored in a compressed format. Compression is often accompanied by re-compression when using audio editing or processing software to tamper the compressed audio. Therefore, audio compression history detection as a digital content authenticity of the previous work is a necessary condition to determine whether the audio has been tampered or forged.

In the history of MP3 audio compression history detection, D'alessandro et al. [1] analyzed the power spectrum of audio at different bit rates and found different distributions in the band of 16 to 20 kHz, thus proposed to detect the true bit rate of MP3 audio through spectrum analysis Methods. Yang et al. [2] found that the number of 1-valued MDCT coefficients in MP3 audio has a significant change before and after compression. Therefore, the proportion of 1-valued coefficients in all frequency coefficients is taken as a distinguishing feature, realized the low bit rate transcoding to high rate MP3 audio detection. Liu et al. [3] achieved uncompressed audio and dual-compressed audio classification by using the ratio of the absolute value of the Modified

Discrete Cosine Transform (MDCT) coefficient to the set threshold, but the threshold was set based on the empirical value of the author and did not have universality. Qiao et al. [4] performed dual-compression audio detection using the features of small MDCT coefficients, the continuity of adjacent frames, and the discrete numerical distribution of coefficients. Luo et al. [5] increased the accuracy of algorithm detection by increasing Mel Frequency Cestrum Coefficient (MFCC), but the feature dimension was higher and the computational cost was increased. Bianchi et al. [6, 7] decoded the test audio and extracted the quantization parameters. The obtained PCM samples were clipped and recompressed using the extracted quantization parameters. The primary and secondary compressed audio after double-compression correction its MDCT coefficient distribution and the distribution before the correction showing a different law to achieve effective detection of double compressed MP3 audio.

In AAC audio compression history detection, Seichter et al. [8] used Convolutional Neural Network (CNN) to classify AAC compressed audio and estimate the original bit rate of compressed audio. Jin et al. [9] used the Huffman codebook index's probability of occurrence and its Markov single-step transition probabilities as features to classify single-compressed and dual-compressed AAC audio. But the recognition rate is lower at compressed audio at the same code rate. Li et al. [10] used the Stacked Automatic Encoder (SAE) based on the frequency components and energy values of AAC during double-compression, but the detection accuracy was low.

This article only addresses AAC audio that has been compressed under two or two times. We found that compressing the audio leaves a significant amount of quantization artifacts, and removing the sample points erases the quantization artifacts. According to the differences in the statistical properties of QMDCT coefficients before and after removing the audio samples, we propose an AAC double-compression audio detection algorithm based on QMDCT coefficients. The algorithm takes the number of occurrences of QMDCT coefficients within $[-10, 10]$ before and after removing the sampling point as the detection feature and classifies the double compressed AAC audio by using LIBSVM. The experimental results show that the algorithm proposed in this paper has high detection accuracy and can effectively detect double compressed AAC audio.

2   The Quantized MDCT Coefficients of AAC Audio

AAC is short for advanced audio coding and is an important part of the ISO/IEC MPEG-2 and MPEG-4 standards [11]. AAC encoding framework as shown in Fig. 1. It uses perceptual audio coding as the basic model to develop. Combined with the psychoacoustic model, the input PCM signal is first time-frequency converted by the filter bank and then quantized by MDCT to quantizing the transformed frequency coefficient. Finally, the bit stream is encapsulated to form the final compressed audio.

The QMDCT coefficient is a quantized value of the PCM signal after MDCT, essentially reflects the characteristics of the original signal. The MDCT coefficient obtained through MDCT of the PCM signal is obtained. After the MDCT coefficient is quantified by the quantization formula, the QMDCT coefficient can be obtained. Quantitative formula is as follows,

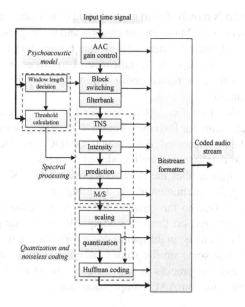

Fig. 1. AAC coding framework

$$x_{\text{quant}} = \left\lfloor \left(\left(|mdct_{\text{line}}| \times 2^{\frac{1}{4}(sf_{\text{decoder}} - 100)} \right)^{\frac{3}{4}} \right) + 0.4054 \right\rfloor \tag{1}$$

$\lfloor \bullet \rfloor$ is rounded down function, sf_{decoder} indicates the quantization step, $mdct_{\text{line}}$ is the pre-quantization MDCT coefficient, x_{quant} is QMDCT coefficient. In the AAC audio coding process, the steps before the quantization is the audio data pre-processing, quantization processing to truly reduce the audio bit rate [11]. The basic goal of the quantization module is to quantize the spectral data to control the quantization noise within the range of perceptual distortion and to make the number of coded bits meet the bit rate requirement. In the AAC coding process, the MDCT coefficients are stored in frequency on the source file. That is, the AAC audio is the data stream after the MDCT coefficients are quantized and encoded. Each subband MDCT coefficient will get the corresponding QMDCT coefficients through the quantization formula. Therefore, the QMDCT coefficients not only reflect the characteristics of the original PCM signal, but also reflect the quantization characteristics. The statistics of the legacy QMDCT coefficients at first compression will still be preserved after the second compression, but there will be fluctuations.

3   AAC Audio Compression Traces

AAC recompression audio is divided into the following three categories: low bit rate transcoding to high bit rate AAC audio, such compressed audio is commonly referred to as fake-quality audio, formed by poor quality (low bit rate) audio transcoding false high quality (high bit rate) audio; the same bit rate compressed AAC audio, the generation of such audio is mostly due to the original compressed audio is tampered, in order not to allow others to doubt the format change, and recompressed at the same rate back to the pre-tampered audio format; high bit rate transcoding to low bit rate AAC audio, although this may happen, the significance of the forensics scene has not yet been proposed. Therefore, compressed audio following this paper default to the first and second types of audio.

In audio compression forensics, researchers tend to use the statistical features of quantized MDCT coefficients for forensics. Figure 2 is a histogram of 500 segments of single-compressed, dual-compressed AAC audio QMDCT coefficients. (The establishment of the sample database will be introduced at the bottom of this section.) As can be seen from the figure, after the AAC compression QMDCT coefficient distribution will be some gully phenomenon, the distribution of the coefficients will be gathered in some value. Due to the quantization of AAC audio coding, the MDCT coefficients are first quantized on the first coding. When decoding these values are truncated and rounded off, that is, in the quantization formula (1), the rounding function is rounded down such that some similar values are quantized to the same value at the second compression and the process is irreversible. Therefore, the phenomenon of Fig. 2, we call this phenomenon AAC compression traces.

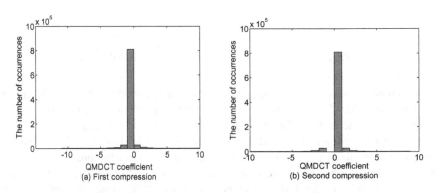

Fig. 2. First compressed and re-compressed AAC audio QMDCT coefficient histogram

Inspired by the idea of image compression correction [12–14], in the image compression detection, the quantization traces of image compression can be erased by removing four pixels. In this paper, it is considered that removing the audio part of sample points will destroy the audio frame structure. After being recompressed, the audio frame undergoes twice compression, but its characteristics (such as spectral coefficient distribution) are similar to the first compression.

To verify the impact of frame structure spoiler on AAC audio, we randomly selected 500 segments 10 s of WAV audio, including country, blues, pop, jazz and other styles. Three types of samples were produced, one of which was single compressed AAC audio, which used the AAC encoder (FAAC/FAAD2) for the original WAV audio and the second was the re-compressed AAC audio, which is decoding-encoding on the basis of a single compressed audio; The third type is destroyed AAC audio frame structure, the type of audio in the single-compressed, dual-compressed audio decompression of the beginning of the WAV audio to remove a number of (remove 1 sample here) sampling points, and then compressed to generate AAC audio. Finally, the histogram of the frequency domain coefficients (QMDCT coefficients) of the frame destruction audio is counted.

It can be seen from Fig. 3 that the QMDCT coefficient distribution of single, double compression after removing the sampling points is highly similar. The audio frame structure in the destruction of the removal of sampling points can remove the audio quantization traces. As can be seen from Figs. 3 and 2, the QMDCT coefficients of single-compressed AAC audio didn't change significantly before and after removing the sampling points, but the QMDCT coefficients of the re-compressed AAC audio had a significant difference before and after removing the sampling points.

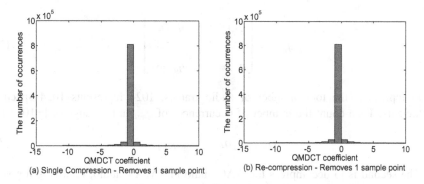

Fig. 3. Frame structure under the destruction of single, double compressed audio

4   Feature Construction and Extraction

4.1   Feature Structure

We use the transformation of audio quantized traces to detect recompressed AAC audio. The core of this algorithm is to analyze the similarity between the histogram of the quantized MDCT coefficients of the AAC audio file under test and the histogram of the quantized MDCT coefficients of the uncompressed AAC audio file. Intuitively, if there is a small difference between the histograms of the two distributions, the AAC audio file to be tested in the analysis is not re-compressed, whereas the audio file will be considered as a re-compressed file.

However, it is difficult to judge whether the audio undergoes recompression operation only from the distribution of the quantized MDCT coefficient histograms. According to the previous analysis, the quantized MDCT coefficient histograms of single and dual compressed audio after removing the sampling points are similar, and we take the difference of QMDCT coefficients of single, double compression before and after removing the sampling points as the feature. Figure 4 is the flow chart of the algorithm of this text, carry on two operations to the test AAC audio. One is to extract its QMDCT coefficient directly, it is recorded as q_{test}.

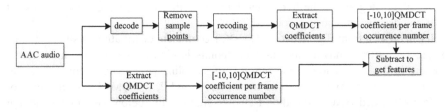

Fig. 4. Algorithm flow chart

$$q_{test} = \begin{bmatrix} q_{1,1} & \cdots & q_{1,1024} \\ \vdots & \ddots & \vdots \\ q_{m,1} & \cdots & q_{m,1024} \end{bmatrix} \quad (2)$$

m represents the total number of audio frames, 1024 represents 1024 spectral coefficients. Then count the number of occurrences of q_{test} in the range of $[-10, 10]$.

$$Q_{test} = [q_1 \quad \cdots \quad q_{21}] \quad (3)$$

The second is to decompress the AAC audio into WAV audio, removing a given number of sampling points from the beginning of the WAV audio. This operation destroys the audio frame structure and removes the quantization artifacts while preserving the original audio characteristics. WAV audio that removes part of the sample points is recompressed to the same bit rate AAC audio as the original audio, to extract its QMDCT coefficients, it is recorded as q_{remove}.

$$q_{remove} = \begin{bmatrix} q'_{1,1} & \cdots & q'_{1,1024} \\ \vdots & \ddots & \vdots \\ q'_{m,1} & \cdots & q'_{m,1024} \end{bmatrix} \quad (4)$$

Then count the number of occurrences of q_{test} in the range of $[-10, 10]$.

$$Q_{remove} = [q'_1 \quad \cdots \quad q'_{21}] \quad (5)$$

The resulting QMDCT coefficients for statistical analysis, calculate the difference that is

$$Q = Q_{test} - Q_{remove} = [Q_1 \quad \cdots \quad Q_{21}] \quad (6)$$

Q is the selected feature of this paper.

The algorithm flow chart will be further explained below.

4.2   Characteristic Analysis

When the audio is encoded for the first time, many small-valued spectral coefficients will become 0 due to quantization distortion, and these zero-valued spectral coefficients can be recovered in the time domain upon decoding. At the second encoding, the zero-valued spectral coefficients quantized in the first encoding will be converted accordingly [2].

Based on the above principles, we make statistical analysis of the QMDCT coefficients of the three types of samples produced in Sect. 3. Figure 5 shows the changes of the zero-valued coefficients in the QMDCT coefficients, before and after the removal of the sampling points. (a) (b) represent the audio code the same-bit-rate compression and from low bit rate transcoding to high bit rate respectively. And show the differences of QMDCT coefficients before and after removing the sampling points. Experiments show that single, double compressed AAC audio before and after the removal of the sampling point QMDCT coefficients appear significant changes in the frequency, and the extent of the change has significant difference.

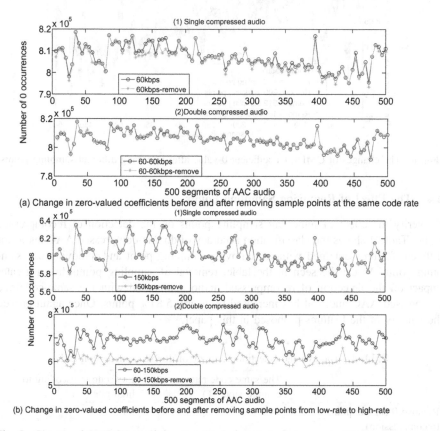

(a) Change in zero-valued coefficients before and after removing sample points at the same code rate

(b) Change in zero-valued coefficients before and after removing sample points from low-rate to high-rate

Fig. 5.   Change of QMDCT coefficient 0 value before and after removing the sampling point

4.3   Remove a Number of Sampling Points

In the experiment above, one sample point was removed, but it is necessary to further discuss whether it is the best.

Take the 60 kbps single-compressed AAC audio in the first class of samples described in Sect. 3, removing a few sample points, 1, 200, 512, 1024, respectively. Figure 6 shows the QMDCT coefficient 0 value comparison between the original audio and after removing a number of sample points. It can be seen from the figure that there is a big difference, but the change of the 0-value coefficient is not obvious for removing different sampling points. Therefore, in the follow-up experiments in this paper, the removal of sampling point is still selected to remove 1 sampling point.

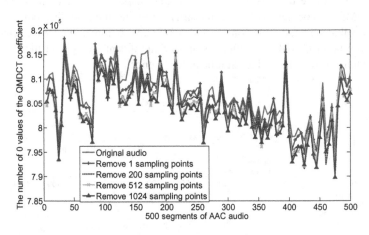

Fig. 6. The changes of QMDCT coefficient 0 value after removing different sampling points

4.4   The Effect of Removing Sampling Points

To verify the effect of removing sampling points on the detection of recompressed audio. Table 1 shows the classification accuracy of double-compressed AAC audio for different features obtained without removing sampling point and removing one sampling point. As can be seen in the table, removal of sampling points has a greater impact on the detection of recompressed audio. Compared with the same-code-rate compressed AAC audio, it has increased by nearly 5.81% points. Once again proved the validity of the features proposed in this paper.

Table 1. The average detection accuracy of double compression audio

	The same code rate compression (%)	Low rate transcoding to high rate (%)
Remove 0 sample point (recompression)	94.5	98
Remove 1 sample point	99.31	99.5

5 Experimental Results and Analysis

5.1 Experimental Setup

The database used in this paper is 2000 segments randomly chosen 10 s long WAV audio. The WAV audio includes a variety of different styles, such as blues, pop, classical, country, folk and so on. The AAC codec used in the experiment was the most widely used open source software, FAAC-1.28 and FAAD2-2.7. The 2000 segments of WAV audio for the above database was compressed using FAAC-1.28 to obtain single compressed AAC audio for a total of seven bit rates of 2000 segments for each of [60, 75, 90, 105, 120, 135, 150] kbps. The double-compressed audio is a single-compressed audio after FAAD2-2.7 decoding again FAAC-1.28 encoded audio, a total of 28 types of secondary compressed audio. The first and second compressed AAC audio obtained above are decompressed to remove one sample point and recompressed to obtain single and dual compressed AAC audio samples with one sampling point removed.

In this paper, LIBSVM is chosen as the classifier, and 70% of the above first and second compressed samples are chosen randomly to train the model, while the remaining 30% are used as the test model.

5.2 Test Results

Table 2 shows the detection results of the feature for recompressed AAC audio in this paper, where BR1 and BR2 represent the code rates set at the first and second compression, and the values in the table represent the specific detection accuracy. Taking the value of the seventh column in the sixth row(99.85%) of the table as an example, the value indicates that the method achieves a combined detection rate of 99.85% for dual-compressed AAC audio that uses 120 kbps and 135 kbps code rate compression (FAAC/FAAD2).

Table 2. Detection accuracy of the characteristics of this paper (%)

BR1	BR2						
	60	75	90	105	120	135	150
60	97.5	100	100	100	99	100	100
75		98.5	99.5	100	99.75	100	99.65
90			99	100	100	100	100
105				99.5	100	99.85	100
120					99.75	99	100
135						98	100
150							98

As can be seen from Table 2, the average correct rate of low bit rate transcoding to high bit rate audio detection is 99.845%, and the average correct rate of the same code rate compression is 98.607%. The feature of this algorithm achieved better detection results at the low code rate transcoding to high code rate, both exceeding 99%. However, for the same rate of compressed audio, the detection rate is relatively low by about 1.238%, which is due to the small QMDCT coefficient change during audio double compression and the relatively small difference before and after removing the sampling point.

5.3   Comparative Experiment

In order to evaluate the AAC compressed audio detection method proposed in this paper more completely, this paper reconstructs and compares the features of Jin et al. [9]. In reference [9], the method of constructing the specific classification features is as follows: There are differences in the usage of the Huffman codebook in the AAC audio primary compression and the secondary compression. Taking the probability of appearance of the Huffman code table index as the first feature, Markov the single-step transition probability is taken as the second feature. The third feature is obtained by fusing the first feature and the second feature, and the single-compressed and dual-compressed AAC audio are classified by LIBSVM. Table 3 compares the experimental detection rate of the reference [9] with the detection rate of the feature in this paper, "+" represents the percentage of the algorithm in this paper which is higher than that of the reference [9], and "−" represents the result of the algorithm is lower than the reference [9] (Table 4).

Table 3. The comparison results between references [9] and this paper (%)

BR1	BR2						
	60	75	90	105	120	135	150
60	+20.33	0	0	0	−1	0	0
75		+21.67	−0.5	0	−0.25	0	−0.35
90			+28	+0.17	0	0	0
105				+25.83	+1.5	−0.15	0
120					+21.08	+1.33	+1.17
135						+17.17	+1.67
150							+14.5

The above results show that the detection rate of Jin's feature is high for AAC audio with low bit rate transcoding to high bit rate, which is not much different from the difference of QMDCT coefficients before and after removal of sampling points in this algorithm. However, the proposed algorithm solves the problem of poor detection in the same code rate in reference [9], and improves the detection accuracy by about 21.22% points. We believe that for the same-rate compression, audio changes little before and after compression, making it difficult to distinguish between. This algorithm uses the difference feature of the audio before and after the sampling point to amplify the difference of the primary and secondary compressed audio. The Jin feature is a primary and secondary compressed audio analysis, and the difference itself is relatively small. Therefore, the accuracy of the algorithm is improved more.

Table 4. The comparison results between references [2] and this paper (%)

BR1	BR2						
	60	75	90	105	120	135	150
60	+27.5	+20.03	+18	+5.03	−1	0	+0.05
75		+15.98	−0.42	0	−0.25	0	−0.35
90			+19.95	+0.32	+0.05	0	+0.1
105				+20.47	+0.54	+0.07	+0.07
120					+21.96	−0.39	+0.22
135						+23.95	+1.43
150							−0.56

This section reconstructs the features of Yang et al. [2]. The results of 0 show that the detection of Yang method for AAC re-compression audio has achieved good detection results at low bit rate transcoding to high bit rate. The detection rate of the same rate compressed audio and 60 → 75 kbps, 60 → 90 kbps is low. The algorithm of this paper solves the poor detection rate, and the rate is obviously improved.

5.4 The Detection Accuracy of Different Duration Audio

In the above experiment, the samples of AAC audio used were 10 s. In order to verify the validity of the features in this paper, this section will discuss the performance of the QMDCT coefficient differences before and after removal of sampling points under different durations audio. Different duration AAC audio samples are obtained from the 2000 segments of 10 s WAV audio in Sect. 5.1 above. For the 2000 audio files, we intercept WAV audio clips of 0.5 s, 1 s, 2 s, 3 s, 4 s, 5 s, 6 s, 7 s and 8 s, re-create of AAC audio sample library with different duration. The AAC audio QMDCT coefficients are extracted respectively and the number of occurrences of the QMDCT coefficients within [−10, 10] is counted. The AAC audio compression is detected by using the difference of the QMDCT coefficients before and after removing the sampling points. Table 5 shows the classification accuracy of AAC audio compression for

Table 5. The accuracy of different duration AAC double compression audio

Duration (s)	The same code rate compression (%)	Low rate transcoding to high rate (%)
0.5	80.45	97.00
1.0	89.14	98.11
2.0	92.28	98.96
3.0	95.03	98.67
4.0	96.03	99.09
5.0	96.80	99.23
6.0	97.20	99.44
8.0	98.45	99.67
10.0	98.60	99.84

different duration of AAC audio. The compression rate of the same code refers to the classification recognition rate when the code rates of the single and the double compression are the same, low code rate transcoding to high code rate refers to the classification recognition rate when the second compression rate higher than the first compression rate.

6 Conclusion

In this paper, AAC compressed audio detection algorithm based on the statistical characteristics of QMDCT coefficients before and after removing the sampling points is proposed for the recompressed AAC audio. By studying the changes of QMDCT coefficients in the compression process, the compressed AAC audio is classified according to the difference of QMDCT coefficients before and after the removal of the sampling points. The experimental results show that the accuracy of AAC audio detection from low bit rate transcoding to high bit rate is up to 99.84%, while the accuracy of detection same code rate compression is also up to 98.60%. Although this algorithm has a high accuracy in detecting the compression history of AAC audio, it has some limitations. Without considering the robustness of the algorithm under attack of other factors such as noise, the compression history detection algorithm of a different encoding algorithm that does not involve the same encoding standard is only applicable to one codec algorithm. Therefore, in the future work will be conducted more in-depth study of these issues.

Acknowledgments. This work was supported by the National Natural Science Foundation of China (Grant No. U1736215, 61672302), Zhejiang Natural Science Foundation (Grant No. LZ15F020002, LY17F020010), Ningbo Natural Science Foundation (Grant No. 2017A610123), Ningbo University Fund (Grant No. XKXL1509, XKXL1503).

References

1. D'Alessandro, B., Shi, Y.Q.: MP3 bit rate quality detection through frequency spectrum analysis. In: Proceedings of the 11th ACM Workshop on Multimedia and Security, MM&Sec 2009, pp. 57–62. ACM, Princeton (2009) https://doi.org/10.1145/1597817. 1597828
2. Yang, R., Shi, Y.Q., Huang, J.: Defeating fake-quality MP3. In: Proceedings of the 11th ACM Workshop on Multimedia and Security, MM&Sec 2009, pp. 57–62, 117–124. ACM, Princeton (2009). https://doi.org/10.1145/1597817.1597838
3. Liu, Q., Sung, A.H., Qiao, M.: Detection of double MP3 compression. Cogn. Comput. 2(4), 291–296 (2010). https://doi.org/10.1007/s12559-010-9045-4
4. Qiao, M., Sung, A.H., Liu, Q.: Improved detection of MP3 double compression using content-independent features. In: IEEE International Conference on Signal Processing, Communication and Computing, pp. 1–4. IEEE, KunMing (2013). https://doi.org/10.1109/icspcc.2013.6664121

5. Luo, D., Luo, W., Yang, R., Huang, J.: Identifying compression history of wave audio and its applications. ACM Trans. Multimed. Comput. Commun. Appl. **10**(3), 1–19 (2014). https://doi.org/10.1145/2575978

6. Bianchi, T., Rosa, A.D., Fontani, M., Rocciolo, G., Piva, A.: Detection and localization of double compression in MP3 audio tracks. Eurasip J. Inf. Secur. **2014**(1), 10 (2014). https://doi.org/10.1186/1687-417X-2014-10

7. Bianchi, T., Rosa, A.D., Fontani, M., Rocciolo, G., Piva, A.: Detection and classification of double compressed MP3 audio tracks. In: Proceedings of the first ACM Workshop on Information Hiding and Multimedia Security, IH&MMSec 2013, pp. 159–164. ACM, Montpellier (2013) https://doi.org/10.1145/2482513.2482523

8. Seichter, D., Cuccovillo, L., Aichroth, P.: AAC encoding detection and bitrate estimation using a convolutional neural network. In: IEEE International Conference on Acoustics, Speech and Signal Processing. IEEE, Shanghai (2016). https://doi.org/10.1109/icassp.2016.7472041

9. Jin, C., Wang, R., Yan, D., Ma, P., Zhou, J.: An efficient algorithm for double compressed AAC audio detection. Multimed. Tools Appl. **75**(8), 1–18 (2016). https://doi.org/10.1007/s11042-015-2552-2

10. Li, H.: AMR and AAC audio double compression detection research. (Doctoral dissertation, South China University of Technology) (2015)

11. Institution, B.S. ISO/IEC 13838-7/FPDAM 1. Information technology. Generic coding of moving pictures and associated audio information. Part 7: advanced audio coding (AAC). amendment 1: signalling of bandwidth extension

12. Fridrich, J., Goljan, M., Hogea, D.: Steganalysis of JPEG images: breaking the F5 algorithm. In: Petitcolas, F.A.P. (ed.) IH 2002. LNCS, vol. 2578, pp. 310–323. Springer, Heidelberg (2003). https://doi.org/10.1007/3-540-36415-3_20

13. Fridrich, J.: Feature-based steganalysis for JPEG images and its implications for future design of steganographic schemes. In: Fridrich, Jessica (ed.) IH 2004. LNCS, vol. 3200, pp. 67–81. Springer, Heidelberg (2004). https://doi.org/10.1007/978-3-540-30114-1_6

14. Kodovský, J., Fridrich, J.: Calibration revisited. In: Proceedings of ACM Multimedia & Security Workshop, pp. 63–74. ACM, Princeton (2009). https://doi.org/10.1145/1597817.1597830

Accurate Hand Detection Method for Noisy Environments

Hang Pan[1], Qingjie Zhu[1], Renjun Tang[2], Jinlong Chen[1,2],
Xianjun Chen[1,3(✉)], Baohua Qiang[1,2], and Minghao Yang[1,4]

[1] Guangxi Key Laboratory of Cryptography and Information Security,
Guilin University of Electronic Technology, Guilin 541004, Guangxi, China
hingini@126.com
[2] Guangxi Colleges and Universities Key Laboratory of Intelligent Processing
of Computer Image and Graphics, Guilin University of Electronic Technology,
Guilin 541004, Guangxi, China
[3] Information Engineering School, Haikou College of Economics,
Haikou 571127, Hainan, China
[4] Institute of Automation, Chinese Academy of Sciences, Beijing 100190, China

Abstract. For the problem of low manual detection accuracy under the conditions of illumination and occlusion, the detection of human hands based on common optical images was explored, and an accurate manual detection method under general conditions was proposed. The method based on skin color model combined with Convolutional Neural Network (CNN) was mainly used. Realize the detection of human hands. Firstly, the skin color model is obtained according to the characteristics of skin color in the HSV (Hue, Saturation and Value) space, which is used to segment skin area. On this basis, a convolutional neural network for the detection of human hand contours is constructed, which is used to extract the human hand contour features to constrain skin region to obtain the hand region. The results show that even in light and shielding, it also has adaptability, which improves the accuracy of hand detection.

Keywords: Hand detection · Skin model · Convolutional Neural Network

1 Introduction

According to statistics, information exchange between the public of seventy percent is through body language or facial expressions, and body language can express human intention more than natural language [1]. In recent years, with the advancement of science and technology and the improvement of people's own needs, human-computer interaction (HCI) technology has also been rapidly developed, and various novels and free interaction methods have also emerged. The efficient human-computer interaction is to let the computer understand body language. Gesture as an important body language, it is a common natural human-computer interaction, but also a simple, free human-computer interaction. The basis of gesture interaction often needs to first determine the position, size, shape, etc. of the human hand, which is often referred to as hand detection.

© Springer Nature Switzerland AG 2018
X. Sun et al. (Eds.): ICCCS 2018, LNCS 11068, pp. 360–368, 2018.
https://doi.org/10.1007/978-3-030-00021-9_33

In gesture recognition or gesture tracking, human hands are often first detected, that is the basis for subsequent gesture recognition and gesture tracking. Therefore, Tompson et al. used the depth camera-based method, combined with the color image tagging method based on optical images to detect the hand [2], and later used depth-based convolutional neural network for gesture tracking. Compared to depth cameras and the use of gloves and other special devices, the ordinary hands under the gloved hands are always rich in expression, relatively free, flexible and convenient. For example, in the field of home or service robots, the detection of human hands under ordinary optical cameras is still very important.

With regard to the research on manpower testing, many scholars have done a lot of related work. The traditional method mainly depends on the features of human hand Haar features, skin color features, and so on. For example, Bilal et al. proposed a human hand detection method combining Haar-like features with Adaboost. They first used Haar-like features to extract information from hand and then used the AdaBoost algorithm to learn [3]. In order to reduce the impact of face detection on human hands, Stenger et al. trained the human hand and face detectors respectively, and used this method to further improve the detection accuracy [4]. These traditional methods can achieve good experimental results under certain conditions. However, when the experimental environment changes greatly, the experimental results tend to be unstable, such as when the light changes. With the release of the Microsoft Kinect depth camera, depth information has also been used as an important feature for human detection research. For example, Liu et al. used a Kinect depth camera to achieve close-range human hand detection and fingertip tracking in complex backgrounds [5]. Sridhar et al. trained a hierarchical random forest classifier to classify each pixel in the depth image and quickly determined the human hand area [6]. With the rapid development of deep learning, the multi-scale Faster-RCNN method proposed by Hoang et al. conducts a manual method. This method uses global and local depth features to encode the human hands in the image to obtain the position of the human hand [7]. These methods are based on pixel-by-pixel clustering combined with the depth image. If the object is held in the hand, there will be a few pixel classification errors because the depth of the object being held is similar to the finger.

Therefore, in order to solve the problem of low manual detection rate in the case of illumination change and occlusion, this paper explores the method of human hand detection based on common optical images, and proposes an accurate human detection method under general conditions, mainly based on skin color models combined with convolution Neural network (Convolutional Neural Network, CNN) method to achieve the detection of human hands. The experimental results show that the method has adaptability and high detection accuracy even in the case of illumination and occlusion.

2 Algorithm Framework

The algorithm proposed in this paper includes two modules: skin color detection and human hand recognition. Among them, the input is a real-time video frame sequence, and the output is a sequence of video frames containing human hand area calibration. In the real-time detection process of the human hand, the interval between the two frames of the video is usually very short, and the algorithm of this paper is low in time complexity, which can satisfy the smooth processing of each frame in real time. Algorithm flow chart shown in Fig. 1:

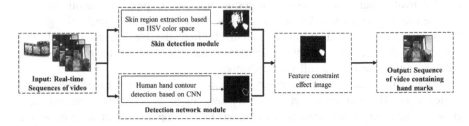

Fig. 1. Hand detection algorithm flow chart. The skin color detection module refers to detecting a skin color region in a video frame based on HSV (Hue, Saturation, and Value) skin color model, and obtaining a skin color mask image. The detection network module extracts the outline features of the human hand through CNN, and uses the outline feature to constrain the skin mask image to obtain the human hand area.

3   Skin Color Detection Based on HSV Space

The human skin color feature is one of the distinctive features that distinguish it from the surrounding environment. After a lot of scientific research, it has been found that human skin color has very good clustering. The human skin color exhibits different clustering characteristics in different color spaces. In order to obtain a cleaner gesture segmentation effect, it is particularly important to select a color space. Usually the image is RGB, where R, G, B represent the brightness information of the red, green, and blue colors, respectively, and there is a certain correlation between them. A slight change in brightness will cause a huge change in the skin color segmentation. It is not suitable for gesture segmentation. It needs to use linear or nonlinear changes to transform it into other color spaces for skin color segmentation. This article uses HSV color space to model skin color. The HSV color model is a color space created by AR Smith in 1978. As shown in Fig. 2:

Regardless of the effects of brightness and saturation, each color has its own hue value in the HSV color space, so the hue dimension in the HSV color space can be used to segment different colors. While performing skin color detection, ambient light often changes, resulting in changes in the brightness and saturation of the human skin; but the hue of human skin generally does not change, so based on the H dimension in the HSV color space can be carried out on the skin color segmentation. First, RGB is normalized, then R, G, B $\in$ [0, 1], then the RGB space is transformed into HSV space, the specific transformation method is as follows:

$$V = max(R, G, B) \tag{1}$$

$$S = \begin{cases} 0 & if\ V = 0 \\ \frac{V - min(R,G,B)}{V} & else \end{cases} \tag{2}$$

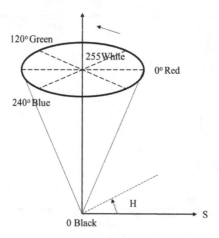

Fig. 2. HSV color space. The angle between the conical bottom radius and the 0° line represents Hue, and the radius of the cone bottom surface represents saturation. The height of the cone represents the value (Value). Their values range from 0 to 360, 0 to 255, and 0 to 255. (Color figure online)

$$r = \frac{V - R}{V - \min(R, G, B)}, \ g = \frac{V - G}{V - \min(R, G, B)}, \ b = \frac{V - B}{V - \min(R, G, B)}$$

$$6H = \begin{cases} NaN & if \ S = 0 \ that \ is \ V = 0 \\ 1 - g & if \ V = R, \min(R, G, B) = B \\ 5 + b & if \ V = R, \min(R, G, B) = G \\ 3 - b & if \ V = G, \min(R, G, B) = R \\ 1 + r & if \ V = G, \min(R, G, B) = B \\ 5 - r & if \ V = B, \min(R, G, B) = G \\ 3 + g & if \ V = B, \min(R, G, B) = R \end{cases} \quad (3)$$

It can be seen from the above formula that if and only if the object color is a gray color (R = G = B), then S = 0; if and only if S = 0, H will be meaningless. This indicates that the color cannot be converted to HSV space when the color is a grayscale color. For this problem, considering that the skin color is not a gray color, this article has added a step judgment, that is, when the color is gray, directly exclude; when the color is not gray, then switch to the HSV skin color space using the skin color model to judge.

In order to detect the human hand, a good skin color model needs to be established. In this paper, the images of human hands under various environmental conditions in this experiment are collected. There are 91 images of human hands collected, a total of 121 skin color areas, and a total of 5910513 pixels. The average gray value of these pixels is 129.12; the average value of the three channels of RGB is 149.21, 124.25, and 101.02, respectively. Here R, G, B ∈ [0,255]. Convert this result to HSV space and observe the H-channel histogram distribution as shown in Fig. 3.

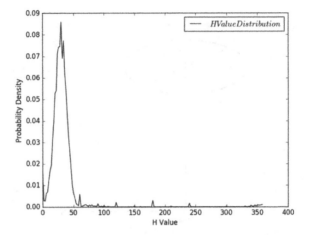

Fig. 3. Skin color H value distribution histogram. H values are evenly distributed in most histograms in the range of 0 to 60 on the left, and a small part of H values are distributed in the vicinity of 80, 180, and 360.

From the HSV to RGB spatial transformation formula (3), it is known that the H value distribution in the range of 0 to 60 represents the normal skin color of the human body under normal conditions, and a very small amount of H values distributed in other regions. Considering its very small probability density and actual conditions, it can be determined that these H values are all caused by noise. In order to make the selected threshold have good anti-noise ability, the H-threshold of the skin color segmentation was selected from 6 to 48 after experimental measurement. Using this range can segment most of the gesture area, and has a good anti-noise performance.

4 Hand Detection Based on Convolutional Neural Network

4.1 Network Structure

Convolutional neural network is a special deep neural network model. It is a new type of artificial neural network. At present, convolutional neural networks have been widely used in various fields such as speech recognition, handwriting recognition, and face recognition. In the image domain, using convolutional neural networks to process images has a natural advantage. Compared with other artificial neural networks, it mainly has the characteristics of local connection, weight sharing, and pooling. These features make it easier to handle image information.

Taking into account the real-time requirements of human detection, the first four layers of the network structure use a full convolutional network and down sample the input image to $160 \times 120 \times 3$ to reduce computational complexity and increase detection speed. The first convolution layer in the network has $64 \times 3 \times 3$ convolution kernels with a step size of 1; the second convolution layer has $128 \times 3 \times 3$ convolution kernels, with a step size of 1; The four convolution layers have

$256 \times 3 \times 3$ convolution kernels, with a step size of 1; 4 full convolution layers followed by 3 fully connected layers with sizes of 1024, 1024, and 4800, respectively; the final output layer is 4800. Converted to an 80×60 image as a prediction result. The details of the network structure are shown in Fig. 4.

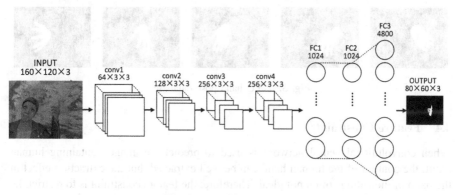

Fig. 4. Network structure.

4.2 Training Data

In this paper, the NYU gesture database [8] is used as a training dataset database, which contains more than 41258 images of 320×320 pixels in size, and gives a hand-tagged image. Since the image in the database is a composite image generated by placing the synthesized human body image in various realistic backgrounds, the synthetic human hand has a certain difference from the real human hand. Therefore, in training, we have the brightness and contrast of the training image., Hue, Saturation for data enhancement.

Because the common real-time image size obtained by common optical cameras is 640×480, in order to better keep the convolutional neural network prediction results consistent with the images obtained by the camera, this paper uses the image of the human hand position of the marker image in the database. Trimming is performed to half the scale of the real-time image 320×240. Taking into account the time-consuming calculation of the network, the original image is further down-sampled to 160×120, and the marked image is down-sampled to 80×60. Some of the training images are shown in Fig. 5.

4.3 Network Training

In the initial state of network training, all network parameters are set to a random initialization state; the Relu function is used as an activation function in all convolution layers of the network, and the Sigmoid function is used as an activation function in the full connection layer including the output layer; The process uses Mean Squared Error (MSE) as a loss function and uses a stochastic gradient descent algorithm to update the network parameters; during the entire iterative training process, the learning rate is set to 0.01.

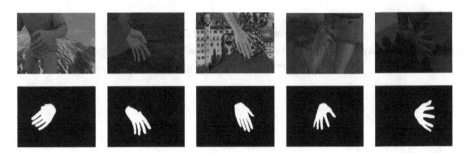

Fig. 5. NYU hand pose database.

4.4 Feature Constraints

When convolutional neural network is used to predict the image containing human input, the contour of the human hand can be well extracted, but the extraction effect in the palm of the palm is often not ideal. Therefore, the feature constraint is to restrict the skin color detection effect based on the HSV according to the outline feature extracted by the CNN, and to obtain the hand area. The specific method is as follows:

$$I_{res} = \begin{cases} 1 & if\ Point_{hsv}\ in\ Contour_{cnn} \\ 0 & else \end{cases} \tag{4}$$

Where I_{res} is the image of the hand obtained by the characteristic constraint, $Point_{hsv}$ is the skin point in the mask image of the skin color detection, and $Contour_{cnn}$ is the outline area obtained by the detection network.

5   Analysis of Results

In order to test the experimental results of this algorithm, this article conducted a manual test related to human hands. The hardware and software environment was: Intel (R) Core(TM) I3 processor, 4G running memory, general optical camera, 64-bit windows 7 operating system, Visual Studio 2013 development environment, OpenCV3.0 image processing library, Caffe deep learning framework. This experiment uses a special color marking method to mark the detected gestures, as shown in Fig. 6, which is an experimental effect chart for this article.

In order to test the experimental results of this algorithm, this article conducted a manual test related to human hands. The hardware and software environment was: Intel (R) Core(TM) I3 processor, 4G running memory, general optical camera, 64-bit windows 7 operating system, Visual Studio 2013 development environment, OpenCV3.0 image processing library, Caffe deep learning framework. This experiment uses a special color marking method to mark the detected gestures, as shown in Fig. 6, which is an experimental effect chart for this article.

At the same time, the human hand detection experiment results of this method are compared with the subjective tests in the literature [9]. The relevant comparison results

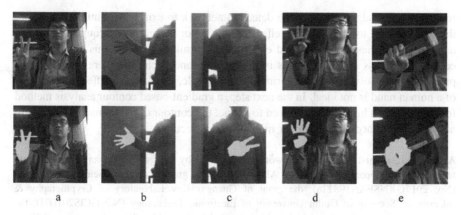

Fig. 6. Experiment effect of hand detection.

are shown in Fig. 7. Where a is the original image in the Dexter database, b is the gesture detection effect in [9], and c is the experimental effect of the method in this paper. It can be seen from the figure that in the blue box area, this method can get better edge effect, but at the wrist of the yellow circular area, the effect of this paper is not particularly ideal. Therefore, it can be concluded that the method in this paper has a relatively good effect on the edge detection of human hands, but the segmentation at the wrist needs further improvement.

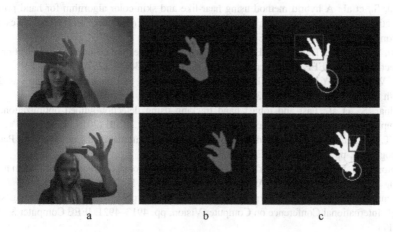

Fig. 7. Experimental comparison. (Color figure online)

6   Conclusion

Gesture is an important body language for intelligent human-computer interaction, and human hand detection is the basis for gesture interaction. This paper proposes a man-hand detection algorithm. Experiments show that the algorithm has good accuracy and robustness. The algorithm uses the detection network to extract the outline features of the human hand to constrain the effect of skin color detection to acquire the human hand area, and has achieved good experimental results. Although this algorithm has certain robustness against changes in illumination and occlusion, there are still some problems to be solved in this algorithm. For example, the detection effect on the wrist of a human hand is not ideal. In the next step, a gradient-based contour analysis method for the wrist of a human hand is used to extract the contour of the human hand so as to achieve a more accurate target for human hand detection.

Acknowledgements. This research work is supported by the grant of Guangxi science and technology development project (No: AB17195053), the grant of Guangxi Science Foundation (No: 2017GXNSFAA198226), the grant of Guangxi Key Laboratory of Cryptography & Information Security of Guilin University of Electronic Technology (No: GCIS201604), the grant of Guangxi Colleges and Universities Key Laboratory of Intelligent Processing of Computer Images and Graphics of Guilin University of Electronic Technology (No: GIIP201602), and the grant of Innovation Project of GUET Graduate Education(2017YJCX55).

References

1. Li, Q., et al.: Gesture segmentation with improved maximum between-cluster variance algorithm. Acta Autom. Sin. **43**(4), 528–537 (2017)
2. Tompson, J., et al.: Real-time continuous pose recovery of human hands using convolutional networks. ACM Trans. Graph. **3**(5), 1–10 (2014)
3. Bilal, S., et al.: A hybrid method using haar-like and skin-color algorithm for hand posture detection, recognition and tracking. In: International Conference on Mechatronics and Automation, pp. 934–939. IEEE (2010)
4. Mita, T., Kaneko, T., Stenger, B., et al.: Discriminative feature co-occurrence selection for object detection. IEEE Trans. Pattern Anal. Mach. Intell. **30**(7), 1257–1269 (2008)
5. Liu, W.H., Fan, Y.Y., Lei, T.: Human fingertip detection and tracking algorithm based on depth image. J. Comput. Appl. **34**(5), 1442–1448 (2014)
6. Sridhar, S., et al.: Fast and robust hand tracking using detection-guided optimization. In: Computer Vision and Pattern Recognition, pp. 3213–3221. IEEE (2015)
7. Le, T.H.N., et al.: Robust hand detection in vehicles. In: International Conference on Pattern Recognition, pp. 573–578. IEEE (2017)
8. Tompson, J., Stein, M., Lecun, Y., et al.: Real-time continuous pose recovery of human hands using convolutional networks. ACM Trans. Graph. **33**(5), 1–10 (2014)
9. Zimmermann, C., Brox, T.: Learnings to estimate 3D hand pose from single RGB images. In: IEEE International Conference on Computer Vision, pp. 4913–4921. IEEE Computer Society (2017)

Adaptive Image Filtering
Based on Convolutional Neural Network

Zehao Ni[1,2(⊠)], Mengxing Huang[1,2], Wei Zhang[3], Le Wang[4],
Qiong Chen[1,2], and Yu Zhang[1,2]

[1] State Key Laboratory of Marine Resource Utilization in South China Sea,
Hainan University, Haikou 570228, China
394864521@qq.com
[2] College of Information Science and Technology,
Hainan University, Haikou 570228, China
[3] A Unit of Shijingshan, Beijing, China
[4] Procuratonal Technology and Information Research Center,
Supreme People's Procuratorate, Beijing, People's Republic of China

Abstract. The process of digital image acquisition and transmission is easy to be polluted by noise. Noises can also cause disturbances, or even misjudgements in the remote sensing image, face recognition, image classification of machine learning and deep learning. Therefore the correctness and safety of image usage is greatly reduced. Different types of noise may occur under various conditions, and the same filtering method has different effects on different types of noise processing, which makes it difficult to select the best way to filtering the image. So the detection and recognition of noise type has always been a hot topic in the field of information security. However, there are lacking solutions to the current noise type identification problem, and the complexity is very high. In this paper, a convolutional neural network(CNN) model which is able to automatically identify salt and pepper noise, Gauss noise and random noise based on deep learning training is proposed. After that, median filter, mean filter and wiener filter are used to filter the corresponding images. The purpose of ensuring correctness and security of the image application is achieved. By simulating the images of different noise and analyzing PSNR, it is proved that this method able to distinguish the noise and filter obviously.

Keywords: Image feature extraction · Convolution neural network
Noise type · Filtering · PSNR

1 Introduction

In recent years, with the rapid development of society, the popularity of all kinds of digital products and digital products has increased greatly. The digital images taken by digital products are likely to be distorted or even not applied to all sorts of noise sources from the early stage to the later stage of transmission, storage and use. As more and more research results in recent years, it is of great significance to estimate the type of noise so that to achieve the best filtering effect.

© Springer Nature Switzerland AG 2018
X. Sun et al. (Eds.): ICCCS 2018, LNCS 11068, pp. 369–379, 2018.
https://doi.org/10.1007/978-3-030-00021-9_34

Nowadays, there are few methods to identify the image noise type, and there are three representative methods. Noise recognition method for the energy distribution of high frequency subband coefficients based on the wavelet domain [1]. The autocorrelation function of white noise is the impulse response. The second method is based on that to distinguish between white noise and colored noise [2]. The third method need to intercept gray histogram in the area of the relative uniformity of the image to analyze [3]. The first and second methods are either analyzed in the frequency domain or with cumbersome formulas. The two methods are both too complicated. Moreover, the third method requires manual selection of the captured image, and the selection of partial images is also unsatisfactory.

In this paper, a model based on convolution neural network in depth learning for automatic identification of salt and pepper noise, Gauss noise and random noise is put forward. The model is used to distinguish the kinds of noise of the image inclusion, then the mean filtering, median filtering or Wiener filtering to filtering. First, feature extraction is performed on the input image, then the CNN model is used to determine the noise type of the image, and finally an appropriate filtering method is applied to filter the image. This method can accurately identify the type of noise in the image and filter the noise by MATLAB.

2   Extract Image Features

The background of the input noise-containing image and the details of the image edge may interfere with the identification of the noise type. Therefore, it is necessary to process the noisy image before creating the model to amplify the noise feature and weaken the image background and edge details. The steps to extract features are as follows, the processed image can be seen to reduce the image background and edge details, so that we can enlarge the noise.

Step1: Imaging processing by Gauss filter. The results are shown in Fig. 1.

Fig. 1. Step 1

Step 2: Subtracting the processed image from the original image. The results are shown in Fig. 2.

Fig. 2. Step 2

Step 3: Using the second-step picture to subtract the minimum value of the pixel in this picture to ensure that the pixel value of the double-type picture is between 0–1. The results are shown in Fig. 3.

Fig. 3. Step 3

3 Convolutional Neural Network

3.1 The Development of CNN

Convolution neural network (CNN) is an efficient recognition method which has been developed in recent years and has attracted much attention of researchers. In 1960s, when Hubel and Wiesel studied the cat's cerebral cortex, they found that the unique network structure for local sensitive and directional selection neurons able to effectively reduce the complexity of the feedback neural network, and then put forward a

CNN. Nowadays, CNN has become one of the research hotspots in many scientific fields, especially in the field of pattern classification. Since the network avoids the complicated pre-processing of images, it can directly input the original image, and thus has been more widely used. The new recognition machine proposed by K. Fukushima in 1980 is the first realization network of convolutional neural networks. Subsequently, more scientific researchers improved the network. One of the representative research results is the "improvement of cognitive machine" proposed by Alexander and Taylor, which combines the advantages of various improved methods and avoids time-consuming error back propagation [4].

3.2   Introduction to CNN

In general, the basic structure of CNN includes two layers. The first layer is the feature extraction layer. The input of each neuron is connected with the local accepted domain of the previous layer and the local features are extracted. Once the local feature is extracted, the positional relationship between it and other features is also determined. The second is the feature mapping layer. Each computation layer of the network consists of multiple feature maps. Each feature map is a plane. The weights of all neurons in the plane are equal. The feature mapping structure uses the sigmoid function with small influence on the function kernel as the activation function of the convolutional network, so that the feature map has displacement invariance. In addition, since the neurons on one mapping plane share weights, the number of network free parameters is reduced. Each convolutional layer in the convolutional neural network is followed by a computational layer for local average and secondary extraction. This unique two feature extraction structure reduces the feature resolution [5].

CNN is mainly employed to identify displacement, scaling and other forms of distortion invariant two-dimensional graphics. Since the CNN feature detection layer learns through training data, when using CNN, it avoids explicit feature extraction, and implicitly learns from training data. And the weights of neurons on the same feature mapping surface are the same, so the network is able to learn in parallel, which is also a great advantage of convolution network relative to neurons connected to each other. Convolutional neural networks have some unique advantages in terms of local recognition of their weights and image processing. Their layout is closer to the actual biological neural network. Weight sharing reduces the complexity of the network, especially the multidimensional image can be a direct input to the network which can avoid the complexity of data reconstruction feature extraction and in the process of classification [6]. Figure 4 shows a CNN model with three input layers, four hidden layers and two output layers.

3.3   Training Process of CNN Model

Step 1:   Setting up training sets and test sets. A total of 1500 pictures of 512*512*3 are used in the CNN model. These images were downloaded from the internet and manually tagged. Of which the training set accounted for 80% and the test set accounted for 20%.

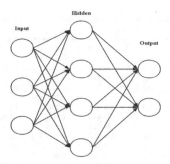

Fig. 4. CNN model

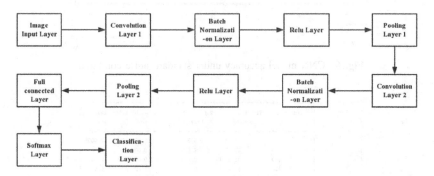

Fig. 5. The structure of the CNN model in this paper

Step 2:   CNN model with structure as shown in Fig. 5 is created. Convolution layer1 is a 2-D convolutional layer with 15 filters of size [7 7]and zero padding of size 2 along all edges of the layer input. Pooling layer 1 is a max pooling layer with pool size [2 2] and stride [2 2]. Convolution layer 2 is a 2-D convolutional layer with 63 filters of size [5 5], and zero padding of size 1 along all edges of the layer input. Pooling layer 2 is a max pooling layer with pool size [2 2] and stride [2 2]. And creates a fully connected layer with an output of 3 in the end.

Step 3:   Creating a set of options for training a network using stochastic gradient descent with momentum. Setting the maximum number of epochs for training to 20and use a mini-batch with 8 observations at each iteration, and starting the training with an initial learning rate of 0.005.

Step 4:   Training the network and test the network.

3.4   Training Results of the CNN Model

In the case of the noise density standard and variance specified by MATLAB, the accuracy of the CNN model in this paper is shown in Fig. 6. As shown in Fig. 7, if we increase the noise density or variance, the accuracy of the model will be greatly improved.

Epoch	Iteration	Time Elapsed (seconds)	Mini-batch Loss	Mini-batch Accuracy	Base Learning Rate
1	1	0.48	8.0295	12.50%	0.0005
2	50	20.30	7.9712	50.00%	0.0005
4	100	40.79	2.2193	75.00%	0.0005
5	150	61.40	0.6639	62.50%	0.0005
7	200	82.15	1.2160	75.00%	0.0005
8	250	102.89	0.7298	87.50%	0.0005
10	300	123.49	0.3090	87.50%	0.0005
11	350	143.97	0.6250	62.50%	0.0005
13	400	164.51	0.6888	75.00%	0.0005
14	450	184.99	0.9433	62.50%	0.0005
16	500	205.54	0.4929	75.00%	0.0005
17	550	226.10	0.8029	75.00%	0.0005
19	600	246.57	0.8665	100.00%	0.0005
20	650	267.13	0.5041	87.50%	0.0005
20	660	271.25	0.8543	37.50%	0.0005

accuracy =

0.7667

Fig. 6. CNN model accuracy under standard noise condition

Epoch	Iteration	Time Elapsed (seconds)	Mini-batch Loss	Mini-batch Accuracy	Base Learning Rate
1	1	0.53	9.9640	37.50%	0.0005
2	50	20.90	2.5694	75.00%	0.0005
4	100	41.53	0.1707	100.00%	0.0005
5	150	62.15	0.3206	75.00%	0.0005
7	200	82.82	2.4386	75.00%	0.0005
8	250	103.51	0.2481	100.00%	0.0005
10	300	124.23	0.6535	87.50%	0.0005
11	350	144.83	2.1618	37.50%	0.0005
13	400	165.65	0.6718	50.00%	0.0005
14	450	186.33	0.4374	75.00%	0.0005
16	500	206.76	0.5590	62.50%	0.0005
17	550	227.16	0.0896	100.00%	0.0005
19	600	247.53	0.1685	87.50%	0.0005
20	650	267.89	0.1126	100.00%	0.0005
20	660	271.97	0.9540	75.00%	0.0005

accuracy =

0.9000

Fig. 7. CNN model accuracy under noise enhancement condition

4   Filtering Methods

4.1   Median Filtering

Median filtering is a non-linear filtering method. This method does not require the use of the statistical characteristics of the image, so it is simple and easy to implement. Median filter required to select all pixels in the appropriate square neighborhood around the target pixel and rank them according to the gray level, then select the intermediate value of the group as the pixel value of the target point output [7].

Some experiments have confirmed that median filtering able to remove salt and pepper noise well [8]. The expression of median filter can be recorded:

$$y(n) = med[x(n - N)...x(n)...x(n+N)] \tag{1}$$

As shown in Fig. 8, if we choose a point with a pixel value of 2 as an input, then the output will be 4 after filtering.

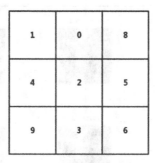

Fig. 8. Pixel grayscale

4.2 Mean Filtering

The mean filtering algorithm is simple and has a good suppression result for noise. The mean filter needs to select the right-sized square neighborhood around the target pixel, and replaces the pixel of the target pixel with the mean of all the pixel sums in the neighborhood [9]. There are experiments to verify that the mean filter can remove Gaussian noise well. The expression of mean filter can be recorded:

$$y(n) = \frac{1}{(2a + 1)} \sum_{k=n-a}^{n+a} x(k) \tag{2}$$

As shown in Fig. 8, if we choose a point with a pixel value of 2 as an input, then the output will be 4 .2 after filtering.

4.3 Wiener Filtering

Wiener filtering is an image filtering method based on the minimum mean square error criterion, that is, minimizing the mean squared error between a noisy image and filtered pictures. Wiener filtering can filter out noise from the interfered signal as much as possible and extract useful signals, so it is also called the best filter [10].

4.4 Color Image Filtering

The filtering method of three-dimensional color image is different from the two-dimensional black and white image. The algorithm uses the method of separating the

RGB three-color channels of the three-dimensional color image, filtering them, and finally combining them. The process is shown in Fig. 9.

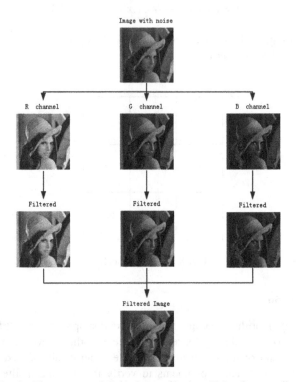

Fig. 9. The process of Color image filtering (Color figure online)

4.5   Image Quality

In the research of image filtering algorithm, the objective evaluation index is needed to be used to measure the quality of the reconstructed image relative to the reference image. In this article, Peak Signal to Noise Ratio (PSNR) is taken as an objective evaluation criterion for images. The formula is as follow, among them, I is the original image, k is the changed image, and i and j are the pixel values corresponding to the images:

$$MSE = \frac{1}{mn}\sum\nolimits_{i=0}^{m-1}\sum\nolimits_{j=0}^{n-1}\|I(i,j) - K(i,j)\|2 \qquad (3)$$

$$PSNR = 20log10(\frac{MAXi}{MSE}) \qquad (4)$$

5   The Algorithm Flow

The algorithm flow is as follows:

Step 1   Inputing images with unknown noise. These images were downloaded from the internet and manually tagged.

Step 2   Extracting image features, which is to reduce the image background and edge details, so that we can enlarge the noise.

Step 3   The processed images in the trained CNN model are put, and then the CNN model is used to judge the noise types in the processed images.

Step 4   If the CNN model shows that the image carries salt and pepper noise, the algorithm will use median filtering to filter out salt and pepper noise. If the CNN model shows that the image carries Gaussian noise, the algorithm will use mean filtering to filter out Gaussian noise. If the CNN model shows that the image carries random noise, the algorithm will use wiener filtering to filter out random noise.

Step 5   Outputting the noise-filtered image (Fig. 10).

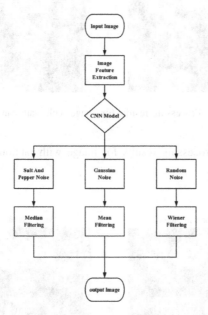

Fig. 10. The algorithm flow

6   Experimental Result

(1) The algorithm's processing results for image with salt and pepper noise are shown in Fig. 11.

Salt and pepper noise   Median filter

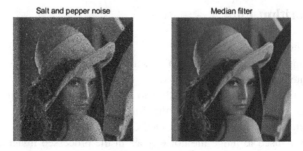

Fig. 11. Processing results for image with salt and pepper noise

(2) The algorithm's processing results for image with Gaussian noise are shown in Fig. 12.

Gaussian noise   Mean filter

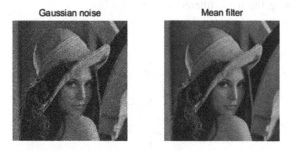

Fig. 12. Processing results for image with Gaussian noise

(3) The algorithm's processing results for image with random noise are shown in Fig. 13 (Table 1).

Random noise   Wiener filter

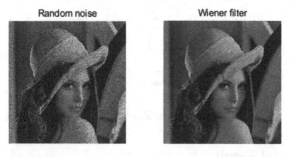

Fig. 13. Processing results for image with random noise

Table 1. PSNR of the noise images and filtered images

Noise type	PSNR of image containing noise (db)	PSNR of filtered image (db)	Improved PSNR (db)
Salt and pepper	20.7025	29.5788	8.8763
Gaussian	22.8248	33.6302	10.8054
Random	22.5951	33.8163	11.2212

7 Conclusion

By simulating pictures with different noise types, it is proved that this method can effectively discriminate salt and pepper noise, Gaussian noise and random noise. The significant increase in PSNR after filtering indicates that this method is conductive of removing the noise well.

Acknowledgments. Foundation item: Natural Science Foundation of Hainan province (Grant#:617062, Grant #: 20156235 and Grant #: 614232), National Natural Science Foundation of China(Grant #: 61462022), the National Key Technology Support Program (Grant #: 2015BAH55F04, Grant #:2015BAH55F01), Major Science and Technology Project of Hainan province (Grant #: ZDKJ2016015), Higher Education Reform Key Project of Hainan province (Hnjg2017ZD-1), Scientific Research Staring Foundation of Hainan University(Grant #: kyqd1610).

References

1. Zhang, Q., Liang, D.Q., Fan, X., Li, W.J.: Idetifying of Noise Types and Edtimating of Noise Level for A Noisy Image in the Wavelet Domain. Infrared Millim, Waves (2004)
2. Yang, Z.G., Ge, W.C., Wu,G.S., Peng, N.: Design of receivers based on noise type recognition. Inf. Technol. **1**, 6 (2010)
3. Ding, S.R., Ma, M.: Image noisetype recognition based on gray relational analysis of histogram information. J. Shaanxi Normal Univ. **39**, 19 (2011)
4. Ye, Y.: Deep Learning & Computer Vision: Algorithms and Examples, 1st edn. China Machine Press, Beijing (2017)
5. Lecun, Y., Bengio, Y., Hinton, G.: Deep learning. Nature **521**, 436 (2015)
6. Alex, K., Iiya, S.: Imagenet classification with deep convolutional neural networks. In: Advances in Neural Information Processing Systems. Nevada, USA (2012)
7. Huang, H.C., Tnomas Lee, C.M.: Data adaptive median filtersfor signal and image denoising using a generalized SURE criterion. IEEE Trans. Image Process. Lett. **13**, 562 (2006)
8. Zhang, Q.L., Ma, Z.P., Xue, R.Z.:Research and analysis of several image denoising based on matlab. Digit.Technol. Appl. **4**, 82 (2015)
9. Ji, X.N., et al.: An effective self-adaptive mean filter for mixed noise. In: ICARM. IEEE (2016)
10. Baselice, F., Ferraioli, G., Johnsy, A.C., pascazio, V., Schirinzi, G.: Speckle reduction based on Wiener filter in ultrasound images. In: EMBC. IEEE (2015)

Aggregated Multimodal Bidirectional Recurrent Model for Audiovisual Speech Recognition

Yu Wen[1]([✉]), Ke Yao[1], Chunlin Tian[2], Yao Wu[1], Zhongmin Zhang[1], Yaning Shi[1], Yin Tian[1], Jin Yang[1], and Peiqi Wang[1]

[1] Experimental Training Base, National University of Defence Technology, Xian 710106, Shaanxi, People's Republic of China
wenyu_80@163.com, yaoke0505@126.com, 610399234@qq.com, zon_8986@126.com, syn573@163.com, 467347796@qq.com, yangjin83202@sina.com
[2] University of Chinese Academy of Sciences, 19A Yuquanlu, Beijing 100049, People's Republic of China
tianchunlin123@gmail.com

Abstract. The *Audiovisual Speech Recognition* (AVSR) most commonly applied to multimodal learning employs both the video and audio information to do *Robust Automatic Speech Recognition*. Traditionally, AVSR was regarded as the inference and projection, a lot of restrictions on the ability of it. With the in-depth study, DNN becomes an important part of the toolkit in traditional classification tools, such as automatic speech recognition, image classification, natural language processing. AVSR often use some DNN models including *Multimodal Deep Autoencoders* (MDAEs), *Multimodal Deep Belief Network* (MDBN) and *Multimodal Deep Boltzmann Machine* (MDBM), which are always better than the traditional methods. However, such DNN models have several shortcomings: Firstly, they can't balance the modal fusion and temporal fusion, or even haven't temporal fusion; Secondly, the architecture of these models isn't end-to-end. In addition, the training and testing are cumbersome. We designed a DNN model—*Aggregated Multimodal Bidirectional Recurrent Model* (DILATE)—to overcome such weakness. The DILATE could be not just trained and tested simultaneously, but alternatively easy to train and prevent overfitting automatically. The experiments show that DILATE is superior to traditional methods and other DNN models in some benchmark datasets.

Keywords: Multimodal deep learning
Audiovisual Speech Recognition

1 Introduction

Automatic Speech Recognition (ASR) has been investigated over several years, and there is a wealth of literature. The recent progress is *Deep Speech2* [2], which

---

Yu Wen, woman, born in 1980, master, lecturer, research direction: information resource management, computer network.

© Springer Nature Switzerland AG 2018
X. Sun et al. (Eds.): ICCCS 2018, LNCS 11068, pp. 380–391, 2018.
https://doi.org/10.1007/978-3-030-00021-9_35

utilizes deep *Convolution Neural Network* (CNN) [8], LSTM [6] and CTC [5], and sequence-to-sequence models [24]. Although ASR achieved excellent result, it had some intrinsical problems including insufficient tolerance of noise and disturbance. Besides, some illusion occurs when the auditory component of one sound is paired with the visual component of another sound, leading to the perception of a third sound [12]. This was described as McGurk effect (McGurk & MacDonald 1976). Robust automatic speech recognition is proposed as a supplement for normal ASR.

Benefited from the multimodal learning, one of the solution for robust automatic speech recognition is *Audiovisual Speech Recognition* (AVSR) that mixes audio and visual information together, and amount of work verified that AVSR strengthened the ASR system [1,14]. When it comes to AVSR, the core part is multimodal learning. In the early decades, many models aimed to fuse the multimodal data more representative and discriminative, of which the representative is multimodal extensions of *Hidden Markov Models* (HMMs). But strong prior assumption limits such models. As the revival of neural networks, some deep models were proposed in multimodal learning. Different from traditional models, deep models usually have two main aspects:

- (1) Many researchers think of *Deep Neural Networks* (DNN) as performing a kind of good representation learning [4], that is, the ability to extract feature of DNN can be exploited for varieties of tasks, especially the CNN for image feature extraction. For aural information, it is refined by some deep models including *Deep Belief Network* (DBN), *Deep Autoencoder* (DAE), *Restricted Boltzmann Machines* (RBMs) and *Deep Bottleneck Features* (DBNF) [11,15,25].
- (2) The other merit of deep models is the well-performed fusion, conquering the biggest disadvantage of traditional methods including *Multimodal DBN* (MDBN) [22], *Multimodal DAEs* (MDAEs) [14] and *Multimodal Deep Boltzmann Machine* (MDBM) [23].

However, the aforementioned deep models have two primary shortcomings:

- (1) They don't balance the modal fusion and temporal fusion, or even haven't temporal fusion. Many methods simply concatenate the features of frames in a single video to do temporal fusion. Besides, in the modal fusion, such methods don't consider the correlation among different frames.
- (2) The architecture of these models isn't end-to-end, the training and testing getting cumbersome.

In order to address the disadvantages, we propose an end-to-end DNN architecture, *Aggregated Multimodal Bidirectional Recurrent Model* (DILATE), for AVSR. The DILATE overcomes the two main weaknesses mentioned before. It is composed of bidirectional recurrent models, projection and recognition, and is trained once. Therefore the modal fusion and temporal fusion are accomplished at the same time, i.e. the modal and temporal fusion are mixed and combined in terms of balance of the two fusion processes. The DILATE is useful for overfitting, besides early stopping [17] and dropout [21] regularization are used to fight against overfitting. Because of the CNN and recurrent networks, DILTATE is also a type of well-known *CNN-RNN architecture*.

We conducted the experiments in three AVSR datasets: AVLetters (Patterson et al., 2002), AVLetters2 (Cox et al., 2008) and AVDigits (Di Hu et al., 2015). The results suggest that DILATE is better than classic AVSR models and some deep models before.

In the following sections, we firstly survey the related work about AVSR in Sect. 2. Section 3 advances the alm-GRU model. In Sect. 4, we conduct AVSR and cross modality speech recognition experiments for evaluating the model on the three datasets, and afterwards the results are displayed and discussed. Section 5 concludes this paper.

2   Related Work

This section reviews the related multimodal models for AVSR historically.

2.1   Traditional AVSR Systems

Humans understand the multimodal world in a seemingly effortless manner, although there are vast information processing resources dedicated to the corresponding tasks by the brain [9]. The early representative work of this field is the multistream HMMs (mHMMs) [13], which has a certain adaptability and flexibility to the modeling sequence and temporal data [18]. But the probability model has some obvious limitations, especially the strong priori. Researchers are also interested in mapping data from different spaces into a space.

The most important part of multimodal learning is multimodal fusion. There are three kinds of fusion strategies: early fusion, late fusion and hybrid fusion. In early fusion, it suffices to concatenate all monomodal features into a single aggregate multimodal descriptor. In late fusion, each modality is classified independently. Integration at decision level, usually based on heuristic rules. Hybrid fusion lies in-between early and late fusion methods and are specifically geared towards modeling multimodal time-evolving data [3,9].

The early representative work of this field is the *multistream HMMs* (mHMMs) [13], which has a certain adaptability and flexibility to the modeling sequence and temporal data [18]. But the probability model has some obvious limitations, especially the strong priori. Researchers are also interested in mapping data from different spaces into a space.

2.2   Deep Learning for AVSR

Deep learning provides a powerful toolkit for machine learning. In AVSR, DNN also shows a significant increase in precision. A pre-trained CNN is used to extract visual features and denoise autoencoders to improve auditory features, and then mHMMs is used for fusion and classification [15]. As I mentioned in Sect. 1, it takes advantage of the feature extraction of DNN.

Some other methods are multimodal fusion based on unsupervised DNN. One type is based on DAEs, the representative work is MDAEs [14]. Others based on Boltzmann Machines, [22] uses MDBN, [23] uses MDBM. In general, the DAEs-based models are easy to train, but lack theoretical support and flexibility. RBM-based models are difficult to train for part of the function, but they are supported in probability models and easy to extend. In addition, they also involve a number of independent training process and testing process that lead to the loss of temporal information in the modal fusion.

3 Proposed Method

The DILATE aims at fusing the audiovisual data at the same time, considering the modal fusion, temporal fusion and the connection between frames simultaneously. In this section, we will introduce the DILATE, and show its simplicity and extensity.

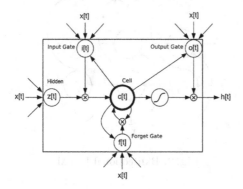

Fig. 1. Simple LSTM

3.1 Bidirectional LSTM

Simple LSTM: There are two widely known issues with properly training vanilla RNN, the vanishing and the exploding gradient [16]. Without some training tricks in training RNN, LSTM [6] uses gates to avoid gradient vanishing and exploding. A typical LSTM often has 3 gates: input gate, output gate and forget gate which slows down the disappearance of past information and makes *Backpropagation through Time* (BPTT) easier. The gates work as follows (Fig. 1):

$$i_t = sigmoid(W_{xi}x_t + W_{hi}h_{t-1} + b_i) \tag{1}$$

$$f_t = sigmoid(W_{xf}x_t + W_{hf}h_{t-1} + b_f) \tag{2}$$

$$c_t = f_t c_{t-1} + i_t tanh(i_t) \tag{3}$$

$$o_t = sigmoid(W_{xo}x_t + W_{ho}h_{t-1} + b_o) \tag{4}$$

$$h_t = o_t tanh(c_t) \tag{5}$$

where i, f, c, o are the input gate, forget gate, cell and output gate.

Bidirectional LSTM: Bidirectional LSTM is a kind of bidirectional recurrent networks [19] which is suitable for language modeling. It uses two recursive neural networks, a recursive neural network compute the implicit vector $\overrightarrow{h}$ from the front, and the other compute the implicit vector $\overleftarrow{h}$ from the back. In this paper, two implicit vectors are combined by formula 6. Figure 2 depicts an unfolding bidirectional LSTM.

$$h = \overrightarrow{h} + \overleftarrow{h} \tag{6}$$

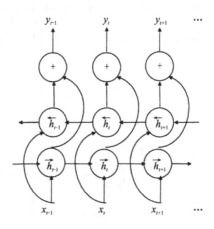

Fig. 2. Bidirectional LSTM

3.2 Aggregated Multimodal Bidirectional Recurrent Model

The *Aggregated Multimodal Bidirectional Recurrent Model* (DILATE) is an extension of bidirectional LSTM which contains two bidirectional LSTMs and some components. The two bidirectional LSTMs are video bidirectional LSTM and audio bidirectional LSTM, the fundamental architecture is same as bidirectional LSTM, the formulae of video bidirectional LSTM are as follows: (the similar formulae can be drawn for the audio bidirectional LSTM.)

$$\overrightarrow{i_t^v} = sigmoid(\overrightarrow{W_{xi}^v}x_t + \overrightarrow{W_{hi}^v h_{t-1}^v} + \overrightarrow{b_i^v}) \tag{7}$$

$$\overrightarrow{f_t^v} = sigmoid(\overrightarrow{W_{xf}^v}x_t + \overrightarrow{W_{hf}^v h_{t-1}^v} + \overrightarrow{b_f^v}) \tag{8}$$

$$\overrightarrow{c_t^v} = \overrightarrow{f_t^v}\overrightarrow{c_{t-1}^v} + \overrightarrow{i_t^v}tanh(\overrightarrow{i_t^v}) \tag{9}$$

$$\overrightarrow{o_t^v} = sigmoid(\overrightarrow{W_{xo}^v}x_t + \overrightarrow{W_{ho}^v h_{t-1}^v} + \overrightarrow{b_o^v}) \tag{10}$$

$$\overrightarrow{h_t^v} = \overrightarrow{o_t^v}tanh(\overrightarrow{c_t^v}) \tag{11}$$

$$\overrightarrow{h_t^v} = \overrightarrow{o_t^v} tanh(\overrightarrow{c_t}) \tag{12}$$

$$\overleftarrow{i_t^v} = sigmoid(\overleftarrow{W_{xi}^v}x_t + \overleftarrow{W_{hi}^v}\overleftarrow{h_{t-1}^v} + \overleftarrow{b_i^v}) \tag{13}$$

$$\overleftarrow{f_t^v} = sigmoid(\overleftarrow{W_{xf}^v}x_t + \overleftarrow{W_{hf}^v}\overleftarrow{h_{t-1}^v} + \overleftarrow{b_f^v}) \tag{14}$$

$$\overleftarrow{c_t^v} = \overleftarrow{f_t^v}\overleftarrow{c_{t-1}^v} + \overleftarrow{i_t^v} tanh(\overleftarrow{i_t^v}) \tag{15}$$

$$\overleftarrow{o_t^v} = sigmoid(\overleftarrow{W_{xo}^v}x_t + \overleftarrow{W_{ho}^v}\overleftarrow{h_{t-1}^v} + \overleftarrow{b_o^v}) \tag{16}$$

$$h_t^v = \overrightarrow{h_t^v} + \overleftarrow{h_t^v} \tag{17}$$

where superscript v denotes modality video, the $\rightarrow$ denotes forward LSTM and $\leftarrow$ denotes backward LSTM (Fig. 3).

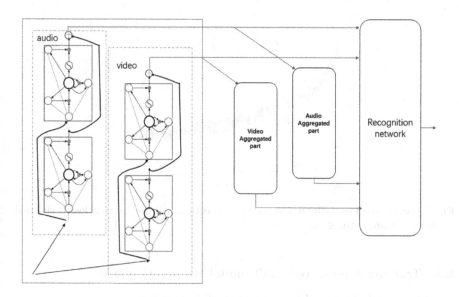

Fig. 3. Aggregated multimodal bidirectional recurrent model

After video bidirectional LSTM and audio bidirectional LSTM, data will be projected into same dimensional space by a projection layer and a activation function thereby. This will also make the model more nonlinear.

$$f_t = g(P_t^v v_t + P_t^a a_t) \tag{18}$$

P^v and P^a are projection matrix trained in the DNN, g is the activation function.

$$g(x) = tanh(x) \tag{19}$$

The features through video bidirectional LSTM, audio bidirectional LSTM and projection could be regarded as well-fused features. The influence of different frames in a single video is summed in both video and audio modalities. Then a recognition network with batch-normalization is used as a classifier.

However, the experiment showed that overfitting is very strong in the architecture aforementioned. Hence, we introduce aggregated connection which accelerates the convergence and prevents overfitting. The aggregated connection lies after video bidirectional LSTM and audio bidirectional LSTM, then data summed and mapped to the target space. In the training, there are three parts taken into account: the main loss, the video aggregated loss and the audio aggregated loss Fig. 4. The implication here is minimizing the audiovisual loss, video loss and audio loss together. The auxiliary networks help the main networks achieve a win-win situation. The aggregated connection conveys information from original networks, which make DILATE consider rich and hierarchy information.

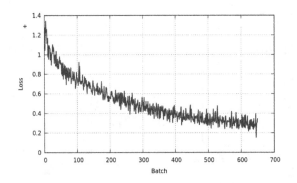

Fig. 4. Batch and loss without aggregated connection. We can see that loss is stopped in about 0.2 since strong overfitting.

3.3   Training Aggregated Multimodal Recurrent Model

To train our DILATE model, we adopt the following loss:

$$
\begin{aligned}
Loss &= loss_{main} + \alpha loss_{aggre}^{video} + \beta loss_{aggre}^{audio} + regularizer \\
&= \frac{1}{n} \sum_{i=1}^{n} [max\{0, (1 - x_{main} + y)^2\} + \alpha max\{0, (1 - x_{aux}^v + y)^2\} \quad (20) \\
&\quad + \beta max\{0, (1 - x_{aux}^a + y)^2\}] + \lambda ||W||_2^2
\end{aligned}
$$

Where *Loss* is the real training loss of DILATE, $loss_{main}$ is the loss of the main part, $loss_{aggre}^{video}$ and $loss_{aggre}^{audio}$ are the loss of aggregated part. α and β are the hyperparameters of the influence from aggregated part, λ is the hyperparameter of the regularizer. y is the classification target. W is the matrices of all components. The aggregated connection is free enough so that the DILATE is flexible and extensive.

4   Experiments and Discussion

In this section, we introduce our experiments details including datasets, data pre-processing, implementation details and some results, indicating that the DILATE is a robust, well-performing and flexible model for AVSR.

4.1   Datasets

We conducted the experiments in 3 datasets: AVLetters (Patterson et al., 2002), AVLetters2 (Cox et al., 2008) and AVDigits (Di Hu et al., 2015).

AVLetters. 10 volunteers saying the letters A to Z three times each. The dataset pre-extracts the lip region of 60 × 80 pixels and *Mel-Frequency Cepstrum Coefficient* (MFCC).

AVLetters2. 5 volunteers spoke the letters A to Z seven times each. The dataset provide raw video and audio in different folders.

AVDigits. 6 speakers saying digits 0 to 9, nine times each. It doesn't pre-extract the video and audio, and provides raw video of long or short time length from 1 s to 2 s (Table 1).

Table 1. Details of the datasets

Datasets	Speakers	Content	Times	Miscellaneous
AVLetters	10	A-Z	3	pre-extracted
AVLetter2	5	A-Z	7	previous split
AVDigits	6	0-9	9	/

4.2   Data Pre-processing

If video and audio are not splitted before, we divide them up, and make video and audio the same length by truncation or closure. Finally, focus the data.

Video Pre-processing. Firstly, the *Viola-Jones algorithm* [27] is used to extract the Region-of-Interest surrounding the mouth. After the area adjusts to 224 × 224 pixels, pre-trained VGG-16 [20] is the tool for extracting the image features. We use the features of the last fully connected layer. Finally, PCA whitening was used to reduce them to 100 principal components.

Audio Pre-processing. The features of the audio signal are extracted as a spectrogram with 20ms Hamming window and 10ms overlap. Using the 251 points *Fast Fourier Transform* of PCA and 50 principal components, the spectral coefficient vector is considered to be the audio features.

Data Augmentation. 4 contiguous audio frames correspond to 1 video frame per time step. We let each video's auditory and visual features simultaneously move 10 frames up and down randomly to double the data. Therefore, the model will have a good extension effect in time domain.

4.3   Implementation Details

The DILATE has two general bidirectional LSTMs with dropout mapping 100 dimensional data to 50. Since the video and audio features have the same dimension, the projection is a identity matrix that could be omitted. The recognition network in main phase has three layers with batch-normalization, together with ReLU activation function. The aggregated parts have simple structure mapping 50 dimensional data to 10 classes prepared for classification. $\alpha = \beta = 0.2$, $\lambda = 0.01$ the training loss is:

$$Loss = \frac{1}{n} \sum_{i=1}^{n} [max\{0, (1 - x_{main} + y)^2\} + 0.2max\{0, (1 - x^v_{aggre} + y)^2\}$$
$$+ 0.2max\{0, (1 - x^a_{aggre} + y)^2\}] + 0.01||W||_2^2 \tag{21}$$

The DILATE is able to be trained and tested once. No redundant training process is needed. The cross modality speech recognition, that is, in the training phase, video and audio modalities are both needed, whereas in the testing phase, only video modality is presented.

4.4   Quantitative Evalution

The evaluation on DILATE is splitted into two parts: AVSR task and cross modality speech recognition. AVSR is evaluated in two modalities and also trained in two modalities. However cross modality speech recognition is evaluated in video but trained in video and audio both. Our experiments on AVSR is conducted in AVLetters2 and AVDigits, cross modality speech recognition is conducted in AVLetters.

Audiovisual Speech Recognition: AVSR is the main task of our work, we conducted the experiments on AVLetters2 and AVDigits, the comparison methods are MDBN, MDAEs, RTMRBM and deep temporal architecture[]. The results indicate that DILATE is better than such models (Table 2).

Cross Modality Speech Recognition: Cross modality lipreading is the secondary task. As mentioned before, we trained DILATE in both modalities but evaluated in visual modality only. The experiments have two modes: only video and cross modality, which show the superiority of cross modality speech recognition. In the experiments in cross modality speech recognition, DILATE performs much better than MDAEs, CRBM, RTMRBM and deep temporal architecture (Table 3).

Table 2. AVSR performance on AVLetters2 and AVDigits. The result indicates that our model performs better than MDBN, MDAEs and RTMRBM.

Datasets	Model	Mean Accuracy
AVLetter2	MDBN [22]	54.10%
	MDAE [14]	67.89%
	RTMRBM [7]	74.77%
	Deep Temporal Architecture [26]	80.11%
	DILATE	**85.11%**
AVDigits	MDBN [22]	55.00%
	MDAE [14]	66.74%
	RTMRBM [7]	71.77%
	Deep Temporal Architecture [26]	78.56%
	DILATE	**81.23%**

Table 3. Cross modality lipreading performance. The experiments suggest that cross modality lipreading is better than single modality. And result of our method performs much better than other model.

Mode	Model	Mean Accuracy
Only Video	Multiscale Spatial Analysis [10]	44.60%
	Local Binary Pattern [28]	58.85%
Cross Modality	MDAEs [14]	64.21%
	CRBM [1]	65.78%
	RTMRBM [7]	66.21%
	Deep Temporal Architecture [26]	70.23%
	DILATE	**73.83%**

5   Conclusion

We proposed an end-to-end deep model for AVSR which increases mean accuracy obviously. Our experiments suggested that DILATE performs much better than other models in AVSR and cross modality lipreading. The benefits of DILATE are trained and tested once; extensibility and flexibility. There are no other training processes needed in training DILATE. Due to DILATE is simple, it could be a tool to model fusion information efficiently. Meanwhile, DILATE considers temporal connection, thus it is suitable for sequence features. In the future, we plan to apply DILATE in other multimodal temporal tasks and make it more flexible.

References

1. Amer, M.R., Siddiquie, B., Khan, S., Divakaran, A., Sawhney, H.: Multimodal fusion using dynamic hybrid models. In: 2014 IEEE Winter Conference on Applications of Computer Vision (WACV), pp. 556–563. IEEE (2014)
2. Amodei, D., et al.: Deep speech 2: End-to-end speech recognition in english and mandarin. In: ICML (2016)
3. Atrey, P.K., Hossain, M.A., El Saddik, A., Kankanhalli, M.S.: Multimodal fusion for multimedia analysis: a survey. Multimed. Syst. **16**(6), 345–379 (2010)
4. Goodfellow, I., Bengio, Y., Courville, A.: Deep Learning. MIT Press (2016). http://www.deeplearningbook.org
5. Graves, A., Fernández, S., Gomez, F., Schmidhuber, J.: Connectionist temporal classification: labelling unsegmented sequence data with recurrent neural networks. In: Proceedings of the 23rd International Conference on Machine Learning, pp. 369–376. ACM (2006)
6. Hochreiter, S., Schmidhuber, J.: Long short-term memory. Neural Comput. **9**(8), 1735–1780 (1997)
7. Hu, D., Li, X., et al.: Temporal multimodal learning in audiovisual speech recognition. In: Proceedings of the IEEE Conference on Computer Vision and Pattern Recognition, pp. 3574–3582 (2016)
8. Krizhevsky, A., Sutskever, I., Hinton, G.E.: Imagenet classification with deep convolutional neural networks. In: Advances in Neural Information Processing Systems, pp. 1097–1105 (2012)
9. Maragos, P., Potamianos, A., Gros, P.: Multimodal Processing and Interaction: Audio, Video, Text, vol. 33. Springer Science & Business Media (2008)
10. Matthews, I., Cootes, T.F., Bangham, J.A., Cox, S., Harvey, R.: Extraction of visual features for lipreading. IEEE Trans. Pattern Anal. Mach. Intell. **24**(2), 198–213 (2002)
11. Mroueh, Y., Marcheret, E., Goel, V.: Deep multimodal learning for audio-visual speech recognition, pp. 2130–2134 (2015)
12. Nath, A.R., Beauchamp, M.S.: A neural basis for interindividual differences in the mcgurk effect, a multisensory speech illusion. NeuroImage **59**(1), 781–787 (2012)
13. Nefian, A.V., Liang, L., Pi, X., Liu, X., Murphy, K.: Dynamic bayesian networks for audio-visual speech recognition. EURASIP J. Adv. Signal Process. **2002**(11), 1–15 (2002)
14. Ngiam, J., et al.: Multimodal deep learning. In: Proceedings of the 28th International Conference on Machine Learning (ICML-2011), pp. 689–696 (2011)
15. Noda, K., Yamaguchi, Y., Nakadai, K., Okuno, H.G., Ogata, T.: Audio-visual speech recognition using deep learning. Appl. Intell. **42**(4), 722–737 (2015)
16. Pascanu, R., Mikolov, T., Bengio, Y.: On the difficulty of training recurrent neural networks. In: International Conference on Machine Learning, pp. 1310–1318 (2013)
17. Prechelt, L.: Automatic early stopping using cross validation: quantifying the criteria. Neural Networks **11**(4), 761–767 (1998)
18. Rabiner, L.R.: A tutorial on hidden markov models and selected applications in speech recognition. Proc. IEEE **77**(2), 257–286 (1989)
19. Schuster, M., Paliwal, K.K.: Bidirectional recurrent neural networks. IEEE Trans. Signal Process. **45**(11), 2673–2681 (1997)
20. Simonyan, K., Zisserman, A.: Very deep convolutional networks for large-scale image recognition. CoRR abs/1409.1556 (2014)

21. Srivastava, N., Hinton, G.E., Krizhevsky, A., Sutskever, I., Salakhutdinov, R.: Dropout: a simple way to prevent neural networks from overfitting. J. Mach. Learn. Res. **15**(1), 1929–1958 (2014)
22. Srivastava, N., Salakhutdinov, R.: Learning representations for multimodal data with deep belief nets. In: International Conference on Machine Learning Workshop, vol. 79 (2012)
23. Srivastava, N., Salakhutdinov, R.R.: Multimodal learning with deep boltzmann machines. In: Advances in Neural Information Processing Systems, pp. 2222–2230 (2012)
24. Sutskever, I., Vinyals, O., Le, Q.V.: Sequence to sequence learning with neural networks. In: Advances in Neural Information Processing Systems, pp. 3104–3112 (2014)
25. Tamura, S., et al.: Audio-visual speech recognition using deep bottleneck features and high-performance lipreading. In: 2015 Asia-Pacific Signal and Information Processing Association Annual Summit and Conference (APSIPA), pp. 575–582. IEEE (2015)
26. Tian, C., Yuan, Y., Lu, X.: Deep temporal architecture for audiovisual speech recognition. In: CCF Chinese Conference on Computer Vision, pp. 650–661 (2017)
27. Viola, P., Jones, M.: Rapid object detection using a boosted cascade of simple features. In: Proceedings of the 2001 IEEE Computer Society Conference on Computer Vision and Pattern Recognition, CVPR 2001, vol. 1, p. I-511. IEEE (2001)
28. Zhao, G., Barnard, M., Pietikainen, M.: Lipreading with local spatiotemporal descriptors. IEEE Trans. Multimed. **11**(7), 1254–1265 (2009)

An Adaptive Construction Test Method Based on Geometric Calculation for Linearly Separable Problems

Shuiming Zhong[1($\boxtimes$)], Xiaoxiang Lu[1], Meng Li[1], Chengguang Liu[1], Yong Cheng[1], and Victor S. Sheng[2]

[1] School of Computer and Software, Nanjing University of Information Science and Technology, Nanjing 210044, China
{smzhong, yongcheng}@nuist.edu.cn, LXX7OKG@163.com,
ml5852912728_2@163.com, LCG7OKG@163.com
[2] Department of Computer Science,
University of Central Arkansas, Conway, AR 72035, USA
ssheng@uca.edu

Abstract. The linearly separable problem is a fundamental problem in pattern classification. Firstly, from the perspective of spatial distribution, this paper focuses on the linear separability of a region dataset at the distribution level instead of the linearly separable issue between two datasets at the traditional category level. Firstly, the former can reflect the spatial distribution of real data, which is more helpful to its application in pattern classification. Secondly, based on spatial geometric theory, an adaptive construction method for testing the linear separability of a region dataset is demonstrated and designed. Finally, the corresponding computer algorithm is designed, and some simulation verification experiments are carried out based on some manual datasets and benchmark datasets. Experimental results show the correctness and effectiveness of the proposed method.

Keywords: Pattern classification · Linear separability · Region datasets
Geometric calculation

1 Introduction

The linearly separable problem is a fundamental problem in pattern classification. The linear separability of the classification task directly affects the choice of classification models. If a linear model such as *Perceptron* [1] and linear *SVM* [4] is used for a linearly inseparable task, it cannot find the solution of the problem; on the contrary, if a nonlinear model such as *MLP* [3] and nonlinear *SVM* is used for a linearly separable task, the generalization performance will be weakened due to the spatial transformation although the solution of the problem can be obtained. In addition, for the nonlinear classification model, although the existence of the problem solution is theoretically proved [2], how to find the problem solution is still difficult in practical applications, which is reflected in the determination of the number of hidden layer neurons in a Neural Network model, and in the selection of the kernel function in a *SVM* model.

© Springer Nature Switzerland AG 2018
X. Sun et al. (Eds.): ICCCS 2018, LNCS 11068, pp. 392–405, 2018.
https://doi.org/10.1007/978-3-030-00021-9_36

Essentially, the difficulty is still the problem of whether the mapping of a classification task from the input space to the hidden space is linearly separable.

The linearly separable problem has drawn more and more researchers' attention, and many results on this issue have been published [11–18]. On the whole, they can be divided into four categories: (1) Methods based on linear programming, in which the most popular ones are the Fourier-Kuhn elimination and the Simplex method [5, 6]. This method tests the linear separability of a dataset by constructing and solving a set of linear inequalities, in which, datasets are linearly separable if there exists a solution; Otherwise, they are not linear separable. Its disadvantage is that the time complexity increases exponentially with the increment of the data size. (2) Methods based on computational geometry, of which the most popular one is the Convex Hall Method [7]. Considering the fact that the convex hull above three dimensions is hardly described and stored, this method is difficult to apply to datasets above three dimensions. (3) Methods based neural networks such as Perceptron [8, 9]. For linearly separable datasets, theoretically, a perceptron can converge after finite iterations. But it is difficult to determine the number of iterations in practical applications. (4) Methods based on quadratic programming, of which the most popular one is *SVM* [4, 10]. The disadvantage of *SVM* is that the computational complexity is high and the choice of kernel functions in practical applications is difficult.

There are two main factors that limit the practical application of existing methods in the linearly separable problem: one is that the time complexity is generally high, especially for high-dimension datasets; the other is that these methods are developed mostly based on ideal two-class datasets with the distribution of two regions. However, in practical applications, the spatial distribution of a dataset is much more complex. More generally, data sets that are linearly inseparable only from the category level are probably linearly separable from distribution level, all or part, which directly limits the practicality of existing methods.

From the perspective of spatial distribution, this paper proposes an adaptive test method based on geometric calculation for the linearly separable problem. The main contributions of this paper are: (1) A new key issue on the linear separable problem, the linear separability of a region dataset, is introduced from distribution level instead of the linear separable issue between two class datasets from the traditional category level, which is more helpful to its application in pattern classification. (2) Based on the computational geometry theory, the corresponding test method for the linear separability of a region dataset, the adaptive construction test method (*ACTM*), is developed, which is simple and practical, with a low time complexity and easy operation.

The rest of the paper is organized as follows: (2) Background knowledge of the linearly separable problem. This section mainly describes related concepts of linearly separable problems and introduces the concept of linear separability of a region dataset which is a new key issue in the linearly separable problem. (3) A region dataset linear separability test method. In this section, a test theorem is proposed and demonstrated, and a test method *ACTM* is designed based on computation geometry. (4) *ACTM* of Region dataset linear separability is programmed. (5) Experimental verification. In this section, experimental verification from *UCI* datasets and some manual datasets are carried out. (6) Conclusion.

2   Background Knowledge About the Linearly Separable Problem

The linearly separable problem is a basic issue in pattern classification research. In general, it mainly refers to the separability between two classes of datasets.

Definition 1. Given two datasets S_1 and S_2, if there exists a linear function $f(\bullet)$, satisfying $f(X) \geq 0(X \in S_1)$ and $f(X) < 0(X \in S_2)$, then S_1 and S_2 are **linearly separable**, denoted as $S_1 \| S_2(f)$, otherwise denoted as $S_1 \nparallel S_2(f)$.

Geometrically, a linearly separable problem can be intuitively expressed as: given two datasets S_1 and S_2, whether there exists a hyperplane f that can split S_1 and S_2 into both sides. As shown in Fig. 1.

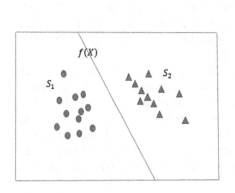

Fig. 1. Linearly separable

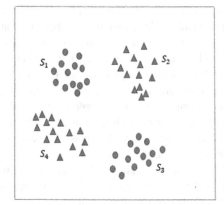

Fig. 2. Linearly inseparable

Traditionally, the test methods for a linearly separable problem are usually deduced and designed based on two classes of datasets which belong to two different regions in space. In fact, the spatial distribution of a dataset is more complicated in practical application, as shown in Fig. 2. In Fig. 2, they are linearly inseparable at the category level, while any two region datasets are linearly separable at the spatial distribution level. Therefore, the linear separability of region datasets is more instructive for pattern classification. The complexity of data space distribution shows that it is more reasonable and significant to discuss "linear separability of a region dataset at the distribution level" than "linear separability between datasets at the category level".

For the convenience of discussion, the related concept of a convex set is introduced as follows:

Definition 2. Assuming a dataset $D \subset R^n$, if it is satisfied $\alpha X_1 + (1 - \alpha)X_2 \in D$ for any two points $X_1, X_2 \in D$ and a real number $\alpha(0 \leq \alpha \leq 1)$, the dataset D is called as a **convex set**. Obviously, if D is a convex set, there exists a set of hyperplanes that can separate D from R^n. Therefore, the dataset D is **linear separability**, denoted as $||D(fs)$, otherwise denoted as $\\D(fs)$.

In fact, the convex set in the strict sense is not required for pattern classification. As long as there exists a convex region that satisfies $S \subseteq G$, it is enough to ensure the linear separability of S. Therefore, this paper focus on a key issue that the linear separability of a region dataset at the distribution level.

Definition 3. In the space R^n, given a region dataset $S = \{X_i | 1 < i < N\}$ and the rest region dataset $\overline{S} = \{Y_j | 1 < j < M\}$. If there exists a convex region G that meets $\alpha X_1 + (1 - \alpha)X_2 \in G$ for any $X_1, X_2 \in S$ and real number $\alpha(0 \le \alpha \le 1)$ and $\overline{S} \cap G = \emptyset$, S is the linear separability, denoted as $||S(fs)$. Otherwise S is the linear inseparability, denoted as $\\S(fs)$.

For the convenience of subsequent derivation, a region dataset's linear separability problem can be further transformed to the linear separable problems between a region dataset and any peripheral point of the region dataset.

Definition 4. In the space R^n, given a region dataset S and its peripheral data point O, if there exists a convex region $G(O \notin G)$ that meets $\alpha X_1 + (1 - \alpha)X_2 \in G$ for any $X_1, X_2 \in S$ and a real number $\alpha(0 \le \alpha \le 1)$, then S and O are linearly separable, denoted as $S||O(f)$; otherwise S and O are linearly inseparable, denoted as $S\\O(f)$.

3 Test Method of Region Dataset Linear Separability

3.1 Theoretical Demonstration of Region Dataset Linear Separability

Decision theorem: In the space R^n, given a region dataset S and its peripheral data point $O(\notin S)$, O and S are linearly separable if and only if there exists a hypercone V with O as the vertex, and it meets $\alpha X_i + (1 - \alpha)X_j \in V$ for any $X_i, X_j \in S$ and real number $\alpha(0 \le \alpha \le 1)$.

Proof:

(1) **Sufficiency:** If there exists a hypercone V with O as vertex, and obviously it meets $\alpha X_i + (1 - \alpha)X_j \in V$ for any $X_i, X_j \in S$ and real number $\alpha(0 \le \alpha \le 1)$, then O and S are linearly separable.

Since hypercone V is a convex polyhedron, and meets $\alpha X_i + (1 - \alpha)X_j \in V$ for any $X_i, X_j \in S$ and real number $\alpha(0 \le \alpha \le 1)$, that is, $S \subset V$. Therefore, there is a hyperplane f passing point O that makes O and S linearly separable.

(2) **Necessity:** If O and S are linearly separable, then there exists necessarily a hypercone V with O as the vertex, and it meets $\alpha X_i + (1 - \alpha)X_j \in V$ for any $X_i, X_j \in S$ and real number $\alpha(0 \le \alpha \le 1)$.

$\because S||O(f)$, Passing the point O, and constructing a hyperplane f with $\overrightarrow{OT}$ as the normal vector. So,

$$\exists f((\forall X_i(X_i \in S) \to f(X_i) \geq 0) \wedge f(O) < 0).$$

Making a hyperplane f' passes O, and satisfying $f' // f$,

$$\because \forall X_i\left(X_i \in S \wedge f'(X_i) > 0\right)$$
$$\therefore \exists V(\forall X_i((X_i \in S) \to (X_i \in V))).$$

(Proof by contradiction) Assuming

$$\exists X_k((X_k \in S) \wedge (X_k \notin V)), \tag{A.1}$$

$$\because f'(X_k) > 0$$
$$\therefore \angle X_k OT < \frac{\pi}{2}. \tag{A.2}$$

By (A.2), we can conclude

$$\therefore \exists V((X_k \in S) \wedge (X_k \in V)). \tag{A.3}$$

Because (A.3) is contradictory with (A.1), the Necessity is correct.

According to the decision theorem above, the inference is as follows:

Corollary: In the space R^n, given a region dataset $S = \{X_i | 1 < i < N\}$ and the rest region dataset $\bar{S} = \{Y_j | 1 < j < M\}$, $\| S(fs)$ if and only if $\forall Y_j(Y_j \in \bar{S}), Y_j \| S(f)$.

Proof:

(1) **Sufficiency:** $\forall Y_j(Y_j \in \bar{S}), Y_j \| S(f) \Rightarrow \| S(fs)$.

$$\because \forall Y_j((Y_j \in \bar{S}) \wedge (Y_j \| S(f)))$$
$$\therefore \exists F = \{f_k | f(X) > 0 \wedge f(Y) \leq 0, 1 \leq k \leq M\}. \tag{B.1}$$

By F in (B.1) compose a close convex region G,

$$\because (S \subset G) \wedge (\bar{S} \cap G = \emptyset). \tag{B.2}$$

According to **Definition 2**, By (B.2), we can conclude

$$Y_j \| S(f).$$

(2) **Necessity:** $\| S(fs) \Rightarrow \forall Y_j(Y_j \in \bar{S}), Y_j \| S(f)$.

$$\because \| S(fs) \tag{C.1}$$

From (C.1), we can conclude that there exists a convex region G,

$$\because (S \subseteq G) \wedge \left(\forall Y_j \left(Y_j \in \overline{S} \right) \wedge \left(Y_j \notin G \right) \right)$$
$$\therefore \forall Y_j \left(\left(Y_j \in \overline{S} \right) \rightarrow \left(Y_j \| S(f) \right) \right).$$

3.2   Test Method Design of Region Dataset Linear Separability

Based on the decision theorem above, as long as there exists a hypercone that meets $S \subseteq V$, then point O and dataset S are linearly separable; otherwise, point O and dataset S are linearly inseparable. Therefore, finding and constructing such a hypercone is the key to determine the linearly separable problem. The method is as follows:

Taking any two points X_i and X_j from dataset S and initializing a hypercone with O as the vertex, $\overrightarrow{OX_i}$ and $\overrightarrow{OX_j}$ as the generatrix. If there exists $X_k \in S \wedge X_k \notin V$, then we should expand V until any $X_k (\in S)$ satisfying $X_k \in V$. The construction method is as follows:

Assuming the original hypercone V with point O as the vertex, $\overrightarrow{OT}$ as the axis, and θ as the angle between the axis and the generatrix. After expanding, the expanded hypercone V' with point O as the vertex, $\overrightarrow{OT'}$ as the axis, and θ' as the angle between the axis and the generatrix. According to the relative position of $X_k (\in S)$ and V, the following three situations are proposed:

Situation 1: $\angle X_k OT < \frac{\pi}{2}$.

(1) Taking $\overrightarrow{OT}$ as the normal vector, and then passing X_k makes a hyperplane f which intersects at one point H with the reverse extension line of $\overrightarrow{OT}$. Connecting X_k and H, $\overline{X_k H}$ or the extension line of $\overline{X_k H}$ intersects at two points Q_1, Q_2 with hypercone V. As shown in Fig. 3.

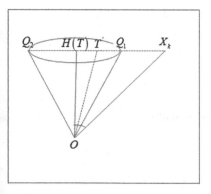

Fig. 3. Situation 1:$\angle X_k OT < \frac{\pi}{2}$

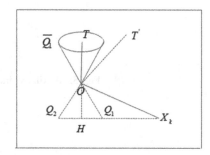

Fig. 4. Situation 2: $\angle X_i OT \geq \frac{\pi}{2}$

(2) Constructing a new hypercone V' with point O as the vertex, $\overrightarrow{OQ_2}$ and $\overrightarrow{OX_k}$ as the generatrix. Then X_k is inside the hypercone V', $V' \supseteq V$.

Situation 2: $\angle X_iOT \geq \frac{\pi}{2}$.

(1) Taking $\overrightarrow{OT}$ as the normal vector, and then passing X_k makes a hyperplane f which intersects at one point H with the reverse extension line of $\overrightarrow{OT}$. Connecting X_k and H, $\overrightarrow{X_kH}$ or the extension line of $\overrightarrow{X_kH}$ intersects at two points Q_1, Q_2 with the reverse of the hypercone V. To make the reverse extension line of $\overrightarrow{OQ_1}$ in hypercone V is $\overrightarrow{OQ_1}$(Fig. 4).

(2) If $\angle X_iOT + \theta < \pi$, then constructing a new hypercone V' with point O as the vertex, $\overrightarrow{OQ_1}$ and $\overrightarrow{OX_k}$ as the generatrix. Similarly, $X_k \in V'$, $V' \supseteq V$.

(3) If $\angle X_iOT + \theta \geq \pi$, the hypercone V' cannot be constructed. There exists no hypercone V' satisfying $X_k \in V'$ or $V' \supseteq V$.The hypercone V' has been constructed above, which correctness is reflected in: $V' \supseteq V$. The proof of this proposition is as follows:

Proof: $X_i \in V \Rightarrow X_i \in V'$.

(For the convenience of following proof, auxiliary drawings is as follows: Constructing a hypercone V'', taking $\overrightarrow{OT}$ as the normal vector, and then passing X_i make a hyperplane f which intersects at one point H with $\overrightarrow{OT}$ and intersects at one point H' with $\overrightarrow{OT'}$, connecting H' and H, $\overrightarrow{HH'}$ or the extension line of $\overrightarrow{HH'}$ intersects at Q with the hypercone V'' and intersects at P with the hypercone V. As shown in Fig. 5.)

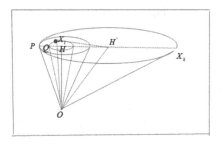

Fig. 5. Auxiliary drawings for proof of $V' \supseteq V$

In $\Delta X_i OH'$,

$$\cos(\angle X_i OH') = \left(|OH'|^2 + |OX_i|^2 - |X_i H'|^2 \right) \Big/ \left(2 \bullet |OH'| \bullet |OX_i| \right). \quad \text{(D.1)}$$

In $\Delta Q_i OH'$,

$$\cos(\angle QOH') = \left(|OH'|^2 + |OQ|^2 - |QH'|^2 \right) \Big/ \left(2 \bullet |OH'| \bullet |OQ| \right). \quad \text{(D.2)}$$

Compared (D.1) with (D.2). Apparently, $|OQ| = |OX_i|, |X_i H'| \leq |QH'|$. So,

$$\cos(\angle QOH') \leq cos\left(\angle X_i OH' \right). \quad \text{(D.3)}$$

From (D.3), we can conclude

$$\angle X_i OH' \leq \angle QOH'. \quad \text{(D.4)}$$

Because of

$$\angle QOH' \leq \angle POH' = \theta', \quad \text{(D.5)}$$

From (D.4) and (D.5), we can conclude

$$\angle X_i OH' \leq \theta'.$$

So, $X_i \in V'$, as the proof shown, $V' \supseteq V$.

4   Test Algorithms of Region Dataset Linear Separability

For the convenience of implement algorithm in computer, we design two algorithms:

Algorithm 1: Linearly Separable test algorithm for the point and the regional dataset.

Input: regional dataset $S = \{X_i \mid 1 \le i \le N\}$, peripheral data point $O \in \overline{S}$.

Begin

1: Taking any two points $X_1, X_2 \in S$,

$\theta = \angle \overrightarrow{OX_1} \overrightarrow{OX_2}/2$, calculate angle divided vector $\overrightarrow{OT}$ between vector $\overrightarrow{OX_1}$ and vector $\overrightarrow{OX_2}$.

2: Constructing a hypercone V with the point O as the vertex, θ as the angle between the axis and the generatrix and $\overrightarrow{OT}$ as axis.

3: For i from 1 to N step 1

3.1: Calculate $\angle \overrightarrow{OX_i} \overrightarrow{OT}$;

3.2: If $\angle \overrightarrow{OX_i} \overrightarrow{OT} \le \theta$, then $X_i \in V$, else step to 4.

4: Calculate $\angle \overrightarrow{OX_i} \overrightarrow{OT}$.

5: If $\angle \overrightarrow{OX_i} \overrightarrow{OT} < \dfrac{\pi}{2}$, then expand the hypercone V according to the expansion method of situation 1 in Section 3.2, and return to step 3.

6: If $\angle \overrightarrow{OX_i} \overrightarrow{OT} \ge \dfrac{\pi}{2}$ and $\angle \overrightarrow{OX_i} \overrightarrow{OT} + \theta < \pi$, then expand the hypercone V according to the expansion method of situation 2 in Section 3.2, and return to step 3.

7: If $\angle \overrightarrow{OX_i} \overrightarrow{OT} + \theta \ge \pi$, then we can't construct a hypercone V, and S is linearly inseparable with O.

End

According to algorithm 1, the linear separability of the points and region datasets can be judged. According to the Corollary in Sect. 3.1, if $\forall Y_j (\in \overline{S})$ is linearly separable with the dataset S, linear separability of the dataset S for the dataset $\overline{S}$. The specific test algorithm is as follow:

Algorithm 2: region dataset linear separability test algorithm.

Input: a region dataset $S = \{X_i \mid 1 \le i \le N\}$, a peripheral dataset $\overline{S} = \{Y_j \mid 1 \le j \le M\}$.

Begin

1: For j from 1 to M step 1

1.1: call algorithm 1 for Y_j;

1.2: If Y_j is lineally separable with S then mark it; Else step to 3.

2: If $j = M + 1$, then S has linear separability, step to end.

3: S is non-linear separability.

End

---

5 Experimental Verification and Analysis

This section mainly verifies the correctness and the rationality of the test method mentioned above. The experimental dataset comes from a manual dataset (low dimension) and *UCI* datasets. The manual dataset is designed to obtain an intuitive visual effect. Table 1 shows the datasets used in this paper.

Table 1. Datasets used in the experiments

No.	Name	Features	Class	Set size
1	two-set1	2	2(1, 2)	30
2	two-set2	2	2(1, 2)	56
3	two-set3	2	2(1, 2)	70
4	two-set4	2	2(1, 2)	101
5	three-set1	3	2(1, 2)	101
6	three-set2	3	2(1, 2)	401
7	three-set3	3	2(1, 2)	500
8	three-set4	3	2(1, 2)	500
9	monks-1	6	2(1, 2)	124
10	iris	4	3(1, 2, 3)	150
11	ionosphere	34	2(1, 2)	270
12	wdbc	30	2(1, 2)	569

5.1 Verification of Test Algorithms Between Points and Region Dataset

To verify the correctness of Algorithm 1 in Sect. 4, some low-dimension datasets, two-set1, three-set1, two-set2, and three-set2 are used. Figures 6, 7, 8 and 9 are the situation of their space distribution, in which "Δ" denotes a peripheral data point, and "$*$" denotes a region data point.

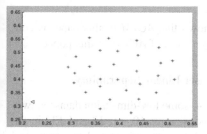

Fig. 6. Distribution of dataset two-set1

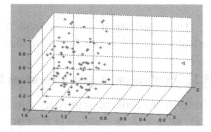

Fig. 7. Distribution of dataset three-set1

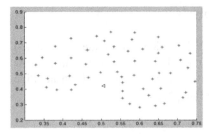

Fig. 8. Distribution of dataset two-set2

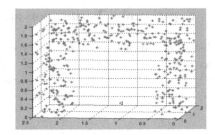

Fig. 9. Distribution of dataset three-set2

In the experiment, S consists of all "$*$" and O denotes as "Δ". The test results of *ACTM* show that O and S are linearly separable on datasets two-set1, three-set1, and O and S are linearly inseparable on two-set2, three-set2. The experimental results based on these datasets are consistent with the intuitive observations from Figs. 6, 7, 8 and 9, which have shown the effectiveness of *ACTM* proposed in this paper.

Linear *SVM* is used to verify the effectiveness of *ACTM* of this paper for some *UCI* datasets. In theory, the accuracy of *SVM* should reach 100% if $S \parallel O(f)$; otherwise the accuracy is less than 100%. The results are shown in Table 2.

Table 2. The results with linear *SVM* and *ACTM* on some *UCI datasets*

No.	Name	Region	linear *SVM*	Algorithm 1
9	monks-1	$2(S_1,S_2)$	$(S_2,O)=98.36\%$	$S_2\|O(f)$
10	iris	$3(S_1,S_2,S_3)$	$(S_2,O)=100\%$ $(S_3,O)=100\%$	$S_2\|O(f)\ S_3\|O(f)$
11	ionosphere	$3(S_1,S_2,S_3)$	$(S_2,O)=100\%$ $(S_3,O)=100\%$	$S_2\|O(f)\ S_3\|O(f)$
12	wdbc	$4(S_1,S_2,S_3,S_4)$	$(S_2,O)=100\%$ $(S_3,O)=100\%$ $(S_4,O)=100\%$	$S_2\|O(f)\ S_3\|O(f)$ $S_4\|O(f)$

The experimental results in Table 2 have shown that *ACTM* of this paper is consistent with *SVM*, which further verified the correctness of *ACTM* of this paper.

5.2   Verification of Test Algorithms for Dataset Linear Separability

To verify the correctness of Algorithm 2 in Sect. 4, some low-dimension datasets, two-set3, three-set3, two-set4, and three-set4 are used. Figures 10, 11, 12 and 13 are the situation of their space distribution, in which "Δ" denotes peripheral data points, and "$*$" denotes region data points.

In the experiment, the dataset S consists of all "*". The test results of *ACTM* showed that datasets of two-set3 and three-set3 are linear separability, and datasets of two-set4 and three-set4 are linear inseparablity. These results are consistent with intuitive observations from Figs. 10, 11, 12 and 13 , which has shown that *ACTM* of this paper is effective.

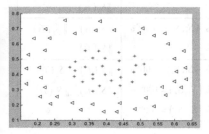

Fig. 10. Distribution of dataset two-set3

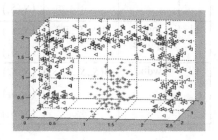

Fig. 11. Distribution of dataset three-set3

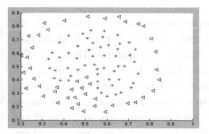

Fig. 12. Distribution of dataset two-set4

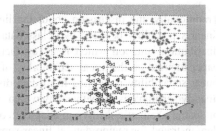

Fig. 13. Distribution of dataset three-set4

Similarly, the linear *SVM* is used to verify the effectiveness of *ACTM* of this paper for *UCI* datasets. According to the definition of the linear separability of a region dataset, *SVM* is used to test the linear separability between a region dataset and it's any peripheral point. The region dataset is linear separability if and only if it and its all peripheral points are linear separable. Otherwise, it is linear inseparability. The experimental results are shown in Table 3.

From the results of Table 3, we can see that the results of *ACTM* proposed in this paper are consistent with the results of *SVM*, which verified the effectiveness of *ACTM*.

Table 3. The results with linear *SVM* and *ACTM* on some *UCI datasets*

No.	Name	Region	Linear *SVM*		Algorithm 2	
9	monks-1	$2(S_1,S_2)$	$(S_1,S_2)=70.96\%$		$\nparallel S_1(fs)$	$\nparallel S_2(fs)$
10	iris	$3(S_1,S_2,S_3)$	$(S_1,S_2)=100\%$ $(S_1,S_3)=100\%$		$\parallel S_1(fs)$	$\nparallel S_2(fs)$
			$(S_2,S_3)=99\%$		$\nparallel S_3(fs)$	
11	iono-sphere	$3(S_1,S_2,S_3)$	$(S_1,S_2)=100\%$ $(S_1,S_3)=100\%$		$\parallel S_1(fs)$	$\parallel S_2(fs)$
			$(S_2,S_3)=100\%$		$\parallel S_3(fs)$	
12	wdbc	$4(S_1,S_2,S_3,S_4)$	$(S_1,S_2)=100\%$ $(S_1,S_3)=100\%$		$\parallel S_1(fs)$	$\parallel S_2(fs)$
			$(S_1,S_4)=100\%$ $(S_2,S_3)=100\%$		$\parallel S_3(fs)$	$\parallel S_4(fs)$
			$(S_2,S_4)=100\%$ $(S_3,S_4)=100\%$			

6   Conclusion

Traditionally, the discussion about the linear separable problem has focused on the linear separability between two class datasets. However, it could not reflect the data distribution situation which is a key factor in pattern classification. Therefore, this paper focused on the linear separability of a region dataset. Firstly, the region dataset linear separability is defined from data distribution level in replace of the traditional linearly separable issue between two datasets from category level. Secondly, by means of spatial geometric theory, an adaptive construction test method has be designed and demonstrated for region dataset linear separability. Lastly, test algorithms carried out some simulation experiments to verify the correctness and the effectiveness of the method.

Compared with the traditional linear separability of data on the category level, the linear separability of a region dataset in distribution level proposed in this paper is more in line with the real situation of the data, and provides a new technology approach to solve the linear separable problem and the pattern classification problem.

We will further improve the research results of this paper. We will focus on investigate the completeness of the method proposed in this paper in theory to further improve the performance and efficiency of the method.

Acknowledgement. This work was supported by the National Natural Science Foundation of China (71373131, 61402236, 61572259 and U1736105), Training Program of the Major Research Plan of the National Science Foundation of China (91546117).

References

1. Rosenblatt, F.: The perceptron: a probabilistic model for information storage and organization in the brain. Psychol. Rev. **65**(6), 386–408 (1958)
2. Minsky, M.L., Papert, S.: Perceptrons: An Introduction to Computational Geometry. The MIT Press, Cambridge (1969)
3. Rumelhart, D.E., Hinton, G. E., Williams, R.J.: Learning representations by back-propagating errors. Neurocomputing: foundations of research. MIT Press (1988)
4. Cortes, C., Vapnik, V.: Support vector network. Mach. Learn. **20**(3), 273–297 (1995)
5. Kuhn, H.W.: Solvability and consistency for linear equations and inequalities. Am. Math. Mon. **63**(4), 217–232 (1956)
6. Bazaraa, M.S., Jarvis, J.J., Sherali, H.D.: Linear programming and network flows. J. Oper. Res. Soc. **29**(5), 510 (1978)
7. Tajine, M., Elizondo, D.: New methods for testing linear separability. Neurocomputing **47**(1), 161–188 (2002)
8. McCulloch, W.S., Pitts, W.: A logical calculus of the ideas immanent in nervous activity. Bull. Math. Biol. **52**(1–2), 99–115 (1990)
9. Mullin, A.A., Rosenblatt, F.: Principles of neurodynamics. Cybern. Syst. Anal. **11**(5), 841–842 (1962)
10. Pang, S., Kim, D., Bang, S.Y.: Face membership authentication using SVM classification tree generated by membership-based LLE data partition. IEEE Trans. Neural Netw. **16**(2), 436 (2005)
11. Elizondo, D.: The linear separability problem: some testing methods. IEEE Trans. Neural Netw. **17**(2), 330 (2006)
12. Rao, Y., Zhang, X.: Characterization of linearly separable boolean functions: a graph-theoretic perspective. IEEE Trans. Neural Netw. Learn. Syst. **28**(7), 1542–1549 (2016)
13. Hochbaum, D.S., Shanthikumar, J.G.: Convex separable optimization is not much harder than linear optimization. J. ACM **37**(4), 843–862 (1990)
14. Bobrowski, L.: Induction of linear separability through the ranked layers of binary classifiers. In: Iliadis, L., Jayne, C. (eds.) AIAI/EANN -2011. IAICT, vol. 363, pp. 69–77. Springer, Heidelberg (2011). https://doi.org/10.1007/978-3-642-23957-1_8
15. Abd, E.K.M.S., Abo-Bakr, R.M.: Linearly and quadratically separable classifiers using adaptive approach. In: Computer Engineering Conference, vol. 26, pp. 89–96. IEEE (2011)
16. Ben-Israel, A., Levin, Y.: The geometry of linear separability in data sets. Linear Algebra Appl. **416**(1), 75–87 (2006)
17. Bauman, E., Bauman, K.: One-class semi-supervised learning: detecting linearly separable class by its mean (2017)
18. Elizondo, D.: Searching for linearly separable subsets using the class of linear separability method. In: IEEE International Joint Conference on Neural Networks, Proceedings, vol. 2, pp. 955–959. IEEE (2004)

An Optimized Resolution Coefficient Algorithm of Gray Relation Classifier

Hui Han[1], Yulong Ying[2(✉)], and Xiang Chen[1]

[1] State Key Laboratory of Complex Electromagnetic Environment
Effects on Electronics and Information System (CEMEE),
Luoyang 471003, Henan, China
[2] School of Energy and Mechanical Engineering,
Shanghai University of Electric Power, Shanghai 200090, China
yingyulong060313@163.com

Abstract. Resolution coefficient of traditional gray relation classifier usually takes a fixed value of 0.5, which greatly limits the adaptive ability, and reduces the effectiveness of this algorithm to identify signals. To solve this problem, an improved optimized resolution coefficient algorithm of gray relation classifier was proposed. Particle swarm optimization (PSO) algorithm was used to calculate the optimized resolution coefficient corresponding to the best classification results under different SNR environment. The adaptive ability of this algorithm was improved by improving the selection method of resolution coefficient and ultimately the classification effect was improved. Simulation results show that, compared with the traditional improved algorithm, it can improve the recognition rate of signals under different SNR environment, and have a good application value.

Keywords: Signal recognition · Classifier design · Gray relation theory
Resolution coefficient · Particle Swarm Optimization (PSO)

1 Introduction

The purpose of communication signal's recognition [1] is to judge the modulation types of communication signals accurately without any modulation information. With the increasingly complex and intensive environment of signals, the modulation mode is more, which will take a lot of resources and much time to process all of the received signal. So determine the modulation of signal first, and then select the signal that the recipient interested to process will greatly improve the timeliness. In this case, it is important and urgent to identify signal's modulation type effectively. An important part of signal's identification—classifier design, get more and more attention of people.

Various pattern recognition methods have been developed for classifier design nowadays, among which the most commonly used ones are artificial neural networks (ANNs) and support vector machines (SVMs). The training of ANNs needs a large number of samples which are not easily obtained in practical application, especially for the fault ones. While, SVMs based on statistical learning theory which is of specialties for a smaller number of samples has better generalization than ANNs and ensures that

© Springer Nature Switzerland AG 2018
X. Sun et al. (Eds.): ICCCS 2018, LNCS 11068, pp. 406–417, 2018.
https://doi.org/10.1007/978-3-030-00021-9_37

the local and global optimal solutions are exactly the same. However, the accuracy of a support vector machine (SVM) classifier is decided by the selection of optimal parameters for SVMs. In order to ensure the diagnostic accuracy, an optimization algorithm or and complex multi-class concept have to be used complementally to improve the effective of SVMs.

Gray theory [2, 3] is a method that quantitatively described and compared the change and develop situation of a system. Its analytical basis is to calculate the distance between reference points and comparison points, and identify the proximities and differences among various factors by the distance. Since the calculation method is relatively simple, it will have a great value if the adaptive capacity and recognition effect is improved.

In recent years, gray relation theory was widely used in many fields. Literature [4] used gray relational analysis to identify IC marking, the identification rate can reach 97.5%, which is an easy and practical method in the field of IC marking inspection. Literature [5] proposed a gas turbine engine fault diagnostic approach with a hybrid of gray relation theory and gas-path analysis, and the fault classification analyses and case studies have shown that the confidence level of the fault classification can reach more than 95%, when single and multiple components are degraded, and the predicted degradations are almost same as that of implanted fault patterns. Literature [6] proposed a rolling bearing fault diagnosis approach based on improved generalized fractal box-counting dimension and adaptive gray relation algorithm.

Literature [7] proposed an algorithm based on a synthetic approach of grey theory for temporal difference learning, it can eliminate all step size parameters and improve data efficiency. Literature [8] mainly discussed the application of grey theory in the non-subsampled contour let domain which can preserve most important information of image. Literature [9] proposed a fault forecasting system using a grey prediction model. Aiming to the problem of poor adaptability, many improved calculation method of weighted value and resolution coefficient value were proposed. Literature [10, 11] used adaptive weight gray relation algorithm to extract signal's features, it improved the recognition results by adaptively setting the weights of every relation coefficients. Based on the literature [10], an adaptive weighted interval gray relation algorithm was proposed by literature [10], distribution intervals of parameter's characteristics were used to achieve the effective recognition. Literature [12–14] improve the adaptive ability of the algorithm by adaptively selecting resolution coefficient values. However, there is no rigorous theoretical basis for selecting the resolution coefficients, and only the distribution range can be obtained. The accurate value of resolution coefficient is necessary for us to further study.

To solve the problems above, this paper presents an improved optimized resolution coefficient algorithm of gray relation classifier. Aim to the problem of poor adaptive capacity of traditional gray relation classifier [15, 16], optimized algorithm was used to select the best resolution coefficient which will lead to better recognition result. Compared with the traditional algorithm, the resolution coefficient is no longer a fixed value. It improves the adaptive ability of the algorithm, and thus improve the recognition performance of classifier.

The rest of this paper is organized as follows. A review of basic theory on PSO is introduced in Sect. 2. The gray relation theory and its optimized algorithm is given in

Sect. 3, followed by Sect. 4 which presents simulation results and analysis by the proposed approach. Finally, conclusions are presented in Sect. 5.

2 Basic Theory

Particle Swarm Optimization (PSO) Algorithm was a biological heuristic algorithm proposed by kennedy and Eberhart which originated from the birds collective behavior. Since its first paper published in 1995, the number of related published articles were growing in exponentially. PSO algorithm is made up of a group of particles, and each particle represents a candidate of solution vector, and each element of particle represents a parameter to be optimized. The particles search the optimal solution with particular speed in the solution space. Each particle has a memory, which can help it track the previous optimum position. The position of each particle are distinguished with extreme individual value *pBest* and extreme group value *gBest*. In the solution space's searching process, the speed of each particle is adjusted with its previous behavior and adjacent particles' behavior. Every movements of particles are mainly affected by memory, current position and group experience. With the process of searching, the particle group is moving towards better search area step by step.

In the searching process, the position and velocity of each particle are updated according to the two following equations with two extreme values (individual extreme value *pBest*, and group extreme value *gBest*) as follows:

$$V_i^{k+1} = W \cdot V_i^k + c1 \cdot r1 \cdot (pBest_i^k - Present_i^k) + c2 \cdot r2 \cdot (gBest^k - Present_i^k) \quad (1)$$

$$Present_i^{k+1} = Present_i^k + V_i^{k+1} \quad (2)$$

In the Eq. (1), $c1$ and $c2$ are accelerated constant and usually $c1 = c2 = 1.2$;
$r1$ and $r2$ are random numbers and their values are between 0 and 1;
W is inertia weight and its value is between 0.1 and 0.9;
V_i^{k+1} is the velocity of the ith particle in the (k + 1)th generation;
$Present_i^k$ is the position of the ith particle in the kth generation;
$pBest_i^k$ is the optimal position of the ith particle in the kth generation;
$gBest^k$ is the optimal position of group particles in the kth generation.

However, the phenomenon of back and forth searching near the global optimal solution easily appears in the traditional PSO algorithm at the end of searching process. To solve this problem, the inertia weight W can be reduced linearly from maximum inertia weight W_{max} to minimum inertia weight W_{min} during searching process shown as below due to that a relative large inertia weight is beneficial for the global searching while a relative small inertia weight is beneficial for the local searching [17].

$$W = W_{max} - iter \cdot \frac{W_{max} - W_{min}}{iter_{max}} \qquad (3)$$

Where W is inertia weight set in the range of 0.1 and 0.9 and can be reduced linearly from maximum inertia weight W_{max} to minimum inertia weight W_{min} during searching process due to that a relative large inertia weight is beneficial for the global searching while a relative small inertia weight is beneficial for the local searching. *iter* is the current generation number; $iter_{max}$ is the total generation number.

After continuous and iterative update of location, the particle group in the solution space is gradually moving towards to the optimal position, and eventually obtain the global optimal solution *gBest*.

Compared with genetic algorithm (GA), PSO algorithm has no crossover and mutation, so the algorithm's structure is simpler, and the computing is faster. From the theoretical analysis above, PSO algorithm can be used to calculate the optimal resolution coefficient values, which provides a good theoretical basis for the proposed algorithm.

3 Optimized Algorithm

3.1 Design Diagram

Resolution coefficient of traditional gray relation classifier usually takes a fixed value of 0.5, which is difficult to adjust the relation degree at any time according to different SNR environment. It is also difficult to improve its adaptive ability to realize accurate recognition. To solve this problem, a particle swarm optimization (PSO) algorithm based gray relation algorithm was proposed, and the basic principle of the improved algorithm was analyzed. According to the optimized results of PSO algorithm under different environments, the optimized resolution coefficient value was selected. The effectiveness of improved algorithm was demonstrated through the calculation and recognition results of parameter's characteristics under different SNR, and the specific design of the system block diagram is shown in Fig. 1.

3.2 The Improved Algorithm

The research of gray relation theory is the foundation of gray system theory, mainly based on the basic theory of space mathematics, to calculate relation coefficient and relation degree between reference characteristic vector and each comparative characteristic vector [10]. Gray relation theory has a good potential to be used in fault classification with four reasons [5, 6]:

It has good tolerance to measurement noise.
It has the ability to assist the selection of characteristic parameters for classification.
It can solve the learning problem with a small number of samples.
Its algorithm is simple and can solve the issue of generality versus accuracy.

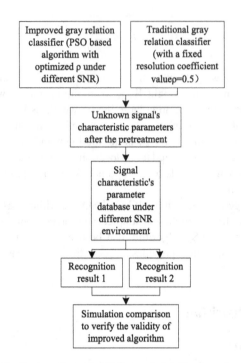

Fig. 1. Design diagram of improved classification algorithm

Based on the traditional gray relation algorithm, an improved algorithm is proposed. The principle is analyzed, simulated and experimental verified. The specific analysis and calculated steps are as follows.

Gray relation algorithm determines the category of signals by comparing the similar degree of sequences to be recognized and the sequences in database, suppose the sequences of system's behavior are:

$$X_0 = (x_0(1), x_0(2), \cdots, x_0(n))$$
$$X_1 = (x_1(1), x_1(2), \cdots, x_1(n))$$
$$\cdots$$
$$X_i = (x_i(1), x_i(2), \cdots, x_i(n)) \tag{4}$$
$$\cdots$$
$$X_m = (x_m(1), x_m(2), \cdots, x_m(n))$$

Where, X_0 represents the reference sequence, $X_1, X_2, \cdots, X_m$ represent the comparative sequences.

First, calculate the initial value X_i' of each sequence:

$$x_i' = \frac{x_i}{x_i(1)} = (x_i'(1), x_i'(2), \cdots, x_i'(n)), \quad i = 0, 1, 2, \cdots, m \tag{5}$$

Where, $i = 0, 1, 2, \cdots, m$ represent the category of signals to be compared in the database, n represents the number of signal's characteristics.

Second, calculate the difference sequence, namely:

$$\Delta x_i(k) = x_0'(k) - x_i'(k), \quad \Delta x_i = (\Delta x_i(1), \Delta x_i(2), \cdots, \Delta x_i(n)), \quad i = 1, 2, \cdots, m \quad (6)$$

$k = 1, 2, \cdots, n$ represents the kth characteristic of signal.

Calculate the extreme maximum value M and the extreme minimum value m:

$$M = \max_i \max_k \Delta x_i(k), \quad m = \min_i \min_k \Delta x_i(k) \quad (7)$$

The relation coefficient value $\gamma_{0i}(k)$ can be obtained:

$$\gamma_{0i}(k) = \frac{m + \rho M}{\Delta x_i(k) + \rho M}, \quad \rho \in (0, 1), \quad k = 1, 2, \cdots, n; \quad i = 1, 2, \cdots, m \quad (8)$$

Generally, the value of ρ is taken as 0.5, in this condition, the algorithm has no adaptive ability. To this problem, PSO algorithm was used to optimize the resolution coefficient values of ρ for each SNR environment, which can further improve the recognition performance of the algorithm. The iterative optimization process of PSO algorithm are shown in Fig. 2.

After the optimization, choose the optimized value of ρ corresponding to the best recognition results, and the optimized ρ can be obtained, the reasons can be analyzed as follows:

In the initialization process of data, generally $m = \min_i \min_k \Delta x_i(k) = 0$, then the Eq. (8) becomes:

$$\gamma_{0i}(k) = \frac{\rho M}{\Delta x_i(k) + \rho M}, \quad \rho \in (0, 1), \quad k = 1, 2, \cdots, n; \quad i = 1, 2, \cdots, m \quad (9)$$

Let $\theta_i(k) = \frac{\Delta x_i(k)}{M}$, the equation above can be transformed into:

$$\gamma_{0i}(k) = \frac{\rho}{\theta_i(k) + \rho}, \quad \rho \in (0, 1), \quad k = 1, 2, \cdots, n; \quad i = 1, 2, \cdots, m \quad (10)$$

Formula (10) shows that, the selection of ρ value, directly affects the final calculation results of relation degree, when $M >> \Delta x_i(k)$, $\theta_i(k)$ is very small. In this situation, if the ρ value is greater, the relation degree is mainly determined by ρ, and the result is close to 1. It is difficult to distinguish the similarity of the signal to be identified with the signal in the database, which directly affect the recognition result. If the communication signal is interfered by random signal which caused mutation, the above situation will occur, so we should try to reduce the value of ρ, and thus weaken the influences of M.

In addition, when the difference of M and $\Delta x_i(k)$ is not large, the value of $\theta_i(k)$ is larger. In this situation, if the value of ρ is small, the relation degree of different signals

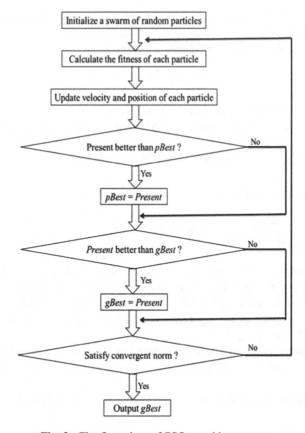

Fig. 2. The flow chart of PSO searching process

will be relatively close, hence, it is difficult to achieve the accurate identification of signal. Therefore, the value of ρ should be increased, to increase the impact of M, which fully reflect the integrity of relation degree. Based on the principle analysis above, literature [12] proposed a new gray relation algorithm, which can determine the range of value ρ according to the value of M and $\Delta x_i(k)$. It achieved a good recognition effect. Although it can determine the scope of ρ, it is still unable to select the exact value of ρ, so PSO based algorithm was proposed above to solve this problem, and optimized the traditional gray relation algorithm.

Finally, calculate the relation degree value γ_{0i}:

$$\gamma_{0i} = \frac{1}{n}\sum_{k=1}^{n} \gamma_{0i}(k), \quad i = 1, 2, \cdots, m \tag{11}$$

γ_{0i} indicates the relation degree, which is the similarity degree of the sequences, according to this calculation results, the signals can be classified.

4 Simulation Results and Analysis

Take six different types of communication modulated signals as examples—AM, FM, PM, ASK, FSK, PSK, the corresponding bandwidth and carrier frequency of the six signals were known. The modulation parameters of these signals were set in Table 1:

Table 1. Modulation parameters of six communication signals

Signals	Parameters' value
AM	$f_z = 2.7 \times 10^8$ Hz, $f_s = 4.32 \times 10^9$ Hz, $f_m = 1.0 \times 10^5$ Hz, $A = 1$, $a = 0.8$
FM	$f_z = 2.7 \times 10^8$ Hz, $f_s = 4.32 \times 10^9$ Hz, $f_m = 1.0 \times 10^5$ Hz, $k_f = 6$
PM	$f_z = 2.7 \times 10^8$ Hz, $f_s = 4.32 \times 10^9$ Hz, $f_m = 1.0 \times 10^5$ Hz, $k_p = 5$
ASK	$f_z = 2.7 \times 10^8$ Hz, $R_b = 1.0 \times 10^5$ bps, 0, 1 keying
FSK	$f_z = 2.7 \times 10^8$ Hz, $R_b = 1.0 \times 10^5$ bps, $f_1 = f_z - \Delta f$, $f_2 = f_z + \Delta f$, $\Delta f = 1.0 \times 10^5$ Hz
PSK	$f_z = 2.7 \times 10^8$ Hz, $R_b = 1.0 \times 10^5$ bps, 0, π binary phase

Where, f_z is the carrier frequency, f_s is the sampling frequency, f_m is the baseband signal frequency, A is the amplitude of AM signal, a is the amplitude modulation index, k_f is the frequency modulation index, k_p is the phase modulation index, R_b is the symbol rate, f_1 and f_2 are the two frequencies of FSK signal, and Δf is the differential frequency.

Then, extract the entropy features [16] (Shannon entropy and Index entropy) of the six signals under different SNR, and the entropy algorithms can be briefly described as follows:

It is an important concept in information theory, which used to measure the uncertainty of system.

Shannon entropy H can be defined as follows:

$$H(p) = H(p_1, p_2, \cdots p_n) = -\sum_{i=1}^{n} p_i \log_2 p_i \qquad (12)$$

Hence, Shannon entropy H can be regarded as a function of n-dimensional probability vectors $p = (p_1, p_2, \cdots p_n)$.

The information content P_i can be expressed as:

$$\Delta I(P_i) = e^{1-P_i} \qquad (13)$$

And index entropy can be similarly defined as:

$$H = \sum_{i=1}^{n} P_i e^{1-P_i} \qquad (14)$$

Entropy analysis method is a method to select valid characteristics using uncertainty property. It does not need to know the specific size and distribution details of the characteristics when uses this method, and it has low calculation, so it is a good feature extraction method.

Through the analysis above, the simulation results are shown in Fig. 3.

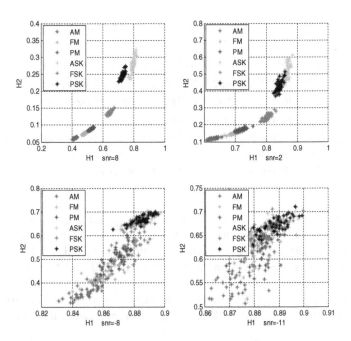

Fig. 3. The extracted entropy features of the six signals

Then using the PSO algorithm based gray relation classifier that proposed in this paper to calculate the gray relation degree (by Eq. (10)) of the unknown signals' entropy features (H1, H2) under different SNR.

Then using the PSO algorithm based gray relation classifier that proposed in this paper to calculate the gray relation degree (by Eq. (10)) of the unknown signals' entropy features (H1, H2) under different SNR, the parameters of PSO based optimized algorithm can be set as in Table 2.

Table 2. Parameters of PSO

Parameters	Value
Population size	5
No. of generation	5
c1	1.2
c2	1.2

After calculating the gray relation degree of the unknown signal with the known signals in the database, consider that the unknown signals should belong to the signals' category with the largest gray relation degree, and then calculate the signals' accurate recognition number which is supposed as λ, and suppose the total number as φ, so the recognition rate can be expressed as:

$$\eta\% = \frac{\lambda}{\varphi} \times 100\% \tag{15}$$

The calculation results reflect the accurate rate of signals' classification.

Compare the recognition results of traditional gray relation algorithm [16, 18–20], and the recognition results of improved gray relation algorithm in literature [12], with the recognition results of the improved algorithm in this paper. Simulation results are shown in Fig. 4. The abscissa represents the SNR, and the ordinate represents the recognition rate η.

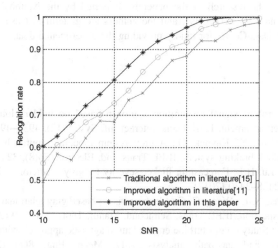

Fig. 4. Recognition rates of different algorithms under different SNR

Simulation results in Fig. 4 show that, under higher SNR environment, the three algorithms all have higher recognition rate. With the decreasing of SNR, the identification effect of traditional classifier in literature [16] is obviously decreasing. And in literature [12], the anti-noise ability of improved recognition algorithm is improved to some extent. The PSO algorithm based gray relation classifier with optimized resolution coefficient proposed in this paper has the best recognition performance.

5 Conclusion

Aiming to the problem that the traditional gray relation algorithm has no adaptive ability, the resolution coefficient value ρ usually takes a fixed value of 0.5. A PSO based algorithm was proposed to optimize the resolution coefficient under different SNR environment. It can improve the adaptive ability and recognition effect of the traditional algorithm. Simulation results show that, compared with the traditional algorithm, the optimized algorithm has a higher recognition rate, which has good application value in the field of classifier design.

In this paper, PSO algorithm was used to design classifier to improve the adaptive ability of gray relation theory, which achieved a relatively good recognition result. Although the improved algorithm is better than the traditional one, if the SNR changes to much lower, the recognition result will be still not good. Thus, how to make the classifier better is still the hot issue for the scholars that studied in the area of signals' recognition.

Acknowledgment. The research of the paper is supported by the National Natural Science Foundation of China (No. 61603239), and the authors are grateful to Case Western Reserve University Bearing Data Center for kindly providing the experimental data.

References

1. Li, J.: A new robust signal recognition approach based on holder cloud features under varying SNR environment. KSII Trans. Internet Inf. Syst. **9**(12), 4934–4949 (2015)
2. Kayacan, E., Oniz, Y., Kaynak, O.: A grey system modeling approach for sliding-mode control of antilock braking system. IEEE Trans. Ind. Electron. **56**(8), 3244–3252 (2009)
3. Chang, G.W., Lu, H.J.: Forecasting flicker severity by grey predictor. IEEE Trans. Power Deliv. **27**(4), 2428–2430 (2012)
4. Jiang, B.C., Tasi, S.-L., Wang, C.-C.: Machine vision-based gray relational theory applied to IC marking inspection. IEEE Trans. Semicond. Manuf. **15**(4), 531–539 (2002)
5. Ying, Y., et al.: Study on gas turbine engine fault diagnostic approach with a hybrid of gray relation theory and gas-path analysis. Adv. Mech. Eng. **8**(1) (2016). 10.1177/1687814015627769
6. Cao, Y., et al.: Study on rolling bearing fault diagnosis approach based on improved generalized fractal box-counting dimension and adaptive gray relation algorithm. Adv. Mech. Eng. **8**(10) (2016) https://doi.org/10.1177/1687814016675583
7. Hwang, K.-S., Lo, C.-Y., Lee, G.-Y.: A grey synthesis approach to efficient architecture design for temporal difference learning. IEEE/ASME Trans. Mechatron. **16**(6), 1136–1144 (2011)
8. Li, H.-J., Zhao, Z.-M., Yu, X.L.: Grey theory applied in non-subsampled Contourlet transform. IET Image Process. **6**(3), 264–272 (2012)
9. Wang, M.H., Tsai, H.H.: Fuel cell fault forecasting system using grey and extension theories. IET Renew. Power Gener. **6**(6), 373–380 (2012)
10. Li, J.: A novel recognition algorithm based on holder coefficient theory and interval gray relation classifier. KSII Trans. Internet Inf. Syst. (TIIS) **9**(11), 4573–4584 (2015)
11. Yun, L.I.N., Xi-cai, S.I., Ruo-lin, Z.H.O.U., Hui, Y.A.N.G.: Application of improved grey correlation algorithm on radiation source recognition. J. Commun. **31**(8A), 166–171 (2010)

12. Zhang, R., Wu, X., Ji, M.: Determination of distinguishing coefficient of gray correlation degree and application in mechanical fault diagnosis. Coal Mine Mach. **34**(3), 291–293 (2013)
13. Dong, Y., Duan, Z.: A new determination method for identification coefficient of grey relational grade. J. Xi'an Univ. Archit. Technol. (Nat. Sci. Edition) **40**(4), 589–592 (2008)
14. Fan, K., Wu, H.: A new method on identification coefficient of relational grade for gray system. J. Wuhan Univ. Technol. **24**(7), 86–88 (2002)
15. Fu, C., Zhang, J., Ji, W., Zhang, Y.: Research on the application of gray correlation theory on multi-sensor radiation recognition system. J. CAEIT **10**(6), 602–606 (2015)
16. Li, J., Guo, J.: A new feature extraction algorithm based on entropy cloud characteristics of communication signals. Math. Probl. Eng. **2015**, 8 (2015)
17. Ying, Y., et al.: Nonlinear steady-state model based gas turbine health status estimation approach with improved particle swarm optimization algorithm. Math. Probl. Eng. **2015**, 12 (2015)
18. Li, J., Cao, Y., Ying, Y., Li, S.: A rolling element bearing fault diagnosis approach based on multifractal theory and gray relation theory. PLoS ONE **11**(12), 1–16 (2016)
19. Ying, Y., Li, J., Chen, Z., Guo, J.: Study on rolling bearing on-line reliability analysis based on vibration information processing. Comput. Electr. Eng. (2017)
20. Ying, Y., Cao, Y., Li, S., Li, J., Guo, J.: Study on gas turbine engine fault diagnostic approach with a hybrid of gray relation theory and gas-path analysis. Adv. Mech. Eng. **8**(1), 1–14 (2016)

Analysis and Research on the Temporal and Spatial Correlation of Traffic Accidents and Illegal Activities

Zhuan Li[1], Xin Guo[2], and Jiadong Sun[3(✉)]

[1] Shandong Public Security Bureau Traffic Police Corps, Tianjin, China
[2] Jinan Haiyi Software Limited Company, Jinan, China
guoxin@haiyisoft.com
[3] Institute of Traffic Management Science,
Ministry of Public Security, Beijing, China
253195895@qq.com

Abstract. The formation of the traffic accidents is always caused by many factors such as the road, the vehicle, the drivers conditions and so on [1, 2]. In order to analyze the various causes of traffic accidents, the feasibility measures should be taken after the accident occurred, and how to prevent the occurrence of related traffic accidents. This paper introduces a novel traffic accident analysis system to analyze traffic accidents, which is mainly composed of seven parts, including accident basic information analysis, accident driver analysis, accident vehicle analysis, accident road analysis, large accident ledger, multi-dimensional accident analysis, and accident analysis report. The suggested framework mainly contains two technology: (1) multi-dimensional analysis which is the core of the data warehouse technology to build the multi-dimensional data model in reservoir management (2) the on-line analytical processing (OLAP) technology in data analysis and display. In addition, Bayesian network is used for multi-dimensional data analysis in this paper. The method proposed in this paper can effectively organize a large number of out of data to get useful information which is convenient for traffic management departments to analyze the reason of traffic accidents and then to take corresponding countermeasures.

Keywords: Traffic accident · Multi-Dimensional analysis · Bayesian network

1 Introduction

Nowadays, the road traffic accidents have seriously affected the national economy [3]. As we all know the triggering of traffic accidents is not only related to the behavior of the drivers, but also has a certain connection with a series of factors such as road environment conditions, weather conditions, traffic conditions and so on. The starting point is how to find the problems from a large number of traffic accident data, then to analyze the accident reasons.

This paper uses multi-dimensional analysis which is the core of the data warehouse technology to build the multi-dimensional data model. The multidimensional data model aims to describe the multidimensional features of the analytical data. In this

© Springer Nature Switzerland AG 2018
X. Sun et al. (Eds.): ICCCS 2018, LNCS 11068, pp. 418–428, 2018.
https://doi.org/10.1007/978-3-030-00021-9_38

model, data is no longer organized by entities and relationships, but is organized by metrics and dimensions. A dimension is a physical feature, which is a basic way to access and express information, and it is generally as an index for identifying data.

Additionally, Bayesian network model is also used to analyze the traffic accidents in this paper. The Bayesian network is a probabilistic network, which is a graphical network based on probabilistic reasoning, and the Bayesian formula is the basis of the probability network, at the same time, is a mathematical model based on probabilistic reasoning. The Bayesian network based on probabilistic reasoning is proposed to solve the problem of uncertainty and incompleteness. It has great advantages in solving the faults caused by the uncertainty and relevance of complex devices.

The rest of this paper is organized as follows. In Sect. 2, we briefly introduce related work about the traffic accident analysis. Then the system function is presented in Sect. 3. Introduction of system principle is presented in Sect. 4. Finally, we conclude in Sect. 5.

2 Related Work

The main purpose of traffic accident analysis is statistical analysis, cause analysis and process analysis of traffic accidents, as well as the influence of various elements of traffic system on traffic safety. Traditional analysis of traffic accidents are adopted by mathematical statistics analysis method to analyze the reasons of accidents, to count the incidence of statistical accidents and to further establish the corresponding model, prediction and evaluation of road safety.

Wang etc. proposed in [1] that ID3 classification strategy tree algorithm in data mining technology is feasible and effective to the cause analysis of traffic accidents. And Wang also suggested in [4] that the association rules in the traffic accident data was got successfully, which further prove that the extraction technology of association rules was valuable [5, 6]. Chu etc. used clustering method to classify the basic data, and data sample of a kind was analyzed from man-vehicle-road link to find out the different effect to traffic accidents by different time and space distribution in [7]. Ye etc. adopted the combination between causality analysis diagram and the analytic hierarchy process (AHP) phase to study on the cause of traffic accident [8]. Lin studied the causes of road traffic accidents, used the principal component analysis theory to analyze the main factors causing road traffic accidents and draw the main contradictions which affect the traffic safety [9].

Recently, the Bayesian network (BN) has become an effective method in the field of artificial intelligence to express the uncertainty of the system and to carry out the probability reasoning. It can conduct two-way uncertain reasoning and widely used in prediction, classification, causality analysis and diagnostic analysis. Analysis of the application of Bayesian network in traffic accident, can directly reflect the relationship between factors and traffic accident graphical expression system, and it is convenient for system analysis of various elements. Furthermore, the application of Bayesian networks with traffic systems has been studied at home and abroad. For example, the United States "IHSDM" is added to the Bayesian network traffic accident prediction module. Kaan Ozbay etc. established Bayesian network model for predicting traffic accident duration.

Some experts in China also used Bayesian network to predict traffic accidents, and established traffic accident Bayesian network for weather, time, traffic volume and speed.

3   System Function

The system mainly consists of three parts: data analysis, data management ledger and accident analysis report. Each part contains several corresponding sub processes. The structure of system is showed in Fig. 1.

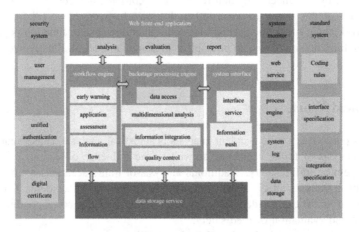

Fig. 1. Overall system architecture diagram

3.1   Data Analysis Process

The data analysis part is mainly used to analyze a series of traffic accident data from simple to complex. First, the mathematical probability analysis of simple accident data is carried out. Then multidimensional model is used to analyze the data in a multidimensional way. Finally, according to data analysis, we get an accident analysis report which can effectively prevent accidents or deal with accidents in time. Next, we will give a detailed introduction to each part.

3.1.1   Analysis of Simple Accident Data

This system can make an accurate analysis of the causes of traffic accidents from many aspects:

(1). Analysis of the basic information of the accident. It mainly analyses some simple accidents or general accidents in the city, including time distribution (hour, day, week), main cause of the accident, accident scene and accident form. In addition, it also analyzes the number of accidents, the number of deaths, the number of injuries and the loss of property in the provinces and cities, and provides the analysis of the year on year, the year-on-year ratio analysis and the accident trend analysis. Two Examples of Analysis of Basic Information of Accidents were showed in Fig. 2.

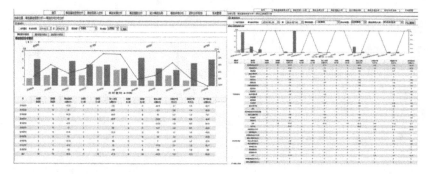

Fig. 2. Analysis of accident time distribution: (day distribution analysis) and The main cause of accident analysis

(2). Analysis of accident road. Based on the accident road, the accident road elements such as accident road administrative grade, accident road type, accident intersection type, and accident road protection facilities were analyzed. The number of accidents, the number of deaths, the number of injuries and the loss of property were analyzed. Furthermore it provides the analysis of the year on year, the year-on-year ratio analysis and the accident trend analysis. Two Examples of Analysis of accident road were showed in Fig. 3.

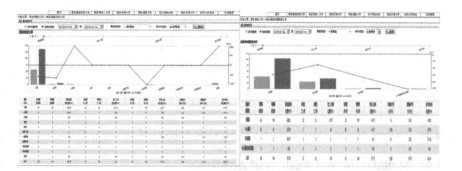

Fig. 3. Accident Road Linear Analysis and Accident road physical isolation analysis

(3). Analysis of accident vehicle. This process is mainly analyzed around traffic accidents, including the type, state, use nature of the vehicle and the situation, location and time of the accident in the province. At the same time, the process also analyzes the distribution of accident vehicles, the number of accidents involved in the accident vehicles, the number of deaths, the number of injuries and the loss of property. What's more, it provides the analysis of the year on year, the year-on-year ratio analysis and the accident trend analysis. Two Examples of Analysis of accident vehicle were showed in Fig. 4.

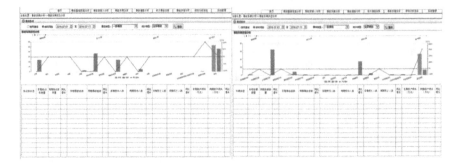

Fig. 4. Accident Vehicle Shape Analysis and Accident vehicle type analysis

(4). Analysis of accident driver. It mainly analyzes the driver's driving age, age, sex, type of person, the number of accidents, the number of deaths, the number of injuries, and the loss of property. In addition, the process also analyzes the training situation of driver school and accident driver, and further understands the details of the driver's training. Two Examples of Analysis of accident driver were showed in Fig. 5.

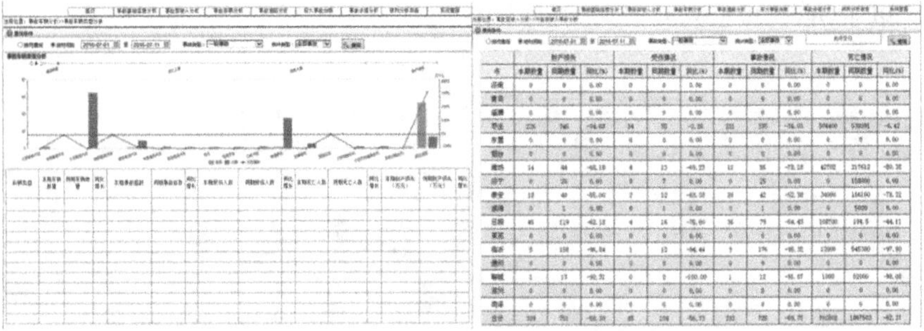

Fig. 5. Accident driving school analysis and Accident Analysis of Drivers in Other Provinces

3.1.2   Multidimensional Analysis of Accident

The system uses multidimensional analysis technology to analyze traffic accident data and establish a corresponding information organization model. Traffic accident data, like business data, are essentially multidimensional. This model is conducive to deep mining the intrinsic relationship between the factors inducing accidents. It is an analysis method supporting decision support. The multidimensional analysis model of the accident data will be introduced in Sect. 4.

3.2   Data Management

The management system can push the large accident data in the province to the subordinate detachment. According to the large accident account information, the team can fill in the accident information (analysis of the causes of the accident, the handling of the driver, the information of the accident information, the investigation of the accident responsibility investigation, the information of the rectification of the work). The report forms a larger accident ledger information and provides a larger accident ledger information export function. Here, as the page number is limited, we only show the two part of the system's ledger information management interface in Fig. 6.

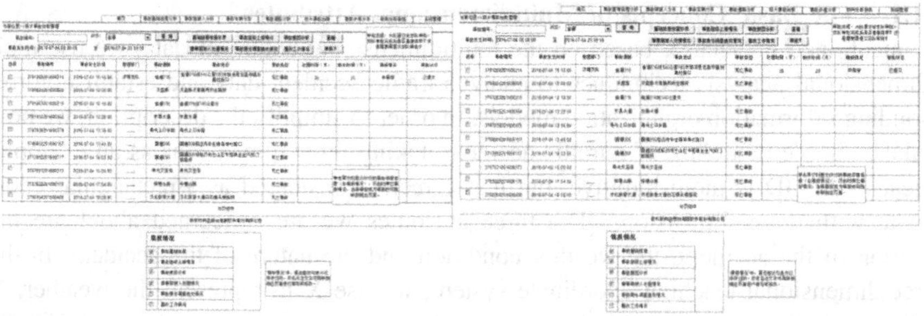

Fig. 6. Management of big accident account information and Account of larger accident.

3.3   Report on the Analysis of the Accident

This part analyzes the traffic accident information by analyzing the number of various types of accidents, deaths, number of injuries, property loss, four accident indicators, and accident data changes during the period of the judgment, as well as the year-on-year, the year-on-year ratio, and overall situation. It automatically generates the presentation as a basic data analysis report for the routine meeting of the accident management department. You can integrate with editing tools such as Word, and edit report style templates required for business generation. For example, which analysis methods are to be displayed (including graphs, tables, or charts). The analysis of an example of a traffic accident is shown in Fig. 7.

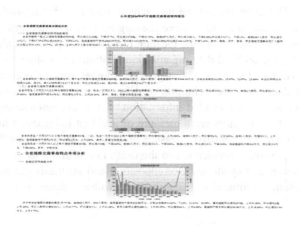

Fig. 7. Report on the analysis of the accident

4   Introduction of System Principle

4.1   Multidimensional Analysis Model

In this section, we will introduce some of the data and mathematical models used in this system in detail.

4.1.1   The Basic Concepts of Multidimensional Attributes

As mentioned in Sect. 3, based on the multidimensional nature of data, we use multidimensional analysis techniques to analyze traffic accident data and establish corresponding information organization models. In order to simplify the description, we now make a simple modeling of a traffic accident, taking three dimensions as an example. Because the 3D is more intuitive, but it is directly considered as a rectangular coordinate with three dimensions. The three attributes we are concerned about are the location of the accident, the weather condition and the nature of the accident. In the three-dimensional teaching coordinate system, we use X to represent the weather, Y indicates the location, and Z indicates the nature of the accident, as shown in Fig. 8.

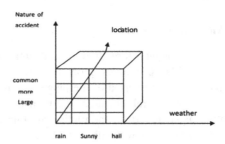

Fig. 8. Cubic Data Modal

The basic concepts of multidimensional attributes:

(1) Hierarchy. The dimension of the hierarchy is based on the detailed requirements of the data organization to achieve the aggregation and decomposition of data from different levels. Taking the location dimension of traffic accident data as an example, the hierarchical data organization relationship is shown in Fig. 9.

(2) Category (Detailed category). Category is another way of organizing multidimensional data. With the definition of dimension, we should further determine how users can retrieve detailed information or how to aggregate data.

(3) Index quantity. Indicators are a measure of accident information in dimensional space. They are a quantitative measure of accident data, such as the number of kilometers of vehicle accidents, and the death rate of millions of kilometers.

(4) Decomposition and synthesis. Decomposition and synthesis can help us further analyze detailed information or observations within a dimension.

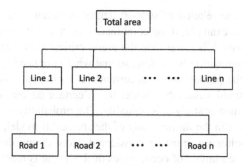

Fig. 9. Positional hierarchy structure

(5) Slice, cut and rotate. In a multidimensional space, the analysis of basic data includes "slicing", "dicing" and "rotation." Slice refers to the action of selecting one-dimensional members in a dimension of a multi-dimensional array. The purpose and effect of cutting is similar to that of slicing. The so-called rotation is to change the display direction of the dimension, such as swapping rows and columns. Rotation can be understood as observing data from different perspectives, which is more convenient for discovering potential problems.

4.1.2 Multidimensional Analysis Module of Accident

The multidimensional analysis of the accident is divided into the following modules:

(1) Accident data statistics. Combing and cleaning traffic accident data, establishing multidimensional and multilevel analysis database of traffic accidents, independently analyzing all factors in traffic accident data, obtaining the proportion and sorting of each factor under each single factor.

(2) Accident trend analysis. The increase analysis of each factor in the accident data was carried out, and the increase and ranking of each factor were obtained. Using Bayesian network analysis algorithm to extract association rules between traffic accident data and generate accident trend statistics.

(3) Focus display. According to the daily work needs, we can set up the analysis rules and set the threshold automatically. The system automatically analyzes the traffic accident data with the customized analysis rules and the set threshold, and pushes the analysis results to the interface of the concerns.

(4) Analysis of the cause of the accident. Based on the analysis of the causes and characteristics of road traffic accidents, the main reasons for a series of accidents can be obtained through multi dimension association mining and analysis of the causes of selected multiple accidents.

(5) Correlation analysis of accident factors. According to the analysis of the characteristics of traffic accidents when the association of multiple dimensions of different causes of the accident of the selected mining analysis, can get the main reason for the formation of a series of accidents, and at the same time, the analysis of factors for the cause of such accidents of support and confidence.

Support degree: The relation of support degree is meaningful under certain probability constraints. For example, if the combination of A and B events is too low in the total transaction records, it is lower than the preset critical value, which means that the number of events combination is too few, so that we do not need to pay attention to it. On the contrary, if the probability of occurrence of this event combination is higher than the preset threshold value, this model has a certain degree of universal significance. We find and further study it is valuable. The probability of the above is 0.

Confidence degree: In the further study of the above AB model, another probability constraint, called confidence, must be considered. Considering that even if A and B occur frequently, if the number of occurrences of this event is much lower than that of A events, it will be lower than the preset threshold value, which means that the occurrence of A is not enough to cause the occurrence of B.

4.2 Bias Network Model

In the multi-dimensional analysis module of the accident, the system uses Bayesian network analysis algorithm to extract association rules between traffic accident data factors to generate and display accident data.

4.2.1 Basic Concepts of Bayesian Networks

The Bias network is a probabilistic network, which is a graphical network based on probabilistic reasoning, and the Bias formula is the basis of the probability network. Below is a brief introduction to the basic formulas related to Bayesian networks:

(1) Conditional probability:
Let A and B be two events, and $P(A) > O$, $P(B|A)$ is called the conditional probability that event B occurs under the condition that event A occurs.

(2) Joint probability:
Let A and B be two events and $P(A) > 0$. Their joint probability is:

$$P(AB) = P(B|A)P(A) \tag{1}$$

(3) Full probability formula:
Suppose that the sample space of test E is S, A is the event of E, B1, B2, ..., Bn is a set of events of E, satisfy: Bl, B2, ... Bn is incompatible with each other; and $P(Bi) > 0$, i - 1, 2, ..., n. There is a full probability formula

$$P(A) = P(A|B1) + P(A|B2) + \cdots + P(A|Bn) = \sum_{t=1}^{n} P(A|B_i|)P(B)_i \tag{2}$$

(4) Bayesian formula
According to the joint probability formula and the full probability formula, the Bayesian formula is derived:

$$P(B|A_i) = \frac{P(A|B_i|)P(B)_i}{\sum_{i=1}^{n} P(A|B_i|)P(B)_i} \tag{3}$$

In addition, we discuss Bayesian network adaptability in accident analysis in Sect. 2. Next we will briefly introduce Bayesian reasoning about accident analysis.

4.2.2 Bayesian Reasoning About Accident Analysis

Bayesian network as a probability-based uncertainty inference method has been widely used in the field of fault diagnosis. Backward reasoning in Bayesian networks is also called diagnostic reasoning. In traffic accidents, there are many causes of accidents that are not recorded at the time, unpredictable causes, or loss of records. At this time, we can use the Bayesian network structure of traffic accidents [10]. Under the conditions of known reasons or certain node conditions, we can conclude that some accidents are mainly crashes, collisions, and roadside cars. The probability of occurrence of accidents such as ditches, collision traffic barriers, and traffic signs.

The essence of Bayesian network reasoning is the joint probability distribution formula in structure and has given evidence of an event, computing the posterior probability of P (X|E), the joint probability distribution of the Bayesian network has been very mature algorithm of computing nodes and in the various kinds of evidence under the conditional probability distribution, and so on after the construction of a Bayesian network system, can be very convenient for the probabilistic safety assessment, including the important degree of probability, the consequences of the various events and other information.

5 Conclusion

In this paper, we introduced a system for analyzing traffic accidents. The system is mainly composed of seven parts, including accident basic information analysis, accident driver analysis, accident vehicle analysis, accident road analysis, large accident ledger, multi-dimensional accident analysis, and accident analysis report. In order to solve the multi-dimensional problem of data, the system adopts a multi-dimensional analysis model which is the core of the data warehouse technology to build the multi-dimensional data model. Further, bayesian network model is also used to analyze the traffic accidents in this paper.

Acknowledgement. This work is partially supported by Open Project of Key Laboratory of Ministry of Public Security for Road Traffic Safety (2017ZDSYSKFKT12-2). The corresponding author of this paper is Jiadong Sun. E-mail: 253195895@qq.com.

References

1. Wang, H.: Application of decision tree algorithm in the analysis of the causes of traffic accident. J. Anhui Sci. Technol. Univ. **27**(6), 74 (2013)
2. Feng, X.: The road traffic accident cause analysis and countermeasure research. Heilongjiangjiaotongkeji **33**(12), 111–112 (2010)
3. Ning, S., Feng, Z.: Analysis on the cause of road traffic accidents. Commun. Stand. **10**, 152–155 (2006)

4. Wang, H.: The Application of the Mining of Association Rules in Analysis of Traffic Accidents. Anhui University (2010)
5. Qi, Z., Tan, D., Meng, H.: Analysis of causes of road traffic accidents based on AHP. Sci. Technol. Inf. **3**, 195–196 (2011)
6. Chen, S.: Application of AHP method in the analysis of the causes of road traffic accidents in the city. Wuxi municipal design and Research Institute (z1), 129–131 (2009)
7. Chu, W.: Analysis of traffic accident mechanism based on clustering method. Automob. Appl. Technol. **4**, 16–18 (2013)
8. Ye, X.: Analysis of the causes of traffic accidents and causal analysis based on AHP method. Highw. Automot. Appl. **3**, 64–67 (2008)
9. Lin, Z.: The cause of traffic accident based on the theory of principal component analysis. J. Shandong Jiao Tong Univ. **14**(1), 55–57 (2006)
10. Liu, L.: Study on Statistic Analysis and Prediction Model of Road Traffic Accident. Chongqing University (2004)

Architecture and Parameter Analysis to Convolutional Neural Network for Hand Tracking

Hui Zhou[1,2(✉)], Minghao Yang[1,2,4], Hang Pan[1,2], Renjun Tang[1,2], Baohua Qiang[1], Jinlong Chen[1], and Jianhua Tao[2,3,4]

[1] Guangxi Key Laboratory of Cryptography and Information Security, Guilin University of Electronic Technology, Guilin 541004, Guangxi, China
zhouwork2017@foxmail.com
[2] National Key Laboratory of Pattern Recognition, Institute of Automation, Chinese Academy of Sciences, Beijing 100190, China
[3] University of Chinese Academy of Sciences, Beijing 100190, China
[4] Research Center for Brain-inspired Intelligence, Institute of Automation, Chinese Academy of Sciences, Beijing 100190, China

Abstract. Currently, the hand tracking based on deep learning has made good progress, but these literatures have less influence on the tracking accuracy of Convolutional Neural Network (CNN) architecture and parameters. In this paper, we proposed a new method to analyze the influence factors of gesture tracking. Firstly, we establish the gesture image and corresponding gesture parameter database based on virtual 3D human hand, on which the convolutional neural network models are constructed, after that we research some related factors, such as network structure, iteration times, data augmentation and Dropout, etc., that affect the performance of hand tracking. Finally we evaluate the objective parameters of the virtual hand, and make the subjective evaluation of the real hand extracted in the video. The results show that, on the premise of the fixed training amount of the hand, the effect of increasing the number of convolutional cores or convolution layers on the accuracy of the real gesture is not obvious, the data augmentation is obvious. For the real gesture, when the number of iterations and the Dropout ratio is about 20%–30%, good results can be obtained. This work provides the foundation for future application research on hand tracking.

Keywords: Hand tracking · Convolutional neural network · Deep learning
Data augmentation · Dropout

1 Introduction

In recent years, the applications based on gesture interaction have extensively been used in somatosensory games, smart home appliances, robot control, augmented reality and other fields. A concise and intelligent Human-Computer Interface (HCI) has become the major research fields for a new generation of intelligent HCI. At present it has formed a theory hot spot, also has made the very big progress [1, 2]. However,

© Springer Nature Switzerland AG 2018
X. Sun et al. (Eds.): ICCCS 2018, LNCS 11068, pp. 429–439, 2018.
https://doi.org/10.1007/978-3-030-00021-9_39

accurate, robust, real-time hand tracking is far more challenging. First of all, the hand pose exists in a high dimensional space because each finger and the palm is associated with several degrees of freedom. Furthermore, the fingers exhibit self-similarity, are flexible and often occlude each other. Secondly, most of images collected by the camera contain Gaussian noise and salt pepper noise, which make it difficult to match the synthetic images. Convolutional neural network can describe the nonlinear mapping process from hand image to hand parameters. Therefore, it is often used in hand tracking process. The CNN model affects directly the accuracy of hand tracking. However, some articles seldom analyze CNN structure and parameters in existing hand tracking methods. Consequently, it is very significant to study the CNN structure and related parameters to improve the accuracy of hand tracking.

Some foreign researchers had also done relevant research and established a hand database in the past few years [3–7]. Some public databases can be used for scientific research. However, there are some problems in hand database and its research: (1) The hand database of reference [3] is collected on the virtual 3D hand model, which avoids the problem of manual data annotation, but the hand model is based on the average of a certain population of the ideal model, the tracking effect of the real hand still remains to be verified. (2) The data collected in reference [4, 5] are real hand, of which reference [4] is the most widely used, most of the hand tracking algorithms are implemented in this database. There are two layers of six CNNs, each CNN contains 7 convolutional layers to hand tracking in [3]. In [4], to extract features of hand images, 3 parallel CNNs are proposed, and then the inverse kinematics algorithm is used to reconstruct the gestures in real time. A three-dimensional coordinate system for human gestures is proposed in [8], a CNN model from gesture images collected in different directions to extract gesture features, and finally fuses features in different directions to track gestures. However, these algorithms do not discuss the impact of different CNN structures and parameters on the accuracy of hand tracking. The thesis mainly analyzes the impact of some important parameters of CNNs, a common hand database based on virtual 3D hand models is built. On the basis of the classical convolutional neural network structure [9], a convolutional neural network model is objectively used to analyze the accuracy of virtual 3D hand tracking, and based on this. Subjective evaluation of the real hand extracted from the video is performed.

We demonstrate that the data augmentation is valid and can improve the hand tracking accuracy for real hand gesture, other factors such as network structure, iteration times, different dropout method and sigmoid activation function has also been used in our method, but the precision and robustness of the algorithm is limited, and is not very obvious.

The rest of this paper is organized as follows. Section 2 briefly describes our model assessment method. The hand database using spatial modeling technology is discussed in Sect. 3. Section 4 introduces the some related parameter and experimental results. Finally, conclusions are presented in Sect. 5.

2 Model Assessment Method

In this paper, the spatial modeling technology is used to build a model based on three-dimensional virtual hands, and the virtual hand image and parameter database are constructed by sampling the 3D hand model. Based on this database, convolutional neural networks are put forward to fit the real gesture data. Through the different network structure and parameter analysis, such as number of iterations, data augmentation, Dropout, etc., we establish the optimal structure and relevant parameters, and the influence of correlative parameter in this model is also evaluated objectively and subjectively. From the subjective stand, we also compare the performance of CNN related parameters on the model's error rate and accuracy by 10-fold cross-validation; and then the real hand images collected in the camera are used as test data, which are fed into the CNN network model subjectively. Through the subjective comparison of the difference between the input gesture and the output gesture, the network model is evaluated to be good or bad. Finally, on the basis of statistics, an optimal algorithm parameter is obtained with defined model. The overall evaluation method of the hand tracking algorithm is described in Fig. 1.

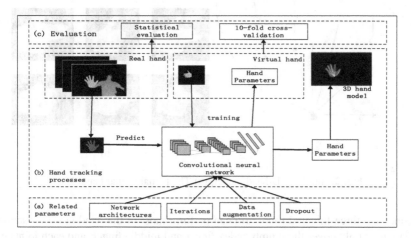

Fig. 1. An overview of the proposed approach for hand tracking. In algorithm, we construct our convolutional neural network based on virtual hand data, and segment the hand in a real-time video. (a) In order to evaluate performance of hand tracking for real hand, some related parameters of convolutional neural network are analyzed with control various methods. (b) the processes of hand tracking. (c) the method evaluation of convolutional neural network.

3 Database

The main difficulty lies in the fact that there is still the lack of training data in hand tracking. The traditional method use 3D sensors as acquisition devices to obtain real hand data [10]. However, with this approach, it is difficult to cover a large number of gestures, and its annotation error is large. Therefore, we present a spatial modeling method to build the synthetic image and parameter database [3, 11]. Because the data is automatically marked by the computer system, the data annotation problem is completely avoided. Accurate annotation can be generated together with the rendering of image. The 3D hand model based on the average size of the human hand within a certain range is constructed, which include 52 degrees of freedom. Each joints can rotate freely in space, and the vector is expressed as: $\theta^w = \left\{ \theta_x^w, \theta_y^w, \theta_Z^w \right\}$, where θ_x^w, θ_y^w and θ_z^w represent the rotation angles around the x, y, z axes. In order to conform to the movement habits of human gestures, corresponding restrictions that $\theta_x^w \in 0, \theta_y^w \in [-90, 0]$ and $\theta_z^w \in [-30, 30]$ are imposed on the rotation range of each joints in the hand model. A 25-dimensional vector is used to represent the movement of the gesture so as to be able to cover the overall movement range of the human gestures, as shown in Fig. 2(a) below.

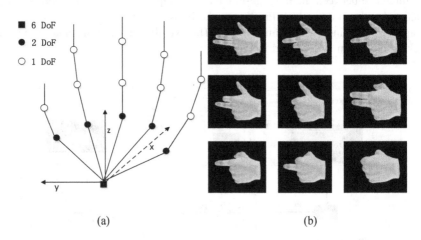

(a)   (b)

Fig. 2. (a) The 3D hand model, (b) The partial virtual hand data.

Since the three-fingered robot arm can perform most of the hand grasping actions, the data may only cover the thumb, index finger and middle finger, and each joints can rotate every 20°. The ring finger and the little finger remain closed. A 25-dimensional vector is created to drive the 3D hand model movement. Hand images can be automatically captured and saved. A total of 15,000 hand images and parameters are collected. To train the network, some hand images are shown in Fig. 2(b). Since the acquired virtual gesture image is composed of various resolution images, our system requires a constant input dimension. Therefore, the picture is down-sampled a fixed resolutions. The network is trained using the pixel values of the gray scaled image. At the same time, the collected gesture angle parameters are normalized and fed into the convolutional neural network together with the virtual gesture images.

Based on the acquired virtual hand database, a convolutional neural network is built. The specific structure of the network and related parameters are described below.

4 Network Structure and Related Parameter Analysis

4.1 Network Architecture

Figure 3 depicts the overall network structure for hand tracking. The network consists of 7 layers, including 2 convolutional layers, 2 down sampling layers and 3 fully connected layers. The output of the last 25-dimensional full-connection layer is sent to the sigmoid activation function, which distributes its result between 0 and 1. The result obtained is inversely normalized and the gesture parameters can be obtained.

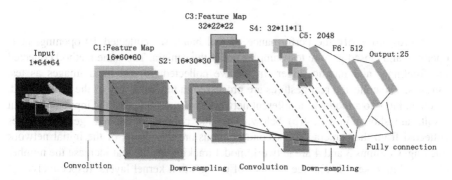

Fig. 3. The main architecture of convolutional neural network for hand tracking.

The first convolutional layer uses 16 cores of size 5×5, to filter a $64 \times 64 \times 1$ input images, the stride is equal to 1, and then down-sampling to reduce the network parameters. The second convolutional layer takes the output of the first convolutional layer and the down sampling layer as its own input, and uses 32 convolution kernels of size 9×9 for filtering. The second convolutional layer is connected to some of the neurons in the previous down sampling layer. All neurons in the fully connected layer are all connected to the neurons in the previous layer. The full connected layer has 2565 neurons in total. The number of neurons in the output layer is 25, as shown in Fig. 3.

In order to verify the influence of the change of the network structure on the accuracy of the gesture tracking, the above-mentioned virtual hand image and parameter database were used in the experiment, and 1500 samples were randomly selected as test sets.

Table 1 shows the training set and validation set error data for different network structures of virtual hand. Model 1 is the initial network model, and models 2 and 3 are the network models that increase the number of convolution kernels and the number of convolution layers, respectively. It can be seen that increasing the number of convolutional kernels and the number of convolutional layers can reduce the error of the training set and the verification set, but it has little impact on the tracking results of the entire network. The reason may be that the number of hand samples is small, it is possible that the changing network structure has little effect on the accuracy of the virtual hand tracking.

Table 1. The influence of different neural network structures on virtual hand

Number	Model 1	Model 2	Model 3
Convolution layers	2	2	4
C1 convolution kernel	16	32	16
C2 convolution kernel	32	64	16
C3 convolution kernel			32
C4 convolution kernel			32
Training set error	0.0576	0.0529	0.0549
Validation set error	0.0591	0.0543	0.0568

In order to verify the performance of real hand, we collected 10 opening, half-opening, and closed gesture test samples under the camera. The same method collected the forefinger and middle finger. In all, we collected 90 real hand images as test samples. The collected real gestures are processed in the same way as the virtual hand, and then input to a model of a different network structure. Some of the input and output results are shown in Fig. 4(b) below. The first column is the real gesture images collected from the camera. The second columns are the results of the initial network tracking. Columns 3 and 4 are network model tracking results that increase the number of convolution kernels and the number of convolution kernel layers, respectively. Let 32 students select which one is the most similar gestures between the input and output. The statistical results are shown in Fig. 4(a) below. As can be seen from the figure, the subjective contrasts of the output of the three models are very similar. After the network structure changes, the subjective comparison results of the real gestures are not clearly distinguished.

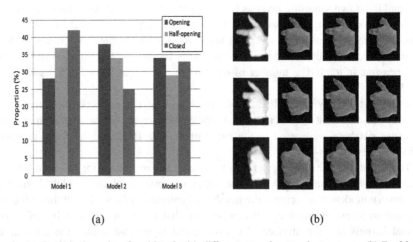

(a)   (b)

Fig. 4. (a) Statistical results of real hand with different neural network structures, (b) Real hand tracking results of different neural network structures.

4.2 Number of Iterations

For the general classification problem [9], with the increasing of iterations, the training error of the model will continuously decrease, and the test error will start to reach a minimum value. After reaching a certain number of iterations, the test error will increase. Once again, we change the iterations number of the network rather than the network parameters under the same data sets, the performance of hand tracking is evaluated from both subjective and objective aspects. The result of the hand tracking is shown in Fig. 5(a). As can be seen from the figure, as the number of iterations increases, the training error and test error of hand tracking continuously decrease from 27% to 2.72%, and the absolute error between the training set and the test set is within 1%. The reason for the analysis may be that the gesture itself has self-occlusion and similarity, so that the discriminative degree between the training set and the test set is small, and the test set tracking error decreases along with the training set.

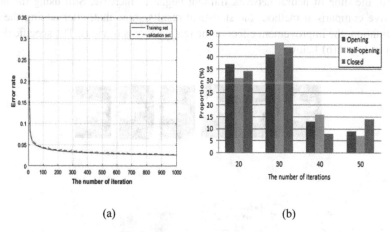

| (a) | (b) |

Fig. 5. (a) Training set error and validation set error for virtual hand, (b) Statistical results of different iterations for real hand.

Using the above real hand as a test set, 90 real hand images are fed into a neural network model under different iteration times. The difference between the subjective contrast input and output is determined. After the subjective evaluation, the statistical experimental results are shown in Fig. 5(b) below. It can be seen that the real hand works best when the number of iterations is 30. As the number of iterations increases, the tracking performance of the real hand drops sharply.

4.3 Data Augmentation

Data augmentation is one of the common methods to avoid over-fitting of the model [12]. Literature [1] adapts to random extraction of the gesture image boundary in units of 10 pixels to adapt to unclear gesture boundaries extracted from the real world. In [3], researchers have proposed a way to shorten the gap between the virtual gestures and the real gestures by adding random Gaussian noise, the above two methods are equivalent to increase the diversity of virtual gesture samples to reduce over-fitting phenomenon indirectly. This article simulates real gesture data by data augmentation, both of which allow transformed images to be from the original images with very little computation, so the transformed images do not need to be stored on disk. In our implementation, the transformed images are generated in Python code on the CPU while the GPU is training on the previous batch of images. So these data augmentation schemes are, in effect computationally free.

We still use the same dataset, and increase the number of sample by the data augmentation. The whole dataset contains 15,000 and 480,000 hand images. Some operations, for example translation, rotation, zoom-in, and zoom-out on the original image, increase the size of the training set by 32 times. Figure 6(a) shows some gesture images after data augmentation. By training data together with the original data, we find that the test error decreases from 5.65% to 4.42%. However, when the data are handled, the time of neural network training began to increase. Still using the above subjective comparison method, the statistical results show that, after adding the data augmentation, the improvement effect of the real gesture is obvious. The specific data is shown in Fig. 6(b) below.

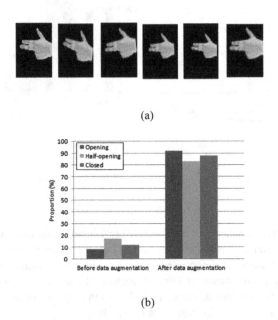

(a)

(b)

Fig. 6. (a) Some partial hand images after data augmentation, (b) Statistical results of data augmentation for real hand.

4.4   Dropout

Over-fitting is a serious problem in deep neural nets. Dropout is a technique for addressing this problem, which is often used to adjust the neural network structure [13,

14]. Consider a neural network with L hidden layers. Let $l \in \{1, \cdots, L\}$ index the hidden layers of network. Let z^l denote the vector of inputs into layer l, y^l denote the vector of outputs from layer l, The neural network can be described as

$$z_i^{l+1} = w_i^{l+1} y^l + b_i^{l+1} \tag{1}$$

$$y_i^{l+1} = f(z_i^{l+1}) \tag{2}$$

where f is activation function, w^l and b^l are the weights and bias at layer l.

With dropout, the neural network becomes

$$r_j^l \sim Bernoulli(p) \tag{3}$$

$$\tilde{y}^l = r^l * y^l \tag{4}$$

$$z_i^{l+1} = w_i^{l+1} \tilde{y}^l + b_i^{l+1} \tag{5}$$

$$y_i^{l+1} = f(z_i^{l+1}) \tag{6}$$

For any layer l, r^l is a vector of independent Bernoulli random variables each of which has probability p of being 1. Let p denotes the probability that the current neuron is discarded, * represents the product of the elements. In back-propagation, it sets the output of the hidden neurons of the hidden layer to 0 with a probability p, thereby it looks like a more "lean" network. Neurons discarded in this way are neither involved in forward propagation nor in reverse propagation. Therefore, every random drop of a neuron is equivalent to learning a different structure for the neural network, which is equivalent to adding a raw hand training sample.

As for Dropout, a corresponding experiment was performed. In the network shown in Fig. 3, the dropout probability of 0.25, 0.5, and 0.75 are added into the second convolutional layer respectively. After the same number of iterations, the result of training set and test set is shown in Fig. 7(a). It can be seen from the figure that for virtual hand, the error of hand tracking increases with the increase of p. This phenomenon show clearly that self-occlusion exists between gestures, which results in little differentiation between gestures. The neural network also considers the test set as train set, so the tracking error of test and training set are rising. For the real hand, the same subjective comparison experiments have been carried out. The statistical results are shown in Fig. 7(b). From the figure, we can see that when p equals 0.25, the best tracking performance can be obtained on real gestures, and continues to increase the p ratio. The hand tracking performance gradually deteriorates.

In summary, the accuracy of real-hand tracking is closely related to the neural network structure and related parameters. Based on the classical LeNet-5 convolutional neural network architecture [9], it can be seen from the experiment that increasing the number of convolutional layers or convolutional kernels has little effect on improving the accuracy of hand tracking, with the amount of training samples being constant.

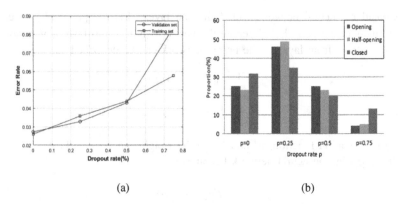

(a)   (b)

Fig. 7. (a) Virtual hand training set and test set error rate, (b) Statistical results of different dropout for real hand

Data augmentation has a significant impact on the promotion of hand tracking. The Dropout ratio and iterations are best when they are approximately 20%–30%.

5   Conclusion

We analyze the influence of different network architecture and parameters, and construct a convolutional neural network model based on the virtual hand database. We find that the accuracy of hand tracking is closely correlated with CNNs structures and parameters statistically. The statistical results showed that: under the certain training amount of samples, increasing the number of convolutional kernel and layers has little influence on hand tracking. However, the effect on improving tracking performance is prominent by using data augmentation, and other factors such as different dropout and activation functions can also alter the accuracy of hand tracking, but these factors have only a small impact on the accuracy. Furthermore, it is reasonable to set the iterations and dropout ratios to 20%–30%. Future work will focus on ways such that system can accurately track by using three cameras when the hand self-occlusion exists. Another line of future work is to improve the accuracy of hand tracking for real hand.

Acknowledgments. This research work is supported by the grant of National key Research and development technology project (2016YFB1001404), 863 plan project (2015AA016305), Guangxi Science and Technology Project (AB17195053), Guangxi Natural Science Fund (2017GXNSFAA198226), National Natural Science Fund (61332017, 61375027, 61273288, 61425017, 61233009), Guangxi Key Laboratory of Trusted Software of Guilin University of Electronic Technology (KX201601), The funding project of the graduate education innovation program of Guilin University of Electronic Technology (2017YJCX55, 2018YJCX43), Guangxi Colleges and Universities Key Laboratory of Intelligent Processing of Computer Images and Graphics of Guilin University of Electronic Technology (No: GIIP201602), Guangxi Key Laboratory of Cryptography & Information Security of Guilin University of Electronic Technology (No: GCIS201601).

References

1. Sharp, T., Keskin, C., Robertson, D., et al.: Accurate, robust, and flexible real-time hand tracking. In: Proceedings of ACM Conference on Human Factors in Computing Systems, pp. 3633–3642 (2015)
2. Dipietro, L., Sabatini, A.M., Dario, P.: A survey of glove-based systems and their applications. IEEE Trans. Syst. Man Cybern. Part C. **38**(4), 461–482 (2008)
3. Sinha, A., Choi, C., Ramani, K.: Deephand: robust hand pose estimation by completing a matrix imputed with deep features. In: Proceedings of Computer Vision and Pattern Recognition, pp. 4150–4158 (2016)
4. Tompson, J., Stein, M., Lecun, Y., et al.: Real-time continuous pose recovery of human hands using convolutional networks. ACM Trans. Graph. **33**(5), 1–10 (2014)
5. Tang, D., Chang, H.J., Tejani, A., et al.: Latent regression forest: structured estimation of 3D articulated hand posture. In: Proceedings of Conference on Computer Vision and Pattern Recognition, pp. 3786–3793(2014)
6. Qian, C., Sun, X., Wei, Y., et al.: Realtime and robust hand tracking from depth. In: Proceedings of Computer Vision and Pattern Recognition, pp. 110–1113 (2014)
7. Song, S., Xiao, J.: Sliding shapes for 3D object detection in depth images. In: Proceedings of European Conference on Computer Vision, pp. 634–651 (2014)
8. Ge, L., Liang, H., Yuan, J., et al.: Robust 3D hand pose estimation in single depth images: from single-view CNN to multi-view CNNs. In: Proceedings of Computer Vision and Pattern Recognition, pp. 3593–3601(2016)
9. Lécun, Y., Bottou, L., Bengio, Y., et al.: Gradient-based learning applied to document recognition. Proc. IEEE **86**(11), 2278–2324 (1998)
10. Navaratnam, R., Fitzgibbon, A.W., Cipolla, R.: The joint manifold model for semi-supervised multi-valued regression. In: Proceedings of International Conference on Computer Vision, pp. 1–8 (2007)
11. Ning, H., Xu, W., Gong, Y., et al.: Discriminative learning of visual words for 3D human pose estimation. In: Proceedings of Computer Vision and Pattern Recognition, pp. 1–8 (2008)
12. Krizhevsky, A., Sutskever, I., Hinton, G.E.: ImageNet classification with deep convolutional neural networks. In: International Conference on Neural Information Processing Systems, pp. 1097–1105 (2012)
13. Srivastava, N., Hinton, G., Krizhevsky, A., et al.: Dropout: a simple way to prevent neural networks from overfitting. J. Mach. Learn. Res. **15**(1), 1929–1958 (2014)
14. Bouthillier, X., Konda, K., Vincent, P., et al.: Dropout as data augmentation. Comput. Sci. **32**(6), 1–11 (2016)

Attention-Based Bidirectional Recurrent Neural Networks for Description Generation of Videos

Xiaotong Du[✉], Jiabin Yuan, and Hu Liu

College of Computer Science and Technology, Nanjing University
of Aeronautics and Astronautics, Nanjing, China
{xtdu,jbyuan,lhu}@nuaa.edu.cn

Abstract. Describing videos in human language is of vital importance
in many applications, such as managing massive videos on line and
providing descriptive video service (DVS) for blind people. In order
to further promote existing video description frameworks, this paper
presents an end-to-end deep learning model incorporating Convolutional
Neural Networks (CNNs) and Bidirectional Recurrent Neural Networks
(BiRNNs) based on a multimodal attention mechanism. Firstly, the
model produces richer video representations, including image feature,
motion feature and audio feature, than other similar researches. Secondly,
BiRNNs model encodes these features in both forward and backward
directions. Finally, an attention-based decoder translates sequential outputs of encoder to sequential words. The model is evaluated on Microsoft
Research Video Description Corpus (MSVD) dataset. The results demonstrate the necessity of combining BiRNNs with a multimodal attention
mechanism and the superiority of this model over other state-of-the-art
methods conducted on this dataset.

Keywords: Video description · Convolutional Neural Networks
Bidirectional Recurrent Neural Networks · Attention mechanism

1 Introduction

Translating open-domain videos to natural language has many applications,
ranging from labeling and managing massive videos on public networks to providing DVS for visually impaired people. Video description research has recently
received considerable interest from computer vision and artificial intelligence
areas, which is simulated by early work in image captioning [1]. An image description method is proposed in [2] which uses a recurrent neural network (RNN) to
train the bidirectional mapping between images and descriptive sentences. These
deep learning methods have also been successfully exploited in video captioning
[3–5]. However, generated description is not as accurate as manual translation
of the video, the improvement of accuracy is still a difficult job.

© Springer Nature Switzerland AG 2018
X. Sun et al. (Eds.): ICCCS 2018, LNCS 11068, pp. 440–451, 2018.
https://doi.org/10.1007/978-3-030-00021-9_40

Typical video description model based on deep learning methods is composed of two networks, namely, CNNs and RNN. The former is used to extract video features and RNN takes these features as input and then outputs sequential words. [4] firstly applied AlexNet, one of CNNs, to extract RGB feature of video representation frames. After mean pooling operation, sequential vectors are input into RNN which is composed of two layers of long short-term memory units (LSTMs). Finally, sequential words are output one by one based on video features and the previous word. This model is effective but not that accurate. [5] proposed a novel end-to-end video description network which extends the RNN model to two stages, encoding and decoding. In addition, it considers optical flow feature as well as static image feature. However, this is a basic model which can make further improvement.

This paper mainly proposes three aspects of improvement. The first is multimodal features. Video contains much more information than image, so that static RGB feature could not fully express the video. In order to obtain as much information as possible, the other three important features are included. Optical flow feature is extracted from ResNet [6], and through 3-dimensional (3D) CNNs [7], C3D feature is added. These two features contain action cues based on visual information while audio feature is another representation of the video. The second improvement is bidirectional RNN which has been used in some researches [8,9]. This model can encode features in both forward and backward directions to capture comprehensive temporal information. Attention-based decoder is the last improvement. [10] creatively applied the attention mechanism on the neural network machine translation (NMT) which is a typical sequence to sequence, namely encoder-decoder model. Because of the similar framework, video description model can introduce this method as well. Former study [8,11] incorporated a soft attention model after feature encoding to increase performance while this paper applies a multimodal attention method in consideration of effective fusion of different modal features.

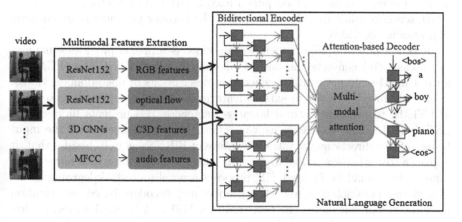

Fig. 1. Attention-based bidirectional video description model (Color figure online)

Figure 1 depicts the whole framework, called attention-based bidirectional video description network (ABiVDN). Firstly, video is converted to parallel multichannel inputs and different modal features (orange rectangles) of the video are extracted from respective models (yellow rectangles). Each feature is represented by sequential vectors and then input into a bidirectional encoder which is composed of three layers of computation units. The first two layers of LSTMs (green rectangles) compute vectors of hidden states of forward and backward feature sequences respectively and the third layer (blue rectangles) combines outputs of these two directions. Finally, hidden states of each modal feature are input into decoding stage which is comprised of an attention-based fusion mechanism and one-layer LSTMs to generate sequential words. ABiVDN has achieved state-of-the-art result on MSVD dataset which can indicate the effectiveness of these improvements.

The remaining sections of this paper are organized as follows. Related work on video description is introduced in Sect. 2, and then Sect. 3 illustrates the architecture and procedure of ABiVDN explicitly. Details of experiment are shown in Sect. 4. Section 5 presents the conclusion, along with advice for future work.

2   Related Work

Automatic video captioning is a high-level semantic understanding of the video which is motivated by the success of image captioning [1,2]. Early work [3] mainly studies video description of fixed actions under simple scenes. [12] uses known sentential templates to generate sentences from detected action class together with knowledge of the participants.

With the development of deep learning techniques, recent study has extended to describe videos with complex and unknown behavior under open scenes [13]. However, most of these methods follow a holistic framework, namely, encoder-decoder architecture, which was originally used in NMT [14]. The main difference is that, the encoder in NMT outputs a fixed-length feature vector of source language sentence while in video description, the encoder produces representation of frames in the video.

Recent study [3–5,15] on open-domain video description provides some useful models. [16] converts the basic CNNs into several fully CNNs (FCNs) to form a multi-scale network for generating descriptions of open-domain videos. It uses improved AlexNet to extract features, and RNNs, especially two layers of LSTMs, to generate natural language sentences. [17] presents bidirectional LSTMs (BiLSTMs) to deeply capture global temporal structure in the input frames of two directions. [8] takes advantage of BiRNNs as well, besides that, it applies a soft attention model in decoding stage to decide on which parts of the input video should be focused. [18] proposes a novel multi-task learning model that shares parameters across the encoders and decoders based on attention mechanism and it achieves the best result on MSVD dataset. However, models above lack of researches on other important video features except raw images and the accuracy of the result remains to be improved.

[7] provides a new video feature, namely, convolution 3D (C3D) feature, which is obtained by training a deep 3-dimensional convolutional network on a large annotated video dataset. It works great on video classification task. In addition, audio is an important characteristic of open-domain videos as well which already has many successful applications, such as audio classification [19] and speech recognition [20]. Some researches [21,22] on video captioning have considered other modal information, like audio or C3D feature. However, they lack sufficient theoretical analysis and do not fully use multimodal information because of the employment of simple one-layer LSTMs in language generation model.

Considering problems above, a general and efficient end-to-end video description model is proposed. Main contributions of this paper are as follows: (1) Making use of multimodal characteristics including RGB images, optical flow, C3D as well as audio feature to improve performance on current study. (2) This paper proposes a novel natural language model by integrating several bidirectional encoders composed of three layers of computation units and an attention-based multimodal decoder. (3) Experimental results on MSVD dataset demonstrate the superiority of this model over other state-of-the-art methods.

3 Approach

The whole model is made up of two parts, namely, multimodal feature extraction and natural language generation (Fig. 1). The second part is composed of bidirectional encoders and an attention-based decoder. This section introduces ABiVDN in detail according to its procedure.

3.1 Multimodal Features Extraction

Feature extraction model makes video as multichannel inputs and incorporates the following features through different models to provide comprehensive representation of the video. Feature extraction is processed by multiple graphics processing units (GPUs). And then these features are input into BiLSTMs respectively.

RGB Image Feature: It is a basic feature in video analysis which is mostly extracted from deep CNNs, especially from AlexNet [5,16] or VGGNet [17,18]. This paper applied the winner model of ImageNet Large Scale Visual Recognition Challenge (ILSVRC) in 2015, ResNet152 [6], to extract static RGB feature. ResNet is much deeper than the other two CNNs models above, therefore it can obtain more strong representations of objects and scenes in frames of the video. ImageNet dataset is used to pre-train the model which can help to recognize more objects in the wild. A 1000 dimensional vector from fc1000 layer of ResNet is chosen as the RGB image feature of each frame in the video.

Optical Flow Feature: This is a normal video feature which contains dynamic information between two image frames. Firstly, fast TV-L1 method [23] is employed to compute optical flow values of two continuous frames. These values indicate the speed of instantaneous movement of each pixel point which are represented as two-dimensional matrices. And then optical flow pictures are obtained by conversing these matrices to gray images. Because the velocity has two directions, each pixel point has two optical flow values, $2 \times (n-1)$ gray pictures are produced from the video has n frames. After that, ResNet152 which is pre-trained on UCF-101 dataset is used to extract features from optical flow images. Finally, by combining two 1000-dimensional vectors of fc1000 layer in both directions of the same frame, a 2000-dimensional vector is obtained to denote optical flow feature of each frame.

C3D Feature: Though optical flow feature has motion information, C3D feature [24] contains action cues over longer sequential frames. It is extracted by a deep 3D CNNs which improves traditional 2D convolution kernel to 3D. For example, the input of model converts from $H \times W$ to $H \times W \times L$ when extending a $k \times k$ kernel to $k \times k \times d$ where $H \times W$ is the size of video frame and L is always bigger than d. Sport-1M dataset is applied to pre-train original 3D CNNs, and then a 4096-dimensional vector is obtained after fc6 layer of the model to represent C3D feature of sequential L ($L = 16$ in this paper) frames in video.

Audio Feature: Previous researches on video processing mainly focus on visual and motion cues but ignore the importance of audio. Most video datasets have no sound including MSVD, therefore, this paper collected existing videos of MSVD from YouTube. Audio contains latent information of people and objects different from features above. Mel-frequency cepstral coefficients (MFCCs) are the most popular audio characteristics which can be indicated by a 13-dimensional vector. Besides these, other 21 values, such as the zero crossing, are added together to form audio feature [25]. Final audio descriptor is represented by average value and standard deviation of audio feature (34 dimensions), namely, a 68 dimensional vector.

3.2 Bidirectional Encoder

Natural language model can be divided into two stages, encoding and decoding. The former part, bidirectional encoder, takes sequences of video representation, that is, feature vectors $F(f_1, f_2, \ldots, f_n)$ as input where f_i indicates i-th feature vector and outputs sequential hidden states. Each modal feature, such as F_{RGB} or F_{C3D}, is entered into a single encoder (Fig. 2).

As seen in Fig. 2, an encoder is composed of three layers of computation units, the first LSTMs layer computes a sequence of hidden states $H^f(h_1^f, h_2^f, \ldots, h_n^f)$ of forward feature sequence, that is, $F(f_1, f_2, \ldots, f_n)$, according to Eq. 1 where the LSTM calculation formula is introduced in [26], the second layer computes for backward feature sequence and outputs $H^b(h_1^b, h_2^b, \ldots, h_n^b)$ (Eq. 2). And then $H^m(h_1^m, h_2^m, \ldots, h_n^m)$ is obtained by combining two directional outputs through the third layer.

$$h_t^f = LSTM(h_{t-1}^f, f_t; \lambda^f) \tag{1}$$

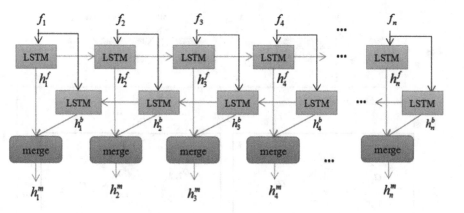

Fig. 2. Bidirectional encoder

$$h_t^b = LSTM(h_{t+1}^b, f_t; \lambda^b) \qquad (2)$$

For a given video, for example, its RGB image feature is $F_1(f_{11}, f_{12}, \ldots, f_{1n})$ where n is the number of representative frames in the video and f_{1i} is a 1000-dimensional vector. After the processing of BiLSTMs, two directions hidden states are produced, H_1^f and H_1^b. Both of them have n J-dimensional vectors where J is the size of each forward or backward hidden state. Then the encoder combines the sequence H_1^f and H_1^b by concatenating vectors according to their positions, such as h_{1i}^f and h_{1i}^b. Finally, a sequence $H_1^m(h_{11}^m, h_{12}^m, \ldots, h_{1n}^m)$ is produced which has n feature vectors and each vector has $2 \times J$ dimensions. Other modal features are handled with similar encoders and numbered in order, so that four modal sequence vectors are obtained, namely, H_1 to H_4.

3.3   Attention-Based Decoder

The second part of natural language model is an attention-based decoder. It takes hidden state vectors of multiple features as input, such as $H_1(h_{11}, h_{12}, \ldots, h_{1n})$ and $H_2(h_{21}, h_{22}, \ldots, h_{2n})$, and outputs a sentence composed of sequential words, that is, $W(w_1, w_2, \ldots, w_m)$.

Figure 3 depicts the decoder which is composed of a multimodal feature fusion method and one-layer LSTMs. Attention mechanism enables the network to focus on hidden states from specific times or spatial regions considering the current context, in order to predict the next word more accurately. This paper uses a multimodal attention mechanism for handling multiple hidden states from parallel encoders. And then feature fusion vectors $D(d_1, d_2, \ldots, d_m)$ are input into LSTMs in sequence to generate the word one by one until the $< eos >$ (end-of-sentence) tag is emitted. Followings are the details of the calculation process.

The multimodal attention mechanism defines attention weights over hidden states throughout the input sequence. For i-th output, each modal feature is

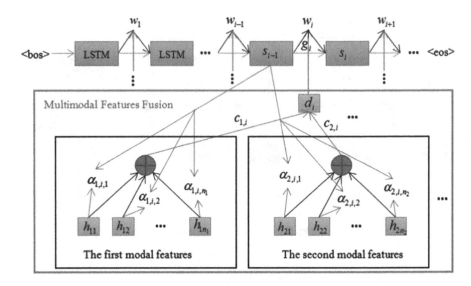

Fig. 3. Attention-based Decode

represented by a weighted sum of all hidden states, see Eq. 3, where $\alpha_{j,i,l}$ is an attention weight between the i-th output word and the l-th hidden state of j-th modal feature. The computation of attention weights can refer to [10].

$$c_{j,i} = \sum_{t=1}^{N} \alpha_{j,i,l} h_{j,t} \tag{3}$$

And then these weighted sums are combined into one vector according to Eq. 4 for feature fusion where W_{cj} indicates weight matric of j-th modal feature ($j \in [1,4]$). In fusion stage, Eq. 5 is computed as the activation vector, in which b_s is the bias value.

$$d_i = W_{c1}c_{1,i} + W_{c2}c_{2,i} + W_{c3}c_{3,i} + W_{c4}c_{4,i} \tag{4}$$

$$g_i = tanh(W_s s_{i-1} + d_i + b_s) \tag{5}$$

Then the probability distribution of output is obtained according to Eq. 6. Finally, word y_i is generated by Eq. 7 where V represents the dictionary produced from sentences of dataset.

$$P(y|s_{i-1}, c_{1i}, c_{2i}, c_{3i}, c_{4i}) = sofymax(W_g g_i + b_g) \tag{6}$$

$$y_i = \operatorname*{argmax}_{y \in V} P(y|s_{i-1}, c_{1i}, c_{2i}, c_{3i}, c_{4i}) \tag{7}$$

The $< bos >$ tag (begin-of-sentence) commands the LSTMs to generate words and the $< eos >$ tag terminates the sentence generation. During testing, the model begins to choose word y_i with the maximum probability after the softmax operation until the $< eos >$ tag is output.

4 Experimental Setup

This section introduces details of the experiment, such as the dataset, evaluation protocols, and parameter settings in the model. At last, results and analysis for ABiVDN compared with other methods are given.

4.1 Dataset

The MSVD dataset is a collection of YouTube clips within 8s to 25s. It contains 85k English descriptions corresponding to 1970 open-domain videos. In order to add audio feature, a total of 1600 existing videos of MSVD are collected from YouTube website for clipping out the audio information.

4.2 Evaluation Protocols

METEOR is originally used in evaluating machine translation results [27], because of analogous evaluation criteria, it is applied in video description model as well. The previous study showed that the results based on METEOR are more highly correlated with manual judgments than those based on precision criteria like Bilingual Evaluation understudy (BLEU) [28]. METEOR precisely compares token matches, stemmed tokens, semantic similarity matches, and paraphrase matches by WordNet synonyms, which guarantees high reliability.

4.3 Implementation Details

The time steps of LSTMs in encoder is set to 80 which has been proved to get a good balance between memory consumption and feature extraction. This paper uses average extraction method over entire video and if the total length of frames is shorter than 80, then filling in blanks with zeros. As a result, each modal feature is represented by a matric $F(f_1, f_2, \ldots, f_{80})$.

For the numbers of training and testing data, except audio information, there are 1570 data for training and 400 data for testing. A total of 1200 audios are randomly chosen for training and the rest 400 audios for testing. The evaluations depend on the testing results. In decoding stage, the batch size is set to 50 and learning rate is automatically set by Adadelta method [29]. The parameters of the network are randomly initialized.

4.4 Results and Discussion

Table 1 shows comparison results of using combinations of different modal features in ABiVDN. It is obvious that the combination of all modal features achieved the best result (METEOR: 37.9%, BLEU-4: 55.5%) on MSVD dataset. The result value represents METEOR value if there is no special mention.

The results above demonstrate that compared with optical flow and C3D features, results are 34.3% and 34.8% respectively, audio plays a more important

Table 1. Performance of combinations different modal features

Features	METEOR(%)	BLEU-4(%)
RGB+Optical Flow	34.3	49.7
RGB+C3D	34.8	50.2
RGB+Audio	35.6	50.9
RGB+Optical Flow+C3D	36.1	51.2
RGB+Optical Flow+C3D+Audio	**37.9**	**55.5**

role, gets 35.6%, when fusing with static RGB image feature. These data proves the necessity of using audio information in video analysis as it performs better than action information in some cases. In addition, it is easy to find that the quality of output is positively related to the quantity of different features. For example, the result of integrating RGB images, optical flow and C3D features as a whole input is 36.1% in METEOR which is higher than only fusing RGB images with optical flow or C3D. BLEU values demonstrate the same conclusions as well.

Table 2. Comparison of ABiVDN with recent advanced models on MSVD

Model	Features	Bidirectional	Attention	METEOR(%)
LSTM-YT$_{coco}$ [4]	RGB	No	No	29.07
S2VT [5]	RGB+Optical Flow	No	No	29.8
Joint-BiLSTM [9]	RGB	Yes	No	30.3
BLSTM [8]	RGB	Yes	Yes	32.6
Multi-Task Model [14]	RGB	Yes	Yes	36
ABiVDN (ours)	**RGB+Optical Flow+C3D+Audio**	**Yes**	**Yes**	**37.9**

Table 2 lists some successful approaches during recent years on video description generation task for comparing with ABiVDN in this paper. [4] translates videos directly to sentences using an unified deep neural network with both convolutional and recurrent structure. [5] proposes the first end-to-end video captioning network incorporating RGB image and optical flow features. BiLSTMs model in [9] deeply capture global temporal information in videos. [8] devises a combination of CNNs and BiRNNs based on a soft attention mechanism. Multi-task model [14] is the state-of-the-art approach as it shares parameters across the encoder and decoder of the unsupervised video prediction and entailment generation tasks.

ABiVDN achieves the best result (37.9%) compared with other advanced methods, in which the best score is 36%. Results prove the efficiency of multimodal attention-based BiRNNs and the superiority of our model. At last, this paper provide a better understanding of the model through several examples shown in Fig. 4.

Videos	Descriptions
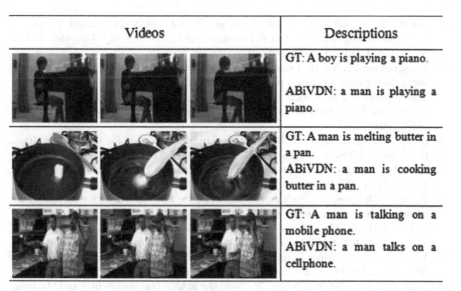	GT: A boy is playing a piano. ABiVDN: a man is playing a piano.
	GT: A man is melting butter in a pan. ABiVDN: a man is cooking butter in a pan.
	GT: A man is talking on a mobile phone. ABiVDN: a man talks on a cellphone.

Fig. 4. Some videos and predicted sentences. (GT) shows the ground truth sentences

5 Conclusion

In conclusion, this paper proposes an end-to-end attention-based bidirectional video description network (ABiVDN). The model could effectively extract multiple features from variable lengths of videos. In addition, attention-based bidirectional language model enables the network to capture more temporal information in entire video. Results on MSVD dataset show the advantage of ABiVDN over state-of-the-art approaches. Additional feature representations of video and improvement in the natural language model could also be explored in the future.

Acknowledgments. This work was supported by Research and Industrialization for Intelligent Video Processing Technology based on GPUs Parallel Computing of the Science and Technology Supported Program of Jiangsu Province (BY2016003-11) and the Application platform and Industrialization for efficient cloud computing for Big data of the Science and Technology Supported Program of Jiangsu Province (BA2015052).

References

1. Kulkarni, G., Premraj, V., Ordonez, V.: BabyTalk: understanding and generating simple image descriptions. IEEE Trans. Pattern Anal. Mach. Intell. **35**(12), 2891–2903 (2013)
2. Chen, X., Zitnick, C.L.: Mind's eye: a recurrent visual representation for image caption generation. In: IEEE Computer Vision and Pattern Recognition, pp. 2422–2431 (2015)

3. Rohrbach, M., Qiu, W., Titov, I., et al.: Translating video content to natural language descriptions. In: IEEE International Conference on Computer Vision, pp. 433–440. IEEE Computer Society (2013)

4. Venugopalan, S., Xu, H., Donahue, J., et al.: Translating videos to natural language using deep recurrent neural networks. Comput. Sci. (2014)

5. Venugopalan, S., Rohrbach, M., Donahue, J., et al.: Sequence to sequence - video to text. In: IEEE International Conference on Computer Vision, pp. 4534–4542. IEEE (2015)

6. He, K., Zhang, X., Ren, S., Sun, J.: Deep residual learning for image recognition. In: Computer Vision and Pattern Recognition, pp. 770–778 (2015)

7. Tran, D., Bourdev, L., Fergus, R., et al.: C3D: Generic Features for Video Analysis. Eprint Arxiv (2014)

8. Peris, A., Bolanos, M., Radeva, P., Casacuberta, F.: Video description using bidirectional recurrent neural networks. In: Villa, A., Masulli, P., Rivero, A. (eds.) ICANN 2016. LNCS, vol. 9887, pp. 3–11. Springer, Cham (2016). https://doi.org/10.1007/978-3-319-44781-0_1

9. Yi, B., Yang, Y., Shen, F., et al.: Bidirectional long-short term memory for video description. In: ACM on Multimedia Conference, pp. 436–440. ACM (2016)

10. Bahdanau, D., Cho, K., Bengio, Y.: Neural machine translation by jointly learning to align and translate. Comput. Sci.(2014)

11. Yao, L., Torabi, A., Cho, K., et al.: Video description generation incorporating spatio-temporal features and a soft-attention mechanism. Eprint Arxiv **53**, 199–211 (2015)

12. Barbu, A., Bridge, A., Burchill, Z., et al.: Video in sentences out. In: Twenty-Eighth Conference on Uncertainty in Artificial Intelligence. arXiv, 274–283 (2012)

13. Yu, H., Wang, J., Huang, Z., et al.: Video paragraph captioning using hierarchical recurrent neural networks. In: Computer Vision and Pattern Recognition, pp. 4584–4593. IEEE (2016)

14. Cho, K., Van Merrienboer, B., Bahdanau, D., et al.: On the properties of neural machine translation: encoder-decoder approaches. Comput. Sci. (2014)

15. Venugopalan, S., Hendricks, L.A., Mooney, R., et al.: Improving LSTM-based video description with linguistic knowledge mined from text. In: Conference on Empirical Methods in Natural Language Processing, Austin, Texas, pp. 1961–1966 (2016)

16. Xu, H., Venugopalan, S., Ramanishka, V., et al.: A multi-scale multiple instance video description network. Comput. Sci. **6738**, 272–279 (2015)

17. Bin Y, Yang Y, Shen F, et al. Bidirectional long-short term memory for video description. In: ACM on Multimedia Conference, pp. 436–440 (2016)

18. Pasunuru, R., Bansal, M.: Multi-task video captioning with video and entailment generation. In: Meeting of the Association for Computational Linguistics, pp. 1273–1283 (2017)

19. Hershey, S., Chaudhuri, S., Ellis, D.P.W., et al.: CNN architectures for large-scale audio classification. In: IEEE International Conference on Acoustics, Speech and Signal Processing. 2379–190X (2017)

20. Abdel-Hamid, O., Mohamed, A.R., Jiang, H., et al.: Convolutional neural networks for speech recognition. IEEE/ACM Trans. Audio Speech Lang. Process. **22**(10), 1533–1545 (2014)

21. Jin, Q., Chen, J., Chen, S., et al.: Describing videos using multi-modal fusion. In: ACM on Multimedia Conference, pp. 1087–1091. ACM (2016)

22. Ramanishka, V., Das, A., Dong, H.P., et al.: Multimodal video description. In: ACM on Multimedia Conference, pp. 1092–1096. ACM (2016)

23. D'Angelo, E., Paratte, J., Puy, G., et al.: Fast TV-L1 optical flow for interactivity. In: IEEE International Conference on Image Processing, pp. 1885–1888. IEEE (2011)
24. Tran, D., Bourdev, L., Fergus, R., et al.: Learning Spatiotemporal Features with 3D Convolutional Networks. eprint arXiv:1412.0767 (2014)
25. Giannakopoulos, T.: pyAudioAnalysis: an open-source python library for audio signal analysis. Plos One **10**(12), e0144610 (2015)
26. Srivastava, N., Mansimov, E., Salakhutdinov, R.: Unsupervised Learning of Video Representations using LSTMs. eprint arXiv:1502.04681 (2015)
27. Denkowski, M., Lavie, A.: Meteor universal: language specific translation evaluation for any target language. In: The Workshop on Statistical Machine Translation, pp. 376–380 (2014)
28. Papineni, K., Roukos, S., Ward, T., Zhu, W.J.: BLEU: a method for automatic evaluation of machine translation. Meeting on Association for Computational Linguistics **4**, 311–318 (2002)
29. Zeiler, M.D.: ADADELTA: an adaptive learning rate method. Comput. Sci. (2012)

Based on Data Analysis and JC Retrofit Scheme of Dam Risk Function and the Simulation Experiment

Chao Zhang[1], Lei Zhang[1], Junmei Wang[1(✉)], Pingzeng Liu[1,2], Yong Zheng[2], and Wanming Ren[2]

[1] Department of Mathematics, Shandong Agricultural University, Tai'an 271018, China
jmwang@sdau.edu.cn
[2] Shandong Provincial Agricultural Information Center, Ji'nan 250013, China

Abstract. The hydropower dam construction and transformation of research involves the social politics, economy, environment and other aspects of content, both in theoretical system and production practice is of great significance in this paper, from the perspective of the cascade reservoirs, the purpose is to use the method of probability theory, analyzing the various factors influencing the design flood of cascade reservoirs, and transformation of cascade reservoirs are studied by using JC method determine the principle of design flood, and using the theory of the zambezi river Carrie and the replacement of the dam for the design of the simulation and experiment.

Keywords: JC model · Harris corner detection · Water diversion strategy for Multi-dam system · MATLAB simulink simulation technology

1 Background

Upstream reservoir flood regulating role changed the design of section downstream natural flood peak discharge and flood process line shape of the actual time, changing the design of the probability distribution of the flood, in order to derive the design flood design section, the most direct way is to measured data according to the reservoir flood discharge and flood regulating rules to simulate flood year by year, calculate in the cross section of the design flood process line, get the statistics after affected by reservoir flood regulating the eigenvalues of the design of flood series, according to the reservoir flood influence after the series of flood frequency calculation will have the practical difficulties, on the one hand, this series of difficult to use any of the known frequency curve line to fit, to achieve the purpose of epitaxy. On the other hand, according to the range according to the experience of the dot frequency is also difficult to use a smooth curve fitting, the extension trend is uncertain "especially analyzed some reservoirs, flood fluctuation mutations in some frequency, frequency curve of experience even modest, is likely to be" there is a big error, therefore, in practice, are seeking under the certain condition of generalized approximate calculation method [1–3].

© Springer Nature Switzerland AG 2018
X. Sun et al. (Eds.): ICCCS 2018, LNCS 11068, pp. 452–463, 2018.
https://doi.org/10.1007/978-3-030-00021-9_41

The design flood calculation of cascade reservoir generally involves the design flood caused by the influence of the upstream reservoir. Two reservoirs of cascade reservoirs is one of the most common, has certain representativeness, because of multistage reservoir can be seen as two levels of various combinations of reservoir "especially in the process of dam alternative multistage series will be directly determined by the total storage capacity of the dam design, sum up, the meaning of design flood should include the following: [4–6]

(1) Water conservancy and hydropower projects, the design flood is the floorboard of the various standards of flood control safety design basis flood" it includes both expressed in frequency flood, also include the possible maximum flood. It includes both the flood and the very operational flood of the normal operation of the permanent waterworks, and the flood that was used during the construction period to design temporary buildings. (2) In the case of flood with frequency, the design flood generally includes flood peak period and flood process line. "The flood control safety mainly depends on the flood peak flow project, such as embankment! The design flood refers to the flood of the flood peak corresponding to the design standard. To control the flood control safety mainly depends on a certain period of time the actual engineering, such as a large reservoir project, the design flood control refers to the time frequency of the corresponding frequency is equal to the design of the actual standard of flood "visible, expressed in the frequency of the meaning of the design flood is closely linked with the characteristics of engineering for flood control" as a result, the design flood refers to the one or a few floods frequency is equal to the design of the characteristics of flood, it could be a flood, also can be a few consecutive floods, according to the specific project and the protective properties of the building " (3) The design flood is usually refers to the flood of a section, the section called design section" for the hydraulic structures, design sections is building site representative sections. For the downstream protection area of engineering, the design section refers to the control section that can represent the flood situation in the protection area. (4) The design flood is usually refers to the natural conditions of flood "does not exist in the natural situation, refers to the basin reservoir to regulate water diversion flood detention dam dramatic change in the form of flood situation such as" if the design project upstream has already built! Built or under construction in the near future are expected to flood regulating role in larger reservoir project, or design engineering itself the flood regulating effect is bigger, and to study design engineering on the downstream area of flood control benefit, the design flood is affected by upstream reservoir to regulate "floods after a set of cascade reservoirs based on the exploration and research method of design flood calculation as the goal, JC method is used for dam alternative to build very reasonable solution is given, and simulation experiments are carried out using cary the dam at the same time.

In the model 1, the JC model is established to consider the flow of the whole river and analyze the flow sources of the multiple small dams, which are divided into the upstream and the incoming water, and the utility function is deduced. The number of smaller dams is 12 when the utility function is zero. However, in order to ensure the flood control capacity, it is recommended to construct 14 smaller dams.

In the model 2, by extracting Zambezi River basin picture and using the Harris corner detection, the 14 dam sites were constructed with the hydro-logical parameters meaning the upstream water and the interval water.

In the model 3, in order to get a reasonable water diversion strategy for multi - dam system, the simulating curve of the whole storage water quantity is obtained by simulink in MATLAB.

2   Basic Assumptions

In this section, we discuss several key assumptions we've made and rationale for making these assumptions.

- Assume that the size and the handling abilities of the rebuilding smaller dams are equivalent.
- Assume that the flow of river water into the reservoir only includes two aspects that are the upstream and inflow of water.
- Assume that precipitation in the basin is normally distributed.

3   Models and Methodology

In this section, we elaborate on our models including data sources, characteristics of indexes and the model to adopt (Table 1).

Table 1. Definition of Model 1

Name	Definition
$Z = h()$	Function
P_s	The probability of completing a scheduled function
P_f	Failure probability
R	Structural resistance
S	Load effect of structure
β	Reliability index
μ	The mean of Z
σ	The variance of Z
$\varphi()$	The density function of normal distribution
$\phi()$	The distribution function of standard normal distribution
X	Upstream reservoir storage floods
Y	Interval flood
Q	The last dam of downstream into the flood

Model 1: JC method
Definition

Introduction
Option 3 requires to remove the Kariba Dam and to replace it with a series of ten to twenty smaller dams along the Zambezi River. We use a cascade dam design, which is

the most common and most representative of the upper and lower reservoirs. However multi stage reservoir can be regarded as the combination of two reservoirs.

As shown in Fig. 1.

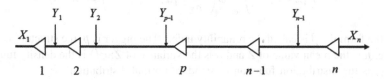

Fig. 1. Multi-dam system schematic diagram

Modeling

We define the utility function

$$Z = h(X_1, X_2, \cdots, X_n) \tag{1}$$

In the formula, X_i is an independent variable. It is necessary to describe the function. When Z is taken positive, the structure is reliable; taken a negative value, the structure is invalid; and when $Z = 0$, it means that the structure is in the limit state. Function called utility function, and also known as the limit state function [7].

With probability to measure structural reliability, the greater the probability of event $(z \geq 0)$, the more reliable it is. We can define P_s: the probability of structures within the prescribed time limit, under specified conditions, the probability of the completion of a predetermined function $(z \geq 0)$ is the structural reliability, namely.

$$P_s = P(Z \geq 0) \tag{2}$$

Event $(z \geq 0)$ and event $(z < 0)$ are a pair of incompatible events. It means that its addition is an inevitable event. Therefore, it can be used to measure the probability of failure, that is

$$P_f = P(Z < 0) = 1 - P(Z \geq 0) = 1 - P_s \tag{3}$$

In this way, the reliability of different structures can be measured by a unified standard.

In practical structural applications, all basic variables are often divided into two categories: one is related with the resistance of the structure, mainly including the performance of the material and the relevant cross-section geometry; the other is related with the load effect of the structure, mainly including the action and load and the associated structural geometry. Generally speaking, it can use simple form to express the structure of the utility function:

$$Z = R - S \tag{4}$$

Assuming that each random variable is a normal distribution, the failure probability is:

$$R = P\{Z<0\} = \int_{-\infty}^{0} \varphi\left(\frac{z-u}{\sigma_{\Sigma}}\right) dz = \phi\left(\frac{-\mu}{\sigma_z}\right) = \phi(-\beta) \tag{5}$$

In the formula, β is called the reliability index. The bigger is β, the structure is more reliable; μ is the mean value of Z and σ is the variance of Z; $\varphi()$ is the density function and $\phi()$ is the distribution function of standard normal distribution.

In solving the problem of reconstructing the number of small dams, we define

$$Q = X + Y \tag{6}$$

Suppose the function is:

$$Z = Q - (X + Y) \tag{7}$$

The limit state equation is: $Z = 0$.

If the last dam of the downstream reservoir is given a definite value $Q_i (i = 1, 2, \ldots, n)$, then the failure probability is the probability that the upstream reservoir discharge flow is combined with the various flood frequencies of the interval flooding.

In order to determine the exact number of small dams that need to be rebuilt, it is important to determine the values of β in (5).

We introduce the method of JC. The method mainly solve two or more than two non-normal distribution of random variables when the distribution of the problem.

For the deduction of β, the method will use $U_i = \frac{(X_i - \mu_{X_i})}{\sigma_{X_i}}$ to transform space X into space U, and you can get:

$$Z = g(U_1, U_2, \cdots, U_n) \tag{8}$$

When $Z = 0$, it is called the limit state equation. The limit state equation is a nonlinear hyper-surface in space. β which is the shortest distance of the space U from the origin $M(O_1, O_2, \ldots, O_n)$ to the limit state hyper-surface [8].

Set the nearest point $P^*(u_1^*, u_2^*, \ldots, u_n^*)$ to the origin, called the design checkpoint. The tangent plane equation of the hyper-surface passing through the point is:

$$Z' = \sum_{i=1}^{n} \frac{\partial g}{\partial U_i} \cdot (U_i - u_i^*) \tag{9}$$

And thus the origin of the distance to the tangent plane is a reliable indicator β.

$$\beta = \frac{-\sum\limits_{i=1}^{n} \frac{\partial g}{\partial U_i} \cdot u_i^*}{\sqrt{\sum\limits_{i=1}^{n} \left(\frac{\partial g}{\partial U_i}\right)^2}} \tag{10}$$

Set

$$\alpha_i = \frac{-\frac{\partial g}{\partial U_i}}{\sqrt{\sum\limits_{i=1}^{n} \left(\frac{\partial g}{\partial U_i}\right)^2}} \tag{11}$$

Then

$$\beta = \sum\limits_{i=1}^{n} \alpha_i \cdot u_i^* \tag{12}$$

And

$$\sum\limits_{i=1}^{n} \alpha_i^2 = 1 \tag{13}$$

Therefore, α_i is the direction of the cosine of the straight line MP^*, which can be:

$$u_i^* = \alpha_i \beta \tag{14}$$

In this way, it can turn from the space U back into space X:

$$X_i^* = \mu_{X_i} + \alpha_i \beta \sigma_{X_i} \tag{15}$$

Because,

$$\frac{\partial g}{\partial U_i} = \frac{\partial h}{\partial X_i} \cdot \sigma_{x_i} \tag{16}$$

Then

$$\alpha_i = \frac{-\frac{\partial h}{\partial X_i} \cdot \sigma_{x_i}}{\sqrt{\sum\limits_{i=1}^{n} \left(\frac{\partial h}{\partial X_i} \cdot \sigma_{x_i}\right)^2}} \tag{17}$$

And

$$Z(X_1^*, X_2^*, \ldots, X_n^*) = 0 \qquad (18)$$

At this point, the reliability index β can be obtained from (15) (17) (18). Therefore, when $Z = 0$, n equals 12. Because we want to ensure the safety of flood control, so we will ensure that the number of small dam is 14 [9–11].

Model 2: Harris corner detector

Introduction

The identification of the human eye on the corner is usually in a local small area or small window to complete. If a small window of this feature is moved in all directions, and the gray scale of the area within the window changes greatly, the corner point will be considered to be encountered in the window. If this particular window is moved in all directions of the image, the grayscale of the image in the window does not change, then there will be no corner point in the window; if the window is moved in a certain direction, Large changes, and in other directions did not change, then the image within the window may be a straight line segment [11, 12] (Figs. 2 and 3).

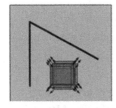 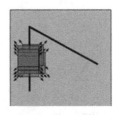 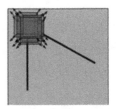

Fig. 2. Corner detection schematic diagram

Modeling

For image $I(x, y)$, the self-similarity after the translation from (x, y) to $(x + \Delta x, y + \Delta y)$, can be given by the autocorrelation function:

$$c(x, y; \Delta x, \Delta y) = \sum_{(u,v) \in W(x,y)} \omega(u, v)(I(u, v) - I(u + \Delta x, v + \Delta y))^2$$

Among them, $W(x, y)$ is a (x, y)-centric window, $\omega(u, v)$ is a weighting function, it can be a constant, it can be a Gaussian weighting function.

According to Taylor expansion, the image $I(x, y)$ after translation in $(\Delta x, \Delta y)$ carries out a first order approximation:

$$\begin{aligned} I(u + \Delta x, v + \Delta y) &= I(u, v) + I_x(u, v)\Delta x + I_y(u, v)\Delta y + O(\Delta x^2, \Delta y^2) \\ &\approx I(u, v) + I_x(u, v)\Delta x + I_y(u, v)\Delta y \end{aligned}$$

Which I_x, I_y is the partial derivative og the image $I(x, y)$, so, auto-correlation function can be simplified as:

Fig. 3. Corner detection of Gaussian weighting function

$$c(x, y; \Delta x, \Delta y) \approx \sum_{\omega} \left(I_x(u, v)\Delta x + I_y(u, v)\Delta y\right)^2 = [\Delta x, \Delta y]M(x, y)\begin{bmatrix} \Delta x \\ \Delta y \end{bmatrix}$$

Among them,

$$M(x, y) = \sum_{\omega} \begin{bmatrix} I_x(x, y)^2 & I_x(x, y)I_y(x, y) \\ I_x(x, y)I_y(x, y) & I_y(x, y)^2 \end{bmatrix} = \begin{bmatrix} \sum_{\omega} I_x(x, y)^2 & \sum_{\omega} I_x(x, y)I_y(x, y) \\ \sum_{\omega} I_x(x, y)I_y(x, y) & \sum_{\omega} I_y(x, y)^2 \end{bmatrix} = \begin{bmatrix} A & C \\ C & B \end{bmatrix}$$

In other words, the auto-correlation function of the image $I(x, y)$ after translation at the point can be approximated as a binomial function:

$$c(x, y; \Delta x, \Delta y) \approx A\Delta x^2 + 2C\Delta x\Delta y + B\Delta y^2$$

Among them,

$$A = \sum_{\omega} I_x^2, B = \sum_{\omega} I_y^2, C = \sum_{\omega} I_x I_y$$

The quadratic function is essentially an elliptic function. The oblateness and size of the ellipse are determined by the eigenvalues λ_1, λ_2 of $M(x, y)$, and the direction of the ellipse is determined by the eigenvectors of $M(x, y)$. As shown in the following figure, the elliptic equation is:

$$[\Delta x, \Delta y]M(x, y)\begin{bmatrix} \Delta x \\ \Delta y \end{bmatrix} = 1$$

The relationship between the eigenvalues of an ellipse and the corners, lines (edges), and planes in the image is shown in the following figure. Can be divided into three situations:

- The line in the image. One eigenvalues is large and the other eigenvalues is small, $\lambda_1 \gg \lambda_2$ or $\lambda_2 \gg \lambda_1$. The auto-correlation function value increases in one direction and decreases in the other direction.
- The image plane. Both eigenvalues are small and approximately equal; the value of the autocorrelation function decreases in all directions.
- Corner of the image. Both eigenvalues are large and approximately equal; the autocorrelation function values increase in all directions.

According to the formula of the eigenvalue of the quadratic function, we can get the eigenvalues of the matrix $M(x, y)$. However, Harris does not need to calculate the eigenvalues, but calculates a corner response value R to determine the corner point. The formula of R is:

$$R = \det M - \alpha(traceM)^2$$

Where, $det\,M$ is the determinant of matrix $M = \begin{bmatrix} A & B \\ B & C \end{bmatrix}$; $trace\,M$ is the straight for the matrix M; α is a constant, and its value range is 0.04 to 0.06. In fact, the feature is implied in $det\,M$ and $trace\,M$, because,

$$det\,M = \lambda_1 \lambda_2 = AC - B^2; trace\,M = \lambda_1 + \lambda_2 = A + C$$

Harris Corner Algorithm

We find the Zambezi River basin picture to deal with the problem of the locations of the smaller dams as shown in Fig. 4.

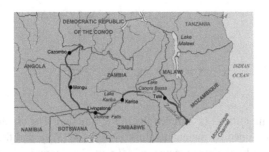

Fig. 4. Zambezi River basin picture

According to the hydro-logical analysis, the dam should be selected in narrow valleys and more curved areas to build in order to ensure adequate supply of water upstream and range of water. We extract Zambezi River basin picture from above figure. Then Harris corner detection method is used to get the whole basin which you can build the dam's address, as shown in Fig. 5.

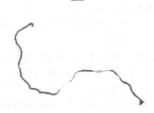

Fig. 5. All selectable dam addresses

And then according to the hydro-logical data meaning upstream and downstream water, we find the most suitable address to build. As shown in Fig. 6.

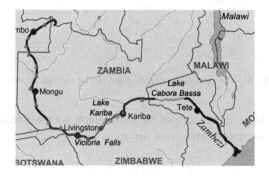

Fig. 6. The most suitable address

Because we do not have all the geographical information of the Zambezi River Basin, We can only get a more suitable address by rough estimation.

Model 3: MATLAB simulink simulation technology
In order to get a reasonable water transferred strategy, we use MATLAB simulink simulation technology. Simulation flow chart is as follows in Fig. 7.

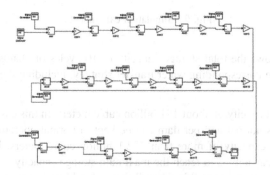

Fig. 7. Simulation flow chart

The signal generator in the figure indicates the inflow of the river source. The signal generator $i(i = 1,2,...,14)$ represents the interval between the two dams. The source water of the river and the incoming water of the interval 1 are superimposed on the total of the dam 1.The amount of water between the two dams is the upstream water, and the amount of water of the dam 1 is superimposed with the signal generator 2 to form the dam 2, and so on. Finally the water quantity of the dam 14 is formed.

Because Zambezi River months flow hydro-graphs shows the shape of the follow Fig. 8.

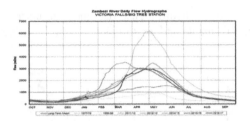

Fig. 8. The time sequence diagram of the storage capacity

And then according to the shape of the above graph, we use sine function to do the simulation experiments and have been the entire water volume curve, as shown in Fig. 9.

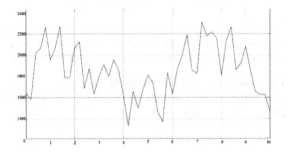

Fig. 9. Simulation experiments

The figure shows the total storage capacity of 10 cycles of change. And different water has been the corresponding water transfer strategy, including the following three cases:

- Water storage capacity of about 181 billion cubic meters. In this case, the amount of water stored is normal and per dam can be kept in normal operation.
- Water storage capacity of more than 232.1 billion cubic meters. In this case, the water storage capacity is to reach the maximum storage capacity. There may be the risk of dam breaking, so at this time all dams should be in the state of maximum water storage capacity.
- Water storage capacity of less than 138.05 billion cubic meters. In this case, the storage capacity reach the minimum storage capacity, through the calculation, we can know that at this time only using 10 dams can achieve the desired effect.

4   Strengths and Weakness

In model 1, to give a more comprehensive assessment of the title of the three programs, we have considered such factors of the environmental, potential costs and benefits.

In model 1, according to the JC risk control function, we determine the minimum number of dams and the number of dams that can cope with the spillage in the multi-dam system design problem. But because there is no more detailed geographic information, we only get a more suitable construction address by a rough estimating.

In model 3, Matlab Simulink simulation makes the appropriate judgments visually, and finally through Harris corner detection determines its location. However, there is no specific function model, we can't get on sensitivity analysis and error analysis.

References

1. Yaqoob, I., et al.: Big data: from beginning to future. Int. J. Inf. Manag. **36**(6), 1231–1247 (2016)
2. Riggins, F.J., Wamba, S.F.: Research directions on the adoption, usage, and impact of the internet of things through the use of big data analytics. In: Proceedings of 48th Hawaii International Conference on System Sciences (HICSS 2015), pp. 1531–1540. IEEE (2015)
3. Bashir, M.R., Gill, A.Q.: Towards an IoT big data analytics framework: smart buildings systems. In: 2016 IEEE 18th International Conference on High Performance Computing and Communications; IEEE 14th International Conference on Smart City; IEEE 2nd International Conference on Data Science and Systems (HPCC/SmartCity/DSS), pp. 1325–1332. IEEE (2016)
4. Lee, C., Yeung, C., Cheng, M.: Research on IoT based cyber physical system for industrial big data analytics. In: 2015 IEEE International Conference on Industrial Engineering and Engineering Management (IEEM), pp. 1855–1859. IEEE (2015)
5. Rizwan, P., Suresh, K., Babu, M.R.: Real-time smart traffic management system for smart cities by using internet of things and big data. In: International Conference on Emerging Technological Trends (ICETT), pp. 1–7. IEEE (2016)
6. Zhang, Q., Zhang, X., Zhang, Q., Shi, W., Zhong, H.: Firework: big data sharing and processing in collaborative edge environment. In: 2016 Fourth IEEE Workshop on Hot Topics in Web Systems and Technologies (HotWeb), pp. 20–25. IEEE (2016)
7. Rathore, M.M., Ahmad, A., Paul, A.: IoT-based smart city development using big data analytical approach. In: IEEE International Conference on Automatica (ICA-ACCA), pp. 1–8. IEEE (2016)
8. Ahlgren, B., Hidell, M., Ngai, E.C.-H.: Internet of things for smart cities: interoperability and open data. IEEE Internet Comput. **20**(6), 52–56 (2016)
9. Pinasco, J.P.: Asymptotic of eigenvalues of the p-Laplace operator and lattice points (2003)
10. Drabek, P., Manasevich, R.: On the closed solutions to some nonhomogeneous eigenvalue problems with p-laplacian. Diff. Int. Equ. **12**(6), 773–778 (1999)
11. Courant, R., Hibert, D.: Methods of Mathematical Physics, vol. 1. Interscience Publishers Inc., New York (1953)
12. Falconer, K.: On the Minkowski measurability of fractals. Proc. Am. Math. Soc. **123**(4), 1115–1124 (1995)

Community-Based Matrix Factorization Model for Recommendation

Cairong Yan[(⊠)], Yan Huang, Yan Wan, and Guohua Liu

School of Computer Science and Technology,
Donghua University, Shanghai, China
cryan@dhu.edu.cn

Abstract. Although matrix factorization has been proven to be an effective recommendation method, its accuracy is affected by the sparsity of the matrix and it cannot resolve the cold start problem. Social recommendation methods have attracted much attention in solving these problems. In this paper, we focus on community discovery rather than individuals' relations in the social network and propose a community-based matrix factorization (CommMF) model. It consists of two parts. One is a community detection algorithm Coo-game, proposed in our previous work and used here to divide the social network of users into multiple overlapping communities. It is based on the game theory and can fast detect overlapping communities. Since the users in the same community share the common interests such as scoring information, some of the null values in the scoring matrix can be filled according to the communities. This will help alleviate the sparsity of the scoring matrix and the cold start problem of new users. The other part is the matrix factorization model, which is used to recommend items to users. The model is trained by a stochastic gradient descent algorithm. The experimental results on real and simulated datasets show that CommMF can get higher accuracy with the help of community information compared with PMF and SocialMF models.

Keywords: Recommender systems · Matrix factorization · Social network
Community

1 Introduction

The recommender systems have been widely used in our lives, which help us find useful information from a large amount of data [1]. These systems include e-commerce recommendation [2], information retrieval [3], and mobile application [4]. Their purposes are to promote products for customers by predicting the users' rating on the items.

Traditional recommendation approaches mainly focus on utilizing users' historical preferences on the purchased products to predict users' interests and they do not consider some information such as the relationship between users [1]. The collaborative filtering recommendation approaches are highly successful in the real world because they are easy to understand, and the relationship between users are considered [5]. However, there are two main weaknesses that affect their accuracy. One is data sparsity

© Springer Nature Switzerland AG 2018
X. Sun et al. (Eds.): ICCCS 2018, LNCS 11068, pp. 464–475, 2018.
https://doi.org/10.1007/978-3-030-00021-9_42

and the other is the cold start problem, e.g. there is no historical purchasing information of new users and new items.

In recent years, due to the development of social networks and the growth of mobile computing, it is very common to use social information to improve the accuracy of the recommender systems. Some social recommendation methods have been proposed by adding the social network information to the recommendation model [6, 7].

Typical social recommender systems are built under a social network among users and the users' rating of the items because users have direct or indirect social relations with each other. One of the most extensively used techniques in these social recommender systems is community detection [8, 9]. The aim of the community detection technique in recommender systems is to find the subgroups among users, and the user' preferences within the group are more similar than the others outside the group. It can help us understand users' collective behavioral patterns better. However, in the recommendation model based on social network, different user relation representation methods will affect the accuracy of recommendation. In our previous work, we have studied the overlapping community detection algorithm based on game theory, which could find a better structure of the community [10].

In this paper, we propose a community-based matrix factorization model (CommMF) for recommendation, which can be used to predict users' preferences via the users' social networks even in the absence of any historical data. Social network aims at establishing the relationships among people and a community is a group of people who share common interests. The community can provide support for the recommendation system. The main contributions of our work are summarized as follows:

- A recommendation model CommMF is proposed, where the community information discovered in the social network is embedded into the matrix factorization (MF) model to alleviate the sparsity of the matrix and add information for new users.
- CommMF is implemented based on our previous work, a community discovery algorithm Coo-game and a Bayesian Probabilistic Matrix Factorization method GBPMF [10, 11].
- We conduct experiments on two datasets, one is a simulation dataset ml-1m-rela, which is produced by integrating a real-life dataset ml-1m and a simulated dataset Lancichinetti-Fortunato-Radicchi which is used to create the social networking relationship, the other is a real-life dataset Epinions [10]. We can obtain good results on both datasets.

The rest of the paper is organized as follows. Section 2 introduces the related work. We propose a community-based recommendation model in Sect. 3. The experimental results are presented in Sect. 4. And finally, we conclude this paper in Sect. 5.

2 Related Work

This section compares the work of traditional commendation methods and social-based recommendation methods.

Traditional Recommendation. The traditional recommendation can usually be divided into collaborative filtering-based approach, content-based approach, and hybrid approach [1]. The collaborative filtering-based approach is directly used to predict user's interest, complex and unexpected patterns from user's past behaviors and recommend items to other users with similar interests and preferences. The content-based approach recommends items to a user based on the description of the item and the profile of the user's interests. The hybrid approach makes use of the advantages of the two approaches.

Social Network-Based Recommendation. Similar to the physical world, people may seek advice from friends before making a purchase decision and their friends always provide good advice [12]. Social relationships can improve the performance of online recommender systems [13]. In order to abstract the most useful information from the social network, some previous studies generally aim at building trust models in light of the social influence theory. Then approaches based on probabilistic matrix factorizations have been proposed to improve the accuracy of recommendation by jointly factorizing a trust network and a user-item matrix [6, 14]. The proposal of the model is to make the social recommendation problem more accurate and more personalized. Hui Li et al. proposed a Social Recommendation (SoRec) [6]. Another social recommendation model is SocialMF [15], and the improved model based on SocialMF is SR [16] model. SocialMF is based on the potential feature vector of friends to learn the user's potential feature vector while SR model improves SocialMF by treating friends with different preferences by taking into account the diversity of each user's friends. PLSA method and MFC method are proposed by taking the community into consideration [17, 18]. Cao et al. also proposed an improved collaborative filtering recommendation algorithm based on community detection [19] and He et al. proposed a topic community-based method via nonnegative matrix factorization (NMF) to get better commendation result [9].

In general, most social-based approaches only consider direct friendships in social networks. When users have few social relationships, these approaches will become less effective. In this paper, the social network is divided into different communities. Supposing that people in the same community may have similar interests, and further made different recommendations for different communities.

3 Community-Based Recommendation

3.1 Community Discovery

One of the most widely accepted definitions of community is given by Girvan and Newman. It is a collection of nodes with similar properties [10]. The community structure means that the network can be naturally divided into node groups with internal dense connections and fewer connections between groups.

Suppose an undirected social network graph $G = (V, E)$, the vertex set $V = \{v_1, v_2, \ldots, v_i\}$ represents all the users and the edge set $E = \{e_1, e_2, \ldots, e_i\}$ represents the relations between users. Let $C = \{c_{ik}\}$ denote the $n \times n$ matrix of G, which is also called the social network matrix. Coo-game, proposed in our previous work, is a game theory based overlapping community detection algorithm, which is used to produce communities from a network. The implementation framework is shown in Fig. 1. Coo-game is an advanced overlapping community detection algorithm based on the game theory which puts the individual game and equilibrium into the community detection process. It can reflect the process of the community formation more vividly from the bottom-up perspective and form a community naturally. It can not only fast detect overlapping communities but also eliminate the unnecessary small clusters. The pseudo-code of Coo-game algorithm is shown as follows.

Algorithm: Coo-game algorithm
Input: G (V, E)   // A graph
Output: File f   // Each line of f contains the member nodes of the i-th community
Begin
Set each node as a single community;
    Initialize community set C;
While the consecutive and unchanged number < Equilibrium point do
    Random select a node;
    Try to add;
    Try to remove;
    Try to move;
    Get the best function value;
    For each C_i in C do
    Get the number of inner edge and outer edge of cluster C_i, P_{in} and P_{out};
    Get the internal and external connection rate of cluster C_i, $\delta_{in}(C_i)$ and $\delta_{out}(C_i)$;
    If $\delta_{in}(C_i) \geq \delta(C)$ and $\delta_{out}(C_i) \leq \delta(C)$ then
        Merge C_i and C_j;
    return community set C;
End

The time complexity of Coo-game algorithm is $O(m^2)$, where m represents the number of edges.

3.2 Matrix Factorization

Matrix factorization model maps both users and items with a joint latent factor space of dimensionality k, such that ratings are modeled as inner products in that space. Accordingly, each user u is associated with a vector $U_i \in R^k$ and each item i is associated with a vector $V_j \in R^k$. A rating is predicted by the rule:

$$\hat{R}_{ij} = U^T V_j \tag{1}$$

The basic MF model shown in Fig. 2 predicts the rating matrix R_{ij} which is the multiplication of the k-dimensional user-feature matrix U_{ik} and the k-dimensional item-feature matrix V_{kj}, where k << min(n, m). In order to learn the vectors U_{ik} and V_{kj} we minimize the regularized squared error:

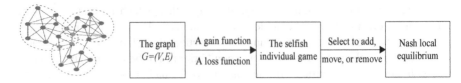

Fig. 1. The framework of Coo-game.

$$\frac{1}{2}\sum_{i=1}^{n}\sum_{j=1}^{m}\left(R_{ij}-U_i^{\mathrm{T}}V_j\right)^2+\frac{\lambda}{2}\left(\|U\|^2+\|V\|^2\right) \tag{2}$$

where $\|\cdot\|^2$ denotes the Frobenius norm. Having potential feature vectors U_i and V_j, and the unknown rating on an item V_j for user U_i can be predicted according to Eq. (1).

3.3 Recommendation Model

The SR model improves rating prediction by imposing similarity constraints between users and their friends. Given a social network, the SR model can quickly be extended to consider all the members of the community where the target user belongs.

In our framework, Coo-game algorithm is adapted, which can detect overlapping communities quickly and can also eliminate the unnecessary small clusters [10]. Our proposed model CommMF, shown in Fig. 3, considers the relationship between users and integrates the community information into the matrix factorization model.

Let $U \in R^{k \times n}$ and $V \in R^{k \times m}$ be the potential user and factor feature matrices, with column vectors U_i and W_k representing user-feature and factor-feature potential feature vectors, respectively. Community C contains the users belonging to a community $(U_i \in C_i)$. User U_i belongs to community C_i and T is the matrix representation of the social network. The loss function to be minimized is:

$$\frac{1}{2}\sum_{i=1}^{n}I_{ij}^R\left(\sum_{j}^{m}R_{ij}-\sum_{j}^{m}U_i^{\mathrm{T}}V_j-\sum_{U_i\in C_{(i)}}I_{ik}^T(U_i^{\mathrm{T}}W_k)-\mu-b_u-b_i\right)^2+\frac{\lambda}{2}\left(\|U\|^2+\|V\|^2+\|W\|^2\right) \tag{3}$$

The constant λ controls the extent of regularization, as usually determined by cross-validation. Minimization is typically performed by either stochastic gradient descent or alternating least squares. Such a pure factor model serves well in capturing the interaction between users and items. However, much of the observed rating values are due to the effects associated with either users or items, independently of their interaction. A prime example is that typical CF data exhibit large user and item biases, i.e., systematic tendencies for some users to give higher ratings than others, and for some items to receive higher ratings than others. We will encapsulate those effects, which do not involve user-item interaction, within the baseline predictors. These baseline predictors tend to capture much of the observed signal. A suitable way to construct a static baseline predictor is as follows. Denote by μ the overall average rating. A baseline

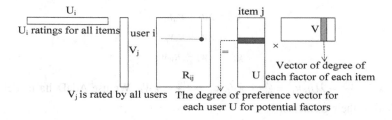

Fig. 2. Matrix factorization model.

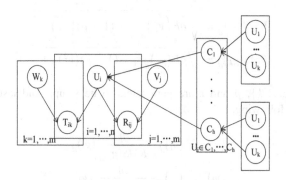

Fig. 3. CommMF model.

predictor for an unknown rating R_{ij} is denoted by b_{ui} and accounts for the user and item main effects: $b_{ui} = \mu + b_u + b_i$. If users U_i and U_k are friends $I_{ij}^T = 1$ and $I_{ij}^T = 0$ otherwise. A local minimum of the above function can be found by performing gradient descent in U_i, V_j and W_k:

$$\frac{\partial E}{\partial U_i} = \left(I_{ij}^R \left(\sum_j^m R_{ij} - \sum_j^m U_i^T V_j \right) - \sum_{U_i \in C_{(i)}} I_{ik}^T (U_i^T W_k) - \mu - b_i - b_j \right) (-V_j - W_k) + \lambda U_i$$

$$\frac{\partial E}{\partial V_j} = \sum_{i=1}^n I_{ij}^R \left(R_{ij} - U_i^T V_j - \sum_{U_i \in C_{(i)}} I_{ik}^T (U_i^T W_k) - \mu - b_i - b_j \right) (-U_i) + \lambda V_j$$

$$\frac{\partial E}{\partial V_j} = \sum_{i=1}^n I_{ij}^R \left(R_{ij} - U_i^T V_j - \sum_{U_i \in C_{(i)}} I_{ik}^T (U_i^T W_k) - \mu - b_i - b_j \right) (-U_i) + \lambda W_k$$

$$(4)$$

In this paper, CommMF is trained by stochastic gradient descent (SGD). In each step, the loss function of a single sample is used to calculate the sub gradient:

$$g_i = \lambda u_i + \kappa_u u_i$$
$$g_j = \lambda v_j + \kappa_v v_j \tag{5}$$
$$g_k = \lambda w_k + \kappa_w w_k$$

where $\kappa_u = \frac{\partial E}{\partial U_i} - \lambda U_i, \kappa_v = \frac{\partial E}{\partial V_j} - \lambda V_j, \kappa_w = \frac{\partial E}{\partial W_k} - \lambda W_k$. We use AdaDelta model [20] to calculate their gradients:

$$RMS(g_i)_d = \sqrt{\rho E(g_i^2)_{d-1} + (1-\rho)(g_i^2)_d + \varepsilon}$$
$$RMS(g_j)_d = \sqrt{\rho E\left(g_j^2\right)_{d-1} + (1-\rho)\left(g_j^2\right)_d + \varepsilon} \tag{6}$$
$$RMS(g_k)_d = \sqrt{\rho E(g_k^2)_{d-1} + (1-\rho)(g_k^2)_d + \varepsilon}$$

where $d = \{1, 2, \ldots k\}$, ρ and ε are parameters to be setup. And lastly, we update u_i, v_j, w_k by the following:

$$(u_i)_d = (u_i)_d - \frac{\eta}{RMS(g_i)_d}(g_i)_d$$
$$(v_j)_d = (v_j)_d - \frac{\eta}{RMS(g_j)_d}(g_j)_d \tag{7}$$
$$(w_k)_d = (w_k)_d - \frac{\eta}{RMS(g_k)_d}(g_k)_d$$

4 Experimental Evaluation

4.1 Experimental Setup

Platform. All experiments are conducted on a server with 8 physical cores on Inter® Core™ i7-7700 CPU @ 3.60 GHz processors and 64 GB memory. The model is implemented in C language and the figures are drawn by Python.

Datasets. In this paper, we use datasets Epinions[1], MovieLens 1M (simply called ml-1m)[2] and ml-lm_rela to evaluate the performance of CommMF. Table 1 shows the statistics of the datasets.

The ml-1m dataset contains 1,000,209 anonymous ratings of approximately 3,900 movies made by 6,040 MovieLens users who joined MovieLens in 2000. The ml-lm_rela dataset is a simulated dataset based on the dataset ml-1m. In order to get the social network of users in ml-1m, we use the Lancichinetti-Fortunato-Radicchi (LFR) benchmark network to establish users' relationship. LFR benchmark can be used

---

[1] http://www.trustlet.org/wiki/Epinions_datasets.

[2] http://grouplens.org/datasets/movielens/1m/.

Table 1. Statistics of the datasets.

	ml-1m	ml-1m_rela	Epinions
Users	6040	6040	49290
Items	3952	3952	139738
Ratings	1000209	1000209	664824
Relation	-	117172	487181
Rating sparsity	95.81%	95.81%	99.99%
Edge sparsity	-	99.36%	99.96%

to produce binary networks with overlapping nodes and we can get different graphs by setting different values of parameters.

Epinions dataset was collected by Paolo Massa in a 5-week crawl (November/December 2003) from the website of Epinions.com. In Epinions, people can write reviews for various products with ratings, and they can also add members to their trust networks or "Circle of Trust". This dataset provides user-item rating information and user-to-user trust networks. The dataset contains 49,290 users who rate a total of 139,738 different items at least once and write 664,824 reviews and 487,181 issued trust statements.

The rating sparsity of a matrix is evaluated by *rating_sparsity*, and the edge sparsity of a matrix is evaluated by *edge_sparsity*. They are defined as:

$$rating\_sparsity = 1 - \frac{|R|}{n \times m}, \ edge\_sparsity = 1 - \frac{2|E|}{n(n-1)} \tag{8}$$

where $|R|$ is the number of ratings, $|E|$ is the number of social connections, m is the number of users, and n is the number of items.

Evaluation Metrics. RMSE is frequently used to value the forecasting or recommendation models. It measures the difference between the values predicted by a model or an estimator and the values actually observed. The RMSE metric is defined as:

$$RMSE = \frac{\sqrt{\sum_{i,j \in T} \left(R_{ij} - \hat{R}_{ij} \right)^2}}{|N_r|} \tag{9}$$

where R_{ij} denotes the rating that user i gives to item j, $\hat{R}_{ij}$ denotes the rating that user i gives to item j, which is predicted by a method, T is the test set, and N_r is the element number of T.

4.2   Result Analysis

In the experiment, the datasets ml-1m_rela and Epinions were randomly divided into training sets and test sets according to the ratio of 8:2. In order to get a better community structure, we set parameter k_c to 1 after several experiments.

For the real dataset Epinions, we firstly set the feature dimension d to 50, the number of iteration e to 1000, and the learning rate η to 0.0001 to adjust the regularization parameter λ. Then, we use the same method to adjust several other parameters.

From Figs. 4 and 5, we can see that when $\lambda = 0.4$ the value of RMSE is the smallest. When d is less than 50, the value of RMSE becomes larger with the increase of d. However, when $d \geq 50$ the value of RMSE decreases substantially with the increase of d, and when $d = 90$ we can get the smallest value. Similarly, when η is set to 0.0001 we can get better results. For all the experiments, we set the number of iterations to 1000 to get these results.

As is shown in Figs. 6 and 7, when $\lambda = 0.05$, RMSE value is the minimum. However, when $d = 10$, RMSE value is the maximum. On the contrary, when $d = 100$, we can get the minimum value. Similarly, when η is set to 0.001 we can get better results. For all the experiments, we set the number of iterations to 1213.

We have compared the following recommendation methods: BaseMF (Basic Matrix Factorization), PMF (Probabilistic Matrix Factorization), CommMF, and SocialMF. PMF, based on MF, further optimized the probability model. Assuming that the feature matrix of user U and item V obeys the Gaussian distribution and the values are obtained from the known value of the rating matrix. It can be used to predict the unknown value in the rating matrix. The RMSE value of the recommended algorithm based on the social network is smaller so we can get that the recommendation accuracy is higher. We tried to preprocess Epinions dataset and experiment on some part of the dataset which has a better community structure (1053 users, 5613 relationships, 6240 ratings, 627 communities), but the effect was not good. The more complete the data, the higher the accuracy.

Whether it is a simulation dataset or a real dataset, CommMF can obtain better accuracy of recommendation compared with other matrix factorization models or social based commendation model. Table 2 shows the difference between them.

5   Conclusion

With the emergence of online social networks, the use of implicit information in the social network to predict the behavior of users has become more and more significant. In this paper, we propose a community-based matrix factorization model for recommendation. The community structure in the social network is to discover the implicit relationship between friends and it is used to improve the quality of recommendation. Experiments on a real-life dataset Epinions and a simulated dataset ml-lm_rela demonstrate that social recommendation methods can effectively improve the recommendation accuracy compared with the basic matrix factorization method BaseMF and probabilistic matrix factorization method PMF. Furthermore, CommMF is superior to

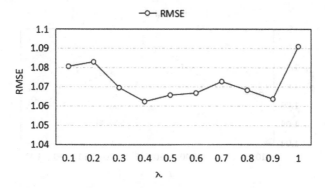

Fig. 4. Comparison of RMSE on Epinions by setting different values of parameter λ.

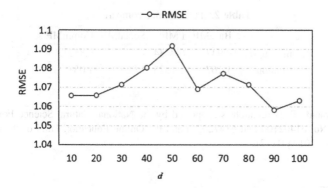

Fig. 5. Comparison of RMSE on Epinions by setting different values of parameter d.

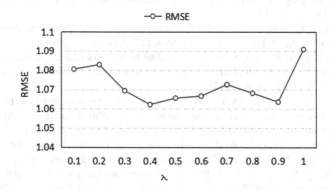

Fig. 6. Comparison of RMSE on ml-1m_rela by setting different values of parameter λ.

the existing social recommendation method SocialMF. In the future, we will focus on researching the effect of communities' size and their affinity.

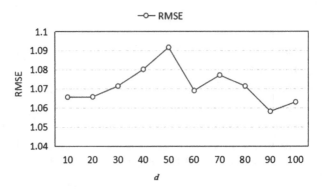

Fig. 7. Comparison of RMSE on ml-1m_rela by setting different values of parameter d.

Table 2. Performance comparison.

	BaseMF	PMF	SocialMF	CommMF
ml-1m_rela	0.947	0.8834	-	0.852
Epinion	1.167	1.1625	1.085	1.058

Acknowledgment. This research is supported by the National Natural Science Foundation of China (grant No. 61402100 and 61472075) and the Online Education Fund of the Ministry of Education (No. 2017YB112).

References

1. Bobadilla, J., Ortega, F., Hernando, A., et al.: Recommender systems survey. Knowl. Based Syst. **46**, 109–132 (2013)
2. Gomez-Uribe, C.A., Hunt, N.: The Netflix recommender system: algorithms, business value, and innovation. ACM Trans. Manag. Inf. Syst. (TMIS) **6**(4), 13 (2016)
3. Okura, S., Tagami, Y., Ono, S., et al.: Embedding-based news recommendation for millions of users. In: 23rd ACM SIGKDD Conference on Knowledge Discovery and Data Mining, Halifax, NS, Canada. ACM (2017)
4. Kazai, G., Yusof, I., Clarke, D.: Personalised news and blog recommendations based on user location, Facebook and Twitter user profiling. In: 39th International ACM SIGIR Conference on Research and Development in Information Retrieval (2016)
5. Lu, Z., Dou, Z., Lian, J., et al.: Content-based collaborative filtering for news topic recommendation. In: 29th AAAI Conference on Artificial Intelligence (2015)
6. Ma, H., Yang, H., Lyu, M.R.: SoRec: social recommendation using probabilistic matrix factorization. In: 17th ACM Conference on Information and Knowledge Management, pp. 931–940. ACM, New York (2008)
7. Huang, S., Zhang, J., Wang, L.: Social friend recommendation based on multiple network correlation. J. IEEE Trans. Multimed. **18**(2), 287–299 (2016)
8. Viktoratos, I., Tsadiras, A., Bassiliades, N.: Combining community-based knowledge with association rule mining to alleviate the cold start problem in context-aware recommender systems. Expert Syst. Appl. **101**, 78–90 (2018)

9. He, C., Li, H., Fei, X.: A topic community-based method for friend recommendation in online social networks via joint nonnegative matrix factorization. In: International Conference on Advanced Cloud & Big Data, CBD, Yangzhou, pp. 28–35. IEEE (2015)
10. Zhao, X., Wu, Y., Yan, C.: An algorithm based on game theory for detecting overlapping communities in social networks. In: 4th International Conference on Advanced Cloud and Big Data, CBD, Chengdu, pp. 150–157. IEEE Computer Society (2016)
11. Yan, C., Zhang, Q., Zhao, X.: A method of Bayesian probabilistic matrix factorization based on generalized Gaussian distribution. J. Comput. Res. Dev. **53**(12), 2793–2800 (2016)
12. Liu, Y., Zhao, P., Liu, X.: Learning optimal social dependency for recommendation (2016). arXiv:1603.04522
13. Reafee, W., Salim, N., Khan, A.: The power of implicit social relation in rating prediction of social recommender systems. PLoS ONE **11**(5), e0154848 (2016)
14. Ma, H., Zhou, D., Liu, C.: Recommender systems with social regularization. In: 4th ACM International Conference on Web Search and Data Mining, pp. 287–296. ACM, New York (2011)
15. Jamali, M., Ester, M.: A matrix factorization technique with trust propagation for recommendation in social networks. In: 4th ACM Conference on Recommender Systems, pp. 135–142. ACM, New York (2010)
16. Shen, Y., Jin, R.: Learning personal + social latent factor model for social recommendation. In: 18th ACM SIGKDD International Conference on Knowledge Discovery and Data Mining, pp. 1303–1311. ACM, New York (2012)
17. Yin, B., Yang, Y., Liu, W.: Exploring social activeness and dynamic interest in community-based recommender system. In: 23rd International Conference on World Wide Web, pp. 771–776. ACM, New York (2014)
18. Li, H., Wu, D., Tang, W.: Overlapping community regularization for rating prediction in social recommender systems. In: 9th ACM Conference on Recommender Systems, pp. 27–34. ACM, New York (2015)
19. Cao, C., Ni, Q., Zhai, Y.: An improved collaborative filtering recommendation algorithm based on community detection in social networks. In: Conference on Genetic and Evolutionary Computation, pp. 1–8. ACM, New York (2015)
20. Yazan, E., Talu, M.F.: Comparison of the stochastic gradient descent based optimization techniques. In: International Artificial Intelligence and Data Processing Symposium, Malatya, Turkey. IEEE (2017)

Composite Descriptors and Deep Features Based Visual Phrase for Image Retrieval

Yanhong Wang[1,2], Linna Zhang[3], Yigang Cen[1,2(✉)], Ruizhen Zhao[1,2], Tingting Chai[1,2], and Yi Cen[4]

[1] Institute of Information Science, Beijing Jiaotong University, Beijing 100081, China
ygcen@bjtu.edu.cn
[2] Key Laboratory of Advanced Information Science and Network Technology of Beijing, Beijing 100081, China
[3] College of Mechanical Engineering, Guizhou University, Guiyang 550025, China
[4] School of Information Engineering, Minzu University of China, Beijing 100081, China

Abstract. Local descriptors are very effective features in bag-of-visual-words (BoW) and vector of locally aggregated descriptors (VALD) models for image retrieval. Different kinds of local descriptors represent different visual content. We recognize that spatial contextual information play an important role in image matching, image retrieval and image recognition. Therefore, to explore efficient features, firstly, a new local composite descriptor is proposed, which combines the advantages of SURF and color name (CN) information. Then, VLAD method is used to encode the proposed composite descriptors to a vector. Third, local deep features are extracted and fused with the encoded vector in the image block. Finally, to implement efficient retrieval system, a novel image retrieval framework is organized a novel image retrieval framework is organized based on the proposed feature fusion strategies. The proposed methods areis verified on three benchmark datasets, i.e., Holidays, Oxford5k and Ukbench. Experimental results show that our methods achieves good performance. Eespecially, the mAP and N-S score achieve 0.8281 and 3.5498 on Holidays and Ukbench datasets, respectively.

Keywords: Composite descriptors · Visual phrase
Vector of locally aggregated descriptors · Feature fusion
Deep feature · Image retrieval

1 Introduction

Resently, VLAD [1] model is one of the most popular models, It attracted many attentions in image retrieval area. The VLAD method is efficient in terms of time and memory consumption, and is applicative to the large-scale image retrieval. The SIFT descriptor is adopted in the original VLAD method. Later, there

---

Supported by organization x.

X. Sun et al. (Eds.): ICCCS 2018, LNCS 11068, pp. 476–486, 2018.
https://doi.org/10.1007/978-3-030-00021-9_43

are a lot of works using more discriminative local features to improve the performance of VLAD [2–4]. In [3], the author used the SURF descriptor to the VLAD method (VLAD-SURF) and compared the performance with VLAD-SIFT and VLAD-rootSIFT. Experimental results showed that VLAD-SURF is better than VLAD-SIFT and VLAD-rootSIFT at aspects of accuracy and computing time. The SIFT and the SURF descriptors only represent the local gradient information of an image, and the color information is not contained. In order to address this problem, many works were proposed to combine color and gradient information [2,4,5]. In [2], the author proposed a SURF-based color feature called CSURF and achieved good results, but the high dimensionality of CSURF is high. In [4], an image descriptor combining global color histogram in HSV space and local rootSIFT feature was introduced. In [5], the author proposed a color-SURF descriptor, which combines SURF with the approximate color local kernel histograms. However, the above local features contain limit spatial contextual information. As we all known, the spatial information is very necessary for image retrieval and matching tasks. In this paper, we propose a new local composite descriptor called SURFCN, which involves in SURF and CN descriptors [15] extracted in a same image interesting resion. The SURFCN descriptor can compensate color information in the gradient features. For an image, it is divided into several small patches, and few patches form a block. Then, in each block, the SURF descriptors are extracted from the image. Thirdly, CN descriptors are extracted from a fixed-size block centered on each SURF descriptor. Finally, the SURF and the CN descriptors are combined as the SURFCN descriptors.

In recent years, the deep features have been successfully employed to image classification [7], object detection [8] and speech recognition [9] etc. In image retrieval area, most of previous works used off-the-shell convolutional neural networks (CNNs) [10] to extract deep features. In order to improve recall and accuracy, deep features are extracted from the image blocks that used for SURFCN descriptors extraction. In each block of image, SURFCN descriptors are encoded into a vector by VLAD model. Also, the deep feature of the block and the VALD vector based on SURFCN are bundled together to represent the image block, where the representation of the block is called as a visual phrase, which boost feature matching accuracy [11].

The rest of this paper is organized as follows. Section 2 introduces related works. Section 3 describes our proposed method. The experimental results are given in Sect. 4 and the conclusions are presented in Sect. 5.

2   Related Work

In this section, some related works are introduced. We first review some related works on local features and visual phrase, and then introduce standardized VLAD model. Finally, dimensionality reduction is simply introduced.

2.1   Local Feature and Visual Phrase

Local features of images play a key role in image retrieval. There are many excellent features such as the SIFT, PCA-SIFT and SURF descriptors etc. For the SIFT descriptor, it is robust against local translation, scaling, rotation and partial invariant for both illumination changes and affine projection of images. It has achieved good performance for image retrieval [12], object recognition [13] etc. However, the high dimensionality of the SIFT descriptor will lead to a high computational cost. SURF descriptor can be regarded as an improved version of the SIFT descriptor. Furthermore, in most instances its performances are comparative with SIFT. Color features are often used for image retrieval, such as HSV color histogram, Color names (CN) and the color boosting Laplacian-of-Gaussian (CLOG) [14] etc. For the HSV color histogram, it only represents the color information, which ignores the color spatial distribution in the image retrieval. Also, the CLOG feature stresses color salience. Color Names, also called as color attributes, were originally proposed in [6]. They are linguistic labels assigned to each pixel of an image. 11 basic color terms of the English language are used to represent color names. Color names are compact and computational efficient. It has been proved that the color feature is effective for image classification and object detection [6,15,16].

For composite features, in [2], a SURF-based color feature (called CSURF) was proposed, and they extacted SURF descriptors from three color pipeline. An image descriptor that combining global color histogram in HSV space and local rootSIFT feature was introduced in [4]. In [5], the author proposed a color-SURF descriptor, which combines SURF with the approximate color local kernel histograms. In information retrieval, representations based on structured visual content can enhance the discriminative ability by combining spatial contextual information. In [17], the author proposed descriptive visual words (DVWs) and descriptive visual phrases (DVPs) as the visual phrase. In [11], they proposed a randomized approach to deriving visual phrase, in the form of spatial random partition. Many algorithms model spatial context information among local features. [18] proposed an improved vocabulary tree based approach by introducing contextual weighting of local features in both descriptor and spatial domains. [19] proposed a one-one spatial relationship method that builds a spatial relationship dictionary embedded with spatial context among local features.

2.2   Vector of Locally Aggregated Descriptors (VLAD)

Vector of locally aggregated descriptors is an efficient encoding method in image retrieval, the process of its implementation is as follows:

(1) Detect interest regions of an image and extract local descriptors, denoted as $x = (x_1, x_2, \ldots, x_n)$.
(2) The local descriptors are quantized to find the nearest visual word on the pre-trained vocabulary $C = (c_1, c_2, \ldots, c_K)$, formula as:

$$NN(x_i) = \arg \min_{k} \|x_i - c_k\|, \tag{1}$$

(3) For each visual word, the differences between the descriptors quantized to it and itself are computed and are summed up, as shown in Eq. (2). Eventually a vector of length $len = Kd$ is obtained and denoted as the VLAD representation, where d represents dimensionality of local descriptors.

$$V_k = \sum_{i:NN(i)=k} (x_i - c_k), \tag{2}$$

(4) The VLAD representation is improved by using power-law normalization [20]. There are two processing steps for computing the VLAD vector V: firstly, a power α is added to the vector with symbol, formulated as Eq. (3), where is a fixed constant. Secondly, the updated vector is l_2-normalized, formula as Eq. (4). This processing operation can reduce the influence caused by visual bursts.

$$V = sign(V)|V|^{\alpha}, 0 \le \alpha < 1 \tag{3}$$

$$V = V/\|V\|_2 \tag{4}$$

3   Methodology

The whole framework of our method is shown in Fig. 1. For a given query, it is divided into several patches. Each block consists few patches, and the SURF descriptors are extracted from each patch. Then, a CN descriptor is extracted in a fixed block centered on each SURF descriptor. After that, the SURF descriptor and its corresponding CN descriptor are combined into a descriptor, called as composite descriptors. Moreover, deep features are extracted in a same block. The composite descriptors in the block are encoded into a vector by VLAD model. The VLAD vector and deep feature of the block are connected into a representation of the block, called as a visual phrase. Thirdly, the visual phrases constitute the representation of the image. Finally, similarities between the query image and the dataset images are measured, and the retrieval results are returned.

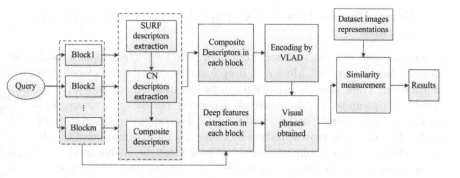

Fig. 1. The whole framework of our method.

3.1 Composite Descriptor

In this paper, we propose a new local descriptor that combines the SURF and the CN descriptors extracted from a same region of the image. The SURF descriptors and the CN descriptors respectively represent the gradient and the color information. Here, our work is similar to [5], however, we use a different color feature, i.e., Color names. There are three reasons to select CN descriptors: Firstly, because in the generation process of CN descriptors several shades of a color are mapped to the same color name, thus, they have a certain amount of photometric invariance. Secondly, the CN descriptor can describe achromatic color such as black, white and gray. Finally, the CN descriptor is a compact representation [6], thus it is very suitable for the composite descriptor. It will be confirmed in our later experiments. Specifically, for an image I, the extracted SURF descriptors are denoted as $x^{SURF} = \left(x_1^{SURF}, x_2^{SURF}, \ldots, x_n^{SURF}\right)$. For an arbitrary SURF descriptor x_i^{SURF}, in the patch of size $p \times p$ around the descriptor, the CN vector corresponding of each pixel in the patch can be obtained. Moreover, the mean of these CN vectors is computed as the CN descriptor corresponding to the patch of the SURF descriptor, denoted as x_i^{CN}. The set of the CN descriptors is denoted as $x^{CN} = \left(x_1^{CN}, x_2^{CN}, \ldots, x_n^{CN}\right)$. Figure 2 shows the extraction process of the CN descriptor. We combine the x_i^{SURF} and x_i^{CN} as a new local descriptor, denoted as x_i^{SC}, as follows:

$$x_i^{SC} = [\omega_1 x_i^{SURF}; \omega_2 x_i^{CN}], \tag{5}$$

where ω_1 and ω_2 are two weight coefficients, $\omega_1 + \omega_2 = 1$. Also, we assume that d^{SURF} and d^{CN} represent the dimensions of the SURF and CN descriptors, respectively. Thus, the dimensionality of composite descriptor x_i^{SC} is $d^{SC} = d^{SURF} + d^{CN}$.

Here, from the process of SURF and CN descriptors extracted, it can be seen that the original two independent features become relevant. Thus, it makes the composite descriptor which combined them be reasonable. Also, since the composite descriptor contains gradient and color information of the same image patch, it can better describe the detail information of the patch.

3.2 Visual Phrases Based on Composite Descriptors and Deep Features

In our proposed composite descriptors, there are local gradient and local color information are involved. Moreover, deep features describe the global structural information. Thus, these information can be mutually compensated to the composite descriptors to a certain extend. To ensure matching accuracy, we divide the image into several patches, and encode the composite descriptors of each patch into a compact representation by using spatial information of the descriptors, called as a visual phrase. Thus, an image can be represented by several visual phrases. Specifically, for an image, it is divided into S blocks. In a block s, the composite descriptors can be obtained according to the processes mentioned in Sect. 3.1, denoted as $x_{(s)}^{SURF} = \left(x_1^{SURF}, x_2^{SURF}, \ldots, x_{n_s}^{SURF}\right)$, and they

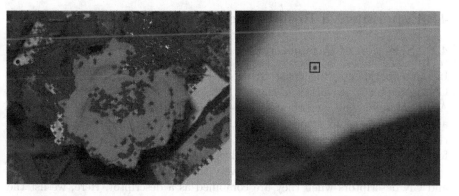

Fig. 2. The process of composite descriptor extracted. (a) The blue keypoints are detected by the SURF algorithm; (b) The black rectangular is the patch of size $p \times p$ around of the SURF keypoint (the blue *). The red circle denotes the CN descriptor corresponding with the SURF descriptor. (Color figure online)

are encoded by VLAD, denoted as $V_{(s)}^{SC}$. Deep features are denoted as $V_{(s)}^{CNN}$. Thus, for the block s, a visual phrase is generated:

$$V_{(s)} = [\lambda_1 V_{(s)}^{SC}; \lambda_2 V_{(s)}^{CNN}], \tag{6}$$

Finally, visual phrases of all blocks form the representation of the whole image, formula as:

$$V = [V_{(1)}, V_{(2)}, \dots, V_{(S)}], \tag{7}$$

3.3 Similarity Measurement

In the image retrieval, similarity measurement depends on the feature matching between images in image retrieval based on local features. Usually, similarity score is obtained by aggregating votes from the matched features. Here, we propose weighted voting method based on visual phrases to measure similarity. Assume two images I_m and I_m, the representations are denoted as $V_{I_m} = [V_{I_m(1)}, V_{I_m(2)}, \dots, V_{I_m(S)}]$ and $V_{I_n} = [V_{I_n(1)}, V_{I_n(2)}, \dots, V_{I_n(S)}]$, where $V_{I_m(i)}$ denotes a visual phrase, i.e., representation of the ith block of image I_m. Assume $V_{I_m(i)}$ and $V_{I_n(i)}$ are two visual phrases, so the score of the block for the image I_m is denoted as:

$$i\_score = g\left(V_{I_m(i)}, V_{I_n(j)}\right), 1 \le j \le S, \tag{8}$$

where $g(\cdot)$ denotes a matching function of two visual phrases. Thus, each block of an image can get a score by similarity measurement with all blocks of the query image, denoted as Eq. (9). After that, the score of the image can be obtained. The results are returned according to the scores of dataset images.

$$score = \sum_{1}^{S} (s\_score), \tag{9}$$

4   Experimental Results and Analysis

4.1   Selection of Parameters

In our experiments, the dense SURF descriptors are extracted from images. CN descriptor is extracted in the 4×4 region around each SURF descriptor. All vocabularies are generated by pre-training on Mirflickr25k [22] dataset by approximate k-means algorithm. Here, we divided each image into 16 patches, then 9 blocks are obtained by sliding 4×4 window with the step of 1. Deep features are extracted by each image block being fed into the VGG-f model [23].

In Eq. (5), ω_1 and ω_2 are respectively the weight parameters of the SURF and CN descriptors when they are combined as a descriptor. Here, we list the retrieval results with different ω_1 and ω_2 on the datasets in Table 1. The better results are marked by bold.

In addition, in Eq. (3), power-law normalization is used, and α is a power exponent of the absolute value of VLAD vector. In our experiments, it is found that the best value of α is between 0.1 and 0.6. we select $\alpha = 0.35$ and $\alpha = 0.4$ for the Holidays and Ukbench datasets respectively, while, on the Oxford5k dataset the best values of α is set to 0.25.

Table 1. The results with different ω_1 and ω_2 on Holidays, Oxford5k and Ukbench datasets.

ω_1	0	0.1	0.2	**0.3**	0.4	**0.5**	0.6	0.7	0.8	**0.9**	1
ω_2	1	0.9	0.8	**0.7**	0.6	**0.5**	0.4	0.3	0.2	**0.1**	0
Holidays (mAP)	0.6286	0.6592	0.6649	0.6723	0.6865	**0.7297**	0.7109	0.7032	0.6896	0.6738	0.6709
Oxford5k (mAP)	0.0862	0.2153	0.2429	0.2766	0.3005	0.3441	0.3605	0.3859	0.3993	**0.3996**	0.3864
Ukbench (N-S score)	3.0825	3.1167	3.1321	**3.1623**	3.1265	3.1217	3.0681	3.0135	2.9500	2.8434	2.7828

4.2   Effectiveness of Visual Phrases

To verify the effectiveness of visual phrases based on composite descriptors and deep features, firstly, we compare the VLAD method based on the composite descriptors with other three different descriptors, denoted as VLAD-SURF, VLAD-CN and VLAD-CSURF. Our composite descriptors (SURFCN) are encoded by VLAD method, denoted as VP-VLAD-SURFCN. The results are shown in Table 2. Here, in our method, only the single vocabulary is adopted and the VLAD vector dimensionality is reduced by the PCA-project operation without whitening operation. The size of vocabulary used in each method of Table 2 is 64. In Table 2, $len = 4800 \times 9$ represents that image representation in our method consists of a matrix of 9 vectors with length of 4800, i.e. 9 visual phrases are selected in our experiments. Moreover, $len' = 128 \times 9$ describes that the dimension of each vector is reduced to 128. It can be seen that our composite descriptors achieve the best performances on Holidays and Oxford5k datasets.

On Ukbench datasets the accuracies of retrieval are slightly worse than VLAD-CSURF. Here, the results look relatively low on Oxford5k dataset. However, it must state that the queries are cropped on Oxford5k for comparing with the results of [2]. Also, the results with * are obtained from [2]. It can be seen that our results obtained for the Holidays and Oxford5k datasets are the best. The results are just acceptable on Ukbench dataset.

Table 2. Comparisons between traditional VLAD-SURF and weighted VLAD-SURF vectors.

Methods		Holidays (mAP)	Oxford5k (mAP) (query cropped)	Ukbench (N-S score)
VLAD-SURF	$len = 4096$	0.6709	0.242	2.689
	$len' = 128$	0.6956	0.2334	2.564
VLAD-CN	$len = 704$	0.6286	–	3.0825
	$len' = 128$	0.6563	–	2.8968
VLAD-CSURF	$len = 12288$	0.717*	0.256*	3.520*
	$len' = 128$	0.697*	0.167*	3.482*
VP-VLAD-SURFCN	$len = 4800 \times 9$	0.7297	0.2638	3.1285
	$len' = 128 \times 9$	0.7009	0.2152	3.0010

In this paper, we adopt visual phrases which consist in local deep features and local VLAD vectors based on composite descriptors. In Eq. (6), λ_1, λ_2 represent the weights of VLAD vector and deep feature respectively when they are fused. The fusion results with different values of λ_1, λ_2 are listed in Table 3, where the vocabularies based on SURFCN descriptors with size 64 are used. It can be seen that the results are the best when λ_1, λ_2 are set to be 0.4 and 0.6 on Oxford5k dataset and 0.5 and 0.5 respectively on Holidays and Ukbench datasets.

Table 3. The fusion results of deep feature and VLAD vectors with different λ_1 and λ_2 on Holidays, Oxford5k and Ukbench datasets.

λ_1	0.1	0.2	0.3	**0.4**	**0.5**	0.6	0.7	0.8	0.9
λ_2	0.9	0.8	0.7	**0.6**	**0.5**	0.4	0.3	0.2	0.1
Holidays(mAP)	0.7387	0.7615	0.7818	0.8017	**0.8186**	0.7952	0.7692	0.7410	0.7234
Oxford5k (mAP)	0.4340	0.4393	0.4509	**0.4597**	0.4569	0.4456	0.4230	0.4077	0.4006
Ukbench (N-S score)	3.4596	3.5349	3.5548	3.5645	**3.5658**	3.3574	3.2689	3.2378	3.2021

The comparison results of our method with ot her methods are shown in Table 4. Here, VP-VLAD-SURFCN denotes image representation (contains local VLAD visual phrases based on composite descriptors), where the vocabulary size is 64. Similar, VP-CNN represents image representation, consisting of visual phrases based on deep features. VLAD-SURFCN expresses that SUR-FCN descriptors are extracted from the whole image and encoded by the VLAD model, and CNN is deep features of the whole image. In Table 4, the results of our proposed visual phrases is better than VLAD-SURFCN and CNN. In Table 4, on the Holidays dataset, the mAPs generated by using VP-VLAD-SURFCN and VP-CNN are 0.7572 and 0.7293, respectively, while the result reaches 0.8281 by fusing VP-VLAD-SURFCN and VP-CNN. It can be seen that our proposed method achieves the best result on the three datasets.

Table 4. Comparison results of our method by fusing of the CNN features and multiple VLAD vectors with other methods.

Methods	Length	Holidays (mAP)	Oxford5k (mAP)	Ukbench (N-S score)
Triangulation embedding [24]	128	0.617	–	3.40
VLAD-CSURF [2]	128	0.738	0.293	3.50
VLAD-SURFCN	128	0.7560	0.3999	2.9975
VP-VLAD-SURFCN	128 × 9	0.7572	0.3996	3.1546
DST-SIFT [26]	128	–	0.3930	–
CNN	128	0.7179	0.3647	3.4203
VP-CNN	128 × 9	0.7293	0.4285	3.4560
Deep fully connected+VLAD [25]	512	0.783	–	–
OUR	128 × 9	**0.8281**	**0.4552**	**3.5498**

5   Conclusion

A composite descriptor consisting of the local gradient information and the local color information of the same image block was proposed in this paper, thus, two irrelevant features become related. Since local features have few the spatial contextual information that is very important for image matching and retrieval, thus, to improve the retrieval accuracy, we proposed a novel retrieval framework that includes partition of image block, generation of visual phrase and similarity measurement, where each visual phrase consists of the deep feature and VLAD vector based on composite descriptor. Since many different features can express different image visual contents, thus, the descriptive ability of the image representation based on visual phrases can be improved when they are bundle together to represent an image. Experimental results showed that compared with other methods, our algorithm obtained better results in three benchmark datasets.

References

1. Jégou, H., Douze, M., Schmid, C., et al.: Aggregating local descriptors into a compact image representation. In: IEEE Computer Society Conference on Computer Vision and Pattern Recognition, pp. 3304–3311. IEEE, San Francisco (2010). https://doi.org/10.1109/CVPR.2010.5540039
2. Spyromitros-Xioufis, E.: A comprehensive study over VLAD and product quantization in large-scale image retrieval. IEEE Trans. Multimed. **16**(6), 1713–1728 (2014)
3. Spyromitros-Xioufis, E., Papadopoulos, S., Kompatsiaris, I.Y., et al.: An empirical study on the combination of surf features with VLAD vectors for image search. In: 13th International Workshop on Image Analysis for Multimedia Interactive Services, pp. 1–4. IEEE, Dublin (2012). https://doi.org/10.1109/WIAMIS.2012.6226771
4. Alzu'bi, A., Amira, A., Ramzan, N., Jaber, T.: Robust fusion of color and local descriptors for image retrieval and classification. In: 2015 International Conference on Systems, Signals and Image Processing (IWSSIP), pp. 253–256. IEEE, London (2015). https://doi.org/10.1109/IWSSIP.2015.7314224
5. Fan, P., Men, A., Chen, M., et al.: COLOR-SURF: a SURF descriptor with local kernel color histograms. In: IEEE International Conference on Network Infrastructure and Digital Content, pp. 726–730. IEEE, Beijing (2009). https://doi.org/10.1109/ICNIDC.2009.5360809
6. Weijer, J.V.D., Schmid, C., Verbeek, J., Larlus, D.: Learning color names for real-world applications. IEEE Trans. Image Process. **18**(7), 1512–1523 (2009)
7. Krizhevsky, A., Sutskever, I., Hinton, G.E.: Imagenet classification with deep convolutional neural networks. In: 25th International Conference on Neural Information Processing Systems, pp. 1097–1105, Curran Associates Inc., Lake Tahoe (2012). https://doi.org/10.1145/3065386
8. Zeiler, M.D., Fergus, R.: Visualizing and understanding convolutional networks. In: Fleet, D., Pajdla, T., Schiele, B., Tuytelaars, T. (eds.) ECCV 2014. LNCS, vol. 8689, pp. 818–833. Springer, Cham (2014). https://doi.org/10.1007/978-3-319-10590-1_53
9. Razavian, A.S., Azizpour, H., Sullivan, J., Carlsson, S.: CNN features off-the-shelf: an astounding baseline for recognition. In: IEEE Conference on Computer Vision and Pattern Recognition Workshops, pp. 512–519. IEEE, Columbus (2014). https://doi.org/10.1109/CVPRW.2014.131
10. Babenko, A., Slesarev, A., Chigorin, A., Lempitsky, V.: Neural codes for image retrieval. In: Fleet, D., Pajdla, T., Schiele, B., Tuytelaars, T. (eds.) ECCV 2014. LNCS, vol. 8689, pp. 584–599. Springer, Cham (2014). https://doi.org/10.1007/978-3-319-10590-1_38
11. Jiang, Y., Meng, J., Yuan, J.: Randomized visual phrases for object search. In: IEEE Conference on Computer Vision and Pattern Recognition, pp. 3100–3104. IEEE, Providence (2012). https://doi.org/10.1109/CVPR.2012.6248042
12. Zheng, L., Wang, S., Liu, Z., Tian, Q.: Packing and padding: coupled multi-index for accurate image retrieval. In: 2014 IEEE Conference on Computer Vision and Pattern Recognition, pp. 1947–1954. IEEE, Columbus (2014). https://doi.org/10.1109/CVPR.2014.250
13. Arandjelovic, R.: Three things everyone should know to improve object retrieval. In: 2012 IEEE Conference on Computer Vision and Pattern Recognition, vol. 157, pp. 2911–2918. IEEE, Providence (2012). https://doi.org/10.1109/CVPR.2012.6248018

14. Vigo, D.A.R., Khan, F.S., Weijer, J.V.D., Gevers, T.: The impact of color on bag-of-words based object recognition. In: 20th International Conference on Pattern Recognition, pp. 1549–1553. IEEE, Istanbul (2010). https://doi.org/10.1109/ICPR.2010.383

15. Khan, F.S.: Modulating shape features by color attention for object recognition. Int. J. Comput. Vis. **98**(1), 49–64 (2012)

16. Bagdanov, A.D.: Color attributes for object detection. In: 2012 IEEE Conference on Computer Vision and Pattern Recognition, vol. 157, pp. 3306–3313. IEEE, Providence (2012). https://doi.org/10.1109/CVPR.2012.6248068

17. Zhang, S.: Generating descriptive visual words and visual phrases for large-scale image applications. IEEE Trans. Image Process. **20**(9), 2664–2677 (2011)

18. Cour, T., Zhu, S., Han, T.X.: Contextual weighting for vocabulary tree based image retrieval. In: 2011 International Conference on Computer Vision, vol. 23, pp. 209–216. IEEE, Barcelona (2011). https://doi.org/10.1109/ICCV.2011.6126244

19. Liu, Z., Li, H., Zhou, W., Tian, Q.: Embedding spatial context information into inverted filefor large-scale image retrieval. In: 20th ACM International Conference on Multimedia, pp. 199–208. ACM, Nara (2012). https://doi.org/10.1145/2393347.2393380

20. Perronnin, F., Liu, Y., Sánchez, J., Poirier, H.: Large-scale image retrieval with compressed Fisher vectors. In: 2010 IEEE Computer Society Conference on Computer Vision and Pattern Recognition, vol. 26, pp. 3384–3391. IEEE, San Francisco (2010). https://doi.org/10.1109/CVPR.2010.5540009

21. Jégou, H., Chum, O.: Negative evidences and co-occurences in image retrieval: the benefit of PCA and whitening. In: Fitzgibbon, A., Lazebnik, S., Perona, P., Sato, Y., Schmid, C. (eds.) ECCV 2012. LNCS, pp. 774–787. Springer, Heidelberg (2012). https://doi.org/10.1007/978-3-642-33709-3_55

22. Huiskes, M.J., Lew, M.S.: The MIR flickr retrieval evaluation. In: 1st ACM International Conference on Multimedia Information Retrieval, pp. 39–43. ACM, Vancouver (2008). https://doi.org/10.1145/1460096.1460104

23. Chatfield, K., Simonyan, K., Vedaldi, A., Zisserman, A.: Return of the devil in the details: delving deep into convolutional nets. (2014). https://doi.org/10.5244/C.28.6

24. Jégou, H., Zisserman, A.: Triangulation embedding and democratic aggregation for image search. In: 2014 IEEE Conference on Computer Vision and Pattern Recognition, pp. 3310–3317. IEEE, Columbus (2014). https://doi.org/10.1109/CVPR.2014.417

25. Gong, Y., Wang, L., Guo, R., Lazebnik, S.: Multi-scale orderless pooling of deep convolutional activation features. In: Fleet, D., Pajdla, T., Schiele, B., Tuytelaars, T. (eds.) ECCV 2014. LNCS, vol. 8695, pp. 392–407. Springer, Cham (2014). https://doi.org/10.1007/978-3-319-10584-0_26

26. Dong, J., Soatto, S.: Domain-size pooling in local descriptors: DSP-SIFT, pp. 5097–5106. eprint arXiv:1412.8556 (2014)

Defect Detection of Alumina Substrate with Adaptive Edge Detection Algorithm

Chaorong Li[1,2(✉)], Liangwei Chen[3], Lihong Zhu[2], and Yu Xue[4]

[1] Center for Information in BioMedicine, Key Laboratory for Neuroinformation
of Ministry of University of Electronic Science and Technology, Chengdu, China
`lichaorong88@163.com`
[2] Department of Computer Science and Information Engineering,
Yibin University, Yibin 644000, China
[3] Department of Information and Engineering, Chengdu Aeronautic Vocational
and Technical College, Chengdu 610100, China
[4] School of Computer and Software, Nanjing University of Information Science
and Technology, Nanjing, China

Abstract. Detecting surface defects of alumina substrate by using computer technique will enhance productivity in industrial manufacture. Edge detection of image is the commonly used technique for the detection of surface defects. However, it is difficult to automatically detect the surface defects of the alumina substrate since the noise and the multiple kinds of defects may exist in a substrate. In this paper, we designed an edge detection algorithm based on Canny detector aiming to automatically detect the surface defects of alumina substrate. Our algorithm can adaptively smooth image as well as adaptively determine the low threshold and high threshold. Experiments show that our algorithm can effectively and automatically detect several kinds of surface defects in the alumina substrate.

Keywords: Alumina ceramic · Surface defect · Defect detection
Canny algorithm · Lifting wavelet · Multilevel Otsu algorithm

1 Introduction

Alumina ceramic is composite material composed of alumina (major component) and other additive materials. It has some excellent properties such as anticorrosion, wear-resistibility, and insulating from electric and it is widely used in many industrial areas. Alumina substrate is a kind of chip made up of alumina ceramic. Ordinarily, defects exist in an alumina substrate and these defects could seriously affect the performance of the alumina substrate. Typical defects in alumina substrate include impurity, crack, big grain and deformation. Among these defects, impurity and crack are the most common defects. Generally, impurity is resulted from nonferrous metal brought in the producing process. Crack may be formed if the alumina substrate bears improper temperature in the sintering process. In Fig. 1(a) shows an alumina substrate with an impurity, a crack as well some glass-like grains (noise). Small grain and other noise are major interfering factors in the processing of automatic inspection using a computer technique.

© Springer Nature Switzerland AG 2018
X. Sun et al. (Eds.): ICCCS 2018, LNCS 11068, pp. 487–498, 2018.
https://doi.org/10.1007/978-3-030-00021-9_44

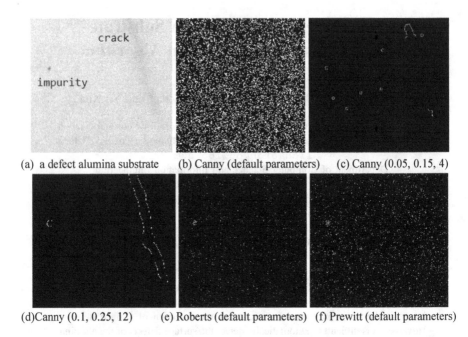

(a) a defect alumina substrate   (b) Canny (default parameters)   (c) Canny (0.05, 0.15, 4)

(d)Canny (0.1, 0.25, 12)   (e) Roberts (default parameters)   (f) Prewitt (default parameters)

Fig. 1. Different edge detectors for alumina defect detection

The defects in substrate alumina, which are inevitable in the producing process, can severely affect the performance of the alumina substrate. Alumina substrates with defects are unqualified and it should be removed from qualified products. Automatic inspection based on the computer vision is an important technique to detect surface defects and it also can increase the efficiency of production lines and improve the quality of product. However, it is difficult to automatically detect the defects by using computer vision technique because of the existence of the noise or glass-like grain in the image of alumina ceramic. So far, the quality of alumina substrate is still largely inspected by human labors. It is well known that the manual inspection is labor tedious, highly cost and is also insufficient to meet the high quality requirement of products.

Some defect detection approaches based on computer vision have been developed during the last two decades. Energy descriptors [1] were utilized to capture feature for inspection of ceramic tiles. An approach based on optimized filters was used to defect detection [2]. Gabor filters were used to enhance the image and then detect the defects of textured material [3]. Wavelet-based methods also are exploited to the defect detection in [4, 5]. The edge information of image is useful in applications such as image segmentation, object extraction, image registration, and image pattern recognition. For example, in [6, 7] edge detection techniques were employed to extract the defects of image.

Canny edge algorithm is a good edge detector. However, it has some drawbacks (e.g., difficult to determine threshold values) which limit its applications to industry. Furthermore, we found that the detecting results are not always satisfactory if we directly apply the edge detectors to an alumina substrate. Figure 1(a) shows a defect alumina substrate image, and Fig. 1(b)–(d) are the results by using Canny edge detector with different parentheses (inside the parentheses, the value are respectively the low threshold, high threshold and sigma). Figure 1(e) and (f) are the results using Roberts and Prewitt edge detector. It is obvious that all the edge detectors are difficultly to detect the three kinds of defects. The Canny edge detector has relatively good performance, but it is sensitive to noise and parameters (including the two thresholds and sigma). Parameter sensitivity of a detecting method is quite negative to automatic detection. Therefore, the aim of this paper is to detect the defects of alumina substrate by using the proposed adaptive Canny.

2 Background

2.1 Canny Edge Detector

First we briefly introduce the original Canny algorithm [10, 12]. The Canny edge detector is developed to discover the optimal edges of image by using multi-stage algorithm. The original Canny edge detector consists of following stages:

a) Smoothing the input image $f(x, y)$ using a Gaussian mask $h(x, y|\sigma)$ with the variance parameter σ: $g(x, y) = h(x, y|\sigma) * f(x, y)$. The Gaussian mask is conducted by Gaussian function. Gaussian function has following express:

$$h(x, y|\sigma) = \frac{1}{2\pi\sigma^2} \exp\left(-(x^2 + y^2)/(2\sigma^2)\right) \tag{1}$$

b) Calculating horizontal gradients $G_X(x, y)$, vertical gradients $G_Y(x, y)$, gradient magnitude $M(x, y)$ and direction $\theta(x, y)$ at each pixel location. They are calculated as:

$$G_X(x, y) = [f(x+1, y) - f(x, y) + f(x+1, y+1) - f(x, y+1)]/2 \tag{2}$$

$$G_Y(x, y) = [f(x, y+1) - f(x, y) + f(x+1, y+1) - f(x+1, y)]/2 \tag{3}$$

$$M(x, y) = \sqrt{G_X(x, y)^2 + G_Y(x, y)^2}, \theta(x, y) = \arctan(G_X(x, y)/G_Y(x, y)) \tag{4}$$

c) Suppressing non-maximal strong edges. Given the image gradient magnitude, a search is then carried out to determine if the gradient magnitude assumes a local maximum in the gradient direction.

d) Computing a low threshold and a high threshold based on the histogram of the gradient magnitudes of the image. This double threshold method is applied to determine possible (potential) edges. In the magnitude map, the pixel value greater than the high threshold is marked as strong; pixel value less than the low threshold is removed and pixel value between the two thresholds is marked as weak.

(e) Performing hysteresis thresholding for connected weak edges by using high and low thresholds. Strong edges can immediately be included in the final edge image. Weak edges are included if and only if they are connected to strong edges.

(f) Applying morphological thinning on the resulting edge map (Fig. 2).

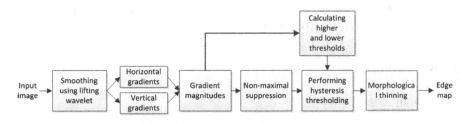

Fig. 2. Flowchart of canny algorithm

2.2   Wavelet Transform and Lifting Wavelet Transform

Wavelet transform is a powerful tool for localized frequency analysis. It decomposes an input image into a smooth part and several detailed parts at different scales. The 2D (two-dimension) wavelet transform which can be used to analyze 2D signal is performed by using a 1D wavelet transformation in term of rows and column respectively. Filter banks implementation of 2D wavelet transform is shown in Fig. 3(a). H(Z) is the low-pass filter and G(Z) is the high-pass filter. The structure of coefficients of 2-level decomposition of image is shown in Fig. 3. The cAi (i = 1, 2) is the low frequency coefficients of the 2-level decomposition, which represents the approximation information of the original image. The cHi, cVi and cDi are the high frequency coefficients, which represent the edges and singularities information at the horizontal directions of, vertical and diagonal of the image.

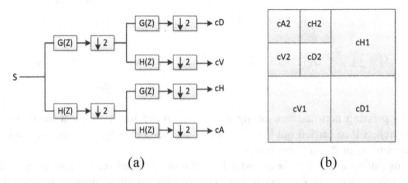

(a)   (b)

Fig. 3. Two-dimension wavelet transform (a) The filter bank implementation of 2D wavelet transform. (b) Coefficients distribution of 2-levels 2D wavelet decomposition.

Lifting wavelet [8] is a memory and computationally efficient implementation of the wavelet transforms, which makes it more suitable for the industrial application. The lifting scheme of wavelet has many advantages compared to filter bank structure, such as lower area, power consumption and computational complexity. The lifting scheme can be easily implemented using hardware because of its significantly reduced computations. Therefore, lifting wavelet is more suitable for detecting the defects of alumina substrate in industrial application. Lifting wavelet is an easiest lifting wavelet and it allows for an in place computation. The decomposition algorithm of lifting wavelet is composed of three steps (see Fig. 4):

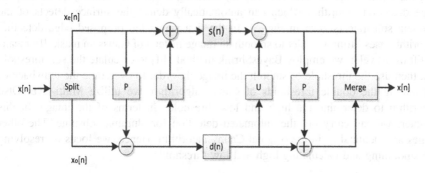

Fig. 4. Lifting wavelet transform

1) **Split**

   In split step the input signals $x(n)$ are separated into two sets of even and odd samples.

   $$x_e(n) = x(2n), \quad x_o(n) = x(2n+1) \tag{5}$$

2) **Prediction**

   The odd samples are predicted by even samples. Prediction step predicts the odd samples using the following equation to produce detail information of the signal.

   $$d(n) = x_o(n) - P[x_e(n)] \tag{6}$$

3) **Update**

   Update step updates the even samples using the following equation to preserve the mean value of samples and generate approximate representation of the signal.

   $$s(n) = x_e(n) + U[d(n)] \tag{7}$$

   $P_i(k)$ and $U_i(k)$ are coefficients depended on wavelet filters.

3   The Proposed Adaptive Edge Detection Algorithm

When applying the canny detector for defect detection, one of the problems is how to determine the high and low thresholds since the different thresholds would lead different detecting results. Another problem is that the noise in an image would degrade the accuracy of the detecting method. Furthermore, although the Canny uses Gaussian mask as smoothing stage (for the purpose of denoising), the variance parameter still need to be preset, which is negative for automatic detection. In recent years, some researchers developed several techniques to compensate for the disadvantages of original Canny edge detector [11, 12]. By referring to these researches, we develop an edge detection algorithm which can automatically detect the surface defects of the alumina substrate (shown in Fig. 5). In the first stage, the proposed edge detecting algorithm uses lifting wavelet to smooth an image instead of Gaussian mask. By means of lifting wavelet, we employ BayesShrink method [14] to calculate the soft threshold and then use the threshold to smooth the image. In order to overcome the drawback of calculating the double thresholds of Canny algorithm, we utilize Multi-level Otsu algorithm to determine the high and low thresholds in terms of the image. In this manner, we can carry out the automated detection for alumina substrate. The other stages are identical as in the original Canny algorithm. Hence, we focus on resolving the smoothing and calculating high and low thresholds.

3.1   Smoothing Image Using Lifting Wavelet Transform

The goal of smoothing is to remove noise from image while retaining as much as possible the edge information of the image. Smoothing algorithms based on the wavelet based method mainly modify the transformed high frequency coefficients by using a threshold and reconstruct the image using those modified coefficients. In this work we smooth alumina substrate image with BayesShrink method [14] which performs soft-thresholding subband-dependent threshold.

Let the noiseless wavelet coefficient be $X = \{x_{ij}, i, j = 1 \cdots, N\}$, the noisy wavelet coefficient be $Y = \{y_{ij} = x_{ij} + v_{ij}, i, j = 1, \cdots, N\}$. Where v_{ij} is additive Gaussian noise signal with variance σ^2. The problem is to estimate X from Y. The soft-threshold function, which is a common estimator of X, is defined as follow [13, 14]

$$\eta_T(t) = \text{sgn}(t) * \max(|t| - T, 0) \tag{8}$$

where T is soft-threshold. With soft-threshold, the estimate of X can be write as: $\tilde{X} = \eta_T(Y)$. The goal of denoising is to find a threshold T by minimizing the mean squared error (MSE)

$$MSE(\tilde{x}) = \frac{1}{N^2} \sum_{i,j=1}^{N} (\tilde{X} - X)^2 = E(\tilde{X} - X)^2 \tag{9}$$

In order to minimize (9), the distribution of wavelet coefficients should be known. In [14] the authors make a detailed study on the statistics of the wavelet coefficients and

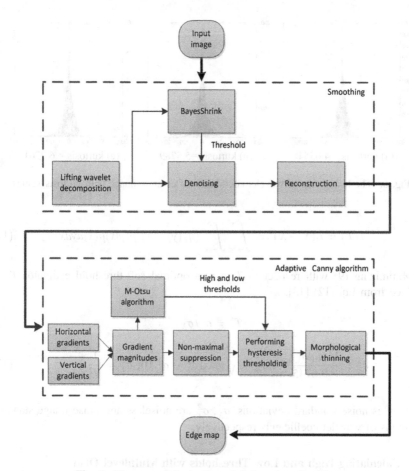

Fig. 5. The proposed adaptive edge detecting algorithm

one of the conclusions shows the subband marginal distributions of natural images in the wavelet domain are highly non-Gaussian. Our experimental results support the conclusion. Figure 6 plots eight histograms of eight directional subbands of a ceramic substrate image with defects. All the kurtosis values are higher than the standards value of 3 for Gaussian distribution. So wavelet coefficients cannot be modeled by Gaussian distribution. In our scheme the *generalized Gaussian distribution* (GGD) is used as the distribution of wavelet coefficients. The GGD is defined as [14]

$$GG_{\beta,\sigma_X}(x) = C(\beta, \sigma_X)\exp - (\alpha(\beta, \sigma_X)|x|)^{\beta} \tag{10}$$

where $C(\beta, \sigma_X) = \frac{\beta\alpha(\beta,\sigma_X)}{2\Gamma(1/\beta)}$ and $\alpha(\beta, \sigma_X) = \sigma_X^{-1}\left[\frac{\Gamma(3/\beta)}{\Gamma(1/\beta)}\right]^{1/2}$; σ_X is the standard deviation and β is the shape parameter. From above two priors can be obtain: $Y|X \sim N(x, \sigma^2)$, $X \sim GG_{\beta,\sigma_x}$. Then the (9) can be written as follow

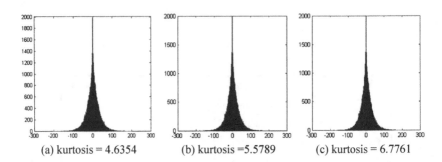

(a) kurtosis = 4.6354   (b) kurtosis = 5.5789   (c) kurtosis = 6.7761

Fig. 6. The histograms of wavelet coefficients of ceramic image with kurtosis values

$$r(T) = E(\tilde{X} - X)^2 = \int_{-\infty}^{\infty} \int_{-\infty}^{\infty} (\eta_T(y) - x)^2 p(y|x)p(x)dydx \tag{11}$$

Minimizing (9) with respect to T, a near-optimal soft-threshold estimator T^* is obtained from Eq. (12) [13].

$$T^* = \sigma^2/\sigma_X \tag{12}$$

$$\sigma^2 = \frac{Median(y_{ij})}{0.6745}, \ \sigma_X = \sqrt{\max(\sigma_Y^2 - \sigma^2, 0)}, \ \sigma_Y^2 = \frac{1}{N^2}\sum_{i,j=1}^{N} y_{ij}^2 \tag{13}$$

where σ^2 is noise standard deviations. σ_X^2, σ_Y^2 are noiseless and noise image standard deviations of wavelet coefficients respectively.

3.2   Calculating High and Low Thresholds with Multilevel Otsu

The goal of Otsu algorithm [9] is to choose the optimal threshold t (image intensity) to segment an image by maximizing the between-class variance. Given an image, the number of pixels with gray level i is denoted n_i. The probability of gray level i is defined as $p_i = n_i/N$. Assuming that an image contains N pixels with gray levels from 1 to L and the pixels are divided into two classes, C_1 with gray levels $[1, \cdots, t]$ and C_2 with gray level $[t+1, \cdots, L]$(where t is the threshold), optimal threshold t^* can be calculated by maximizing between-class variance as follow

$$t* = \arg\max_t \left(\sigma_M^2(t)\right) \tag{14}$$

Inspired by Otsu algorithm, we divided the gradient magnitudes into three classes, C_1 C_1 for $[1, \ldots, t_1]$, C_2 for $[t+1, \cdots, t_2]$, C_3 for $[t_2+1, \cdots, L]$. C_1, C_2 and C_3 represent the weak, moderate and strong sections of threshold value respectively. Multilevel Otsu algorithm is formulated as follow:

$$\sigma_M(t_1, t_2) = \sum_{k=1}^{3} \omega_k(t)(\mu_k - \mu_T)^2 \tag{15}$$

where the mean of the whole image $\mu_T = \sum_{k=1}^{3} \omega_k(t)\mu_k$. μ_k is the mean of class C_k, $k = 1, 2, 3$.

$$\mu_1 = \sum_{i=1}^{t_1} ip_i/\omega_1(t), \ \mu_2 = \sum_{i=t_1+1}^{t_2} ip_i/\omega_1(t), \ \mu_3 = \sum_{i=t_2+1}^{L} ip_i/\omega_2(t) \tag{16}$$

where $\omega_1(t) = \sum_{i=1}^{t_1} p_i$, $\omega_2(t) = \sum_{i=t_1+1}^{t_2} p_i$, $\omega_3(t) = \sum_{i=t_2+1}^{L} p_i$, satisfy the condition of $\sum_{i=1}^{3} \omega_i(t) = 1$. Then the high threshold t_1^* and low threshold t_2^* can be computed from Eq. (22)

$$(t_1^*, t_2^*) = \arg\max_{t_1, t_2} \sigma_M^2(t_1, t_2) \tag{17}$$

Calculating t_1^* and t_2^* using (17) is time-consuming. For improving the efficiency of computation, we can resort the fast multilevel thresholding developed in [15] to obtain the optimal thresholds.

4 Experimental Results

In this section, several experiments are used to detect the defects of alumina substrates by employing the proposed improved Canny algorithm. The improved Canny method is implemented at the Matlab environment. First the "circuit" and "eight" pictures are used for testing and the output images are shown in Fig. 7. The output of original Canny [Fig. 7(b)] shows more edges but also appears more fake edge than improved Canny.

Two types of defects, crack and impurity [see Fig. 1(a)], are selected from an alumina product plant for the experiments. Figure 8 shows three sample images with crack and impurity defects. The second row of Fig. 8 is the output images by using original Canny algorithm with presented parameters (low threshold = 0.16, high threshold = 0.4, sigma = 2) and the third row is the output images by using improved Canny algorithm without parameters. Note that the edges of original Canny output images have some fractures, while the output images of improved Canny show better edges.

Finally, we make an analysis to the computing time of our method. Because the proposed edge detection algorithm uses complexity algorithms for smoothing image and selecting the double thresholds, it will consume more computing time than Canny algorithm. In Fig. 9(a) three smoothing methods including lifting wavelet, Gaussian filter and wavelet are compared (the wavelet filter is "db4"). It can be seen that lifting wavelet consumes less time than traditional wavelet, and the method consumes the least time is the Gaussian filter. Hence the lifting wavelet but not wavelet is employed in our method. The total computational time of improved Canny is also longer than Canny algorithm, as seen in Fig. 9(b).

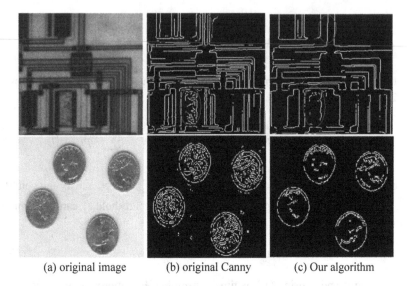

(a) original image   (b) original Canny   (c) Our algorithm

Fig. 7. Output images by using our algorithm

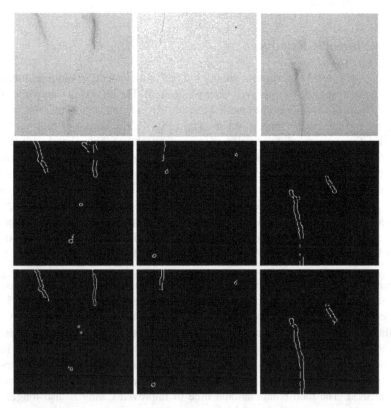

Fig. 8. Output images of original canny and our algorithm on alumina substrates

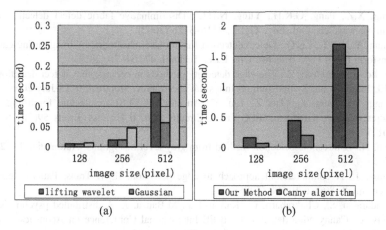

Fig. 9. Computing time comparison. (a) Computational time of three smoothing methods; (b) Computational time of two canny algorithms.

5 Conclusions

In this paper, an adaptive edge detection algorithm for detecting surface defects of alumna substrate was developed by focusing on obtaining the characteristic of automatic detection and the good detecting effect. The main advantages of our detecting algorithm are it can adaptively smooth image as well as automatically determine the low threshold and high threshold. By this manner, the proposed detecting method has high practical value in surface defect detection. The satisfying performance of the proposed detecting algorithm was obtained from the experimental results.

Acknowledgements. This work is supported by the China Postdoctoral Science Foundation (No. 2016M602675), the Foundation of Central Universities in China (No. ZYGX2016J123), and the Project of Education Department of Sichuan Province (No. 16ZA0328), PhD research startup foundation of Yibin University (No. 2015QD08), and Sichuan Science and Technology Program (No. 2018JY0117).

References

1. Habib, H.A., Yousaf, M.H., Mohibullah, M.: Modified laws energy descriptor for inspection of ceramic tiles. In: National Conference on Emerging Technologies, vol. 34, no. 5, pp. 138–140 (2004)
2. Kumar, A., Pang, G.K.H.: Defect detection in textured materials using optimized filters. IEEE Trans. Syst. Man Cybern. Part B Cybern. **32**(5), 553–570 (2002)
3. Kumar, A., Pang, G.K.H.: Defect detection in textured materials using Gabor filters. IEEE Trans. Ind. Appl. **38**(2), 425–440 (2002)
4. Li, W.-C., Tsai, D.-M.: Wavelet-based defect detection in solar wafer images with inhomogeneous texture. Pattern Recognit. **45**(2), 742–756 (2012)

5. Yang, X.Z., Pang, G.K.H., Yung, N.H.C.: Discriminative fabric defect detection using adaptive wavelets. Opt. Eng. **41**(12), 3116–3126 (2002)
6. Zhang, Y., Li, T., Li, Q.: Defect detection for tire laser shearography image using curvelet transform based edge detector. Opt. Laser Technol. **47**, 64–71 (2013)
7. Vasilic, S., Hocenski, Z.: The edge detecting methods in ceramic tiles defect detection. In: IEEE International Symposium on Industrial Electronics, Montreal, 9–13 July 2006
8. Zhang, W., Jiang, Z., Gao, Z., Liu, Y.: An efficient VLSI architecture for lifting-based discrete wavelet transform. IEEE Trans. Circuits Syst. II Express. Briefs **59**(3), 158–162 (2012)
9. Otsu, N.: A threshold selection method from gray-level histograms. Automatica **11**, 23–27 (1975)
10. Canny, J.: A computational approach to edge detection. IEEE Trans. Pattern Recognit. Mach. Intell. **8**(6), 679–698 (1986)
11. Varadarajan, S., Chakrabarti, C., Karam, L.J., M.Bauza, J.: A distributed psycho-visually motivated Canny edge detector. In: IEEE International Conference on Acoustics, Speech, and Signal Processing, Dallas, pp. 14–19 (2010)
12. McIlhagga, W.: The Canny edge detector revisited. Int. J. Comput. Vis. **91**(3), 251–261 (2011)
13. Mihcak, M.K., Kozintsev, I., Ramchandran, K., Moulin, P.: Low complexity image denoising based on statistical modeling of wavelet coefficients. IEEE Signal Process. Lett. **6**(12), 300–303 (1999)
14. Chang, S.G., Yu, B., Vetterli, M.: Adaptive wavelet thresholding for image denoising and compression. IEEE Trans. Image Process. **9**(9), 1532–1546 (2000)
15. Liao, P.-S., Chen, T.-S., Chung, P.-C.: A fast algorithm for multilevel thresholding. J. Inf. Sci. Eng. **17**(5), 713–727 (2001)

Disseminating Quality-Based Analysis
of Microblog Users' Influencing Ability

Ziqi Tang$^{(\boxtimes)}$, Junyong Luo, Meijuan Yin, Xiaonan Liu,
and Yan Zheng

China State Key Laboratory of Mathematical Engineering
and Advanced Computing, Zhengzhou, China
690245411@qq.com

Abstract. In fact, microblog users' influencing ability is the same thing to their spreadability. The research of microblog users' spreadability has received much attention in the past years, towards which most of the existing advanced methods are based on the spread range of users' blogs. However, those methods neglect the blogs' disseminating quality, we find that only the spread range of those blogs with disseminating quality could precisely indicate the spreadability of microblog users, yet those without will jeopardise the precision of the analysis of users' spreadability. In addition, the information dissemination in microblog mainly relies on the followers' reposting behavior, yet the existing methods have not taken much into consideration of the factors that affect the followers' reposting behavior. In this paper, the blogs' disseminating quality in microblog is thoroughly studied. In addition, we propose a method to measure microblog users' spreadability based on the forecast of the spread range of users' blogs possessing disseminating quality. In the analysis, we innovatively combine the users' attention degree received from their followers and interest similarity between them. We conducted several experiments on the real data set of Sina Weibo, a very common and popular microblog in China, and the results prove the accuracy of our method.

Keywords: Spreadability · Microblog · Disseminating quality

1 Introduction

Many researchers have been studied the influential node in complex network since 1980s, which laid a firm theoretical foundation for the latter research of identifying influentials in social network. In 1972, Bonacich [1] proposed degree centrality and eigenvector Eigenvector centrality, he believed the importance of a node depends both on the number and the importance of its neighbor nodes. In 1983, Burt [2] pointed out that the importance of nodes in the network is equivalent to the importance of the connections with its neighbor nodes. Currently, most of the methods measuring the influence of microblog users are based on the network topology importance, yet microblogs are social medias, where users influence others by spreading information, thus in microblog, the most influential users are those with highest spreadability.

X. Sun et al. (Eds.): ICCCS 2018, LNCS 11068, pp. 499–514, 2018.
https://doi.org/10.1007/978-3-030-00021-9_45

At present, the main indicator of microblog users' spreadability is the average spread range of their blogs, but we find that some users with high spreadability sometimes post some blogs that will nerver be reposted, which seriously affect the analysis precision of users' spreadability. As shown in Fig. 1, microblog user u has posted blog A, which possess disseminating quality, it also has posted blog B and blog C, which do not, yet user v has only posted blog A. Trees in Fig. 1 correspond to the dissemination cascades of each blog respectively triggered by user u and user v.

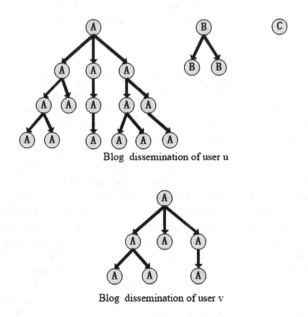

Fig. 1. The dissemination cascades of users' blogs

As can be seen from Fig. 1, for blog A, the spread range triggered by user u is obviously bigger than that triggered by user v, apparently user u has higher spreadability than user v, because the other two blogs posted by user u do not possess disseminating quality. This two blogs will not cause apparent spread range no matter who post it, however, if we do not consider disseminating quality of each blog and simply measure the users' spreadability via average spread range, the calculated result will tell that user u has lower spreadability because of blog B and blog C. This kind phenomenon is quite normal in microblog, thus when analysing the spreadability of microblog users, we take blogs' disseminating quality into consideration.

Moreover, the current methods measuring microblog users' spreadability have not consider the factors that affect the followers' reposting behavior in the calculation of followers' reposting probability, which decreases the calculation precision. In a microblog, such as Sina Weibo, the most influential factors of microblog users' reposting behavior are attention degree and interest similarity [3, 4]. Attention degree means the degree a follower pays attention to a user, which can be seen from the follower's behavior towards the user, such as thumb-up, comment and repost.

Obviously the higher the follower's attention degree towards the user, the higher the probability that the follower repost the user' blogs. In addition, interest similarity refers to the similarity between the topics of the follower's blogs and the topic of users', obviously, the follower with same interest to the user is more inclined to repost the user's blogs than the user's other follower.

In this paper, we thoroughly analyse the blogs' disseminating quality in microblog, and try to find the features of blogs possessing it, based on which we obtain a pure data set of blogs with disseminating quality. Then we combine the attention degree and interest similarity to calculate the followers' reposting probability, with which the spread range of user's blogs can be forecasted, then we take the spread range expectation of users' blogs as the final indicator to measures their spreadability.

The remainder of the paper is organized as follows. We review the related work in Sect. 2. In Sect. 3 we analyse the disseminating quality of blogs in microblog. In Sect. 3, we present a model of spreadability. Section 4 introduce the experiment we conducted on the data set of Sina Weibo. Finally, in Sect. 5 we Summarize this paper and our future work.

2 Related Work

In 2003, Kempe et al. [5] studied the "influence maximization" problem in social network like microblog under a parameter-given model, they searched for the best combination of seed users, which maximized the spread range of influence, yet they have not studied how to infer the correct parameters for the model, therefore their method can not be directly used to measure the spreadability of microblog users. In 2005, Borgatti et al. [6] proposed method to measure the users' influence in a social network based on their contribution to the network cohesion. In 2008, Zhai et al. [7] combined the user interest with PageRank algorithm to identify the opinion leader in the network constructed by the comment relations among users in BBS.

This early studies are mainly based on network topology, via which the found influentials are those with many followers, however, Cha [8] pointed out that micro-blog users with many followers may not be able to trigger more reposting behavior, which means they can not be used to measure the users' influencing ability in social network.

In the social media like microblog, users' spreadability can better represent their influencing ability. In 2011, Bakshy [9] proposed a method to forecast the average size of the dissemination cascades of users' blogs to measure their influencing ability, yet this method selected static indicators from the history data, which brings limitations to the forecast precision in the dynamic microblog network. In 2013, Ding et al. [10] believed that the users' reposting behavior features and the user's network location and has a strong correlation with users' spreadability, and combined these two factors to comprehensively measure users' spreadability, of which the experiment results turned out to be good, but this method still needs improvement for the lack of thorough studies users' reposting behavior, without which the users' reposting probability can not be calculated correctly, yet the reposting probability is the key to the measurement of users' spreadability. In 2014, In the microblog network, Mao et al. [11] introduced reading and reposting behavior into their model, based on which they forecast the spread range of users' blogs to measure their spreadability, their method has achieved good results, but they neglected the follower's interest and their attention degree towards the users they follow when calculating their reposting probability. In 2016, Liu et al. [12] combined the user interests and blogs' attributes to forecast microblog users' reposting behavior and achieved good results, but they did not calculate the users' reposting probability, but still, their method inspire us a lot.

All the above spreadability-measuring methods neglect a significant factor, the disseminating quality of the information spread by users, which will lead to considerable deviation to the measurement of users' spreadability.

In this paper, we thoroughly study the disseminating quality in microblog, and analyse the features of blogs possessing disseminating quality, based on which the experimental data sets are filtered. In the pure disseminating quality-possessing blogs data set, we calculate the users' reposting probability with interest similarity and attention degree, based on which, we calculate the spread range expectations of users' blogs to measure their spreadability.

Analysis of Disseminating Quality

Microblog users influence others via the dissemination of their blogs' information, thus in order to accurately measure the user's influencing ability, we need to focus on those blogs possessing disseminating quality. First of all, we must answer two critical questions below:

- What is disseminating quality?
- What are the features of blogs with disseminating quality?

1. What is dissemination quality?

For the first question, this paper gives a vague explanation about disseminating quality: The higher a blog's disseminating quality, the bigger the probability that the blog get reposted. We divide the blogs into four types, life-recording, entertaining, advertising and thoughts-expressing. Then, we randomly selected 100 users in Sina Weibo and obtain 45363 blogs they have posted, in the meantime, we randomly crawled 100000 blogs, of which each has been reposted at least 100 times. At last, we draw the distribution pictures for the 4 types of blogs of this two data set.

As can be seen from Figs. 2 and 3, 35% of the blogs in the first data set are life-recording, while in another dataset, in which each blog has been reposted a least 100 times, those blogs undoubtedly possess disseminating quality, yet only 1% of them are life-recording. The comparison tells the fact that in microblog a considerable amount of blogs do not possess disseminating quality and would nerver be reposted. However, to the best of our knowledge, this important fact is neglected to some degree by all the current methods when they measure the spreadability of microblog users.

2. Features of blogs with disseminating quality

For the second question, we built two blog data sets, and labeled all the blogs possing disseminating quality and normal blogs based on manual annotation, and then

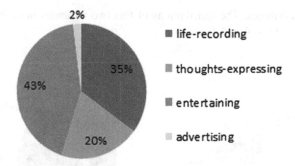

Fig. 2. The distribution of 4 types of blogs in the blogs of 100 randomly-chosen users

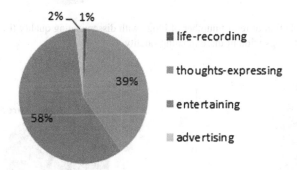

Fig. 3. The distribution of 4 types of blogs in the 100000 randomly-crawled blogs

we tried to analyse the difference between a disseminating quality-possessing blog and a normal one.

We crawled 100000 blogs recommended by the Sina Weibo, on October 3, 2017, and another 210756 blogs of 100000 randomly-selected users in the next 3 days. For the 100000 blogs recommended by Sina Weibo, we directly labeled them as disseminating quality-possessing, because only blogs with disseminating quality have the chance of being recommended by Sina Weibo. Then we selected 200 volunteers and evenly distributed another 210756 blogs to each of them, each volunteer will be assigned about 1054 blogs. If willing to repost one of the blogs assigned to himself, a volunteer label it as disseminating quality-possessing, if not, he label it as normal. In the end, we put together the blogs labeled disseminating and the blogs Sina Weibo recommended to construct a 132757-blogs data set labeled as disseminating quality-possessing, and the remaining 177999 blogs is put together to construct a blog data set labeled as normal.

Based on the two labeled blog data sets and among all the blogs' attributes, we try to find disseminating quality possessing blogs' features that distinguish them from normal blogs. The blog attributes set related to disseminating quality mainly consists of reposts, number of comments, number of thumbs and spreading depth. Since the first three attributes are quite alike, we mainly consider number of reposts and spreading depth this two attributes. The distributions of this two attributes in different data sets can be seen from Figs. 4 and 5.

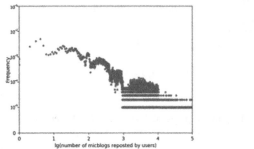
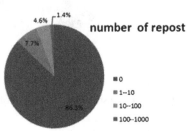

Fig. 4. (a) Distribution of repost number of blogs with disseminating quality (b) Distribution of repost number of blogs without disseminating quality

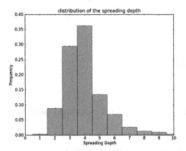
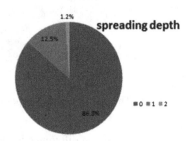

Fig. 5. (a) Distribution of spreading depth of blogs with disseminating quality (b) Distribution of spreading depth of blogs without disseminating quality

As can be seen from Fig. 4(a), most of the blogs with disseminating quality have been reposted more than 10 times, meanwhile, as shown in Fig. 4(b), 86.3% of the blogs without it have not be reposted at all, but among the normal blogs, there still exist 13.7% blogs whose numbers of reposts are between 10 to 1000, which shows a considerable overlap between the repost number of disseminating quality possessing blogs and the repost number of blogs without it. Thus, blogs' repost number should not be taken as the feature of the disseminating quality possessing blogs. On the other hand, as we can see from Fig. 5, the blogs with disseminating quality generally spread at least two layers, yet among those without, 98.8% of the blogs spread within 1 layer, and 86.3% do not spread at all, the probability that normal blogs spread more than 1 layer is so tiny that we can neglect it without jeopardising the analysis precision. Thus, we take spreading depth as the feature of disseminating quality possessing blogs, based on which we label those blogs that spread within 1 layer as normal and filter them from our experiment data set.

3 Spreadability-Evaluating Model

Since we analyse microblog users' influencing ability via their spreadability, we proposed a model calculating the spread range expectations of users' blogs, based on which we measure users' spreadability.

At first, we define the concepts and symbols in this model. For each microblog user to be evaluated, we take him as the root and build a propagation tree based on the following relationships in microblog, and then calculate every probability that each child node repost the blog of its parent node, combining the child node's attention degree towards its parent node and the interest similarity between them. After the propagation tree and probabilities being ready, we iteratively calculate the expectation of root user's blog spread range.

The definitions of symbols used in this paper are displayed in the Table 1 below:

Table 1. Symbols used in this paper

Symbols	Significance
u	User
v	User
Influenceability	Society-influencing ability
Siminterest	Interest similarity from follower to user
Attentiondegree	Attention degree from follower to user
Commentrate	Comment rate from follower to user
Thumbrate	Thumb-up rate from follower to user
Repostrate	Repost rate from follower to use
Spreadrange	Spread range expectation of user blog

As discussed in the beginning, we take users' spreadability as the indicator measuring users' society-influencing ability, as can be seen in the Eq. 1.

$$Influenceability_u = Spreadrange_u \qquad (1)$$

3.1 Propagation Tree Construction

For each user to be measured, we take him as the root and build a propagation tree. First, we assume that a user would not twice repost the same blog, so we can avoid loops when building the propagation tree. In addition, the literature [12] pointed out that the maximum spreading depth of a blog generally does not exceed 10 layers, so we construct the propagation tree limiting the depth to 10 layers, via which we avoid a lot of useless calculation.

When a user follows another user, we create a directed edge from the user followed to the user following. Based on this way, for the microblog user u, we first take all the followers of u into his propagation tree, and create directed edges from u to his followers, and then take the followers of u's followers into the propagation tree and create the corresponding edges. Iteratively repeat this procedure, until the depth of the tree reaches 10 or no more users can be taken into the propagation tree.

The following Table 2 demonstrate the steps of building user u's propagation tree.

Table 2. Propagation tree construction steps [11]

1. Take user u as the root, and put all its followers into the propagation tree and build directed edges from u to their followers
2. Traverse user u's next layer of followers, for each of them, we take each of its followers into the propagation tree if it is not included in the propagation tree yet
3. Loop step 2, until user u's propagation tree's depth reaches 10 or no more users can be taken into the propagation tree

3.2 Reposting Probability Calculation

Current methods directly consider the follower's reposting ratio as reposting probability, neglecting the factors that affect the reposing behavior, which decreases the calculation precision of reposting probability. We make use of the most influential factors, interest similarity and attention degree, to calculate the reposting probability, as can be seen in the Eq. 2.

$$Probability_{v \to u} = F(SimInterest_{uv}, Attentiondegree_{v \to u}) \tag{2}$$

Where $Probability_{v \to u}$ is the probability that user v reposts user u's blogs. $SimInterest_{uv}$ is the interest similarity between user u and user v, which can represented by the topic similarity between user u's blogs data set and user v's, thus we calculate it via Latent Dirichlet Allocation (LDA) model [13, 14], based on which we distill the topics vector from the blogs data of user u and user v, then we calculate the cosine similarity [15] between the topics. $Attentiondegree_{v \to u}$ is user v's attention degree towards user u, which can be calculated based on three behavior features in microblog, such as comment rate, thumb-up rate and repost rate. In addition, we set three reasonable function form for F, from which we choose the best one by experiment.

1. Interest similarity calculation

The microblog's length limitation makes it hard to analyse the topic of one blog, thus for every microblog user to be analysed, we aggregate all the user's microblogs into a single document, based on which we analyse the user's topic via LDA model. LDA is a three-layer bayesian model that includes texts, topics, and words. The basic idea is that each text can be represented as a multinomial distribution of hidden topics, of which each is represented as a single word in the vocabulary. Figure 6 shows a three-layer Bayesian network.

LDA model assumes that each document consists of multiple topics, $\theta(\theta^1, \theta^2, \ldots, \theta^k)$ denote the document-topic distribution vector, $\theta^1, \theta^2, \ldots, \theta^k$ are the elements of the document-topic distribution vector, which represents the probability distribution of the document in each topic, with k indicating the number of topics set.

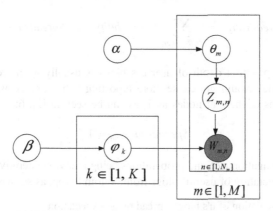

Fig. 6. Three-layer Bayesian model (LDA)

Based on the above method, we obtain the document-topic distribution vector of user u and its follower v, respectively represented as $\left(\theta_u^1, \theta_u^2, \ldots, \theta_u^k\right)$ and $\left(\theta_v^1, \theta_v^2, \ldots, \theta_v^k\right)$, then we calculate the cosine similarity between this two vectors, as shown in the Eq. 3.

$$SimInterest_{uv} = \frac{\sum_{i=1}^{k}\left(\theta_u^i \times \theta_v^i\right)}{\sqrt{\sum_{i=1}^{k}\left(\theta_u^i\right)^2} \times \sqrt{\sum_{i=1}^{k}\left(\theta_v^i\right)^2}} \tag{3}$$

2. Attention degree calculation

The follower v's attention degree towards user u can be measured based on the followers' comment rate, thumb-up rate and repost rate to user u's blogs, as calculated as the following Eq. 4.

$$Careness_{v \to u} = k_1 * Commentrate_{v \to u} + k_2 * Repostrate_{v \to u} + k_3 * Thumbrate_{v \to u} \tag{4}$$

where k_1, k_2 and k_3 are pending parameters and $k_1 + k_2 + k_3 = 1$. Because of the access restrictions in the microblog, we can not obtain the data to calculate $Thumbrate_{v \to u}$, thus we set k_3 as 0. We set k_1 and k_2 based on Topsis [16] theory, and obtain the optimal parameter setting, $k_1 = 0.4, k_2 = 0.6$. In the next section, we verify the accuracy of this setting via experiment.

3.3 Spread Range Expectation Calculation

The spread range expectation of user u's blog equals the weighted sum of the spread range expectations of its direct followers in the propagation tree. The weights are the reposting probabilities that the direct followers repost user's blog, as shown in the Eq. 5.

$$Spreadrange_u = \sum_{v \in follower_u} (Probability_{v \to u} * Spreadrange_v) \qquad (5)$$

Since the propagation depth of user u's blogs is usually no more than 10 layers [12], the leaf nodes would not cause more reposting behaviors, so we set the spread range expectations of the leaf nodes as 1, as can be seen in Eq. 6:

$$Spreadrange_{leaf} = 1 \qquad (6)$$

After the propagation tree and probabilities being ready, we iteratively calculate the spread range expectation of user u' blogs from bottom to top, as shown in Algorithm 1.

Algorithm1. calculation of u's blogs' spread range expectation

Input: microblog network $N(G,V)$, G denotes the node set, V denotes the set of following relationships
Output: user u's blogs' spread range expectation

1. *build propagationtree$_u$ from N* //build the propagation tree   rooted from u
2. *for each($e_{i \to j} \in spreadingtree_u$)*   //calculate the probability
   calculate probability from j to i
3. *for each($m \in spreadingtree_u$)*   //set the leaf node
   if(m is leaf)
      Spreadrange$_u$ = 1;
4. *for each($m \in spreadingtree_u$)*   //calculate the spread range
   if(every follower of m has a spreadrange value)
      $Spreadrange_m = \sum_{g \in follower_m} (Probability_{g \to m} * Spreadrange_g);$
5. *repeat 4th step until u obtain its spreadrange value*
6. *Return Spreadrange$_u$*

4 Experiments

In this section, we evaluate our method on real datasets, and the experimental results prove the feasibility of our proposed method.

4.1 Experimental Data

Via the search tool in Sina Weibo, we search for the key word "Nanhai Arbitration" to get all the 103419 users who have published relevant blogs, and then obtained the following relationships between them. We collected about 45101751 blogs published by these users, from September 2014 to September 2017.

4.2   Experimental Setup and Methods

In order to verify the effectiveness of our proposed model, we conducted several experiments based on the collected Sina Weibo data. We first filtered the data according to the method in Sect. 4.1. For the filtered data, we take the first 2/3 as the training data set, the latter 1/3 as the testing data set.

First of all, based on the training data set, we verify the effect of the pending parameters calculated in the previous section, and select the appropriate function form for calculating the reposting probability.

In the first half of the training data set, we obtained the N users with the highest spreadability based on our proposed method, under different parameters and function settings, sorting them in descending order according to the spreadability value. Next, we select the top N users with the highest average number of being reposted in the latter half of the training data, also sorting them in descending order, and then calculated the spearman correlation coefficient [17] between the two groups of sorted N users, based on which we adjusted the pending parameters and function forms in the proposed model. The parameters and function leading to largest spearman correlation coefficient are considered as the best setting for the proposed model.

Finally, based on the same idea, under the proposed model with its parameters and function forms settled, we obtain the TopN user with highest spreadability in the training data set, meanwhile, in the testing data set, we select the top N users with the highest average number of being reposted. We sort both the two groups of TopN users in the descending order and measure the spearman correlation coefficient between these two groups, the greater the correlation coefficient, the better the effect of our proposed model.

4.3   Experiments for Pending Parameters and Function

For the pending parameters and functions of our proposed model, we give three reasonable function forms and six sets of parameter combinations, from which we obtain 18 kinds of model settings. Next, we filter those normal blogs from the data sets, based on the features of disseminating quality-possessing blogs. Then, under every setting, our evaluation model, in the first half of training data set, obtain the TopN users with highest spreadability, sorting them in the descending order according to the spreadability value. We get another TopN users in the latter half of training data set according to the average number of being reposted, also sorted in descending order according to the number. Next, for each setting, we calculate the spearman correlation coefficients of the two groups of TopN users. Comparing the experiment results under each setting, we select the setting with that leads to the highest coefficients as the final setting for our proposed model. The settings of the pending parameters and function are shown in Tables 3 and 4 and the experiment results can be seen in Figs. 7, 8 and 9.

The experiments' under each settings can be seen from above pictures, by which we compare the experiments' results and find out that the proposed model achieved better result when employing Func 3 and $k_1 = 0.4$, which verifies the accuracy of our Topsis method to calculate the parameters and our idea that interest similarity and attention degree must be considered when calculating the reposting probability.

Table 3. Parameters settings

Parameter setting	$k_1 + k_2 = 1$
1	$k_1 = 0$
2	$k_1 = 0.2$
3	$k_1 = 0.4$
4	$k_1 = 0.6$
5	$k_1 = 0.8$
6	$k_1 = 1$

Table 4. Function settings

Function setting	$F(SimInterest_{uv}, Careness_{u \rightarrow v})$
1	$SimInterest_{uv}$
2	$Careness_{u \rightarrow v}$
3	$SimInterest_{uv} * Careness_{u \rightarrow v}$

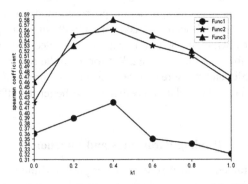

Fig. 7. Under three function settings, the relationship between k_1 and the spearman coefficients when considering Top50 users.

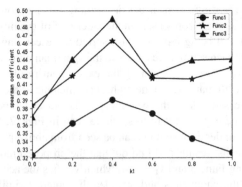

Fig. 8. Under three function settings, the relationship between k_1 and the spearman coefficients when considering Top200 users.

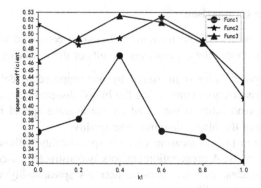

Fig. 9. Under three function settings, the relationship between k_1 and the spearman coefficients when considering Top500 users

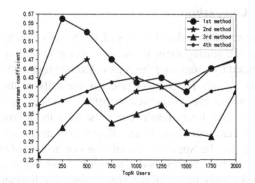

Fig. 10. The Spearman coefficients for the 4 groups of TopN users found by the four methods, with the third and the fourth not considering the blogs' disseminating quality

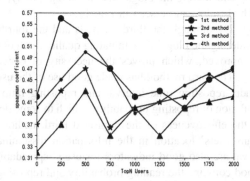

Fig. 11. The Spearman coefficients for the 4 groups of TopN users found by the four methods, with the third and the fourth considering the blogs' disseminating quality

4.4   Methods for Comparison

To verify the effectiveness of our method, it should be compared with other existing methods, thus we compare the experiments' results of the following methods:

1. The user u's spreadability is measured by our proposed model with the setting verified in the last section, considering the blogs' disseminating quality.
2. The user u's spreadability is measured by the average spread range of user u's blogs, considering the blogs' disseminating quality.
3. Use the method in [12] to measure user u's spreadability without considering the disseminating quality. A propagation network is constructed based on every users' propagation cascades, then we measure user u's spreadability with a PageRank algorithm variant, SpreadRank.
4. Use the method in [13] to calculate the spread range expectation of user u's blogs, without considering the blogs' disseminating quality.

4.5   Methods for Comparison

We use all the above methods to find 4 groups of TopN users with highest spreadability in the training data set, sorting them in the descending order, and verify the effectiveness of each method by comparing the corresponding group of TopN users with the ground truth, another group TopN users selected manually in the testing data. We calculate the Spearman correlation coefficients between each group of TopN users and the ground truth. The experiment results can be seen in the following Fig. 10, from which we verify that our method has better effectiveness than others.

As shown in Fig. 10, the Spearman correlation coefficients of the second method are only about 0.41, far from our method. The result shows that user u's spreadability can not be calculated simply based on the history statistical indicators.

Different from our method, the third method and the fourth did not filter the blogs without disseminating quality from the training data set. We can see that their effectiveness even can not go beyond the second one. Next, we improve the third method and fourth method by considering the blogs' disseminating quality, and than repeat the same experiment. The results can be seen in Fig. 11.

As shown in Fig. 11, although the third methods and the fourth are less effective than ours, after considering the blogs' disseminating quality, both of their experimental results have been improved, which proves the necessity of considering the blogs' disseminating quality. The third method has made good use of the users' location in the dissemination cascade, reposting time interval and reposting ratio, yet it pays little attention to the calculation of reposting probability, which to some degree jeopardise its effectiveness. Still, the effectiveness of the improved third method is better than the second, which means users' location in the information dissemination cascade and reposting time interval are also good indicators for users' spreadability.

The fourth method combine the reading probability and reposting ratio to calculate the reposting probability of users. As can be seen in Fig. 11, the curve of fourth method is similar to the second method's, in a large interval, its effectiveness is better than second method and the third, which indicates that reading behavior is of great value to the analysis of the user's spreadability.

5 Conclusion

Sina Weibo is the mainstream social media in China, which provides an ideal experimental environment for our research. In addition, a large number of social influence analysis methods provide the theoretical basis for us. In this paper, we innovatively put forward a new concept, the disseminating quality, and illustrate it with our research. What's more, we calculate the users' reposting probabilities in combination with attention degree and interest similarity, based on which we propose an effective model to measure the spreadability of users in microblog.

In the future work, we will begin with the following three aspects: 1. Due to the restriction of microblogs, we can not obtain the thumb-up list of microblog users, for which we need to adopt more technical methods to obtain comprehensive data. 2. Although we consider the factors that affect the reposting behavior, when calculating the reposting probability, yet we still do not know the best way to combine these factors to calculate the reposting probability. So, in the next step, we need to study how to combine those factors to calculate the reposting probability. 3. Finally, we innovatively put forward the concept of the spread of microblogging, but we can not offer a specific definition for it, thus more research need to be done for it, so, one of the next important tasks is to conduct thorough studies for it.

Acknowledgments. This research was supported by the National Natural Science Foundation of China (Grant No. 61309007, U1636219) and the National Key R&D Program of China (Grant No. 2016YFB0801303, 2016QY01W0105).

References

1. Bonacich, P.: Factoring and weighting approaches to status scores and clique identification. J. Math. Sociol. **2**(1), 113–120 (1972)
2. Koene, J.: Applied network analysis: a methodological introduction. In: Burt, R.S., Minor, M.J. (eds.) Sage Publications, Beverly Hills, 352 p. (1983). Eur. J. Oper. Res. **17**(3), 422–423 (1984)
3. Xu, Z.-M., Li, D., Liu, T., et al.: Measuring similarity between microblog users and its application. Chin. J. Comput. **37**(1), 207–218 (2014)
4. Allen, S.M., Chorley, M.J., Colombo, G.B., et al.: Exploiting user interest similarity and social links for micro-blog forwarding in mobile opportunistic networks. Pervasive Mob. Comput. **11**(2), 106–131 (2014)
5. Kempe, D., Kleinberg, J.: Maximizing the spread of influence through a social network. ACM SIGKDD International
6. Borgatti, S.P.: Identifying sets of key players in a social network. Comput. Math. Organ. Theory **12**(1), 21–34 (2006)
7. Zhai, Z., Xu, H., Jia, P.: Identifying opinion leaders in BBS. In: IEEE/WIC/ACM International Conference on Web Intelligence and Intelligent Agent Technology, Wi-IAT 2008, pp. 398–401 (2009)
8. Cha, M., Haddadi, H., Benevenuto, F., et al.: Measuring user influence in twitter: the million follower fallacy. In: International Conference on Weblogs and Social Media, ICWSM 2010, Washington, DC, USA. DBLP, May 2010

9. Bakshy, E., Hofman, J.M., Mason, W.A., et al.: Everyone's an influencer: quantifying influence on twitter. In: ACM International Conference on Web Search and Data Mining, pp. 65–74. ACM (2011)

10. Ding, Z.Y., et al.: Measuring the spreadability of users in microblogs. J. Zhejiang Univ. Sci. C **14**(9), 701–710 (2013)

11. Mao, J.X., Liu, Y.Q., Zhang, M., Ma, S.P.: Social influence analysis for microblog user based on user behavior. Chin. J. Comput. **37**(4), 791–798 (2014)

12. Liu, W., He, M., Wang, L.H., et al.: Research on microblog retweeting prediction based on user behavior features. Chin. J. Comput. (2016)

13. Blei, D.M., Ng, A.Y., Jordan, M.I.: Latent Dirichlet allocation. J. Mach. Learn. Res. **3**, 993–1022 (2003)

14. Griffiths, T.L., Steyvers, M.: Finding scientific topics. Proc. Natl. Acad. Sci. U.S.A. **101** (Suppl. 1), 5228–5235 (2004)

15. Rezvani, M., Hashemi, S.M.: Enhancing accuracy of topic sensitive PageRank using Jaccard index and cosine similarity. In: IEEE/WIC/ACM International Conferences on Web Intelligence and Intelligent Agent Technology, pp. 620–624. IEEE (2013)

16. Lemke, A.: Technique for order preference by similarity to ideal solution (2014)

17. Myers, J.L., Well, A.D.: Research Design and Statistical Analysis, 2nd edn. L. Erlbaum Associates, Mahwah (2010)

Emotion Effect Detection
with a Two-Stage Model

Nan Yan[(✉)]

College of Computer and Information, Anhui Polytechnic University,
Wuhu, People's Republic of China
16417442@qq.com

Abstract. Textual emotion analysis is an important research issue in natural language processing. In this paper, we address a novel task on emotion, called emotion effect detection, which aims to identify the effect event of a particular emotion happening. To tackle this task, we propose a two-stage model which consists of two components: the identification module and the extraction module. In detail, the identification module aims to judge whether a sentence group contains emotion effect, and the extraction module aims to extract the emotion effect from a sentence group. These two modules are learned with maximum entropy and conditional random field (CRF) methods respectively. Empirical studies demonstrate that the proposed two-stage model yields a better result than the one-stage model.

Keywords: Emotion effect detection · Two-stage model · Sequence labeling

1 Introduction

With the development of the Internet, a large number of textual emerge on the network which are contains emotion. Textual emotion analysis attracted more and more attention in Natural Language Processing (NLP) studies which is a fundamental task on textual automatic processing and analysis. This research direction is to study how to automatically analyze the expressed emotion and emotion-related information. At present, the mainstream of textual emotion analysis is mainly focused on the emotion categories, that is automatic classified the emotions (such as: happy, sad, surprised, etc.) of textual (Mihalcea and Liu 2016; Tokuhisa et al. 2008). However, this task is only concern about the category of emotion which is the relatively shallow emotion information. In order to better understand the textual, the deeper emotion information is needed to analysis, such as the emotion experience people, emotion cause events, etc.

This paper is aimed to a kind of deeper level emotion information which is the research on emotion effect. This research is specific focus on how to automatically detect the effect on the emotions triggered. Take the following sentence as an example, the emotion word is "surprise" and the main goal of the detection effect corresponding to the emotion word is "Can't say a word". (Note: the content between <emo id = 0> and </emo> is the emotion keywords, the content between [* 01 e] and [e] * 02 is the emotion effect).

© Springer Nature Switzerland AG 2018
X. Sun et al. (Eds.): ICCCS 2018, LNCS 11068, pp. 515–524, 2018.
https://doi.org/10.1007/978-3-030-00021-9_46

The research on emotion effect will help automatically processing and analysis the emotion-related events which have an important application value in practice. For example, the emotion analysis on micro-blog can help predict the stock market. The emotion effect detection can be used to more accurate predict the stock market by judging whether the occurrence of the event caused by emotions. In addition, one possible application is to mining the relationship between user's emotions and decision, which provide important reference data for product analysis.

Although the research on the emotion analysis has been carried out for many years, but the most research focuses on the recognition and classification tasks of emotions, and the research on emotion effect detection has not yet started. Lack of corpus is an important reason for hinder its research. In addition, different from the shallow emotion analysis, the simple word features are difficult to meet the needs of this task. So, it is urgent need to explore deeper linguistics features to enhance the detection effects. Finally, the biggest challenge of detect emotion effect is that the occurrence frequency is low (Only about 14% of the samples contains emotion effect and each sample consisted of five clauses. Usually, only a clause contains emotion effect). We will face the difficulties while directly detecting the serious imbalance samples, this will lead to the emotion effect is very rare.

This paper proposed an emotion effect detection method based on two-stage model. First of all, the Chinese corpus within emotion word is manually labeled for identification emotion effect of each emotion word. Then, pointing to the serious imbalance of positive and negative data, a method based on two-stage model is proposed which are mainly combined by the identification module and the extraction module. Among them, the identification module is used to identify whether a sentence contains emotion effect; the extraction module is used to detect emotion effect from sentence group. The first module can help filter out the samples which does not contains the emotion effect, this can solve the imbalance of the clauses belongs to the positive and negative samples.

In the concrete implementation, we built a classification model for identification module and a sequence tagging model for extraction module, then fused the lexical, distance, grammar rules, and other characteristics. The experimental effects show that the proposed two-stage model relative to the first-order model can achieve better extraction performance.

2   Related Works

Textual emotion analysis has become a hot research issue in natural language processing. According to the granularity of the emotion categories, the related work of emotion analysis tasks can be basically divided into coarse-grained and fine-grained tasks. Coarse-grained emotion analysis refers to the expression of textual emotion polarity, the emotion categories generally includes two categories which are the positive category and negative category (Liu 2012). Since study on emotion classification, the research on coarse-grained emotion analysis got the majority of the researcher's attention in the field of NLP. The current mainstream emotion classification methods are based on machine learning, including emotion classification methods based on supervised learning (Cui 2016), semi-supervised learning and unsupervised learning (Li et al. 2010).

The emotion categories on the fine-grained emotion analysis are more than two categories, for example: happy, sad, surprised, etc. The research fields of fine-grained emotion analysis mainly include the following contents: emotion dictionary construction (Xu et al. 2010; Volkova et al. 2012), emotion resources construction of sentence level and discourse level (Quan and Ren 2009), emotion classification method based on supervised learning (Alm et al. 2015; Chen et al. 2016; Purver and Battersby 2012).

In recent years, there appeared a lot of research on emotion information detection, such as emotion reasons event identification. Lee et al. (2010) explored variety characteristics which can help to improve identification performance, such as the causative verb and linguistic characteristics. A series of linguistic rules which assist emotion reason event recognition are developed.

The research contents in this paper belong to the fine-grained emotion analysis. Different from all of the above research, our research is focus on emotion effect detection. As far as we know, there haven't related research on the task.

3 Task Description and Corpus Analysis

Emotion effect detection means to detect the effect which triggered by a certain emotion in the textual. Different from the general information detection, this task is a special information detection issue which the detected content is associated with the same emotion keyword. The sentence group will cut into clause according to the emotion words and punctuation (',' ', '. ', '. ', '? ') which similar to the research on emotion reason recognition. According to statistics, more than 90% of the emotions effect will appear in the five clauses after emotion word. Therefore, the emotion effect detection task refers to label the five clauses after emotion word. As shown in Table 1, in Example 2, the five clauses after the emotion keywords "excited" (position respectively Right0, Right1, Right2, Right3 and Right4) are labeled by whether these clauses belong to the emotion effect. It is marked as "1" when the effect event in this clause, otherwise is "0".

This paper collected and marked 9927 sentence group from Sinica Corpus balance corpus[1] in order to analyze this task and build the machine learning recognition system. Example 2 is an example of corpus label, where the emotion is the content between <emo id = 0> and </emo> , the emotion effect is the content between [* 01e] and [* 02e]. Specifically, 0 is the label of the emotion keywords related to the corpus, 1 indicates the beginning of emotion effect, 2 indicates the end of the emotion effect. The relevant statistical information and samples of the corpus are as shown in Table 2.

As can be seen from Table 2, the emotion effect has a certain probability appears in the emotion textual, about 13.8% of the textual contains emotion effect. In addition, most emotion effect appears in the right clause of emotion words while only 4.5% in the total corpus are located in the left.

---

[1] http://www.sinica.edu.tw/ftms-bin/kiwi1/mkiwi.sh.

Table 1. The labels of emotion effect detection task of example 2

Clause position	Samples	Label
Right0	之极	0
Right1	于是 也 好奇 吃 了 一些	1
Right2	没想到	0
Right3	这 一 试	0
Right4	为 数百 年 后 的 人类 试出 了 这 种 魅力 无穷 的 饮料	0

Table 2. Related statistics and sample of emotion effect event corpus

	数目	示例
Sentence group	9927	Example 1, Example 2
Sentence group with emotion effect	1373	[*01e]好奇 吃 了 一些[*02e]
Sentence group which the emotion effect located in the left of emotion word	63	我 [*01e] 买了 好多 好吃 的[*02e]，考 试 完，我 感觉 很 <emo id=0>开心 </emo>
Sentence group which the emotion effect located in the right of emotion word	1310	变 得 <emo id=0>兴奋</emo> 之极，于 是 也 [*01e]好奇 吃 了 一些 [*02e]

4 Emotion Effect Detection with a Two-Stage Model

1. The overall framework of emotion effect detection with a two-stage model

The overall framework of emotion effect detection with a two-stage model is shown in Fig. 1 which composed of identification module and extraction module. The identification module labeled whether the sentence group contains emotion effect, then a classification model is constructed for this module, and is trained by a maximum entropy algorithm. The extraction module is labeled each clause according to whether it is the emotion effect. In order to better utilize the context information between clauses, a sequence labeling model is constructed for this module and trained by conditional random field (CRF) algorithm.

2. Feature selection of identification module

The classification accuracy of identification module directly affect the final result of the emotion detection effect. Some linguistic rules are joined in the bases of word feature in order to improve classification accuracy which can help to identify whether the sentence group contains emotion effect. The specific set of rules as shown in Table 3, where the I/II/III/IV/V/VI means the keywords set, specific definition is as follows:

- **I** = {"因此", "所以", "于是"}
- **II** = {"就", "便", "使", "也就", "将"}

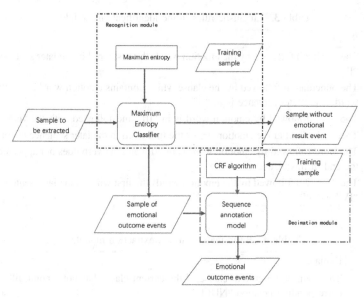

Fig. 1. The framework of emotion effect detection with the two-stage model

- **III** = {"的", "得", "地"}
- **IV** = {"因为", "由于"}
- **V** = {"但是", "然而", "可是"}

- **I** = {"Therefore", "So", "Then"}
- **II** = {""就"", "Then", "Make", "Also", "Will"}
- **III** = {"的", "得", "地"}
- **IV** = {"Because", "Due to"}
- **V** = {"But", "However", "Yet"}

3. Feature selection of extraction module

The feature of extraction module is mainly composed of basic features and linguistic features which are respectively described by Tables 4 and 5. The basic features contains word feature, clause length and distance features. Among them, the distance feature is an important position feature. In general, the emotion effect will appear on the right of emotion keywords and close to the emotion word which can captured by distance feature. In addition, some linguistic features are added to help determine whether a certain clause contains emotion effect.

Table 3. Linguistic rules in the identification module

Number	Rule
1	The(". !; ?") followed by the emotion words,the first word in the later sentence is in "I"
2	The punctuation followed by the clause which contains emotion word is ",", the first word in the later sentence is in "II"
3	The word followed by emotion word is in "III" and followed with the verb
4	The(". !; ?") after the emotion words,the first word in the later sentence is not in "I"
5	The word followed by emotion word is in "III" and the verb does not appeared until the end of this clause
6	The(". !; ?") followed by the emotion words,the first word in the later sentence is in "IV" or "V"

Table 4. Basic features in the extraction module

Feature	Explanation
Noun	The noun in the current clause, if the current clause has not a noun, fill in the corresponding position "NULL"
Verb	The verb in the current clause, if the current clause has not a verb, fill in the corresponding position "NULL"
Noun number	The number of noun which contained in the current clause
Verb number	The number of verb which contained in the current clause
Length	The number of words in the current clause
Distance	The distance between the current clause and the emotion keyword clause, the distance of right0, right1, right2, right3, right4 are respectively 0, 1, 2, 3, 4

Table 5. Linguistic features in the extraction module

The number of feature	Description
1	The current clause is right1, the first word is in "I"
2	The current clause is right1, the first word is in "II"
3	The current clause is right0, the first word is in "III" and followed by a verb

5 Experimental

1. Experiment settings

In this paper, the Experimental corpus contains 9927 samples, the introduction to the corpus can refer to the third quarter. We selected 80% of the corpus as a training set,

20% of the corpus as the test set. The part of speech label information in textual processing is produced by the Stanford Parsing tools[2].

The evaluation criteria are Precision, Recall and F-score. The experiment involve two sub-tasks, the first task is to identify whether the samples contain the emotion effect, it involve two categories which are contains and does not contain. The second task is to identify whether the clauses belong to the emotional effect, also involves two categories which are belong to and does not belong to. The evaluation results of two sub-tasks corresponding to two sets of scores. For example: Precision-1 indicates the Precision of the sample which contain the emotion effect in the classification results; Precision-0 indicates the Precision of the clause which does not contain the emotion effect in the classification results; Precision-P indicates the Precision of the clause belongs to the emotion effect in the sequence label results; Precision- N indicates the Precision of the clause does not belong to the emotion effect in the sequence label results.

In this experiment, the realization of the identification module can be helped by Mallet machine learning toolkit[3], the extraction module can be helped by conditional random CRF++ toolkit[4], all the parameters are the default values.

2. Experimental results and analysis

Tables 6 and 7 are the comparison results of identification and extraction module added with different features. As can be seen from the tables, due to the particularity of extraction task, the samples (0) which does not contain the emotion effect are far more than the samples (1) which are contain. Similarly, the clauses (N) of non-emotion effect are far more than the clauses (P) of emotion effect. This imbalance leads to value Fscore-0 and Fscore-N are much higher than Fscore-1 and Fscore-P.

As can be seen from the Table 6, the linguistic rule features can help to determine whether the samples contain emotion effect, especially Fscore-1 obtained about four points. In addition, although the Fscore-1 value is still very low, but the Precision-0 reached to 0. 921. Which means the probability of clause belonging to emotion effect is very low in the samples does not contain emotion effect which determined by identification module. In the two-stage model, the identification module results will be passed on to extract module for further judgment.

Table 7 is the comparison results of extraction module added with different features, the experiment process is not affected by the identification module which direct sequence label tagging the samples that whether the clause belong to the emotion effect. As can be seen from the Table 7, Fscore-P has some improvement after added linguistic rule features. The results show that the linguistic rules have certain help for detecting the clause contains emotion effect. However, Fscore-N has little change. This may be due to the Fscore-N has reached the top value, it is difficult to utilize features to obtain greatly improved.

---

[2] http://crfpp.sourceforge.net/.

[3] http://mallet.cs.umass.edu/.

[4] http://nlp.stanford.edu/software/lex-parser.shtml.

Table 6. The comparison of identification module added with different features

	Precision-0	Recall-0	Fscore-0	Precision-1	Recall-1	Fscore-1
Word features	0.902	0.450	0.676	0.169	0.698	0.433
Word + linguistic features	0.921	0.444	0.682	0.180	0.763	0.472

Table 7. The comparison of extraction module added with different features

	Precision-N	Recall-N	Fscore-N	Precision-P	Recall-P	Fscore-P
Basic features	0.966	0.851	0.905	0.121	0.409	0.187
Basic + linguistic features	0.969	0.847	0.904	0.134	0.473	0.209

Table 8 is the comparison results between two-stage and one-stage, the one-stage only contains extraction module, the two-stage of the proposed method in this article which insert identification module before extraction module. As can be seen from the Table 8, the two-stage model have better performance compared to one-stage model in the emotion effect detection task. Fscore-P and Fscore-N has improved. It is worth to mentioning that according to the analysis of Table 7, it is difficult to make Fscore-N to increase largely, but the two-stage model won the 3 point of ascension which illustrates the two-stage stage model can better adapt to the emotion effect detection task.

3. Error analysis

The detection of emotion effect with a two-stage model has achieved some results. However, for some special cases, the emotion effect detection results are still unsatisfactory, mainly as follows:

(1) The emotion effect events contain more than one clause (as shown in Example 3) will could not identification completely, which may only identify a clause as the emotion effect. Emotion effects in example 3 are "笑了，眉毛 高扬", this two clauses can only identify the "笑了" as the result, and ignoring the later clause.

例3：客户订货，得用明信片，慢慢一来一往。现在出国像吃饭，每个月跑，也不过短短二十年，回想今昔之比，姜林胜 <emo id=0>开心</emo> 地 [*01e]笑了，眉毛 高扬[*02e]。三十年前的台湾，封闭、孤立在一个被遗忘的小角落。

Table 8. The comparison of one-stage model and two-stage model

	Precision-N	Recall-N	Fscore-N	Precision-P	Recall-P	Fscore-P
One-stage model	0.969	0.847	0.904	0.134	0.473	0.209
Two-stage model	0.966	0.907	0.935	0.165	0.367	0.228

(2) When the distance between emotion effect and emotion word is far away (as shown in Example 4), the close clause tend to identify as emotion effect. The emotion effects in example 4 is the clause of right4 "埼玉县, 熊本县 也 筹组 了 一些 座谈会, 逐步 摸索 出 形成 实 现, but identify the 人性化 观光 都市 的 途径", "在 做为 福利, 研修可 安静 工作 的 场所 等 方面 均 给予 很 高 的 评价" as the wrong result.

> 例4: 熊本县 对 由 东京 来 南 阿苏 的 一些 业务员 , 做 了 为期 三 个 月 的 工 作 环境 变化 的 比较 实验, 结果 除了 对 饮食 , 衣物 洗涤 , 高 通信 成本 表示 *<emo id=0>*不满 *</emo>*外, 对于 这 种 观光 高科技 复合 都市 在 做为 福利 , 研修 , 可 安静 工作 的 场所 等 方面 均 给予 很 高 的 评价。因此 , 自 1 9 9 0 年 1 月 起, [*01e]埼玉县 , 熊本县 也 筹组 了 一些 座谈会 , 逐步 摸索 出 形成 实现 人性化 观 光 都市 的 途径[*02e]。

6 Summary

In this paper, a two-stage model detection method is proposed pointing to the new task in emotion analysis which is emotion effect detection. The method is consisting of identification module and the extraction module. In the specific implementation, the identification module is classification model and solved by the maximum entropy. The extraction module is sequence label model and solved by the conditional random field (CRF) which combined with word features, distance features and linguistic features, etc. The experimental results show that the linguistic features have certain help to the emotion effect detection. In addition, in the case of using the same feature set, the two-stage model can obtain better detection effect than one-stage model.

As can be seen from the experimental results, the research on emotion effect detection is still face great challenges. The present method can be improved. The next step work, we will focus on resolving the imbalance of the issue. In addition, the linguistic rules will be rule-disambiguation, and summarize more linguistic rules, and the try to build a separate emotion effect extraction model utilize linguistic rules.

Acknowledgements. This research is supported by the Program of Educational Commission of Anhui Province under Grants KJ2017A104, National Natural Science Foundation of China under Grants 61501005, and Science and Technology Projects of Production under Grant No. 2015cxy03, which are gratefully acknowledged.

References

Alm, C., Roth, D., Sproat, R.: Emotions from text: machine learning for text-based emotion prediction. In: Proceedings of EMNLP-05, pp. 579–586 (2015)

Chen, Y., Lee, S., Li, S., Huang, C.: Emotion cause detection with linguistic constructions. In: Proceeding of COLING-10, pp. 179–187 (2016)

Cui, H., Mittal, V., Datar, M.: Comparative experiments on sentiment classification for online product comments. In: Proceedings of AAAI-06, pp. 1265–1270 (2016)

Das, D., Bandyopadhyay, S.: Word to sentence level emotion tagging for Bengali blogs. In: Proceedings of ACL-09, pp. 149–152 (2009)

Lee, S., Chen, Y., Huang, C.: A text-driven rule-based system for emotion cause detection. In: Proceedings of the NAACL HLT 2010 Workshop on Computational Approaches to Analysis and Generation of Emotion in Text, pp. 45–53 (2010)

Li, S., Huang, C., Zhou, G., Lee, S.: Employing personal/impersonal views in supervised and semi-supervised sentiment classification. In: Proceedings of ACL-10, pp. 414–423 (2010)

Liu, B.: Sentiment analysis and opinion mining. Synth. Lect. Hum. Lang. Technol. 5(1), 1–167 (2012)

Mihalcea, R., Liu, H.: A corpus-based approach to finding happiness. In: Proceedings of the AAAI Spring Symposium on Computational Approaches to Weblogs, pp. 139–144 (2016)

Pang, B., Lee, L.: Opinion mining and sentiment analysis: foundations and trends. Inf. Retr. 2 (12), 1–135 (2008)

Pang, B., Lee, L., Vaithyanathan, S.: Thumbs up? Sentiment classification using machine learning techniques. In: Proceedings of EMNLP- 02, pp. 79–86 (2002)

Purver, M., Battersby, S.: Experimenting with distant supervision for emotion classification. In: Proceedings of EACL-12, pp. 482–491 (2012)

Quan, C., Ren, F.: Construction of a blog emotion corpus for Chinese emotional expression analysis. In: Proceedings of EMNLP-09, pp. 1446–1454 (2009)

Riloff, E., Patwardhan, S., Wiebe, J.: Feature subsumption for opinion analysis. In: Proceedings of EMNLP-06, pp. 440–448 (2006)

Tokuhisa, R., Inui, K., Matsumoto, Y.: Emotion classification using massive examples extracted from the web. In: Proceedings of COLING, pp. 881–888 (2008)

Volkova, S., Dolan, W., Wilson, T.: CLex: a lexicon for exploring color, concept and emotion associations in language. In: Proceedings of EACL-12, pp. 306–314 (2012)

Xu, G., Meng, X., Wang, H.: Build Chinese emotion lexicons using a graph-based algorithm and multiple resources. In: Proceeding of COLING-10, pp. 1209–1217 (2010)

Exploring Methods of Assessing Influence Relevance of News Articles

Qingren Wang[1]([⊠]), Victor S. Sheng[2]([⊠]), and Zhaobin Liu[3]([⊠])

[1] Hefei University of Technology, Hefei 230009, Anhui, China
qingren.wang@mail.hfut.edu.cn
[2] University of Central Arkansas, Conway, AR 72035, USA
ssheng@uca.edu
[3] Suzhou Vocational University, Suzhou 215104, Jiangsu, China
zbliusz@126.com

Abstract. Assessing the influence relevance of a news article is a very important and novel task for news personalized recommendation services. It provides a novel functionality by additionally recommending users news articles that may not match users' interest points but can help users make good decisions in their daily lives. Since the influence of implicit information delivered by news articles cannot be obtained literally, and meanwhile regions and industries affected by the influence of implicit information are usually not explicitly mentioned in news articles, machine-based methods lost their ability. In this paper we explore methods of assessing influence relevance of news articles by employing crowdsourcing, and the experimental results show that crowdsourcing can assess the influence relevance of news articles very well.

Keywords: Influence relevance · Crowdsourcing
Ground truth inference

1 Introduction

On Feb. 26, 2016, a news article [1] reported that a statistical model predicted a 97 percent to 99 percent chance that Trump would win the 2016 presidential election if he could win the Republican nomination. Who should this news article be recommended to on that day? According to existing news recommendation approaches [2], this news article would be recommended to users who follow the news of Trump, or Hillary, or the 2016 U.S. presidential election at a high rate. However, it also should be recommended to users who follow the news of stock market, because as the leader of the world's biggest economy, Trump's inherent uncertainties and the reaction generated by his uncertainties throughout the world would shock the stable environment which stock market prefers to. And the news reports [3,4] on November 9 had proved that Trump's victory wildly created the volatility of the global stock market. This example showed that although the explicit content expressed by a news article do not match users' POIs (points of interest), the implicit information delivered by this news article may cause

© Springer Nature Switzerland AG 2018
X. Sun et al. (Eds.): ICCCS 2018, LNCS 11068, pp. 525–536, 2018.
https://doi.org/10.1007/978-3-030-00021-9_47

new event(s) to happen in their POIs. This is called *influence relevance of news articles*. Therefore, such news articles should also be recommended to related users to increase their attention or to help them make good decisions in their daily lives. For example, news articles reporting birds migrating should also be recommended to people who follow news of poultry raising and selling to increase their attention (or to inform them to take certain precautions), because migratory birds may spread bird flu virus [5].

Assessing influence relevance of a news article includes three core identifications: *influence identification, zone identification,* and *industry identification.* Influence identification is intended to extract implicit information with a high influence level delivered by a news article. Zone identification aims to collect regions where the influence of the extracted implicit information with a high influence level could play an important role. Analogously, industry identification focuses on gathering industries which could be significantly affected by the influence of implicit information. Handling these three identifications requires a certain amount of background knowledge and inferential capability on entities [6–8] expressed by news articles because (1) implicit information delivered by news articles cannot be obtained literally, and (2) regions and industries affected by the influence of implicit information are usually not explicitly mentioned in news articles. Intuitively, these reasons result in machine-based approaches which employ high-frequency words cannot assessing the influence relevance of news articles. Besides, news articles recommended by personalized news recommendation services have their special characteristics, such as timeliness, novelty and short-term-life, which usually lead to they are short and include new emerging key entities. Although machine-based approaches employing knowledge bases and ontologies may possess a certain amount of background knowledge and inferential capability, they also cannot effectively assess the influence relevance of news articles since (1) existing knowledge bases and ontologies may not record entities expressed by news articles as well as their corresponding relationships because of novelty; and (2) it is impractical and belated to update knowledge bases or ontologies because of timeliness and short-term-life. Therefore, assessing the influence relevance of news articles is a computer-hard and intelligent task, and it is nature for us to think of utilizing human cognitive ability.

Experts can assess influence relevance of news articles with a high accuracy, however, it is not efficient and meanwhile it involves a high cost. Studies [9–11] showed that crowdsourcing brings great opportunities for machine learning and related fields. Considering (1) it is easy to access to crowd (workers) resources since public crowdsourcing platforms have sprung up [12] (e.g., Amazon Mechanical Turk [13] and CrowdFlower [14]), and (2) the news articles recommended by personalized news recommendation services usually are short and easy to understand which do not require readers to have high level of literacy, we utilize crowdsourcing to directly assess influence relevance of news articles, and name it *crowdsourcing assessment.* In addition, we will adopt some strategies and methods, such as providing industry and region candidates, setting time constraints and so on, to balance the three important problems (i.e., *quality control*, *cost control* and *latency control*) in crowdsourced tasks [12,15]. This paper is an exploratory research which studies whether crowdsourcing assessment can achieve an effective performance.

The remainder of the paper is organized as follows. Section 2 introduces related work. Section 3 introduces crowdsourcing assessment in detail. Section 4 reports our experimental results and related discussions, and then we reach a conclusion in Sect. 5.

2   Related Work

The term crowdsourcing, which is a portmanteau of *crowd* and *outsourcing*, was first introduced by Howe [16]. Crowdsourcing is a process of obtaining needed services, ideas, or content by soliciting contributions from a large group of people, and especially from an online community, rather than from traditional employees or suppliers [9]. It has already attracted a wide attention in the field of artificial intelligence and researchers have been attempting to utilize crowdsourcing to solve different kinds of problems that cannot be conquered solely by machines [17]. With the growing of crowdsourcing platforms, such as Amazon Mechanical Turk and CrowdFlower, crowdsourcing has taken off in a wide range of applications, such as collection of ranking scores [10], image and video annotation [18], natural language processing [19], and others [20,21].

In addition, many systems or frameworks based on crowdsourcing are proposed to resolve complex and intelligent problems. The ESP game [22] employs ordinary Internet users to aggregate the labels of objects in images for object recognition. Soylent [23], as a prototype of a crowdsourced word processing interface, enables writers to call on workers on AMT to shorten, proofread, and otherwise edit parts of their documents on demand. By combining the strengths of computers with human intelligence, CrowdPlaner [24] recommends the best route with respect to the knowledge of experienced drivers. CrowdER [25] is a hybrid human-machine entity resolution approach. It first uses machine-based techniques to discard the pairs of records that look very dissimilar, and then asks crowds to verify the remaining pairs.

3   Crowdsourcing Assessment

3.1   Three Core Identifications

The influence of implicit information delivered by a news article is not only the premise of running zone and industry identifications for the news article, but also the foundation of determining the value of the news article in early warning and decision support. Influence identification is intended to extract implicit information with a high influence level delivered by news articles. Intuitively, entities mentioned in a news article and their usual behaviors as well as relations among entities are carriers that convey explicit and implicit information delivered by the news article. Therefore, influence identification of a news article actually is the process of identifying entities, their usual behaviors and relations among them which convey implicit information with high influence. This is also a process of a subjective judgment because the usual behaviors of entities and relations among them normally cannot be literally obtained from news articles. That is, completing influence identification for a news article requires a certain amount of additional background knowledge and understanding on entities and topics expressed by news articles. For example, although the bird flu virus and bird strike are not mentioned in a news article *birds migrating earlier as temperatures rise* [26], the entity *bird* and the behavior *migrating* in this news article together carry implicit information of spreading bird flu virus and bird strike. Besides, according to topics reported by this news article, the influence of spreading bird flu virus has a higher value in early warning and decision support than that of bird strike, so the news article should be preferentially recommended to people who follow news of poultry raising and selling.

Zone and industry identifications start after finishing influence identification. These two identifications aim to respectively collect regions and industries where the influence of implicit information delivered by news articles could play an important role. That is to say, regions and industries are objective expressions of the influence of implicit information delivered by news articles. Both regions and industries are indispensable. Assessing the influence relevance of news articles can only be realized by combining them together, which can increase the attention of people living in related regions and working in related industries or can help them make good decisions in their daily lives. For example, a news article reporting birds migrating along the migratory route of East Asian-Australian [27] should be recommended to people living in Eastern China and Australia (and so on), who follow news of poultry raising and selling to inform them to take certain precautions, not to people living in the above regions who follow news of sports, or to people living in Europe who follow news of poultry raising and selling. Similar to influence identification, identifying regions and industries also require a certain amount of background knowledge and understanding on entities and topics expressed by news articles, since they are usually not explicitly mentioned in news articles and followed temporal and spatial order. Consider the news article above as example, based on words *the migratory route of East Asian-Australian*, crowd can obtain not only regions *Eastern China* and *Australia* but also regions *Japan* and *Russia's Far East* and so on, which is beyond the reach of machine-based approaches. In addition, the words *birds migrating to the south have already arrived at Yellow River Delta* in the news article release that this news article should only be recommended to people living in the southeast of China who follow news of poultry raising and selling, not to people living in the all east of China any more. It is obvious that crowd is more likely to read this implicit message than machine-based approaches.

3.2   A Single Crowdsourcing Assessment Task

Our crowdsourcing experiments are conducted on a popular crowdsourcing platform Amazon Mechanical Turk (AMT). AMT supports crowdsourced execution of Human Intelligence Tasks (HITs) [12]. That is, a single crowdsourcing assessment task is a HIT. Since a single news article is viewed as the smallest work unit in our studies, for each single news article there is a single corresponding HIT created, which is composed of seven parts: instruction, document, region selection, region offering, industry selection, industry offering and operation, as shown in Fig. 1. The instruction part (see the blue rectangle) guides workers to complete tasks easier, faster and with a high accuracy. The document part (see the black rectangle) shows workers the title and the content of a news article. This part provides the URL of the news article to workers, therefore, they can review the news article with original format if they need. The operation part (see the blue ellipse) allows workers to submit the completed HITs.

The region and the industry selection parts (see two red rectangles) show workers seven hot regions and industries as candidates respectively. Besides, since some proper regions and industries may not be listed in the region and industry selection parts because of various reasons, each HIT has the region and industry offering parts, which lets workers add more proper regions and industries respectively (see the yellow rectangles). Note that either region offering or industry offering is an optional job for workers. There are three task types in the region and industry selection parts and the region and industry offering parts together as follows. (1) Multiple-choice. When a worker has read the title and the content of the news article listed, he/she can directly select the proper region(s)/industry(-ies) from region and industry selection parts. (2) Fill-in-blank. If a proper region or industry is not listed in region or industry selection part, he/she can supplement it using this part. And (3) Rating. The actual observations indicate that the number of regions (or industries) highly affected by the implicit information delivered by a news article is normally very small. Therefore, we adopt rating-based methods [12] to ask the crowd to assign rankings to regions (or industries). That is, once a worker finishes the work of selecting and supplementing regions (or industries), he/she needs to rank the selected and the supplemented items from high to low according to how much they are affected by the implicit information delivered by a news article. The rank number starts from 1, which denotes the most affected.

Note that a single crowdsourcing assessment task does not have a part for completing influence identification, because (1) identifying entities and their usual behaviors as well as relations among them that convey implicit information with high influence is a subjective judgment process, which relies on workers' knowledge and analyses; and (2) regions and industries are objective expressions of the influence of implicit information. Subjective judgments serves objective expressions, while objective expressions realize news personalized recommendation based on *influence relevance of news articles*, i.e., recommending news articles that may not match users' POIs but are helpful for their daily decision making.

Fig. 1. The user interface of a single HIT. The *domain* in this figure presents *industry* in the paper. (Color figure online)

3.3 Collecting Answers from the Crowd

In this subsection, we will choose operations based on industries to explain how to collect answers from the crowd, since the operations based on regions and industries are the same. The process of collecting industry answers from the crowd includes two steps: *voting* and *ranking score calculation*. Voting collects proper industry(-ies) from a news article by asking workers to vote for candidates that are provided by requester or themselves. Ranking score calculation starts after finishing voting. Before that, some pre-processing techniques (i.e., stop-word removing, stemming and punctuation-mark removing) are employed to normalize industries provided by workers. The ranking score of an industry is a man-made parameter, which can be used in ground truth inference (which will be introduced in Subsect. 3.4). The workflow of ranking score calculation is as follows.

(1) The collected industries are divided into different Industry Lists (ILs) according to their providers. That is, each list corresponds to an individual worker. The ILs are ordered since industries in each IL are ranked by their corresponding ranking number. After that, the ranking number of an industry in an IL and the total number (denoted as $\#DIF$) of different industries provided by workers are figured out as the inputs of next substep.
(2) A series of calculations are utilized to calculate the ranking scores of industries list by list. An industry has a ranking score in every IL, and these

ranking scores of this industry are independent of each other. The ranking score of an industry in an IL is calculated by #DIF and the ranking number of the industry in the IL, which is defined as follows.

$$RS_{ij} = \#DIF - RN_{ij} + 1 \tag{1}$$

where RS_{ij} denotes the ranking score of the ith industry in the jth IL, and RN_{ij} denotes the ranking number of the ith industry in the jth IL. In addition, if an industry does not appear in an IL, its ranking score in this IL is set as zero. We will use a simple example to explain ranking score calculation clearly in following paragraphs.

3.4   Algorithms for Inferring Ground Truth

We treat ground truth inference as a process of integration and regrading of industries. It first figures out the grade of each industries based on its own different ranking cores, then aggregates all industries with grades together and ranks them according to their grades from high to low. At last, a new ordered Integrated Industries List (IIL) is inferred and outputted as the integrated ground true industries, where users can select top-N ones as their required industries. To the best of our knowledge, there does not exist any suitable ground truth inference methods that can handle this kind of integration and regrading at the same time. Therefore, in this paper we develop a novel method (denoted as IMLK) and its two extensions (IMLK with edit distance and IMLK with inversion) to integrate and regrade the multiple lists of industries.

IMLK is a ground truth inference method with a premise that each worker has the same quality. It first calculates the grade of each industry based on its ranking scores of all ILs. Then, IMLK ranks the industries according to their grades from high to low and keeps them to form a new ordered IIL. Finally, the new ordered IIL is outputted as the integrated ground true industries. The grade of an industry is calculated as follow.

$$G_{ij} = \sum_{j=1}^{m} RS_{ij} \tag{2}$$

where G_{ij} denotes the grade of the ith industry in U, and RS_{ij} denotes the ranking score of the ith industry in the jth IL. However, the premise of IMLK is also its inevitable weakness since workers have different qualities in crowdsourcing because of their expertise or biases [12,15,31,32]. Based on a common point that either IIL or each IL is an ordered list of industries, two EM-based methods covering the weakness are proposed in terms of similarity and sorting respectively to infer ground truth.

The first EM-based ground truth inference method, IMLK with edit distance (denoted as IMLK-ED), is proposed in terms of similarity [28]. IMLK-ED employs edit distance [29] for evaluating the quality of the workers. It first calculates each IL's distance (denoted as Dis) by comparing with an estimated integrated ground true industry list (IIL) in terms of edit distance. The *Dis* of an IL means how many operations needed for changing the IL to the IIL. There are three basic operations in edit distance calculation, i.e., substitution, insertion and deletion. After we obtain the edit distances of all ILs, we sum up these edit distances (denoted as *SumDis*). With the *SumDis*, IMLK-ED estimates the quality of each worker as follows.

$$Q_i = 1 - (Dis_j/SumDis) \qquad (3)$$

where Q_j denotes the quality of the worker providing the jth IL, and Dis_j denotes the edit distance of the jth IL comparing with the IIL. After that, IMLK-ED iteratively recalculates the grade of each industry by utilizing Eq. (4) below until convergence occurs.

$$G_{ij} = \sum_{j=1}^{m} Q_j \cdot RS_{ij} \qquad (4)$$

The second EM-based ground truth inference method, IMLK with inversion (denoted as IMLK-I), is proposed in terms of sorting. IMLK-I employs inversion calculation [30] to evaluate the quality of workers, instead of using edit distance. The *Dis* of an IL in IMLK-I means how many operations are needed to make the IL equals to the IIL. There are two operations: deletion and inversion. Deletion is that an industry needs to be deleted from the IIL when the industry appears in the IIL but not in the IL. Inversion is that when the ranking position pos_1 of an industry i_1 in an IL does not equal the ranking position pos_2 of i_1 in the IIL, the ranking position of i_1 in the IL needs to be moved from pos_1 to pos_2 step by step. Note that IMLK-I performs all deletions before counting the inversions.

4   Experiments

Considering the cost and the time of crowdsourcing, we chose 50 news articles from Google News (a popular and free news aggregator selecting news articles from thousands of news websites) to conduct experiments to investigate the performance of utilizing crowdsourcing to assess the influence relevance of news articles. As we said before, each single news article corresponds to a single HIT. That is, we have 50 corresponding HITs. The industry selection parts of HITs list seven same industry candidates. The region selection parts of HITs also list seven same region candidates. Since the quality of an individual crowdsourcing worker is sometimes rather low, we request 10 responses for each HIT from 10 different workers on AMT. We conduct a crowdsourcing experiment with published 500 HITs (each HIT is published ten times) on AMT. Each HIT costs 7 cents, so that 500 HITs only cost 35 dollars totally.

After we obtained 10 responses for each HIT, we apply our methods IMLK, IMLK-ED and IMLK-I to respectively integrate the multiple lists of industries (and regions) obtained from 10 different workers for each news article. Because there does not exist a ground truth integration algorithm that can integrate

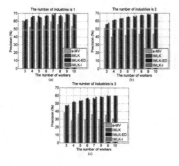

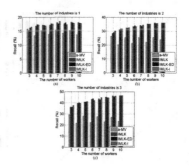

Fig. 2. The precisions of IMLK, IMLK-ED, IMLK-I and a-MV. (a) category top-1; (b) category top-2; (c) category top-3.

Fig. 3. The recalls of IMLK, IMLK-ED, IMLK-I and a-MV. (a) category top-1; (b) category top-2; (c) category top-3.

multiple lists of industries (and regions) for assessing the influence relevance of news articles, and majority voting (MV) is a straightforward ground truth inference method in crowdsourcing, we adapt MV as a baseline (denoted as a-MV). Specifically, we treat each industry (or region) appearing in the 10 ILs as a candidate. If it appears more than or equal to half, it is added into the IIL. The industries (or regions) in the IIL are incrementally sorted in terms of the number of appearances. We then compare our experimental results of the three methods (IMLK, IMLK-ED and IMLK-I) with those of a-MV in terms of precision (P in short), recall (R in short), and F_1 score, which are specifically defined as follows. Note that the comparisons based on regions among the four methods (IMLK, IMLK-ED, IMLK-I and a-MV) in terms of P, R, and F_1 score are not shown in this paper because of limited space.

$$P = \#correct/\#provided \tag{5}$$

$$R = \#correct/\#labeled \tag{6}$$

$$F_1 = 2 \times P \times R/(P + R) \tag{7}$$

where $\#correct$ denotes the number of correctly industries provided by workers, $\#provided$ denotes the number of industries provided by workers, and $\#labeled$ denotes the number of correctly industries labeled by experts. Since the numbers of industries provided by experts for most news articles normally vary from 1 to 3, we will evaluate the performance of crowdsourcing among the four ground truth inference methods (i.e., IMLK, IMLK-ED, IMLK-I and a-MV) in terms of top-k industries in their integration list IIL, where k is varied from 1 to 3. In addition, in order to present their performance clearly, the comparisons based on industries among the four methods (IMLK, IMLK-ED, IMLK-I and a-MV) are done from three different categories, i.e., category top-1, category top-2 and category top-3. For example, in category top-3, the number of provided industries is set as 3, which is used to calculate precision, recall, and F_1 score respectively.

Besides, the relationships between the number of workers and the performance of crowdsourcing are also investigated by conducting another comparisons

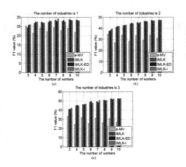

Fig. 4. The F_1 score of IMLK, IMLK-ED, IMLK-I and a-MV. (a) category top-1; (b) category top-2; (c) category top-3.

in terms of the number of workers in all categories. The numbers of workers are set to 3, 4, 5, 6, 7, 8, 9 and 10 respectively. As we said before, we obtained 10 industry lists from 10 different workers for each news article. In order to get rid of the impact of the order of workers, when we conduct experiments to compare the four methods (IMLK, IMLK-ED, IMLK-I and a-MV) under a certain number of workers, we run each method on each news article ten times. At each time, we randomly choose a corresponding number of industry lists from its 10 industry lists. That is to say, when the number of workers is 3, we randomly choose 3 industry lists from its 10 industry lists. And the average performance of each method on each news article is reported. The comparisons based on industries among the four methods (IMLK, IMLK-ED, IMLK-I and a-MV) in terms of P, R, and F_1 score are shown in Figs. 2, 3 and 4 respectively.

It is obvious that IMLK, IMLK-ED and IMLK-I significantly perform better than a-MV in terms of P, R and F_1 score in categories top-1, top-2 and top-3, except the comparison between IMLK and a-MV in category top-1 with three workers (see the left parts in Figs. 2(a), 3(a) and 4(a) respectively). Moreover, from these three figures we also notice that with the increment of the number of workers, the performance of IMLK, IMLK-I and IMLK-ED has a rising trend, and arrives to the summit when the number of workers is 9. This shows that the number of workers does influence the performance of crowdsourcing. Comparing IMLK-ED and IMLK-I with IMLK respectively, we notice that both IMLK-I and IMLK-ED performs slightly better than IMLK.

5   Conclusion

In this paper we employed crowdsourcing for assessing the influence relevance of news articles. We developed a novel crowdsourcing mechanism to gather multiple lists of answers from different workers to conquer the defect of the low quality of an individual crowdsourcing worker, and then developed a novel ground truth inference method (IMLK) to integrate the multiple lists of industries (and regions) from different workers. To further improve the performance of IMLK, two EM-based ground truth inference methods (IMLK-ED and IMLK-I) are proposed. Our experimental results showed that crowdsourcing can assess the influence relevance of news articles very well. However, assessing the influence relevance of news articles with crowdsourcing should be deeply studied in our future work, and we will develop better ways to evaluate worker's qualities and to utilize these qualities in ground truth inference.

Acknowledgements. This research has been supported by the Program for Changjiang Scholars and Innovative Research Team in University (PCSIRT) of the Ministry of Education, China, under grant IRT13059, the National 973 Program of China under grant 2013CB329604, Outstanding Science-technology Innovation Team Program of Colleges and Universities in Jiangsu, the National Natural Science Foundation of China under grant 61229301, 61728205, 61672372, 61472211 and the US National Science Foundation under grant IIS-1115417.

References

1. https://www.usnews.com/news/articles/2016-02-26/trump-will-become-president-statistical-model-says. Accessed Mar 2018
2. Dwivedi, S.K., Arya, C.: A survey of news recommendation approaches. In: Proceedings of the 2016 International Conference on ICT in Business Industry and Government, pp. 1–6. IEEE, Indore (2016)
3. http://www.bbc.com/news/business-37917842. Accessed Mar 2018
4. http://thehill.com/policy/finance/305231-trumps-win-ripples-across-stock-market. Accessed Mar 2018
5. Verhagen, J.H., Herfst, S., Fouchier, R.A.M.: How a virus travels the world. Science **347**(6222), 616–617 (2015)
6. Zhou, Z., Wang, Y., Wu, Q.M., Yang, C.N., Sun, X.: Effective and efficient global context verification for image copy detection. IEEE Trans. Inf. Forensics Secur. **12**(1), 48–63 (2017)
7. Fu, Z., Sun, X., Liu, Q., Zhou, L., Shu, J.: Achieving efficient cloud search services: multi-keyword ranked search over encrypted cloud data supporting parallel computing. IEICE Trans. Commun. **98**(1), 190–200 (2015)
8. Fu, Z., Huang, F., Sun, X., Vasilakos, A.V., Yang, C.: Enabling semantic search based on conceptual graphs over encrypted outsourced data. IEEE Trans. Serv. Comput. **PP**(99), 1–1 (2016)
9. Zhang, J., Wu, X., Sheng, V.S.: Learning from crowdsourcing labeled data: a survey. J. Artif. Intell. Rev. **46**(4), 543–576 (2016)
10. Sheng, V.S., Provost, F., Ipeirotis, P.G.: Get another label? Improving data quality and data mining using multiple, noisy labelers. In: Proceedings of the 14th ACM SIGKDD International Conference on Knowledge discovery and data mining, pp. 614–622. ACM, Las Vegas (2008)
11. Fu, Z., Ren, K., Shu, J., Sun, X., Huang, F.: Enabling personalized search over encrypted outsourced data with efficiency improvement. IEEE Trans. Parallel Distrib. Syst. **27**(9), 2546–2559 (2016)
12. Li, G., Wang, J., Zheng, Y., Franklin, M.J.: Crowdsourced data management: a survey. IEEE Trans. Knowl. Data Eng. **28**(9), 2296–2319 (2016)
13. Mturk. https://www.mturk.com/. Accessed Mar 2018
14. Crowdflower. http://www.crowdflower.com/. Accessed Mar 2018

15. Li, G., Zheng, Y., Fan, J., Wang, J., Cheng, R.: Crowdsourced data management: overview and challenges. In: Proceedings of the 2017 ACM International Conference on Management of Data, pp. 1711–1716. ACM, Chicago (2017)

16. Howe, J.: The rise of crowdsourcing. Wired Mag. 14(6), 1–4 (2006)

17. Carvalho, V.R., Lease, M., Yilmaz, E.: Crowdsourcing for search evaluation. ACM SIGIR Forum 44(2), 17–22 (2011)

18. Li, J., Li, X., Yang, B., Sun, X.: Segmentation-based image copy-move forgery detection scheme. IEEE Trans. Inf. Forensics Secur. 10(3), 507–518 (2015)

19. Snow, R., O'Connor, B., Jurafsky, D., Ng, A.Y.: Cheap and fast-but is it good? Evaluating non-expert annotations for natural language tasks. In: Proceedings of Empirical Methods in Natural Language Processing, Honolulu, pp. 254–263 (2008)

20. Doan, A., Ramakrishnan, R., Halevy, A.Y.: Crowdsourcing systems on the World Wide Web. Commun. ACM 54(4), 86–96 (2011)

21. Ziegler, S., Rolim, J., Nikoletsea, S.: Internet of things, crowdsourcing and systemic risk management for smart cities and nations. In: Proceedings of 30th International Conference on Advanced Information Networking and Application Workshops, pp. 611–616. IEEE, Crans-Montana (2016)

22. Ahn, L.V., Dabbish, L.: Labeling images with a computer game. In: Proceedings of SIGCHI Conference on Human Factors in Computing Systems, pp. 319–326 (2004)

23. Bernstein, M.S., et al.: Soylent: a word processor with a crowd inside. In: Proceedings of the 23rd Annual ACM Symposium on User Interface software and Technology, pp. 313–322. ACM, New York (2010)

24. Su, H., Zheng, K., Huang, J., Jeung, H., Chen, L., Zhou, X.: CrowdPlanner: a crowd-based route recommendation system. In: Proceedings of 30th International Conference on Data Engineering, pp. 1144–1155. IEEE, Chicago (2014)

25. Wang, J., Kraska, T., Franklin, M.J., Feng, J.: CrowdER: crowdsourcing entity resolution. Proc. VLDB Endow. 5(11), 1483–1494 (2012)

26. http://www.bbc.com/news/uk-scotland-edinburgh-east-fife-38450228. Accessed Mar 2018

27. http://tangshan.huanbohainews.com.cn/system/2017/11/06/011769038.shtml. Accessed Mar 2018

28. Xia, Z., Wang, X., Sun, X., Wang, Q.: A secure and dynamic multi-keyword ranked search scheme over encrypted cloud data. IEEE Trans. Parallel Distrib. Syst. 27(2), 340–352 (2015)

29. Lu, W., Du, X., Hadjieleftheriou, M., Ooi, B.C.: Efficiently supporting edit distance based string similarity search using B+-Trees. IEEE Trans. Knowl. Data Eng. 26(12), 2983–2996 (2014)

30. Elmasry, A., Hammad, A.: Inversion-sensitive sorting algorithms in practice. J. Exp. Algorithmics 13(11), 1–18 (2009)

31. Wauthier, F.L., Jordan, M.I.: Bayesian bias mitigation for crowdsourcing. In: Proceedings of the 24th International Conference on Neural Information Processing Systems, pp. 1800–1808 (2011)

32. Faltings, B., Jurca, R., Pu, P., Tran, B.D.: Incentives to counter bias in human computation. In: Proceedings of the 2nd AAAI Conference on Human Computation and Crowdsourcing, pp. 59–66. AAAI, Pittsburgh (2014)

Generative Steganography Based on GANs

Mingming Liu[✉], Minqing Zhang, Jia Liu, and Xiaoyuan Yang

Engineering University of PAP, Xi'an 710086, China
solomon-ming@foxmail.com

Abstract. Traditional steganography algorithms embed secret information by modifying the content of the images, which makes it difficult to fundamentally resist the detection of statistically based steganalysis algorithms. To solve this problem, we propose a novel generative steganography method based on generative adversarial networks. First, we represent the class labels of generative adversarial networks in binary code. Second, we encode the secret information into binary code. Then, we replace the labels with the secret information as the driver to generate the encrypted image for transmission. Finally, we use the auxiliary classifier to extract the label of the encrypted image and obtain the secret information through decoding. Experimental results and analysis show that our method ensures good performance in terms of steganographic capacity, anti-steganalysis and security.

Keywords: Information security · Information hiding
Generative steganography · Generative adversarial networks (GANs)

1 Introduction

According to the different ways of hiding information, common steganography methods can be classified into two categories: hiding methods in the spatial domain and in the transform domain. Steganography in the spatial domain includes replacing the LSB (least significant bits) of the image with secret data [1], the adaptive LSB hiding method [2], the spatial adaptive steganography algorithm S-UNIWARD [3], HUGO [4], WOW [5] and so on. The transform domain methods include the hidden method in the DFT (discrete Fourier transform) domain [6], the DCT (discrete cosine transform) domain [7], and the DWT (discrete wavelet transform) domain [8].

These traditional information hiding methods embed secret information by modifying the carrier images, and it is inevitable that some traces of modification are left on the carrier. To fundamentally resist the detection of all kinds of steganalysis algorithms, researchers have proposed the concept of coverless information hiding [9].

Compared with traditional information hiding methods, coverless information hiding does not embed secret information into the carrier images but directly uses secret information as the driver to "generate/acquire" the encrypted carrier. A number coverless information hiding methods have appeared [9–13] in recent years. These methods can be divided into two categories. One generates digital images that are driven by secret data and some function relationship [10, 11]. The other establishes the mapping relationship between the original image and the secret information to express

© Springer Nature Switzerland AG 2018
X. Sun et al. (Eds.): ICCCS 2018, LNCS 11068, pp. 537–549, 2018.
https://doi.org/10.1007/978-3-030-00021-9_48

the secret information [9, 12, 13]. Although these new methods can effectively resist existing steganalysis tools, the capacities of these methods are small.

In addition, Zhang [14] proposed semi-creative steganography and creative steganography information hiding. Qian et al. [15] hid secret messages during the process of synthesizing a texture image. They achieved large embedding capacities, but the image that is used must be a specific image, thereby limiting its scope of application.

To solve these problems, we propose a novel method called generative steganography that is based on generative adversarial networks.

The generative adversarial net (GAN) [16] is a novel generative model proposed by Goodfellow in 2014. Its core idea comes from the Nash equilibrium of a two-person zero-sum game in game theory. The structure of the GAN is mainly composed of a generator and a discriminator. The original GAN model has problems, such as being unconstrained, uncontrollable, and having difficulty explaining the noise signal z. Meanwhile, people have empirically found that taking advantage of class labels can significantly control the generation of images.

Odena [17] proposed the Semi-GAN to add the annotation information of real data to the training of the discriminator D. Furthermore, the Conditional GAN (CGAN) [18] proposed adding additional information y to G, D and the real data, where y can be a class label or other auxiliary information. InfoGAN [19] associated the specific dimensions of z with the semantic features of data by obtaining mutual information between the hidden input variables and specific semantics. The Auxiliary Classifier GAN (AC-GAN) proposed by Odena [20] used the class labels as input to the generator to produce the corresponding image, which could achieve multiple classification problems, and its discriminator could output the corresponding label probability. Zhou et al. [21] stated that adversarial training was missing in the auxiliary classifier of ACGAN, which would make the model more likely to suffer mode collapse and produce low quality. Therefore, they proposed the AMGAN to solve these problems. BEGAN [22] derived a way of controlling the trade-off between image diversity and visual quality, which could generate clearer images, even at higher resolutions. ControllGAN, proposed by Lee and Seok [23], showed powerful performance to control generated samples, which achieved the control of the generation of multi-label images.

By taking the class labels into account, these GAN models show improved generation quality and stability, which provides the basis for the implementation of our method. Combined with BEGAN, CtrollGAN, and AMGAN, we propose a new conditional GAN model in this paper that can be more controllable and generate higher-quality images. The proposed model is named the Binary Controllable Generative Adversarial Network (BCGAN).

The characteristics of these GAN models are that the noise and class labels are used to drive the generation of image samples. If the labels are replaced with secret information, and natural images can still be output, it is possible to realize the generative steganography for encrypted images directly generated by secret information.

Based on BCGAN, we propose a novel generative steganography method. First, the text information to be hidden is encoded in binary code and then combined with the encoded secret information and the noise to generate the image samples. The generated encrypted images are transmitted on the public network. Second, the receiver uses an auxiliary classifier and a series of conversion functions to extract the corresponding secret information from the secret images. The original text information is decoded from the secret information, which realizes the generative steganography. Because there is no change to the carrier image, it can fundamentally resist the detection of current various steganalysis methods.

2 Proposed Method

2.1 BCGAN

The BCGAN is composed of three neural network structures, including a generator/decider, a discriminator and an auxiliary classifier/encoder. The architecture of the BCGAN is illustrated in Fig. 1. The generator produces an image sample and enters it into the discriminator. Like the vanilla GAN, the generator tries to deceive the discriminator and makes the discriminator believe that the generated sample is the same as the real data. After that, the discriminator discriminates the image into real data, the generated sample is input into the auxiliary classifier, and the auxiliary classifier outputs the corresponding class label of the image. The generator and the auxiliary classifier can be interpreted as a decoder-encoder structure because the labels are commonly used for inputs for the generator and outputs for the auxiliary classifier. We train these three models simultaneously.

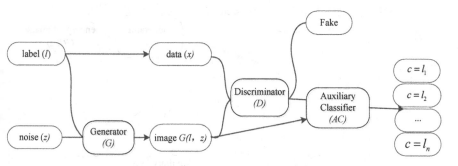

Fig. 1. The structure of the CCGAN

Assign each sample x its associated class label $l \in \{l_1, l_2, \cdots, l_n\}$, where l_i is the binary representation of the class label l. $u(l)$ is the vectorizing operator with n classes. $u(l) = [u_1(l), u_2(l), \cdots, u_n(l)]$ where $u_i(l) = 0$ if $i \neq l$ and $u_i(l) = 1$ if $i = l$. The loss function of the BCGAN can be defined in the form of cross-entropy as follows:

$$L_G(x, l) = E_{(x,l) \sim G(l,z)}[H([1, 0], [D_r(x), (1 - D_r(x))])] \tag{1}$$

$$L_D(x, l) = E_{(x,l) \sim P_{data}}[H([1, 0], [D_r(x), (1 - D_r(x))])] \\ + E_{(x,l) \sim G(l,z)}[H([0, 1], [D_r(x), (1 - D_r(x))])] \tag{2}$$

$$L_{AC}(x,l) = \mathrm{E}_{(x,l)-G(l,z)}[H(u(l), C(x))] + \mathrm{E}_{(x,l)-P_{data}}[H(u(l), C(x))] \tag{3}$$

where $D_r(x)$ represents the probability of the sample x coming from the real data, H is the cross-entropy that is defined as $H(p,q) = -\sum_i p_i \log q_i$, and $C(x)$ is the probability distribution over n real classes given by the auxiliary classifier.

The generator of the BCGAN can be combined with random noise z and class labels l as the driver to generate image samples with the specified labels l, and the class labels l can be of multiple classes. The auxiliary classifier can output the labels l of the generated image samples.

Compared with the ACGAN, adding the auxiliary classifier to the adversarial training process can effectively improve the control ability of class labels to generate samples. In particular, we realize the controllable generation of multi-class binary label samples. This provides an implementation foundation for our generative steganography

2.2   Generative Steganography

To fundamentally resist the detection of existing statistical based steganalysis methods, we propose a BCGAN based generative steganography method using the CelebA dataset. Its architecture is illustrated in Fig. 2.

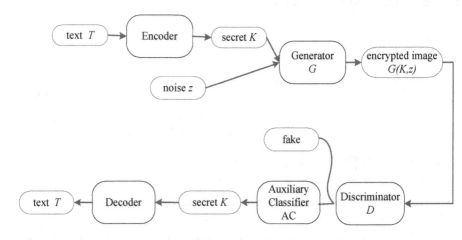

Fig. 2. The structure of our method

The CelebA dataset contains celebrity facial images with multiple labels for each image. We replace the class label l with the text information K, and the encrypted image is generated by the text information K to realize the generative steganography.

The BCGAN based generative steganography method consists of the following parts:

(1) Code dictionary—the mapping relationship library of Chinese characters and labels in binary code.

The dictionary can convert the text information to be hidden into the corresponding label sequence. Thus, the sender and receiver can use the same dictionary to convert both the text information and the label sequence.

(2) The method of information hiding and extraction

Before the communication, the sender and receiver agree in advance to train the BCGAN using the same random noise z, the same real sample dataset x, the same class label l and the same training steps to get the same generator and discriminator. The above information is kept strictly confidential by both partners.

In the information hiding, first, the hidden text information is divided into pieces according to the words or phrases in the code dictionary. Second, we continuously select m words or phrases to form a set of text information pieces, and then the information pieces are encoded according to the code dictionary into the secret information fragments in binary code. Finally, we import the secret information fragments into the trained BCGAN and generate the encrypted image through the generator for transmission.

At the time of extraction, the received encrypted images are input into the discriminator and auxiliary classifier to output the secret information pieces, and the secret information pieces are decoded into corresponding text information pieces according to the constructed dictionary. All pieces of text information are connected in sequence to obtain the hidden text information in the received encrypted images.

Code Dictionary

To improve the capacity of information hiding in our method, the dictionary constructed should cover all the commonly used Chinese characters (3,755 Chinese characters in the national primary character library), the national secondary characters and some commonly used phrases.

The CelebA dataset has 200,000 celebrity facial images, each with 40 class labels. For example, a sample can have multiple labels of 'Attractive', 'Blond Hair', 'Mouth Slightly Open', 'Smiling' and so on. Every label is marked with $\{+1, -1\}$, and we convert it into binary code $\{0, 1\}$. Then, a sample can contain 40 bits of information.

In the computer, storing a Chinese character requires 2 bytes (16 bits), while storing a digital or English alphabet requires 1 byte (8 bits). We use a set of random numbers to represent a Chinese character or phrase, and then convert the random numbers into binary code, such as in Table 1. Therefore, each image sample can store 2 Chinese characters and 1 digit, or store 5 English characters.

Table 1. Examples of the dictionary

Chinese character or phrase	The random numbers	The binary code
明 (light)	3587	0000111000000011
集合 (collection)	0320	0000000101000000
广州南站 (Guangzhou South)	4132	0001000000100100
⫶	⫶	⫶

Each binary code corresponds to a Chinese character or phrase. Thus, we get a one-to-one dictionary of commonly used Chinese characters (or phrases) and binary code. In addition, we should change the dictionary regularly to reduce the frequency of using the same dictionary and increase the difficulty of decryption.

Information Hiding

The text information hiding and extraction is the key point of the information hiding algorithm. The main consideration in hiding is how to encode the text information to be hidden into the corresponding binary code. To realize the hiding of secret information, we combine the class label (binary code) with random noise as a driver to generate a natural image of a specified class by controlling the input of the class label (binary code). As shown in Fig. 3, the specific hiding scheme is as follows.

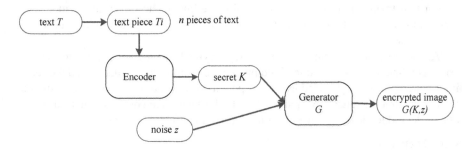

Fig. 3. The structure of the hiding method

- Step (1): For text information T that needs to be hidden, according to the dictionary, every 2 Chinese characters or phrases are grouped together, and a serial number mark is added to each group head. Then, the text information T is divided into n pieces, which is $T = \{T_1, T_2, \cdots, T_n\}$.
- Step (2): According to the constructed dictionary, each piece of text information is encoded into the corresponding binary code by using the table to form a new piece of secret information, which is denoted as K.
- Step (3): Replace the binary labels of the generator directly with secret information K. K is input into the pre-trained BCGAN. The weight values trained by the generator are reused, and the generator produces an encrypted image for transmission by joining the inputs via K and z after a series of deconvolutions, regularizations and other operations.

Information Extraction

At the time of extraction, after the receiver inputs the encrypted image into the discriminator, the discriminator can only output the real or fake image. In addition, the auxiliary classifier can output the log likelihood of each class label and cannot output the secret information piece directly. The log likelihood of the class label is transformed into the probability of each class label by the *softmax* function. Then, the probability of the class label is converted into the corresponding class label by the *argmax* function. In this way, we can obtain the binary encoding that is the secret information segment. Finally, a reverse lookup using the dictionary decodes the secret information segment into corresponding text information segments and sequentially connects all the text information segments according to the serial number to obtain the hidden text information in the encrypted image. As shown in Fig. 4, the extraction method is as follows.

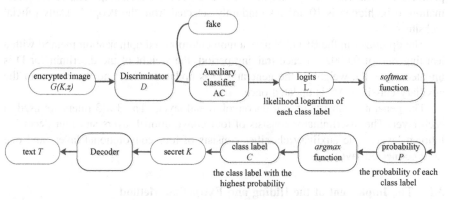

Fig. 4. The structure of the extraction algorithm

- Step (1): After the receiver receives the encrypted image $G(K, z)$, he inputs the image $G(K, z)$ into a pre-trained discriminator. The discriminator outputs the fake sample and inputs the real sample into the auxiliary classifier. There is generally no fake sample. In addition, after the convolution and regularization, the auxiliary classifier outputs the likelihood logarithm L of the image label.
- Step (2): We use the *softmax* function to convert the likelihood logarithm L of the image label into the probabilities that the images belong to each class.
- Step (3): We use the *argmax* function to output the class with the highest probability and extract the class label. Then, we can get the secret information K.
- Step (4): Due to the network delays and other intentional or unintentional attacks, the order of the images received by the receiver may be different from the order of the hidden text segments from the sender. Therefore, we first need to extract the serial number in the head of the secret information K from the received image.
- Step (5): The secret information K is sorted by the serial number. According to the constructed code dictionary, the secret information K is decoded into the corresponding text information fragments in turn through the reverse lookup dictionary. Then, all the text information fragments are sequentially connected to obtain the text information T, which is hidden in the received image. The text information T is the same as the sender's text information, and thus we achieve the generative steganography.

3   Experiment and Analysis

The BCGAN network training settings for the sender and receiver are as follows: the random noise z is uniformly distributed on $(-1,1)$, the real sample data set is the CelebA celebrity face set, and the number of training steps is 10,000. The experimental platform is Tensorflow v1.3, and the GPU is an NVIDIA Titanxp. The secret information to be hidden is 10 articles randomly selected from the People's Daily official website.

The optimizer in the BCGAN uses a momentum-based optimization method with a learning rate of 0.0002. In each training period, the weight of the discriminator D is updated once, the weight of the generator G is updated twice, and the weight of the auxiliary classifier AC is updated once.

The generator consists of four deconvolutional layers. The 3×3 filters are used in each layer. The discriminator consists of four convolutional layers and four deconvolutional layers. The auxiliary classifier consists of four convolutional layers and one fully connected layer.

3.1   The Implement of the Hiding and Extraction Method

Hiding
Suppose that the information T to be transmitted is "明天 8 时,广州南站集合 (Tomorrow 8:00 Guangzhou South Station Collection)". According to the dictionary, every 2 Chinese characters or phrases are a group. Then, 明天8时 and 广州南站集合. The sequence number is added to the head of each piece of information. For example, we query from the dictionary to get the binary code of T_2 as $K_2 = 00100100000$ 100000010010000000000101000000. Its labels are 'Attractive', 'Bangs', 'Brown_Hair', 'Heavy_Makeup', 'Mouth_Slightly_Open', 'Smiling', and 'Wavy_Hair'.

As we described, the BCGAN can generate multi-label samples by inputting multiple labels into the generator. We can generate the encrypted image of the labels K_2 with the generator trained by the CelebA dataset. The results are shown in Fig. 5. In Fig. 5, the 'No Label' image is generated only with random noise z, and the input label is set to a zero vector of length 40, such as $l = [0, 0,\ldots, 0]$. The '+ Attractive' image is generated by the same z and the binary representation of the 'Attractive' label. Then, add labels in order. In this manner, the last image is generated by the same z and the seven different labels.

| No label | +Attractive | +Heavy_Makeup | +Brown_Hair | +Bangs | +Mouth_slightly_Open | +Smiling | +Wavy_Hair |

Fig. 5. The generated encrypted pictures

Every time we train the BCGAN network 100 times in the experiment, we conduct a test that generates a secret image using secret message K and extracts secret message K from the encrypted image.

Extraction

The number of extracted error class labels is shown in Fig. 6. After 1000 training iterations, although the extracted class labels can be completely correct, there are very rare cases where a class label extraction error occurs. For example, during the 4900th training iteration, the second to last label that was extracted by the discriminator was incorrect.

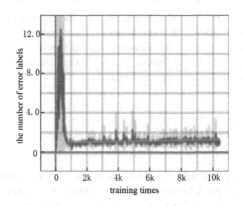

Fig. 6. The number of error class labels extracted

2018-01-24T11:05:50.231032: step 4900, d_loss 1.09119, g_loss 0.644074

('class_loss_fake', array([0, 0, 1, 0, 0, 1, 0, 0, 0, 0, 0, 1, 0, 0, 0, 0, 0, 0, 1, 0, 0, 1, 0, 0, 0, 0, 0, 0, 0, 0, 1, 0, 1, 0, 0, 0, 0, **1**, 0]))

In this case, the correctness of the decoding can be guaranteed by adding an error correction code during encoding. From this, we can also see that the traditional information hiding modifies the carrier without changing the secret information. In generative steganography, the secret information is allowed to have errors in the covert communication process, and the correctness of decoding can be ensured by adding an error correction code.

After extracting the labels (secret information segment K_2), we can get the original textual information segment T_2 by reverse lookup in the dictionary.

It can be seen from the above that we can generate the corresponding images according to the specified label arrangement, and correctly extract the selected label arrangement from the image. Therefore, the text information to be hidden can be decoded according to that, and we realize the generative steganography of text information hiding and extraction. In addition, because there is no need to make any modifications to the carrier, it can resist the detection of the steganalysis algorithms more effectively.

3.2   Capacity

According to Sect. 2.2, each image has 40 labels (meaning 40 bits of binary information), and each Chinese character is represented by 16 bits. Since the resolution of each image generated is not high (e.g., 128×128 pi), if 16 images of size 128×128 pi are used to form a 512×512 pi joint image, each joint image contains $40 \times 16 = 640$ labels (meaning 640 bits of information). We conducted hidden capacity test experiments according to 3 different word segmentation methods. The experimental results are shown in Table 2.

Table 2. Experimental results for the hiding capacity test

Average word length of dictionary (Chinese characters/words)	Number of words and phrases in dictionary	The capacity of Wu and Wang's [10] method (Chinese characters/image)	The capacity of our method (Chinese characters/image)	The capacity of our method (Chinese characters/joint-image)
0	0	1	2	39
2	100	1.57	3.6	70.2
3	100	1.86	3.9	74.1

(1) We do not use the word segmentations in the dictionary but directly divide the text information into single Chinese characters. Hidden experiments are performed on the textual information. The 8-bit labels in the header of the image are combined as a serial number. The hidden capacity of each image is $(40 - 8)\%16 = 2$ words. The hidden capacity of each joint image is $(640 - 8)\%16 = 39$ words. Since no word segmentation dictionary is used, the number of phrases in the dictionary and the average word length are zero.

(2) Select the first 100 Chinese phrases of length 2 from the selected articles to build a phrase dictionary (100 phrases where the average length is 2). The dictionary at this time includes both the binary codes corresponding to the words in the national primary and secondary characters libraries, and the phrases in the phrase dictionary. Then, the word segmentation is performed according to the dictionary using the forward maximum matching method when hidden. That is, if the secret information contains a phrase in the phrase dictionary, the words are divided into the phrase. Otherwise, it is divided into a single word. Randomly select 100 text segments. The experimental results show that the average hidden capacity of each image is 3.6 words, and the hidden capacity of each joint image is 70.2 words.

(3) The others are similar to (2) except that the average length of the phrases is 3. The experimental results show that the average hidden capacity of each image is 3.9 words, and the hidden capacity of each joint image is 74.1 words.

Theoretically, the hidden capacity of a single image is the number of Chinese characters corresponding to 40 labels. The average information hiding capacity of multiple images is the average length of the secret information fragments after word segmentation:

$$\overline{C} = \frac{\sum_{i=1}^{n} C_i}{n} \tag{4}$$

where n is the number of secret information fragments, and C_i is the length of the i-th secret information fragment.

From the experimental results, it can be seen that increasing the average length of words in the phrase dictionary can increase the average hidden capacity of each image. In addition, the use of multiple images with smaller resolution to form a joint image with a larger resolution can also significantly increase the hidden capacity.

According to Table 2, compared with Wu and Wang [10], the capacity of our method has been greatly improved in joint images. The reason is that Wu and Wang [10] only used one visual keyword with the highest frequency to hide the secret information in an encrypted image, and the resulting capacity was relatively small. In our method, all the labels of an encrypted image are used to hide secret information so that it can effectively increase the hidden capacity.

To further improve the information hiding capacity of each image, we can construct a more perfect dictionary according to commonly used contents of the communication parties. In addition, we can increase the number of words in the phrases dictionary so that the secret information fragments after the word separation could contain as many words as possible. Second, using more images to form a joint image can also significantly increase the hidden capacity.

3.3   Anti-detection

For steganalysis experiments, we used the S-UNIWARD algorithm to obtain 60,000 celebrity face embedded images at an embedding rate of 0.4 bpp. In addition, we also use the BCGAN to generate 10,000 celebrity face encrypted images. We use the SCNN method with the steganalysis detection accuracy rate of 96% for the S-UNIWARD proposed by Liu et al. [24]. We respectively select 50,000 celebrity face original images and embedded images as training set A, the remaining 10,000 celebrity face original images and embedded images make up test set B, and 10,000 generated encrypted images and celebrity face original images make up test set C. Steganalysis test results are shown in Table 3.

Table 3.   Accuracy of the steganalysis tested on 2 test sets

Test set	Detection accuracy of SCNN
B	0.961
C	0.509

From the result of test set C, we can see that the detection rate is close to 0.5, and the steganalysis detector almost cannot distinguish between the generated encrypted image and the original image. The reason for this is that our encrypted image is generated directly by BCGAN. Therefore, during the embedding of the text information and the transmission of the encrypted image, the encrypted image is not modified at all. Therefore, it can effectively resist the detection of the human eye, and it can also fundamentally resist the detection of the statistics-based information hiding analysis algorithms.

3.4 Security

This study concerns generative steganography. The encrypted image is a natural image that is generated directly by the BCGAN without any modification. From Sect. 3.3, it is difficult for the detector to distinguish generated images from natural images in statistics. It can be seen from Fig. 5 that the generated image is very realistic. It is difficult for the human eye to distinguish the difference compared with the natural image, and it can be better disguised as a commonly used image transmitted in the usual manner. Therefore, compared with the traditional methods of encryption and information hiding, our method is more difficult for the attacker to detect and can covertly conduct secret communications.

Assume that the attacker suspects that the transmitted image contains secret information. Because he does not have the same BCGAN model as the communicating parties, it is difficult to extract the secret information from the encrypted images by the discriminator. Even if the attacker accidentally extracts the secret information, he cannot decode the secret information into the original text information because he does not know the code dictionary. Therefore, we can ensure the security of the covert communications.

4   Conclusion

We propose a new generative steganography method by using the characteristics of BCGAN that can join input noise and class labels to generate natural images, which are difficult to distinguish from natural images in statistics. In addition, we combine it with the idea of coverless information hiding that generates secret images that are directly driven by secret information. Theoretical analysis and experiments show that this method can effectively resist the detection of the existing steganalysis methods, and it can also provide large hidden capacity and good security. We will use more complex networks to generate clearer natural pictures in our next work.

References

1. Tirkel, A.Z., Rankin, G.A., Schyndel, R.V.: Electronic watermark. In: Digital Image Computing, Technology and Applications (1993)
2. Yang, C.H., Weng, C.Y., Wang, S.J.: Adaptive data hiding in edge areas of images with spatial LSB domain systems. IEEE Trans. Inf. Forensics Secur. 3(3), 488–497 (2008)
3. Holub, V., Fridrich, J., Denemark, T.: Universal distortion function for steganography in an arbitrary domain. EURASIP J. Inf. Secur. 2014(1), 1 (2014)
4. Pevný, T., Filler, T., Bas, P.: Using high-dimensional image models to perform highly undetectable steganography. In: Böhme, R., Fong, Philip W.L., Safavi-Naini, R. (eds.) IH 2010. LNCS, vol. 6387, pp. 161–177. Springer, Heidelberg (2010). https://doi.org/10.1007/978-3-642-16435-4_13

5. Holub, V., Fridrich, J.: Designing steganographic distortion using directional filters. In: 2013 IEEE International Workshop on Information Forensics and Security, pp. 234–239. IEEE (2013)

6. Ruanaidh, J.O., Dowling, W.J., Boland, F.M.: Phase watermarking of digital images. In: 1996 International Conference on Image Processing, pp. 239–242 (1996)

7. Cox, I.J., Kilian, J., Leighton, F.T.: Secure spread-spectrum watermarking for multimedia. IEEE Trans. Image Process. **6**(12), 1673–1687 (2010)

8. Lin, W.H., Horng, S.J., Kao, T.W.: An efficient watermarking method based on significant difference of wavelet coefficient quantization. IEEE Trans. Multimed. **10**(5), 746–757 (2008)

9. Zhou, Z.L., Cao, Y., Sun, X.M.: Coverless information hiding based on bag-of-words model of image. J. Appl. Sci. **34**(5), 527–536 (2016)

10. Wu, K.C., Wang, C.M.: Steganography using reversible texture synthesis. IEEE Trans. Image Proc. **24**(1), 130–139 (2015)

11. Xu, J., Mao, X., Jin, X.: Hidden message in a deformation-based texture. Vis. Comput. **31**, 1653–1669 (2015)

12. Chen, X., Sun, H., Tobe, Y., Zhou, Z., Sun, X.: coverless information hiding method based on the chinese mathematical expression. In: Huang, Z., Sun, X., Luo, J., Wang, J. (eds.) ICCCS 2015. LNCS, vol. 9483, pp. 133–143. Springer, Cham (2015). https://doi.org/10.1007/978-3-319-27051-7_12

13. Zhou, Z., Sun, H., Harit, R., Chen, X., Sun, X.: Coverless image steganography without embedding. In: Huang, Z., Sun, X., Luo, J., Wang, J. (eds.) ICCCS 2015. LNCS, vol. 9483, pp. 123–132. Springer, Cham (2015). https://doi.org/10.1007/978-3-319-27051-7_11

14. Zhang, X.P., Qian, Z.X., Li, S.: Prospect of digital steganography research. J. Appl. Sci. **34**(5), 475–489 (2016)

15. Qian, Z., Zhou, H., Zhang, W., Zhang, X.: Robust steganography using texture synthesis. Advances in Intelligent Information Hiding and Multimedia Signal Processing. SIST, vol. 63, pp. 25–33. Springer, Cham (2017). https://doi.org/10.1007/978-3-319-50209-0_4

16. Goodfellow, I., et al.: Generative adversarial nets. In: Proceedings of the 2014 Conference on Advances in Neural Information Processing Systems 27, pp. 2672–2680. Curran Associates, Inc., Montreal, Canada (2014)

17. Odena, A.: Semi-supervised learning with generative adversarial networks. arXiv preprint arXiv:1606.01583 (2016)

18. Mirza, M., Osindero, S.: Conditional generative adversarial nets. arXiv preprint arXiv:1411.1784 (2014)

19. Chen, X., et al.: InfoGAN: Interpretable representation learning by information maximizing generative adversarial nets. In: Advances in Neural Information Processing Systems, pp. 2172–2180 (2016)

20. Odena, A., Olah, C., Shlens, J.: Conditional image synthesis with auxiliary classifier GANs. arXiv preprint (2016)

21. Zhou, Z., et al.: Activation Maximization Generative Adversarial Nets. arXiv preprint arXiv:1703.02000 (2017)

22. Berthelot, D., Schumm, T., Metz, L.: BEGAN: Boundary equilibrium generative adversarial networks. arXiv preprint arXiv:1703.10717 (2017)

23. Lee, M., Seok, J.: Controllable Generative Adversarial Network. arXiv preprint arXiv:1708.00598 (2017)

24. Liu, M., Zhang, M., Liu, J., Gao, P.: A steganalysis method based on shallow convolution neural network. J. Shandong Univ. (Nat. Sci.) **03**, 63–70 (2018)

How the Variance of Hotel Dominance Attribute Affects the Consumer Recommendation Rate: An Empirical Study with the Data from Ctrip.com

Bingjia Shao[1], Shasha Liu[1,2(⊠)], Yuan Gao[3,5,6], Xingyang Lyu[4],
and Zhendong Cheng[1]

[1] School of Economics and Business Administration,
Chongqing University, Chongqing 400030, China
{shaobingjia,liushasha}@cqu.edu.cn, czd.
huai.nan@163.com
[2] Chongqing Jadun Economics and Management Academy,
Chongqing 400030, China
[3] Xichang Satellite Launch Center, Xichang 615000, China
[4] School of Business Administration,
Southwestern University of Finance and Economics, Chengdu, China
lvxingyang@swufe.edu.cn
[5] China Defense Science and Technology Information Center,
Beijing 100142, China
[6] Department of Electronic Engineering,
Tsinghua University, Beijing 100084, China
yuangao08@tsinghua.edu.cn

Abstract. The influence of consumer reviews on hotel reservation has been addressed in both practical and theoretical fields. Most previous studies focus on the volume and score of reviews, little about the score of hotel attributes. This paper focuses on that how the variance of the hotel dominance attribute ratings affects the consumer recommendation rate to economy hotels and luxury hotels respectively. Research model has been developed based on Elaboration Likelihood Model and tested with the data from Ctrip.com in China. The results show that the variance of economy hotels has positive effect on the consumer recommendation rate, while that of luxury hotels has negative effect. Furthermore, results also indicate that the volume and score of reviews have different moderating effect.

Keywords: Variance · Dominance attribute · Consumer recommendation rate

1 Introduction

Online word of mouth (WOM) such as consumer reviews has played an increasingly important role with the fast development of electronic commerce [1]. Prior studies show that consumers rely on reviews when purchasing experience goods versus search goods, which makes WOM especially important for hotels [2]. Many studies have

© Springer Nature Switzerland AG 2018
X. Sun et al. (Eds.): ICCCS 2018, LNCS 11068, pp. 550–562, 2018.
https://doi.org/10.1007/978-3-030-00021-9_49

shown the volume of reviews and review score significantly affect consumer cognition towards product quality [3]. Empirical research provides little about the information of specific product attribute.

Previous studies pay more attention on the variance of the review score [4–6]. For example, some hotels get five stars, while some get two stars. The review score of a hotel represents consumers' overall perception of the hotel [7]. This failed to reflect consumers' evaluation on the differences of hotel attributes. Take Ctrip.com for instance, consumers need to rate the location of the hotel, the facilities of the hotel, the service of the hotel and the cleanliness of the hotel respectively. Then the system generate the arithmetic mean as review score which represents consumers' evaluation on the hotel (see Fig. 1). Compared with the review score, the score of each attribute is also very easy to be received and used by consumers and give more intuitive information of specific hotel attributes. This study mainly focuses on the difference of dominance attribute. Some hotels have large variance of the dominance attribute, while some have minor variance.

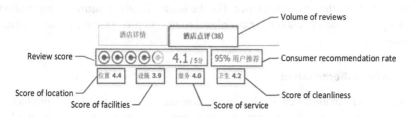

Fig. 1. Example of a hotel review on Ctrip.com.

This paper proposes the difference of dominance attribute affect consumer recommendation rate based on the framework of Elaboration Likelihood Model. The influence is inconsistent referred to the economy hotels and the luxury hotels. We investigate the moderating effect of hotel reviews features (characterized by the volume of reviews and review score) on the relationship between the difference of dominance attribute and consumer recommendation rate [8, 9].

The rest of the paper is organized as follows. We review the related literature in Sect. 2 and develop our hypotheses in Sect. 3. We describe the data collection process in Sect. 4 and the empirical model in Sect. 5. Main findings are presented and discussed next, and the paper ends with a discussion of limitation and future research.

2 Literature Review

2.1 Elaboration Likelihood Model (ELM)

The Elaboration Likelihood Model is proposed by Petty and Cacioppo [10]. This model suppose combinations of factors are viewed as determining people's motivation (e.g. interests and needs) and ability (e.g. knowledge and experience) to think carefully about the merits of the information for a hotel [11]. They have suggested that there are "central" and "peripheral" routes to process the information, with the "central route" representing the processes involved when elaboration likelihood is high and the "peripheral route" typifying the processes operative when elaboration likelihood is low. When the consumer's motivation and ability is both high, the elaboration likelihood is high. When either motivation or ability is low, the elaboration likelihood is low. When the elaboration likelihood is high, consumers will try their best to do a series of serious attempts to evaluate the information in a cognitive way. When the elaboration likelihood is low, consumers tend to the peripheral route and are more likely to adopt a strategy wherein they draw a simple inference in an affective way. In the high-speed internet era, consumers have rich knowledge and experience when booking hotels. So consumers' ability of processing information is high. Consumers' motivation is different when booking the economy hotels and luxury hotels. Compared to the luxury hotel consumers, consumers' expectation of the economy hotels is lower and the budget is limited [12]. The economy hotel consumers are willing to spend more time to process the information of reviews and try their best to find out better hotel from various economy hotels. The dominance attribute of economy hotel can attract consumers who have the same preference. For the luxury hotels, consumers' motivation is low, they are inclined to choose the peripheral route and prefer simple or non-difference information.

2.2 Hyper-differentiation

In today's information-rich environment, consumers can comparison product, get product reviews from other consumers and become very well informed about what is available in the market. If your products are not differentiated, pure price competition will be more extreme than ever before. Michael E. Porter proposed that differentiation strategy is to make enterprise products, services and image different from competitors, in order to gain competitive advantage. The hotel as an experience product, it is very important for consumers to perceive the overall hotel quality. So the differentiation strategy of hotels need the overall quality of hotel keep in a high level. This is called hyper- differentiation. It refers to the enterprise focus on enhancing the dominance attribute while keep the overall quality of product in an upward level.

The motivation of economy hotel consumers is high. They are willing to spend more time to compare the difference of the attributes and find out the dominance attribute which is consistent with their preference. They tend to choose the hotel with dominance attribute while the overall quality keep in an upward level.

2.3 Attribute Balance

To deal with the increasing number and complexity of products available to consumers, many companies have begun to describe their offerings using aggregate attributes [13]. Consumers use attribute balance as a reason for choice. Attribute balance emphasize the equilibrium relationship among the attributes. Consumers suppose the hotel with balanced attributes is better and reasonable. There is no obvious difference among the attributes.

The motivation of luxury hotel consumers is low. They tend to avoid effortful thinking the difference information and prefer to the hotel with balanced attributes.

In this study, the motivation of economy hotel consumers and luxury hotel consumers is different, then consumers will choose different routes to process information. In the central route, the economy hotel consumers positively process information and prefer the difference of dominance attribute. In the peripheral route, the luxury hotel consumers negatively process information and prefer the balanced attributes (see Fig. 2).

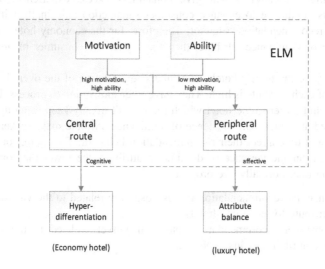

Fig. 2. Research model.

3 Hypothesis Development

The product of hotel contained a set of attributes, such as location, facilities, service and cleanliness. Consumers will give score to each attribute. Due to the existence of various attributes, the distribution of hotels' attribute score is different when the review score is the same. There are three hotels, hotel A, hotel B, hotel C. The volume and score (4.2) of reviews is the same, but the score of location, facilities, service and cleanliness is different. The score of hotel A attributes are (4.8, 4, 4, 4). The score of hotel B attributes are (4, 4.4, 4.4, 4). The score of hotel C attributes are (4.2, 4.2, 4.2, 4.2). The difference of dominance attribute is measured by the score of dominance attribute minus the review score (the average score of four attributes). The variance of dominance attribute is 0.6(4.8-4.2), 0.2(4.4-4.2) and 0(4.2-4.2) respectively. From the review score, it is no difference among the three hotels. Referred to the variance of dominance attribute, they are different. When the three hotels' review score is the same, the variance of hotel A' dominance attribute is maximum and the hotel C is minimum.

3.1   The Variance of Dominance Attribute and Consumer Recommendation Rate

The customers of economy hotels and luxury hotels have difference in consumption ability and psychological expectation [14]. Consumers' expectation of the economy hotels is lower and their budget is limited. They are willing to spend more time to process the information of reviews and try their best to find out the hotel which has dominance attribute consistent with their preference.

According to the theory of hyper- differentiation, the dominance attribute consistent with consumers' preference will give consumers excess experience. The excess experience is conducive to enhance consumer satisfaction and finally will affect the consumer's recommendation behavior. Therefore, for the economy hotels, the greater the variance of dominance attribute, then the higher the consumer recommendation rate.

However, for the luxury hotels, consumers' expectation of the overall quality and the quality of each attribute is high. They have litter motivation to process the variance information and prefer to the hotel which the overall quality keep in an upward level with balanced attributes. The existence of dominance attribute may weaken consumer satisfaction and then affect their recommendation behavior. Therefore, for the luxury hotels, the greater the variance of dominance attribute, the lower the consumer recommendation rate. Formally, we propose:

H1a: Consumer recommendation rate is positively related to the variance of dominance attribute for economy hotels.

H1b: Consumer recommendation rate is negatively related to the variance of dominance attribute for luxury hotels.

3.2   The Review Score

The review score refers to values towards the products. It reflects the overall quality or performance of products based on a variety of consumers' preferences [15]. Since consumers take reviews as a relatively credible source of information, the review score has a strong effect on consumer judgment. Consumers trust sellers with high review score, which are signals of superior reputation. The high review score of products also can help products sales [16]. Some studies have found that the book review score of Amazon have a positive impact on its sales and rankings [5].

Referred the attributes affect on the consumer recommendation rate, consumers prefer to the hotel which have a higher review score [17]. Therefore, the positive effect of review score can enhance the relation between the attributes (the dominance attribute or balanced attributes) and consumer recommendation rate. Formally, we propose the following:

H2: The relation between the variance of dominance attribute and consumer recommendation rate is moderated by the review score.

H2a: The positive relation between the variance of dominance attribute and consumer recommendation rate will become stronger when the review score of economy hotel is high.

H2b: The negative relation between the variance of dominance attribute and consumer recommendation rate will become stronger when the review score of luxury hotel is high.

3.3 The Volume of Reviews

The volume of reviews refers to the number of reviews provided by consumers [18]. It is regarded as an indicator of the intensity of reviews that plays a dominant role in driving revenues [19]. Some researchers argue that the volume of reviews reflects the momentum of the product [20]. A larger number of reviews may increase the objectivity and be trusted more by potential consumers. On the other hand, with the accumulation of the volume of produces reviews, consumers need to spend more energy to find out the information they need. Consumers' burden of processing information is hard [21]. In recent years, researchers pay more attention on the information overload. It has been well documented that consumer's ability to process information is restricted when the amount of information is extremely large [22, 23].

Despite the inconsistent findings in the literature, we follow the theory that the information overload play a dominant role, based on the following considerations. It is difficult for consumers to extract relevant and useful information from a large amount of reviews. Consumers can not distinguish the authenticity and usefulness of attribute information. Therefore, the negative effect of review volume can weaken the relation between the attributes (the dominance attribute or balanced attributes) and consumer recommendation rate. Formally, we propose the following:

H3: The relation between the variance of dominance attribute and consumer recommendation rate is moderated by the volume of reviews.
H3a: The positive relation between the variance of dominance attribute and consumer recommendation rate will become weaker when the volume of economy hotel reviews is high.
H3b: The negative relation between the variance of dominance attribute and consumer recommendation rate will become weaker when the volume of luxury hotel reviews is high.

4 Methodology

4.1 Data Source

The data for this study is collected from Ctrip.com, one of the most popular product review sites in China, which enables us to obtain a large sample. We selected restaurants from 18 popular cities. There are 86,683 economy hotels and 1,233 luxury hotels of 18 popular cities. In order to compare and analyze the economy hotels and the luxury hotels, we randomly selected 1,921 hotels from the 86,683 economy hotels. For this sample, we gathered all available information for each hotel using an original web crawler tool from June 23rd to September 1st, 2017. For each hotel, we collect basic information, including hotel name, whether it is a brand hotel, the open time or the latest renovation time, whether it is weekend when grabbing data and so on. We also collect the consumer recommendation rate, the review score, the volume of reviews, and the score of each attribute. In order to ensure the integrity of the data, we excluded the missing data from this sample. The final data set consists of 116,752 items of 1,818 economy hotels and 73,627 items of 1,216 luxury hotel.

The descriptive statistics of variables for economy hotel and luxury hotel are respectively shown in Tables 1 and 2.

Table 1. Descriptive statistics of variables for economy hotel.

Variable	Mean	SD	Min	Max
Consumer Recommendation Rate	0.943	0.038	0.73	1
Score	4.179	0.249	3.7	5
Volume	484	622	10	7010
Variance	0.14	0.091	0	0.65

Table 2. Descriptive statistics of variables for luxury hotel.

Variable	Mean	SD	Min	Max
Consumer Recommendation Rate	0.965	0.023	0.8	1
Score	4.556	0.167	3.8	5
Volume	3238	2903	15	37572
Variance	0.104	0.066	0	0.475

4.2   Variables

4.2.1   Dependent Variable

Consumer recommendation rate. When consumers write reviews for a hotel, Ctrip.com inquires whether they would recommend the hotel to others and use the individual data to calculate the overall guest recommendation rate.

4.2.2   Independent Variables

The variance of dominance attribute (balanced attributes means that the variance of dominance attribute is trending to zero). In this paper, we view the attribute with the highest score among the four attributes as the dominance attribute. The variance of dominance attribute is that the score of dominance attribute minus the review score (the average score of four attributes).

4.2.3   Moderator Variable

(1) The review score. (2) The volume of online reviews.

4.2.4 Control Variables

(1) Brand. (2) Weekend. (3) The open time or the latest renovation time.

4.3 Empirical Model

In order to determine the appropriate model to apply, we first check the guest recommendation rate. This dependent variable is normally distributed, hence the multivariable linear regression model would be appropriate. For hotel i at time t:

$$Consumer\ Recommandation\ Rate_{i,t}$$
$$= \Theta + \beta_1 Score_{i,t-1} + \beta_2 lnVolume_{i,t-1} + \beta_3 Variance_{i,t-1}$$
$$+ \beta_4 Score_{i,t-1} * lnVolume_{i,t-1} + \beta_5 Score_{i,t-1} * Variance_{i,t-1}$$
$$+ \beta_6 lnVolume_{i,t-1} * Variance_{i,t-1} + \mu_{it}$$

$$\Theta = \alpha_0 + \alpha_1 Weekend + \alpha_2 Brand + \alpha_3 Opentime$$

$$Variance_{i,t-1} = max\left[Sl_{i,t-1} - \overline{S_{i,t-1}}, Sf_{i,t-1} - \overline{S_{i,t-1}}, Ss_{i,t-1} - \overline{S_{i,t-1}}, Sc_{i,t-1} - \overline{S_{i,t-1}} \right]$$

In this model, the dependent variable *Consumer Recommandation Rate*$_{i,t}$ represents the recommendation rate of hotel i at time t. There is a time lag between the time consumers checking in and posting comments. $Score_{i,t-1}$ is the review score of hotel i at time t−1. $Volume_{i,t-1}$ is hotel i's number of reviews of at t−1。 $Variance_{i,t-1}$ is the hotel i's variance of dominance attribute at t−1. $\overline{S_{i,t-1}}$ means hotel i's the average score of the four attributes at t−1.

$Sl_{i,t-1}$, $Sf_{i,t-1}$, $Ss_{i,t-1}$, $Sc_{i,t-1}$ represent the hotel i's score of location, facilities, service and cleanliness at t−1 respectively. $Score_{i,t-1} * Variance_{i,t-1}$ and $Volume_{i,t-1} * Variance_{i,t-1}$ represent the moderating effect of score and volume on the variance for hotel i at time t−1 respectively. The lack of subscript t shows *Brand* and *Opentime* may differ among hotels but do not change overtime.

5 Results and Discussion

5.1 Results

We run two models for the economy hotel, and two models for the luxury hotel. Tables 3 and 4 present the regression results.

5.2 Discussion

Tables 3 and 4 reports the estimation results for the proposed research model. Model 1 and Model 3 is base the model with the main effects and control variables. Model 2 and 4 add the moderating effects and interaction effects. With the comparison with the results of Tables 3 and 4, we have a discussion.

Table 3. The regression result of economy hotel model.

	Model 1	Model 2
Constant	81.7(0.247)***	73.45(2.059)***
$Variance_{i,t-1}$	0.91(0.065)***	1.01(0.135)***
$LnVolume_{i,t-1}$	0.63(0.012)***	0.66(0.049)***
$Score_{i,t-1}$	2.05(0.055)**	2.18(0.981)**
$LnVolume_{i,t-1}*Variance_{i,t-1}$		−9.16(2.148)**
$Score_{i,t-1}*Variance_{i,t-1}$		9.14(2.147)***
$Score_{i,t-1}*LnVolume_{i,t-1}$		9.03(2.15)***
Weekend	0.001	0.001
Brand	0	0
OpenTime	0	0
R^2	0.26	0.32
F	7784.99	7742.59
Number of Obs.	106,625	103,851
Number of Groups	1,821	1,788

Note: ***$p < 0.005$, **$p < 0.05$, *$p < 0.1$, standard errors are reported in parenthesis.

Table 4. The regression result of luxury hotel model.

	Model 3	Model 4
Constant	49.27(0.321)***	69.32(3.205)***
$Variance_{i,t-1}$	−0.34(0.106)***	−3.08(0.247)***
$LnVolume_{i,t-1}$	1.11(0.018)***	1.82(0.098)***
$Score_{i,t-1}$	8.50(0.059)**	15.14(1.284)***
$LnVolume_{i,t-1}*Variance_{i,t-1}$		12.66(2.964)***
$Score_{i,t-1}*Variance_{i,t-1}$		−12.37(2.962)**
$Score_{i,t-1}*LnVolume_{i,t-1}$		−17.78(2.977)***
Weekend	0.01*	0.01*
Brand	0	0
OpenTime	0	0
R^2	0.43	0.41
F	366.72	331.81
Number of Obs.	75,543	74,993
Number of Groups	1,167	1,166

Note: ***$p < 0.005$, **$p < 0.05$, *$p < 0.1$, standard errors are reported in parenthesis.

In Model 1, we find that the effects of variance (0.91), volume(0.63) and score (2.05) on the consumer recommendation rate are positive and significant for economy hotels. The effect of variance on the consumer recommendation rate is greater than the effect of score. In Model 2, after verifying the main effects, then add the moderating effects (LnVolume $_{i,t-1}$*Variance $_{i,t-1}$ and Score $_{i,t-1}$* Variance $_{i,t-1}$) and the interaction effect(Score$_{i,t-1}$* LnVolume $_{i,t-1}$). The results show that the main effects is still significant and even much stronger. It indicates the main effects has good robustness. In addition, the volume of reviews negatively moderate the effect of variance on the consumer recommendation rate (−9.16), and the review score positively moderate the effect of variance on the consumer recommendation rate (9.14).

Hypothesis 1a posits that consumer recommendation rate is positively related to the variance of dominance attribute for economy hotels. The results in Model 1 and 2 indicate that the coefficient for the relationship is positively significant(0.91 and 1.01). Hence, Hypothesis 1a is supported.

Hypothesis 2a predicts that the positive relation between the variance of dominance attribute and consumer recommendation rate will become stronger when the review score of economy hotel is high. The results in Model 2 suggest the coefficient for the moderating between the variance and consumer recommendation rate is positively significant (9.14), which lends support to Hypothesis 2a.

Hypothesis 3a postulates that the positive relation between the variance of dominance attribute and consumer recommendation rate will become weaker when the volume of economy hotel reviews is high. The results in Model 2 suggest the coefficient for the moderating between the variance and consumer recommendation rate is negatively significant (−9.16). Therefore, Hypothesis 3a is supported.

In Model 3, we find that the effect of variance (−0.34) on the consumer recommendation is negative and the effects of volume (1.11) and score (8.50) are positive for luxury hotels. The effect of variance on the consumer recommendation rate is weaker than the effect of score and volume. In Model 4, after verifying the main effects, then add the moderating effects (LnVolume$_{i,t-1}$*Variance $_{i,t-1}$ and Score $_{i,t-1}$* Variance $_{i,t-1}$) and the interaction effect(Score$_{i,t-1}$* LnVolume $_{i,t-1}$). The results show that the main effects is still significant and even much stronger. It indicates the main effects has good robustness. In addition, the review score positively moderate the effect of variance on the consumer recommendation rate (−12.37) and the volume of reviews negatively moderate the effect of variance on the consumer recommendation rate (12.66).

Hypothesis 1b assumes that consumer recommendation rate is negatively related to the variance of dominance attribute for luxury hotels. The results in Model 3 and 4 indicate that the coefficient for the relationship is negatively significant (−0.34 and −3.08).Hence, Hypothesis 1b is supported.

Hypothesis 2b proposes the negative relation between the variance of dominance attribute and consumer recommendation rate will become stronger when the review score of luxury hotel is high. The results in Model 4 suggest the coefficient for the moderating between the variance and consumer recommendation rate is positively significant (−12.37), which lends support to Hypothesis 2b.

Hypothesis 3b states that the negative relation between the variance of dominance attribute and consumer recommendation rate will become weaker when the volume of luxury hotel reviews is high. The results in Model 4 suggest the coefficient for the moderating between the variance and consumer recommendation rate is negatively significant (12.66). Therefore, Hypothesis 3b is supported.

The goodness of fit was tested by R^2 for the four models. The results showed that R^2 are 0.43, 0.41, 0.26 and 0.32 respectively. The results were in an acceptable range.

6 Conclusion and Implications

6.1 Conclusion

Previous studies mainly focus on the volume of reviews and the review score. Litter studies research the score of each attribute and it is blank in studying the variance of dominance attribute. Through mining the data from Ctrip.com, we proposed that the variance of dominance attribute affect consumer recommendation rate. The influence was inconsistent referred to the economy hotels and the luxury hotels. We also investigated the moderating effect of hotel reviews features (characterized by volume and score of hotel reviews) on the relationship between the variance of dominance attribute and consumer recommendation rate.

First, we found that the variance of dominance attribute positively affect consumer recommendation rate for economy hotels, and the review score positively moderate the relationship while the volume of reviews negatively moderate it. The prominent dominance attribute can help to improve the consumer recommendation rate for economy hotels. In the high-speed internet era, consumers can get a lot of information from internet, so the heterogeneity of economy hotels is higher, it may be more easily to avoid direct competition from other hotels. It is worth noting that economy hotel managers should focus on highlighting the dominance attribute, at the same time have to take into account other attributes, so as to promote the positively effect of dominance attribute. With increasing in the volume of reviews, the bonus from the dominance attribute will be reduced. So in the early days of the hotel online business, the volume of reviews is small, the economy hotel managers should pay more attention on the differentiation of dominance attribute.

Second, to luxury hotels, balanced attributes positively affect consumer recommendation rate, and the review score positively moderate the relationship while the volume of reviews negatively moderate it. It is worth noting that luxury hotel managers should focus on highlighting the balanced attributes, at the same time have to keep the quality of other attributes in a high level, so as to promote the positively effect of balanced attributes. In the early days of the hotel online business, the volume of reviews is small, the luxury hotels should adopt the balanced attributes strategy to operate hotel.

6.2 Limitations and Future Research

We conclude by addressing the limitations of our study and discussing future research directions. One limitation of this study is that using a single website (Ctrip.com in this paper) can limit the generalizability of our results. It will be interesting to extend our framework to other websites. Second, this study only based on the panel data. If it is possible, it's best to do experiments to verify the relationship between the variance of dominance attribute and consumer decision-making. Future studies may consider using experimental method to test this mechanism.

Acknowledgments. This research was supported by the National Social Science Foundation of China (No. 14AGL023) and the Plan of Ten Thousand Tourism Excellence launched by National Tourism Administration (No. WMYC20171080). We would like to thank all the reviewers for their kind suggestions to this work.

References

1. Yin, D., Bond, S.D.: Anxious or angry effects of discrete emotions on the perceived helpfulness of online reviews. MIS Q. **38**, 539–560 (2013)
2. Ye, Q., Law, R.: The impact of online user reviews on hotel room sales. Int. J. Hosp. Manag. **28**(1), 180–182 (2009)
3. Wang, M., Lu, Q.: How word-of-mouth moderates room price and hotel stars for online hotel booking an empirical investigation with expedia data. J. Electron. Commer. Res. **16**(1), 72–80 (2015)
4. Provencher, J.F.: Quantifying ingested debris in marine megafauna: a review and recommendations for standardization. Anal. Methods **9**(9), 1454–1469 (2017)
5. Sun, M.: How does the variance of product ratings matter. Manag. Sci. **58**(4), 696–707 (2012)
6. Huang, A.H., Chen, K.: A study of factors that contribute to online review helpfulness. Comput. Hum. Behav. **48**(C), 17–27 (2015)
7. Liu, Z.W., Sangwon, P.: What makes a useful online review? Implication for travel product websites. Tourism Manag. **47**(47), 140–151 (2015)
8. Li, Z.: A survey of link recommendation for social networks: methods, theoretical foundations, and future research directions. ACM Trans. Manag. Inf. Syst. **9**(1) (2018)
9. Liu, Y.: Recommendation in a changing world: exploiting temporal dynamics in ratings and reviews. ACM Trans. Web **12**(1), 3 (2018)
10. Petty, R.E., Cacioppo, J.T.: The elaboration likelihood model of persuasion. Adv. Consum. Res. **19**(4), 123–205 (1986)
11. Cheung, M.Y., Sia, C.L.: Is this review believable? A study of factors affecting the credibility of online consumer reviews from an ELM perspective. J. Assoc. Inf. Syst. **13**(8), 618–635 (2012)
12. Liu, S.W., Law, R.: Analyzing changes in hotel customers' expectations by trip mode. Int. J. Hosp. Manag. **34**(1), 359–371 (2013)
13. Kim, D., Perdue, R.R.: The effects of cognitive, affective, and sensory attributes on hotel choice. Int. J. Hosp. Manag. **35**, 246–257 (2013)
14. Mao, M.: Multirelational social recommendations via multigraph ranking. IEEE Trans. Cybern. **47**(12), 4049–4061 (2017)
15. Duan, W., Gu, B.: Do online reviews matter? An empirical investigation of panel data. Decis. Support Syst. **45**(4), 1007–1016 (2008)
16. Zhu, F., Zhang, X.M.: Impact of online consumer reviews on sales: the moderating role of product and consumer characteristics. J. Market. **74**(2), 133–148 (2010)
17. Sparks, B.A., Browning, V.: The impact of online reviews on hotel booking intentions and perception of trust. Tourism Manag. **32**(6), 1310–1323 (2011)

18. Baka, V.: The becoming of user-generated reviews: looking at the past to understand the future of managing reputation in the travel sector. Tourism Manag. **53**, 148–162 (2016)
19. Duan, W., Gu, B.: The dynamics of online word-of-mouth and product sales—an empirical investigation of the movie industry. J. Retail. **84**(2), 233–242 (2008)
20. Flanagan, A.J., Metzger, M.J.: Trusting expert- versus user-generated ratings online: the role of information volume, valence, and consumer characteristics. Comput. Hum. Behav. **29**(4), 1626–1634 (2013)
21. Park, D.H., Lee, J.: eWOM overload and its effect on consumer behavioral intention depending on consumer involvement. Electron. Commer. Res. Appl. **7**(4), 386–398 (2008)
22. Zhang, S.: The recommendation system of micro-blog topic based on user clustering. Mob. Netw. Appl. **22**(2), 228–239 (2017)
23. Park, J.Y., Jang, S.C.: Confused by too many choices? Choice overload in tourism. Tourism Manag. **35**(4), 1–12 (2013)

Image Recovery via Truncated Weighted Schatten-p Norm Regularization

Lei Feng[1]([✉]) [iD] and Jun Zhu[1,2] [iD]

[1] Jinling Institute of Technology, Nanjing 211169, China
fenglei4923272780126.com
[2] Nanjing University of Science and Technology, Nanjing 210094, China

Abstract. Low-rank prior knowledge has indicated great superiority in the field of image processing. However, how to solve the NP-hard problem containing rank norm is crucial to the recovery results. In this paper, truncated weighted schatten-p norm, which is employed to approximate the rank function by taking advantages of both weighted nuclear norm and truncated schatten-p norm, has been proposed toward better exploiting low-rank property in image CS recovery. At last, we have developed an efficient iterative scheme based on alternating direction method of multipliers to accurately solve the nonconvex optimization model. Experimental results demonstrate that our proposed algorithm is exceeding the existing state-of-the-art methods, both visually and quantitatively.

Keywords: Compressive sensing
Truncated weighted schatten-p norm
Alternating direction method of multipliers

1 Introduction

Compressive Sensing (CS) [1–5] draws recently much more attention in the field of image processing. Compared with the traditional scheme of sampling followed by compressing, CS carries out the above two steps at the same time. From fewer measurements than required by Nyquist theorem, CS can efficiently reconstruct images under the condition that they satisfy the sparsity.

Traditional CS algorithms often exploit the sparsity in some transform domains [6–11]. Lately, the intrinsic low-rank property exploited by self-similarity and nonlocal operation, has widely used in many research fields, such as face recognition [12–14], image inpainting [15] and compressive sensing [16,17]. These methods based on low-rank property have shown competitive performances in each area.

The success of these low-rank regularization based CS methods depends on the solution of the low-rank regularization problem. Unfortunately, the low-rank regularization problem is NP-hard and there is no method to solve it directly. Many methods use different substitution functions to approximate the rank function [18–20]. [18,19] selected convex nuclear norm and employed singular value

© Springer Nature Switzerland AG 2018
X. Sun et al. (Eds.): ICCCS 2018, LNCS 11068, pp. 563–574, 2018.
https://doi.org/10.1007/978-3-030-00021-9_50

thresholding [21] to efficiently resolve the rank regularization problem. Compared with the original rank definition has the fact that all nonzero singular values play the same important role, the nuclear norm based approaches minimized the summarization of all the singular values. [16] chose logdet function (the logarithm sum of all the singular values) and can obtain better results than nuclear norm. However, logdet function is fixed and essentially deviates from the rank function. In order to obtain a competitive solution of low-rank regularization problem, many methods adopt distinct schemes and treat each singular value differently [22–25]. Weighted nuclear norm [22] assigned larger weights to larger singular values and smaller weights to smaller ones. So smaller singular values are penalized more than larger ones. Since the largest r (the rank) singular values will not impact the rank, in our previous work, truncated schatten-p norm [24] abandoned them and only minimized the summation of surplus singular values to the power of p.

In this paper, truncated weighted schatten-p norm (TWSP), which is taking advantages of both weighted nuclear norm and truncated schatten-p norm, has been firstly proposed toward better exploiting low-rank property in image CS recovery. At last, we further propose an efficient iterative scheme based on alternating direction method of multipliers to accurately solve the nonconvex optimization model.

The reminder is organized as follows. Section 2 simply reviews the weighted nuclear norm based image CS model and truncated schatten-p norm based image CS model. In Sect. 3, our proposed TWSP and an efficient iterative scheme for the optimization model are given in details. In Sect. 4, the effectiveness of our method is proved by several experiments. Finally, we summarize our proposed model in Sect. 5.

2   Related Work

In this section, we will review low-rank regularization based image CS recovery model. Suppose an image is defined as $x \in R^n$ and its sampling matrix is $\Phi \in R^{m \times n}(m \ll n)$, the purpose of CS is to reconstruct the image x from the measurement $y \in R^m$ ($y = \Phi x$) than suggested by traditional Nyquist sampling theorem.

Usually, natural images have a large number of repetitive structures and these blocks with repetitive structures are located in the global scope of the images. So the rank of each block matrix grouped by corresponding nonlocal similar blocks is low. The intrinsic low-rank property exploited by self-similarity and nonlocal operation, has widely used in face recognition, compressive sensing and image denoising. These methods based on low-rank property have shown competitive performances in each area.

Suppose $x_j \in R^d$ is a block, we query for h most similar blocks from all image blocks. $R_j x = [R_{j_1} x, R_{j_2} x, \cdots R_{j_h} x] \in R^{d \times h}$ (R_{j_k} is the corresponding extraction matrix) is the j-th block matrix formed by these similar blocks. Then the CS recovery problem is formulated as follows:

$$(x, L_j) = \arg\min_{x, L_j} \|y - \Phi x\|_F^2 + \lambda \sum_j rank\, (R_j x) \, . \tag{1}$$

where $\| \cdot \|_F^2$ is the square sum of all elements.

Weighted nuclear norm [22] assigned larger weights to larger singular values and smaller weights to smaller ones. So smaller singular values are penalized more than larger ones. So the weighted nuclear norm based image CS model is represented as follows:

$$x = \arg\min_x \|y - \Phi x\|_F^2 + \lambda \sum_j \sum_{i=1}^{min(d,h)} w_i \delta_i\, (R_j x) \, . \tag{2}$$

where $w_i = \rho\sqrt{h}/\left(\delta_i\left(A_j^s\right) + \varepsilon\right)$, ρ is a normal number and $\varepsilon = 10^{-16}$.

Since the largest r (the rank) singular values will not impact the rank, truncated schatten-p norm [24] abandoned them and only minimized the summation of surplus singular values to the power of p. Then the truncated schatten-p norm based image CS model is defined as

$$(x, A_j, B_j) = \arg\min_{x, A_j, B_j} \|y - \Phi x\|_F^2 + \lambda \sum_j \sum_{i=1}^{min(d,h)} \delta_i^p\, (R_j x) \cdot \left(1 - \delta_i\left(B_j^T A_j\right)\right) \, . \tag{3}$$

Assume $U \Delta V^T$ is the singular value decomposition of L_j, where $\Delta \in R^{d \times h}$, $U = (u_1, \ldots u_d) \in R^{d \times d}$ and $V = (v_1, \ldots v_h) \in R^{h \times h}$, then $A \in R^{r \times d}$ and $B \in R^{r \times h}$ are the corresponding transposition of former r columns from U and V respectively.

3   Truncated Weighted Schatten-p Norm for Image Compressive Sensing Recovery

In this paper, to obtain better results of low-rank regularization problem, truncated weighted schatten-p norm regularization, which is taking advantages of both weighted nuclear norm and truncated schatten-p norm, is presented toward better exploiting low-rank property. Specially, we only minimize the summation of few smallest singular values to the power of p multiplied by the certain weights. From the above analysis, our method can be modeled as

$$(x, A_j, B_j, w_i) = \arg\min_{x, A_j, B_j, w_i} \|y - \Phi x\|_F^2 + \lambda \sum_j \sum_{i=1}^{min(d,h)} w_i \delta_i^p\, (R_j x) \left(1 - \delta_i\left(B_j^T A_j\right)\right) \, . \tag{4}$$

Except for the compressive measurements, all the other information cannot be known. We introduce auxiliary variables and address the above problem by alternating direction method of multipliers, where the image x, the block group

$R_j x$ and the corresponding auxiliary variable L_j are computed in turn. Then Eq. (4) can be reformulated as

$$
\begin{aligned}
(x, A_j, B_j, w_i, L_j) = \underset{x, A_j, B_j, w_i, L_j}{\arg\min} \ \|y - \Phi x\|_F^2 + \\
\lambda \sum_j \left(\sum_{i=1}^{\min(d,h)} w_i \delta_i^p (L_j) \left(1 - \delta_i \left(B_j^T A_j \right) \right) + \beta \left\| R_j x - L_j \right\|_F^2 \right) .
\end{aligned}
\tag{5}
$$

Equation (5) contains the following four subproblems.

$$
\left(A_j^{t+1}, B_j^{t+1} \right) = \underset{A_j, B_j}{arg max} \sum_{i=1}^{\min(d,h)} w_i^t \delta_i^p (L_j) \delta_i \left(B_j^T A_j \right) .
\tag{6}
$$

$$
w_i^{t+1} = \underset{w_i}{\arg\min} \sum_{i=1}^{\min(d,h)} w_i \delta_i^p (L_j) \left(1 - \delta_i \left(\left(B_j^{t+1} \right)^T A_j^{t+1} \right) \right) .
\tag{7}
$$

$$
L_j^{t+1} = \underset{L_j}{\arg\min} \sum_{i=1}^{\min(d,h)} w_i^{t+1} \delta_i^p (L_j) \left(1 - \delta_i \left(\left(B_j^{t+1} \right)^T A_j^{t+1} \right) \right) + \beta \left\| R_j x^t - L_j \right\|_F^2 .
\tag{8}
$$

$$
x^{t+1} = \underset{x}{\arg\min} \|y - \Phi x\|_F^2 + \lambda \beta \sum_j \left\{ \left\| R_j x - L_j^{t+1} \right\|_F^2 \right\} .
\tag{9}
$$

3.1 $\{A_j, B_j\}$ Subproblem

According to the definition of truncated schatten-p norm [24], when A^{t+1} and B^{t+1} are calculated based on singular value decomposition of L_j^t, Eq. (6) gets the maximal value. Given intermediate estimated value L_j^t, we first calculate the singular value decomposition of L_j^t ($[U_j^t, \Delta_j^t, V_j^t] = svd(L_j^t)$), and then estimate A^{t+1} and B^{t+1} by the following formula.

$$
A^{t+1} = \left(u_{j_1}^t, \dots u_{j_r}^t \right)^T, \quad B^{t+1} = \left(v_{j_1}^t, \dots v_{j_r}^t \right)^T .
\tag{10}
$$

3.2 w_j Subproblem

Since the larger singular values are corresponding to the energy of the major components, they are more important than the smaller ones. According to the definition of weighted nuclear norm [22], we set

$$
w_i^{t+1} = \rho \sqrt{h} / \left(\delta_i \left(L_j^t \right) + \varepsilon \right) .
\tag{11}
$$

3.3 L_j subproblem

Although L_j subproblem is nonconvex, we can obtain a suboptimal solution through a local minimization method referred to [4,16,24]. $g(\delta) = w_i^{t+1}\delta_i^p (L_j) \left(1 - \delta_i \left(\left(B_j^{t+1}\right)^T A_j^{t+1}\right)\right)$ can be approximated using first-order Taylor expansion.

$$g(\delta) = g(\delta^k) + \left\langle \nabla g\left(\delta^k\right), \delta - \delta^k \right\rangle. \tag{12}$$

Suppose $\delta^{t+1,k} = \delta\left(L_j^{t+1,k}\right)$ is the k-th iteration solution. Therefore, neglecting the constant term, Eq. (12) can be solved with by iteratively computing

$$L_j^{t+1,k+1} =$$
$$\arg\min_{L_j} \sum_{i=1}^{\min(d,h)} w_i^{t+1} p(\delta_i^k)^{p-1} \left(1 - \delta_i \left(\left(B_j^{t+1}\right)^T A_j^{t+1}\right)\right)\delta_i + \beta \left\| R_j x^t - L_j \right\|_F^2.$$
$$\tag{13}$$

Equation (13) denotes the weighted nuclear norm and has an analytical solution [4,16,24].

3.4 x Subproblem

Equation (9) is a quadratic problem and has a closed-form solution.

$$x^{s+1} = \left(\Phi^T\Phi + \lambda\beta\sum_j R_j^T R_j\right)^{-1} \left(\Phi^T y + \lambda\beta\sum_j R_j^T L_j^{t+1}\right). \tag{14}$$

When an estimated image x is obtained, the variables w_j, A_j, B_j and L_j can be updated. Then L_j is used to obtain a better estimated image. This process continues to iterate until convergence. The algorithm is summarized as bellows.

Algorithm 1. Image Recovery via Truncated Weighted Schatten-p Norm Regularization

---

Input: an initial image x^0 (DCT based CS method), λ, β, $p = 0.6$, $r = 4$;
    while stopping criteria unsatisfied *do*
        (a) constructing group matrix $R_j x^t$: grouping several similar blocks for x_j^t;
        (b) solving $\{A_j, B_j\}$ subproblem via Eq. (10);
        (c) solving w_j subproblem via Eq. (11);
        (d) solving L_j subproblem via Eq. (13);
        (e) solving x_j subproblem via Eq. (14);
    end while
Output: final reconstructed image $\hat{x}$.

---

4   Experimental Results

In order to prove the effectiveness of our model, TWSP is compared with total variation based method (TV) [25], low-rank regularization based method (NLR) [16], weighted nuclear norm based method (WNN) [22] and truncated schatten-p norm based method (TSPN) [24]. Note that TV exploits the gradient sparsity; NLR, WNN and TSPN all employ nonconvex substitution function to exploit nonlocal low-rank property; TSPN shows the current state-of-the-art performance.

The parameters are set as follows: random sampling rate is $\frac{100m}{n}$%; the size of block is 6×6 and the number of similar blocks is 45; we divide the image into overlapping blocks into reference blocks for every five pixels; the regularization parameter p is 0.6, r is 4, λ and β are tuned separately for each sampling rate. Eight test natural images are used which are shown in Fig. 1. The Peak Signal-to-Noise Ratio (PSNR) is employed to evaluate the different recovery results.

4.1   Experiments on Noiseless Measurements

The PSNR comparison when the sampling rates are 2.5%, 5%, 10%, 15% and 20% is provided in Table 1. From Table 1, we can see that (1) WNN, TSPN and TWSP outperform NLR for almost all the situations; (2) on average, WNN and TSPN get similar recovery results; (3) TWSP obtains the highest PSNRs in all the cases; (4) The average PSNR gains of TWSP over TV, NLR, WNN and TSPN are 3.66 dB, 1.57 dB, 0.39 dB and 0.36 dB respectively with 2.5% sampling rate. The visual results of three images are provided as Figs. 2, 3, and 4. We can see that TWSP can better exploit the nonlocal low-rank property and shows better performance than NLR, WNN and TSPN.

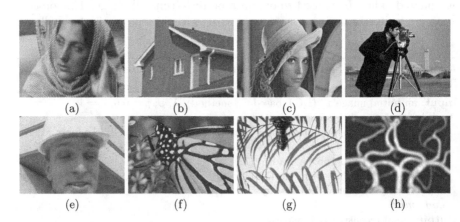

(a)	(b)	(c)	(d)
(e)	(f)	(g)	(h)

Fig. 1. Eight test images. (a) Barbara; (b) House; (c) Lena; (d) Cameraman; (e) Foreman; (f) Monarch; (g) Leaves; (h) Vessels.

Table 1. The PSNR (dB) results on noiseless measurements

Image	Method	Sampling Rate				
		2.5%	5.0%	10%	15%	20%
Barbara	TV	21.56	22.79	24.78	26.72	28.87
	NLR	24.25	29.79	35.47	38.17	40.00
	WNN	25.02	30.54	35.67	38.26	40.13
	TSPN	24.98	30.63	35.64	38.17	40.06
	TWSP	25.21	30.81	35.85	38.40	40.38
House	TV	29.31	30.50	33.63	35.54	37.20
	NLR	32.43	34.80	38.39	40.62	42.49
	WNN	33.20	35.13	38.72	40.77	42.63
	TSPN	33.04	35.08	38.73	40.84	42.62
	TWSP	33.37	35.22	38.81	40.95	42.78
Lena	TV	25.02	26.48	29.63	32.32	34.74
	NLR	26.84	30.69	35.75	38.95	41.38
	WNN	27.55	31.15	35.95	39.09	41.47
	TSPN	27.52	31.26	36.08	39.17	41.44
	TWSP	27.76	31.48	36.31	39.40	41.69
Cameraman	TV	22.16	25.09	28.63	31.48	34.20
	NLR	24.72	28.36	32.30	36.10	39.16
	WNN	25.66	28.67	32.38	36.18	39.29
	TSPN	25.61	28.68	32.67	36.21	39.33
	TWSP	25.91	28.95	32.94	36.50	39.72
Foreman	TV	30.21	32.50	36.02	38.34	40.49
	NLR	33.34	35.70	39.39	41.98	44.02
	WNN	34.63	36.82	39.85	42.34	44.38
	TSPN	34.56	36.87	40.07	42.52	44.49
	TWSP	34.80	37.15	40.29	42.86	44.81
Monarch	TV	20.93	24.21	28.78	31.93	34.84
	NLR	23.76	28.85	34.30	37.78	40.31
	WNN	24.91	29.19	34.44	37.95	40.42
	TSPN	24.74	29.23	34.46	37.86	40.16
	TWSP	25.32	29.36	34.68	38.32	40.82
Leaves	TV	18.23	21.53	25.89	30.03	32.35
	NLR	18.24	27.14	33.80	38.26	41.51
	WNN	20.87	27.66	34.14	38.60	41.96
	TSPN	21.27	27.33	33.87	38.34	41.49
	TWSP	21.56	27.92	34.12	38.86	42.31
Vessels	TV	17.20	20.18	25.03	29.04	32.19
	NLR	17.80	26.09	32.82	37.97	40.95
	WNN	18.96	26.74	33.41	38.11	41.19
	TSPN	19.30	26.56	33.01	38.00	41.48
	TWSP	20.02	27.31	33.94	38.56	42.05
Average	TV	23.08	25.41	29.05	31.93	34.36
	NLR	25.17	30.18	35.28	38.73	41.23
	WNN	26.35	30.74	35.57	38.91	41.43
	TSPN	26.38	30.71	35.57	38.89	41.38
	TWSP	**26.74**	**31.03**	**35.87**	**39.23**	**41.82**

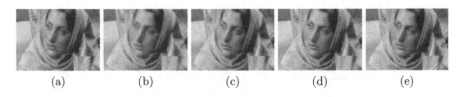

Fig. 2. Recovered Barbara with 5% sampling rate. (a) Original image; (b) NLR recovery (29.79 dB); (c) WNN recovery (30.54 dB); (d) TSPN recovery (30.63 dB); (e) TWSP recovery (30.81 dB).

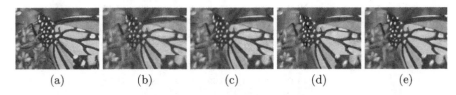

Fig. 3. Recovered Monarch with 2.5% sampling rate. (a) Original image; (b) NLR recovery (23.76 dB); (c) WNN recovery (24.91 dB); (d) TSPN recovery (24.74 dB); (e) TWSP recovery (25.32 dB).

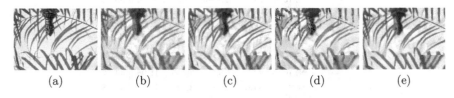

Fig. 4. Recovered Leaves with 2.5% sampling rate. (a) Original image; (b) NLR recovery (18.24 dB); (c) WNN recovery (20.87 dB); (d) TSPN recovery (21.27 dB); (e) TWSP recovery (21.56 dB).

4.2   Experiments on Noisy Measurements

In this subsection, experiments with noisy measurements are carried out to verify the robustness of TWSP approach to Gaussian White noise. The sampling rate is 20%. The signal-to-noise ratio ($SNR = 20 * \log \frac{\bar{A}}{\bar{D}}$), where $\bar{A}$ is the average value and $\bar{D}$ is the standard derivation of noise, varies from 15dB to 35 dB. The PSNR comparisons when SNR is 15 dB, 20 dB, 25 dB, 30 dB and 35 dB are provided in Table 2. TWSP achieves the highest PSNR results among all the methods. The average PSNR gains of TWSP over TV, NLR, WNN and TSPN can be as much as 5.07 dB, 2.80 dB, 1.80 dB and 1.82 dB respectively when SNR=15dB. Some visual results are shown in Figs. 5, 6 and 7, which verify the superiority of our proposed TWSP approach.

Table 2. The PSNR (dB) results of different methods on noisy measurements

Image	Method	SNR				
		15dB	20dB	25dB	30dB	35dB
Barbara	TV	20.91	24.56	28.13	32.79	34.31
	NLR	22.90	26.91	30.42	35.66	37.56
	WNN	23.86	28.43	31.86	36.85	38.26
	TSPN	23.80	28.35	32.00	36.41	37.82
	TWSP	25.64	30.24	33.93	37.80	38.65
House	TV	20.31	24.71	28.87	33.45	36.75
	NLR	23.24	27.98	32.47	35.95	39.64
	WNN	23.61	28.47	33.01	36.71	39.89
	TSPN	23.67	28.53	32.96	36.48	39.77
	TWSP	25.58	30.50	35.11	38.56	41.14
Lena	TV	21.31	24.56	29.30	33.03	34.62
	NLR	23.35	27.59	32.08	36.30	38.43
	WNN	23.93	28.43	33.17	37.21	38.88
	TSPN	23.87	28.34	32.95	36.84	38.63
	TWSP	25.87	30.54	35.44	38.94	40.08
Cameraman	TV	20.14	23.46	27.19	30.49	32.34
	NLR	23.21	26.74	29.85	33.89	35.77
	WNN	23.92	28.32	32.18	35.58	37.04
	TSPN	23.91	28.30	31.90	35.27	36.79
	TWSP	25.88	30.46	34.31	37.22	38.11
Foreman	TV	18.07	22.49	27.59	32.12	35.81
	NLR	22.24	26.02	29.99	35.47	40.52
	WNN	22.81	27.65	32.43	37.16	41.72
	TSPN	22.78	27.58	32.37	36.96	41.37
	TWSP	24.66	29.54	34.50	39.27	42.43
Monarch	TV	21.42	25.01	28.17	31.15	32.01
	NLR	23.33	27.15	30.95	35.42	37.58
	WNN	24.40	28.65	32.79	36.59	38.16
	TSPN	24.33	28.55	32.28	36.00	37.81
	TWSP	26.24	30.69	34.83	38.01	39.00
Leaves	TV	17.89	21.86	24.83	27.55	30.42
	NLR	19.01	22.63	26.26	31.58	35.80
	WNN	20.38	24.70	29.06	33.85	36.73
	TSPN	20.49	24.83	28.92	33.43	36.32
	TWSP	21.85	26.16	30.68	35.69	38.29
Vessels	TV	22.86	27.03	29.44	31.27	32.30
	NLR	23.78	27.99	33.12	37.85	39.93
	WNN	26.14	30.50	35.06	38.28	40.46
	TSPN	26.03	30.40	34.65	38.09	40.24
	TWSP	27.73	32.83	37.40	39.83	40.79
Average	TV	20.36	24.21	27.94	31.48	33.57
	NLR	22.63	26.63	30.64	35.27	38.15
	WNN	23.63	28.14	32.45	36.53	38.89
	TSPN	23.61	28.11	32.25	36.19	38.59
	TWSP	**25.43**	**30.12**	**34.53**	**38.17**	**39.81**

Fig. 5. Recovered Cameraman with SNR = 35 dB. (a) Original image; (b) NLR recovery (35.77 dB); (c) WNN recovery (37.04 dB); (d) TSPN recovery (36.99 dB); (e) TWSP recovery (38.11 dB).

Fig. 6. Recovered Foreman with SNR = 30 dB. (a) Original image; (b) NLR recovery (35.47 dB); (c) WNN recovery (37.16 dB); (d) TSPN recovery (36.96 dB); (e) TWSP recovery (39.27 dB).

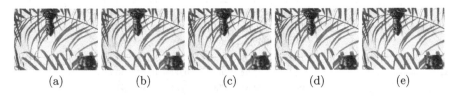

Fig. 7. Recovered of Leaves with SNR = 35 dB. (a) Original image; (b) NLR recovery (35.80 dB); (c) WNN recovery (36.73 dB); (d) TSPN recovery (36.32 dB); (e) TWSP recovery (38.29 dB).

5   Conclusion

In this paper, we have presented a new approach toward image recovery via truncated weighted schatten-p norm which is taking advantages of both weighted nuclear norm and truncated schatten-p norm. Truncated weighted schatten-p norm can better exploit the nonlocal low-rank property than current CS methods based on low-rank regularization. In addition, we also propose an efficient iterative scheme based on alternating direction method of multipliers to accurately solve the nonconvex optimization model. Experimental results demonstrate that our proposed algorithm is exceeding the existing state-of-the-art methods, in terms of subjective and objective qualities.

Acknowledgments. The authors would like to express their gratitude to the anonymous referees as well as the Editor and Associate Editor for their valuable comments which lead to substantial improvements of the paper. This work was supported by

High-level Talent Scientific Research Foundation of Jinling Institute of Technology (No. jit-b-201801), National Natural Science Foundation of China (No. 61772272), Doctor Initial Captional of Jinling Institute of Technology Nanjing (No. jit-b-201508), Jiangsu Key Laboratory of Image and Video Understanding for Social Safety (Nanjing University of Science and Technology) (No. 30916014107).

References

1. Donoho, D.L.: Compressed sensing. IEEE Trans. Inf. Theory **52**, 1289–1306 (2006)
2. Cand, E.J., Wakin, M.B.: "people hearing without listening:" an introduction to compressive sampling. IEEE Signal Process. Mag. **25**, 21–30 (2008)
3. Feng, L., Sun, H.: Blind compressive sensing method via local sparsity and nonlocal similarity. J. Nanjing Univ. Sci. Technol. **41**, 399–404 (2017)
4. Feng, L., Sun, H., Sun, Q., Xia, G.: Compressive sensing via nonlocal low-rank tensor regularization. Neurocomputing **216**, 45–60 (2016)
5. Zou, X., Feng, L., Sun, H.: Robust compressive sensing of multichannel eeg signals in the presence of impulsive noise. Inf. Sci. **429**, 120–129 (2018)
6. Zhang, J., Zhao, D., Zhao, C., Xiong, R., Ma, S., Gao, W.: Compressed sensing recovery via collaborative sparsity. In: Data Compression Conference, pp. 287–296 (2012)
7. Yao, X., Han, J., Zhang, D., Nie, F.: Adaptively determining regularization parameters in non-local total variation regularization for image denoising. Electron. Lett. **51**, 144–145 (2015)
8. Bioucas-Dias, J.M., Figueiredo, M.A.T.: A new twist: Two-step iterative shrinkage/thresholding algorithms for image restoration. IEEE Trans. Image Process. **16**, 2992 (2007)
9. Becker, S., Bobin, J., Cands, E.J.: Nesta: A fast and accurate first-ordermethod for sparse recovery. SIAM J. Imaging Sci. **4**, 1–39 (2009)
10. Javaherian, A., Soleimani, M., Moeller, K., Movafeghi, A., Faghihi, R.: An accelerated version of alternating direction method of multipliers for tv minimization in eit. Appl. Math. Model. **40**, 8985–9000 (2016)
11. Bertalmio, M., Caselles, V., Roug, B., Sol, A.: Tv based image restoration with local constraints. J. Sci. Comput. **19**, 95–122 (2003)
12. Wang, Y.C.F., Wei, C.P., Chen, C.F.: Low-rank matrix recovery with structural incoherence for robust face recognition. In: Computer Vision and Pattern Recognition, pp. 2618–2625 (2012)
13. Wei, C.P., Chen, C.F., Wang, Y.C.F.: Robust face recognition with structurally incoherent low-rank matrix decomposition. IEEE Trans. Image Process. **23**, 3294–3307 (2014)
14. Nguyen, H., Yang, W., Shen, F., Sun, C.: Kernel low-rank representation for face recognition. Neurocomputing **155**, 32–42 (2015)
15. Han, J., Quan, R., Zhang, D., Nie, F.: Robust Object Co-Segmentation Using Background Prior. IEEE Trans. Image Process. **27**, 1639–1651 (2018)
16. Dong, W., Shi, G., Li, X., Ma, Y.: Compressive sensing via nonlocal low-rank regularization. IEEE Trans. Image Process. **23**, 3618–3632 (2014)
17. Wang, H., Zhao, R., Cen, Y.: Rank adaptive atomic decomposition for low-rank matrix completion and its application on image recovery. Neurocomputing **145**, 374–380 (2014)

18. Cabral, R., Torre, F.D.L., Costeira, J.P., Bernardino, A.: Unifying nuclear norm and bilinear factorization approaches for low-rank matrix decomposition. In: IEEE International Conference on Computer Vision, pp. 2488–2495 (2014)

19. Toh, K.C., Yun, S.: An accelerated proximal gradient algorithm for nuclear norm regularized least squares problems. Pac. J. Optim. **6**, 615–640 (2009)

20. Wang, J., Wang, M., Hu, X., Yan, S.: Visual data denoising with a unified schatten-p norm and lq norm regularized principal component pursuit. Pattern Recognit. **48**, 3135–3144 (2015)

21. Cai, J.F., Candes, E.J., Shen, Z.: A singular value thresholding algorithm for matrix completion. SIAM J. Optim. **20**, 1956–1982 (2008)

22. Gu, S., Zhang, L., Zuo, W., Feng, X.: Weighted nuclear norm minimization with application to image denoising. In: IEEE Conference on Computer Vision and Pattern Recognition, pp. 2862–2869 (2014)

23. Xie, Y., Gu, S., Liu, Y., Zuo, W., Zhang, W., Zhang, L.: Weighted schatten p-norm minimization for image denoising and background subtraction. IEEE Trans. Image Process. **25**, 4842–4857 (2015)

24. Feng, L., Sun, H., Sun, Q., Xia, G.: Image compressive sensing via truncated schatten-p norm regularization. Signal Process. Image Commun. **47**, 28–41 (2016)

25. Zhang, J., Liu, S., Xiong, R., Ma, S., Zhao, D.: Improved total variation based image compressive sensing recovery by nonlocal regularization. In: IEEE International Symposium on Circuits and Systems, pp. 2836–2839 (2013)

Improving Semantic Annotation Using Semantic Modeling of Knowledge Embedding

Yuhua Fan[(✉)][iD], Liya Fan, and Jing Yang

School of Mathematical Sciences, Liaocheng University, Liaocheng, China
angelfyh@gmail.com

Abstract. Semantic annotation has attracted a growing interest in the information retrieval and computer vision. Existing methods have typically focused on several visual cues and semantic context information with an image itself using different frameworks, neglecting the prior knowledge constraints about the real world. However, strong prior knowledge embedding should be considered to improve the performance of semantic annotation tasks. Note that semantic objects will interact each other during the semantic prediction stage, and the support visual relationships can affect the recall and accuracy of semantic annotations. In this paper, we exploit a novel method to semantic modeling with prior knowledge embedding to jointly find the semantic objects and the corresponding support relationships in the images. Inference in the model can be conducted exactly via graph modeling and knowledge embedding, and the parameters can be learned at the supervised learning stage. The extensive experiments on COCO15 and Stanford Visual Relationship data sets confirm the benefits of semantic annotation for the objects for the knowledge embedding.

Keywords: Image annotation · Knowledge embedding · Optimization

1 Introduction

Semantic annotation is playing very important role in computer vision and information retrieval. It aims at providing detailed semantic information about the unseen images, such as the semantic type, the corresponding visual relationships and so on. In essence, the ability to assign semantic labels to objects and their relationships is very important [1–3]. Algorithms like neural networks are often used to construct graphs for scene representations and semantic annotations [4,5]. By using RNs method, semantic objects set can be identical and shared computations across the groups. Exploiting contextual relationships

Supported by Research Start-up Fundation for the Doctoral Program of Liaocheng University (318051654) and Shandong Province Higher Education Science and Technology Program (J18KA390) and Natural Science Foundation of Shandong Province (ZR2016AM24, ZR2018BF010).

© Springer Nature Switzerland AG 2018
X. Sun et al. (Eds.): ICCCS 2018, LNCS 11068, pp. 575–585, 2018.
https://doi.org/10.1007/978-3-030-00021-9_51

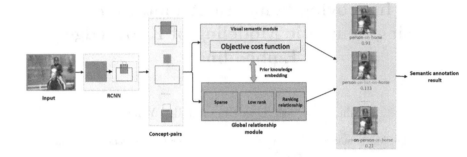

Fig. 1. Operation flowchart, showing the pipeline of the proposed method.

among objects in scenes has also been explored in various applications of computer science and classification tasks.

In graphs, a number of approaches have been to capture scene structure, such as energy models [6], graphical and mixture models [7], probabilistic programs [8]. Graphs also have been increasingly utilized in the characterization of complex networks from diverse origins, including different kinds of semantic networks and semantic embedding [9–11]. Here we use the knowledge graph to leverage an inverted index along with a complementary uninverted index to represent nodes and edges to improve the performance of semantic prediction. This can provide indirection between each pair of nodes and their relative corresponding relationships.

Our method is also related to some existing approaches that apply NN to graphs [12–14]. Critically, we aim to construct the objective function, where several prior knowledge are incorporated to learn the relationships better. Then we optimize the model to solve and obtain the reliable parameters. Finally, we conduct the proposed approach on public data set, demonstrating the ability of the suggested models to rapidly discover semantics and relationships for semantic annotations. The overall framework is summarized in Fig. 1.

2   Problem Formulation

Based on the regions with CNN features framework [15], we can obtain the objects in images. Suppose $O = \{o_i^1, o_i^2, \cdots, o_i^n\}$ to be the set of n-dimensional features encoding the corresponding properties, each belonging to one of L semantic classes. And let X be the k-dimensional space representation and $D \in R^{n \times k}$ be the dictionary. Then the standard dictionary learning strategy can be defined as follows:

$$< D, O > = argmin_{D,O} ||O - DX||_2^2 + \lambda_1 ||O||_1, \tag{1}$$

with the regularization parameter λ_1. To take the attributes into account, the objective function can be extended with an additional term $L(X)$ as:

$$< D, O > = argmin_{D,O} ||O - DX||_2^2 + \lambda_1 ||O||_1 + \lambda_2 L(X). \tag{2}$$

2.1 Knowledge Constrained

To learn the visual relationships among entities from different semantic classes, we can map the original feature cues into the visual relationship space. Define the matrix $Q \in R^{n \times m}$ with the elements that containing the structured visual relationships of all objects in O. Let W be an $L \times L$ matrix, then $S_{l,l'}$ can represent the degree of semantic consistency between concepts l and l'. According to the natural characteristic, W will be symmetric. When $l = l'$, $W_{l,l'}$ can capture the self-consistency, which is a meaningful measure since multiple instances of the same object can appear in the same image.

In order to find the transformation of O and Q, similar function [16] can be used to learn the weighting matrix $W = [W_1^T, W_2^T, \cdots, W_M^T]$. Let A represent the transformation from X to Q, we can define the following function as:

$$argmin_A ||Q - AX||_2^2 = argmin_A ||WO - AX||_2^2. \qquad (3)$$

Then our goal is to find the matrix W, which map the relative sparse semantic relationship space to the corresponding object space Q with a minimum distance measurement. The loss term can be defined as follows:

$$< D, O >= argmin_{D,O,A} ||O - DX||_2^2 + \lambda_1 ||X||_1 + \lambda_2 ||WO - AX||_2^2. \qquad (4)$$

From the first term, we can see that $O \approx DX$. Note that A can be learned at the learning stage. So we aim to conduct a new matrix $\tilde{W}$ by integrating knowledge into the matrix W. For the semantic annotation, we wish predict the label for o as $\hat{l} = argmax_l \tilde{W}_{o,l}$ efficiently. After the attribute dictionary is learned, the goal is to obtain a sparse and effective visual relationship representation for the input data. Then we can transfer the problem as an sparse coding issue that can be described and solved as [17]. The illustration of the transformation from different spaces is showing in Fig. 2.

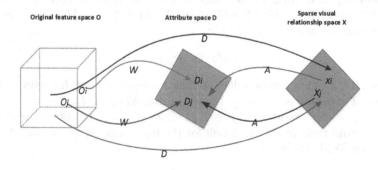

Fig. 2. Illustration of information transformation from different spaces.

2.2 Knowledge Integration

Our goal is to produce a matrix $\tilde{W}$ by integrating knowledge into the initial matrix W. Then $\tilde{W}$ will be rich and knowledge-aware enhancement of W.

Cost Function. The key intuition is that two objects with better semantic consistency are more likely to appear in the same class image with comparable probability. That is, for two objects owning a higher semantic occurring probability, one can support the semantic annotation for the other one. Let P_{o_i,l_i} represent the probability of object o_i with its semantic label l. $\tilde{W}_{i,l''}$ represents the prediction based on the knowledge that enrich on the matrix $\tilde{W}$. The cost function can be given as follows:

$$
\begin{aligned}
E(\tilde{P}, P) &= (1-\epsilon) \sum_{i=1}^{m} \sum_{i' \neq 1}^{m} \sum_{l=1}^{L} \sum_{l' \neq 1}^{L} W_{i,l''} \left(\tilde{P}_{i,l} - \tilde{P}_{i',l} \right)^2 \\
&+ \epsilon \sum_{i=1}^{m} \sum_{l=1}^{L} D(\left\| W_{i,l''} \right\|_1 + \left\| W_{i,l''} \right\|_*) \left(\tilde{P}_{i,l} - P_{i,l} \right)^2
\end{aligned}
\tag{5}
$$

where $\epsilon \in (0,1)$. The above equation shows the constraints on the semantic consistency and the attribution: the first term gives semantic consistency constraint through the minimizing the objective function and the second term gives the knowledge-aware characters of the approach. When $W_{l,*}$ is large, the $P_{b,l}$ and $P_{b',l'}$ will become smaller. Otherwise, $P_{b,l}$ and $P_{b',l'}$ will be different to say the semantic consistency for two concepts. Note that the $\|W_{i,*}\|_1$ balances the difference between two objects and $\|W_{i,*}\|_*$ gives the semantic sparse constraints on the whole semantic space. The overall trade-off between the terms is controlled by the parameter ϵ, which can be chosen a given valid set.

Relationship Ranking. For semantic objects, the relationship ranking can be learned through the ranking functions w_M for $m = \{1, \ldots, M\}$. The predicted relative concepts can be computed by:

$$
r_m(x_i) = w_m^T x_i.
\tag{6}
$$

When (O_i, O_j) is a pair of ordered semantic pairs with label l_i having a strong presence of attribute a_m than l_j, then we define $\forall (i,j) \in T_m : w_m^T x_i > w_m^T x_j$. Otherwise, we can consider $\forall (i,j) \in T_m : w_m^T x_i \doteq w_m^T x_j$. To obtain the ranking vector w_m and their relative ordering for the input images, we use the strategy just like an SVM classifier:

$$
\begin{aligned}
&min(\frac{1}{2}\|w_m^T\| + c(\sum \xi_{ij} + \sum \gamma_{ij})) \\
&s.t. \begin{cases} w_m^T(o_i - o_j) \geq 1 - \xi_{ij}, \forall (i,j) \in Q_m \cdot \\ |w_m^T(o_i - o_j)| \leq \gamma_{ij}, otherwise \end{cases}
\end{aligned}
\tag{7}
$$

2.3   Optimization

To minimize the Eq. (7), we find its stationary point where its gradient w.r.t $\tilde{P}_{b,l}$ is zero, then we can transfer the problem as follows:

$$\frac{\partial E(\tilde{P}, P)}{\partial \tilde{P}_{b,l}} = 4(1 - \epsilon) \sum_{i'=1}^{m} \sum_{l'=1}^{L} W_{i,l'} \left(\tilde{P}_{i,l} - \tilde{P}_{i',l'} \right)$$
$$+ 4\epsilon D \left(\|W_{i,*}\|_1 + \|W_{i,*}\|_* \right) \left(\tilde{P}_{i,l} - P_{i,l} \right) \tag{8}$$

Setting the above to zero, we will obtain an equivalent configuration over optimal $\tilde{P}_{b,l}$ as follows:

$$\tilde{P}_{b,l} = (1 - \epsilon) \frac{\sum_{b'=1}^{m} \sum_{l'=1}^{L} W_{i,l'} \tilde{P}_{b',l'}}{\sum_{b'=1}^{m} \sum_{l'=1}^{L} W_{i,l'}} + \epsilon P_{b,l}. \tag{9}$$

It can be shown that the exact solution for the above equation is the limit of the series in the following equation for $i = \{1, 2, \cdots\}$. In particular, for any arbitrary initialization $\tilde{P}_{b,l}^0$ and $\tilde{P}_{b,l}^i$ always converges to the same solution when $\rightarrow \infty$. Then we can obtain as:

$$\tilde{P}_{b,l}^i = (1 - \epsilon) \frac{\sum_{b'=1}^{m} \sum_{l'=1}^{L} W_{i,l'} \tilde{P}_{b',l'}^{i-1}}{\sum_{b'=1}^{m} \sum_{l'=1}^{L} W_{i,l'}} + \epsilon P_{b,l}. \tag{10}$$

Note that the solution can be computed in polynomial time. The computation complex is $O(D^2 L^2) I$, where I is the number of iterations of the algorithm. Because the characters of the semantic space, a near-perfect approximate solution can be obtained over a subset of labels.

3   Experiment

3.1   Datasets

We evaluate the proposed model on COCO15 dataset [18] and Stanford Visual Relationship dataset [19]. For COCO15, we combine the training and validation sets for training the baseline method, except for a subset of 5000 images named minival. We further split minival into two subsets with 1000 and 4000 images, named minival-1k and minival-4k respectively. We also use minival-1k to choose hyperparameters and minival-4k for offline evaluation. Online evaluation is performed on test-dev and test-std sets. On Stanford Visual Relationship dataset, we use the same learning rate and iterations set as the [20].

We employ the state-of-the-art [4,19,22] as the baseline. Models on two datasets are trained using the corresponding parameters set as original references.

3.2   Evaluation Metrics

To evaluate performance of the suggested method, we use the maximum weighted coverage scheme as [21], defined over the ground-truth $\mathcal{S}$ and its predicted semantic label $\mathcal{S}'$ as follows:

$$Coverage_w(\mathcal{S}, \mathcal{S}') = \frac{1}{|\mathfrak{I}|} \sum_{j=1}^{\mathcal{S}} |r_j^S| max_{1,\dots,|\mathcal{S}'|} IoU(r_j^S, r_i^{S'}), \qquad (11)$$

where $|\mathfrak{I}|$ is the total number of pixels in the set of ground-truth object region, and r_j^S is the number of pixels in ground-truth object region j.

The semantic annotation accuracy on the testing data set can be computed over all the per-class accuracy and compute the average over all the classes. For the support visual relationship accuracy, we can use the precision and recall of the positive support types on pairs of semantic objects. Note that the hidden object regions will not be considered if they are not detected available during the detection stage.

3.3   Training

At the training stage, we mainly compute the parameters using stochastic descent strategy. And a learning rate of 1e-3 and 1e-4 for the first and the second iterations respectively as the [18]. We use a learning rate of 1e-4 for the first 4000K iterations, followed by 1e-5 for another 160K iterations for Stanford Visual Relationship dataset.

To obtain the better semantic annotation results, we re-optimize the semantics label by RCNN to retain them of high confidence, requiring the scores of at least 1e-6. Select the parameter ϵ on the validation set for $\epsilon \in \{0.3, 0.55, 0.85\}$, then we run the learned model for 30 iterations to ensure the convergence completely. To construct the semantic consistency, a small of set (less than 10%) will be considered as the noise to guarantee the corrections when on training set. For the random walk restarting probability, we set the same parameters as the comparison methods. And the main metrics computed are mean average precision (MAP) and recall at top 100.

3.4   Results

Semantic Object Annotation. For semantic annotation tasks, we consider the different types of settings with eliminating the errors for the semantic labels predictions. We report the experimental results on COCO15 in Table 1. We can see that the approaches are significantly increase recall @100 over the baseline method, respectively. Note that the proposed method is consistently better than other three methods on COCO15 at different situations. We can find that the prior knowledge integrated in the presented model can mitigate the semantic ambiguity among different objects. Especially under the condition of region overlapping in images and the very small region object occurring. The support isual relationship will supply the correct information to mitigate the semantic onfuse during the semantic annotation and improve the performance of recall percentage.

Table 1. Comparison of semantic object annotation among our method with other methods on COCO15.

Task	MAP	Recall		Recall@100 by area		
Evaluation	@100	@10	@100	Small	Medium	Large
Minival-4K						
[22]	24.1	35.6	41.6	17.4	47.6	63.3
[4]	25.2	36.7	42.1	18.8	48.2	64.6
[19]	24.5	37.5	42.8	18.9	50.0	64.3
Our method	26.1	38.4	44.1	19.8	52.0	66.2
Test-dev						
[22]	23.3	36.0	38.4	14.0	43.1	60.2
[4]	24.6	37.1	39.4	15.2	44.3	61.7
[19]	24.3	36.2	38.6	14.1	43.3	60.1
Our method	25.1	37.6	40.2	16.1	45.4	62.2
Test-std						
[22]	24.3	36.1	38.1	14.0	43.8	59.8
[4]	24.7	36.8	39.3	14.7	44.0	60.5
[19]	24.1	36.2	38.6	13.9	43.3	59.9
Our method	25.4	37.4	39.6	15.3	44.7	62.7

Inferring Relations from Models. For inferring visual relations from the models, we use the same settings as [4, 22]. Similar to [22], we also conduct the experiments for visual relationship detection, triple detection and predicate detection. At the training stage, we hold out 5% of the nonzero triples as a validation set. And we determine the optimal prediction methods based on the hold-out set.

We report Recall at 50 and 100 for four different validation settings in the experiments in Table 2. The first row shows the regularization terms are added to the visual model when training, which are described in more detail in [19]. For the proposed method, we can see that the recall at top 100 is better than at top 50, however the difference is much small than other three models. This shows that much more correctly triples are detected and ranked to obtain much better experimental results. For the relationship detection, which is the most challenging setting, our method also works best for the top 100 and top 50 results respectively. Since we take no account the overlapping, the scores are higher for several methods for triple detection.

Table 2. Comparison among different methods for detection of visual relationship detection.

Task	Phrase Dec.		Rel. Det.		Predicate Det.		Triple Det.	
Evaluation	R@100	R@50	R@100	R@50	R@100	R@50	R@100	R@50
[22]	17.03	16.17	14.70	13.86	47.87	47.84	18.11	17.11
[4]	16.14	16.51	16.22	14.23	51.71	51.69	20.03	19.55
[19]	18.72	17.33	17.01	15.03	53.02	53.01	21.06	19.03
Our method	20.21	18.9	18.04	16.25	54.8	53.6	22.1	20.1

Zero-Shot Learning. We evaluate the models to reveal the ability of generalization for the semantic model on COCO15 for zero-shot learning tasks. Note that here we only evaluate on triples, which had not been occurred in the training data. The test set contains 1877 of triples. For the recall, we count how many of the unseen triples are detected successfully using the models.

The test triples consisted of objects with images from 5 randomly selected and they do not occur from previous unseen classes. Table 3 shows the results for the zero-shot learning using different methods. For the first three settings, the best performing method, which is almost retrieves twice as many correct triples as the [19]. Especially, for the predicate detection, which assumes the objects to be given, a relatively high recall percent can be reached as can be seen in Table 3. In the zero-shot setting for the predicate detection, our method shows significantly better performance than other three state-of-the-art methods. These results clearly show that the suggested model is able to infer also new likely triples, which have not been observed in the training data. And this will be big benefits for the semantic annotations.

Table 3. The results for the zero-shot learning tasks on COCO15.

Task	Phrase Dec.		Rel. Det.		Predicate Det.		Triple Det.	
Evaluation	R@100	R@50	R@100	R@50	R@100	R@50	R@100	R@50
[22]	4.05	4.01	3.51	3.41	8.79	8.52	6.13	5.36
[4]	6.84	6.23	6.57	6.33	16.25	16.10	6.54	6.41
[19]	6.91	6.43	6.70	6.81	17.03	17.01	6.73	6.67
Our method	7.21	7.26	6.77	6.78	17.66	17.60	6.81	6.81

The recall at 50 on the zero-shot test set as a function of the rank is given as the Fig. 3. We can see that the methods tend to be overfitting in the zero-shot setting if the rank is too high enough. Under the condition of limited rank, the visual relationships will be more important for the performance of the approaches, which can improve the generalization characteristic of the model. Note that the resented method has more parameters due to the complex semantic modeling procedure, performs better than other several methods and reaches the maximum value at the rank of around 16.

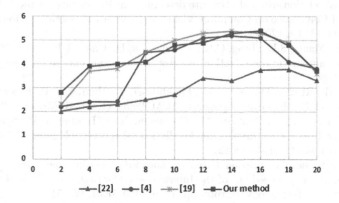

Fig. 3. Recall at 50 as a function of the rank for the zero-shot setting.

4 Conclusion

n this paper, we address the problem of improving semantic annotation using emantic modeling of knowledge embedding. Compared to existing methods vhich focus on features and context semantic information in images, we proose to leverage the knowledge information integration and model the semantic ues. We conduct the semantic modeling with prior knowledge embedding to ointly find the semantic objects and the corresponding support relationships in he images. And inference in the model exactly via graph modeling and knowledge embedding by learning the parameters at the supervised learning stage. The extensive experiments on COCO15 and Stanford Visual Relationship data sets onfirm the benefits of semantic annotation for the objects for the knowledge mbedding.

References

1. Lake, B.M., Ullman, T.D., Tenenbaum, J.B., Gershman, S.J.: Building machines that learn and think like people. Behav. Brain Sci. **40**, e253 (2017)
2. Grainger, T., AlJadda, K., Korayem, M., Smith, A.: The semantic knowledge graph: a compact, auto-generated model for real-time traversal and ranking of any relationship within a domain. In: Proceedings of the IEEE International Conference on Data Science and Advanced Analytics, Montreal, pp. 420–429. IEEE (2016)
3. Shalaby, W., Zadrozny, W., Jin, H.: Beyond word embeddings: learning entity and concept representations from large scale knowledge bases (2018). arXiv preprint: arXiv:1801.00388

4. Raposo, D., Santoro, A., Barrett, D., Pascanu, R., Lillicrap, T., Battaglia, P.: Discovering objects and their relations from entangled scene representations (2017). arXiv preprint: arXiv:1702.05068

5. Liang, X., Lee, L., Xing, E.P.: Deep variation-structured reinforcement learning for visual relationship and attribute detection. In: Proceedings of the IEEE International Conference on Computer Vision and Pattern Recognition, Honolulu, pp. 4408–4417. IEEE (2017)

6. Yu, L.F., Yeung, S.K., Tang, C.K., Terzopoulos, D., Chan, T.F., Osher, S.J.: Make it home: automatic optimization of furniture arrangement. ACM Trans. Graph. **30**, 86:1–86:12 (2011)

7. Fisher, M., Ritchie, D., Savva, M., Funkhouser, T., Hanrahan, P.: Example-based synthesis of 3D object arrangements. ACM Trans. Graph. **31**(6), 135 (2012)

8. Yeh, Y.T., Yang, L., Watson, M., Goodman, N.D., Hanrahan, P.: Synthesizing open worlds with constraints using locally annealed reversible jump MCMC. ACM Trans. Graph. **31**(4), 56 (2012)

9. Fan, Y.: Scene classification based on knowledge sharing and latent structural constraints. In: Proceedings of the International Conference on Computer Science and Network Technology, Harbin, pp. 1356–1360. IEEE (2015)

10. Narayanan, A., Chandramohan, M., Venkatesan, R., Chen, L., Liu, Y., Jaiswal, S.: Graph2vec: learning distributed representations of graphs (2017). arXiv preprint: arXiv:1707.05005

11. Duran, A.G., Niepert, M.: Learning graph representations with embedding propagation. In: Advances in Neural Information Processing Systems, pp. 5125–5136 (2017)

12. Nickel, M., Murphy, K., Tresp, V., Gabrilovich, E.: A review of relational machine learning for knowledge graphs. Proc. IEEE **104**, 11–13 (2016)

13. Kipf, T.N., Welling, M.: Semi-supervised classification with graph convolutional networks (2016). arXiv preprint: arXiv:1609.02907

14. Edwards, M., Xie, X.: Graph based convolutional neural network (2016). arXiv preprint: arXiv:1609.08965

15. Girshick, R., Donahue, J., Darrell, T., Malik, J.: Rich feature hierarchies for accurate object detection and semantic segmentation. In: Proceedings of the IEEE International Conference on Computer Vision and Pattern Recognition, Ohio, pp. 580–587. IEEE (2014)

16. Babaee, M., Wolf, T., Rigoll, G.: Toward semantic attributes in dictionary learning and non-negative matrix factorization. Pattern Recogn. Lett. **80**, 172–178 (2016)

17. Hackel, T., Usvyatsov, M., Galliani, S., Wegner, J.D., Schindler, K.: Inference, learning and attention mechanisms that exploit and preserve sparsity in convolutional networks (2018). arXiv preprint: arXiv:1801.10585

18. Lin, T.-Y.: Microsoft COCO: common objects in context. In: Fleet, D., Pajdla, T., Schiele, B., Tuytelaars, T. (eds.) ECCV 2014, Part V. LNCS, vol. 8693, pp. 740–755. Springer, Cham (2014). https://doi.org/10.1007/978-3-319-10602-1_48

19. Lu, C., Krishna, R., Bernstein, M., Fei-Fei, L.: Visual relationship detection with language priors. In: Leibe, B., Matas, J., Sebe, N., Welling, M. (eds.) ECCV 2016, Part I. LNCS, vol. 9905, pp. 852–869. Springer, Cham (2016). https://doi.org/10.1007/978-3-319-46448-0_51

20. Yuan, F., Kingsley, K., Jie, L., Cheston, T.: Object detection meets knowledge graphs. In: Proceedings of the Twenty-Sixth International Joint Conference on Artificial Intelligence, Melbourne. IEEE (2017)

21. Zhuo, W., Salzmann, M., He, X., Miaomiao, L.: Indoor scene parsing with instance segmentation, semantic labeling and support relationship inference. In: Proceedings of the International Conference on Computer Vision and Pattern Recognition, Honolulu. IEEE (2017)
22. Baier, S., Ma, Y., Tresp, V.: Improving visual relationship detection using semantic modeling of scene descriptions. In: Proceedings of the International Conference on Semantic Web, Vienna, pp. 53–68. IEEE (2017)

JSPRE: A Large-Scale Detection of Malicious JavaScript Code Based on Pre-filter

Bingnan Hou[1], Jiaping Yu[2], Bixin Liu[3(✉)], and Zhiping Cai[1]

[1] National University of Defense Technology, Changsha, China
[2] Chang'an University, Xi'an, China
[3] Academy of Military Science, Beijing, China
liu_bi_xin@sina.com

Abstract. Malicious web pages that use drive-by-download attacks or social engineering technique have become a popular means for compromising hosts on the Internet. To search for malicious web pages, researchers have developed a number of systems that analyze web pages for the presence of malicious code. Most of these systems use dynamic analysis. That is, the tools are quite precise, the analysis process is costly. Therefore, performing this analysis on a large-scale of web pages can be prohibitive. In this paper, we present JSPRE, an approach to search the web more efficiently for pages that are likely malicious. JSPRE proposes a malicious page collection algorithm based on guided crawling, which starts from an initial URLs of know malicious web pages. In the meanwhile, JSPRE uses static analysis techniques to quickly examine a web page for malicious content. We have implemented our approach, and we evaluated it on a large-scale dataset. The results show that JSPRE is able to identify malicious web pages more efficiently when compared to crawler-based approaches.

Keywords: Web security · Web client side malicious script
Web crawler · Pre-filter

1 Introduction

Coupled with the development of internet, the web applications have been used more and more prevalently. Web application refers to the application developed based on Web, and is composed of server side and client side. The running environment of client side program mainly refers to Web browsers, such as Internet Explorer, FireFox, Chrome, etc., and development techniques mainly include JavaScript, VBScript, CSS, etc. The running environment of server side program includes Web server, application server and database server, and development techniques mainly include ASP/ASP.NET, PHP, Java, etc. The communication protocol between server side and client side is based on HTTP. In early period, the function of Web browser is only to obtain content from server and display

© Springer Nature Switzerland AG 2018
X. Sun et al. (Eds.): ICCCS 2018, LNCS 11068, pp. 586–599, 2018.
https://doi.org/10.1007/978-3-030-00021-9_52

t to user, which lacks interactivity between user and server. With development of Web technology, and appearance of dynamic webpage technologies such as JavaScript, etc. current Web can provide users with multifarious information and functions, such as online bank, email, file storage, multimedia recreation and e-business, etc. Web browser has developed from previous display tool of HTML content into an execution environment that can execute distributed application. Besides, as malicious code on web pages of Web client side evolved as the malicious code form with the most comprehensive hazard and the best communication effect, the focus of network attack has been shifted from Web server side to Web client side. The security threats to client side mainly include two aspects: the first is that the drawbacks of client side script development techniques such as JavaScript and VBScript are prone to be utilized by malicious code; the second is that the drawbacks of Web browsers themselves result in execution of malicious code.

Among numerous attack means for client side, the webpage Trojan is one of the attack forms that spread most widely and have the most severe hazard [1]. It is essentiality a HTML webpage with malicious JavaScript attack script. Once the webpage is accessed by user, the malicious script would be executed automatically, and attack the programs with vulnerabilities on client side, such as browser or browser plugins, to finally download, install and execute malicious code without being known by the user. This attack pattern also goes by the name of drive-by download exploiting [2]. The most efficient tools of choice for the identification of malicious web pages are high-interaction or low-interaction honeyclients [3]. These honeyclients, such as the MITRE Honey Client, Microsoft's Honey Monkey or Google Safe Browsing, run a web browser on a real or simulative operating system inside a virtual machine. However, the analysis times ranging from seconds to a few minutes for a single page. As a result, it becomes very costly to analyze millions of URLs in a day on the Internet.

In this paper, we propose an approach that improves the efficiency of identification of malicious web pages. More precisely, we propose a system, called JSPRE, which is a method to collect and detect malicious script in mass data in network environment in a large scale. The JSPRE firstly extracts the known features of malicious page, according to which, seed URLs of crawler are produced. With these seed URLs as initial value, page grabbing is conducted, then the collected pages were treated with prefiltering algorithm based on classification of static features of pages. The algorithm analyzes the return head information, HTML source code and JavaScript script of webpage, to extract webpage features via static detection. As the static detection only resolves the code structure of webpage source code and does not execute code, such feature extraction is quick. Then the extracted page feature vector is placed in the classification model deduced via machine learning to classify pages. The web pages classified as normal pages are filtered out, which will filter out most of pages that are nearly impossible to be malicious pages, thereby significantly raising the collection efficiency of malicious pages.

2   Related Work

Currently, a great many detection methods have been suggested for detection of malicious JavaScript that targets client side, being mainly static and dynamic ones. The well-known traditional anti-virus software ClamAV [4] just recognizes malicious documents using static detection technique. However, the malicious JavaScript script usually hides the attack codes in webpage via various obfuscating and encryption mechanisms, so the static detection method represented by ClamAV tend to fail to effectively detect malicious script. Thus, the detection tools for malicious web pages usually adopt dynamic detection, which mainly uses honey pot technology [5]. The honey pot is a computer system that runs on the internet with design purpose of attracting and capturing the attackers attempting to intrude in others' computer systems. The traditional honey pot technology mainly refers to server-side honey pot. The honeyclient was firstly proposed by Lance Spitzner in 2004. Different from the server-side honey pot, the honeyclient actively starts the software of client side according to possible vulnerabilities of software on client side, to access server and monitor abnormal behavior, track and analyze malicious programs, thereby capturing attack. The currently developed honey pot systems mainly include HoneyMonkey [9], Spycrawler [11], Captutre-HPC [12] etc.

There are some other detection tools based on analysis of JavaScript script. The Caffeine Monkey [18] in which, the installation and invoking of vulnerability control can be simulated and the operations of malicious method invoking and parameter assignment by control can be monitored. Cujo [19] extracts static and dynamic features of script and combines machine learning to differentiate between malicious script and normal script. zozzle [20] extracts the features of expression and variable declaration nodes in abstract syntax tree AST generated by malicious script in execution process of interpreter to form feature set. The JODW [21] is a tool specially detecting the obfuscation degree of JavaScript script. Due to large use of obfuscation technology in malicious JavaScript script, JODW can serve as a means for preliminary detection.

The researches show that malicious code detection techniques for Web client side mainly includes static detection technique, high-interaction honeyclient, low-interaction honeyclient and detection technique based on script feature analysis [22], which have respective advantages and disadvantages. The static detection technique does not execute webpage script, but only detect via the static features shown by page source code, URL or domain name, with quick detection speed yet low accuracy. The advantages of high-interaction honeyclient and low-interaction honeyclient are ability to detect attack behavior and high accuracy, yet with drawbacks of large resource consumption and difficulty in applying to large-scale webpage detection. The detection technique based on script feature analysis combines extraction of static and dynamic features of script with machine learning to classify the to-be-detected page, with detection efficiency higher than that of the honeyclient technology, yet it is not sensitive to the new features of malicious web pages, hence higher missdetection rate and omission rate.

3 System Overview

In this section, we describe in detail the goals of our work, and we provide a brief overview of the overall approach and the components of our system.

3.1 System Goal

The crawler program can collect tens of thousands of web pages every day, while most of which are normal ones without malicious code. Large resources are consumed if dynamic detection is made for each page, thereby significantly lowering the detection efficiency. To cope with this problem, the paper proposes a pre-filtering algorithm based on classification of static features to rapidly find and collect malicious webpage, This algorithm firstly extracts page properties via static detection, then translates the page properties into a multidimensional feature vector. Lastly the pages are divided into normal and suspicious ones via machine learning according to specific classification model, while the pages classified as suspicious ones are submitted to detection program for determination of malicious webpage.

3.2 System Architecture

The general architecture of JSPRE is shown in Fig. 1. The overall architecture of JSPRE contains four modules: page collection module, prefiltering module, page detection module, data storage module. The system starts from a crawler generating seed URL according to specific strategy, i.e. webpage collection module. Then the to-be-detected page is submitted to prefiltering module, which realizes prefilter algorithm based on classification of static features of webpage, and extracts static features of webpage to predict whether the page is a suspicious malicious page. The page determined as suspicious by webpage filtering module is submitted to page detection module, which realizes the malicious webpage determination method based on analysis proposed herein and combines the detection technique based on simulation of vulnerabilities to successfully recognize the malicious script which has been obfuscated with high detection accuracy.

Seed Generator. The generation of seeds in seed generator is based on two crawling strategies: One is the seed generation strategy based on guided crawling, and another is seed generation strategy based on random crawling. In the seed generation strategy based on guided crawling, the seed generator firstly extracts such feature information as page URL, page title, page text keywords, etc. from the known malicious page, then combines these features with Google advanced operator to form search entries, lastly the Google search API is invoked to search for entries. The returned URL is just seed URL. The strategy of guided crawling aims to find out the similar malicious pages in network at the quickest speed. In the seed generation strategy based on random crawling, the seed generator firstly invokes Google Trend API to obtain the hot trends that day, then invokes API (Google keyword search API) provided by search engine to search for hot trends. The return value is just seed URL.

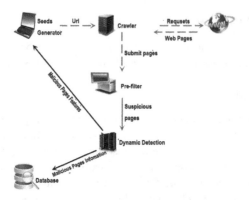

Fig. 1. JSPRE overview

Page Classifier. The goal of JSPRE is to classify pages collected by a web crawler as either likely malicious or likely benign. To perform this classification task, JSPRE uses a set of models that evaluate the features extracted from a page. These models are derived using supervised machine-learning techniques. Based on the test result of existing training set, the Naive Bayesian Classifier model has the lowest rate of missing report. Thus JSPRE adopts the classifier trained by Naive Bayesian Classifier. The model learning process is further explained in Sect. 3.4.

Page Determinant. The webpage detection module determines the malicious web pages. The system adopts detection method based on Bytecode analysis and detection method based on simulation of vulnerabilities to detect the suspicious pages. The detection method based on Bytecode analysis is established on script execution, thus the substrate needs a script operating environment. For this, the system realizes operating environment of script by rewriting open-sourced JavaScript engine SpiderMonkey.

3.3   Guided Crawling

Malicious web pages suffuse the internet. However, their proportion to massive normal pages is very small, and to collect malicious script by grabbing web pages randomly without using certain search strategies is nothing else than looking for a needle in a bottle of hay. Although some issuing sites of malicious domain names regularly publicize the URL list of malicious sites, yet the malicious sites usually have short lifetime, and their URLs fail before long if not collected in time, leading to inability to visit to obtain source code sample of malicious webpage, which is also one of reasons for difficulty in collecting data source of malicious script. The massive network resources can be regarded as infinite for the conventional webpage collection tools. To raise the number of malicious web pages in unit time, JSPRE uses a malicious web pages collection algorithm based n guided crawling to rapidly find and collect malicious web pages. Standing apart from the collection system based on random crawling, the guided crawling is designed to find out new pages similar to the known malicious web pages. It firstly extracts the feature set of known malicious webpage. The feature set mainly contains the URL information, title message, keyword information and server version information of malicious page, which are combined with Google advanced operators to generate query entries. Lastly, the Google Search API is invoked to index the entries, and the return value serves as seed URL for guided crawling. Algorithm 1 shows the pseudocode for guided crawling, in the algorithm URL represents malicious page url, TITLE represents title of malicious page, CONTENT represents text keywords of malicious page, SERVER represents server version of malicious page.

Algorithm 1. Malicious Pages Collection based on Guided Crawling.

Input:
    Malicious pages set $P = \{page_1, page_2, \ldots, page_n\}$;
Output:
    URL seed set $S = \{seed_1, seed_2, \ldots, seed_m\}$;
1: $S = \varnothing$;
2: $i = 0$;
3: **while** $i \neq n$ **do**
4:     extract   malicious   feature   set   of $page_i$ M_i =
       $\{page_i.url, page_i.title, page_i.content, page_i.server\}$;
5:     M_i combines with Google senior operator creating the query set $Query_i$ =
       $\{$"*link*": + $page_i.url$, "*int itle*": + $page_i.title$, "*all int ext*": + $page_i.content$,
       "*intitle: index of*": + $page_i.server\}$
6:     **for all** q such that $q \in Query_i$ **do**
7:        $seed_i = +GoogleSearch(q)$;
8:     **end for**
9:     $seed = +seed_i$
0:     $i = i + 1$
1: **end while**

Seed Generator Based on URL. The basis of realization of search algorithm of malicious pages based on guided crawling is a malicious web sample set, which contains two types of pages. The first is a web page created directly by hackers, which typically contains malicious scripts. The second type of page does not contain a malicious script itself, but contains an external link to the first type of page, usually this page is released by the sites that are attacked by hackers. The study found that pages containing links to malicious pages are also likely to be malicious pages. So the guided crawling algorithm uses a search engine to retrieve URLs that contain links to malicious pages and use them as the seed URL for crawlers. The specific process is to extract the URL and its sublink of the malicious pages, then use the senior operator Link of Google to form a search term with the URL of the malicious page or its sub-link, and use Google Search API to query, its search parameter is a URL or server name, its form is *link:<MALICIOUS URL>*.

Seed Generator Based on Title. To improve access to malicious pages, hackers often use hot topics to attract users to their malicious sites. Hackers, for example, write hot topics in the title of their web pages, making it easier for search engines to retrieve their published sites. To this, guided crawling algorithm firstly extracts known malicious page title, and then use Google senior operators Intitle and malicious page titles to form search terms, and use the Google Search query API to query. The Intitle operator is that search engine is limited in the page title, and its form is *intitle:<TITLE>*.

Seed Generator Based on Keywords. Like the malicious page titles, text content of malicious page HTML is also more likely to be reused by hackers. Therefore, the guided crawling algorithm uses the keyword extraction technology to extract the text content of the malicious page. Keywords extraction uses information retrieval and natural language processing and other technologies, and it is based on the calculation of the frequency of the phrase in the text. The extracted keywords are then indexed by the Google senior operator, Allintext, the returned URL is used as a crawling seed of crawlers, and the form is *allintext:<KEY WORD>*.

Seed Generator Based on Server. Hackers frequently use Google Hacking to find vulnerable targets in the Web, and these vulnerable servers are also the key objects of the guided crawling algorithm. For example, if your query "index of the/etc/", search engines will return some Apache Web servers that their security information is not banned from Google. These sensitive search terms related to server versions are also known as Google Dork, and Google Dork search was first proposed by Johnny Long, and its online database and some penetration testing tools have been produced. After the guided crawling algorithm gets the server version, it queries by virtue of the search engine API, and its terns form is *intitle: index of <SERVER VERSION>*.

3.4   Classification of Page Static Feature

Pre-filtering algorithm based on web page classification of static features firstly extracts the static features of the page to be detected, including HTML text features of web pages, script feature of JavaScript and features contained in the return header information. In this way, the page to be tested is transformed into an eigenvector containing its attribute information, and by the classification mode that was built to predict and classify, if the classification is a malicious page, it will be submitted to the next malicious web decision system, otherwise it was filtered directly.

The basis of predictive classification of the prefiltering algorithm based on the static feature classification of web pages is the classification model that derived from the known training sample set. Because the purpose of the pre-filtering algorithm is to make the initial screening of the page, it pays special attention to the quality of the omission factor in the process of the derivation of the model. In this paper, by observing the experimental results of the training sample set, a classification model with the lowest omission rate is applied to the pre-filtering algorithm based on the static feature classification of web pages. Φ refers to the classification model function, N_i refers to the static eigenvector of the page to be classified. Because the model is a binary classification model, classification set is recorded as $C = suspicious, normal$, then, the prediction classification model of page to be classified satisfies formula

$$\Phi(N_i) = \begin{cases} suspicious \\ normal \end{cases}$$

Algorithm 2 shows the pseudocode for pre-filter, in the algorithm, H_i represents text feature vector of page HTML, J_i represents script eigenvector of page JavaScript, U_i represents eigenvectors of page return header information.

Algorithm 2. Pre-filter Pages based on the Classification of Page's Static Characteristics.

Input:
  Pages to be detected $P = \{page_1, page_2, \ldots, page_n\}$;
Output:
  Suspicious pages set $S = \{s_1, s_2, \ldots, s_m\}$;
1: $S = \varnothing$;
2: $i = 0$;
3: **while** $i \neq n$ **do**
4:    extract the static characteristics of $page_i$ $N_i = [H_i, J_i, U_i]$;
5:    **if** $\Phi(N_i) == suspicious$ **then**
6:      $S = +page_i$;
7:    **end if**
8:    $i = i + 1$
9: **end while**

HTML Features. The extraction of HTML features is based on the statistical information of the page and the parsing information of the page structure. As to hide attack behavior, hackers will usually hide malicious JavaScript in hidden elements in web page. The concrete implementation is to calculate the area size of div, iframe or object tag. External link are also counted for script, iframe, frame, embed, form, object, and other tags. JSPRE also collects the vulnerability information of ActiveX from the vulnerability information database such as CVE [38], and manually records the classid, classname and method of the vulnerability to check if the HTML contains these information.

JavaScript Features. The extraction of JavaScript script features comes from two aspects, one is the contents of the text/JavaScript tag within the page, and the other is the contents of external script documents that the script tag src attribute points to. Script confusion is an effective method to avoid static detection of web pages. Many of the JavaScript code auto-obfuscation tools that exist in the network make this approach very easy to be used, while automatic obfuscation tools typically use JavaScript language built-in functions or DOM object methods like eval(), document.write(), and so on. Therefore, the algorithm uses these functions as the sensitive function of the key tracking.

Features of Return Header Information. Page redirection is also an important feature of malicious web pages. After some malicious sites receive a client request, they will obtain the user operating system or browser version information by detecting request header, and they will conduct page redirection to return to different pages according to different operating system or browser version. There are also some malicious sites detect the Referrer attribute in the request header information to avoid the page capture of the detection system. If the attribute value is empty, it shows that the request is from the web site that the user directly enter from address bar, or request from a crawler, the website will return to a normal page or return to a malicious web page.

By observing the differences between malicious web pages and the static characteristics of web pages, JSPRE conduct feature extraction of static attributes from 13 aspects.

Derivation of Classification Model. This section describes the derivation of the classification model of the prefiltering algorithm based on the static feature classification of web pages. Generation and assessment of the classification model requires data set, and the experiment selects the top 100 web sites from Alexa as a seed, grabs the web page and uses the Google Safe Browsing API to remove the malicious web pages by crawlers module, then randomly selects 39315 pages as the normal web data set. Then selects 800 pages as malicious web data sets from web sites with malicious domain names such as MDL and previous malicious pages. A total of 40115 data samples were established and evaluated through the WEKA machine learning platform. In the classification feature selection, using information gain to sort out eigenvalues, selecting 10 kinds of features with the largest information gains from 13 features as the eigenvectors of training sets in order to reduce the noise of the training sample set. The experiment mainly evaluates classification and prediction model from three indicators: accuracy rate, error rate and omission rate.

$$Accuracy\ rate = \frac{TP + TN}{TP + TN + FP + FN} \times 100\%$$

$$Error\ rate = \frac{FP}{FP + TN} \times 100\%$$

$$Omission\ rate = \frac{FN}{TP + FN} \times 100\%$$

The accuracy rate indicates the percentage of pages that are correctly classified as the total number of pages, the omission rate represents the percentage of the total number of malicious web pages classified as normal. The error rate indicates the percentage of normal web pages classified as malicious web pages.

The experiment evaluates the advantages and disadvantages of classification model by 10-times cross validation, the inspection process is that all data samples are divided into 10 roughly equal shares, training and test will be conducted for 10 times, 9 copies will be used each time, 1 is used to test, the experimental results are shown in Table 1.

Table 1. Performance of classification algorithm

Index	Classification			
	Naive-Bayes	SVM	J48	Logistic
Confusion matrix	$\begin{bmatrix} 720 & 80 \\ 967 & 38348 \end{bmatrix}$	$\begin{bmatrix} 413 & 387 \\ 197 & 39118 \end{bmatrix}$	$\begin{bmatrix} 506 & 294 \\ 218 & 39097 \end{bmatrix}$	$\begin{bmatrix} 404 & 396 \\ 170 & 39145 \end{bmatrix}$
Omission rate	10.0%	48.4%	36.7%	49.5%
Error rate	2.5%	0.5%	0.6%	0.4%
Accuracy rate	97.4%	98.5%	98.7%	98.6%

By calculating the index, the naive Bayes classification model of the training sample set has the lowest omission rate and acceptable error rate. Therefore, pre-filtering algorithm based on the static feature classification of web pages proposed by this paper select the page suspicious prediction.

3.5 Limitations

In the pre-filtering algorithm based on static feature classification of web pages, the derivation of page classification model is based on the existing training sample set. If there is one type of large number of malicious samples in the training set, the classification model will only be sensitive to this type of malicious page. When a new type of malicious page appears, the detection method becomes invalid, so it is necessary to update and expand the type and number of malicious samples in the training sample.

4 Evaluation

In this section, we evaluate the effectiveness and performance of JSPRE. More precisely, we fist discuss whether the guided crawling approach used in JSPRE is effective at locating malicious pages. Then, our paper evaluates the effectiveness of the JSPRE pre-filter module for the large-scale webpage detection from the two aspects of filtration efficiency and omission rate.

4.1   Effectiveness of Guided Crawling

This section tries to verify whether the malicious web search algorithm based on guiding crawling proposed in this paper can improve the efficiency of malicious web search of crawlers, so the object of the experiment is a random crawler. In the experiment, the web pages collected by crawlers with two different crawling strategies will be submitted to the malicious web testing program. As for malicious web detection programs, this article uses the malicious web detection API provided by VirusTotal [37]. In the experiment, there are two ways to collect the malicious web pages that are required to guide crawling. One is a total of 204 local malicious web pages collected previously. The other is to collect 400 web URLs that are marked as malicious domain names from the malicious domain name site MDL (malwaredomainlist.com). In order to improve the generalization of the seed URL for the crawlers using random crawling strategies, this paper uses the hot terms of Google trend as the search term to generate the seed URL, and then the two crawlers were then run for 30 days on an Intel Core i7 processor, 4G memory, Ubuntu12.04, and 64-bit operating system.

The comparison results are shown in Table 2, in which the guided crawling group generated 2,740 search terms by extracting 604 malicious page feature information, and these search terms returned a total of 82391 URLs, a total of 71,272 pages were collected within 30 days. This is because part of the URLs are duplicate URLs or the URLs have expired. A total of 1097 pages were malicious webpages in the collected 71272 pages, and the malicious page collection rate was 1.53%. At the same time, the Random Crawling Group generated a total of 300 search terms through Google Trends. These search terms returned a total of 83,510 URLs, of which 80,510 were collected. Of the 80,510 collected pages, 47 were malicious pages. Its malicious page collection efficiency is 0.058%.

It can be seen from the comparison test data that the collection efficiency of guided crawling malicious pages is significantly higher than that of random crawling malicious web pages. This proves that the malicious web collection method based on guided crawling is an effective method to quickly collect malicious web pages. But random crawling is still an essential crawling strategy for malicious web pages, because random crawling is one of the most important ways to find new malicious pages with different types of malicious web pages.

4.2   Performace of Pre-filter

This section will test the filtering performance of the prefiltering algorithm based on the static feature classification of web pages. In the experiment, the proposed page feature classification model is configured after the crawler program with random crawling strategy, and the suspicious page will be alarmed. In the experiment, crawlers that did not use the guided crawling strategy because the malicious pages grabbed by the crawlers with guided crawling strategies have the high similarity, so the eigenvectors show very high similarity. While the prefiltration algorithm is based on the classification model algorithm, so eigenvalue with a high similarity does not have universal meaning, which can lead to the leviation of the index evaluation. Therefore, we choose crawlers with random crawling strategies that are meaningful to grab web pages samples.

Table 2. Comparison of guided crawling and random crawling

Index	Crawling strategy	
	Guided crawling	Random crawling
Malicious URLs	604	0
Generated search terms	2740	300
Total number of access URLs	82391	83510
Total number of valid pages	71272	80510
Collection of malicious pages	1097	47
Malicious pages collection rate	1.53%	0.06%

The algorithm is evaluated with a large scale web prefiltering performance, as shown in Table 3. The crawler program collected 81157 valid pages after 30 days of operation, and 1679 of the alarm pages accounted for 2.07%, that is 97.93% of the filtration efficiency. After that, the alarm pages was tested through the VirusTotal in the experiment, 45 pages were malicious pages, and the error detection rate of the pre-filter was calculated at 97.3%. It is worth noting that the error rate of the prefilter is not the error detection rate of the final detection program, but it is indicated from the side that the feature constraint can be strengthened to improve the filter efficiency of the prefilter. As for the calculation of omission factor, due to the large amount of sample data. The experiment took 10 percent of the pages from the filtered pages and tested it through the VirusTotal API, we found that only one malicious web page was detected, and the estimated error rate was 0.013%.

Table 3. Performance evaluation table of pre-filter

Index	Value
Number of valid pages	81157
Number of alarm pages	1679
Actual number of malicious pages	45
Percentage of suspicious pages	2.07%
Filtration efficiency	97.93%
Error rate	97.3%
Omission rate	≈0.013%

It can be concluded from the experimental data that the pre-filtering algorithm based on the static feature classification of web pages has low leak detection rate and high error detection rate and filtration efficiency, so it is considered that the algorithm is effective. This is because the prefiltering algorithm only serves as the criterion to determine whether a web page is a suspicious page, instead of the criterion whether the web page is the final judgment of malicious web page, so it can accept higher false detection rate. At the same time, the low leakage rate ensures the probability that the page is determined by malicious web page. If the web filtering module is configured before a large-scale web page detection system, it will achieve more than 97% filtering efficiency and greatly improve the system detection efficiency. Therefore, the prefiltering algorithm based on the static feature classification of web pages is an effective method for the detection of large-scale malicious web pages.

5   Conclusions

More and more hackers are using Internet for drive-by-download exploiting, whose invisibility of diffusion means and process largely threaten users. For script of drive-by-download exploits, currently most of detection systems adopt static detection or dynamic detection, while the obfuscating and encryption technique of script tend to successfully dodge the static detection. The dynamic detection submits the webpages to real browser or simulated environment of browser to observe whether the malicious act exists in script execution, leading to high cost and failure to apply it to large-scale detection. An effective method for large-scale detection is to pre-filter the normal pages, The dynamic detection only detect the suspicious pages. Based on this, JSPRE realizes a large-scale detection of webpages based on guided crawling and pre-filter via static detection. The experimental result shows that JSPRE can effectively improve the collection efficiency of malicious pages and filter out a large number of normal pages. thereby providing an important reference for detection, analysis and research of malicious JavaScript.

References

1. Bichhawat, A., Rajani, V., Garg, D., Hammer, C.: Information flow control in WebKit's JavaScript bytecode. In: Abadi, M., Kremer, S. (eds.) POST 2014. LNCS, vol. 8414, pp. 159–178. Springer, Heidelberg (2014). https://doi.org/10.1007/978-3-642-54792-8_9
2. Shindo, Y., et al.: Lightweight approach to detect drive-by download attacks based on file type transition. ACM (2014)
3. Jensen, S.H., Madsen, M., Moller, A.: Modeling the HTML DOM and browser API in static analysis of JavaScript web applications. ACM (2011)
4. Thinh, T.N., et al.: Memory-efficient signature matching for ClamAV on FPGA (2014)
5. Flores, R.: How Blackhat SEO became big. Technical report, Trend Micro (2010)
6. Spitzner, L.: The honeynet project: trapping the hackers. IEEE Secur. Priv. 1(2), 15–23 (2003)
7. Gang, Z., Peng, W., Xin, W.: The detection method for two-dimensional barcode malicious URL based on the decision tree. Inf. Secur. Technol. 2, 12 (2014)

8. Choi, J., et al.: Efficient malicious code detection using n-gram analysis and SVM. IEEE (2011)

9. Wang, Y., et al.: Automated web patrol with strider honeymonkeys (2006)

0. Kaur, R., Singh, M.: Efficient hybrid technique for detecting zero-day polymorphic worms. IEEE (2014)

1. Moshchuk, A., et al.: A crawler-based study of spyware in the web (2006)

2. Seifert, C., Steenson, R.: Capture-honeypot client (capture-HPC) (2006)

3. Nazario, J.: PhoneyC: a virtual client honeypot. USENIX Association (2009)

4. Keane, J.K.: Using the Google safe browsing API from PHP. Mad Irish, 7 August 2009

5. Dean, J., Ghemawat, S.: MapReduce: simplified data processing on large clusters. Commun. ACM **51**(1), 107–113 (2008)

6. Seifert, C., Welch, I., Komisarczuk, P.: Honeyc-the low-interaction client honeypot. In: Proceedings of the 2007 NZCSRCS, Waikato University, Hamilton (2007)

7. Friedrichs, O., Huger, A., O'Donnell, A.J.: Method and apparatus for detecting malicious software using machine learning techniques. US Patent (2015)

8. Feinstein, B., Peck, D., Secureworks, Inc.: Caffeine monkey: automated collection, detection and analysis of malicious JavaScript. Black Hat USA (2007)

9. Rieck, K., Krueger, T., Dewald, A.: Cujo: efficient detection and prevention of drive-by-download attacks. ACM (2010)

0. Curtsinger, C., et al.: ZOZZLE: fast and precise in-browser JavaScript malware detection (2011)

1. Choi, Y.H., Kim, T.G., Choi, S.J., Lee, C.W.: Automatic detection for JavaScript obfuscation attacks in web pages through string pattern analysis. In: Lee, Y., Kim, T., Fang, W., Ślęzak, D. (eds.) FGIT 2009. LNCS, vol. 5899, pp. 160–172. Springer, Heidelberg (2009). https://doi.org/10.1007/978-3-642-10509-8_19

2. Long, J.: Google Hacking for Penetration Testers. Syngress (2011)

3. Pilgrim, M.: Dive Into Python [EB/OL] (2000). http://www.diveintopython.com/

4. Hartstein, B.: Jsunpack: an automatic JavaScript unpacker (2009)

5. Page, L., et al.: The PageRank citation ranking: bringing order to the web (1999)

6. Das Sarma, A., et al.: Fast distributed PageRank computation. Theor. Comput. Sci. (2014)

7. Polychronakis, M., Anagnostakis, K.G., Markatos, E.P.: Network-level polymorphic shellcode detection using emulation. In: Büschkes, R., Laskov, P. (eds.) DIMVA 2006. LNCS, vol. 4064, pp. 54–73. Springer, Heidelberg (2006). https://doi.org/10.1007/11790754_4

8. Daniel, M., Honoroff, J., Miller, C.: Engineering heap overflow exploits with JavaScript. WOOT **8**, 1–6 (2008)

9. Hallaraker, O., Vigna, G.: Detecting malicious JavaScript code in Mozilla. IEEE (2005)

0. Shkapenyuk, V., Suel, T.: Design and implementation of a high-performance distributed web crawler. IEEE (2002)

Multilevel Features Fusion in Deep Convolutional Neural Networks

Yi-Fan Zhuo and Yi-Lei Wang[✉]

College of Mathematics and Computer Science,
Fuzhou University, Fuzhou, Fujian, China
yilei@fzu.edu.cn

Abstract. The convolution neural networks (CNNs) can extract the rich feature of the image. It was widely used in the field of computer vision (CV) and made great breakthroughs. However, most of the existing CNNs models only utilize the features out put by last layer, the representation of features is not comprehensive enough. In this paper, we propose a multilevel features fusion method, in order to make full use of the intermediate layer features. This method can strengthen feature propagation and improve the accuracy of downstream tasks. We evaluate our method through experiments on two image classification benchmark tasks: CIFAR-10 and CIFAR-100. The experimental results show that our method is able to significantly improve the accuracy of VGG-like model. The improved model is better than most existing models.

Keywords: Convolutional neural networks · Feature fusion · Deep learning

1 Introduction

Deep convolutional neural network has widely usesd for image and video recognition, and achieved good results [1–3]. As more and more image datasets such as ImageNet [4] are made public, and high computing performance GPUs are popularized, we can train deeper models with more data. Deep convolutional neural network connects different levels of feature extractors and classifiers for end-to-end training. However, the most of the existing convolutional neural networks (CNNs) [5, 6] used for image classification are trained in a top-down fashion. Get the output of the previous layer and as the input of the next layer. This means that when trained in the last layer of the network, some information contained in many intermediate levels will lost.

In recent years, papers [7] had explored for why deep convolutional neural network performed so well, or how they might be improved. Zeiler [1] introduced a visualization technique to understand the functionality of intermediate layers, and show that during CNNs training, different layers of network can extract different levels of features. All of these features are beneficial to downstream tasks. Inspired by this, we attempt to improve the traditional CNNs by fusion multilevel feature.

In this paper, we propose a variety of multilevel features fusion methods. The central idea is to concatenate the output of intermediate layers with the original final output, and multilevel features will be fusion in the final output layer. Figure 1 illustrates the layout of our model. We use Tensorflow [8] and make some experiments on

© Springer Nature Switzerland AG 2018
X. Sun et al. (Eds.): ICCCS 2018, LNCS 11068, pp. 600–610, 2018.
https://doi.org/10.1007/978-3-030-00021-9_53

CIFAR [9] dataset. Moreover we use techniques like dropout [10] and batch normalization [11], which are widely used to improve the effect of model. The experiment results show that our multilevel features fusion method significantly outperforms a few popular alternatives.

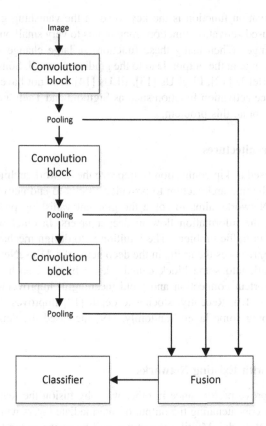

Fig. 1. Extracted features from the intermediate layer and fusion.

The rest of the paper is divided into these parts: In Sect. 2, we introduced the relevant work in recent years and compared with our model. In Sect. 3, we introduced the implementation details of the model. In Sect. 4. we compare basic model and our model on CIFAR image classification task. In Sect. 5, we conclude this paper.

2 Related Works

In recent years, many methods of deep learning were proposed. As the model changes from AlexNet [2] to VGG [5], GoogLeNet [6] and ResNet [3], the performance becomes better and better. Unfortunately, vanishing gradient problem still exists in gradient based methods. Especially, as the network deepens, the parameters of the earlier layer in the network are difficult to adjust. In order to overcome these difficulties, more research has been done on optimizing technology and network architecture of neural network.

2.1   Optimization Techniques

The choice of activation function is the key to solve the vanishing gradient problem. Many commonly used activation functions map inputs to very small output ranges from very non-linear range. When using these functions, a large change in the input will produce a small change in the output, lead to the gradient is small. Some new activation functions such as ReLU [12], PReLUs [13], ELUs [14] does not have these problems. They widely replace activation function such as Sigmoid and Tanh. good initialization [15] can also ameliorate this problem.

2.2   Network Architectures

Recent work has used a skip connection to improve the network architecture. Highway Networks [16] is the first architecture to provided an end-to-end networks of over 100 layers. Highway Networks aims to solve the gradient vanishing problem, especially when exacerbated the information flow in deeper layers. In other words, the information is blocked in traffic problem. The intuition is to design mechanism, and set up special path that rejuvenates the traffic in the deep networks. DenseNet [17] divided the deep neural network into some block called "dense blocks", each block is densely connected with shortcut connection and yield meaningful improvements in accuracy (96.54% on CIFAR-10). Recently, stochastic depth [18] improves the deep residual networks by skipping some layers randomly. [19] increased the depth beyond 1200 layers.

2.3   Compared with Existing Networks

We attempt to improve performance in other ways by fusion the features of intermediate layers, which concatenating the output of intermediate layers with the final output of the original CNN model. Multilevel features will be fusion in the final output layer and improve efficiency. Compared with DSN [20], we build an end-to-end networks without the extra classifiers to supervise the training of intermediate layer. Compared with DenseNet [17], DenseNet had densely connected in each block, without connection from intermediate layer to final layer. We only fusion the feature map learned by intermediate layers and final layer. The main purpose of DenseNet is to alleviate the vanishing-gradient problem and train deeper network, but the main purpose of our method is to the full use multilevel features.

3   Multilevel Features Fusion

Traditional convolutional neural networks are overlapped by the pooling layers [21] and the convolution layers. Only adjacent layers are connected and train through the top-down fashion. Outputs of the final layer is used as features of the original input.

This results in the features learned by intermediate layers, which contain rich discriminative information, are not directly used for downstream tasks.

We attempt to improve the traditional CNNs by fusion the features of intermediate layers. The central idea is to fusion the features of intermediate layers into new feature and used for downstream tasks. Consider a neural network has a layer which is a top-down architecture, and each layer has a non-linear activation function $f(x)$. The convolution layer use ReLU [12] as the activation function and use Batch Normalization [11] for optimization. A convolution block consists of multiple convolutional layers. The whole network is divided into several blocks, all blocks are ended with a max-pooling layer. We denote the output of the ith pooling layer as x_i, where i is used to index the pooling layer of the model. We fusion the features of all preceding pooling layers:

$$x = fusion(x_1, \ldots, x_n) \tag{1}$$

where x refers to the new feature obtained through fusion. Then use this new feature image classification task.

3.1   Network Architectures

In order to compare with the traditional top-down network, we have tested various VGG-like nets and our model. Two models are describing as follows.

Our baseline model named VGG-like (Fig. 2, left) was inspired by the VGG [5] network. We divide the whole network into three blocks, and each block has one to five convolutional layers, each block ends with a max-pooling layers. Then through the fully-connected (FC) layer. The network ends with a 10-way or 100-way fully-connected layer with softmax.

Based on the above VGG-like network, we fusion all outputs of the pooling layers (Fig. 2, right). which turn the network into its counterpart our VGG-F model version.

3.2   Fusion Method

We designed several multilevel feature fusion methods, We assume the extracted features of intermediate layer are $x_1, \ldots, x_n$, we fusion these features into a new feature x.

Accumulation Method. The model using this method is called VGG-Fa. The multilevel features we have obtained are converted into features of the same dimension by using fully connected layers. After that, we add up these features to a new feature.

$$x_i' = fully\_connected(x_i, new\_dimension) \tag{2}$$

$$x = \sum_{i=1}^{n} x_i' \tag{3}$$

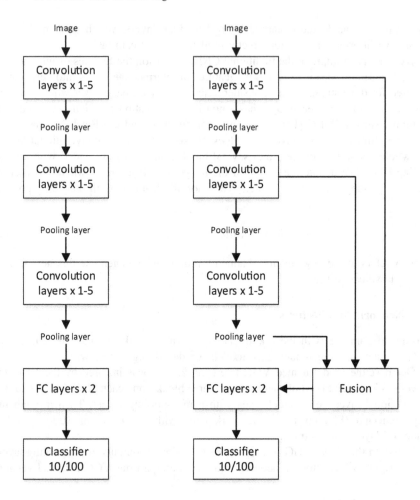

Fig. 2. VGG-like model (left) and VGG-F model (right).

Concat Method. The model using this method is called VGG-Fc. We flatten the features of different levels into a one-dimensional vector and then concat these vectors into a new feature:

$$x_i' = flatten(x_i) \tag{4}$$

$$x = concat(x_1, \ldots, x_n) \tag{5}$$

Set Weight Method. The model using this method is called VGG-Fw. Intuitively, The features of the different layers will lose some information. Therefore, different levels of features should be set with different weights:

$$x = fusion(x_1 w_1, \ldots, x_n w_n) \tag{6}$$

We assume that upper features will lose more information, vice versa. We're setting the coefficients $\{w_1, w_2, \ldots, w_n\}$ as parameters in neural network and the parameter is decreasing.

3.3 Implementation Details

We implement model using Tensorflow and train model using stochastic gradient descent with momentum. As an example of Fig. 2, let $32 \times 32 \times 3$ (width 32, height 32, 3 color channels R,G,B) image passes through the convolution blocks. The convolutional layers mostly have 3×3 filters (3×3 conv) and output dimension doubles in turn from 64. For each convolution layer use batch normalization [11], then ReLU [12]. And then passed a size of 2×2 kernel for pooling. It will take down sampling operation in the space dimension. Due to the additional parameters have been extended in the network, we apply dropout [10] to the each fully-connected layer in 4096 dimension to avoid overfitting. All feature output by intermediate layers are flattened before fused.

4 Experiments

In order to evaluate the effect of our model, we perform experiments on two image classification task datasets: CIFAR10 and CIFAR100 [8]. By comparing the accuracy, we verify that our model is valid. We performed all experiments using the Tensorflow framework [9]. Experiment with the basic VGG-like model. We also compare with some other existing models, such as ResNet, Highway network.

4.1 Datasets

Each dataset contains 60000 colored natural scene images, with 32×32 pixels each. Consist of 10,000 test images and 50,000 training images. The CIFAR10 dataset is divided into 10 classes. The CIFAR100 dataset is divided into 100 classes. We randomly select 5,000 training images as a validation images, and the remaining 45000 pictures for real training. We refer a standard data augmentation scheme for this training set. For each image, we created a 20-flod augmentation by cropping and flipping. we set the size of crop equal to the input of the CNN architecture and generated 5 crops from the center and four corners. For each crop, we created a 4-flod by flipping about the x-axis and y-axis. By doing this, we can get a new dataset which is about hundred times the size of the original. We add the "+" to represent data augmentation (e.g., C10+, C100+).

4.2 Configurations

As shown in Table 1, shows the VGG-like network configurations evaluated in this paper. all networks are similar to VGG [5]. We divide the model into five categories by layer number: A, B, C, D, E. The whole network is divided into 3 blocks, difference blocks have difference width of convolution layers.

Table 1. The configuration of basic VGG-like

Networks configuration				
A	B	C	D	E
6 layers	9 layers	12 layers	15 layers	18 layers
Input (32*32 RGB image)				
conv3-64	conv3-64 × 2	conv3-64 × 3	conv3-64 × 4	conv3-64 × 5
conv3-128	conv3-128 × 2	conv3-128 × 3	conv3-128 × 4	conv3-128 × 5
conv3-256	conv3-256 × 2	conv3-256 × 3	conv3-256 × 4	conv3-256 × 5
Max-pooling				
FC-4096 × 2				
FC-10/FC-100				
Softmax				

For training parameters setting. There are 300 epochs for each dataset (C10, C10+, C100, C100+). Use stochastic gradient descent with batch size 128. Initialization learning rate is 0.01 and decay is 0.9.

4.3 Results

We experiment with our VGG-Fa, VGG-Fc, VGG-Fw models on benchmark datasets: C10, C10+, C100, C100+. Calculating accuracy through image classification tasks. We will show the experimental results in detail in the following.

Table 2 shows the performance of basic VGG-like model. Obtain the baseline accuracy: 88.95% accuracy on C10, 92.49% on C10+, 62.22% on C100, 67.82% on C100+.

Table 2. Accuracy on basic VGG-like model

VGG-like	c10	c10+	c100	c100+
A	83.00	87.34	50.21	62.55
B	82.14	90.98	58.62	66.84
C	88.64	91.83	60.67	67.79
D	**88.95**	92.14	62.14	67.09
E	88.93	**92.49**	**62.22**	**67.82**

Table 3 shows that our VGG-Fa model preliminarily improves the accuracy. We found that the model achieved the preferably effect on the version of D (15 layers).

Table 3. Accuracy on VGG-Fa model.

VGG-Fa	c10	c10+	c100	c100+
A	85.67	88.03	59.61	63.43
B	88.34	92.20	63.21	69.20
C	90.16	92.27	64.02	70.68
D	**90.55**	**92.57**	**64.40**	**71.71**
E	89.21	92.50	64.26	70.86

Table 4 shows that the accuracy of our VGG-Fc model is further improved. Experiments show that with the increase number of network layers, the accuracy is improved. This model is more robust than the VGG-Fa model.

Table 4. Accuracy on VGG-Fc model.

VGG-Fc	c10	c10+	c100	c100+
A	84.10	87.98	60.51	62.81
B	88.89	92.04	65.33	69.24
C	88.95	92.59	65.37	70.28
D	89.02	92.71	65.51	71.37
E	**89.10**	**93.22**	**65.52**	**71.77**

Comparison Tables 2, 3 and 4, Our feature fusion method has significantly improved the accuracy of basic model of VGG-like. And VGG-Fc is better than VGG-Fa in most cases.

Table 5 shows we further improve the accuracy of image classification on VGG-Fw model. We try to set the feature weights coefficients. w = $\{0.5, 0.3, 0.2\}$ on the basis of VGG-Fc model. We achieves better performance than previous models: 90.55% accuracy on C10, 93.39% accuracy on C10+, 65.69% on C100 and 72.19% on C100+.

Table 5. Accuracy on VGG-Fw model.

VGG-Fw	c10	c10+	c100	c100+
A	85.38	88.65	61.02	65.15
B	89.48	92.21	64.55	70.32
C	89.51	92.71	64.98	71.13
D	90.31	93.02	65.33	71.68
E	**90.55**	**93.39**	**65.69**	**72.19**

Figures 3 and 4 shows our VGG-Fw model compared with the basic VGG-like model, the accuracy was improved significantly. Our model also achieves better image classification accuracy with the increase of network layer number. In addition, the original basic model is superimposed on all layers, and our method is an effective method.

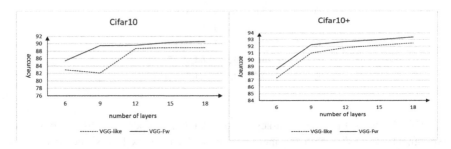

Fig. 3. Compare VGG-like and VGG-Fw on Cifar10 and Cifar10+ dataset.

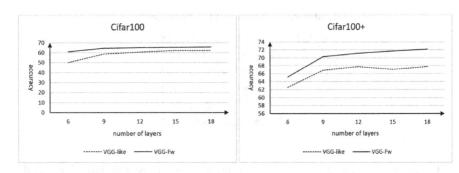

Fig. 4. Compare VGG-like and VGG-Fw on Cifar100 and Cifar100+ dataset.

Table 6 compare performance of our model with Maxout [22], NIN [23], DSN [20] and FractalNet [24] on CIFAR-10. All methods are with augmentation. We achieves an accuracy of 93.39%, outperforms most of recent models.

Table 6. Accuracy on cifar-10, with data augmentation.

Model	Accuracy (%)
Maxout	91.62
MIN	91.19
DSN	92.03
FractalNet	94.76
VGG-Fw	**93.39**

Table 7 compare performance of our model with FitNet [25], Highway [16] and original ResNet [3] on CIFAR10. All methods are with data augmentation. Our CIFAR-10 accuracy is close to that of the best ResNet with less layers.

Table 7. Accuracy on cifar-10, with data augmentation.

Model	Layers	Accuracy (%)
FitNet	19	91.61
Highway	19	92.46
Highway	32	91.20
ResNet	20	91.61
ResNet	32	92.49
ResNet	44	92.83
ResNet	56	93.03
ResNet	110	93.57
VGG-Fw	6	88.65
VGG-Fw	9	92.21
VGG-Fw	12	92.71
VGG-Fw	15	93.02
VGG-Fw	18	**93.39**

Conclusion

In this paper, we designed a variety of multilevel features fusion methods using in the basic VGG-like model. The method obtained significant improvements VGG-like networks which are trained from the top-down. Through fusion features of intermediate layers in order to make full use multilevel features at the same time. We showed that our method extended naturally to many layers, and have no optimization problem. In our experiments, with growing number of parameters, the accuracy of is improve, there is no problem of fitting and degradation.

References

1. Zeiler, M.D., Fergus, R.: Visualizing and understanding convolutional networks. In: Fleet, D., Pajdla, T., Schiele, B., Tuytelaars, T. (eds.) ECCV 2014. LNCS, vol. 8689, pp. 818–833. Springer, Cham (2014). https://doi.org/10.1007/978-3-319-10590-1_53
2. Krizhevsky, A., Sutskever, I., Hinton, G.E.: ImageNet classification with deep convolutional neural networks. In: Advances in Neural Information Processing Systems, pp. 1097–1105 (2012)
3. He, K., Zhang, X., Ren, S., Sun, J.: Deep residual learning for image recognition. In: Proceedings of the IEEE Conference on Computer Vision and Pattern Recognition, pp. 770–778 (2016)
4. Deng, J., et al.: ImageNet: a large-scale hierarchical image database. In: Proceedings of the IEEE Conference on Computer Vision and Pattern Recognition, pp. 248–255 (2009)

5. Simonyan, K., Zisserman, A.: Very deep convolutional networks for large-scale image recognition. arXiv preprint arXiv:1409.1556 (2014)
6. Szegedy, C., Liu, W., Jia, Y., Sermanet, P., Reed, S., Anguelov, D., et al.: Going deeper with convolutions. In: Proceedings of the IEEE Conference on Computer Vision and Pattern Recognition, pp. 1–9 (2015)
7. Yosinski, J., Clune, J., Nguyen, A., Fuchs, T., Lipson, H.: Understanding neural networks through deep visualization. arXiv preprint arXiv:1506.06579 (2015)
8. Krizhevsky, A., Hinton, G.: Learning multiple layers of features from tiny images (2009)
9. Abadi, M., et al.: Tensorflow: large-scale machine learning on heterogeneous distributed systems. arXiv preprint arXiv:1603.04467 (2016)
10. Srivastava, N., Hinton, G., Krizhevsky, A., Sutskever, I., Salakhutdinov, R.: Dropout: a simple way to prevent neural networks from overfitting. J. Mach. Learn. Res. **15**, 1929–1958 (2014)
11. Ioffe, S., Szegedy, C.: Batch normalization: accelerating deep network training by reducing internal covariate shift. In: Proceedings of the International Conference on Machine Learning, pp. 448–456 (2015)
12. Nair, V., Hinton, G.E.: Rectified linear units improve restricted boltzmann machines. In: Proceedings of the International Conference on Machine Learning, pp. 807–814 (2010)
13. He, K., Zhang, X., Ren, S., Sun, J.: Delving deep into rectifiers: surpassing human-level performance on imagenet classification. In: Proceedings of the IEEE International Conference on Computer Vision, pp. 1026–1034 (2015)
14. Clevert, D.A., Unterthiner, T., Hochreiter, S.: Fast and accurate deep network learning by exponential linear units (elus). arXiv preprint arXiv:1511.07289 (2015)
15. Glorot, X., Bengio, Y.: Understanding the difficulty of training deep feedforward neural networks. In: Proceedings of the International Conference on Artificial Intelligence and Statistics, pp. 249–256 (2010)
16. Srivastava, R.K., Greff, K., Schmidhuber, J.: Highway networks. arXiv preprint arXiv:1505.00387 (2015)
17. Huang, G., Liu, Z., van der Maaten, L., Weinberger, K.Q.: Densely connected convolutional networks. In: Proceedings of the IEEE Conference on Computer Vision and Pattern Recognition, pp. 4700–4708 (2017)
18. Huang, G., Sun, Yu., Liu, Z., Sedra, D., Weinberger, Kilian Q.: Deep networks with stochastic depth. In: Leibe, B., Matas, J., Sebe, N., Welling, M. (eds.) ECCV 2016. LNCS, vol. 9908, pp. 646–661. Springer, Cham (2016). https://doi.org/10.1007/978-3-319-46493-0_39
19. He, K., Zhang, X., Ren, S., Sun, J.: Identity mappings in deep residual networks. In: Leibe, B., Matas, J., Sebe, N., Welling, M. (eds.) ECCV 2016. LNCS, vol. 9908, pp. 630–645. Springer, Cham (2016). https://doi.org/10.1007/978-3-319-46493-0_38
20. Lee, C.Y., Xie, S., Gallagher, P., Zhang, Z., Tu, Z.: Deeply-supervised nets. arXiv preprint arXiv:1409.5185 (2015)
21. LeCun, Y., Bottou, L., Bengio, Y., Haffner, P.: Gradient-based learning applied to document recognition. Proc. IEEE **86**(11), 2278–2323 (1998)
22. Goodfellow, I.J., Warde-Farley, D., Mirza, M., Courville, A., Bengio, Y.: Maxout networks. arXiv preprint arXiv:1302.4389 (2013)
23. Lin, M., Chen, Q., Yan, S.: Network in network. arXiv preprint arXiv:1312.4400 (2013)
24. Larsson, G., Maire, M., Shakhnarovich, G.: Fractalnet: ultra-deep neural networks without residuals. arXiv preprint arXiv:1605.07648 (2016)
25. Romero, A., et al.: Hints for thin deep nets. arXiv preprint arXiv:1412.6550 (2014)

Personality Trait Prediction Based on 2.5D Face Feature Model

Jia Xu[1,2], Weijian Tian[1(✉)], Yangyu Fan[1], Yuxuan Lin[2],
and Chengcheng Zhang[2]

[1] School of Electronics and Information, Northwestern Polytechnical University,
Xi'an, Shaanxi, China
Xujiajia_2008@163.com, tianweijian@sina.com
[2] North China University of Science and Technology, Tangshan, Hebei, China

Abstract. The assessment of individual personality traits plays a crucial role in important social events such as interpersonal relationships, job search, crime fighters, and disease treatment. In this paper, a multi-view (frontal and profile view, 2.5D) facial feature extraction model is proposed to evaluate the possible correlation between personality traits and face images. Our main contribution and innovation are threefold: Our primary contribution is the development of a 2.5D hybrid personality computational model in order to gain a more comprehensive understanding of one's personality traits; the second is that we have established two datasets. Datasets of people over 35 years of age are compared with those of 16–35-year-olds. We focus on the relationship between personality traits in human face and age; Finally, on a dataset of 500 facial images preprocessed from our face database and an personality score dataset collected from human testers, we evaluate the model through the application of support vector regression (SVR). Result shows that the prediction performance of the 2.5D feature model is better than that of the 2D model. We show that the 2.5D model performs well with low statistic error (MSE = 0.4991) and good predictability (R^2 = 0.5638).

Keywords: Face recognition · Personality prediction · 2.5D
Geometric features

1 Introduction

Since the time of the four ancient civilizations, people have tried to establish the relationship between facial morphological characteristics and individual personality traits [1]. This is called physiognomonica. Not only the East, but people of all eras in both East and West have discussed this field and their attitudes have been mixed. The physiognomonica chapter in Aristotle's Complete Works suggests that face can reflect certain personality traits [2]. At present, psychological research shows that faces play a central role in people's daily assessment of others. Humans more or less intuitively judge human character traits from their facial features, which play a crucial role in interpersonal relationships, job search, crime fighters, and disease treatment. Todorov, Roberts, Blair [3–5], et al.'s studies have shown that in terms of criminal tracking,

© Springer Nature Switzerland AG 2018
X. Sun et al. (Eds.): ICCCS 2018, LNCS 11068, pp. 611–623, 2018.
https://doi.org/10.1007/978-3-030-00021-9_54

election campaigns, and medical care, certain dimensions of personality traits can be reliably inferred from faces.

So far, there have been many researches on the realization of personality trait prediction based on face using machine learning. Among them, Rojas et al. [6, 7] constructed an automatic facial feature predictor based on facial structure and appearance descriptors. Wolhechel et al. [8] studied the relationship between the personality traits revealed by the questionnaire and the first impression of people. They used the Cubics assessment scale to measure participants' personality traits. The results show that some personality traits in the 17 dimensions can be predicted from the faces to some extent. In general, almost all of the current research in personality trait prediction is designed for 2D faces, especially for 2D frontal view of faces [9]. However, simply relying on 2D frontal images will lose much valuable information relevant to personality. At the same time, facial features were extracted manually to match facial traits with personality traits. The results did not form a guiding significance in personality prediction.

Our main contribution and innovation are threefold: Our primary contribution is the development of a 2.5D hybrid personality computational model in order to gain a more comprehensive understanding of one's personality traits; the second is that we have established two datasets. Datasets of people over 35 years of age are compared with those of 16–35-year-olds. We focus on the relationship between personality traits in

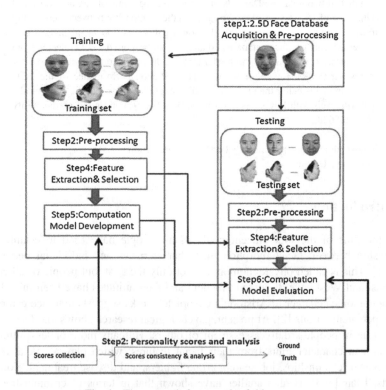

Fig. 1. The research framework of this paper.

uman face and age; finally, on a dataset of 500 facial images pre-processed from our ace database and a personality score dataset collected from human testers, we evaluate he model through the application of support vector regression (SVR).

Our experimental results show that: 1. Some personality traits can be reliably redicted from face images. 2. Prediction performance of 2.5D hybrid model is better han 2D. 3. The relationship between face and personality of people over 35 is more losely compared to people aged 16–35. The overview of the general framework of this aper is given in Fig. 1.

2 Establishment of Datasets

Ve constructed two datasets to investigate the correlation between personality traits ind face images. It contains stereoscopic facial photos and personality measurement esults data.

2.1 The Establishment of Face Dataset

)ur dataset was designed for East Asian races and is different from existing works [9] or Caucasian races. Dataset I contains facial images of 500 (250 men and 250 women) i5–60 year olds. Dataset II contains facial images of 500 (250 men and 250 women) .6–35 year olds. Participants provided photos of the front and side of the neutral xpression. The partial data set one and two pictures are shown in Fig. 2.

Fig. 2. Partial face dataset used in the experiment.

2.2   Personality Dataset

We used the theory of the Big Five Personality [10], known as the ocean of personality. This theory was proposed after the researchers reached a consensus on the personality description model. The five major factors of Big Five include: Conscientiousness, Agreeableness, openness, Neuroticism, and Extraversion. The five dimensions are like five rulers, and each person's character will fall on a certain point of the ruler. This point is close to a certain endpoint, which means that individuals have certain preferences. The score value of each dimension is set to 0–60 points. For example, in the dimension of Agreeableness, the higher the individual score the more Agreeable the personality is and the more pleasant [11, 12].

In the specific measurement content, the Chinese simplified version of the Big Five Personality Test Scale was selected from Costa and McCrea's improved NEO-PI-R with a total of 60 items. The scale used in this article contains 60 questions in five dimensions: personal information and Conscientiousness, Agreeableness, openness, Neuroticism, and Extraversion. The reliability of the scale used in this article was tested using the Cronbach$^\alpha$ coefficient. The five dimensions of the scale used are basically above the 0.65–0.80 level, and the effectiveness of the scale can be verified.

This article uses SPSS analysis tools for descriptive statistical analysis of relevant data. The data analyzed by SPSS20.0 can clearly see the scores of each subject in five dimensions (Table 1 describe the big five personality traits of the testee.), and analyze the personality characteristics of each subject according to the score. A comparison table of Big Five personality traits for the three testers is shown in Fig. 3.

Table 1. Big five personality traits description table

Low neuroticism Calm, dull, safe, guiltless	Rational <20.4 points	Stability	Sensitive >38.8 points	High neuroticism Excited, alert, reactive
Low extraversion	Introversion	Neutral	Neutral	**Highly extroverted**
Conservative, independent, incommensurable	<26 points		>42 points	Enthusiastic, sociable, enthusiastic
Low openness	Conservative	Moderate	Open	**High openness**
Introverted, conservative, professional	<32 points		>47 points	Hobbies, pursuit of new ideas, freedom, passion
Low agreeableness	Aggressive	Mediation	Accommodated	**Highly pleasant**
Attacking, unfriendly, distrustful, skeptical	<32 points		>47 points	Cooperative, inclusive and modest
Low conscientiousness	Not concentrated	Balanced	Concentrated	**High conscientiousness**
Spontaneous, divergent, unorganized	<32 points		>47 points	Organized, planned, and cautious

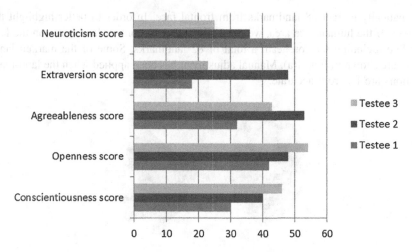

Fig. 3. Comparative analysis of big five personality traits.

.3   Moral Statement

'articipants are required to verbally agree to participate in the study, and all data is ollected after obtaining the consent. The data agreed to be measured was used for this tudy. In addition, we have numbered each participant and the data of the personality valuation report will be conducted anonymously in the form of numbers.

•   Improved 2.5D Face Feature Model

▲ 2D frontal view was used to establish the relationship between face and personality aits proposed by scholars such as Professor Hu [13] team at the State Key Laboratory or Pattern Recognition at the Institute of Automation at the Chinese Academy of ciences, and Qin [14] in China University of Science and Technology. However, imply relying on 2D frontal images will lose much valuable information relevant to ersonality.

Geometric features are the most commonly used features in Personality prediction esearch. The fundamental step in measuring facial geometry depends on the accurate ocalization of landmarks on the prominent facial regions like face contour, eyebrows, yes, nose, mouth and chin [15]. In fact, the frontal and profile view of faces are aturally complementary. Therefore, a multi-view (frontal and profile view, 2.5D) of aces is expected to provide a more comprehensive description. We use the term 2.5D" in the rest of the paper to refer to the combination of frontal and profile view.

.1   Front View Feature Extraction

▲ccurate localization of prominent facial landmarks is a fundamental step in measuring acial geometry. In this work, landmarks are chosen according to our previous work. he Asmlibrary implementation, based on active shape model (ASM) [16], is used to automatically extract 68 landmarks from frontal face. In order to better highlight the features of the human face area, we manually added 14 contour landmarks on the face half line including the forehead, a total of 82 landmarks. Some of the marked landmarks are shown in Fig. 4(a). Manual adjustment has been applied when the land-mark locations are far from accurate.

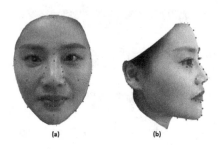

Fig. 4. Facial landmarks used in this paper. (a) 82 frontal landmarks; (b) 40 profile landmarks

For the selection of features, we chose as much data as possible for training. Due to the different size of each picture and the distance of the shooting distance, using the distance as a feature is not representative. Therefore, we calculate the ratio of feature pixels to face pixels and the aspect ratio of features as feature values. This gives 22 2D facial features. The meanings and symbols of the 22 facial features are shown in Table 2.

Table 2. The description and symbols of the 22 facial features

Feature symbol	Description	Feature symbol	Description
Rf	face length-width ratio	Rfn	distance from the forehead to the tip of the nose accounts for the length of the face
Rvl	left eyebrow length-width ratio	Rfm	ratio of the distance from the center of the forehead to the mouth to the length of the face
Rvr	right eyebrow length-width ratio	Rvel	ratio of the distance between the left eyebrow and the eye to the length of the face
Rvf	ratio of the distance between the eyebrows to the width of the face	Rver	ratio of the distance between the right eyebrow and the eye to the length of the face
Rel	left eye length-width ratio	Rvln	ratio of the distance between the left eyebrow to the nose to the length of the entire face
Rer	right eye length-width ratio	Rvrn	ratio of the distance between the right eyebrow to the nose to the length of the entire face
Ref	ratio of the distance between the pupils to the width of the face	Reln	ratio of the distance from the pupil of the left eye to the nose to the entire face
Rn	node length-width ratio	Rern	ratio of the distance from the pupil of the right eye to the nose to the entire face

(continued)

Table 2. (*continued*)

Feature symbol	Description	Feature symbol	Description
Rnhf	Ratio of nose to face length	Rnm	ratio of the distance between the nose and mouth to the entire face
Rm	mouse length-width ratio	Rnf	ratio of the distance between the nose and chin to the entire face
Rfv	ratio of the forehead to the length of the face	Rmf	ratio of the distance between mouth and chin to the entire face

3.2 Profile View Feature Extraction

For the profile view, we want to highlight the multi-dimensional features highlighted by the profile view. For the profile view, the points are mainly located on the face contour line, the jaw line, and the nose wing with a total of 40 feature points. Some marked feature points are shown in Fig. 4(b). Angles have been used to capture the symmetry and shape information in the frontal face, as well as profile contour and shape quality of individual facial regions in the profile face.

Use angles to capture certain stereoscopic information of a human face which cannot be represented on the frontal face, thereby improving the quality of describing facial features. We extracted three typical angles as feature values. They are: the angle between the forehead and brow line and the vertical line of the face ($\partial 1$), the angle between the wing connection ($\partial 2$) and the angle between the chin lines ($\partial 3$), as shown in Fig. 5.

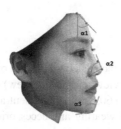

Fig. 5. Examples of angles on profile face.

In this way we have established the definition of the 25 features of the sample. 22 features come from frontal view and 3 angle features come from profile view. The 25 feature values calculated from the three test samples are shown in Tables 3, 4 and 5.

Table 3. Selected facial features

No	Rf	Rvl	Rvr	Rvf	Rel	Rer	Ref	Rn	Rnhf
1	0.736	0.200	0.200	0.183	0.455	0.455	0.275	0.952	0.092
2	0.738	0.186	0.186	0.274	0.340	0.336	0.317	0.855	0.117
3	0.751	0.128	0.129	0.260	0.444	0.444	0.315	0.826	0.101

Table 4. Selected facial features

No	Rm	Rfv	Rfn	Rfm	Rvel	Rver	Rvln	Rvrn	Rnm
1	0.393	0.399	0.313	0.558	0.779	0.780	0.286	0.233	0.245
2	0.362	0.362	0.298	0.528	0.755	0.755	0.227	0.227	0.170
3	0.385	0.385	0.302	0.538	0.769	0.770	0.2483	0.249	0.237

Table 5. Selected facial features

No	Reln	Rern	Rnf	Rmf	$\alpha 1$	$\alpha 2$	$\alpha 3$
1	0.675	0.687	0.166	0.160	0.333	0.911	0.672
2	0.699	0.706	0.167	0.167	0.344	0.675	0.578
3	0.710	0.698	0.154	0.154	0.245	0.789	0.594

4 Evaluation of Personality Prediction Effectiveness Based on SVR Regression Model

Many machine learning-based and statistical-based methods have been adapted to map the representative features of a face to personality evaluation. In this paper, the personality prediction is formulated into a standard regression problem in order to evaluate the effectiveness of the extracted features. After preliminary experimentation with several regression algorithms, and wide spread and success of SVR in many different applications, it is found that epsilon-SVR (ϵ-SVR) with a radial basis function (RBF) kernel performs the best.

4.1 Testing Dataset

In this paper, we established two face database used as our experimental database. Both contain 3D face models (frontal view and profile view) of 250 Chinese males and 250 Chinese females, aged from 16 to 60, with almost neutral expression. The faces are in a frontal upright position, without wearing any accessories and cosmetic products. The hair above the forehead and ears has been almost removed. We are divided into two groups according to age one: group is 16–35 years old, the other group is 35–60 years old, based on this, we analyze the relationship between facial features and personality of people of different ages. Figure 6 shows some example images from our dataset.

For the purpose of facial attractiveness prediction, our dataset is partitioned into a training dataset and a testing dataset. The training set contains the frontal and profile images of 400 randomly selected subjects. The testing set includes frontal and profile images of the remaining 100 subjects. Both sets have equal number of males and females. In our implementation (see Fig. 1), steps of geometric feature selection and computational model development are performed on training set only. The trained computational model is then evaluated on the non-overlapped testing data [17].

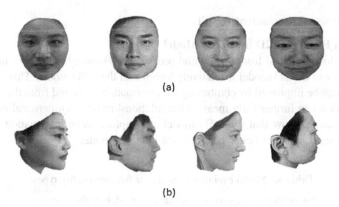

(a)

(b)

Fig. 6. Sample images from our dataset in the (a) frontal view; (b) right-side view.

4.2   Prediction Model Evaluation

The Libsvm implementation [18] is employed to develop a $\epsilon-$SV model for personality prediction, we manually set $\epsilon = 0.001$ and a RBF kernel. The SVR model is trained on 400 frontal and profile training images respectively under the conduct of five-fold cross validation. As mentioned in Sect. 3, the inputs of SVR model are the extracted principal components of 25 geometric features. We compare the 22 features of the front image with the 25 features of the frontal side as inputs. The ground truth labels of SVR model are Scores from five different personality dimensions for each image. The coarse-to-fine grid search is adopted to find the optimal penalty parameter C in cost function and optimal parameter γ in RBF kernel function (see details in [19]). The model performance is evaluated on the non-overlapped 90 frontal and profile testing images by two metrics, i.e., mean square error (MSE) and coefficient of determination (R^2). We have:

$$\text{MSE} = \frac{1}{100} \sum_{i=1}^{100} (\hat{y}_i - l_i)^2 \tag{1}$$

$$R^2 = 1 - \frac{\sum_{i=1}^{100} (\hat{y}_i - l_i)^2}{\sum_{i=1}^{100} (l_i - \bar{l})^2} \tag{2}$$

Where l_i and $\hat{y}_i$ are the ground-truth score and the SVR predicted score for ith testing face respectively, and l is the average score over all testing faces. The smaller MSE and the higher R^2 indicate better prediction. A MSE of 0 and an R^2 of 1 indicate the perfect prediction.

4.3   Analysis of Assessment Results

Evaluation Results of 2D and 2.5D Model
The evaluation results of frontal (2D) and profile (2.5D) model are shown in Table 6. The accuracy of the 2D model is relatively lower than the 2.5D model. This shows that the results can be improved by combining the information extracted from the two views (2.5D). In order to further fully measure the relationship between personality and face view. Our results show that the 2.5D model can capture some information related to personality traits, and get better performance than 2D model.

Table 6. Model evaluation results for five personality types.

Personality dimension	Computational model	MSE	R^2
Conscientiousness	Frontal	0.5317	0.5389
	2.5D Hybrid	0.4972	0.5748
Neuroticism	Frontal	0.5324	0.5213
	2.5D Hybrid	0.4867	0.5674
Extraversion	Frontal	0.5547	0.5234
	2.5D Hybrid	0.5374	0.5456
Openness	Frontal	0.5211	0.5498
	2.5D Hybrid	0.4672	0.5878
Agreeableness	Frontal	0.5517	0.5114
	2.5D Hybrid	0.5072	0.5435
Average value	Frontal	0.5383	0.5290
	2.5D Hybrid	0.4991	0.5638

Figure 7 shows a comparative analysis of the two models' predictive personality and actual scores (take the "Conscientiousness" dimension as an example). Strong linear tendency shows up in the two sub-figures, where in Fig. 7(b) points associate more tightly. This indicates again that our extracted features have good correlation with the personality traits. Similar results were also obtained in the other four dimensions (Neuroticism, Extraversion, Openness and Agreeableness).

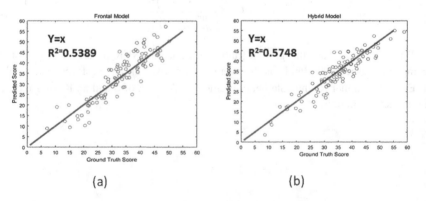

(a)   (b)

Fig. 7. Conscientiousness Score prediction results for (a) frontal model; (b) 2.5D hybrid model.

valuation Results for Different Age Group Dataset

wo groups of different age datasets were evaluated and the results are shown in able 7. Here we use the 2.5D model for evaluation. We found that the assessment ccuracy of 16–35 age group on "Conscientiousness", "Agreeableness", "Extraversion", and "Neuroticism" is slightly lower than that of 35–60 age group. Only in the openness" dimension, the 16–35 age group is slightly higher than the 35–60 age roup. This also further explains the saying that "State outside is based on mind aside", with the growth of age and the maturity of the mind, people's faces tend to be table and their personality is gradually stable.

Table 7. Two different age groups evaluation results for five personality types.

Personality dimension	Computational model	MSE	R^2
Conscientiousness	Age of 16–35	0.5227	0.5312
	Age of 35–60	0.5122	0.5548
Neuroticism	Age of 16–35	0.5314	0.5233
	Age of 35–60	0.5142	0.5574
Extraversion	Age of 16–35	0.5497	0.5214
	Age of 35–60	0.5334	0.5436
Openness	Age of 16–35	0.5011	0.5398
	Age of 35–60	0.5272	0.5178
Agreeableness	Age of 16–35	0.5217	0.5134
	Age of 35–60	0.4872	0.5335
Average value	Age of 16–35	0.5253	0.5294
	Age of 35–60	0.5148	0.5414

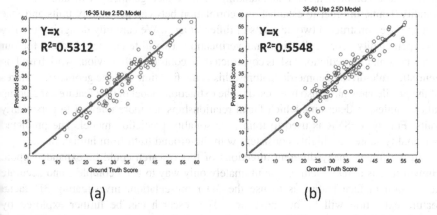

(a)   (b)

ig. 8. Conscientiousness Score prediction results for (a) 16–35 age group; (b) 35–60 age roup.

Figure 8 shows the comparison of the predicted and actual scores of the 2.5D model on two different age datasets. Strong linear tendency shows up in the two subfigures, where in Fig. 6(b) points associate more tightly. This shows that the personality's traits of people over the age of 35 are more closely related to the human face.

Evaluation Results of Different Personality Dimensions

Table 8 lists the results of different five-dimension assessments, we have found that the relationship between different personality traits and people's faces is not the same, and the relationship between Conscientiousness and face is even closer.

Table 8. Personality prediction accuracy and error rate

Personality type	Correctly number of samples	Correct rate	Error number of samples	Error rate
Conscientiousness	84	84%	16	16%
Neuroticism	82	82%	18	18%
Extraversion	83	83%	17	17%
Openness	76	76%	24	24%
Agreeableness	78	78%	22	21%
Average	403	80.6%	97	19.4%

However, in general, the regression model we use has a good effect on the prediction results of Big Five traits on the premise of providing 2.5D face features.

5   Conclusions

The purpose of this paper is to develop a 2.5D hybrid facial feature extraction model to gain a more comprehensive understanding of how face geometry will affect its personality Traits. In order to establish the correlation between personality traits and face and age, we constructed two data sets of different ages. We carefully designing the Big Five personality score collection and verification, two different age datasets for our facial personality prediction task is constructed. In contrast with previous work based on heuristics rule-driven geometric features, this is the first time that the geometric features of the profile view have also been used in the extraction model of face features, including ratios, angles, to determine which facial relationships are more relevant to personality traits. Finally, ϵ-SVR is used to train a personality prediction model. The predicted personality scores are highly consistent with the ground truth from human raters.

In the future, many different directions of this research could be expanded upon. Human face is a 3D structure. The ultimately only way to get a complete and accurate description of face feature is to use the 3D representation. Investigating 3D facial feature extraction will be our next step. The research can be further explored by analyzing the differences of judging criteria in terms of different gender, ethnicity, and age groups of human raters.

Acknowledgment. This work is supported in part by the National Natural Science Foundation of China under Grant 61402371, Science and Technology Innovation Engineering Plan in Shaanxi Province of China under Grant 2013SZS15-K02, Natural Science Basic Research Plan in Shaanxi Province of China under Grant 2015JM6317.

References

1. McNeill, D.: The Face: A Natural History. Back Bay Books, NewYork (2000)
2. Aristotle, Litian, M.: Compiled, Aristotle's Complete Works. Renmin University of China Press, Beijing (1997)
3. Ballew II, C.C., Todorov, A.: Predicting political elections from rapid and unreflective face judgments. Proc. Natl. Acad. Sci. U.S.A. **104**(46), 17948–17953 (2007)
4. Little, A.C., Burriss, R.P., Jones, B.C., Roberts, S.C.: Facial appearance affects voting decisions. Evol. Hum. Behav. **28**(1), 18–27 (2007)
5. Blair, I.V., Judd, C.M., Chapleau, K.M.: The influence of afrocentric facial features in criminal sentencing. Psychol. Sci. **15**(10), 674–679 (2004)
6. Rojas, Q.M., Masip, D., Todorov, A., Vitrià, J.: Automatic point-based facial trait judgments evaluation. In: Proceedings of IEEE Conference on Computer Vision and Pattern Recognition, San Francisco, USA, pp. 2715–2720. IEEE (2010)
7. Rojas, Q.M., Masip, D., Todorov, A., Vitria, V.: Automatic prediction of facial trait judgments: Appearance vs. structural models. PLoS ONE **6**(8), e23323 (2011)
8. Wolhechel, K., et al.: Interpretation of appearance: the effect of facial features on first impressions and personality. PLoS ONE **9**(9), e107721 (2014)
9. Laurentini, A., Bottino, A.: Computer analysis of face beauty: a survey. Comput. Vis. Image Underst. **125**, 184–199 (2014)
10. Qu, L., Wang, X.: On Personality Psychology and Big Five Personality Theory. Youth Science (2009). (10)
11. Peng, Y.: General Psychology. Beijing Normal University Press, Beijing (2012)
12. Huang, H.: Face recognition algorithm based on Haar feature. Comput. Disk Softw. Appl. (23), 88 (2013)
13. Zhang, T.: Physiognomy: personality traits prediction by learning. Int. J. Autom. Comput. **14**(4), 386–395 (2017)
14. Qin, R.: Personality Analysis Based on Face Image. Chinese Academy of Sciences University, Beijing (2016)
15. Liu, S., Fan, Y., Samal, A., Guo, Z.: Advances in computational facial attractiveness methods. Multimed. Tools Appl. **75**(23), 16633–16663 (2016)
16. Wei, Y.: Research on Facial Expression recognition and synthesis. Master Thesis, Nanjing University (2009)
17. Liu, S.: A landmark-based data-driven approach on 2.5D facial attractiveness computation. Comput. Neurocomput. **238**, 168–178 (2017)
18. Schmid, K., Marx, D., Samal, A.: Computation of face attractiveness index based on neoclassic canons, symmetry and golden ratio. Patt. Recognit. **41**(8), 2710–2717 (2008)
19. Kagian, A., Dror, G., Leyvand, T., Cohen-Or, D., Ruppin, E.: A humanlike predictor of facial attractiveness. In: Proceedings of the Advances in Neural Information Processing Systems, pp. 649–656 (2006)

Recaptured Image Detection Through Enhanced Residual-Based Correlation Coefficients

Nan Zhu[1](✉) and Zhao Li[2]

[1] Department of Electronic Information Engineering, Xi'an Technological University, Xi'an 710021, China
nanzhu.xatu@foxmail.com
[2] School of Electronic Engineering, Xidian University, Xi'an 710071, China

Abstract. With the rapid development of image display technology and digital acquisition device, recapturing the copies of images from LCD screens with high quality becomes rather convenient and easy. Such recaptured images post severe security threats in image credibility and bio-authentication. In order to alleviate such security problems, in this paper, we propose a simple yet effective method to detect the images recaptured from LCD screens based on enhanced residual-based correlation coefficients. Specifically, we first extract the blocks which contain only one edge with pre-defined criteria. Then, pixel-wise sharpness is used to enhance the discriminability of the extracted single-edge blocks. Finally, pixel-wise correlation coefficients in the residual of the enhanced single-edge blocks are adopted as features. Extensive experiments on three high-resolution and high-quality recaptured image databases demonstrate the superior of our proposed method when compared with the state-of-the-art approaches.

Keywords: Image forensics · Recaptured Image Detection
Image credibility · Bio-authentication · Correlation coefficients

1 Introduction

Image display technology has flourished over the past years, thus we can see high-quality images displayed everywhere. By photographing them with various capturing device, people can easily obtain the copies of these displayed images. This process, called image recapture, can be modeled in Fig. 1. In this figure, the left dashed box illustrates the process of generating real-scene images while the right dashed box exhibits the process of image recapture. Such recaptured images have negative influences on image credibility and bio-authentication. On one hand, recapture can be utilized to hide image tampering traces. Attacker can recapture the edited image to bypass the current image tampering detection technologies [1,2] which are based on searching specific statistical inconsistencies introduced by manual tampering. Another threat brought by recaptured images

© Springer Nature Switzerland AG 2018
X. Sun et al. (Eds.): ICCCS 2018, LNCS 11068, pp. 624–634, 2018.
https://doi.org/10.1007/978-3-030-00021-9_55

playback attack, also called spoofing. Nowadays, face recognition systems are widely used in access control, ATM, and smart phone. However, some of these systems are vulnerable to face spoofing, i.e., the attacker can easily fool these systems with a recaptured facial image of the target user. Therefore, it is very essential for a face recognition system to own the ability of distinguishing a genuine user from a recaptured facial image. Besides face authentication, similar threats exist in other biometric authentication device such as iris and fingerprint recognition systems.

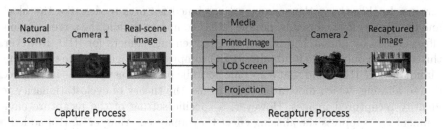

Fig. 1. The process of generating the real-scene images (left dashed box) and the recaptured images (right dashed box).

Recaptured image detection (RID) technologies aim to distinguish recaptured images from the real-scene ones. The problem of detecting recaptured images from LCD screens and printed materials received large attention in recent years and a growing number of literatures can be found in this area. Generally, the approaches for RID rely on the classifiers trained from discriminated features extracted from spatial and/or transform domain(s). According to the media projected during recapture, the existing approaches can be divided into two categories. The first category focuses on identifying the images recaptured from printed materials. As the pioneers, Yu *et al.* [3] found that the spatial distribution of specularity of images can be utilized to separate recaptured images from the authentic ones, which inspired them to use the high-frequency spatial variations in the specular component as features for RID. The same finding was also utilized in [4] to resist face spoofing. Later, a set of Markov process based features which extracted from the DCT coefficients arrays were utilized in [5] to identify recaptured images. The work in [6] utilized texture features including local binary patterns variance (LBPV) and relative-contrast to identify the images recaptured from printed materials. This method works well on low quality recaptured images.

In comparison, more approaches have been proposed for detecting the images recaptured from LCD screens as the quality of the images recaptured from LCD screens can be very high under a professional image recapture environment setting (c.f. Fig. 2). Cao *et al.* [7] designed several sets of features including texture, loss-of-detail, and color features to detect finely recaptured images. The work in [8] utilized noise features and MBFDF (mode based first digit features) [9] for RID. However, MBFDF only works for double JPEG compressed images. Thongkamwitoon *et al.* [10] used edge profiles and structured dictionary learning to detect recaptured images from LCD screens. A crucial limitation of this method is that the detection performance depends on the interest regions selected by users. The same group then solved this problem by extracting proper blocks owning a single sharp edge automatically in [11]. Furthermore, they trained two dictionaries with KSVD and used the smallest error in sparse representation as metric for RID. More recently, they further extended their work in [12] by using dictionary approximation errors combined with mean edge spread width as features to detect high-quality recaptured images from LCD screens. In [13], the authors proposed combined features to describe the block and blurriness effect caused by double JPEG compression, and the screen aliasing effect caused by unmatched frequency of screen and camera for RID. However, this approach only works for double JPEG compressed images. At the same time, Mahdian *et al.* [14] found that a specific periodic patterns usually was introduced due to aliasing, which motivated them to use the theory of cyclostationarity to identify recaptured images. However, a specific setting of the recapture environment can suppress the aliasing effect they analyzed. Yang *et al.* [15] added a Laplacian filter layer into CNN (convolutional neural networks) to strengthen the difference between real-scene images and recaptured ones. However, although the Laplician layer can represent the high-frequency information loss, a filter with fixed coefficients will ignore some other distortions in color and luminance. More recently, the pixel-wise correlation coefficients in image differential domain were adopted as features for RID [16]. However, all the over-lapping blocks are utilized to calculate the correlation coefficients, which inevitably introduces some redundant information.

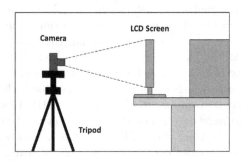

Fig. 2. Professional image recapture environment

In this paper, we address the problem of detecting the images recaptured from LCD screens. Motivated by the effectiveness of the correlation coefficients for RID [16], we propose a RID approach based on enhanced residual-based correlation coefficients. Specifically, due to the fact that the blurriness and aliasing artifacts introduced by recapture are not clear in the blurred and flat regions, only the single-edge blocks are utilized for calculating, which can eliminate the

edundant information in these regions. On the other hand, the pixel-wise sharp-
ess is used to enhance the discriminability of the single-edge blocks before cal-
ulating the correlation coefficients. Extensive experiments on three high-quality
ecaptured image databases demonstrate the superior of our proposed method
·hen compared with some representative approaches.

The remainder of this paper is organized as follows. Section 2 elaborates our
·roposed approach for RID. Experimental results and discussions are given in
·ect. 3. The last section concludes this paper by specifying some open issues to
·e solved and providing an outlook in the future.

! Proposed Method

n this section, we present the technical details of our proposed method. Figure 3
llustrates the whole framework. The following subsections will give descriptions
n detail.

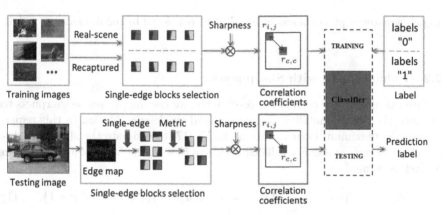

Fig. 3. The framework of our proposed approach.

!.1 Single-Edge Blocks Selection

iven an image, we first extract the single-edge blocks. Specifically, we first
onvert it into grayscale and detect the edges with Canny detector. Then, the
·locks of the input image which center at edge points with size $W \times W$ and
ontain only one single running-across (near) horizontal or vertical sharp edge
·re detected. Here, W is experimentally set as 15. In order to avoid obtaining
·oo many similar blocks, we extract the blocks at every ten edge points. Figure 4
llustrates some examples of blocks which are detected (a and b) and discarded
·c and d). Here, both blocks (a) and (b) contain only one running-across edge.
·lock (c) does not contain a running-across edge while block (d) contains two
·dges, which leads to that both (c) and (d) would be discarded. Next, only

the blocks whose contrast values fall into the top largest 20% of the calculated values of all the obtained blocks are selected. Here, the contrast of a block is measured by its variance. This step enables us to obtain the most prominent regions to reveal the blurriness and aliasing artifacts introduced by recapture. Finally, we normalize the extracted single-edge blocks into the same direction via rotation. In consequence, we can obtain a set of single-edge blocks $\mathbf{B} = \{B^{(1)}, B^{(2)}, \ldots, B^{(K)}\}$, where K is the total number of the blocks.

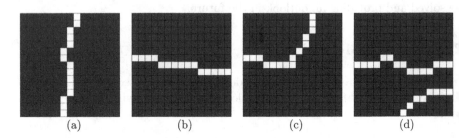

(a)   (b)   (c)   (d)

Fig. 4. Some examples of blocks which are detected (a and b) and discarded (c and d).

2.2 Enhancement with Sharpness

Before calculating the correlation coefficients, we use the pixel-wise sharpness to enhance the discriminability of the extracted single-edge blocks. In this paper, we use the maximum local variation (MLV) [17] to estimate the sharpness distribution of each block. For a block with size $U \times V$, the MLV of a pixel $I_{u,v}$ in a block is defined as

$$\phi(I_{u,v}) = \{\max |I_{u,v} - I_{s,t}|, s = u - 1, u, u + 1; t = v - 1, v, v + 1\}. \quad (1)$$

Based on the fact that the pixels with large MLV values have more influence in sharpness estimation, the sharpness values can be corrected by assigning different weights to the MLV values as

$$\Phi(I) = \begin{pmatrix} w_{1,1}\phi(I_{1,1}) & \cdots & w_{1,V}\phi(I_{1,V}) \\ \vdots & \ddots & \vdots \\ w_{U,1}\phi(I_{U,1}) & \cdots & w_{U,V}\phi(I_{U,V}) \end{pmatrix}, \quad (2)$$

where $w_{u,v} = e^{\eta_{u,v}}$ and $\eta_{u,v}$ stands for the ranking order of $\phi(I_{u,v})$ in an ascending sequence. Then, the enhanced single-edge blocks $E^{(k)}$ can be calculated as

$$E^{(k)} = B^{(k)}. * \Phi^{(k)}, \quad (3)$$

where k is the index of a block and '.*' means pixel-wise multiplication. As a result, we can obtain a set of enhanced single-edge blocks $\mathbf{E} = \{E^{(1)}, E^{(2)}, \ldots, E^{(K)}\}$.

.3   Feature Selection

or each enhanced single-edge block $E^{(k)}$, the residual $R^{(k)}$ of this block can be alculated as

$$R^{(k)} = trim(E^{(k)} - E^{(k)} * \mathbf{f}). \tag{4}$$

Here, '$*$' means convolution and the function $trim(\cdot)$ removes the first and the ist rows and columns. As we have normalized the enhance single-edge blocks ito the same direction, only a horizontal convolution kernel $\mathbf{f}$ is used, which efined as

$$\mathbf{f} = [0\ 0\ 0;\ 0.5\ 0\ 0.5;\ 0\ 0\ 0]. \tag{5}$$

We concatenate the residual blocks along the third dimension and denote iem as $\{R^{(1)}, R^{(2)}, \ldots, R^{(K)}\}$. The elements in each block are denoted as $r_{i,j}^{(k)}$ ith $i, j \in \{1, 2, \ldots, 13\}$ and $k \in \{1, 2, \ldots, K\}$. Then, the correlation coefficient $r_{i,j}$ between each index $\{i, j\}$ to the central index $\{c, c\}$ can be defined as

$$C_{i,j} = \frac{\sum_{k=1}^{K} \left(r_{c,c}^{(k)} - \overline{r_{c,c}}\right)\left(r_{i,j}^{(k)} - \overline{r_{i,j}}\right)}{\sqrt{\sum_{k=1}^{K}\left(r_{c,c}^{(k)} - \overline{r_{c,c}}\right)^2}\sqrt{\sum_{k=1}^{K}\left(r_{i,j}^{(k)} - \overline{r_{i,j}}\right)^2}}, \tag{6}$$

'here $\overline{r_{i,j}}$ is the mean value of the elements $\{r_{i,j}^{(1)}, r_{i,j}^{(2)}, \ldots, r_{i,j}^{(K)}\}$. In consequence, 'e can obtain a 13×13 feature matrix. We only retain the correlation coefficients i the upper triangle of the matrix due to symmetry. Besides, we remove the :ntral element from the feature matrix as it is always equal to 1. Finally, we an obtain a 90-D feature for an image.

Experiments

1 this section, we present the experimental results of our proposed approach n three public recaptured image databases in comparison with a dictionary-:arning-based method [12] and an image-statistics-based method [16] along with ome useful discussions.

.1   Databases

'o evaluate the effectiveness of our proposed approach and compare the perfor-1ance with other algorithms, we conduct a set of experiments on the following hree public databases.

- **NTU-ROSE Database:**[1] The database constructed in [7] contains 2776 recaptured images and 2712 real-scene images acquired by high-resolution

---

http://rose1.ntu.edu.sg/Datasets/recaptureImages.asp.

DSLR (digital single lens reflex) cameras. The resolutions of both the real-scene images and the corresponding recaptured versions range from 2048 × 1536 to 3264 × 2448 pixels with JPEG format. Figure 5 shows some examples in this database. Slight colour distortion and misalignment are introduced during recapture process. Specifically, this database contains some recaptured tampered images which are visually very convincing (seeing the last two columns for example).

– **BJTU-IIS Database:**[2] The database constructed in [13] contains 706 recaptured images and 636 real-scene images acquired with high-resolution DSLR cameras. The resolutions of both the real-scene images and the corresponding recaptured versions range from 3456 × 2304 to 6016 × 4016 pixels with JPEG format. Figure 6 shows some examples in this database. Some images in this database have black and/or white box(es) caused by misalignment (seeing the first two columns for example). Furthermore, slight aliasing artifacts can be found in some recaptured images from this database.

– **ICL-COMMSP Database:**[3] The database constructed in [12] contains 1035 real-scene images and 2520 recaptured images captured by high-resolution DSLR cameras. However, only 900 real-scene images and 1440 recaptured images are freely available. The resolutions of the recaptured images range from 1778 × 1326 to 2286 × 1522 pixels with PNG format, while the resolutions of real-scene images range from 2576 × 1932 to 5472 × 3684 pixels with JPEG format. Figure 7 shows some examples in this database. The images in this database have perfect alignment but slight colour distortions are introduced during recapture process. Furthermore, the aliasing artifact in this database is the weakest among these three databases.

Fig. 5. Example images from NTU-ROSE database. The first row illustrates some real-scene images and the second row presents the corresponding recaptured versions.

---

[2] http://iis.bjtu.edu.cn/download/database_IWDW2015.rar.
[3] http://www.commsp.ee.ic.ac.uk/~pld/research/Rewind/Recapture/.

Fig. 6. Example images from BJTU-IIS database. The first row illustrates some real-scene images and the second row presents the corresponding recaptured versions.

Fig. 7. Example images from ICL-COMMSP database. The first row illustrates some real-scene images and the second row presents the corresponding recaptured versions.

2 Experimental Setting

For each database mentioned above, 20% of the real-scene and recaptured images are used for training while the rest images are used for testing. Unlike the work in [12,16] rescaled all the images into a fixed width of 2048 pixels and [12] used further selection of the training set, in this paper, to be as fair as possible, we randomly select images for training without any additional operation. The SVM (support vector machine) with RBF (radial basis function) kernel is utilized as classifier. The SVM hyper-parameters are determined by using 5-fold cross validation on the training set. The performance is evaluated with the accuracy of recaptured images, real-scene images, and the overall images. We use the mean results obtained from 50 runs as the final accuracy.

3 Results and Discussions

Tables 1, 2 and 3 present the comparison results on NTU-ROSE, BJTU-IIS, and ICL-COMMSP databases, respectively. From these tables we can see that our proposed method outperforms the others on a whole. Specifically, all the methods perform at the same level on NTU-ROSE and BJTU-IIS databases as the recaptured images from these two databases have comparable quality. On average, our proposed method improve the detection accuracy in about 1.01%, 2.13%, and 1.55% for recaptured, real-scene, and the whole images respectively on these two databases, which verifies the good discriminability of our proposed statistical feature. In comparison, the recaptured images from ICL-COMMSP database are a little more difficult to detect by our method and [16] due to the very high image quality. However, when compared with [12] on this database, although our method has a lower accuracy on recaptured images, a higher accuracy can be obtained from real-scene images, which still leads to a slightly higher overall accuracy than this method. It can be contributed to that [12] makes strong prior knowledge of blurriness effect in the edge regions of the recaptured images. A few parameters are empirically fixed in particular for the edge extraction, which could lead to performance loss on some practical cases.

Table 1. Detection results on NTU-ROSE database.

Method	Acc. recaptured	Acc. real-scene	Acc. overall
Thongkamwitoon *et al.* [12]	0.9257	0.9078	0.9169
Wang [16]	0.9325	0.9073	0.9200
Proposed	0.9417	0.9284	0.9351

Table 2. Detection results on BJTU-IIS database.

Method	Acc. recaptured	Acc. real-scene	Acc. overall
Thongkamwitoon *et al.* [12]	0.9226	0.9047	0.9141
Wang [16]	0.9235	0.9114	0.9178
Proposed	0.9344	0.9328	0.9336

Table 3. Detection results on ICL-COMMSP database.

Method	Acc. recaptured	Acc. real-scene	Acc. overall
Thongkamwitoon *et al.* [12]	0.9389	0.8959	0.9224
Wang [16]	0.9123	0.9046	0.9093
Proposed	0.9227	0.9236	0.9230

Conclusion

ı this paper, a simple yet effective method to detect the images recaptured from CD screens based on enhanced residual-based correlation coefficients is proosed. Extensive experimental results on three high-resolution and high-quality atabases demonstrate that the proposed method is capable of dealing with nage recapture detection task. However, we believe that our method has a reat room for improvement. To further improve the performance, the resoluon of image would be considered first. In our proposed approach, the block size set to a fixed value. However, in a very high-resolution image, neighboring ixels tend to have high similarity, which inevitably decreases the effectiveness f the residual-based correlation coefficients. In order to alleviate this problem, self-adaption rescaling algorithm can be utilized before extracting features ɔ better describe the statistical difference between recaptured and real-scene nages. Secondly, we will attempt to optimize the coefficients in the filter kernel ɔr better performance. Finally, the color and luminance distortions introduced y recapture should be studied.

References

1. Birajdar, G.K., Mankar, V.H.: Digital image forgery detection using passive techniques: a survey. Digit. Invest. **10**, 226–245 (2013)
2. Korus, P.: Digital image integrity - a survey of protection and verification techniques. Digit. Signal Process. **71**, 1–26 (2017)
3. Yu, H., Ng, T.-T., Sun, Q.: Recaptured photo detection using specularity distribution. In: IEEE International Conference on Image Processing, pp. 3140–3143 (2008)
4. Bai, J., Ng, T.-T., Gao, X., Shi, Y.-Q.: Is physics-based liveness detection truly possible with a single image? In: IEEE International Symposium on Circuits and Systems, pp. 3425–3428 (2010)
5. Yin, J., Fang, Y.: Markov-based image forensics for photographic copying from printed picture. In: ACM International Conference on Multimedia, pp. 1113–1116 (2012)
6. Zhai, X., Ni, R., Zhao, Y.: Recaptured image detection based on texture features. In: International Conference on Intelligent Information Hiding and Multimedia Signal Processing, pp. 234–237 (2013)
7. Cao, H., Kot, A.C.: Identification of recaptured photographs on LCD screens. In: IEEE International Conference on Acoustics, Speech and Signal Processing, pp. 1790–1793 (2010)
8. Yin, J., Fang, Y.: Digital image forensics for photographic copying. In: Proceedings of the SPIE 8303, Media Watermarking, Security, and Forensics 2012, pp. 83030F-1–83030F-7 (2012)
9. Li, B., Shi, Y.-Q., Huang, J.: Detecting doubly compressed JPEG images by using mode based first digit features. In: IEEE International Workshop on Multimedia Signal Processing, pp. 730–735 (2008)
0. Thongkamwitoon, T., Muammar, H., Dragotti, P.L.: Identification of image acquisition chains using a dictionary of edge profiles. In: European Signal Processing Conference, pp. 1757–1761 (2012)

11. Thongkamwitoon, T., Muammar, H., Dragotti, P.L.: Robust image recapture detection using a K-SVD learning approach to train dictionaries of edge profiles. In: IEEE International Conference on Image Processing, pp. 5317–5321 (2014)
12. Thongkamwitoon, T., Muammar, H., Dragotti, P.L.: An image recapture detection algorithm based on learning dictionaries of edge profiles. IEEE Trans. Inf. Forensics Secur. **10**(5), 953–968 (2015)
13. Li, R., Ni, R., Zhao, Y.: An effective detection method based on physical traits of recaptured images on LCD screens. In: Shi, Y.-Q., Kim, H.J., Pérez-González, F., Echizen, I. (eds.) IWDW 2015. LNCS, vol. 9569, pp. 107–116. Springer, Cham (2016). https://doi.org/10.1007/978-3-319-31960-5_10
14. Mahdian, B., Novozámský, A., Saic, S.: Identification of aliasing-based patterns in re-captured LCD screens. In: IEEE International Conference on Image Processing, pp. 616–620 (2015)
15. Yang, P., Ni, R., Zhao, Y.: Recapture image forensics based on laplacian convolutional neural networks. In: Shi, Y.Q., Kim, H.J., Perez-Gonzalez, F., Liu, F. (eds.) IWDW 2016. LNCS, vol. 10082, pp. 119–128. Springer, Cham (2017). https://doi.org/10.1007/978-3-319-53465-7_9
16. Wang, K.: A simple and effective image-statistics-based approach to detecting recaptured images from LCD screens. Digit. Invest. **23**, 75–87 (2017)
17. Bahrami, K., Kot, A.C.: A fast approach for no-reference image sharpness assessment based on maximum local variation. IEEE Signal Process. Lett. **21**(6), 751–755 (2014)

Reducing the Computational Complexity of the Reference-Sharing Based Self-embedding Watermarking Approach

Dongmei Niu[1,2], Hongxia Wang[1(✉)], and Minquan Cheng[3]

[1] Southwest Jiaotong University, Chengdu 610031, China
hxwang@home.swjtu.edu.cn
[2] Southwest University of Science and Technology, Mianyang 621010, China
[3] Guangxi Normal University, Guilin 541004, China

Abstract. Reference-sharing based self-embedding watermarking schemes had been shown to be an effective way to avoid the tampering coincidence and the reference waste problems. Typical reference-sharing based schemes adopt pseudo-random binary matrices as the encoding matrices to generate the reference information. This paper investigate to reduce the computational complexity of the reference-sharing based self-embedding watermarking approach by using the sparse binary matrices as the encoding matrices. Experimental results demonstrate the proposed approach can reduce the computational complexity significantly while maintaining the same tampering restoration capability as the traditional.

Keywords: Self-embedding watermarking · Computational complexity
Tamper detection and recovery · Sparse matrices

Introduction

Self-embedding watermarking scheme has the functions of detecting the tampered image regions and recovering the tampered image information. There are usually two watermarks to be embedded in the original image. They are the authentication watermark and the recovery watermark. The recovery watermark is always the compression of the original image block. In some schemes, for example in [1–6], according to the block-mapping the recovery watermark of an image block is embedded into another different image block. In this case, if both the image block and the image block that store its recovery watermark are tampered, the recovery will fail. This phenomenon is called tampering coincidence [7]. To alleviate this problem, one easy method is to copy the recovery watermark and embed them all in the original image [8, 9]. In this way, the probability of the tampering coincidence will be greatly reduced. But the effectiveness of watermark payload is reduced at the same time.

To settle the tampering coincidence problem, the more effective way is to design the reference-sharing based self-embedding schemes. The reference-sharing mechanism has been explained in detail in [10]. In the scheme, the 5 MSB of all the pixels are permuted and divided into subsets. The subsets are encoded in sequence to generate the

© Springer Nature Switzerland AG 2018
X. Sun et al. (Eds.): ICCCS 2018, LNCS 11068, pp. 635–643, 2018.
https://doi.org/10.1007/978-3-030-00021-9_56

reference information. The reference information is the recovery watermark. The reference information will be permuted and divided into subsets, which will be embedded in an image block with the authentication information. Permutation and encoding make each bit of the reference information shared by multiple image blocks as recovery information. In this way, the problem of tampering coincidence can be alleviated effectively. To recover MSBs of the tampered image blocks, lots of systems of linear equations whose coefficient matrix is the sub-matrix of the pseudo-random binary matrix are needed to be solved. This thought of reference sharing is also reflected in many other schemes [7, 11–17]. In [15], the overlapping block-wise mechanism for tampering localization and the pixel-wise mechanism for content recovery are combined. Reference bits are derived from the mean value of each overlapping block through the information interleaving. The scheme can achieve better quality of recovered image. In [16], reference sharing mechanism is adopted. The binary bits in the adopted MSB layers are scrambled and individually interleaved with different extension ratios according to their importance to image visual quality. The hierarchical recovery strategy was adopted to improve the visual quality recovered results. In [17], the reference sharing method is improved. The content reconstruction problem is modeled as a communication over an erasure channel. The reference information are generated by encoding the reference symbols blocks of all the image blocks based on Random Linear Fountain (RLF) codes. The reference information embedded in an image block will be shared by all the image blocks, which allows for working with higher tampering rates than other self-embedding schemes with the same rate of reference information per image block.

Reference-sharing based self-embedding watermarking schemes has been shown to be an effective way to avoid the tampering coincidence and the reference waste problems, and it can achieve good recovery performance even higher tampered rate. In the process of executing the program, the matrix multiplication and especially solving systems of linear equations account for the computational complexity. If the encoding matrix is more sparse ones, the computational complexity will be expected to be reduced. For that, in this paper, we discuss to improve the computational complexity of the reference sharing based self-embedding watermarking scheme in [10] by employing the sparse matrices as the encoding matrices. Experimental results demonstrate the proposed approach can reduce the computational complexity significantly while maintaining the same tampering restoration capability as the traditional.

2 Related Work

The procedure of the reference sharing based self-embedding watermarking scheme in [10] includes the watermark embedding procedure and the tampering detection and content recovery procedures. To facilitate understanding, we describe the procedures as follows. More details can refer to [10].

The watermark embedding procedure including the following steps:

Step 1: Given an 8-bit gray-level image, the total number of its pixels is denoted as N. The 5 MSB of each pixel are collected to form a set that includes 5 N bits.

Step 2: The 5 N bits is permuted based on the secret key, and divided into M subsets, each of which containing L bits. For each subset, the reference data generation is performed by

$$\left(r_{m,1}, r_{m,2}, \ldots, r_{m,L/2}\right)^{\mathrm{T}} = A_m \left(c_{m,1}, c_{m,2}, \ldots, c_{m,L}\right)^{\mathrm{T}}, \quad m = 1, 2, \ldots, M \quad (1)$$

where A_m is the encoding matrix, a pseudo-random binary matrix sized $L/2 \times L$, $\left(c_{m,1}, c_{m,2}, \ldots, c_{m,L}\right)$ is the mth subset. There are a total of 5 $N/2$ reference bits.

Step 3: The 5 $N/2$ reference bits are permuted based on the secret key and divided into $N/64$ groups, each of which containing 160 bits. The host image is divided into $N/4$ blocks sized 8×8. For each block, 320 bits in the 5 MSB-layers and the 160 reference-bits in the corresponding group are fed into a hash function to generate 32 hash bits. According to the secret key, permute the 160 reference-bits and 32 hash-bits pseudo-randomly. These 192 bits are used to replace the three LSB planes of the block, producing a watermarked image.

Step 1: The received image will be divided into blocks with the same size as the original image. For each image block, the 192 bits taken from the three LSB-layers are decomposed into two parts, 160 reference bits and 32 hash-bits, using the same key. If the hash of the 320 bits in the 5MSB-layers and the 160 extracted reference-bits differs from the extracted 32 hash-bits, the block is said to be "tampered". Otherwise, we say it is a "reserved".

Step 2: According to the step 1 and the step 2 of the watermark embedding procedure, the MSB of the image blocks are processed to get the M subsets, paying attention to mark the MSB of the tampered blocks as the unknowns. The extracted reference-bits are connected and permuted inversely and divided into M subsets, paying attention to mark the reference-bits of the tampered blocks as the unknowns too. Then, the equations in (1) will be reconstructed. For each equations, the invalid equations that the reference-bit is unknown is removed,

$$\left(r_{m,e(1)}, r_{m,e(2)}, \ldots, r_{m,e(v)}\right)^{\mathrm{T}} = A_m^{(E)} \left(c_{m,1}, c_{m,2}, \ldots, c_{m,L}\right)^{\mathrm{T}}, \quad m = 1, 2, \ldots, M \quad (2)$$

where the $\left(r_{m,e(1)}, r_{m,e(2)}, \ldots, r_{m,e(v)}\right)^{\mathrm{T}}$ and $A_m^{(E)}$ are the constant vector and the coefficient matrix after removing the invalid equations. Then reformulate the equations for the standard system of equations as follows,

$$\left(r_{m,e(1)}, r_{m,e(2)}, \ldots, r_{m,e(v)}\right)^{\mathrm{T}} - A_m^{(E,R)} C_R = A_m^{(E,T)} C_T, \quad m = 1, 2, \ldots, M \quad (3)$$

where $A_m^{(E,T)}$ is the coefficient matrix of the standard system of equations.

Step 3: When each system of equations containing the unknowns in (3) has unique solution, all the MSB of the tampered blocks can be successfully restored. The probability of restoration is dependent upon tampering rate α, image size N, and system parameter L, which has been deduced in [10]. By combining the MSB in reserved blocks and the recovered MSB in tampered blocks, the principal image content can be reconstructed.

It can be seen a large number of matrix multiplication and solving systems of linear equations must be executed in (1) and (3). Therefore, the more sparse the encoding matrix is, the more little the computation load of (1) and (3) will be. In this article we try to reduce the computational complexity by using the sparse matrices as the encoding matrices. In the next sections the feasibility and efficiency will be proved by extensive experimental studies.

3   Sparse Binary Random Matrices Generation

Denote the probability of 1 in the binary random matrix as p. In the traditional reference sharing based self-embedding watermarking scheme [10], which had been sketched in Sect. 2, it can be seen that $p = 0.5$. The more little the probability of is, the more sparse the matrix will be. So we can generate the sparse binary random matrices by reduce the probability of 1 in the binary random matrix. Algorithm 1 illustrates the procedure of generating the sparse binary random matrices.

Algorithm 1 Generating the sparse binary random matrix

```
Input: The probability p, the number of rows t, the number of
columns n,
Output: The sparse binary random matrix A_{t×n}
for i from 1 to t
for j from 1 to n do
   A_{i,j} ∈ {0,1} and let A_{i,j}=1 independently with probability p
end
end
```

The important question is if the matrix becomes a sparse one, will the probability of the tampered blocks being successfully restored be equivalent to the previous. It had been said in Sect. 2 that if each system of equations in (3) has unique solution, all the MSB of the tampered blocks can be successfully restored. Each system of equations in (3) has the unique solution if and only if the columns of $A_m^{(E,T)}$ are linearly independent. Because the tampering is random, $A_m^{(E,T)}$ could be any sub-matrix of the binary random matrix A. Of course, it's columns may be not independent. That is, the columns of $A_m^{(E,T)}$ are linearly independent will be probabilistic. So, for a random binary matrix sized $i \times j(i \geq j)$, the probability of its columns being independent is mainly responsible for the successful recovery. We can conduct experiments to compare this probability.

For any sub-matrix of the binary random matrix, it's size is $i \times j(i \geq j)$. Denote the probability of its columns being independent as $P_p(i,j)$. First, we generate the same size random matrix when $p = 0.5$ and $p < 0.5$. Second, we extract i rows of the matrices randomly. Third, we extract $j(j \leq i)$ columns of the i rows to generate the sub-matrix. Last, verify if the extracted sub-matrix is independent. Repeat the experiments to obtain to the statistical values of $P_p(i,j)$.

Tables 1, 2 and 3 gives the experiment results. In Table 1, we select $p = 0.24$, ,18, 0.06, 0.03 and 0.5. For each p, the size of binary random matrices is 128 × 256. irst, for each p, generate the binary random matrices $A_{128 \times 256}$, then extract ($i = 121,115,108,102,96,89$) rows randomly, and then for each i, randomly extract $i \geq j$) columns of the i rows to get the sub-matrix A_{ij} for 100 times. Each time verify ⁄hether the columns of the sub-matrices A_{ij} is linearly independent. In this way, we btain the statistical values of $P_p(i, j)$.

'able 1. The statistical values of $P_p(i, j)$ ($j \leq i$) for the size of random matrixes is 128 × 256

Numbers of extracted rows i	The statistical values of $P_p(i, j)$ with different p				
	$p = 0.24$	$p = 0.18$	$p = 0.06$	$p = 0.03$	$p = 0.5$
121	1.00	1.00	1.00	0.94	1.00
115	1.00	1.00	1.00	0.97	0.96
108	1.00	1.00	1.00	0.94	1.00
102	0.99	1.00	0.99	0.82	1.00
96	0.99	0.96	1.00	0.87	0.99
89	0.60	1.00	0.99	0.76	0.99

In Table 2, we still select $p = 0.24, 0.18, 0.06, 0.03$ and 0.5. For each p, the size of inary random matrices is 256 × 512. First, for each p, generate the binary random ιatrices $A_{256 \times 512}$, then randomly extract i ($i = 243, 232, 220, 208, 196, 184$) rows of the ιatrices, and then for each i, randomly extract j ($i \geq j$) columns of the i rows to get the ub-matrix A_{ij} for 100 times. Each time verify whether the columns of the sub-matrices $_{ij}$ is linearly independent. In this way, we obtain the statistical values of $P_p(i, j)$.

In Table 3, we still select $p = 0.24, 0.18, 0.06, 0.03$ and 0.5. For each p, the size of inary random matrices is 512 × 1024. First, for each p, generate the binary random ιatrices $A_{512 \times 1024}$, then randomly extract i ($i = 486, 460, 435, 409, 384, 358$) rows of ιe matrices, and then for each i, randomly extract j ($i \geq j$) columns of the i rows to get ιe sub-matrix A_{ij} for 100 times. Each time verify whether the columns of the sub-ιatrices A_{ij} is linearly independent. In this way, we obtain the statistical values of $P_p(i, j)$.

It can be seen from Table 1, when $p = 0.03$ and $i = 102,96,89$, $P_{0.03}(i, j)$ is smaller ιan $P_{0.5}(i, j)$. But in Table 2 and Table 3, even $p = 0.03$, $P_{0.03}(i, j)$ is still comparable ɔ that when $p = 0.5$. This shows when the matrix is too sparse, the number of extracted ɔws should not be too little.

Experimental Results

n this section, we use the sparse binary random matrices to implement the reference-haring based self-embedding watermarking scheme in [10]. The sparse matrices with = 0.03 are used. Experiments were conduct to compare the detection and restoration apability and the computational complexity (in terms of running time) of the proposed ɔproach with that of [10]. The two approaches were implemented using the Matlab

Table 2. The statistical values of $P_p(i, j)$ ($j \leq i$) for the size of random matrixes is 256 × 512

Numbers of extracted rows i	The statistical values of $P_p(i, j)$ with different p				
	$p = 0.24$	$p = 0.18$	$p = 0.06$	$p = 0.03$	$p = 0.5$
243	1.00	1.00	0.99	1.00	1.00
232	1.00	1.00	0.99	1.00	1.00
220	1.00	1.00	1.00	1.00	0.98
208	1.00	0.99	1.00	0.98	0.99
196	1.00	0.99	1.00	1.00	0.99
184	1.00	0.99	0.98	1.00	0.99

Table 3. The statistical values of $P_p(i, j)$ for the size of random matrixes is 512 × 1024

Numbers of extracted rows i	The statistical values of $P_p(i, j)$ with different p				
	$p = 0.24$	$p = 0.18$	$p = 0.06$	$p = 0.03$	$p = 0.5$
486	1.00	1.00	0.99	1.00	1.00
460	1.00	1.00	0.99	0.99	0.98
435	0.99	1.00	1.00	1.00	1.00
409	1.00	1.00	1.00	1.00	1.00
384	0.99	1.00	1.00	1.00	1.00
358	1.00	0.99	1.00	1.00	1.00

R2013a programming language and run on a PC with an Intel Core i3-2310 M 2.10 GHz CPU and a 6 GB RAM.

8-bit gray scale image Crowd sized 512 × 512 (Fig. 1(a)) is used as the test image. The parameter $L = 512$. So the binary random matrices sized 256 × 512 will be generated as the encoded matrices. We generated the reference-bits and embedded the watermark in the image, the value of PSNR due to watermark embedding is 37.8 dB which is same as that of [10]. Then, the watermarked image were altered by substituting their partial contents with the fake contents. The tampered watermarked images are shown in Fig. 1(b). There are about 23.7% of the image blocks are tampered, the rate is the maximum tampering rate allowed in [10].

The identification and restoration results are given in Fig. 1(c) and (d). All the tampered image blocks can been identified and the PSNR in the restored area is about 37.5 dB when regarding the watermarked version as the reference, which is also equal to that of [10]. So, the restoration capability of the two schemes is equivalent. However, the run time of the proposed is 349.0 s, and the run time is 639.5 s when the algorithm of [10] is performed, which is nearly twice that of the proposed.

We also made a comparison over 50 gray images sized 512 × 512 with $L = 512$. The 50 images are embedded watermarks using binary random matrices and the sparse binary random matrices with $p = 0.03$ as the encoding matrices respectively. We calculated the average values of PSNR due to watermark embedding, both they are 38.25 dB. We tampered each watermarked images with the tampering rate from 0.05 to 0.45 with a 0.05 step. The tampering pattern is the same for all the tests. We implement

(a)   (b)

(c)   (d)

Fig. 1. Tampered watermarked image, identification and restoration results of the proposed method. (a) Watermarked image Crowd (b) Tampered watermarked Crowd, with tampering rate = 23.7%. (c) Identification result of tampered blocks. (d) Restored version of (b).

the two procedures of identification and restoration for each tampered watermarked images. We calculate and average the probability of successful restoration under the selected tampering rate, which are shown in Fig. 2. We can seen that the performance of restoration is equivalent. We also collect and average the run time of the two schemes, including the time of watermark embedding, tampering identification and restoration. The comparison results is shown in Fig. 3. It can be seen the run time of the proposed scheme is significantly lower than that of [10].

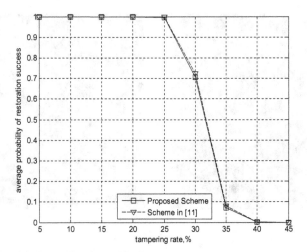

Fig. 2. Comparison of average probability of restoration success over 50 gray images

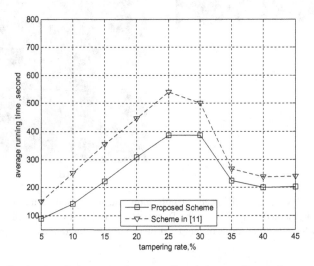

Fig. 3. Comparison of average running time over 50 gray images

5 Conclusions

In this paper, we improve the reference sharing mechanism based watermark self embedding scheme by using the sparse matrices as the encoding matrices. The proposed approach has been compared with the traditional. The experimental results demonstrate the proposed approach has much better performance on the computational complexity, but the restoration capability is same as the traditional.

Acknowledgment. This research is supported in part by the National Natural Science Foundation of China (NSFC) (No. U1536110).

References

1. Fridrich, J., Goljan, M.: Images with self-correcting capabilities. In: International Conference on Image Processing, ICIP 1999 Proceedings, vol. 3, pp. 792-796. IEEE (1999)
2. Dadkhah, S., Abd Manaf, A., Hori, Y., Ella Hassanien, A., Sadeghi, S.: An effective SVD-based image tampering detection and self-recovery using active watermarking. Sig. Process. Image Commun. **29**(10), 1197–1210 (2014)
3. Zhang, X., Xiao, Y., Zhao, Z.: Self-Embedding Fragile Watermarking Based on DCT and Fast Fractal Coding. Kluwer Academic Publishers, Hingham (2015)
4. Qin, C., Chang, C.C., Chen, P.Y.: Self-embedding fragile watermarking with restoration capability based on adaptive bit allocation mechanism. Sig. Process. **92**(4), 1137–1150 (2012)
5. He, H., Chen, F., Tai, H.M., Kalker, T., Zhang, J.: Performance analysis of a block-neighborhood-based self-recovery fragile watermarking scheme. IEEE Trans. Inf. Forensics Secur. **7**(1), 185–196 (2012)
6. Singh, D., Singh, S.K.: Effective Self-Embedding Watermarking Scheme for Image Tampered Detection and Localization with Recovery Capability. Academic Press, Inc., Orlando (2016)
7. Zhang, X., Qian, Z., Ren, Y., Feng, G.: Watermarking with flexible self-recovery quality based on compressive sensing and compositive reconstruction. IEEE Trans. Inf. Forensics Secur. **6**(4), 1223–1232 (2011)
8. Lee, T.Y., Lin, S.D.: Dual watermark for image tamper detection and recovery. Pattern Recogn. **41**(11), 3497–3506 (2008)
9. Li, C., Wang, Y., Ma, B., Zhang, Z.: A novel self-recovery fragile watermarking scheme based on dual-redundant-ring structure. Comput. Electr. Eng. **37**(6), 927–940 (2011)
10. Zhang, X., Wang, S., Qian, Z., Feng, G.: Reference sharing mechanism for watermark self-embedding. IEEE Trans. Image Process. **20**(2), 485–495 (2011)
11. Zhang, X., Wang, S.: Fragile watermarking with error-free restoration capability. IEEE Trans. Multimed. **10**(8), 1490–1499 (2008)
12. Zhang, X., Wang, S.: Fast communication: fragile watermarking scheme using a hierarchical mechanism. Sig. Process. **89**(4), 675–679 (2009)
13. Qin, C., Wang, H., Zhang, X., Sun, X.: Self-embedding fragile watermarking based on reference-data interleaving and adaptive selection of embedding mode. Inf. Sci. **373**, 233–250 (2016)
14. Qin, C., Ji, P., Wang, J., Chang, C.C.: Fragile image watermarking scheme based on VQ index sharing and self-embedding. Multimed. Tools Appl. **76**(2), 2267–2287 (2017)
15. Qin, C., Ji, P., Zhang, X., Dong, J., Wang, J.: Fragile image watermarking with pixel-wise recovery based on overlapping embedding strategy. Signal Process. **138**(C), 280–293 (2017)
16. Cao, F., An, B., Wang, J., Ye, D., Wang, H.: Hierarchical recovery for tampered images based on watermark self-embedding. Displays **46**, 52–60 (2017)
17. Korus, P., Dziech, A.: Efficient method for content reconstruction with self-embedding. IEEE Trans. Image Process. Publ. IEEE Signal. Process. Soc. **22**(3), 1134 (2013)

Research on Cascading Failures
in Complex Network

Yu Nan[(⊠)], Yaohui Hao, Fengjuan Zhang, and Gang Zhou

China State Key Laboratory of Mathematical Engineering
and Advanced Computing, Zhengzhou 450002, China
ddappl32011@163.com

Abstract. The study on the cascading failure of complex network is an important branch in the complex network researches. In this paper, the attack strategies used in the researches on the cascading failure of complex network at home and abroad have been summarized. At the same time, the different characteristics of the new attack strategies and the traditional attack strategies have been analyzed. The modeling principles and the methods of the cascading failure model of complex network have been proposed. Furthermore, the research progress of the cascading failure in the complex network is reviewed. The existing problems as well as the future development trends have been pointed out.

Keywords: Complex network · Attack strategy · Cascading failure
Model

1 Introduction

The complex network refers to the network with self organization, self similarity, attackor, small world and partial or total properties in free scale (defined by Qian Xuesen). If the constituent elements in system are abstracted as the nodes in network and the interaction (relation) between elements is abstracted as the edge of network, a large number of functional systems in the real world can be described over the web. For example, the human society is a huge social network [1]; Internet is also a typical complex network [2]; the similar networks include the terrorist organization network [3], the transportation network [4], the scientists' cooperative network [5], the power network [6], the logistics network [7], the brain nerves network [8] and the hardware network [9], etc. It can be said that the real world is full of networks and the network has more and more influenced our work and life and brought us great convenience and shortcut.

In these networks, there are lots of streams (also known as payloads) that are closely related to human life. These streams can be information, energy or matters, etc. Therefore, the nodes/edges in network are loaded. As the endurance capacity of each node/edge is limited, if one or a small number of nodes/edges in the network is not available, the streams or loads in network will be redistributed, which may cause other nodes/edges in trouble due to excessive load. The fault will be gradually spread and the cascading effects will be appeared. Finally, a number of nodes in network and even the

hole network will be collapsed. This phenomenon is called the cascading failure.
rom the aspects of the attack strategy in complex network and the cascading failure2
1odel in complex network, the main research progress of the vulnerability attack of the
omplex network has been summarized and compared. Finally, the suggestions have
een provided for the study of the cascading failure in complex networks.

Typical Complex Network Structure Model

.1   Random Network

.t the end of 1950s, Erdos and Renyi have considered that the network is not regular,
ut random through the study on the communication field. Afterwards, the Random
etwork model, also known as the ER network model[44, 101-103], has been proosed. In the ER Random network G(N, p) with fixed edge probability, the total
umber of edges is not fixed. The probability of having one edge between any two
ifferent nodes in N nodes is fixed as p. In Fig. 2.1, three instances of a Random
etwork have been presented when N = 12, p = 0, 0.1, 0.2.

.2   Small-World Network

ccording to the analysis of interpersonal interaction, Milgram, an American psy-
hologist, has found that people are not only acquainted with their neighbors and
olleagues in real life, but also know some friends far away (in a foreign country). On
1e basis of this study, Milgram has proposed the famous "six-degree separation"
1eory that shows that the average distance between people is 6. In other words, only
ve people are needed to contact anyone in the world. The World Wide Web
WWW) contains 153127 nodes[44] and the average path length of the network is only
.67. The phenomenon that the scale of network is large and the average path length is
mall is called the "small-world" effect. These small-world features that are evident in
eal networks cannot be described and simulated by the Random network or the regular
etwork. Based on this, Watts and Strogtz published articles in Nature in 1998 and the
mall-world network model has been proposed. The small-world network is also
nown as the WS network model[104-108].

.3   Scale-Free Network

common feature of the ER random graph and the WS small-world network model is
1at the distribution of the network node degree can be approximately represented by
oisson distribution. The Poisson distribution has a peak value at the average value
k> and then it has been exponentially and rapidly decayed. However, the Barabasi
eam has studied the World Wide Web (WWW) and found that the in-degree and the
utdegree distributions of WWW can be well described by the power law distribution,
vhich deviates from the Poisson distribution of the ER Random network and the WS
mall-world network. On the basis of this research, in 1999, Barabasi and Albert
ublished their papers in Science on the growth and the priority connection mechanism

based on power law distribution. It is proposed that the Scale-free network is also known as the BA network model[109-116].

3   Research and Analysis on the Attack Strategy of Complex Network

3.1   Random Attack Strategy and the Deliberate Attack Strategy [10]

The attack strategies used in the research field of complex networks usually employ the random attack strategy and the deliberate attack strategy proposed by Barabasi et al. [10]. The random attack strategy completely and randomly selects some nodes in the network and removes them from the network. The deliberate attack strategy sorts the nodes in the network from large to small according to the degree value and starts with removing the node with the highest medium value in the network. In the use of these two attack strategies, assuming that the proportion of the number of removed nodes in the total number of the nodes in original network is f, Barabasi team has studied the Scale-free network and the Random network and found if the deliberate attack strategy is adopted, the connectivity of the whole Scale-free network will be greatly affected through removing a small number of nodes with greater degree value in Scale-free network. The Scale-free network can be quickly split into the isolated islands which cannot communicate with each other, resulting in the network communication paralysis. However, if the random attack strategy is employed and a large number of nodes are randomly removed in Scale-free network, that is, when the value of f is very large, the Scale-free network can still keep the basic connectivity in Scale-free network.

After the research of Barabasi, the representative research results of the attack strategy are the four deliberate attack strategies proposed by Holme through taking the network centrality metrics of degree and betweenness as basis and considering the changes of the degree value and the betweenness value of each node in the network before and after the attack [11]:

ID (Initial Degree): based on the degree value of each node in the initial network, the nodes are removed from large to small;

RD (Recalculated Degree): based on the current network, the nodes are removed from large to small according to the new degree values of the nodes after recalculating the degree value of each node;

IB (Initial Betweenness): based on the betweenness value of each node in the initial network, the nodes are removed from large to small;

RB (Recalculated Betweenness): based on the current network, the nodes are removed from large to small according to the new betweenness values of the nodes after recalculating the betweenness value of each node.

It is found that RD and RB attack strategies have more damage to the network connectivity than ID and IB attack strategies and the Scale-free network is very vulnerable under the four attack strategies. In addition, considering that there is usually a line (edge) getting out of order in the network instead of removing all adjacent edges of a node and taking the edge removal attack strategy in the network as the basis, Guillaume et al. [12] has obtained the conclusion that the network will be not bound to ollapse when the random attack strategy and the deliberate attack strategy remove the ame number of connection edges.

In recent years, the representative research results in this direction include: Nie t al. have proposed two attack strategies based on Homle's research: IDB (Initial egree and Betweenness) and RDB (Recalculated Degree and Betweenness) [13], in hich the attack effectiveness of RDB attack strategy has been increased by 20% ompared with RD attack strategy proposed by Homle. The attack effectiveness of IDB ttack strategy has been increased by 40% compared with ID attack strategy. Pu et al. ave proposed the approximate longest path attack strategy starting from the large roportions of node failure in public transport networks caused by the natural disasters ich as hurricanes. The RPA (the Random Longest Path Augmenting Approach) pproximate longest path attack generation algorithm [14, 15] is employed. The iter- tive method is adopted in which one RPA approximate longest path in the network is :moved in the network until there is no remaining path. At the same time, the vul- erabilities of Random and Scale-free networks have been analyzed and it is found that nder the RPA approximate longest path attack strategy, the maximum path attack eration number Step of Random network increases linearly with the network density k>. However, the maximum path attack iteration number Step of Scale-free network icreases exponentially with the network density <k>. Under the path attack strategy, ie more uniform the degree distribution of the network is, the more vulnerable the etwork will be. Shao et al. started from the destructive nature of seismic waves and roposed LA (Localized Attacks) strategy [16, 17]. It is found that bi-Poisson and iaussian are more vulnerable under LA attacks than random attacks. Dong et al. have nalyzed the dependent network by using LA attack strategy [18] and proposed the nproved LA attack strategy [19]. When the nodes (root nodes) in the random selection re attacked, the root node will be not removed, but the unprotected nodes around the)ot node will be removed. According to the research on the complex network of andom and Scale-free, it is believed that the increase of the network connection ensity helps to significantly improve the robustness of network.

.2   Problems of Common Attack Strategies

he proposition of these attack strategies has well extended the understanding of the ehavior characteristics of complex network. However, on the one hand, some of the ew attack strategies proposed in recent years have only analyzed the vulnerability of ie complex network structures without considering the load and cascading failure :udy in complex network is not available; on the other hand, these attack strategies are uite different from the ones in the real world. Through the analysis of these new etwork attack methods, it is found that there are many differences between these new etwork attack methods and the traditional network attack methods. The comparison is nown in Table 1.

In Table 1, it can be found that these new attack methods always have a series of teps such as the investigation, the invasion and the attack and these methods are well rganized, persistent and targeted. When the attacker successfully invades a node in the etwork, the node will be not immediately destroyed. The attacker will continue to use iis node as the starting node to invade other nodes connected to it. When the attack

Table 1. Comparison of the new network attack methods and the traditional network attack methods

Threat characteristics	Traditional attack	New attack
Financial support	It may be not sufficient	Funds are sufficient and political resources may be available
Attack target	It is random and the system that is easily broken can be selected as the attack target	There is a clear target of attack, whether it is easily destroyed or not
Executive patience	There is little patience	Very patient
Coordinated execution	A single action is common	Multiple individuals are organized to implement the attacks
Preliminary investigation	There is a small amount f investigation	Investigations are extensive and adequate

target set by the intruder is reached or a certain condition or opportunity is satisfied, the attacker will launch an attack. Once the attacker launches an attack, all the nodes under attack can be destroyed at the same time. That is, the nodes/edges destroyed by these new attack strategies in network are always adjacent. However, for the random and the deliberate attack strategies proposed by Barabasi, ID, IB, RD and RB attack strategies put forward by Holme, IDB and RDB attack strategies proposed by Nie, these nodes and edges are not required to be adjacent when selecting to remove the multiple nodes or edges in the network. In addition, the key nodes with maximum degree value and betweenness value in network are the key protection objects. For example, the server nodes in Internet network, which are often protected by the focus, are difficult to be directly invaded/destroyed. However, for the nodes with small degree value and betweenness value in network, the preventive measures are relatively weak and they are easily invaded/destroyed. Therefore, some of the current attackers will firstly invade/destroy the neighbor nodes with relatively small degree value and betweenness value around the nodes with great degree value and betweenness value, and then invade/destroy the nodes with maximum degree value and betweenness value or make the nodes with maximum degree value and betweenness value become the isolated nodes that cannot play the roles.

Thus it can be seen that the new attack strategies used in the real world show disparate features compared with the traditional random and deliberate attack strategies. The attack models employed in the current network are more complex and diverse than those used in the past. In this realistic situation, when facing these new attack methods, it is required to analyze the characteristics and the steps of these new attack methods, construct the new attack strategy that accords with the real attack characteristics and conduct the modeling description for the new attack methods from the network form.6 At the same time, it is necessary to implement the new attack strategies in the complex network models with different features and analyze the cascading failure behaviors of the complex network with different features under the new attack strategies. Then, the obtained dynamic research results of the complex network behaviors have more practical significance, which can provide the valuable and theoretical support for the security protection of network and the design of high reliability network.

4 Analysis on the Cascading Failure Modeling in Complex Network

4.1 Cascading Failure Model in Typical Complex Networks

At present, many researchers at home and abroad have conducted extensive modeling researches on the cascading failure of complex network from many angles. The most classical model is the "load-capacity" model proposed by Motter and Lai. This model considers the linear relationship between the node capacity C and the load L and the proportional coefficient is the fault-tolerant parameter. Assuming that the load redistribution employs the shortest path principle and the maximum connected graph G of network is used to measure the network performance. It is found that the greater the heterogeneity of load distribution is, the greater the influence on the network performance under deliberate attack strategy will be, but the impact of the random attack is less. When the load distribution is homogeneous, the random attack and the deliberate attack are not easy to cause the cascading failure.

Moreno et al. have studied the cascading failure problems caused by the node overload in Scale-free network through introducing the fiber beam model [24] and assuming that the initial load of the node is the same and the load of the fault node is redistributed to its neighbor nodes. It is found that the network performance becomes worse with the increase of initial load and the network with uniform capacity distribution is more robust to the cascading failure. Moreno et al. have studied the cascading failure caused by the side overload in Scale-free network [25] and found that the possibility of the cascading failure will be increased with the increase of the network average load. Since then, some researchers have studied the cascading failure behaviors of the complex network with different features based on the fiber beam model and revealed some phase transition phenomenon in the cascading failure process of network [26, 27].

The sand-pile model is a widely-used model in the cascading failure study of complex network. This model assumes that each node starts with no load, and then the nodes are randomly selected to perform the load increase operations. At the same time, the method that the load of the overloaded nodes is redistributed to some of their neighbor nodes. Bonabeau, Goh et al. took the lead in introducing the sand-pile model into the cascading failure analysis of Random network and Scale-free network [28, 29] and analyzed the influence of the load growth on the self-organized critical behavior before the network collapse. Goh et al. have continued further research and verified that the scale and the duration of Scale-free network collapse process have the power law property from the aspects of numerical simulation and theoretical analysis [30]. Based on the sand-pile model, Huang et al. have studied the robustness of Scale-free network embedded by weighted grid [31]. It is found that in the Scale-free network with the regional restrictions, the more tightly the local connection of network is, the more vulnerable the network collapse will be.

Dobsond et al. have proposed the OPA model [34] and the Cascade model [35] in view of the features of power grid. In recent years, many scholars have introduced new technologies and methods into the field of cascading failure models and some improved cascading failure models have been proposed. For example, Sun et al. have introduced the data mining technology into the research field of cascading failure mode [36] and used the cluster analysis model to analyze the relationship between the intermediate data and the results of the failure chain, which has provided a prediction for the potential propagation path of cascading failure as well as reduced the risk of catastrophic events. Yan et al. have determined the load of power through combining the features of network structure with the electrical characteristics and an extended medium model has been proposed [37]. Through adjusting the different tolerance systems, the cascading failure behavior of the power network under different loads and overloads has been analyzed. Fang et al. have introduced the concept of neighbor chain [38] and analyzed the cascading failure behaviors of Random network, directed Scale-free network and IEEE 118 network.

4.2   Problems of the Cascading Failure Model in Complex Networks

It is not difficult to find that the construction of the suitable cascading failure model of complex network according to the characteristics of cascading failure dynamics of real networks as well as the research and the evaluation of the cascading failure behaviors of complex network with different features under different attack strategies has become the important and effective method to understand and control the cascading failure behaviors of network. In the research on the cascading failure of complex network, how to model the network is a very important problem. In fact, the construction of the model is to solve three basic problems: how to define the initial load of node/edge, how to define the capacity of node/edge and how to redistribute the load of node/edge after the failure.

To sum up, the research on the cascading failure of complex network has obtained great progress and many valuable conclusions have been got. The obtained results have greatly changed and expanded the understanding of cascading failure behavior of network to a great extent. Many valuable network protection strategies have been also provided. However, the load-capacity definition and the load redistribution method used in these studies are all for the static networks without considering the time and the space attributes of nodes/edges. The time refers to the continuity and the sequence of the process of material movement and the space refers to the extensibility of the existence of matter that is inseparable from the moving matters. The time and the space together constitute the two basic forms of the existence of the moving matters and there is no time and space separated from the movement of matter. And there is no matter that is not moving in time and space. Without considering the effects of time and space, the current cascading failure study of complex network is only for the static network, while all networks are dynamic in reality. For example, the nodes (people) in social network will be in different places at different times; the maximum load of the nodes (station) in transportation network is closely related to the time value. Due to the crease of the additional staff and the temporary train in holidays, the maximum load f each node will be higher than that of the normal working day. Therefore, taking the ynamic network in the real world as the background, considering the space-time factor f node/edge, establishing a more accurate cascading failure model and analyzing the ascading failure behavior of the dynamic complex network with different character-tics under the new attack strategies are very meaningful.

Conclusion and Prospects

ased on the above introduction, it can be found that the results of the cascading failure searches in complex networks have greatly changed and expanded our understanding f the cascading failure phenomenon. However, in view of these researches, there are e following aspects that should be discussed in depth:

) It is required to design the attack strategy that accords with the real situation: according to the real attack behavior characteristics obtained by analysis, it is necessary to conduct the model description for the attack strategies of real scene and construct the new attack strategies that conform to the characteristics. Based on the new attack strategies, it is demanded to analyze the cascading failure behavior of complex network.

) It is necessary to design the cascading failure model of dynamic complex network: starting from the temporal and spatial characteristics of node/edge changes of dynamic complex network, it is required to build the cascading failure model of complex network with space-time factors through considering the temporal and spatial environment of each node/edge in dynamic networks.

With the continuous improvement and development of the complex network the-ry, it will be very meaningful to systematically and deeply study the cascading failure ehaviors in complex network in view of the emerging problems.

References

1. Apicella, C.L., Marlowe, F.W., Fowler, J.H., et al.: Social networks and cooperation in huntergatherers. Nature **481**(7382), 497–501 (2011)
2. Albert, R., Jeong, H., Barabási, A.L.: Internet: diameter of the world-wide web. Nature **401** (6749), 130–131 (1999)
3. Krebs, V.E.: Mapping networks of terrorist cells. Connections **24**(3), 43–52 (2001)
4. Hossain, M.M., Alam, S.: A complex network approach towards modeling and analysis of the Australian airport network. J. Air Transp. Manag. **60**, 1–9 (2017)
5. Newman, M.E.: The structure of scientific collaboration networks. Proc. Natl. Acad. Sci. U. S.A. **98**(2), 404–409 (2000)
6. Hu, J., Yu, J., Cao, J., et al.: Topological interactive analysis of power system and its communication module: a complex network approach. Physica A **416**, 99–111 (2014)
7. Zhou, Y., Wang, S.: Generic model of reverse logistics network design. J. Transp. Syst. Eng. Inf. Technol. **8**(3), 71–78 (2008)

8. Stam, C.J.: Modern network science of neurological disorders. Nat. Rev. Neurosci. **15**(10), 683 (2014)

9. Bjornson, E., Matthaiou, M., Debbah, M.: Massive MIMO with non-ideal arbitrary arrays: hardware scaling laws and circuit-aware design. IEEE Trans. Wirel. Commun. **14**(8), 4353–4368 (2015)

10. Albert, R., Jeony, H., Barabasi, A.L.: Attack and error tolerance in complex networks. Nature **406**(6794), 387–482 (2000)

11. Holme, P., Kim, B.J., Yoon, C.N., et al.: Attack vulnerability of complex networks. Phys. Rev. E **65**(5 Pt 2), 056109 (2002)

12. Guillaume, J.-L., Latapy, M., Magnien, C.: Comparison of failures and attacks on random and scale-free networks. In: Higashino, T. (ed.) OPODIS 2004. LNCS, vol. 3544, pp. 186–196. Springer, Heidelberg (2005). https://doi.org/10.1007/11516798_14

13. Nie, T., Guo, Z., Zhao, K., et al.: New attack strategies for complex networks. Physica A **424**, 248–253 (2015)

14. Pu, C.L., Cui, W.: Vulnerability of complex networks under path-based attacks. Physica A **419**, 622–629 (2015)

15. Pu, C., Li, S., Michaelson, A., et al.: Iterative path attacks on networks. Phys. Lett. A **379** (28–29), 1633–1638 (2015)

16. Shao, S., Huang, X., Stanley, H.E., et al.: Percolation of localized attack on complex networks. New J. Phys. **17**(2), 1–11 (2015)

17. Yuan, X., Shao, S., Stanley, H.E., et al.: How breadth of degree distribution influences network robustness: comparing localized and random attacks. Phys. Rev. E **92**(3), 032122 (2015)

18. Dong, G., Hao, H., Du, R., et al.: Localized attack on clustering networks, p. 14 (2016) arXiv:1610.04759

19. Dong, G., Du, R., Hao, H., et al.: Modified localized attack on complex network. EPL **113** (2), 28002 (2016)

20. Sood, A.K., Enbody, R.J.: Targeted cyberattacks: a superset of advanced persistent threats. IEEE Secur. Priv. **11**(1), 54–61 (2013)

21. Xenakis, C., Ntantogian, C.: An advanced persistent threat in 3G networks: attacking the home network from roaming networks. Comput. Secur. **40**(2), 84–94 (2014)

22. Marchetti, M., Pierazzi, F., Colajanni, M., et al.: Analysis of high volumes of network traffic for advanced persistent threat detection. Comput. Netw. **109**, 127–141 (2016)

23. Motter, A.E., Lai, Y.C.: Cascade-based attacks on complex networks. Phys. Rev. E **66**(6) 065102 (2002)

24. Moreno, Y., Gomez, J.B., Pacheco, A.F.: Instability of scale-free networks under node breaking avalanches. EPL **58**(4), 630–636 (2002)

25. Moreno, Y., Pastor Satorras, R., Vazquez, A.: Critical load and congestion instabilities in scalefree networks. Europhys. Lett. **62**, 292–298 (2003)

26. Kim, B.J.: Phase transition in the modified fiber bundle model. EPL **66**(6), 819–825 (2004)

27. Kim, D.H., Kim, B.J., Jeong, H.: Universality class of the fiber bundle model on complex networks. Phys. Rev. Lett. **94**, 025501 (2005)

28. Bonabeau, E.: Sandpile dynamics on random graphs. J. Phys. Soc. Jpn. **64**, 327–328 (1995)

29. Goh, K.I., Lee, D.S., Kahng, B., et al.: Sandpile on scale-free neworks. Phys. Rev. Lett. **91** 148701 (2003)

30. Lee, D.S., Goh, K.I., Kahng, B., Kim, D.: Sandpile avalanche dynamics on scale-free networks. Physica A **338**, 84–91 (2004)

31. Huang, L., Yang, L., Yang, K.Q.: Geographical effects on cascading breakdowns of scale-free networks. Phys. Rev. E **73**, 036102 (2006)

2. Holme, P., Kim, B.J.: Vertex overload breakdown in evolving networks. Phys. Rev. E **65**(6), 066109 (2002)
3. Holme, P.: Edge overload breakdown in evolving networks. Phy. Rev. E **66**(3), 036119 (2002)
4. Dobson, I., Carreras, B.A., Lynch, V.E., et al.: An initial model for complex dynamics in electric power system blackouts. In: 34th HICSS (2001)
5. Dobson, I., Carreras, B.A., Newman, D.E.: A probabilistic loading-dependent model of cascading failure and possible implications for blackouts. In: 36th HICSS (2003)
6. Sun, Q., Shi, L., Ni, Y., et al.: An enhanced cascading failure model integrating data mining technique (2017)
7. Yan, J., He, H., Sun, Y.: Integrated security analysis on cascading failure in complex networks. IEEE Trans. Inf. Forensics Secur. **9**(3), 451–463 (2016)
8. Fang, X., Yang, Q., Yan, W.: Modeling and analysis of cascading failure in directed complex networks. Saf. Sci. **65**(3), 1–9 (2014)

Research on Dynamic Performance and Road Performance of Dense-Gradation Asphalt Mixture

Congrong Tang[1,2(✉)], Xin Xu[3], and Haiyan Ding[3]

[1] Nanjing Sutong Road and Bridge Engineering Co., Ltd.,
Nanjing 211200, China
tcr751101@163.com
[2] Engineering Nanjing Tech University, Nanjing 211200, China
[3] Kunshan Dengyun College of Science and Technology, Suzhou 215300, China
711593419@qq.com, 534468911@qq.com

Abstract. The scientific construction of technical specifications for construction of highway asphalt pavement puts forward higher requirements on the performance and grade of construction materials such as asphalt and other materials. The performance of asphalt mixture has an important impact on the quality of pavement engineering. In this paper, we research and analyze different whetstones and different gradations of dense-graded asphalt mixture by applying computer technology and the Marshall test. the results of the Marshall test show that the properties of dense-graded asphalt mixture are within the scope of the index under a reasonable gradation, and dynamic stability and residual stability meet the specifications, and the dynamic performance and road performance of dense-mixed materials meet the requirements by the comprehensive testing.

Keywords: Densegrade · Asphalt mixture · Dynamic and road performance

1 Introduction

The weight of a new type of scientific asphalt concrete pavement is getting bigger and bigger in highway construction, there is a scientific and practical value about the research and analysis of densely asphalt mixture. The porosity Vv of dense grade asphalt mixture after mechanical compaction is generally small, usually Vv is within the range of 0.02–0.1. After Asphalt Concrete mixes, they form a dense structure with bonds through the mixing of bitumen and minerals with different particle sizes. At the same time, there is enough space that is between the same particle size mineral material in Asphalt Concrete to be filled by low-grade mineral materials, due to a lower level. The existence of voids between the extrusion of the mineral material and the same-grade ore material makes it impossible to directly contact the larger-sized ore materials. But the large-size mineral materials can't directly contact each other because the extrusion of the low-grade mineral materials and the presence of pores between the same particle size mineral material, the smaller particle-size minerals can be fully mixed with asphalt to fill voids to form a suspension-compact structure [1]. The

X. Sun et al. (Eds.): ICCCS 2018, LNCS 11068, pp. 654–664, 2018.
https://doi.org/10.1007/978-3-030-00021-9_58

iternal friction angle is smaller because the Large grain size aggregates of Suspended-ompact structure can not form skeletons. The cohesion of suspended-compact struc-ire is higher because the small grain sizes can fully fill voids. Only reasonable design f Asphalt Concrete gradation can obtain extremely high adhesive force and internal iction, better compactness, good dynamic performance and good road performance. ' 1 this article, we use the computer application technology and technical standards and elect three gradations as well as five asphalt aggregate ratios to conduct the Marshall st of AC-13, AC-16, AC-25 three kinds of asphalt mixture. At the same time, we search and analyze the dynamic performance and road performance of Asphalt oncrete through the test data.

Raw Material Technical Indicators and Test Results

1 Road Asphalt

According to the relevant requirements of highway design and the engineering survey f the region, we choose SBS modified bitumen for AC-13 and AH-70 ordinary asphalt or AC-16 as well as AC-25, When researching and analyzing the matching, dynamic erformance and road performance of the Asphalt Concrete. According to the regu-itions of the "Standard Test Methods of Bituminous and Bituminous Mixtures for lighway Engineering" (JTGE20-2011) [2], we conducted a technical determination to ie selected two types of asphalt respectively, The results are shown in Table 1. We ompared and analyzed according to the regulations of the "Standard Test Methods of iituminous and Bituminous Mixtures for Highway Engineering" (JTGE20-2011) [2] nd the results of technical measurement in the Tables 1 and 2. We can see that the elected two types of asphalt can meet the technical requirements of the standard [2].

Table 1. SBS modified asphalt technical indicators

ndex	Technical indicators	The measurement results	Experiment method
Penetration (0.1 mm) (25 °C, 5 s, 100 g)	40–60	53	T0604
Ductility (5 cm/min, 5 °C) (cm)	≥ 20	28	T0605
Softening Point (Ring and Ball Method) (°C)	≥ 75	79	T0606
Elastic recovery (25 °C, 10 cm) (%)	≥ 75	81	T0662
Relative density of asphalt (25 °C)g/cm3	Recorded	1.037	T0603
Quality change (%)	$\leq \pm 1.0$	−0.082	T0609
5 °C ductility (cm)	≥ 15	17	T0605
Residual Penetration Ratio (10 °C) (%)	≥ 65	76	T0604

Table 2. AH-70 technical indicators for road petroleum asphalt

Index	Technical indicators	The measurement results	Experiment method
Penetration (0.1 mm) (25 °C, 5 s, 100 g)	60–80	64	T0604
Penetration index PI	(−1.5) + (1.0)	−1.02	T0604
Softening Point (Ring and Ball Method)	≥ 46 °C	51 °C	T0606
60 °C dynamic viscosity (Pa.s)	≥ 180	259	T0620
15 °C ductility (cm)	≥ 100	132	T0605
Relative density of asphalt (25 °C)g/cm3	Recorded	1.035	T0603
Quality change (%)	≤ ± 0.8	0.34	T0609
Residual Penetration Ratio (%)	≥ 61	63	T0604
Residual ductility (10 °C) (cm)	≥ 6	8.3	T0605
Residual ductility (15 °C) (cm)	≥ 15	21.1	T0605

2.2 Aggregate

According to the regulations of the "Standard Test Methods of Bituminous and Bituminous Mixtures for Highway Engineering" (JTGE20-2011) [2] and the project overview of the area, we choose the basalt with the particle-sizes of 9.5 mm to16 mm as well as 4.75 mm to 9.5 mm and the limestone with the particle-sizes of 2.36 mm to 4.75 mm as well as 0 to 2.36 mm as aggregates of the AC-13 mixture, and choose the limestone with the particle-sizes of 9.5 mm to 19 mm, 4.75 mm to 9.5 mm as well as 0 to 4.75 mm as aggregates of the AC-16 mixture, choose the limestone with the particle-sizes of 19 mm to 26.5 mm, 9.5 mm to 19 mm, 4.75 mm to 9.5 mm as well as 0 to 4.75 mm as aggregates of the AC-25 mixture, When researching and analyzing the matching, dynamic performance and road performance of the Asphalt Concrete. The Requirements of the Coarse and fine aggregates are clean and dry, no weathering impurities, the surface should be rough [3]. According to the regulations of the "Standard Test Methods of Bituminous and Bituminous Mixtures for Highway Engineering" (JTGE20-2011) [2], we did tests of the density and screening for the above several aggregates respectively, The results are shown in Tables 3 and 4.

Analyze the screening results of the mineral mixtures in Tables 3 and 4, All of them can meet the technical requirements for the gradation range of intensive asphalt concrete mix and the density of mineral materials specified in the Technical Specifications for Construction of Highway Asphalt Pavements.

Table 3. Mineral density test results

Particle size index		19–26.5	9.5–19	4.75–9.5	2.36–4.75	0–2.36	Slag	Lime
AC-13	Ad	/	2.884	2.879	2.36-4.75	0–2.36	2.703	2.455
	γ_{sb}	/	2.844	2.827	2.818	2.748	/	/
AC-16	Ad	/	2.732	2.736	2.715	2.68	2.703	
	γ_{sb}	/	2.678	2.68	2.72		/	
AC-25	Ad	2.72	2.73	2.745	2.658		2.704	
	γ_{sb}	2.681	2.684	2.694	2.725		/	

Note: Ad. apparent density; γ_{sb}. gross volume relative density. (same as below)

able 4. Screening results and grading ranges of AC-13, 16, 25 various minerals and ore fines

Types	Particle size sieve	26.5	19	16	13.2	9.5	4.75	2.36	1.18	0.6	0.3	0.15	0.075
						Through the sieve (square hole sieve, mm) percentage (%)							
AC-13	19–26.5	/	/	/	/	/	/	/	/	/	/	/	/
	9.5–19	/	/	100	93.6	16.6	0.5	0.1	0.1	0.1	0.1	0.1	0.1
	4.75–9.5	/	/	100	100	92.9	2.1	0.3	0.1	0.1	0.1	0.1	0.1
	2.36–4.75	/	/	100	100	100	85.0	1.4	1.0	1.0	1.0	0.9	0.7
	0–2.36	/	/	100	100	100	97.3	71.9	48.8	36.3	28.4	16.6	12.1
	Slag	/	/	100	100	100	100	100	100	100	100	100	76.0
	lime	/	/	100	100	100	100	100	100	100	100	100	98.0
AC-16	9.5–19	100	90.5	63.1	32.6	6.5	2.4	2.3	2.2	2.1	1.9	1.7	1.5
	4.75–9.5	100	100	100	100	88.4	40.3	14.1	7.3	4.8	4.2	3.5	3.1
	0–4.75	100	100	100	100	100	95.3	67.2	45.1	28.2	18.2	13.9	12.2
	Slag	100	100	100	100	100	100	100	100	100	100	95.4	78.7
AC-25	19–26.5	100	94.0	15.4	3.7	1.0	0.4	0.4	0.4	0.4	0.4	0.4	0.4
	9.5–19	100	100	90.5	69.9	46.0	16.7	5.3	2.7	2.6	2.5	2.3	2.2
	4.75–9.5	100	100	100	100	96.6	79.1	38.7	6.7	3.4	2.8	2.7	2.5
	0–4.75	100	100	100	100	100	100	98.4	74.0	53.0	31.9	20.1	15.4
	Slag	100	100	100	100	100	100	100	100	100	100	100	97.8

Mineral Mixture Gradation Design

According to the Highway Engineering Industry Standards of the "Specifications for Design of Highway Asphalt Pavements" (JTG D50-2017) and "Standard Test Methods f Bituminous and Bituminous Mixtures for Highway Engineering" (JTG E20-2011) 1, 2] and combined with engineering practice, we choose initial asphalt aggregate ratio f 4.8%, 4.9% as well as 4.0% to separately make Marshall specimens for AC-13, AC-6, and AC-25 for grading adjustment and initial volumetric analysis through studying nd analyzing the above Table 4, and measure the relevant performance indicators of 1e clearance rate, saturation, VMA [2], In the test process, we choose three levels that 3:27:10:27:1.5:1.5, 30:28:10:29:1.5:1.5 as well as 28:28:10:31:1.5:1.5 to make

Marshall specimens for AC-13, and choose three levels that 33:39:27:1, 30:40:29:1 a
well as 27:41:31:1to make Marshall specimens for AC-16, and choose three levels tha
20:33:23:23:1, 19: 33:20.5:26.5:1 as well as 22:24:25:28:1 to make Marshall speci
mens for AC-25. The results are shown in Tables 5, 6 and 7.

Table 5. AC-13 design grading test results

Gr	AAR (%)	MS (KN)	FL (mm)	VV (%)	VMA(%)	VFA (%)	γ_f	TMD
1	4.8	13.56	2.83	4.67	14.68	68.16	2.488	2.610
2	4.8	13.52	2.86	4.45	14.48	69.26	2.491	2.609
3	4.8	13.47	2.89	4.26	14.27	70.14	2.494	2.606
Claim	/	≥ 8.0	2–5	4.0–5.5	≥ 14	65–75	/	/

Note: Gr. grading; AAR. Asphalt aggregate ratio; MS. Stability; FL. Flow value; VV.
Porosity; VMA. Mineral material clearance rate; VFA. Asphalt saturation; γ_f. gross
volume relative density; TMD. theoretical maximum relative density (same as below)

Table 6. AC-16 design grading test results

Gr	AAR (%)	MS (KN)	FL (mm)	VV (%)	VMA(%)	VFA (%)	γsb	TMD
1	4.9	12.60	3.2	3.9	13.7	71.5	2.422	2.520
2	4.9	13.26	3.5	3.5	13.3	73.8	2.431	2.519
3	4.9	12.77	3.3	3.0	12.8	77.0	2.445	2.519
Claim	/	≥ 8.0	2–4	3–5	/	65–75	/	Measured

Table 7. AC-25 design grading test results

Gr	AAR (%)	MS (KN)	FL (mm)	VV (%)	VMA(%)	VFA (%)	γsb	TMD
1	4.0	12.60	3.4	6.2	14.0	55.8	2.399	2.557
2	4.0	13.35	3.1	4.7	12.6	62.5	2.436	2.557
3	4.0	13.58	3.0	5.4	13.3	59.4	2.418	2.556
Claim	/	≥ 8	1.5–4	3–6	/	65–75	/	Measured

According to the mineral gradation range of dense-graded bituminous mixtures [2
and the results of test, we plot separately the distribution curves of AC-13, AC-16, anc
AC-25, and the results are shown in Figs. 1, 2 and 3.

According to the Highway Engineering Industry Standards of the "Specifications
for Design of Highway Asphalt Pavements" (JTG D50-2017) and "Standard Tes
Methods of Bituminous and Bituminous Mixtures for Highway Engineering" (JTC
E20-2011) [1, 4], we can see that the grading meets the basic requirements througl
studying and analyzing the Tables 5, 6 and 7 and Figs. 1, 2 and 3.

In order to make the more reasonable grading and the better technical performance
according to Tables 5, 6 and 7 and Figs. 1, 2 and 3, we use the gradation2 that close to the
limit median as the test grading, The best design grade of its mixtures is shown in Table 8

Table 8. Best Design Mix Ratio of AC-13, 16, 25

The mass percentage (%) passing through the following sieves(square sieve, mm)

Type	Gr	31.5	26.5	19.0	16.0	13.2	9.5	4.75	2.36	1.18	0.6	0.3	0.15	0.075
AC-13	1	/	/	/	100	97.9	70.6	38.6	23.5	16.3	12.9	10.5	7.6	5.9
AC-16	2	/	/	100	90.9	80.8	67.5	45.5	26.8	17.6	11.7	8.5	6.9	6.1
AC-25	3	100	98.9	80.8	71.8	62.7	49.3	36.8	23.0	16.7	10.9	7.7	6.4	5.3

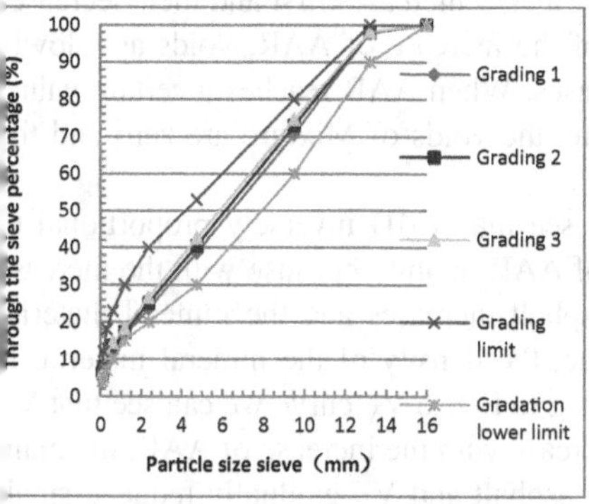

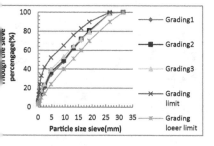

Fig. 1. AC-13 design grading diagram 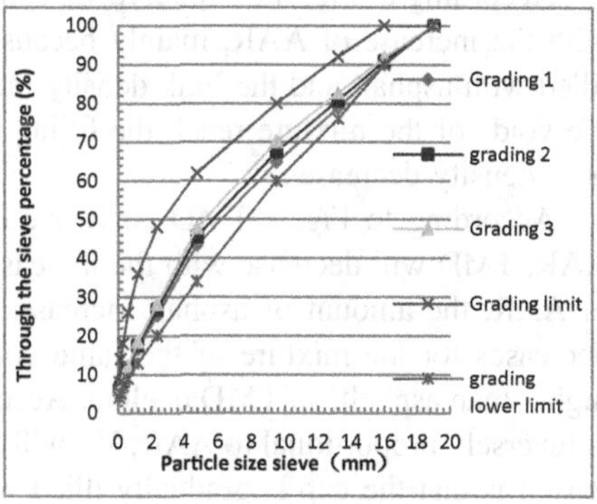   **Fig. 2.** AC-16 design grading diagram

Fig. 3. AC-25 design grading diagram 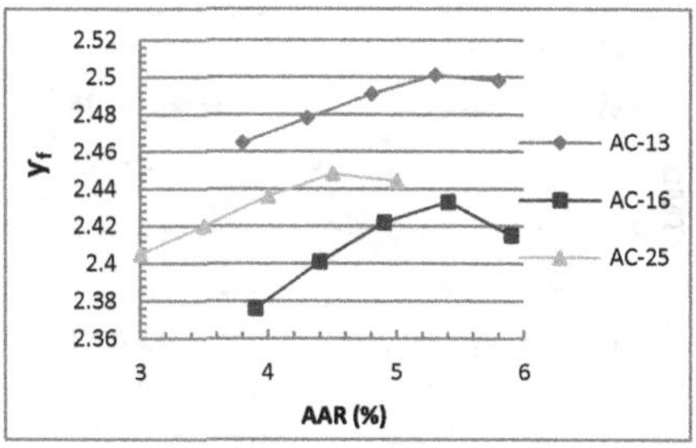   **Fig. 4.** γ_f curve

Dynamic Performance Test

.1 Marshall Stability Test and the Relationship Between the Amount of Asphalt and the Physical and Mechanical Indexes

he asphalt mixture is prepared to a cylindrical test piece of a predetermined size, and
e test piece is horizontally placed in two semicircular press molds so that the test
iece is subjected to a certain lateral limit. At the specified temperature and loading
peed, the specimen is subjected to pressure, the pressure and deformation curve of the
pecimen are recorded.

The main mechanical parameters are Marshall stability and flow values. For the tes
specifications and requirements, we see "Standard Test Methods of Bituminous an
Bituminous Mixtures for Highway Engineering" (JTG E20-2011) [2]. The Marshal
stability test was carried out according to the ratio of the designed mineral materials
and the ratio of five kinds of oil and stone was used.

According to the Marshall stability test results, plots of density, stability, flow
value, voidage, saturation, VMA, and oil/rock ratios are plotted in Figs. 4, 5, 6, 7, 8, 9
and 10.

According to Fig. 4 of γ_f curve we can see that γ_f increases first and then decrease
with the increase of AAR, mainly because of the increase of AAR, voids are slowly
filled with asphalt and the bulk density increases. When AAR reaches a certain value
the voids of the mixture reach the filling state, the voids of Mixture are zero and the
bulk density decreases.

According to Fig. 5 TMD curve we can see that TMD inversely proportional to
AAR, TMD will decrease with the increase of AAR, mainly because with the increase
of AAR, the amount of asphalt increases, asphalt increases and the mineral materia
decreases for the mixture of the same volume, the density of the mineral material is
higher than asphalt, so TMD decline; According to Fig. 6 V_V curve we can see that V_V
is inversely proportional to AAR, V_V will decrease with the increase of AAR, the main
reason is that the gap is gradually filled with asphalt and V_V gradually reduced small
with the increase of AAR; According to Fig. 7 VMA curve we can see that VMA

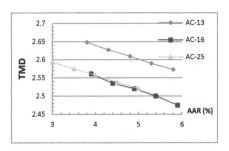

Fig. 5. TMD curve

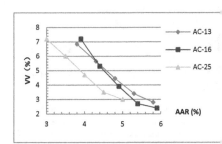

Fig. 6. VV curve

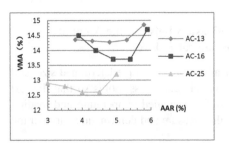

Fig. 7. VMA curve

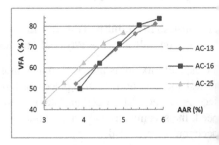

Fig. 8. VFA curve

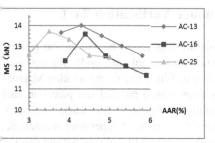

Fig. 9. MS curve

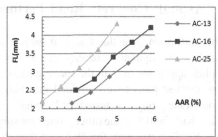

Fig. 10. Flow curve

ncreases with the increase of AAR, the reason is that the movement force between ninerals gradually increases, minerals closer together, and VMA decreases with the ncrease of AAR, When the AAR exceeds a certain limit, the asphalt becomes satuated, and gradually produces external tension to separate mineral, so VMA increase; According to Fig. 8 VFA Curve, Fig. 9 MS curve and Fig. 10 Flow curve, we can see nat asphalt content in the mixture increases with the increase of AAR, and MS ncreases first and then decrease with the increase of AAR, this indicates that the sphalt mixture fully combines, and the strength increases, and the bearing capacity ncreases with the increase of AAR. When the AAR exceeds a certain limit, the asphalt •ecomes saturated, and the internal structure of the asphalt mixture is destroyed, and ne strength is reduced, and the force drops. Simultaneously FL is proportional to AAR, nobility is also increasing as AAR increases.

.2   The Choice of the Best Mix Ratio

According to the results of the Marshall stability test and the above-mentioned raphs 4–10, we can detect the amount of asphalt corresponding to a_1, a_2, a_3 and a_4 for ne maximum amounts of stability, the maximum density, the median value of the sphalt saturation range, and the median value of the air gap. Calculating the optimal sphalt ratio using formula $OAC_1 = (a_1 + a_2 + a_3 + a_4)/4$, and calculating range OAC_{min}, OAC_{max}) of dosage for the asphalt which all indicators meet the specification equirements, calculating OAC_2 by formula $OAC_2 = (OAC_{min} + OAC_{max})/2$, deternining OAC according to formula $OAC = (OAC_1 + OAC_2)/2$, verify OAC, and letermining the best synthesis gradation [2, 4].

According to the mapping method, OAC_1 for AC-13, AC-16 and AC-25 are espectively 4.83%, 4.87% and 4.15%; OAC_2 are respectively 5.15%, 4.8% and 4.46%;)AC are respectively 4.99%, 4.84% and 4.2%. According to experience, the best sphalt aggregate ratios are 4.8%, 4.9%, and 4.2% respectively, which met the design equirements.

5   Asphalt Concrete Road Performance Verification Test

The performance of the designed asphalt mixture was tested by testing the residual stability and dynamic stability of the designed asphalt mixture under the optimum asphalt aggregate ratio in the soaking Marshall test. When testing the soaking Marshall test, the test pieces were divided into two groups with 6 parallel test pieces in each group. One group was tested for Marshall stability S_1 after being maintained in a 60 °C water bath for 0.5 h; the other group was subjected to constant temperature maintenance in a 60 °C water bath for 48 h and then tested for Marshall stability S_2; the residual stability was calculated as $S_0 = S_2/S_1 \times 100$. Test specifications and requirements are listed in the "Standard Test Methods of Bituminous and Bituminous Mixtures for Highway Engineering" (JTG E20-2011) [1, 2]. The test results are shown in Table 9.

Table 9. Test of each performance index under the best ratio of oil and stone

| Asphalt mixture | | Residual stability (%) | | Dynamic stability (times/mm) | |
Mix type	AAR	Test results	Design requirements	Test results	Design requirements
AC-13	4.8	89.0	≥ 85	4860	≥ 3000
AC-16	4.9	87.1	≥ 80	1455	≥ 1000
AC-25	4.2	85.5	≥ 80	1728	≥ 1000

According to the relevant verification test in Table 9, the dynamic stability of the AC-13, AC-16, and AC-25 ordinary asphalt mixture and the stability of the flooding Marshall test are all accordant with the design documents.

6   Conclusion and Suggestion

Through the previous tests and analysis, dense-graded asphalt concrete has better dynamic performance and road performance, and can effectively improve the engineering quality of asphalt concrete road surface. The dense-assured asphalt concrete has high stability, low temperature crack resistance, good water stability, and long-term durability. The main reason is that the internal gradation of the asphalt concrete is suspended in the structure, and the fine aggregate fully fills the gaps. Fine particles and asphalt cementitious materials fully fused, the porosity is small, there is a certain gap between the coarse aggregates, the internal frictional resistance is small, the mutual cohesion force is large, compaction degree after compaction molding is high. However, the high temperature properties depend on the quality of the asphalt material itself, the viscosity of the asphalt decreases, and the high temperature stability of the dense grade asphalt concrete also decreases. At the same time, dense grade asphalt concrete is mainly composed of fine aggregates, and the coarse aggregate suspension minerals are combined, and the construction process The medium-fine aggregate sinks into the interior of the structure, and part of the coarse aggregate floats on the surface of the structure. Although the compactness of the concrete increases and the voidage ecreases, the surface of the structure is not smooth enough, and the high-temperature ability and water damage resistance of the asphalt concrete pavement are both high. It as a great impact, and at the same time, the characteristics of gradation of dense-raded asphalt concrete can easily lead to the production of segregation sites, and it will lso have a certain impact on the bleeding performance of asphalt concrete.

References

1. Research institue, H.M.O.F.: Specifications for design of highway asphalt pavements. JTG (D50), 5–48 (2017)
2. Research institue, H.M.O.F.: Standard test methods of bituminous and bituminous mixtures for highway engineering. JTG (E20), 12–77 (2011)
3. Research institue, H.M.O.F.: Highway engineering aggregate test regulations. JTG (E42), 14–55 (2005)
4. Feiteira Dias, J.L., Picado-Santos, L.G., Capitão, S.D.: Mechanical performance of dry process fine crumb rubber asphalt mixtures placed on the Portuguese road network. Constr. Build. Mater. **73**, 247–254 (2014)
5. Fazaeli, H., Samin, Y., Pirnoun, A., Dabiri, A.S.: Laboratory and field evaluation of the warm fiber reinforced high performance asphalt mixtures (case study Karaj-Chaloos Road). Constr. Build. Mater. **122**, 273–283 (2016)
6. Kırbaş, U., Karaşahin, M.: Performance models for hot mix asphalt pavements in urban roads. Const. Build. Mater. **116**, 281–288 (2016)
7. Pasetto, M., Baldo, N.: Experimental evaluation of high performance base course and road base asphalt concrete with electric arc furnace steel slags. J. Hazard. Mater. **181**(1–3), 938–948 (2010)
8. Adam, G.P., Anaya-Lara, G.O., Burt, G.: Dynamic performance and transient response during ac network disturbances. In: 6th IET International Conference on Power Electronics Machines and Drives (PEMD 2012), pp. 1–5 (2012)
9. Darji, P.B., Kulkarni, A.M.: Dynamic performance of a modular multi-level converter based HVDC terminal under unbalanced AC grid conditions. In: International Conference on Ac & Dc Power T, pp. 1–6 (2013)
10. Yang, X.B., Yuan, C.M., Yao, D.W., Yang, C., Yue, C.Y.: Dynamic performance of series multiterminal HVDC during AC faults at inverter stations. In: 16th European Conference on Power Electronics Power Electronics and Applications, pp. 1–9. Machines and Drives (2014)
11. Adam, G.P., Anaya-Lara, G.O., Burt, G.: STATCOM based on modular multilevel converter: dynamic performance and transient response during AC network disturbances. In: 6th IET International Conference on Power Electronics, pp. 1–5 (2012)
12. Darji, P.B., Kulkarni, A.M.: Dynamic performance of a modular multi-level converter based HVDC terminal under unbalanced AC grid conditions. In: 10th IET International Conference on AC and DC Power Transmission, pp. 1–6 (2013)
13. Roiu, D., Bojoi, R., Limongi, L.R., Tenconi, A.: Dynamic performance of grid connected AC/DC Voltage Source Converter under voltage dips transient conditions. Energy Conversion Congress & Exposition, pp. 2794–2800 (2009)

14. Kumar, T.A., Krishna, V.S., Ramana, N.V.: Improvement of dynamic performance of three area thermal system under deregulated environment using AC tieline parallel with HVDC link. In: International Conference on Power & Energy Systems, pp. 1–6 (2011)
15. Ziari, H., Amini, A., Goli, A., Mirzaeiyan, D.: Predicting rutting performance of carbon nano tube (CNT) asphalt binders using regression models and neural networks. Constr. Build Mater. **160**, 415–426 (2018)

Research on Image Classification of Marine Pollutants with Convolution Neural Network

Tingting Yang[1], Shuwen Jia[2], Huanhuan Zhang[3(✉)],
and Mingquan Zhou[3]

[1] Institute of Information and Intelligence Engineering,
University of Sanya, Sanya, Hainan, China
[2] Teaching Management Office, University of Sanya, Sanya, Hainan, China
[3] Collage of Information Science and Technology,
Beijing Normal University, Beijing, China
ytt1202@126.com

Abstract. The good marine ecological environment is the basis for the sustainable development and utilization of marine resources. However, humans have also severely damaged the marine environment while utilizing marine resources. Therefore, image classification for marine pollution is beneficial to the protection and development of the ocean. In recent years, with the rise of convolution neural networks, this algorithm is rarely used in the classification of marine pollutants. This paper will apply the design of 6-layer convolution neural network to image classification of marine pollution (called for short MP-net). Experiments show that Alex net, VGG(11) and MP-net are learning and training in the same data set, and the accuracy rates respectively are 89.17%, 86.25%, and 90.14%. Therefore, in the image classification of marine pollutants using convolution neural networks, the network can adapt to image scenes, automatically learn features, and have good classification results.

Keywords: Image classification · Marine pollution · CNN

Introduction

With developing of science and technology, the relationship between human and ocean becoming more and closer. Establishing good marine ecosystem environment is the Marine resources sustainable exploitation and utilization to hold on to the bottom line, to the protection of Marine environment is more important. However, in the process of using the marine environment, human use it as a trash can to discharge waste, which leads to the pollution of the ocean and its surrounding environment and brings great inconvenience to human life.

Marine pollution as defined by the Group of Experts on the Scientific Aspects of Marine Pollution (GESAMP), as part of the basic framework of the UN Convention on the Law of the Sea (UNCLOS) 1982 (Article 1.4), is: "the introduction by man, directly or indirectly, of substances or energy into the marine environment (including estuaries) resulting in such deleterious effects as harm to living resources, hazards to human health, hindrance to marine activities including fishing, impairment of quality for use of

© Springer Nature Switzerland AG 2018
. Sun et al. (Eds.): ICCCS 2018, LNCS 11068, pp. 665–673, 2018.
https://doi.org/10.1007/978-3-030-00021-9_59

sea water, and reduction of amenities." Based on the previous definition of marine pollutants, this research used the designed MP-net classification algorithm to classify over 700 oceanographic (Fig. 1. difference of oceanographic) images and achieved good experimental results.

a. Image of no-marine pollutants

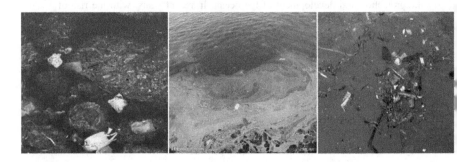

b. Image of marine pollutants

Fig. 1. Difference of oceanographic

2 Relate Work

The traditional image feature extraction algorithm is more specific to specific problems and is specially set manually. This method has weak generalization ability, poor portability, and relatively poor accuracy. In the 1960s, Hubel researched the visual cortex of the cat's brain and found that the biological vision system was achieved through layer-by-layer excitation of the Receptive Field. An in-depth study of the animal's visual mechanism inspired researchers to think about whether similar algorithms could be designed to give the machine the ability to recognize images, so CNN was born. Convolutional neural networks rely on the network itself to learn about training data and learn to extract data features. With the arrival of the era of big data, CNN shows its irreplaceable advantages in image processing, Image recognition, target

letection, image segmentation, target tracking and other fields have been achieved
adical progress.
The structure of the current convolutional neural network is constantly optimized.
'or example, the accumulation of The Convolutional Deep Belief Network was created
hrough a combination of a network and a trusted network, which is successfully
pplied to face feature extraction as an unsupervised model of generation, Alex Net
chieved breakthrough results in the massive image classification field; R-CNN suc-
eeded in the target detection field based on regional feature extraction, and Fully
onvolutional network realized end-to-end image segmentation, and the accuracy was
reatly improved, which surpass the traditional semantic segmentation algorithm. After
everal experiments, it has been shown that CNN is the best for the secondary clas-
ification of marine pollutant images.

The Data Set

he images of marine pollutants are collected from the internet. These images were
rawled using a web crawler program. A total of more than 1,300 images were crawled.
mage sizes are normalized to 256 × 256 pixels, and there were more than 760 images
vith useful values, of which more than 521 were for training sets and 239 were for test
ets (Table 1).

Table 1. Data set.

	Marine pollutants	No-marine pollutants
Training set	181	340
Testing set	75	164

Image Classification of Marine Pollutants Based on CNN

.1   The Basic Architecture of the Convolution Neural Network

Convolutional neural network includes input layer, convolution layer, pooling layer,
ull connection layer and classification. The convolutional neural network structure
hown in Figs. 2 and 3.
The convolutional layer is the core building block of a CNN. The convolutional
xpression in calculus is:

$$y(t) = \int h(s - t)x(t)dt \tag{1}$$

While the expression is the earliest type, it is used by Sylvestre François Lacroix on
age 505 of his book entitled Treatise on differences and series. The main use of
onvolution in engineering is in describing the output of a linear, time-invariant
LTI) system. The input-output behavior of an LTI system can be characterized via

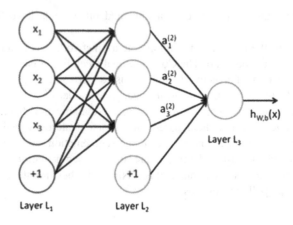

Fig. 2. Neural network structure

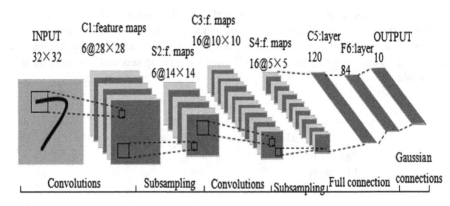

Fig. 3. Architecture of the convolution neural network

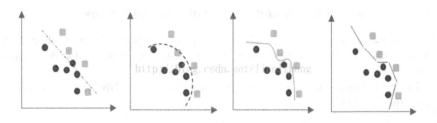

Fig. 4. Different function to fit (the linear cannot fit anything)

its impulse response, and the output of an LTI system for any input signal x(t) can be expressed as the convolution of the input signal with the system's impulse response. Namely, if the signal x(t)x(t) is applied to an LTI system with impulse response h(t)h(t) then the output signal is y(t).

If it is a two-dimensional convolution, the expression is:

$$s(i,j) = (X * W)(i,j) = \sum_m \sum_n x(i-m, j-m)w(m,n) \qquad (2)$$

The layer's parameters consist of a set of learnable filters (or kernels), which have a small receptive field, but extend through the full depth of the input volume.

$$x_j^{l-1} = f(u_j^l)$$
$$u_j^i = \sum_{i \in M_j} x_i^{l-1} * w_{ij}^l + b_j^l \qquad (3)$$

Where f ($\cdot$) represents an activation function, then x_i^{l-1} represents a certain pixel value of a feature image of the previous layer, w_{ij}^l represents a convolution kernel, * represents a convolution operation, and M_j represents a sub-image of a feature image of an upper layer participating in the operation set; b_j^l stands for bias term, superscript l for the l layer.

The activation function (Fig. 5 shows) is used to add nonlinear factors, because the linear model is not expressive enough (Fig. 4). The standard way to model a neuron's output f as a function of its input x is with f(x) = tanh(x)() or f(x) = $(1 + e^{-x})^{-1}$. However, the two activation functions have certain disadvantages, that is, the gradient value is very small when saturated and the output value is not centered on 0. So now the research generally use Alexnet's activation function f(x) = max(0,x) (refer to neurons with this nonlinearity as Rectified Linear Units (ReLUs)).

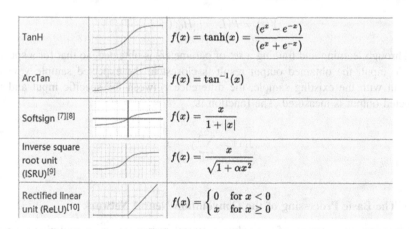

TanH		$f(x) = \tanh(x) = \dfrac{(e^x - e^{-x})}{(e^x + e^{-x})}$
ArcTan		$f(x) = \tan^{-1}(x)$
Softsign [7][8]		$f(x) = \dfrac{x}{1 + |x|}$
Inverse square root unit (ISRU)[9]		$f(x) = \dfrac{x}{\sqrt{1 + \alpha x^2}}$
Rectified linear unit (ReLU)[10]		$f(x) = \begin{cases} 0 & \text{for } x < 0 \\ x & \text{for } x \geq 0 \end{cases}$

Fig. 5. Activation function

The pooling layer reduces the dimension of the image by different pooling operations, and improves the invariant characteristics of the image features. Commonly used pooling operations include maximum pooling and average pooling. After alternating convolution and pooling layers, highly abstract feature images have been obtained. For example, Max pooling is to find the maximum value in each area, and finally extract the main features in the original feature map to get the right image (as the Fig. 6 show).

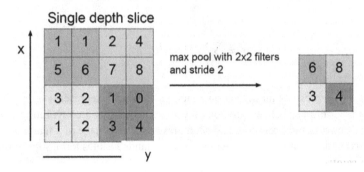

Fig. 6. Max pooling

Convolutional neural networks classify extracted features based on a fully connected network and obtain input-based probability distributions as Y. As shown in formula 2, the convolutional neural network essentially makes the original matrix (H0 transformed or reduced by multiple layers of data and mapped to a new mathematical model of feature representation.

$$Y(i) = P(L = l_i | H_0; (w, b)) \tag{4}$$

Through learning and training a set of parameters is obtained, so that for a specific sample input, the obtained output result is closest to the expected sample y value wherein with the existing sample, the difference between the specific input and the expected output is measured. The function is:

$$J(x) = \sum_{i=0}^{n} y_i - x_i \tag{5}$$

4.2   The Basic Processing of the Convolution Neural Network

The learning and training of convolution kernel parameters in convolutional neural networks is implemented by a gradient back propagation algorithm, which is a supervised learning algorithm. Assuming that the training of the network is not yet complete, there will be some errors between the training output and the actual output of the input signal. The error propagates layer by layer in the gradient descent algorithm and updates the network parameters layer by layer.

4.3   Constructing CNN Architecture for Image Classification of Marine Pollutants (MP-Net)

For the image classification problem of marine pollutants, the architecture of MPnet in this paper is shown in Fig. 7. The network has 6 layers, the first 4 layers are convolution layers, and the last two layers are fully connected layers. In order to prevent network overfitting from affecting the model's generalization by referring to the dropout technique, and Nair and Hinton proposed the relu function which is used to increase the non-neutrality between neural networks. Linear relationships make neural networks better able to solve more complex problems.

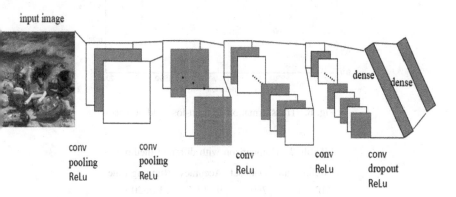

Fig. 7. CNN architecture for image classification of marine pollutants

In the paper the first convolutional layer has convolutional kernels of size 11*11*3 with a stride of 4 pixels; The second layer uses a convolution kernel of 5*5, and the convolution kernel behind it uses a convolution kernel of 3*3. All convolution kernels act on all feature maps of the corresponding previous layer at the same time, and the same convolution kernel is inconsistent with the weights of different feature maps of the previous layer, and the four convolution layers abstractly extract different features layer by layer.

5   Result

The environment used in this experiment is: linux-64 operating system, and Caffe's development framework, Inter(R) CPU2, 40 GHZ, 32 GB of memory, 8 GB of video memory. During the experimental process, the image resolution was first preprocessed. If the resolution is too low, the useful information of the image will be lost; If it is too high, it will cause a huge computational cost. Therefore, in the experiment, considering the memory and CNN architecture limitations, the resolution was finally adjusted to 256 * 256. As shown in Fig. 8, we can clearly see the train-loss, test-loss and accuracy experimental results. The convolutional neural network designed (MP-net) in this research and the classical CNN of Alexnet and VGG(11) networks have made comparisons on this classification problem. The accuracy of MP-net and the other two classical structures of this design on the test set are 90.14%, 89.17%, and 86.25% respectively, as shown in Table 2.

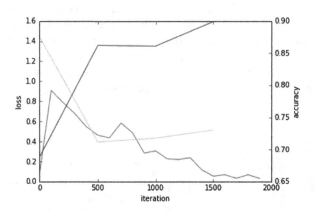

Fig. 8. Transformation of train-loss and accuracy

Table 2. Comparison with different methods.

Architecture	Data set	Accuracy	Running time
MP-net	760	90.14%	13 m 20 s
Alexnet	760	89.17%	19 m 52 s
VGG(11)	760	86.25%	51 m 15 s

6 Conclusion

This paper mainly explores the method of deep learning convolutional neural network and applies the classification of images of marine pollutants. The dataset used in the experiment collects from the network in which there are a total of 760 images, and Combined with the popular convolutional neural network methods such as Rectified Linear Units (ReLU) and random dropout in recent years, the paper research classification problem of marine pollutants by designed 6-layer convolutional neural network (referred to as MPnet). Comparing with the classic convolutional neural network structure alexnet, VGG(11), in the experiment, the convolutional layer and the fully connected layer of the MP-net structure are reduced by one layer at a time. Therefore the running time is greatly shortened, but the accuracy rate is not reduced but higher. The experiments show the network structure designed (MP-net) according to specific problems in the data set of marine pollutants can obtain higher accuracy.

Acknowledgement. This work is supported by Hainan Provincial Natural Science Foundation of China (project number: 20166235), Hainan provincial university scientific research funding project (project number: Hnky2017-57).

References

1. Clark, R.B.: Marine Pollution, 5th edn. Oxford University Press, Oxford (2002)
2. Fukushima, K., Miyake, S., Ito, T.: Neocognitron: a neural network model for a mechanism of visual pattern recognition. IEEE Trans. Syst. Man Cybern. SMC **13**(5), 826–834 (1983)
3. Hinton, G.E., Osindero, S., Teh, Y.W.: A fast learning algorithm for deep belief nets. Neural Comput. **18**(7), 1527–1554 (2006)
4. Le Cun, Y., Boser, B., Denker, J.S., et al.: Backpropagation applied to handwritten zip code recognition. Neural Comput. **1**(4), 541–551 (1989)
5. Krizhevsky, A., Sutskever, I., Hinton, G.E.: Imagenet classification with deep convolutional neural networks. In: Advances in Neural Information Processing Systems, pp. 1097–1105 (2012)
6. Hinton, G.E., Srivastava, N., Krizhevsky, A., et al.: Improving neural networks by preventing co- adaptation of feature detectors. Comput. Sci. **3**(4), 212–223 (2012)
7. Le Cun, Y., Huang, F.J., Bottou, L.: Learning methods for generic object recognition with invariance to pose and lighting. In: Proceedings of the 2004 IEEE Computer Society Conference on Computer Vision and Pattern Recognition (CVPR 2004) (2004)
8. Girshick, R., Donahue, J., Darrell, T., et al.: Rich feature hierarchies for accurate object detection and semantic segmentation. In: Proceedings of the IEEE Conference On Computer Vision and Pattern Recognition, pp. 580–587 (2014)
9. Simonyan, K., Zisserman, A.: Very deep convolutional networks for large-scale image recognition. In: Proceedings of ICLR 2015 (2015)
10. Mensink, T., Verbeek, J., Perronnin, F., Csurka, G.: Metric learning for large scale image classification: generalizing to new classes at near-zero cost. In: Fitzgibbon, A., Lazebnik, S., Perona, P., Sato, Y., Schmid, C. (eds.) ECCV 2012. LNCS, pp. 488–501. Springer, Heidelberg (2012). https://doi.org/10.1007/978-3-642-33709-3_35
11. Russell, B.C., Torralba, A., Murphy, K.P., Freeman, W.T.: LabelMe: a database and web-based tool for image annotation. Int. J. Comput. Vis. **77**(1), 157–173 (2008)
12. Nair, V., Hinton, G.E.: Rectified linear units improve restricted boltzmann machines. In: Proceedings of the 27th International Conference on Machine Learning (2010)
13. LeCun, Y., Huang, F.J., Bottou, L.: Learning methods for generic object recognition with invariance to pose and lighting. In: Computer Vision and Pattern Recognition(CVPR 2004) (2004)
14. Endres, I., Hoiem, D.: Category independent object proposals. In: Daniilidis, K., Maragos, P., Paragios, N. (eds.) ECCV 2010. LNCS, vol. 6315, pp. 575–588. Springer, Heidelberg (2010). https://doi.org/10.1007/978-3-642-15555-0_42
15. Wang, X., Yang, M., Zhu, S., Lin, Y.: Regionlets for generic object detection. IEEE Trans. Pattern Anal. Mach. Intell. **37**(10), 2071–2084 (2015)
16. Zeiler, M., Taylor, G., Fergus, R.: Adaptive deconvolutional networks for mid and high level feature learning. In: Computer Vision and Pattern Recognition (CVPR2011) (2011)
17. Howard, A.G.: Some improvements on deep convolutional neural network based image classification. In: Proceedings of the ICLR2014 (2014)
18. Perronnin, F., Sánchez, J., Mensink, T.: Improving the fisher kernel for large-scale image classification. In: Daniilidis, K., Maragos, P., Paragios, N. (eds.) ECCV 2010. LNCS, vol. 6314, pp. 143–156. Springer, Heidelberg (2010). https://doi.org/10.1007/978-3-642-15561-1_11
19. Fei-Fei, L., Fergus, R., Perona, P.: Learning generative visual models from few training examples: an incremental bayesian approach tested on 101 object categories. Comput. Vis. Image Underst. **106**(1), 178–187 (2007)
20. Simonyan, K., Zisserman, A.: Very deep convolutional networks for large-scale image recognition. In: ICLR2015 (2015)

Robust Manifold Learning Based Ordinal Discriminative Correlation Regression

Qing Tian[1,2,4(✉)], Wenqiang Zhang[1,2], and Liping Wang[3]

[1] School of Computer and Software, Nanjing University of Information Science and Technology, Nanjing 210044, China
tianqing@nuist.edu.cn
[2] Collaborative Innovation Center of Atmospheric Environment and Equipment Technology, Nanjing University of Information Science and Technology, Nanjing 210044, China
[3] Department of Mathematics, Nanjing University of Aeronautics and Astronautics, Nanjing 210016, China
[4] School of Electrical and Electronic Engineering, The University of Manchester, Manchester M13 9PL, UK

Abstract. Canonical correlation analysis (CCA) is a typical learning paradigm of capturing the correlation components across multi-views of the same data. When countered with such data with ordinal labels, the accuracy performance yielded by traditional CCA is usually not desirable because of ignoring the ordinal relationships among data labels. In order to incorporate the ordinal information into the objective function of CCA, the so-called ordinal discriminative CCA (OR-DisCCA) was presented. Although OR-DisCCA can yield better ordinal regression results, its performance will be deteriorated when the data are corrupted with outliers because the ordered class centers easily tend to be biased by the outliers. To address this issue, in this work we construct robust manifold ordinal discriminative correlation regression (rmODCR) by replacing the traditional (l_2-norm) class centers with l_p-norm centers in objective optimization. Finally, we experimentally evaluate the effectiveness of the proposed method.

Keywords: Canonical correlation analysis · Ordinal regression
l_p-norm centers · Manifold learning

1 Introduction

Canonical correlation analysis (CCA) was first proposed in 1936 [18] to find projection vectors along which the correlation of two sets of variables is mutually maximized. However, the original CCA can only handle such data with two views of features. In order to analyze multi-view data, Kettenring generated its multi-view counterpart [11]. Motivated by the work of [11], a variety of variants of CCA were successively proposed. For example, Kernel CCA [13,15], Sparse CCA [2,17], Probabilistic CCA [9], etc. It can be found from the aforementioned works

© Springer Nature Switzerland AG 2018
X. Sun et al. (Eds.): ICCCS 2018, LNCS 11068, pp. 674–683, 2018.
https://doi.org/10.1007/978-3-030-00021-9_60

hat the supervised label information is not incorporated in their objectives. To vercome such drawbacks, supervised discriminative counterpart of CCA was roposed by minimizing the inter-class cross-view correlation while maximizng the intra-class cross-view correlation in the objective function [24,25]. In ddition, more general semi-supervised [5], sparse unsupervised [4] and spectral mbedding [3] based multi-view learning were also introduced in CCA modelng. The above reviewed CCA and its variants have wide applications in image rocessing [6,7], multimedia analysis [21,22,26], information retrieval [28], text lassification [20], etc.

Although the aforementioned methods can yield promising results on their oncerned problems, their performance will be dramatically reduced when faced vith so-called ordinal data whose ground-truth labels are discrete and orderly nonotonous. This is because in their learning the ordinality characteristic of lata labels sequence was not taken into account. For the sake of clarification, ve take age estimation as an example, which is a typical ordinal estimation roblem. Age 16 is much closer to age 15 than to age 20, and the severity of nisclassifying the face aged 16 to age 15 is less than to age 20. But, if we disegard such an ordinal relationship and assign them with same severity weight, he estimation will be seriously unreliable. To address such ordinal data tasks vith multi-view feature representations, Kawashima et al. [10] proposed to first erform multi-view fusion by CCA and then conduct ordinal regression in the used space. Although the ordinality relationship of data labels was specially preerved, the multi-view fusion and subsequent decision making are performed in a eparate manner, leading to non-optimal performance. To incorporate both the liscriminative and ordinality information in the CCA objective function, Zhou t al. [31] proposed the so-called ordinal discriminative CCA (i.e. OR-DisCCA) oy explicitly modeling both the supervised label information and the ordinalty relationships between the class labels. Although the OR-DisCCA method generated comparatively better regression results, it will be degenerated if the lata are corrupted with outliers. Through analyzing the objective function of)R-DisCCA, we can find that the ordinal constraints are imposed on the class enters derived from l_2-norm which is sensitive to the outliers [29]. As a result, f the data are corrupted with outliers or noise samples, these l_2-norm centers vill be biased by them and thus subsequent ordinal regression accuracy will be educed. In addition, the discriminative within-class scatters are incorporated in he objective function, which also easily tends to be biased by the outliers far rom the true distributions. To overcome these drawbacks, with similar motivaion to the work of [29], we in this paper propose a novel l_p-norm class centers omputing algorithm to replace the traditional l_2-norm centers. By the above tep, a robust manifold ordinal discriminative correlation regression (rmODCR) an be constructed. Finally, we experimentally evaluate the effectiveness of the nethod.

2 Background

Without loss of generality, assume a set of N training samples with two rep
resentation views $X := \{x_i\}_{i=1}^N \in \mathbb{R}^{p \times N}$ and $Y := \{y_i\}_{i=1}^N \in \mathbb{R}^{q \times N}$ from K
ordinal classes are provided. The classical CCA aims to seek two projection vec
tors $w_x \in \mathbb{R}^p$ and $w_y \in \mathbb{R}^q$ such that the correlations between $w_x^T X$ and $w_y^T Y$ is
maximized as follows

$$\max_{w_x^T w_x = 1, w_y^T w_y = 1} \frac{w_x^T X Y^T w_y}{\sqrt{w_x^T X X^T w_x}\sqrt{w_y^T Y Y^T w_y}}. \tag{1}$$

Essentially, Eq. (1) can be equivalently rewritten as

$$\min_{w_x, w_y} \quad \|w_x^T X - w_y^T Y\|_2^2$$
$$s.t. \quad w_x^T X Y^T w_y = 1, \ w_y^T Y Y^T w_y = 1. \tag{2}$$

Motivated by Eq. (2) and the KDLOR method [23], Zhou et al. [31] proposed
the OR-DisCCA model to handle multi-view ordinal regression tasks, which was
formulated as follows

$$\min_{w, \rho} \quad \|w_x^T X - w_y^T Y\|_2^2 + \lambda_1 w^T S_w w - \lambda_2 \rho$$
$$s.t. \quad w^T (m_{k+1} - m_k) \geq \rho, \ k = 1, ..., K - 1, \tag{3}$$

where ρ is the margin scale, $w = \begin{pmatrix} w_x \\ w_y \end{pmatrix}$, $m_k = \begin{pmatrix} m_{x,k} \\ m_{y,k} \end{pmatrix}$ with $m_{x,k} =$
$\frac{1}{N_k} \sum_{x \in X_k} x$ and $m_{y,k} = \frac{1}{N_k} \sum_{y \in Y_k} y$ being the k-th class centers of X and
Y, respectively. And, the total within-scatter $S_w = \begin{pmatrix} S_w^x & 0 \\ 0 & S_w^y \end{pmatrix}$ with $S_w^x =$
$\frac{1}{N} \sum_{k=1}^K \sum_{x \in X_k} (x - m_{x,k})(x - m_{x,k})^T$ and $S_w^y = \frac{1}{N} \sum_{k=1}^K \sum_{y \in Y_k} (y - m_{y,k})^T$, and λ_1 and λ_2 are nonnegative tradeoff parameters. After solving Eq. (3)
in a similar manner to [23], the projection vector $w = \begin{pmatrix} w_x \\ w_y \end{pmatrix}$ can be obtained.
Usually, projection just along one direction w is not enough for desirable perfor
mance, multiple directions are required. To this end, the authors extended Eq.
(3) to its multi-direction counterpart as

$$\min_{w_d, \rho} \quad \|w_x^T X - w_y^T Y\|_2^2 + \lambda_1 w^T S_w w - \lambda_2 \rho + \lambda_3 \sum_{i=1}^{d-1}(w_i^T w_d)^2$$
$$s.t. \quad w_d^T (m_{k+1} - m_k) \geq \rho, \ k = 1, ..., K - 1, \tag{4}$$

in which the previous $d-1$ projection directions $w_1, ..., w_{d-1}$ can be generated in
the same manner as w_d $(d \leq \{p, q\})$. Equation (4) can be simplified as

$$\min_{w_d, \rho} \quad w_d^T M_d w_d - \lambda_2 \rho$$
$$s.t. \quad w_d^T (m_{k+1} - m_k) \geq \rho, \ k = 1, ..., K - 1, \tag{5}$$

n which $M_d = \begin{pmatrix} X \\ -Y \end{pmatrix}\begin{pmatrix} X \\ -Y \end{pmatrix}^T + \lambda_1 S_w + \lambda_3 \sum_{i=1}^{d-1} w_i w_i^T$. Equation (5) is a quadratic programming (QP) problem and can be easily solved using the off-the-shelf optimization algorithms [14,19]. With the obtained $w = \{w_1, ..., w_d\}$, one first map a test instance alongside them and then perform ordinal regression decision.

3 Proposed Method

3.1 Robust Class Centers Derived from l_p-norm Against Outliers

Through analyzing Eq. (5), we can find that the class centers $\{m_k\}_{k=1}^K$ are involved in both the objective function (see the within-scatter term) and the ordinal margin constraints. For $\{m_k\}_{k=1}^K$ defined in Eq. (4), they are essentially derived from the l_2-norm as follows

$$
\begin{aligned}
(m_k)^* &= arg\min_{m_k} \sum_{x\in X_k, y\in Y_k} \left\| \begin{pmatrix} m_{x,k} \\ m_{y,k} \end{pmatrix} - \begin{pmatrix} x \\ y \end{pmatrix} \right\|_2^2 \\
&= arg\min_{m_k} \sum_{x\in X_k, y\in Y_k} \left(\begin{pmatrix} m_{x,k} \\ m_{y,k} \end{pmatrix} - \begin{pmatrix} x \\ y \end{pmatrix} \right)^T \left(\begin{pmatrix} m_{x,k} \\ m_{y,k} \end{pmatrix} - \begin{pmatrix} x \\ y \end{pmatrix} \right) \quad (6) \\
&= \frac{1}{N_k} \sum_{x\in X_k, y\in Y_k} \begin{pmatrix} x \\ y \end{pmatrix},
\end{aligned}
$$

where $m_k = \begin{pmatrix} m_{x,k} \\ m_{y,k} \end{pmatrix}$, X_k and Y_k denote the k-th class training set from the two representation views, respectively. Unfortunately, l_2-norm is sensitive to outliers [29], resulting in that the performance of OR-DisCCA tends to be deteriorated if the training data are corrupted with outlier samples. To overcome this drawbacks with the motivation from the work of [29], we propose to derive the class centers from l_p-norm instead of l_2-norm. Specifically, the l_p-norm based class centers can be generated by optimizing the following objective function

$$
(m_k)^* = arg\min_{m_k} \sum_{x\in X_k, y\in Y_k} \left\| \begin{pmatrix} m_{x,k} \\ m_{y,k} \end{pmatrix} - \begin{pmatrix} x \\ y \end{pmatrix} \right\|_p^p, \ p \in (0,2], \quad (7)
$$

in which $\|x\|_p^p = \sum_{i=1}^d |x_i|^p$ with x_i being the i-th element of x. Because the distributions of outliers are typically unknown and without rules, the parameter $0 < p \le 2$. Although Eq. (7) has no closed-form solution (except for $p = 2$), we can construct its analytical-type solutions in an iterative manner, which is summarized in Table 1, where $f(t)$ indicates the t-th iteration objective value of Eq. (7), and $\{(m_k^{lp})^{(t)}\}_{k=1}^K$ denote the generated centroid corresponding to the data classes.

By comparing the definitions of l_p-norm and l_2-norm aforementioned, we can see that l_2-norm is covered by l_p-norm. In other words, the l_p-norm based models

Table 1. An iterative optimization algorithm for l_p-norm based two-view class centers

Input: Training data $\{X_k\}_{k=1}^{K} \subseteq R^p$ and $\{Y_k\}_{k=1}^{K} \subseteq R^q$, parameter p, and convergence threshold ε.
Output: $\{m_k\}_{k=1}^{K}$

1. for $k = 1, \ldots, K$ do
2. $\quad t = 1;$
3. $\quad (m_k)^{(t)} = \begin{pmatrix} m_{x,k} \\ m_{y,k} \end{pmatrix}^{(t)} = \dfrac{1}{N_k} \sum_{x \in X_k, y \in Y_k} \begin{pmatrix} x \\ y \end{pmatrix};$
4. $\quad f(t-1) = 1e^{10},\ f(t) = \dfrac{1}{N_k} \sum_{x \in X_k, y \in Y_k} \left\| \begin{pmatrix} m_{x,k} \\ m_{y,k} \end{pmatrix}^{(t)} - \begin{pmatrix} x \\ y \end{pmatrix} \right\|_p^p$
5. $\quad$ while $\dfrac{f(t-1) - f(t)}{f(t-1)} > \varepsilon$ do
6. $\quad\quad f(t-1) = f(t);$
7. $\quad\quad$ for $i = 1, \ldots, N_k$ do
8. $\quad\quad\quad (D_i)^{(t)} = diag\left\{ \left\| \begin{pmatrix} m_{x,k} \\ m_{y,k} \end{pmatrix}^{(t)} - \begin{pmatrix} x_i \\ y_i \end{pmatrix} \right\|^{p-2} \right\};$
9. $\quad\quad$ end for
10. $\quad\quad (m_k)^{(t+1)} = \begin{pmatrix} m_{x,k} \\ m_{y,k} \end{pmatrix}^{(t+1)}$

$\quad\quad\quad = \arg\min_{m_k} \sum_{i=1}^{N_k} \left(\left(\begin{pmatrix} m_{x,k} \\ m_{y,k} \end{pmatrix}^{(t)} - \begin{pmatrix} x_i \\ y_i \end{pmatrix} \right)^T (D_i)^{(t)} \left(\begin{pmatrix} m_{x,k} \\ m_{y,k} \end{pmatrix}^{(t)} - \begin{pmatrix} x_i \\ y_i \end{pmatrix} \right) \right)$

$\quad\quad\quad = \left(\sum_{i=1}^{N_k} (D_i)^{(t)} \right)^{-1} \left(\sum_{i=1}^{N_k} (D_i)^{(t)} \begin{pmatrix} x_i \\ y_i \end{pmatrix} \right);$
11. $\quad\quad f(t+1) = \dfrac{1}{N_k} \sum_{x \in X_k, y \in Y_k} \left\| \begin{pmatrix} m_{x,k} \\ m_{y,k} \end{pmatrix}^{(t+1)} - \begin{pmatrix} x \\ y \end{pmatrix} \right\|_p^p;$
12. $\quad\quad t = t + 1.$
13. $\quad$ end while
14. end for

can handle more complex data distributions even with unknown types of outliers (or say noises) and consequently alleviate the influence of outliers to the true data distributions than the l_2-norm based models. It is just the superiority of l_p-norm.

3.2   Robust Cross-View Ordinal Discriminative Correlation Regression

To make the OR-DisCCA (see Sect. 2) robust (or insensitive) against outliers, we propose to remodel it by replacing the class centers with the proposed l_p-norm centers in the objective function of OR-DisCCA. More concretely, Substitute Eq. (7) in Eq. (3) result in the proposed robust manifold ordinal discriminative correlation regression (coined as rmODCR) as follows

$$\min_{w_d,\rho} \quad \|w_x^T X - w_y^T Y\|_2^2 + \lambda_1 w^T S_w w - \lambda_2 \rho + \lambda_3 \sum_{i=1}^{d-1} (w_i^T w_d)^2 \tag{8}$$

$$s.t. \quad w_d^T(m_{k+1}^* - m_k^*) \geq \rho, \ k = 1, ..., K-1,$$

where m_k^* and m_{k+1}^* are the proposed l_p-norm class centers via the proposed algorithm. For the sake of optimization, it can be simplified as

$$\min_{w_d,\rho} \quad w_d^T M_d w_d - \lambda_2 \rho \tag{9}$$

$$s.t. \quad w_d^T(m_{k+1}^* - m_k^*) \geq \rho, \ k = 1, ..., K-1,$$

where $M_d = \begin{pmatrix} X \\ -Y \end{pmatrix} \begin{pmatrix} X \\ -Y \end{pmatrix}^T + \lambda_1 S_w + \lambda_3 \sum_{i=1}^{d-1} w_i w_i^T$. In order to solve our method more efficiently, we resort to optimize its dual problem which is derived as follows

$$\min_{\alpha} \quad \sum_{k=1}^{K-1} \alpha_k (m_{k+1}^* - m_k^*)^T M_d^{-1}(m_{k+1}^* - m_k^*) \tag{10}$$

$$s.t. \quad \alpha_k \geq 0, \ \sum_{k=1}^{K-1} \alpha_k = \lambda_2.$$

The dual problem in Eq. (10) is also quadratic programming and can be solved using the same algorithms as the OR-DisCCA method. When the α are generated, we can obtain $w_d = \frac{1}{2} M_d^{-1} \sum_{k=1}^{K-1} \alpha_k (m_{k+1}^* - m_k^*)$. With the obtained d projection vectors $w = [w_1, ..., w_d]$, we can calculate the projections along them for a test instance with two representation views x_t and y_t through $w^T \begin{pmatrix} x_t \\ y_t \end{pmatrix} = [w_1, ..., w_d]^T \begin{pmatrix} x_t \\ y_t \end{pmatrix}$, and thus make final regression decision.

4   Experiment

To evaluate the proposed method, we are in position to perform comparative experiments on the MFD and USPS datasets. The motivation of choosing these databases are that they are collected for different tasks, and more importantly that they all are representative datasets widely used for ordinal regression estimation. For the comparative methods, we take sepOrCCA [10], OR-DisCCA [31] and the proposed rmODCR for comparison.

4.1   MFD

MFD is a multi-feature handwritten digit ("0" to "9") database [1], in which each digit has 200 samples to account for a total of 2000 samples. Each of the digit samples is represented in six types of features, i.e., *Fou, Fac, Kar, Pix, Zer,*

Mor, etc. We select any two sets of the features as two feature views and thus generate totally 15 combinations for experiment. For experimental setup, all the hyper-parameters are tuned via 5-fold cross-validation in $\{1e_{-1}, 0, 1e_1, 1e_3, 1e_5\}$ And, we randomly take 50% of the data set as training set and the remaining for test. We uniformly take the widely used *Mean Absolute Error* (MAE) (MAE $= \frac{1}{N} \sum_{i=1}^{N} |\widehat{l_i} - l_i|$ with l_i and $\widehat{l_i}$ denoting the ground-true and regressed values respectively) as performance criterion (*the lower the better*). We uniformly make final decisions by performing nearest class center regression. To evaluate the performance of the compared methods against outlier samples (i.e. noise), we corrupt the training set with different ratios of sample noises. Finally, we run the experiments 10 times and report the averaged results in Fig. 1. We can see from the results that Generally, the MAE values of the proposed rmODCR are lowest among the methods, especially against OR-DisCCA. These results clearly demonstrate the effectiveness of the proposed methodology.

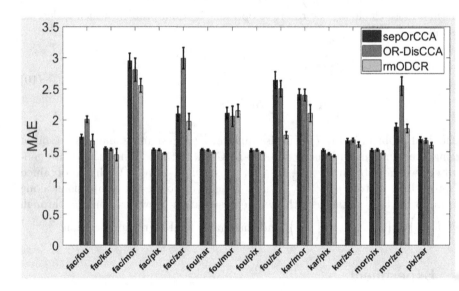

Fig. 1. Experiment on MFD with 20% noise corruption.

4.2   USPS

USPS is a handwritten digital database consisting of 11000 digits from 0 to 9 with 1100 for each. Some image examples from the database are shown in Fig. 2 Unlike the MFD database, USPS is originally collected with single view images That is, it is a single view database. To perform multi-view correlation evaluation, we extract pixel-values and HoG parameters [12] as two types of view representations. We also conducted comparative experiments on the extracted feature sets of the database with the same setting as in Sect. 4.1. The experimental results are provided in Fig. 3. It can be found from the results that, with

Fig. 2. Image examples from the USPS dataset.

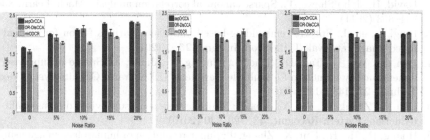

(a)   Training Percentage: 10%   (b) Training Percentage: 30%   (c)   Training Percentage: 50%

Fig. 3. Experimental results on USPS.

ncreased noise ratios in each of the subfigures, the MAEs of all methods are enerally increasing. It shows that noise samples (i.e., outliers) hinder improv-ng the regression accuracy of the methods, because the spatial structure of raining samples are biased from their true distributions, especially when large atios of outliers are involved. Moreover, the MAEs of the proposed rmODCR re the lowest, which shows the effectiveness of the proposed method.

Conclusion

n this paper, we proposed a novel type of l_p-norm class centers deriving lgorithm to replace the traditional l_2-norm centers involved in OR-DisCCA. Through the above steps, we constructed a robust ordinal discriminative corre-ation regression (rmODCR). Finally, we experimentally demonstrated the effec-iveness of the proposed method, and robustness relative to compared methods. n the future, we will consider to extend the method to deep learning based ross-heterogeneous-database scenarios [8,27] by combining cross-database sam-les with deep model structures [16,30] to further generalize the performance of he estimators.

Acknowledgment. This work was partially supported by the National Natural Sci-nce Foundation of China under grant 61702273, the Natural Science Foundation of iangsu Province under grant BK20170956, the Natural Science Foundation of the iangsu Higher Education Institutions of China under grant 17KJB520022, a Project unded by the Priority Academic Program Development of Jiangsu Higer Education

Institutions, and the Startup Foundation for Talents of Nanjing University of Informa
tion Science and Technology.

References

1. Breukelen, M.V., Duin, R.P.W., Tax, D.M.J., Hartog, J.E.D.: Handwritten digi
   recognition by combined classifiers. Kybern. Praha **34**, 381–386 (1998)
2. David, H., John Shawe, T.: Sparse canonical correlation analysis. Mach. Learn. **83**
   331–353 (2011)
3. Feng, L., et al.: Spectral embedding-based multiview features fusion for content
   based image retrieval. J. Electron. Imaging **26**, 1 (2017)
4. Han, Y., Wu, F., Tao, D., Shao, J., Zhuang, Y., Jiang, J.: Sparse unsupervised
   dimensionality reduction for multiple view data. IEEE Trans. Circuits Syst. Video
   Technol. **22**, 1485–1496 (2012)
5. Hou, C., Zhang, C., Wu, Y., Nie, F.: Multiple view semi-supervised dimensionality
   reduction. Pattern Recognit. **43**, 720–730 (2010)
6. Huang, H., He, H., Fan, X., Zhang, J.: Super-resolution of human face image using
   canonical correlation analysis. Pattern Recognit. **43**, 2532–2543 (2010)
7. Ji, H., Shen, X., Sun, Q., Ji, Z.: Sparse discrimination based multiset canonical
   correlation analysis for multi-feature fusion and recognition. In: British Machine
   Vision Conference, pp. 141.1–141.9 (2015)
8. Juefei-Xu, F., Pal, D.K., Savvides, M.: NIR-VIS heterogeneous face recognition via
   cross-spectral joint dictionary learning and reconstruction. In: Computer Vision
   and Pattern Recognition Workshops, pp. 141–150 (2015)
9. Kamada, C., Kanezaki, A., Harada, T.: Probabilistic semi-canonical correlation
   analysis. In: ACM International Conference on Multimedia, pp. 1131–1134 (2015
10. Kawashima, T., Ogawa, T., Haseyama, M.: A rating prediction method for e
    commerce application using ordinal regression based on LDA with multi-modal
    features. In: Consumer Electronics, pp. 260–261 (2013)
11. Kettenring, J.R.: Canonical analysis of several sets of variables. Biometrika **58**
    433–451 (1971)
12. Kobayashi, T., Otsu, N.: Image feature extraction using gradient local auto
    correlations. In: Forsyth, D., Torr, P., Zisserman, A. (eds.) ECCV 2008. LNCS
    vol. 5302, pp. 346–358. Springer, Heidelberg (2008). https://doi.org/10.1007/978
    3-540-88682-2_27
13. Lai, P.L., Fyfe, C.: Kernel and nonlinear canonical correlation analysis. Int. J
    Neural Syst. **10**, 365–377 (2000)
14. Lawrence, C.T.: A computationally efficient feasible sequential quadratic program
    ming algorithm. Soc. Ind. Appl. Math. **11**, 1092–1118 (2000)
15. Melzer, T., Reiter, M., Bischof, H.: Appearance models based on kernel canonical
    correlation analysis. Pattern Recognit. **36**, 1961–1971 (2003)
16. Meng, R., Rice, S.G., Wang, J., Sun, X.: A fusion steganographic algorithm based
    on faster R-CNN. Comput. Mater. Contin. **55**, 1–16 (2018)
17. Parkhomenko, E.: Sparse canonical correlation analysis. Stat. Appl. Genet. Mol
    Biol. **8**, 1 (2008)
18. Pearson, E.S.: Relations between two sets of variates. Biometrika **28**, 321–37
    (1936)
19. Radoslav, L.: Sequential Quadratic Programming. Springer, Boston (2006)
    https://doi.org/10.1007/978-0-387-40065-5

20. Rupnik, J., Grobelnik, M.: Cross-lingual search over 22 european languages. In: International ACM SIGIR Conference on Research and Development in Information Retrieval, pp. 883–883 (2008)

21. Sargin, M.E., Erzin, E., Yemez, Y., Tekalp, A.M.: Multimodal speaker identification using canonical correlation analysis. In: Proceedings of IEEE International Conference on Acoustics, Speech and Signal Processing, ICASSP 2006, pp. 613–616 (2006)

22. Sargin, M.E., Yemez, Y., Erzin, E., Tekalp, A.M.: Audiovisual synchronization and fusion using canonical correlation analysis. IEEE Trans. Multimed. **9**, 1396–1403 (2007)

23. Sun, B.Y., Li, J., Wu, D.D., Zhang, X.M., Li, W.B.: Kernel discriminant learning for ordinal regression. IEEE Trans. Knowl. Data Eng. **22**, 906–910 (2009)

24. Sun, T., Chen, S., Yang, J., Shi, P.: A novel method of combined feature extraction for recognition. In: Eighth IEEE International Conference on Data Mining, pp. 1043–1048 (2008a)

25. Sun, T.K., Chen, S.C., Jin, Z., Yang, J.Y.: Kernelized discriminative canonical correlation analysis. In: International Conference on Wavelet Analysis and Pattern Recognition, pp. 1283–1287 (2008b)

26. Tae-Kyun, K., Roberto, C.: Canonical correlation analysis of video volume tensors for action categorization and detection. IEEE Trans. Pattern Anal. Mach. Intell. **31**, 1415–1428 (2009)

27. Tian, Q., Chen, S.: Cross-heterogeneous-database age estimation through correlation representation learning. Neurocomputing **238**, 286–295 (2017)

28. Vinokourov, A., Shawe-Taylor, J., Cristianini, N.: Inferring a semantic representation of text via cross-language correlation analysis. In: Advances of Neural Information Processing Systems, pp. 1497–1504 (2002)

29. Wang, L., Chen, S.: Joint representation classification for collective face recognition. Pattern Recognit. **63**, 182–192 (2017)

30. Zeng, D., Dai, Y., Li, F., Sherratt, R.S., Wang, J.: Adversarial learning for distant supervised relation extraction. Comput. Mater. Contin. **55**, 1–16 (2018)

31. Zhou, H.X., Chen, S.C.: Ordinal discriminative canonical correlation analysis. J. Softw. **25**, 2018–2025 (2014)

Signal Subtle Feature Extraction Algorithm Based on Improved Fractal Box-Counting Dimension

Xiang Chen[1], Jingchao Li[2(✉)], and Hui Han[1]

[1] State Key Laboratory of Complex Electromagnetic Environment Effects
on Electronics and Information System (CEMEE),
Luoyang 471003, Henan, China
[2] College of Electronic and Information Engineering,
Shanghai Dianji University, Shanghai 201306, China
lijc@sdju.edu.cn

Abstract. Aiming at the limitations of traditional fractal box-counting dimension algorithm in the application of subtle feature extraction of radiation source signals, an improved generalized fractal box-counting dimension algorithm is proposed in the paper. Firstly, the signal is preprocessed, and the real and imaginary data of the signal after Hilbert transform is extracted to obtain the instantaneous amplitude of the signal; Then, the improved fractal box-counting dimension of signal instantaneous amplitude is extracted as the first eigenvector; At the same time, the improved fractal box-counting dimension of the signal without Hilbert transform is extracted as the second eigenvector; Finally, the dual improved fractal box-counting dimension eigenvectors form the multi-dimensional eigenvectors to form a new fractal box-counting dimension eigenvector as signal subtle features, for radiation source signal recognition. By establishing a dual improved fractal box-counting dimension feature space, 11 different practical radiation source signals are classified, compared with the traditional box-counting dimension algorithm, and the recognition rate is calculated. The experimental results show that compared with the traditional fractal box-counting dimension algorithm and the single improved fractal box-counting dimension algorithm, the proposed dual improved fractal box-counting dimension algorithm, can better reflect the signal subtle distribution characteristics under the different reconstruction phase space, and has a better recognition effect with good real-time performance.

Keywords: Radiation source signal · Subtle features
Traditional fractal box-counting dimension
Improved fractal box-counting dimension · Gray relation algorithm

1 Introduction

Radiation source signal recognition technology is an emerging field of research in information warfare. Exploring the effective signal feature extraction technology at a lower SNR and realizing the identification of different radiation source signals is the

X. Sun et al. (Eds.): ICCCS 2018, LNCS 11068, pp. 684–696, 2018.
https://doi.org/10.1007/978-3-030-00021-9_61

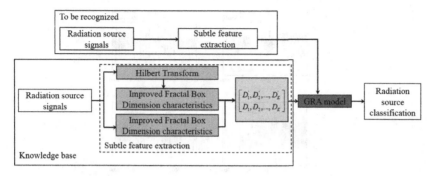

Fig. 1. Radiation source signal recognition based on signal subtle feature extraction

technical basis for the development of a new generation of electronic counterintelligence reconnaissance equipment. Owing to the complexity, importance and urgency of individual identification of radiation sources, research in this area is a key and difficult research topic in the field of information warfare. Therefore, it is necessary to develop a reliable and effective signal subtle feature extraction algorithm for radiation source signal recognition. Currently, many signal processing techniques have been applied to signal subtle feature extraction. However, due to many nonlinear factors, radiation source signal will exhibit nonlinear and unsteady characteristics [1]. Due to the usual large background noise, slight radiation source signal information is easily submerged in background noise and difficult to extract. Therefore, conventional time-domain and frequency-domain methods do not allow for an accurate assessment of radiation source signal subtle feature [2]. With the development of nonlinear dynamics, many nonlinear analytical techniques have been applied to identify and predict the complex dynamic nonlinearities of radiation source signal [3]. Among them, the most typical one is to extract the characteristic frequency from the radiation source signal through the combined usage of some advanced signal processing techniques and further evaluate the radiation source signal by comparing with the theoretical characteristic frequency value. These methods need to be combined with the expert's judgment. With the development of Artificial Intelligence (AI) [4], Radiation source signal recognition technology is more and more introduced into the category of pattern recognition. And the validity and reliability of radiation source signal recognition technology are mainly taken from the selection of dominant eigenvectors that characterize the signal subtle feature [5]. Recently, some entropy-based methods have been proposed for extracting dominant eigenvectors that characterize signal subtle feature from radiation source signal and have achieved some effect. After signal subtle feature, a pattern recognition technique is needed to automate the radiation source signal recognition. Nowadays, a variety of pattern recognition methods have been used in radiation source signal recognition, of which the most widely used are support vector machines (SVMs) [6] and artificial neural networks (ANNs) [7]. Among them, the artificial neural network (ANN) training requires a large number of samples, which is difficult or even impossible in practical applications. Support Vector Machines (SVMs) are based on statistical learning theory (especially suitable for training small samples), which have

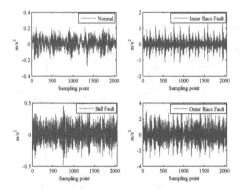

Fig. 2. The radiation source signals of rolling bearing normal operating condition and various fault conditions with fault diameter 7mils

better generalization ability than artificial neural networks (ANNs) and ensure that local optimal solutions and global optimal solutions consistent [8]. However, the accuracy of support vector machine (SVM) classifiers depends on the choice of their optimal parameters. In order to ensure the accuracy of radiation source signal recognition, some optimization algorithms and/or the design of complex multi-class structures [9] often need to be made to improve the effectiveness of support vector machines (SVMs). This paper aims to solve the problem that the traditional time and frequency domain method is not easy to make an accurate assessment of signal subtle feature extraction, and an improved generalized fractal box-counting dimension algorithm is proposed in the paper. Firstly, the signal is preprocessed, and the real and imaginary data of the signal after Hilbert transform is extracted to obtain the instantaneous amplitude of the signal; Then, the improved fractal box-counting dimension of signal instantaneous amplitude is extracted as the first eigenvector; At the same time, the improved fractal box-counting dimension of the signal without Hilbert transform is extracted as the second eigenvector; Finally, the dual improved fractal box-counting dimension eigenvectors form the multi-dimensional eigenvectors to form a new fractal box-counting dimension eigenvector as signal subtle features, for radiation source signal recognition.

2   Methodology

2.1   Hilbert Transform

Hilbert transform is widely used in signal processing to obtain an analytic representation of the signal, which allows calculation of instantaneous amplitude, phase and frequency.

Given an actual radiation source signal $f(t)$, its Hilbert transform is defined as follows:

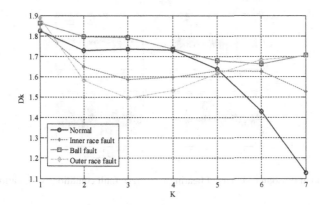

(a) without Hilbert Transform

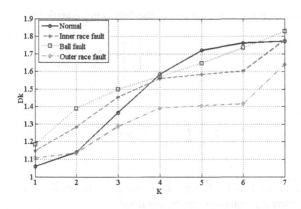

(b) with Hilbert Transform

Fig. 3. Improved generalized fractal box-counting dimension of a random chosen sample from the radiation source signals of bearing normal condition and different fault conditions with fault size 7 mils

$$h(t) = \frac{1}{\pi} P \int_{-\infty}^{\infty} \frac{f(\tau)}{t - \tau} d\tau \qquad (1)$$

where P is a Cauchy Lord value.

It can be seen from Eq. (1) that the independent variable is not changed as the result of Hilbert transform, so the output $h(t)$ is also a time dependent function. Furthermore, $h(t)$ is a linear function of $f(t)$. It is obtained from $f(t)$ by applying convolution with $(\pi t)^{-1}$ which is shown in the following relationship:

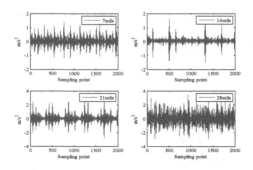

Fig. 4. The radiation source signals of bearing inner race fault conditions with various severities

$$h(t) = \frac{1}{\pi t} * f(t) \tag{2}$$

Then Fourier transform is used to get the following equation:

$$F\{h(t)\} = \frac{1}{\pi} F\left\{\frac{1}{t}\right\} F\{f(t)\} \tag{3}$$

Since

$$F\left\{\frac{1}{t}\right\} = \int_{-\infty}^{\infty} \frac{1}{x} e^{-j2\pi fx} dx = -j\pi \, \mathrm{sgn} f \tag{4}$$

where
    if $f > 0$, $\mathrm{sgn} f$ is +1, if $f = 0$, $\mathrm{sgn} f$ is 0, and if $f < 0$, $\mathrm{sgn} f$ is −1.
    Then the following equation can be obtained:

$$F\{h(t)\} = -j \, \mathrm{sgn} f F\{f(t)\} \tag{5}$$

In the frequency domain, the result is then obtained by multiplying the spectrum of $f(t)$ and j (+$\pi/2$) for negative frequencies and $-j$ ($-\pi/2$) for positive frequencies. The time domain result can be obtained over performing an inverse Fourier transform. Therefore, the Hilbert transform $h(t)$ of the original function $f(t)$ represents its harmonic conjugate.

Hilbert transform can be used to create an analytic signal from a practical signal. The $\pm\pi/2$ phase-shift operator is the basic property of Hilbert Transform. Thus the Hilbert Transform of a practical signal $f(t) = \cos(2\pi f_0 t)$ is given by $h(t) = \sin(2\pi f_0 t)$. Therefore they form an analytic signal where the instantaneous amplitude is:

$$|z(t)| = \sqrt{f^2(t) + h^2(t)} = \sqrt{\cos^2(2\pi f_0 t) + \sin^2(2\pi f_0 t)} = 1 \tag{6}$$

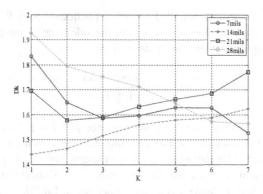

(a) without Hilbert Transform

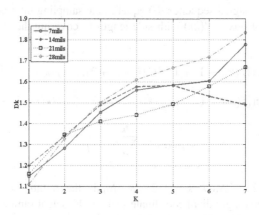

(b) with Hilbert Transform

Fig. 5. Improved generalized box-counting dimension of a random chosen sample from the radiation source signals of bearing inner race fault condition with different levels of severity

2.2   Traditional Fractal Box-Counting Dimension

Fractal theory is one of the most important branches for contemporary nonlinear science [10], and is suitable for processing all types of nonlinear and nonstationary phenomenon and may also be suitable for subtle feature extraction from radiation source signal. Fractal box-counting dimension algorithm has the advantage of simple calculation compared with other fractal dimension algorithms. The conventional algorithm of fractal box-counting dimension has been widely used in the fields of image analysis [11], electromagnetic fault diagnosis and biomedicine, which have strict self-similar signals.

Suppose A is a nonempty bounded subset of Euclidean space R^n to be calculated, and $N(A, \varepsilon)$ is the least number of boxes with the side length ε covering A. Then the fractal box-counting dimension can be defined as:

$$D = \lim_{\varepsilon \to 0} \frac{\log N(A, \varepsilon)}{\log(1/\varepsilon)} \tag{7}$$

For the actual radiation source signal sequence $f(i), i = 1, 2, \ldots, N_0$, there is no meaning for $\varepsilon \to 0$ to calculate the box counting dimension as the sampling interval σ is the highest resolution for the signal due to the existence of the sampling frequency. It is often made the minimum side length of the box $\varepsilon = \sigma$. Consider the actual sampled radiation source signal sequence $f(i)$ as the closed set of Euclidean space R^n, and the calculation process of fractal box-counting dimension is described as follows:

Use the approximate method to make the minimum side length of the box covering the radiation source signal sequence $f(i)$ equal to the sampling interval σ. And calculate the least number of boxes $N(k\varepsilon)$ with side length $k\varepsilon$ covering the signal sequence $f(i)$, thus:

$$p_1 = \max\{f(k(i-1)+1), f(k(i-1)+2), \ldots, f(k(i-1)+k+1)\} \tag{8}$$

$$p_2 = \min\{f(k(i-1)+1), f(k(i-1)+2), \ldots, f(k(i-1)+k+1)\} \tag{9}$$

$$p(k\varepsilon) = \sum_{i=1}^{N_0/k} |p_1 - p_2| \tag{10}$$

Where $i = 1, 2, \ldots, N_0/k$, $k = 1, 2 \ldots K$. N_0 is the number of sampling points, $K < N_0$. $p(k\varepsilon)$ is the longitudinal coordinate scale of the actual sampled radiation source signal sequence $f(i)$. Thus $N_{k\varepsilon}$ can be defined as:

$$N(k\varepsilon) = p(k\varepsilon)/k\varepsilon + 1 \tag{11}$$

Select a fitting curve $\log k\varepsilon \sim \log N(k\varepsilon)$ with good linearity as a scale-free zone, and the fitting curve can be defined as:

$$\log N(k\varepsilon) = a \log k\varepsilon + b \tag{12}$$

Where $k_1 \leq k \leq k_2$ and k_1 and k_2 are the start and end of the scale-free zone, respectively.

Generally, a least square method is used to calculate the slope of the fitting curve, which is the fractal box-counting dimension D of the actual sampled radiation source signal sequence $f(i)$:

$$D = \frac{(k_2 - k_1 + 1) \sum \log k \cdot \log N(k\varepsilon) - \sum \log k \cdot \sum \log N(k\varepsilon)}{(k_2 - k_1 + 1) \sum \log^2 k - (\sum \log k)^2} \tag{13}$$

.3 Improved Generalized Fractal Box-Counting Dimension

However, for the actual radiation source signal, they do not satisfy the self-similar structure of fractal theory to some degree. Therefore, when using the traditional fractal box-counting dimension algorithm to calculate box-counting dimension of the radiation source signal, the fitting curve often do not have good linear structure. Aiming at this issue, an improved generalized fractal box-counting dimension algorithm was developed to overcome the defect of the conventional fractal box-counting dimension algorithm. The specific calculation procedure is as follows:

) Resample the actual radiation source signal sequence $f(i)$, $i = 1, 2, \ldots, N_0$, and properly increase the sampling points to reduce the minimum side length ε, to improve the calculation accuracy of the fractal box-counting dimension of the signal sequence $f(i)$. the phase space of the signal sequence $f(i)$ is reconstructed, and the number of iterated dimension of the reconstructed phase space is determined according to the number of sampling points.

) Suppose the number of sampling points of the signal sequence $f(i)$ is $N_0 = 2^n$. To improve the calculation accuracy, resample the actual radiation source signal sequence $f(i)$, and suppose the number of sampling points of the signal sequence $f(i)$ is $N = 2^K$ ($K > n$). The reconstruction dimension of the phase space of the signal sequence $f(i)$ is set respectively as $m = K + 1 = 2, 3, 4, \ldots, \log_2 N + 1$.

) The derivate process of the number of boxes covering the actual radiation source signal sequence $f(i)$ can be described as follows:
When $k = 1$:
$p_1 = \max\{f(i), f(i+1)\}$, $p_2 = \min\{f(i), f(i+1)\}$, $i = 1, 2, \ldots, N/k$. In this case, the reconstructed phase space dimension is 2.
When $k = 2$:

$$p_1 = \max\{f(2i-1), f(2i), f(2i+1)\}, \quad p2 = \min\{f(2i-1), f(2i), f(2i+1)\},$$

$i = 1, 2, \ldots, N/k$. In this case, the reconstructed phase space dimension is 3.
When $k = 3$:
$p_1 = \max\{f(3i-2), f(3i-1), f(3i)f(3i+1)\}$,
$p_2 = \min\{f(3i-2), f(3i-1), f(3i)f(3i+1)\}$, $i = 1, 2, \ldots, N/k$. In this case, the reconstructed phase space dimension is 4.
When $k = K$:
$p_1 = \max\{f(Ki - K + 1), f(Ki - K + 2), \ldots, f(Ki + 1)\}$,
$p_2 = \min\{f(Ki - K + 1), f(Ki - K + 2), \ldots, f(Ki + 1)\}$, $i = 1, 2, \ldots, N/k$. In this case, the reconstructed phase space dimension is $m = K+1$.

) It can be seen from the above deduction that, during reconstructing the phase space of the radiation source signal sequence $f(i)$ K times, the corresponding $\log N_{k\varepsilon}$ can be obtained at each time. And then the relation curve of $\log N_{k\varepsilon} \sim \log k\varepsilon$ can be drawn. Since the fitting curve does not have strict linear relationship, take the derivation of the relation curve at these K points over the improved generalized fractal box-counting dimension algorithm. The slopes $D_1, D_2, D_3 \ldots D_K$ at these K points from the relation curve are the fractal box-counting dimensions in the different reconstructed phase space. Take the slopes $D_1, D_2, D_3 \ldots D_K$ obtained as the K characteristic parameters for the fault feature vector extracted from the signal sequence $f(i)$, which characterizes the signal subtle features.

2.4   Gray Relation Theory

The research of gray relation theory is the foundation of gray system theory, mainly based on the basic theory of space mathematics, to calculate relation coefficient and relation degree between reference characteristic vector and each comparative characteristic vector. Gray relation theory has a good potential to be used in radiation source signal recognition with four reasons [12–15]: it has good tolerance to measurement noise; its algorithm is simple and can solve the issue of generality versus accuracy; it can solve the learning problem with a small number of samples; it has the ability to assist the selection of characteristic parameters for classification.

Suppose the feature vectors $\left[D_1', D_2', \ldots, D_K', D_1, D_2, \ldots, D_K\right]$ (i.e., the dual improved generalized fractal box-counting dimension eigenvectors) extracted from radiation source signal, to be identified are as follows:

$$B_1 = \begin{bmatrix} b_1(1) \\ b_1(2) \\ b_1(3) \\ \cdots \\ b_1(2K) \end{bmatrix}, B_2 = \begin{bmatrix} b_2(1) \\ b_2(2) \\ b_2(3) \\ \cdots \\ b_2(2K) \end{bmatrix}, \ldots, B_i = \begin{bmatrix} b_i(1) \\ b_i(2) \\ b_i(3) \\ \cdots \\ b_i(2K) \end{bmatrix}, \ldots \qquad (14)$$

Where $B_i(i = 1, 2, \ldots)$ is a certain radiation source signal type to be recognized.

Assume that the knowledge base between the radiation source signal type and signal subtle features based on a part of samples is as follows:

$$C_1 = \begin{bmatrix} c_1(1) \\ c_1(2) \\ c_1(3) \\ \cdots \\ c_1(2K) \end{bmatrix}, C_2 = \begin{bmatrix} c_2(1) \\ c_2(2) \\ c_2(3) \\ \cdots \\ c_2(2K) \end{bmatrix}, \ldots, C_j = \begin{bmatrix} c_j(1) \\ c_j(2) \\ c_j(3) \\ \cdots \\ c_j(2K) \end{bmatrix}, \ldots \qquad (15)$$

where $C_j(j = 1, 2, \ldots)$ is a known radiation source signal type and $c_j(j = 1, 2, \ldots)$ is a certain feature parameter.

$$\text{For } \rho \in (0, 1): \ \xi\big(b_i(k), c_j(k)\big)$$
$$= \frac{\min\limits_{j} \min\limits_{k} \big|b_i(k) - c_j(k)\big| + \rho \cdot \max\limits_{j} \max\limits_{k} \big|b_i(k) - c_j(k)\big|}{\big|b_i(k) - c_j(k)\big| + \rho \cdot \max\limits_{j} \max\limits_{k} \big|b_i(k) - c_j(k)\big|} \qquad (16)$$

$$\xi\big(B_i, C_j\big) = \frac{1}{2K} \sum_{k=1}^{2K} \xi\big(b_i(k), c_j(k)\big), \quad j = 1, 2, \ldots \qquad (17)$$

Where ρ is the distinguishing coefficient; $\xi(b_i(k), c_j(k))$ is the gray relation coefficient of k_{th} feature parameter for B_i and C_j; $\xi(B_i, C_j)$ is the gray relation degree for B_i and C_j. Thereafter B_i is categorized to a certain radiation source signal type where the maximal $\xi(B_i, C_j)(j = 1, 2, \ldots,)$ is calculated.

2.5 Proposed Approach

Totally, the process of the proposed method for radiation source signal recognition is as follows, and the flow chart is illustrated in Fig. 1.

Step 1: A variety of target radiation source signals are sampled, to establish the knowledge base.
Step 2: The subtle feature vectors are extracted from the sample knowledge base through the dual improved generalized fractal box-counting dimension eigenvectors.
Step 3: The sample knowledge base for GRA is established based on the signal symptom (i.e., the extracted subtle feature vectors $[D_1', D_2', \ldots, D_K', D_1, D_2, \ldots, D_K]$) and the signal pattern (i.e., the known radiation source signal type).
Step 4: The subtle feature vectors extracted from radiation source signals to be identified are input into GRA, and the recognition results are output.

3 Application and Analysis

In order to verify the properties of dual improved fractal box-counting dimension eigenvectors, 11 different radiation source signals were used to test the recognition effect, compared with the traditional fractal box-counting dimension and the single improved generalized fractal box-counting dimension. In the paper, the radiation source signals for testing are from Case Western Reserve University Bearing Data Center [16]. The motor drive end rotor is supported by a test bearing, where a single point of failure is set through discharge machining. The radiation source signals of bearing vibration data used for analysis are obtained under the motor speed of 1797 r/min and load of 0 horsepower. An accelerometer is installed on the motor drive end housing with a bandwidth of up to 5000 Hz, and the vibration data for the test bearing under different fault patterns is collected by a recorder as radiation source signals, in which the sampling frequency is 12 kHz. The fault types contain outer race fault, the inner race fault, and the ball fault, and the fault diameters, i.e., fault severities, contain 28 mils, 21 mils, 14 mils and 7 mils. Totally 11 types of radiation source signals of bearing vibration data considering different fault categories and fault severities are analyzed. Each data sample is made up of 2048 time series points. For those 550 data samples, 110 data samples are chosen randomly for the establishment of the knowledge base, with the rest 440 data samples taken as testing data samples (Table 1).

The subtle feature vectors extracted from radiation source signals of rolling bearing normal operating condition and different fault conditions with 7 mils fault diameter (seen in Fig. 2) based on dual improved generalized fractal box-counting dimension eigenvectors were shown in Fig. 3. And the subtle feature vectors extracted from the

Table 1. Traditional fractal box-counting dimension of a random chosen sample from radiation source signals of bearing normal condition and different fault conditions with fault size 7 mils

Signals	Normal	Inner race fault	Ball fault	Out race fault
Traditional box-counting dimension	1.5718	1.6173	1.7511	1.6000

radiation source signals of bearing inner race fault condition with various severities (seen in Fig. 4) based on dual improved generalized box-counting dimension eigenvectors were shown in Fig. 5.

From Table 2, it is can be seen that the features extracted by traditional box-counting dimension method are limited, and the distances between different types of radiation source signals are close which are not easily to be classified by a pattern recognition technique.

From Figs. 3 and 5, it is interesting to see that the dominant subtle feature vectors $[D_1', D_2', \ldots, D_K', D_1, D_2, \ldots, D_K]$ extracted from the radiation source signals of rolling element bearing vibration signals with different fault types and severities through the dual improved generalized fractal box-counting dimension eigenvectors show apparent differences, in particular for the extracted improved fractal box-counting dimension characteristics $[D_1, D_2, \ldots, D_K]$. The sample knowledge base for GRA is established based on the signal symptom (i.e., the extracted subtle feature vectors $[D_1', D_2', \ldots, D_K', D_1, D_2, \ldots, D_K]$) and the signal pattern (i.e., the known radiation source signal type). The subtle feature vectors $[D_1', D_2', \ldots, D_K', D_1, D_2, \ldots, D_K]$ extracted based on the radiation source signals of the testing rolling bearing vibration signals to be identified input to GRA, and the recognition results are output, shown in Table 3.

Table 2. Traditional box-counting dimension of a random chosen sample from radiation source signals of bearing inner race fault condition with different levels of severity

Signals	7mils	14mils	21mils	28mils
Traditional box-counting dimension	1.6173	1.5795	1.6356	1.6491

From Table 3, the recognition results of the proposed method illustrate that the total recognition success rate can reach 98.86%, which shows a certain improvement in the recognition accuracy after the application of dual improved fractal box-counting dimension eigenvectors in the signal subtle feature extraction, compared with the methods from references [17] and [18]. The time cost of the methods over a laptop computer with a 4.0 GHz dual processor for one Test Case is only 0.027 s and the time consumption of the proposed approach is encouraging.

Table 3. The recognition results by the proposed method compared with results from references [17] and [18]

Label of classification	The number of testing samples	The number of misclassified samples			Testing accuracy (%)		
		[17]	[18]	Proposed	[17]	[18]	Proposed
1	40	0	0	0	100	100	100
2	40	0	0	0	100	100	100
3	40	0	2	1	100	95	100
4	40	3	0	0	92.5	100	100
5	40	0	0	0	100	100	100
6	40	2	3	2	95	92.5	100
7	40	3	0	3	92.5	100	87.5
8	40	3	4	0	92.5	90	100
9	40	0	0	0	100	100	100
10	40	0	3	0	100	92.5	100
11	40	4	0	1	90	100	100
In total	440	15	12	7	96.59	96.9697	98.86

4 Conclusion

Fractal dimension is an important tool to describe the complexity of fractal body. In this paper, the box-counting dimension algorithm in fractal theory is improved, and an improved generalized fractal box-counting dimension algorithm is proposed. The improved generalized fractal box-counting dimension algorithm can effectively characterize the box-counting dimensionality of radiation source signal under different reconstructed phase space conditions. The experimental results show that compared with the traditional fractal box-counting dimension algorithm and the single improved fractal box-counting dimension algorithm, the proposed dual improved fractal box-counting dimension algorithm, can better reflect the signal subtle distribution characteristics under the different reconstruction phase space, and has a better recognition effect with good real-time performance.

Acknowledgment. The research of the paper is supported by the National Natural Science Foundation of China (No. 61603239), and the authors are grateful to Case Western Reserve University Bearing Data Center for kindly providing the experimental data.

References

1. Zhang, D.D.: Bearing fault diagnosis based on the dimension–temporal information. Proc. Inst. Mech. Eng. Part J. Eng. Tribol. **225**(8), 806–813 (2011)
2. Sun, W., Yang, G.A., Chen, Q., et al.: Fault diagnosis of rolling bearing based on wavelet transform and envelope spectrum correlation. J. Vib. Control **19**(6), 924–941 (2013)

3. Wang, H., Chen, J., Dong, G.: Fault diagnosis of rolling bearing's early weak fault based on minimum entropy de-convolution and fast Kurtogram algorithm. Proc. Inst. Mech. Eng. Part C: J. Mech. Eng. Sci. (2014). https://doi.org/10.1177/0954406214564692
4. Lin, Y., Wang, C., Wang, J., Dou, Z.: A novel dynamic spectrum access framework based on reinforcement learning for cognitive radio sensor networks. Sensors 16, 1–22 (2016)
5. Zhu, K., Li, H.: A rolling element bearing fault diagnosis approach based on hierarchical fuzzy entropy and support vector machine. Proc. Inst. Mech. Eng. Part C: J. Mech. Eng. Sci. (2015). https://doi.org/10.1177/0954406215593568
6. Dong, S., Xu, X., Liu, J., et al.: Rotating machine fault diagnosis based on locality preserving projection and back propagation neural network-support vector machine model. Meas. Control 48(7), 211–216 (2015)
7. Jayaswal, P., Verma, S.N., Wadhwani, A.K.: Development of EBP-Artificial neural network expert system for rolling element bearing fault diagnosis. J. Vib. Control 17(8), 1131–1148 (2011)
8. Ao, H.L., Cheng, J., Yang, Y., et al.: The support vector machine parameter optimization method based on artificial chemical reaction optimization algorithm and its application to roller bearing fault diagnosis. J. Vib. Control (2013). https://doi.org/10.1177/1077546313511841
9. Hsu, C.W., Lin, C.J.: A comparison of methods for multiclass support vector machines. IEEE Trans. Neural Networks 13(2), 415–425 (2002)
10. Liu, Shuai, Weina, Fu, He, Liqiang, Zhou, Jiantao, Ma, Ming: Distribution of primary additional errors in fractal encoding method. Multimed. Tools Appl. 76(4), 5787–5802 (2017)
11. Liu, Shuai, Pan, Zheng, Cheng, Xiaochun: A novel fast fractal image compression method based on distance clustering in high dimensional sphere surface. Fractals 25(4), 1–11 (2017)
12. Li, J., Guo, J.: A new feature extraction algorithm based on entropy cloud characteristics of communication signals. Math. Problems Eng. 2015, 8 (2015)
13. Li, J.: A new robust signal recognition approach based on holder cloud features under varying snr environment. KSII Trans. Internet Inf. Syst. 9(11), 4934–4949 (2015)
14. Li, J.: A novel recognition algorithm based on holder coefficient theory and interval gray relation classifier. KSII Trans. Internet Inf. Syst. (TIIS), 9(11), 4573–4584 (2015)
15. Ying, Yulong, Cao, Yunpeng, Li, Shuying, Li, Jingchao, Guo, Jian: Study on gas turbine engine fault diagnostic approach with a hybrid of gray relation theory and gas-path analysis. Adv. Mech. Eng. 8(1), 1–14 (2016)
16. The Case Western Reserve University Bearing Data Center. http://csegroups.case.edu/bearingdatacenter/pages/download-data-file. Accessed 11 Oct 2015
17. Li, J., Cao, Y., Ying, Y., Li, S.: A rolling element bearing fault diagnosis approach based on multifractal theory and gray relation theory. PLoS ONE 11(12), 1–16 (2016)
18. Ying, Y., Li, J., Chen, Z., Guo, J.: Study on rolling bearing on-line reliability analysis based on vibration information processing. Comput. Electr. Eng. 69, 842–851 (2017)

Study on Topic Intensity Evolution Law of Web News Topic Based on Topic Content Evolution

Zhufeng Li, Zhongxu Yin[✉], and Qianqian Li

Zhengzhou Science and Technology Institute, Zhengzhou 450001, China
20086538@qq.com, yinzhxu@163.com

Abstract. The Time Pre-discretized model is firstly adopted to extract web news topic, then a model of topic content evolution is adopted based on the analysis of topic clusters, on which basis a quantification method of topic content is proposed. Experiments on the data sets from social web media find a Pearson correlation coefficient (PCC) of 0.74 between the sequence of topic intensity and that of topic content complexity based on the above quantification method, and a more than 71.5% chance of the simultaneous increase/decrease is observed, showing the "increase or decrease together" law of topic intensity evolution based on topic content evolution.

Keywords: Topic intensity evolution · Topic content evolution Relevance

1 Introduction

In the Internet era, the booming development of new online media such as Weibo, WeChat and news websites has gradually changed the mode of information dissemination and people's communication. After the emergency broke out, netizens highly participated in the comment and forwarding of news topics on the Internet and gradually produced influential trends in public sentiment and political attitudes. As a result, they formed a powerful social media force –online public opinions [1]. Studying the evolution of topic intensity and the evolution of topic content, and the timely monitoring of topic content migration and the increase or decrease of topic intensity will automatically analyze public opinion and provide adequate response time for public opinion guidance and decision-making. Therefore, the evolution of topic intensity and the evolution of topic content has important practical significance.

The intensity of Weibo and other online media is directly reflected in the "headline", "hot search" and other rankings, thus we can directly obtain the quantitative indicators of topic intensity, which provides a more convenient channel for the analysis of public opinion. However, there are many types of news websites, there is no direct measure of topic intensity, and their background data are often not disclosed, which brings great difficulty to topic intensity analysis and prediction, and also highlights its theoretical research value.

© Springer Nature Switzerland AG 2018
X. Sun et al. (Eds.): ICCCS 2018, LNCS 11068, pp. 697–709, 2018.
https://doi.org/10.1007/978-3-030-00021-9_62

The related research of topic evolution analysis starts from the TDT (Topic Detection and Tracking) research project established and funded by DARPA of United States. However, time information of corpus is not effectively used in TDT research.

With the rise of the topic model, how to introduce the time information of the text corpus and study the evolution of the topic over time has become a research hotspot in the field of machine learning and text mining [2–7].

According to the introduction of time information, there are mainly three types of research on topic evolution models at home and abroad: Time Post-discretized, Time Pre-discretized and Time Variable Joint.

In the field of topic evolution, LDA topic evolution model has a wider range of applications, because this approach considers the order of topics, and can better reflect the connections between the former topic and the latter topic. However, it requires researchers to construct a quantitative model of the topic relevance measurement in different time slices according to the research purpose. Meanwhile, the method also needs to solve the topic alignment in different time slices.

At present, many literatures [8–10] are focused on the construction of the topic model and the tracking of the hot topics. But few articles discuss the relationship between the topic intensity evolution and the topic content evolution. In the field of the evolution of Weibo topic, there are precedents for predicting the Weibo topic's intensity using linear regression prediction models [11], while in the field of the evolution of online news, there are relatively few related studies because the prediction of the intensity of news topics is different from that of Weibo. The method is quite difficult because of the low participation of users in the network news platform, the difficulty of measuring the intensity, the uneven data, the lack of sufficient user data to support the regression prediction model, and the difficulty of fitting through the regression method. Therefore, it's necessary to analyze the promotion of the topic content evolution to the topic intensity evolution, and use the evolution of the topic content to predict the topic intensity. This study attempts to explore the relevance between topic intensity evolution and topic content evolution and provide a theoretical basis for predicting topic intensity of network news. In a word, the research of topic intensity evolution should focus on topic semantic features, thus study the inner function of topic intensity in nature.

The correlation between the evolution of topic intensity of online news and the evolution of topic content is firstly studied, and then topic intensity evolution law of web news topic based on topic content evolution is secondly studied. It builds the LDA topic model in different time slices of the network news texts, and clusters the topic using K-Means algorithm. Then the content evolution model is used to quantify the evolution of the topic content. Based on the quantification of the topic intensity, it studies the correlation mechanism between topic content evolution and topic intensity evolution ("increase or decrease together"), which provides a theoretical basis for predicting the topic intensity of the next time slice using the topic content evolution. As shown below (Fig. 1):

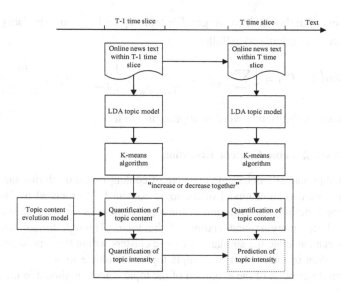

Fig. 1. Research approach.

2 Analysis of Topic Content Evolution and Quantification of Topic Intensity

2.1 Topic Extraction and Clustering

The LDA model is adopted to extract topic. According to the LDA model, the document can be represented as a mixed distribution of topics, while topics can also be represented as a mixed distribution of words, whose essence is a three-level Bayesian probability model, including words, topics and documents. In the model, there are two Bayesian probability mappings among words, topics and documents, so we can use unsupervised learning method to identify the topics contained in the corpus.

The subject words are used to represent the topic of the text, using ten keywords by default. The topic representation represents the "bag of words" model of online news texts as low-dimensional space formed by subject words, thus paving the way for topic clustering.

The task of topic clustering is to classify the relevant texts together without knowing the category, which is an unsupervised machine learning process. Compared with the K-Means clustering algorithm based on cosine distance, the K-Means clustering algorithm based on relative entropy can better identify the noise points, so K-Means clustering method based on relative entropy is adopted in this paper. The algorithm assumes that the number of clusters is k, and k documents are selected in advance as the initial clustering kernel. Then, the similarity between the remaining documents and the clustering starting document is compared, the highest similarity document is selected and grouped into corresponding clusters. Finally, we iterate the above process until the result converges. For topic T_i^m and T_j^n, topic similarity based on relative entropy is calculated as follows:

$$\text{Sim}\left(T_i^m, T_j^n\right) = \frac{1}{2}\sum_{w \in V} p_w \log \frac{2p_w}{q_w + p_w} + \frac{1}{2}\sum_{w \in V} q_w \log \frac{2q_w}{q_w + p_w} \quad (1)$$

q_w is the probability that word w appears in the topic.

2.2   Analysis of Topic Content Evolution

In order to automatically determine the state of content evolution during the life cycle of the topic, the evolution model of the topic content [12] proposed by Hu Weili is adopted, which defines the evolution of the topic content as six basic states: creation, split, drift, keep, merging and ending of the topic. Through formal descriptions, researchers can calculate the similarity of topic clusters within the time slices, and sort out the evolution of the content of a single topic or multiple topics.

A formal description of the evolution of the topic content is shown in the following Table 1:

Table 1. The discriminant conditions of topic content evolution.

Status	Condition
Creation	for all topic A_{t-1}, $\text{Sim}(A_{t-1}, A_t) <= \sigma$
Split	$\text{Sim}(A_t, B_{t+1}) > \sigma$, $\text{Sim}(A_t, C_{t+1}) > \sigma$, $\text{Sim}(B_{t+1}, C_{t+1}) < \varepsilon$
Drift	$\varepsilon > \text{Sim}(A_t, B_{t+1}) > \sigma$
Keep	$\text{Sim}(A_t, B_{t+1}) > \varepsilon$
Merging	$\text{Sim}(A_t, B_{t-1}) > \sigma$, $\text{Sim}(A_t, C_{t-1}) > \sigma$, $\text{Sim}(B_{t-1}, C_{t-1}) < \varepsilon$
Ending	for all topic A_{t+1}, $\text{Sim}(A_{t+1}, A_t) <= \sigma$

There are two important thresholds ε and σ in the evolution of the topic content, which are the criteria for judging the state. At present, there are mainly two methods for setting the threshold: one is to select the thresholds that fit the data better through multiple tests based on the experience of the researcher; the second method is to use the machine learning method to set thresholds with the support of reliable learning corpus. Because the thresholds are different in the different fields, the manual setting of the threshold is selected in the research, and set initial threshold for the system. At the same time, the threshold setting interface is opened to the user, allowing the user to adjust the sensitivity of the topic state judging.

Since the two thresholds ε and σ are both in the interval of $(0,1)$ and $\varepsilon > \sigma$, the two thresholds are determined by grid searching after many data tests. In an open text environment, the topic data of different fields are randomly extracted. After two rounds of iterative tests with 0.1 and 0.01 spans respectively, the threshold values ε and σ are adjusted continuously until a clear topic content evolution can be generated for the vast majority of topics. In the end, we choose $\sigma = 0.20$ and $\varepsilon = 0.38$ as the parameters, which can basically determine the state of all nodes and form a complete evolution of topic content.

On the basis of the topic content evolution model, the online news text is divided according to the granularity of the certain time slice to generate the evolution graph of the topic content. The topic content evolution graph is the directed empowerment graph, which describes the life cycle of the evolution of the topic content. It has a natural time attribute, and is irreversible in the time dimension, that is, each edge of the graph is a unidirectional edge, forming a directed non-cyclic graph. The nodes in the graph are topic clusters, representing subtopics. In order to facilitate the display, nodes are represented by numbers in the system. The edges in the figure represent the relationship of the clusters of related topics, the assignment of which is the similarity value of the clusters of related topics, and represent the semantic differences of the clusters of related topics.

The network news texts of "Tianjin Port Explosion" are extracted and clustered in the research. According to the topic content evolution model, the "Tianjin Port Explosion" topic evolution graph and topic feature evolution word vector is shown as follows (Fig. 2):

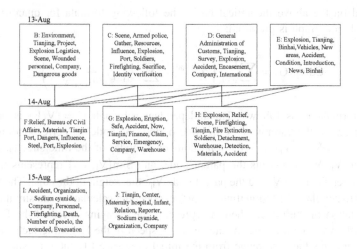

Fig. 2. Distributed representations of words in content evolution of topic "Tianjin Port Explosion".

The topic evolution graph consists of a point set, an edge set and a weight set. The set of points of the directed empowerment graph embodies topic clusters. The set of edges embodies the semantic association and topic evolution between the topic clusters. The weight set reflects the degree of semantic similarity between the topic clusters. In this paper, the topic evolution graph is quantified in order to find out the rule of the evolution of the topic content and try to sort out the influence of the topic content evolution on the topic intensity evolution.

Based on the graph theory and news dissemination theory, the following theoretical basis is proposed:

(1) If two graphs are isomorphic, that is, the pattern of point set and edge set is isomorphic, the smaller the edge weight is, the lower the semantic relation between the predecessor topic and the succeeding topic is. Thus, we assume that the probability of a new topic appearing is higher, and the probability of topic intensity increasing is higher.
(2) If two graphs aren't isomorphic, the graph that has more points, or topic clusters, has greater probability of the topic intensity increasing.
(3) Based on the principle of news distribution and human forgetting curve, people will gradually forget past topics and turn their interest to new topics. Therefore, we assume that the topic cluster of different time slices has different influence and contribution to the future topic. The shorter the time slice is, the greater the impact of past topic clusters on the future topic intensity is. This article summarizes this factor as "forgetting factor".

Based on the above theoretical basis, the following formula for quantifying the topic evolution graph is proposed:

$$\text{Comp}(G) = \sum\nolimits_{t_0=1}^{T} \left(\alpha^{\lambda|t-t_0|} \times \sum\nolimits_{i=0,t=t_0}^{n} \frac{1}{\text{sim}(v_i, v_{ip})} \right) \quad (2)$$

The formula is as follows: The independent subgraph $G = (V, E)$ is the topic evolution graph, the variable T is the time period, the node set corresponding to the time slice t_0 is $V = (V_i)$, n is the total number of nodes of the time slice t_0. For any element in V_i, V_{ip} represents the parent node, and $\text{Sim}(V_i, V_{ip})$ represents the similarity between the node V_i and the parent node V_{ip}, the weight of the edge. The variable α is used to simulate the "forgetting factor", exponential calculation can simulate long-tail attenuation of the topic, where λ represents the decaying speed of the forgetting factor. If the variable λ is greater, the decaying speed of the forgetting factor is faster. $|t - t_0|$ represents the time range from the initial time slice t to the time slice t_0.

Through data analysis and experiment, the paper set the default value of α as 20%, λ as 1. The specific methods are as follows: we collected news texts of various topics, generated topic evolution graph, quantified the graph by using the above quantification formula, adopted a manual filtering method of "forcing", and finally concluded that 20% can simulate the forgetting factor in most topics. Users can also adjust the value of α according to specific topic.

2.3   Quantification of Topic Intensity

The topic intensity is the level of interest that a topic received for a certain period of time. The topic intensity is mainly measured from media's intensity and user's intensity. The two aspects has different perspectives: the former measures the topic intensity from the sender of the news report, that is, the frequency of the related reports and the distribution of the reports; The latter measures the topic intensity from the receiver of reports, the indicators include the browser number, the comment number and so on. Topic intensity is mainly measured from the perspective of media's intensity. Because the network news media do not have the characteristics of high comment rate and high forwarding rate of short text media such as Weibo, users usually do not comment and forward the online news. Besides, most websites are not open programming interface, so we can only get the rough value of user's intensity.

In previous researches, Chen et al. [13] considered that the topic intensity is mainly related to three aspects: the relevance between the topic and the previous topic, the frequency of report of the topic within certain time slice, and the comments on the topic. However, it is not suitable for this paper to quantify the topic intensity from user's intensity(number of forwarding and comments).

He and Li [14] and Xu et al. [15] quantified the topic intensity using the topic document support rate. The definition is as follows: According to the result of LDA topic model, the topic distribution of a document is not uniform, that is, the contribution of each document to the same topic is different. They proposed the hypothesis, which is if a document has at least 10% words which is generated by the topic z, the document is the support document of the topic z, the document support rate of topic z in the time range t is calculated as follows:

$$S(z, t) = \frac{|D_z^t|}{|D^t|} \tag{3}$$

$|D_z^t|$ represents the number of supported documents for topic z in time range t, and $|D_z^t|$ represents the total number of documents in this time period.

After comprehensively considering the above reasons, this article draws on the topic document support rate to quantify the topic intensity.

3   Study on Topic Intensity Evolution Law of Web News Topic Based on Topic Content Evolution

According to the basic view of journalism, during the dissemination of topic A, there will be a marked increase in the topic intensity with the increase of the number of followers and the topic intensity will peak in a short period of time. If the topic A has no content evolution (creation, split, merging or drift of topic), with the appearance of topic B, the attention of public will be turned to topic B (because of the public forgetting factor), topic A will gradually decrease until it reaches zero. If the content of topic A evolves, it will cause the topic intensity to rise in a short period of time. And after reaching a peak value, it will gradually decrease until it reaches zero.

3.1   Analysis of Topic Intensity Evolution Without Changes in Topic Content

In this paper, crawler software is used to crawl Jingzhou Elevator Accident, Chai Jing Event, Heiung Feng Accident and Tianjin Port Explosion online news texts, quantify the topic intensity, shift four events into the same time dimension, smooth the data, and draw the following (Fig. 3):

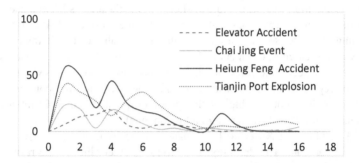

Fig. 3. Topic intensity evolution of four illustrational topics

The analysis of Tianjin Port Explosion is as follows: Tianjin Port Explosion happened at 10 pm, August 12, 2015, then the accident aroused widespread public concern on August 13, the topic intensity rose sharply. From August 14 to 16, the topic intensity slowly decrease. On August 17, Supreme Procuratorate began to investigate the accident, and the Prime Minister issued the relevant instructions, which aroused public concern, thus topic intensity reached the second peak. In the time period when topic content does not evolve, the evolution of topic intensity follows the chi-squared distribution. From the analysis, the intensity peak is accompanied by the evident change of topic content. If no significant changes in the topic content is observed, the topic intensity will decrease.

3.2   Analysis of Topic Intensity Evolution with Changes in Topic Content

This article collects the related news reports about "Tianjin Port Explosion". Based on the quantification of topic content evolution and topic intensity evolution, the following Fig. 4 is drawn:

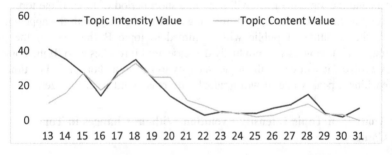

Fig. 4. Topic content value and intensity value of "Tianjin Port Explosion"

It can be seen from the figure above that in the "Tianjin Port Explosion", there is a clear correlation between the topic content value and the topic intensity. In order to prove this point of view, we use the Pearson correlation coefficient to measure the correlation between topic content evolution and topic intensity evolution.

The Pearson correlation coefficient is an index that describes the degree of correlation between two discrete series of values and is used to determine whether the changes in the two values are linearly related. The correlation coefficient is calculated as:

$$\rho(X, Y) = \frac{Cov(X, Y)}{\sqrt{Var(X)Var(Y)}} \tag{4}$$

Var (X) is the variance of X, Cov (X, Y) is the covariance of X and Y. Pearson's correlation coefficient results in the interval of [−1.0, +1.0], with 0 as the boundary. The closer the calculated value is to 1, the higher the positive correlation between the two discrete sequences is. The closer to −1, the higher the negative correlation is. The correlation coefficient is highly correlated in the range of 0.8–1.0, strong in the range of 0.6–0.8, moderate in the range of 0.4–0.6, soft in the range of 0.2–0.4, and weak in the range of 0.0–0.2.

In this topic, ρ (topic content evolution value, topic intensity value) = 0.776034, which means that the topic content evolution value sequence and the topic intensity sequence are strongly related in this topic.

Due to the instability of topic features in the early stage of topic evolution, the model designed in this paper has the characteristic of cold start-up, that is, the fitting degree of the topic in the early stage of evolution is not high. However, as the topic continues to develop, the fitting effect of the model becomes better and better, and ultimately remain in a highly performed stable fit, as shown in the following Table 2:

Table 2. The pearson correlation coefficient of "Tianjin Port Explosion" within different time slices

Date	Pearson correlation coefficient
13-Aug	0.776034
14-Aug	0.838399
15-Aug	0.853551
16-Aug	0.90602
17-Aug	0.904841
18-Aug	0.850106

In order to get more accurate statistics, six independent topics is collected under the open text environment according to the random sampling method. These topics belong to different fields and have a wide range of representation.

The Pearson Correlation Coefficients were calculated from the third time slice of the topic and the following Table 3 was drawn:

Table 3. The pearson correlation coefficient of four illustrational topics

Topic	Pearson correlation coefficient	Corpus scale
Tianjin Port Explosion	0.853551	520
"Eastern Star" Capsized	0.7887603	569
Heiung Feng Missile Accident	0.792665	314
Russian Anniversary of WWII	0.722894	161
JingzhouElevator Accident	0.543766	112
Renminbi's adding to the SDR	0.740715	406

It can be seen from the above table that after the third time slice, the correlation coefficients of most topics are above 0.7. We take the average of these correlation coefficients, and the average is 0.740392, that is, the topic content evolution and topic intensity evolution have strong correlations.

Based on the strong correlation between the topic content value and the topic intensity, the symbolic function model is adopted to quantify the phenomena of "increase or decrease together" between the topic content value and the topic intensity.

The principle of the symbolic function model is as follows: Take the symbolic function value of the first-order derivative of the topic content evolution as an independent variable, and take the symbolic function value of first-order derivative of the topic intensity as dependent variable. If the first derivative is positive, the sign function value is 1. If the first derivative is negative, the function value is −1. If the independent variable and the dependent variable have the same sign, the increase (or decrease) of the topic content value is thought to cause an increase (or decrease) in the topic intensity and vice versa.

Symbolic function model can be expressed as follows:

$$\text{sgn}(a) = \begin{cases} 1 & a > 0 \\ 0 & a = 0 \\ -1 & a < 0 \end{cases} \tag{5}$$

After referring to the state-based verification method, we propose a fitting validity measure suitable for Boolean expression, which is defined as follows: Suppose [T1, T2] is the time interval, t = 1,2,..., n are n test points, At is the right fitting probability of a single test point. The fitting validity m defined in the time interval [T1, T2] can be represented by the following formula:

$$m = \frac{1}{N} \sum_{i=1}^{N} A_t \tag{6}$$

The positive correlation between the curve of topic content and intensity can further prove that the evolution of topic content and intensity can be studied under the same model, which can also provide data verification for the topic intensity prediction based on content evolution. The positive correlation is concluded as "increase or decrease" phenomena, That is to say, when the value of the topic content increases, the topic intensity will also increase. When the value of the topic content decreases, the topic intensity will also decrease. The phenomena of "increase or decrease together" does not happen in the same time slice, but within several time slices. There is a time interval between the increase or decrease process. The following diagram can roughly explain the hypothesis (Fig. 5):

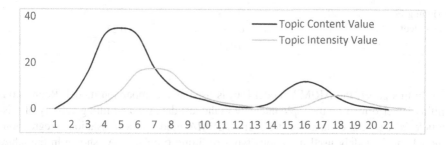

Fig. 5. "Increase or Decrease Together" Phenomena.

If the product of all symbolic function value within certain time slices is greater than or equal to zero, the phenomena of "increase or decrease together" for the test point can be proved. If the fitting validity is quite high, the phenomena of "increase or decrease together" can be verified during the whole period of the topic.

4 Experiment Results and Analysis

The hypothesis is validated by the following experiment. Firstly, preprocess the data of the randomly selected independent topics. Secondly, calculate the symbolic function value of first-order derivative of the topic intensity—sgn(a) and that of topic content—sgn(b). Thirdly, calculate the product of sgn(b) and sgn(a) which is one or two time slices later than sgn(b). Finally, calculate the fitting validity of the product, in order to verify the hypothesis of "increase or decrease together". According to the experimental procedure, the following results are as follows (Table 4):

It can be seen from the experimental results that when the time slice between the topic content value and topic intensity is 1, the average fitting validity of "increase or decrease" phenomena is over 0.715, which can effectively prove the rationality of the hypothesis, and to some extent reveal the mechanism of the correlation between the topic content evolution and topic intensity evolution. Why the validity is highest when time slice is 1? Because the Internet news media cannot immediately response to the evolution of topic content, the topic intensity cannot immediately change with the topic content evolution.

Table 4. The results of sign function

Topic	Time slice distance	Validity (using our model)	Validity (using ARIMA model)
Tianjin Port Explosion	0	0.6	0.2
	1	0.73	0.25
	2	0.87	0.44
"Eastern Star" Capsized	0	0.3	0.3
	1	0.75	0.37
	2	0.95	0.42
Heiung Feng Accident	0	0.476	0.17
	1	0.667	0.27
	2	0.714	0.31

In this paper, the ARIMA model [16] is used as a comparison model. Regression fitting is performed on the topic intensity in the test data set, and fitting validity of this article is used for comparison test. The ARIMA model is a translational regression model and is widely used in various types of fitting problems. As shown in the table above, the performance of the ARIMA model is poor, which demonstrates that we can't get good results using regression models for short observation sequences.

5 Conclusion

The correlation between the topic content evolution and topic intensity evolution of web news is mainly studied. The whole process is realized from the acquisition of open web news to LDA topic extraction and K-Means topic clustering, from the creation and quantification of topic content evolution model to the quantification of topic intensity, and from correlation hypothesis to experiment and verification.

The main contributions of this paper are as follows: First, under the premise that the topic content has not evolved, the topic intensity evolution curves conform to the chi-square distribution; Second, under the premise that the topic content has evolved, the topic intensity and topic content value will increase or decrease together within several time slices. Experiment results demonstrates that the Pearson correlation coefficient achieves 0.74, and the fitting validity of "increase or decrease together" phenomena reaches up to 0.715, which to some extent prove the two hypotheses.

Based on the current research results and existing shortcomings, the next step is to predict the topic intensity of next time slice on the basis of correlative mechanism between topic content evolution and topic intensity evolution. In terms of project implementation, the measure to set threshold will be improved and the topic content evolution model will be optimized.

References

1. Chen, F.J., Zheng, X.X.: Research on the knowledge model of government facing online public opinions (in Chinese). Libr. Inf. Serv. **56**(8), 123–127 (2012)
2. Shan, B., Li, F.: A survey of topic evolution based on LDA (in Chinese). J. Chin. Inf. Process. **24**(6), 43–50 (2010)
3. He, J.Y., Chen, X., Min, D.U.: Topic evolution analysis based on improved online LDA model. J. Cent. South Univ. **46**(2), 547–553 (2015)
4. Yu, B., Wang, L., Zhang, W.: Topic evolution analysis based on dual-OLDA model under Chinese semantic environment. In: International Conference on Big Data Analysis, pp. 658–664. IEEE (2017)
5. Wang, J., Wu, X., Li, L.: Semantic connection based topic evolution. In: AAAI, pp. 5001–5002 (2017)
6. Zhou, H., Yu, H., Hu, R.: Topic evolution based on the probabilistic topic model: a review. Front. Comput. Sci. **11**(5), 1–17 (2017)
7. Wei, W., Guo, C., Chen, J.: Textual topic evolution analysis based on term co-occurrence: a case study on the government work report of the State Council (1954–2017). In: International Conference on Intelligent Systems and Knowledge Engineering, pp. 1–6. IEEE (2018)
8. Chen, T., Wang, X.Y., Qu, F.: Research on method of public opinion topic evolution analysis based on time sliced topic (in Chinese). J. Cent. China Norm. Univ. (Nat. Sci.) **50**(5), 672–676 (2016)
9. Chu, K.M., Li, F.: Topic evolution based on LDA and topic association (in Chinese). J. Shanghai Jiaotong Univ. **44**(11), 1501–1506 (2010)
10. Zhao, X.J., Yang, C.M.: A topic evolution mining algorithm of news text based on feature evolving (in Chinese). Chin. J. Comput. **37**(4), 819–832 (2014)
11. Zhao, L.W., Gong, R.T., Chen, M.Y.: Hotness prediction research of microblog topics based on the participation of opinion leaders (in Chinese). J. Intell. **12**, 42–46 (2013)
12. Hu, Y.L., Bai, L., Zhang, W.M.: Modeling and analyzing topic evolution (in Chinese). Acta Autom. Sin. **38**(10), 1690–1697 (2012)
13. Chen, T., Qu, F., Chen, F.J.: Dynamic evolution model based on time slices of the topic (in Chinese). J. Cent. China Norm. Univ. (Nat. Sci.) **49**(6), 890–894 (2015)
14. He, L., Li, F.: Topic discovery and trend analysis in scientific literature based on topic mode (in Chinese). J. Chin. Inf. Process. **26**(02), 109–115 (2012)
15. Xu, J.J., Yang, Y., Yao, T.F.: LDA based hot topic detection and tracking for the forum (in Chinese). J. Chin. Inf. Process. **30**(01), 43–49 (2016)
16. Stoean, R., Stoean, C., Sandita, A.: Evolutionary regressor selection in ARIMA model for stock price time series forecasting. In: Czarnowski, I., Howlett, R.J., Jain, L.C. (eds.) IDT 2017. SIST, vol. 73, pp. 117–126. Springer, Cham (2018). https://doi.org/10.1007/978-3-319-59424-8_11

Team Formation in Social Networks Using Imperialist Competitive Algorithm

Wenan Tan[1,2](✉) and Ting Jin[1](✉)

[1] Nanjing University of Aeronautics and Astronautics, Nanjing, China
wtan@foxmail.com, tingj@nuaa.edu.cn
[2] Shanghai Polytechnic University, Shanghai, China

Abstract. With the prevalence of various social sites and the rapid development of Internet communication, the problem of team formation in social networks has aroused the enthusiasm of many scholars. Previous research concentrates on raising the variants of this problem and most of them rely on designing approximation optimization algorithms, whose disadvantage is lacking extensibility. In this paper, we deal with the team formation problem for finding a cooperative team within a social network to perform a specific task that requires a set of skills and minimizing the communication cost among team members. In the light of its NP-hard nature, Imperialist Competitive Algorithm (ICA), an evolutionary algorithm for optimization inspired by the imperialistic competition, has been utilized for this problem with different ways of measuring the communication cost. We design a discrete version of ICA by introducing genetic operator in our application, imperialist mutation and imperialist crossover with similarity detection are proposed to avoid a local optimum. Comprehensive experiments on a real-world dataset indicate the performance of the ICA algorithm obtains high-quality results with the comparison of some state-of-the-art ones.

Keywords: Social networks · Team formation · Imperialist
Competitive Algorithm

1 Introduction

With the development of Internet technology, innumerable interactive Web applications and social network sites have emerged, which shorten the distance between people, and break down the geographical constraints on the formation of teams. Nowadays people's social activities have been closely integrated with the network, online cooperation and communication have become a new trend people who can cover all required capabilities from different geographical locations are easily connected. Team Formation (TF) in online social networks plays a significant role in several applications and sets off a wave of research.

The traditional problem of team formation only needs to find a set of members that cover the required skills without considering the communication cost

© Springer Nature Switzerland AG 2018
X. Sun et al. (Eds.): ICCCS 2018, LNCS 11068, pp. 710–722, 2018.
https://doi.org/10.1007/978-3-030-00021-9_63

between members. Nevertheless, The success of a project in the real-world application depends not only on the members' professional skills but also on effective communication between team members, the relationship between team members greatly influences the progress and quality of the task. Lappas et al. [1] firstly considered the problem of finding a team of experts in the context of an expertise social network to accomplish a project. The team formation problem was proved to be NP-hard, and two approximation algorithms were introduced to solve two instantiations of the communication-cost function, diameter and sum of the weights of minimum spanning tree respectively. Later, in the last ten years of research, there have been a series of studies on team formation in social networks, a range of deformation problems have arisen in order to adapt to different limitations and specific application scenarios. For example, TF for generalized tasks [2] generalizes basic problem by associating each required skill with a specific number of experts. TF based on skill grading [3] usually distinguishes skill level of experts. With consideration of the existence of leader in practical situation, who is responsible for supervising and coordinating the project, TF with a leader was also discussed in literature [4]. It can be seen from the above research that the current work on team formation in social networks mostly focuses on problem innovation. Various solutions have been come up according to specific problems and different methods of measuring the communication cost, and most studies tend to solve NP-hard TF problems with approximation algorithms. However, for the NP-hard problem, the approximate solution of the problem can be worked out by approximate algorithm and heuristic algorithm. Heuristic algorithms are developed by simulating the operational mechanisms of social systems, physical systems, biological systems and so on that obtain a satisfactory solution in an acceptable cost. Some renowned heuristics such as Genetic Algorithm, Particle Swarm Optimization, Simulated Annealing, and Ant Colony Optimization have come into wide use for different optimization problems.

In this paper, Imperialist Competition Algorithm (ICA) [5], a meta-heuristic algorithm for optimization which has inspired from socio-political process of imperialistic competition, is introduced as an approach to team formation problem. Colonies movement toward their correlative imperialist and imperialistic competition among the empires are the core parts of the ICA while the latter tells ICA from other evolutionary algorithms. The original ICA is used for function optimization problems with continuous variables. This paper modifies some parts of this algorithm and designs a discrete version of ICA for the TF problem.

The remainder of this paper is organized as follows: some related prior work in the areas of team formation and ICA is reviewed in Sect. 2; in Sect. 3, some preliminaries and problem statements are presented; we provide an introduction to ICA and its variant for team formation in Sect. 4; experimental results and analysis compared to other algorithms are exhibited in Sect. 5 followed by the conclusion in which the research direction in the future is given.

2   Related Work

Previous work can be roughly divided into two categories: team formation and ICA algorithm.

2.1   Team Formation

There has been a great deal of research on team formation in operational research. Under such a model that does not consider the social network among people, the TF problem only concentrates on the assignment of required skills to candidates. Existing approaches basically tend to transform the team formation problem into integer programming, and then find out the optimal match. In the last 10 years, increasing studies have been devoted to discover a team of experts from a social network. TF in social networks involves considering effectiveness and efficiency of the team simultaneously, in other words, besides the need to match the skill requirements of a task, extra attention should be paid on a more vital respect that whether experts in the team co-ordinate and communicate with one another in an efficient manner. Lappas et al. [1], as described in *Introduction*, pioneered TF problem with consideration of cost in communication. For large-scale tasks usually need to be partitioned in the actual application, Sun et al. [6] aimed at TF problem with Grouping Task, multiple search strategies and algorithms were designed based on different communication models including the interior-group and inter-group communication cost criterion. Then they subsequently put forward that there are a large number of practical requirements for the weak relationship between members [7] and proved TF with weak ties in social networks is NP-hard. Xie et al. [8] introduced a relational model using the relationship categories between individuals in social networks and the similarity of social attributes among individuals to further quantify the strength of the relationship among team members.

Nonetheless, solutions involved in mentioned research are not easily extensible and most of them are approximate algorithms. Thus, this paper intends to apply ICA algorithm to address the basic issue of TF in social networks faced with diverse communication costs.

2.2   ICA Work

The study of imperialist competition algorithm can be classified into two kinds: one pays close attention to the improvement of the algorithm and the other is concern with how to solve problems with this algorithm. On the one hand, Lin et al. [9] were dedicated to improving competition operation for weak interaction among empires. In order to enhance the impact of the competition operation, two ways were raised. The first way constructs a new artificial imperialist that uses the information of all imperialists, and the second one strengthens the interaction among all imperialists by imperialist states crossover. Bahrami et al. [10] proposed a novel chaotic ICA algorithm, using chaotic maps to adjust the moving direction for the assimilation operation, they also provided an adaptive movement radius using the probabilistic model to reinforce the search ability for global optimum [11]. Guo et al. [12] presented two improved ICAs motivated by biological evolution, namely ICADE and ICACE. The former incorporates differential evolution operator into ICA to avoid losing better colonies, the latter introduces clone evolution operator so as to effectively guide the algorithm to search for the global optimum solution. On the other hand, ICA has been successfully applied to solve many optimization problems, ranging from scheduling to machinery design issues. Zandieh et al. [13] solved the two-stage assembly flowshop scheduling problem with ICA where the array of country denotes a sequence of jobs. Mostafaei et al. [14] used ICA to extend the network lifetime in a deployed network that has achieved a better performance than existing algorithms.

This paper elaborates how to adapt the ICA algorithm for team formation problem. One more thing to note is that the ICA is not only applicable to different varieties of the communication cost, but also can be extend to deal with the generalized task.

3   Notion and Notation

We now introduce the notion and notation of the TF problem. Suppose that there is a pool of N candidate experts, denoted as $C = \{c_1, c_2, \cdots, c_N\}$, and a collection of M specified skills $S = \{s_1, s_2, \cdots, s_M\}$. Each expert c_i is associated with a set of skills, represented as $S(c_i)$, $S(c_i) \subseteq S$. $C(s_k)$ indicates the set of experts grasping skill s_k, and therefore $C(s_k) \subseteq C$. We say that a subset of experts $X' \subseteq C$ has skill s_j if there is at least one in X' that possesses s_j. A task $T = \{s_i, \cdots, s_j\} \subseteq S$ is defined as a set of skills required to satisfy. A subset of individuals X' is said to be feasible for task T, if and only if, the following expression is satisfied: $\forall s_j \in T, \exists x_i \in X', s_j \in S(x_i)$. In Addition, people are participating in a social circle along with the popularity of social networks in the world, and the close relationship between people guarantees effectiveness for cooperation. A network of social relations among all candidate experts, modeled as an undirected and weighted graph $G(V, E)$, can be extracted from LinkedIn, Xing, and GitHub. The nodes in the graph stand for experts in some skills. Each edge connecting two nodes represents the corresponding two experts have a certain social relationship. The edges' weight is determined by previous collaboration frequency, which characterizes the strength of relationships or the communication cost between two experts. The lower the edge weight, the lower the communication cost is, the more easily experts work with each other.

Definition 1. (TF problem) Team Formation problem in social networks is to find a team of experts from G so that the selected experts cover the skills required by a given task and minimize communication cost of the whole team.

Definition 2. (Communication cost)

Communication Cost Between Arbitrary Two Experts. Any two vertices in a graph are either directly connected or joined by several intermediate vertices (any unconnected pairs of nodes are not considered in this paper since the experimental data come from the maximum connected component extracted from real-world datasets). If two experts v_i, v_j are adjacent, i.e., their communication cost is simply the weight of $(v_i, v_j) \in E$, otherwise the communication cost is given by the weight of their shortest path $sp(v_i, v_j)$ [1].

Total Communication Cost of Team. The two types of communication cost among a crew of professionals in social networks are defined as follows for we believe they are representative, one only takes into account the maximum communication cost between all pairs of experts to avoid excessive communication cost, the another is more stable to slight changes in the social network since it considers the interactions between the holders of each pair of the required skills.

Cc-D(X). The communication cost of team X on radius distance is defined as the largest shortest path between any two experts in team, also known as diameter cost. CC-D(X)= $max_{v_i, v_j \in X} sp(v_i, v_j)$ [1].

Cc-SD(X). A team of experts for a task $T = \{s_1, \cdots, s_p\}$ is $\{(s_1, c_{s_1}), (s_2, c_{s_2}), \cdots, (s_p, c_{s_p})\}$, where c_{s_j} $(j = 1, \cdots, p)$ is an expert mastering skill s_j, (s_j, c_{s_j}) means that expert c_{s_j} is responsible for skill s_j for $j = 1, \cdots, p$. The communication cost of team X is defined as the sum of the shortest distances between the experts responsible for each pair of skills: Cc-SD(X)=$\sum_{i=1}^{p-1} \sum_{j=i+1}^{p} d\left(c_{s_i}, c_{s_j}\right)$, it is also referred to as Sum-Distances cost through this paper [4].

4   Imperialist Competitive Algorithm and Collaborative Team Formation Problem

4.1   Imperialist Competitive Algorithm

Imperialist Competitive Algorithm (ICA) is a population-based evolutionary algorithm which is inspired by a socio-human phenomenon. The following is a brief introduction to the concept of ICA.

Empires Initialization. For a D-dimensional minimization problem, the initial population is a D-dimensional vector set of size N, i.e., $P = (country_1, country_2, \cdots, country_N)$. Each individual in the population indicates a country, $country = (x_1, x_2, \cdots, x_D)$. After calculating the cost of each country, select a user-specified number of the countries (denoted by N_{imp}) with the lowest cost as the imperialists. The imperialists, depending on their power, divide the remaining countries into colonies to generate the initial empires. The more powerful the imperialists are, the more colonies they possess.

Colonies Movement. The imperialists spread their own language, customs, and arts to their colonies. The colonies are gradually developed by assimilation, and the ICA algorithm models the assimilation process by moving all the colonies to their relevant imperialist. The colonies move toward the imperialist by x units which obeys uniform distribution: $x \sim U(0, \beta \times d)$, where $\beta \in (1,2]$ is the assimilation coefficient, and d is the Euclidean distance between imperialist and colony. In the meantime, a deviation angle θ is used to adjust the movement direction of the colonies to expand the search range, and $\theta \sim U(-\gamma, \gamma)$, $0 < \gamma < \pi$. Therefore, new position of each colony is determined jointly by the approaching distance and the angle. Additionally, Ref. [15] introduced colony revolution operation in order to increase population diversity, replacing a part of the colonies with the same number of randomly created new candidate individuals. The number of colonies to be replaced is calculated as follows:

$$RC_{.k} = initialRevoluteRate \times dampRation \times NC_{.k} \qquad (1)$$

initialRevoluteRate is the initial rate of revolution, *dampRatio* is a positive number less than 1. $NC_{.k}$ is the number of colonies owned by the k_{th} empire. As the number of iterations increases, a gradual reduction in revolution rate helps to strengthen the local search capabilities of the population. All colonies reach a new position after assimilation and revolution operation, if there are some colonies whose cost is lower than that of the imperialist state, then the colony with the lowest cost rise to rulership and the imperialist country is forced to become a colony.

Empires Union. Ref. [15] also stated that the two empires should be merged if the distance between the two imperialists is less than a specified threshold. If imperialist a and imperialist b in the search space are too close to each other, imperialist a, whose cost is lower, becomes the leader of the united empire and owns all other colonies of the imperialist b.

Imperialistic Competition. All imperialists attempt to capture the colonies of other empires to extend their territory. Competition among all empires is achieved by picking the weakest colony or a randomly selected colony from the weakest empire and distributing it to a chosen empire. The stronger an empire is, the more likely it is to take possession of the colony. The competition leads to a development of the powerful empires and a decline of the powerless ones. When the last colony of an empire is seized by another empire, it will be eliminated. *Competition Pressure* is added to control the probability of competition so as to prevent weak empires from losing colonies too quickly and protect the diversity of the population.

4.2   ICA for Cooperative Team Formation Problem

In this section, the details of how to apply ICA to solve the collaborative team formation problem are described.

Country Representation. The term country in ICA which is equivalent to the chromosome in genetic algorithm(GA) is a team of experts for a given task. Assume a task needs skills $\{s_1, s_2, \cdots s_k\}$, a candidate solution in the ICA algorithm $country_i$ $(i = 1, \cdots, N)$ is a $1 \times k$ array. For example, given a task that must meet requirements of algorithms, software engineering, distributed systems, web programming. Experts a, b, c are available with the following expertise, $S(a) = \{$algorithms, distributed systems$\}$, $S(b) = \{$web programming, software engineering$\}$, $S(c) = \{$algorithms, software engineering$\}$. Figure 1 depicts a country from initial population. Each gene in the country marks the selected expert for skill s_i. For example, the third gene corresponds to the skill named distributed systems, so the possible genic value can only be a.

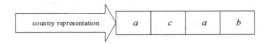

Fig. 1. Country representation.

Moving the Colonies of an Empire Toward the Imperialist. It is noteworthy that the assimilation method involved in ICA is only valid for the numerical variables, based on the distance between the colonies and the imperialist plus an alteration vector. For team formation problem the genes indicate expert ids, the subtraction of two linear vectors makes no sense, therefore the genetic operator is used to move the position of countries. During assimilation process, all colonies in an empire move toward their imperialist to develop themselves, the crossover operator is introduced to help colonies obtain the good characteristics of the imperialist. A single point crossover is applied to produce two new individuals, a randomly selected position splits the colony and the imperialist in two, the first offspring solution combines the first part from the colony with the second one from the imperialist. The other offspring solution forms the opposite sub-individuals. After applying the crossover, the mutation operator, the counterpart of the alteration vector, is applied to these two new solutions to increase probability of escaping from a local optimum. The mutation operator randomly selects a skill position p and replace the current member in skill p with an expert at random from support set of p. At last, select the better of two candidates as the new colony position. In addition, we know that if an imperialist in an empire relapses into a local area, then the algorithm can be easily fall into the local optimum as all colonies in the same empire are pulled toward the surrounding of the imperialist state by absorption policy, so the mutation operation is also adopted for the imperialists.

Unite Empires. The distance between two imperialists used to judge whether two empires are united into one is meaningless in our application. For a D-dimensional country whose elements are expert ids, we present a new strategy that if the number of identical genes of the two imperialist countries is greater than a specified value, they are thought to be very similar, then we unite the empires dominated by these two imperialists.

Imperialists Crossover. Since the competition operation in the original ICA has a minor influence, Lin et al. imposed a crossover operation on the imperialists to improve the quality of interaction among all empires [9], the same way appears in this paper while exists some differences. The added interaction step randomly selects two imperialists p_i^{imp}, p_j^{imp} from empire i and j to perform crossover and generates their two descendants q_1, q_2, the best and the second best of p_i^{imp}, p_j^{imp}, q_1 and q_2 are assigned as the new imperialists. However, here we introduce similarity detection to avoid converging fast, a simple example is presented to explain why the similarity detection is offered and how it works. For example, there are two imperialists p_i^{imp}, p_j^{imp} as parents with cost c_i, c_j, randomly select gene blocks in the same location from parents and exchange them, then two chromosomes q_1, q_2 with cost c_{q_1}, c_{q_2} are produced. Suppose a better quality solution is created after crossover operation and $c_{q_1} < c_i < c_j < c_{q_2}$, it means the new chromosome with cost c_{q_1} substitutes for the parent imperialist p_j^{imp} while q_1 carries more excellent genes from p_i^{imp}. In such a circumstance, the algorithm has a great chance of getting into the local optimal solution because of the diversity loss. Thus, the similarity detection is proposed to protect population diversity, we make a judgement about which imperialist the offspring is more like with similarity detection as introduced in the part of unite empires. If offspring A is more like imperialist A, compare their costs and the country with a lower cost takes the role of dominator. For the above example q_1 and p_i^{imp} are similar to each other, imperialists crossover with similarity detection forbids them to become the imperialists at the same time.

5   Experimental Evaluation

In this section the performance of our proposed algorithm is evaluated and compared with the other algorithms using the scientific-collaboration network which is extracted from the DBLP server. Experiments show that our algorithm for TF problem provides good quality results with regard to two representative definitions of the communication cost and the cardinality of the team.

5.1   The DBLP Dataset

DBLP offers open bibliographic information in the field of computer science that contains papers published in international journals and conferences, etc. The experimental data can be acquired using the same method of processing data as [1]. Abstract records published in some major conferences on Database (DB), Data mining(DM), Artificial intelligence (AI) and Theory (T) areas. For each paper, we make a note about its authors, title, the conference where it was published. The authors who have published at least three articles are recognized as experts, corresponding to nodes in the scientific-collaboration graph. The skillset of each author consists of the terms that appear in at least two titles of papers that he/she has co-authored. Two experts are connected if they have co-published at least two articles, the weight of an edge connecting two experts is defined as Jaccard distances.

5.2   Other Algorithms and Algorithms Setting

We implemented two algorithms introduced in [1] and [4] for contrast. Besides, we make a modification of the algorithm involved in [16], for convenient for comparing, we call this algorithm RareFirstGreedy.

RareFirst. RareFirst algorithm is proposed by Lappas for the team formation with diameter communication cost [1].

BEST-SD. An approximation algorithm is designed for the team formation with communication function Cc-SD by Kargar [4].

RareFirstGreedy. RareFirstGreedy algorithm stems from the algorithm for finding a group of diverse experts in [16]. It is very similar to RareFirst but there are a few points to note: this algorithm sorts all skills in ascending order according to their supporters cardinality. The skill with least supporters is granted the top authority to assign a specialist, then the second least, and so on. At each step pick the expert that minimizes the communication cost of the whole team while RareFirst only considers the distance from seed expert.

We set the skill number $D = 4,6,8$. For each number of skills, 30 random tasks have been generated. We take the average over 30 tasks as the final result of approximation algorithms mentioned above. ICA, as a meta-heuristic algorithm, runs for 20 times for each task, the communication cost of each task is determined by the average of the results found in 20 runs. The average result over 30 tasks is computed and employed as the final result of ICA algorithm to make the results more convincing. For ICA algorithm, the same setting is adopted as [15]. A small threshold for uniting makes ICA converge fast and easily gets a local optimal solution while a bigger value hinders the convergence speed of the algorithm, the value is taken half of the number of required skills to make a tradeoff. The rate of mutation and crossover are 0.4.

5.3   Results

Communication Cost. Tables 1 and 2 exhibit the maximum, minimum and average diameter and Sum-Distances costs of the solutions obtained by RareFirst, RareFirstGreedy, BEST-SD, and ICA. The best values are highlighted in bold. It draws a conclusion that, with regard to the diameter cost, the ICA algorithm has the best experimental performance, followed by RareFirstGreedy, but the results of RareFirstGreedy is barely satisfactory with regard to communication function Cc-SD. The ICA algorithm also gets better experimental

Table 1. Average diameter cost of RareFirst, RareFirstGreedy, ICA Algorithms.

Task	Meas	RareFirst	RareFirstGreedy	ICA
4 skills	Max	3	**2**	**2**
	Min	**1**	**1**	**1**
	Mean	1.921	1.733	**1.606**
6 skills	Max	4	3	**2.942**
	Min	2	**1.862**	**1.862**
	Mean	3.116	**2.308**	2.327
8 skills	Max	4	3.625	**3.090**
	Min	4	**2**	2.79
	Mean	4	3.023	**2.949**

Table 2. Average Sum-Distance cost of BEST-SD, RareFirstGreedy, ICA Algorithms.

Task	Meas	BEST-SD	RareFirstGreedy	ICA
4 skills	Max	**8**	**8**	**8**
	Min	**4**	**4**	**4**
	Mean	5.819	5.946	**5.601**
6 skills	Max	**26.25**	27.751	26.786
	Min	**14.8**	14.875	**14.8**
	Mean	19.941	19.926	**19.249**
8 skills	Max	52.006	54.125	**49.544**
	Min	39.168	37.598	**35.717**
	Mean	45.331	45.826	**43.367**

results than others and the BEST-SD algorithm outperforms RareFirstGreedy where the communication cost is measured by Sum-Distances. To sum up, our proposed algorithm is the best of all algorithms with the capability of forming a team that is able to accomplish a given task with low communication efforts. It is also general-purpose for different communication cost definitions not limited to these defined in the paper.

Cardinality of the Team. Since the size of the team often maintains a positive proportion with the expenses of a task, we evaluate the cardinality of the teams formed by above TF algorithms. The results in Figs. 2 and 3 demonstrate that the ICA algorithm generally forms a smaller group than the others for both communication cost measurements. Note that RareFirst algorithm sometimes produces a relatively small team than others in the presence of some tasks. The reason is that it generates a small cardinality team with high communication cost, this can be explained by picking an expert into team just considering the distance between the expert and the seed expert with the initial skill but ignoring the objective optimization.

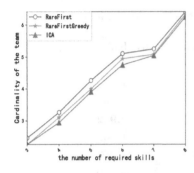

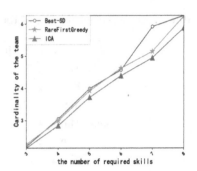

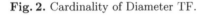

Fig. 2. Cardinality of Diameter TF.

Fig. 3. Cardinality of Sum-Distances TF.

Impact of Imperialists Crossover. The imperialist, as the best country in one empire, their crossover promotes more useful information exchange between empires. To study the impact of imperialist crossover operation with similarity detection on the performance, we keep the same with the original experimental setting except for the imperialist crossover operation, which choose the two best individuals as the imperialists. The experimental results are show in Figs. 4 and 5, we witness the great effect of our proposed imperialists crossover which can always gain a lower communication cost on both functions. The reason for the superiority is that it effectively protects population diversity and reduce the possibility of getting stuck in locally optimal value.

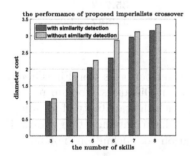

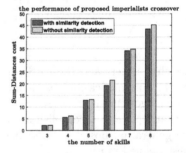

Fig. 4. The performance of proposed imperialist crossover on diameter cost.

Fig. 5. The performance of proposed imperialist crossover on Sum-Distances cost.

6   Conclusion and Future Work

In this paper, we study the basic form of team formation problem. Former work in TF paid more attention to problem variants, and most solutions are approximate algorithms. Here we intend to use heuristic algorithm with the complexity of TF problem. With consideration of the ability of ICA algorithm in handling different optimization problems, we introduced ICA and provided a discrete version to solve TF problem by defining a new assimilation method with genetic operator and imperialist crossover operation with similarity detection. The experimental results show the effectiveness and superiority of ICA algorithms in comparison with RareFirst, RareFirstGreedy and BEST-SD algorithms. However, there exist some other factors that we need to considered but not mentioned in this paper, such as personnel cost and workload balance. In the future, we will extend the ICA algorithm to address multi-objective TF problem for generalized task.

Acknowledgments. The paper is supported in part by the National Natural Science Foundation of China under Grant No. 61672022, Key Disciplines of Software Engineering of Shanghai Second Polytechnic University under Grant No. XXKZD1604, and Graduate Innovation Program No. A01GY17F022.

References

1. Lappas, T., Liu, K., Terzi, E.: Finding a team of experts in social networks. In: Proceedings of the 15th ACM SIGKDD International Conference on Knowledge Discovery and Data mining, pp. 467–476. ACM, New York (2009)
2. Li, C.-T., Shan, M.-K.: Team formation for generalized tasks in expertise social networks. In: 2010 IEEE Second International Conference on Social Computing, pp. 9–16. IEEE, New York (2010)
3. Farhadi, F., Sorkhi, M., Hashemi, S., Hamzeh, A.: An effective expert team formation in social networks based on skill grading. In: Proceedings of 2011 IEEE 11th International Conference on Data Mining Workshops, pp. 366–372. IEEE, New York (2011)
4. Kargar, M., An, A.: Discovering top-k teams of experts with/without a leader in social networks. In: Proceedings of the 20th ACM International Conference on Information and knowledge management, pp. 985–994. ACM, New York (2011)
5. Atashpaz-Gargari, E., Lucas, C.: Imperialist competitive algorithm: an algorithm for optimization inspired by imperialistic competition. In: Proceedings of 2007 IEEE Congress on Evolutionary Computation, pp. 4661–C4667. IEEE, New York (2007)
6. Sun, H., Jin, M., Liu, J., Yu, G.: Methods for team formation problem with grouping task in social networks. J. Comput. Res. Dev. **52**(11), 2535–2544 (2015)
7. Sun, H., Fu, S., Liu, J., Yu, G., Xu, H.: Team Formation with weak Ties in Social Networks. J. Front. Comput. Sci. Technol. **10**(6), 773–785 (2016)
8. Xie, X., Han, S., Chen, M., Zhang, Z., Li, Y., Pan, H.: Research on team formation method in social network. Chin. J. Comput. **40**(3), 712–728 (2017)
9. Lin, J.-L., Tsai, Y.-H., Yu, C.-Y., Li, M.-S.: Interaction enhanced imperialist competitive algorithms. Algorithms **5**(4), 433–448 (2012)
10. Bahrami, H., Faez, K., Abdechiri, M.: Imperialist competitive algorithm using chaos theory for optimization (CICA). In: Proceedings of the 12th International Conference on Computer Modelling and Simulation, pp. 98–103. IEEE Computer Society, USA (2010)
11. Bahrami, H., Abdechiri, M., Meybodi, M.-R.: Imperialist competitive algorithm with adaptive colonies movement. Int. J. Intell. Syst. Appl. **4**(2), 940–945 (2012)

12. Guo, W., Ye, D.: Evolutionary optimization of imperialist competitive algorithm. J. Front. Comput. Sci. Technol. **8**(4), 473–482 (2014)

13. Shokrollahpour, E., Zandieh, M., Dorri, B.: A novel imperialist competitive algorithm for bi-criteria scheduling of the assembly flowshop problem. Int. J. Prod. Res. **49**(11), 3087–3103 (2011)

14. Mostafaei, H., Shojafar, M., Zaher, B., Singhal, M.: Barrier coverage of WSNs with the imperialist competitive algorithm. J. Supercomput. **12**, 1–24 (2017)

15. Atashpaz-Gargari, E.: Imperialist competitive algorithm, (ICA). http://www.mathworks.com/matlabcentral/fileexchange/22046-imperialist-competitive-algorithm-ica. Accessed 10 Jan 2012

16. Yin, H., Cui, B., Huang, Y.: Finding a wise group of experts in social networks. In: Tang, J., King, I., Chen, L., Wang, J. (eds.) ADMA 2011. LNCS (LNAI), vol. 7120, pp. 381–394. Springer, Heidelberg (2011). https://doi.org/10.1007/978-3-642-25853-4_29

The Ship Struck by Lightning Indirect Effect Simulation and Data Analysis

Li Cui[✉], Zhiwei Gao, and Shuai Zhang

School of Information Science and Technology, Shijiazhuang Tiedao University,
Shijiazhuang 050043, China
18832117771@163.com, 1040745658@qq.com,
1732257070@qq.com

Abstract. Lightning strike simulation ships, ship body inside and outside surface current distribution of transient and frequency domain, the ship to hold various points transient and frequency domain the electric field and magnetic field distribution and ship to warehouse internal cables on the induction of transient impulse voltage and current and its frequency spectrum. Based on transmission line matrix, the indirect effect of lightning striking the ship is analyzed by CST (Computer Simulation Technology) according to GJB1389A and SAE-ARP5414 relative standards. In this paper, two kinds of lightning stroke paths are simulated by the high current injection. The simulation results show while the lightning stroke paths is not same, the transient magnetic field distribution and current distribution on the surface of the ship is different as well. Moreover, the research method can be used for further study on the protection of the lightning indirect effects and related research. The method can effectively simulate the lightning the lightning indirect effect of ships, for ship lightning protection design and relevant experiment provided the basis and method, has the important value of engineering application.

Keywords: Lighting strikes · CST · Ship · High current injection
Indirect effect

1 Introduction

Lightning is a common natural discharge phenomenon of high voltage and large current, which occurs in summer in China. In the earth's atmosphere, an average of about eight million lightning strikes occur every day. Its damage includes thermal effect and mechanical effect, electromagnetic effect, electrostatic induction effect, electromagnetic radiation effect and back flashover, the shock wave effect, etc. Lightning is one of the ten natural disasters, ship accidents caused by lightning strike also occur frequently [1]. The ship is the main transport vehicle at sea. In order to improve the comprehensive performance of ships, modern large ships are using advanced composite materials more and more. Modern electronic equipment is used in the large scale integrated circuit to replace the vacuum tube, with their advantages of great integration and high running speed. However, the microelectronics equipment working voltage is low and its ability of resisting overvoltage, overcurrent and lightning electromagnetic pulse is poor, therefore it can be infringed by the lightning easily. The mighty

© Springer Nature Switzerland AG 2018
X. Sun et al. (Eds.): ICCCS 2018, LNCS 11068, pp. 723–732, 2018.
https://doi.org/10.1007/978-3-030-00021-9_64

Microelectronic device is sensitive to strong lightning electromagnetic pulse, so the lighting brings huge loss and bad effects, and even leads to indirect loss which is incalculable. The thunder and lightning disasters is mainly concentrated on the equipment of microelectronic device [2]. In a very short time (usually only a few tens of microseconds to hundreds of microseconds) can amount to thousands of kv, even with a few kv voltage peak current can be up to tens of thousands or even hundreds of thousands of Ann, the lightning is commonly thousands of meters in length, the longest up to 400 km. This results in a series of lightning strike effects, namely, the direct strike effect and the inductive effect (or secondary effect). Different damages are caused when the light stroke different parts of the system equipment [3].

Ships are the main means of transport on sea transportation. When navigating in the electromagnetic environment, the ship will encounter complicated surroundings. When the ship encounters lightning struck, the electrical and electronic equipment of the ship will be seriously damaged by the overvoltage or overcurrent that induced by the strong electromagnetic pulse by which the discharges of the lightning companied [4]. The biggest natural problem that can interfere with the system is lightning. Cloud-to-ground lightning can cause damage in two ways: by a direct strike or by induction effects resulting from an ear by strike. Occasionally lightning can strike far from an object and still affect it. Indirect strikes can also affect the detection system, but are not as severe as direct strikes. In this case, the wave is conducted to the object by other means, for instance, conducting systems and power lines. The most relevant properties of the lightning that cause damage are peak current and maximum rate of current change. The largest currents are produced by return peak currents when the struck object presents a resistive load. The typical value for a peak current is about 30 kA. The simulation experiment is in the CST cable studio environment.

2   The Simulation Environment Setup

2.1   The Ship Model Construction

Based on CST (Computer Simulation Technology) full wave 3d electromagnetic Simulation software, modeling and Simulation of lightning ships are carried out. CST is an electromagnetic simulation software based on Finite Integration Technology (FIT), which has certain advantages in time domain calculation. FIT is a time-domain Maxwell equation discretization algorithm, not only ensure the precision of the model calculation, and save the calculation time and calculation of the model space, so this article selected CST when modeling software. CST software package with Cable (Cable) Studio Studio, Microwave Studio (Microwave Studio, MWS), and other studios, including Microwave Studio has certain advantages in the field of high frequency applications, is used for the design and analysis of transmission line, the high frequency Microwave passive components such as electromagnetic device package, the simulation calculation for the antenna has strong ability, combined with the simulation model of demand, this paper choose Microwave Studio on the simulation modeling. In the CST microwave studio package, there are many types of solvers, Time Domain Solver and frequency domain Solver, and the Solver is set as the Time Domain Solver.

The simulation experiment is intended to calculate the surface current of the ship model under the impact of EMP (electromagnetic pulse). The length of a ship is 130 m, and the whole ship is made up of PEC (ideal dielectric conductor). The sea level uses the CST specific thin panel material to simplify the sea level model without having to build the whole ocean, which is still accurately full-wave electromagnetic simulation, greatly improving the simulation speed. The transmission matrix method (TLM) is combined with compact models in CST, which in other lightning simulations has absolute advantage. A compact model with a width of 5 mm and a depth of 5 mm is set up at the deck of the ship. Because it does not need large numbers of grid subdivision calculation in the vicinity of the slot, improving the simulation efficiency (Fig. 1).

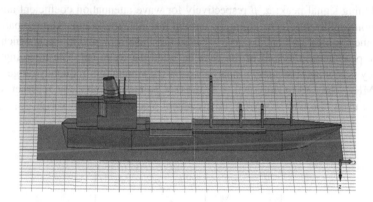

Fig. 1. The ship model

2.2 Lightning Signal Setting

Electromagnetic pulse is a transient electromagnetic phenomenon [5], along the steep rise in time domain, short action time and other characteristics, can be in the form of electromagnetic waves in a very short time would spread to the distance, its powerful energy in frequency domain for spectrum range, large scope, etc. The source of electromagnetic pulse can be divided into natural source and artificial source. Natural sources include lightning, electrostatic discharge, lightning, etc., the artificial source has various power of the radar generation of electromagnetic pulse, high-voltage power grid switch operation and so on. Among them, the common Electromagnetic Pulse type has Electro-Static Discharge Pulse, ESD EMP, High Altitude Electromagnetic Pulse (HEMP), Lightning Electromagnetic Pulse (LEMP) [6], etc.

In order to analyze the effect of electromagnetic pulse, the protection technique of electromagnetic pulse, the international electrotechnical commission (IEC) in the electromagnetic pulse effect and protection in the standard (such as IEC61000 series standard, etc.) [7] gives the ESD, HEMP, LEMP, different types of the typical electromagnetic pulse waveform parameters, such as that most of them use the double exponential function describing electromagnetic pulse, the other in the American military standard (such as MIL - STD - 464 electromagnetic environment effects the system requirements, etc.) [8] most also use the electromagnetic pulse double exponential function model research. According to the related references [9], for indirect effects caused by lightning striking, the waveform of the lightning signal is shown in Fig. 2. The experiment simulated the effects of severe lightning striking on the ship. The lightning current signal rises exponentially with time, and then decreases exponentially with time. The experimental waveform is called double exponential function, whose mathematical expression is:

$$i(t) = I_0(e^{-\alpha t} - e^{-\beta t}) \tag{1}$$

$$I_0 = 218810 \text{ A}, \alpha = 11354 \text{ s}^{-1}, \beta = 647256 \text{ s}^{-1}.$$

Lightning signal peak; α, β respectively for wave attenuation coefficient and coda attenuation coefficient; i(t) for lightning current instantaneous value. The left part of the peak of the double exponential curve is called the wavefront, and this part which drops from the peak current to half of the peak is called the wave tail. The lightning signal frequency is low and the energy is large, so set the simulation frequency range from 0 to 100 MHz. The 130-m ship, with 1 V and 0 V points on both sides, represents cloud discharge using the CST EMS-Es finite element electrostatic field solver.

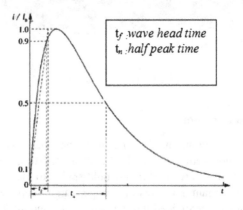

Fig. 2. Double exponential function

2.3   The Grid Settings

CST electromagnetic simulation grid setting determines the accuracy of the results of simulation. The smaller the grid is, the smaller the structure is, but it takes the longer time to do the simulation. Therefore, the setting of the grid need to consider factors both the accuracy and simulation time.

Manual setting of hexahedral grid:

(1) sufficient condition setting, for microstrip structure, set 35/35/50; For the waveguide structure, set 25/25/30.

(2) maximization of min. Mesh step. The smaller the number, the longer the simulation time. This number is doubled, and the simulation time is doubled in all other conditions. On the contrary, the number of times doubled, and the simulation time doubled. So the bigger the better. If this number is comparable to the minimum spacing in the key structure, it is set. If this number is far less than the minimum spacing of the structure, the option to limit the smallest mesh step must be adopted.

The setting principle of minimum grid step is equal to the minimum size of the simulation key structure times 0.5 to 0.8. If the most fine structure is 0.25, the minimum grid step should be set at about 0.17.

(3) set the smallest mesh step. Just changing this number to 0.17 makes the total grid number drop five times. In addition, the minimum grid increased 1.7 times, and the simulation speed will be 5 * 1.7 times faster than before.

If after the above Settings, there are still a lot of small grid, the grid can be very close to the minimum, you can into the grid is the Special menu, open the Fixpoints page, will change the default of 1000.

The hexahedral mesh is used in the experiment. Then the minimum grid element is 0.0598 m, while the maximum grid element is 0.596 m, and the number of grids is 300491730. The background is set up normal air, and the boundary condition is open.

Because the simulation needs to analyze the surface current of the ship, the experiment sets up the field monitor to observe the simulation of the lightning signal frequency in the 10 MHz. Simulation time which is too long will lead to a longer operation time, but too short time will lead to incomplete simulation results. With comprehensive analysis, the simulation time is set up 10 us.

3   The Transmission Matrix Theory

The simulation uses TLM solver. The TLM theory is based on Maxwell electromagnetic field theory. In the 3D TLM theory, it puts forward the symmetrical condensed node (SCN) model, which is shown in Fig. 3. There are 6 directions in each node, and the transmission lines in each direction are represented by two voltage components that are perpendicular to each other. In the calculation period, there are twelve voltage changes in which, the electric field can change the magnetic field, repeating the process again and again, so the process of electromagnetic wave propagation can be simulated in space [10].

TLM USES a three-dimensional transmission line network to describe the spatial discrete model of the electromagnetic field, which is propagated along these transmission lines as an excitation voltage pulse and is reflected at the node.

FITD grid vs. TLM grid.

(1) Both are rectangular hexahedral mesh (HEX).
(2) FITD's HEX is like a rubik's cube, with each small cuboid unit, and the electromagnetic field propagating between adjacent cuboids.
(3) The HEX of TLM is the same as the steel bar in reinforced concrete, with the line of every pull.

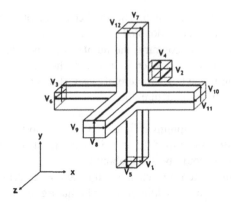

Fig. 3. Symmetrical condensed TLM nodes

(4) TLM's HEX can be large, such as 100 or even thousands, and FITD's best is within 100.

(5) TLM supports simplified model library, especially for EMC simulation; FITD applies to other applications, such as antennas, RCS, and so on.

The main advantage of TLM method is that it can deal with the most complex model simply Meanwhile the TLM theory avoids the calculating equation, there are no convergence verification and stability problems (Fig. 4).

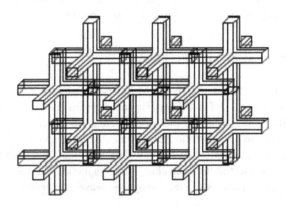

Fig. 4. The spatial discrete model established by TLM

4   The Results of Simulation and Analysis

4.1   Ship Surface Current Distribution

Lightning coupling intrudes into the ship's path, and lightning coupling intrudes into the ship channel, but there are several main types: (1) direct lightning strike by the ship surface equipment directly. (2) lightning electromagnetic radiation formed by direct lightning from lightning conductor. (3) inductive lightning strikes the strong electro-magnetic radiation of the ship's surface equipment. (4) inductive lightning electro-magnetic radiation is introduced into the cabin by the antenna feeder, pipeline and waveguide. (5) inductive lightning electromagnetic radiation shall be penetrated into the cabin by the openings and feeders, pipes and waveguides of the network holes, doors and Windows that are inevitably existing in the ship.

The simulation of the indirect effect of ship lightning strikes is based on the large current injection method. The experiment sets up two kinds of lightning path comparison: path A as shown in Fig. 5, by the current source type discrete port A hitting; path B as shown in Fig. 5, by the current source type discrete port B hitting. The two groups of experiments only set the distinct paths, the other parameters are consistent. Under different lightning stroke paths, the ship's surface current at f = 10 MHz is shown in Figs. 5 and 6: By way of contrast, it can be seen that when the lightning current path is different, the surface current distribution of the ship is diverse. The rule of the simulation is consistent with the literature [11]. The test results show that the point of the lightning attachment is mainly distributed in the area with high electric field intensity, such as the tip of the wing horizontal tail and the vertical tail, and the front cone (pitot tube). That is consistent with theoretical analysis, because after cal-culated approximation of the plane, always in these areas, with a strong electric field, an induction of the surrounding air ionization, easy to form on the forerunner, to attract calculated in these parts attached.

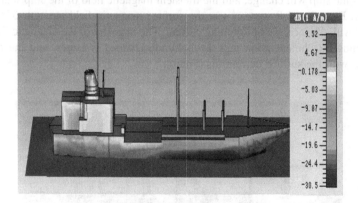

Fig. 5. Lighting A

When the path A, the current density of the cabin which is as a lightning current channel is relatively large, and then the current density around the cabin and the boat deck gap is relatively large too, but there is relatively small current density at the lower part of the hull. The Fig. 7 show that when the path B is used, the current density of the ship column which is as the lightning current channel is the largest, the current density at the gap of the ship deck is second, and the current density of other parts is relatively small. Therefore, in the design and maintenance process, the lightning attachment point and lightning current channel should be specially strengthened. Please try to avoid

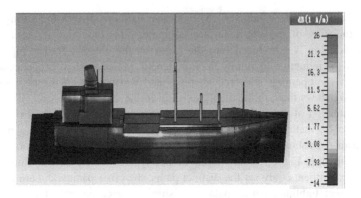

Fig. 6. Lighting B

rasterized images for line-art diagrams and schemas. Whenever possible, use vector graphics instead.

4.2   The Ship on the Surface of the Transient Magnetic Field Distribution

Magnetic patterns from a moving target provide the basic for researching the character a moving target. If the lightning stroke path is changed, the current distribution on the surface of the ship will change, and the transient magnetic field of the ship will change too. From Figs. 7 and 8 we can see, the surface magnetic field strength of the ship increased with the increase of lightning current; The intensity of the magnetic field near the lightning attachment point and the lightning channel is larger, and the result is consistent with the surface current distribution.

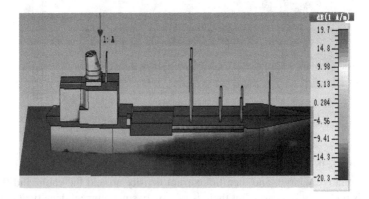

Fig. 7. H-field (A)

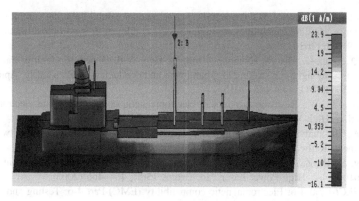

Fig. 8. H-field (B)

5 Conclusion

The numerical simulation of indirect effect of ship lightning strike has important research value. The key of numerical simulation is to establish the calculation model, and then simplify equivalent treatment reasonably. The experiment analyses the ship surface current and transient electromagnetic field distribution under lightning striking the boat. It provides the basis and method for the design of the ship lightning protection and the related experiments, and has important application value in life.

The lightning protection design of the ship is divided into five steps:

1. Establishment of lightning environment;
2. Finding systems and components that are vulnerable to lightning damage;
3. Determine the lightning protection standards for different systems and components;
4. Design the lightning protection of the system and parts;
5. The rationality of lightning protection is tested by test.

Acknowledgment. The research work of this paper is done under the guidance of the supervisor Gao. I would like to express my sincere thanks to my teacher for the first time. I also want to thank Ms. Hao, Mr. Zhang and Mr. Su for their help during the research work. In addition, I would like to thank all the professors and teachers for their valuable comments and suggestions.

References

1. Zhou, Y., Qie, X., Soula, S.: A study of the relationship between cloud-to-ground lightning and precipitation in the convective weather system in China. Ann. Geophys. **20**(9), 107–113 (1999)
2. Lizano-Díez, X., Alentorn-Geli, E., León-García, A., Marqués-López, F.: Fracture of a tapered femoral neck after total hip arthroplasty and lightning strike. Case report. Acta Orthopaedica et Traumatologica Turcica (2015)

3. Malcolm, N., Aggarwal, R.: The significance of median natural lightning current strokes on the energy handling capabilities of surge arresters employed in wind farms. Renew. Energy **85**, 319–326 (2016)

4. Wu, Q., Qian, G., Hu, B., Huang, S., Dou, X., Hao, W.P.: A new trip fault of transmission line caused by lightning striking to ground wire and conductor simultaneously. Appl. Mech. Mater. **3682**(701), 443–445 (2015)

5. Liu, S., Liu, W.: Research progress in electromagnetic compatibility and electromagnetic protection. High Volt. Technol. **40**(6), 1605–1613 (2014)

6. Jia, M.: The analysis and countermeasures of transient impulse interference of railway signal equipment. Railw. Commun. Signal Eng. Technol. **1**, 87–89 (2013)

7. Sheng, S., Bi, Z., Tian, M.: A new analytical expression of current waveform in standard IEC 61000-4-2. High Power Laser Part. Beams **15**(5), 464–466 (2003)

8. IEC. IEC61000-4-6: Electromagnetic compatibility (EMC)-Part 4-6: Testing and measurement techniques-Immunity to conducted disturbances, induced by radio-frequency fields (2008)

9. SAE. ARP5414 Aircraft Lightning Zoning. Society of Automotive Engineers, Warrendale (2005)

10. Johns, P.B.: A symmetrical condensed node for the TLM method. IEEE Trans. Microwav. Theor. Tech. **35**(4), 370–377 (1987)

11. Guo, F., Zhou, B., Gao, C.: Analysis for lightning indirect effects of the aircraft by numerical stimulation. Chin. J. Radio Sci. **27**(06), 1129–1135 (2012)

Discriminative Dictionary Learning with Local Constraints for Face Recognition with Occlusion

Tao Zhang[1(⊠)], Zhuoqun Yang[1], Yaqi Xu[1], Bin Yang[2],
and Wenjing Jia[3]

[1] Jiangsu Provincial Engineering Laboratory of Pattern Recognition
and Computational Intelligence, Jiangnan University, Wuxi, China
taozhang@jiangnan.edu.cn
[2] Department of Design, Jiangnan University, Wuxi, China
[3] Faculty of Engineering and Information Technology,
University of Technology Sydney, Ultimo, Australia

Abstract. Facial occlusion, such as sunglasses, mask etc., is one important factor that affects the accuracy of face recognition. Unfortunately, faces with occlusion are quite common in the real world. In recent years, sparse coding becomes a hotspot of dealing with face recognition problem under different illuminations. The basic idea of sparse representation-based classification is a general classification scheme in which the training samples of all classes were taken as the dictionary to represent the query face image, and classified it by evaluating which class leads to the minimal reconstruction error of it. However, how to balance the shared part and class-specific part in the learned dictionary is not a trivial task. In this paper we make two contributions: (i) we present a new occlusion detection method by introducing sparse representation-based classification model; (ii) we propose a new sparse model which incorporates the representation-constrained term and the coefficients incoherence term. Experiments on benchmark face databases demonstrate the effectiveness and robustness of our method, which outperforms state-of-the-art methods.

Keywords: Face recognition · Occlusion detection · Sparse representation

1 Introduction

Automatic face recognition with occlusion has been a hot topic in the area of computer vision and pattern recognition due to the increasing need for real-world applications. Various approaches have been proposed, including subspace mapping algorithm [1–3], feature extraction [4–6] and kernel models [7–10]. However, all these method used the reconstructed images for classification, considering the fact that the reconstructed images might remove some useful information and introduce some redundant information, therefore, whether the reconstructed images are suitable for occluded face recognition needs study.

To avoid over-fitting, a regularization term is generally imposed upon the LR model. There are two widely-used constraints: the L2-normand the L1-norm. While

© Springer Nature Switzerland AG 2018
X. Sun et al. (Eds.): ICCCS 2018, LNCS 11068, pp. 733–744, 2018.
https://doi.org/10.1007/978-3-030-00021-9_65

L1-norm regularizer is a traditional model for sparse representation. Recently proposed sparse representation classification (SRC) algorithms have obtained promising performance on image classification and image super-resolution tasks, etc. [11–17]. Since sparse representation classification approaches obtained competitive performance in face recognition area [18], it has attracted researchers' attention in image classification. Sparse representation classification model has shown the robust ability to deal with sparse random pixel corruption and block occlusion. Nevertheless, a discriminative dictionary for both sparse data representation and classification is still a difficult learning problem.

Some recent work, on the other hand, began to investigate the role of sparsity in face recognition [10, 19–21]. Liu et al. [21] introduce the dual form of dictionary learning and provided some theoretical proof. They argued that it is L1 constraint together with L2 that makes SRC more effective. To overcome high residual error and instability, Zeng et al. [20] analyzed the main principle of SRC and believed that the collaborative representation strategy can enhance the interpretability. They presented a collaborative representation classifier (CRC) based on Ridge regression. CRC can be thus considered as a special case of the SRC algorithm, however, does not provide a mechanism for noise removal, so it is not robust to detect occluded face.

Face recognition with occlusion algorithm need to be robust against arbitrary occlusions. Despite the emergence of a large number of face detection algorithms, most of the existing algorithm are focused on partial occlusion. In the early years, Wen et al. proposed a face occlusion detection method using Gabor filter function [22]. In order to use the temporal feature, some algorithm based on spatial-temporal information were used to find frontal faces [23–25]. Some skin color-based detection approaches are used to find faces [26, 27]. Interestingly, other researchers focus on the popular "recognition by parts" scheme, whose main aim is to predict the head position by determining the appropriate human body model of other parts, such as a probabilistic weighted retrieval [28], locally salient ICA information [29], a new learning algorithm PRSOM (Probabilistic Self-Organizing Model) [30], discriminative and robust subspace model [31], dynamic similarity function [32], local non-negative matrix factorization [33], holistic PCA model [34], SVM model [35], Markov Random Field method [36], optimal feature selection model [37], confidence weighting model [38], embedded hidden Markov method [39]. These approaches can cope with the partial occlusion cases through extracting other features of the non-occluded parts. However, for the severe occluded cases, the performance of these algorithm will be reduced. Other head detection approaches are also a hot research area in surveillance application, such as color model-based approaches, contour-based approaches and matching-based approaches, and these can also be regarded as a different application of face detection. Color model-based approaches [40, 41] determine face regions by extracting hair and face color information. The computational complexity of these algorithm is very low, but when the region of head is severely covered, these methods will not work. Matching-based approaches [42, 43] detect head by comparing the similarity of training template and the current area. Contour-based approaches [44, 45] adequately use complex geometric curves to depict face contour feature. This kind of algorithm can deal with severe occlusion problem, but the computational cost is high. Also, it is hard to work in a low-resolution image. In this paper, we try to detect head regions by a novel and robust algorithm.

It is worth mentioning that the convolutional neural networks methods, such as DeepID [46] and WebFace [47], are proved to handle face recognition with various variations. However, they exploit lots of information with very complex image variations to assist the training process, so the main drawbacks contribute to the high computational complexity and complex parameter tuning. Thus, they are not suitable to treat with undersampled face recognition, especially for face occlusion problem.

Note that the residual image (a difference between the raw and reconstructed image) contains most of the occluded information as shown in Fig. 1. It is obviously that the occluded region in the residual image is very intuitive. In this paper, we propose a discriminative sparse coding model to deal with recognition task. With the same setting as [20, 21], we consider the scenario that only one non-occluded training sample is available for each subject of interest, which is close to many real application scenarios such as security, video surveillance et al. Compared with some related methods, the advantages of our proposed model are highlighted as follows:

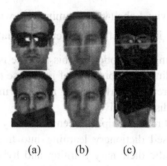

(a)   (b)   (c)

Fig. 1. Examples of raw images, reconstructed images and residual images. (a) The raw images. (b) The reconstructed images. (c) The residual images.

- An occlusion variation dictionary is learned for representing the possible occlusion variations between the training and testing samples. Different from SRC, our proposed model extracts the features from the covariance of occlusion variations based on deep networks to construct the occlusion variation dictionary. Experimental results show that the learned dictionary can efficiently represent the possible occlusion variations.
- Proposing novel measurements strategy to improve sparsity, robustness and discriminative ability. Different from traditional sparse representation which task is to minimize the reconstruction error only, in this proposed model, two terms, the similarity constrain term and the coefficient incoherence term are introduced to ensure that the learned dictionary has the powerful discriminative ability.

The reminder of the paper is organized as follows: Sect. 2 presents some related works. Section 3 describes our proposed model. Section 4 shows experiment results and Sect. 5 draws conclusions.

2   Related Work

In SRC [15], Wright et al. proposed a general classification scheme in which the training samples of all classes were taken as the dictionary to represent the query face image, and classified it by evaluating which class leads to the minimal reconstruction error of it. Since SRC scheme has shown impressive performance in FR, how to design a framework and algorithm to learn a discriminative dictionary for both sparse data representation and classification are attracting a great deal of attention.

Wright et al. [15] proposed the sparse representation based classification (SRC) scheme for robust face recognition (FR). Given K classes of subjects, and let $D = [A_1, A_2, \cdots, A_K]$ be the dictionary formed by the set of training samples, where A_i is the subset of training samples from class i. Let y be a test sample. The algorithm of SRC is summarized as follows.

(a)   Normalize each training sample in A_i, $i = 1, 2, \cdots, K$.

(b)   Solve l_1-minimization problem: $\hat{x} = \text{argmin}_x \left\{ \|y - Dx\|_2^2 + \gamma \|x\|_1 \right\}$, where γ is scalar constant.

(c)   Label a test sample y via: $\text{Label}(y) = \text{argmin}_i \{e_i\}$, where $e_i = \|y - A_i \hat{\alpha}^i\|_2^2$, $\hat{x} = [\hat{\alpha}^1, \hat{\alpha}^2, \cdots, \hat{\alpha}^K]^T$ and $\hat{\alpha}^i$ is the coefficient vector associated with class i.

Obviously, the underlying assumption of this scheme is that a test sample can be represented by a weighted linear combination of just those training samples belonging to the same class. Its impressive performance reported in [15] showed that sparse representation is naturally discriminative.

According to predefined relationship between dictionary atoms and class labels, we can divide current supervised dictionary learning into three categories: shared dictionary learning, class-specific dictionary learning and hybrid dictionary learning. In shared dictionary learning, a dictionary shared by all classes is learned, meanwhile the discriminative power of the representation coefficients is also mined [48, 49]. In generally, in this scheme, a shared dictionary and a classifier over the representation coefficients are together learned. However, there is no relationship between the dictionary atoms and the class labels, and thus no class-specific representation residuals are introduced to perform classification task.

In the class-specific dictionary learning, a dictionary whose atoms are predefined to correspond to subject class labels is learned and thus the class-specific reconstruction error could be used to perform classification [50, 51].

The hybrid dictionary models which combines shared dictionary atoms and class-specific dictionary atoms have been proposed [52, 53]. However, the shared dictionary atoms could encourage learned hybrid dictionary compact to some extent, how to balance the shared part and class-specific part in the hybrid dictionary is not a trivial task.

3   Proposed Model

Machine learning algorithm are often used in computer vision due to their ability to leverage large amounts of training data to improve performance. For face recognition task, the deeply learned features are required to be generalized enough for identifying new unseen classes without label prediction. In order to enhance the discriminative power of the deeply learned features, wen etc. propose new supervision signal, called center loss. Specifically, the center loss simultaneously learns a center for deep features of each class and penalizes the distances between the deep features and their corresponding class centers [54]. It is encouraging to see that their CNNs achieve the state-of-the-art accuracy. Therefore, in this paper, we adapt this deep network model to extract occluded face feature.

Recently proposed sparse representation classification (SRC) algorithms have obtained promising performance on image classification and image super-resolution tasks, etc.. For a detailed introduction to sparse representation, which can be found in [15–17]. Since sparse representation classification approaches obtained competitive performance in face recognition area [18], it has attracted researchers' attention in image classification. Nevertheless, a discriminative dictionary for both sparse data representation and classification is still a pending problem.

To address these difficulties, we propose a modified sparse model for this purpose. Different from traditional sparse representation which task is to minimize the reconstruction error only, in this proposed model, two terms, the representation-constrained term and the coefficient incoherence term are introduced to ensure that the learned dictionary has the powerful discriminative ability.

3.1   Proposed Sparse Classification Model

The representation-constrained term is used to project each descriptor into its local coordinate system which captures the correlations between similar descriptors by sharing dictionary. On the other hand, the coefficients incoherence term ensures that samples from different classes can be built by independent dictionary.

In the class-specific dictionary learning, each dictionary atom $D = [D_1, D_2, L, D_K]$ indicate class label, where D_i is the sub-dictionary of class i. In our experimental settings, corresponding training deep feature samples set $\{a_{ij} | i = 1, 2, L, \ k; j = 1, 2, L, N.\}$, where a_{ij} indicates the j-th sample of class i, K is the number of classes, and N denotes the number of training samples in each class. Let $A = [A_1, A_2, L, A_i] \in R^{n \times N}$, where $A_i = [a_{i1}, a_{i2}, L, a_{iN}]$, n is the deep feature dimension. Our purpose is to contain the classification error as a term in the objective function for dictionary learning for purpose of making the lexicon be optimal for classification. Sparse code Z can be directly utilized as a characteristic for classification. Let $Z = [Z_1, Z_2, L, Z_i]$, denote the learned dictionary by $D = [d_1, d_2, L, d_k] \in R^{n \times k}$ ($k > n$ and $k < N$). We propose the following novel sparse model:

$$\langle D, W, Z \rangle = \arg\min\{\|A - DZ\|_F^2 + \lambda_1\|Z\|_1 + \lambda_2\|Z - m\|_F^2 + \gamma_1\|WZ - B\|_F^2 + \gamma_2\|W\|_F^2\} \tag{1}$$
$$s.t.\|d_c\|_2 \leq 1, \forall c \in \{1, 2, \cdots, k\}$$

Where $m = [m_1, m_2, L, m_i] \in R^{k \times N}$, m_i denotes mean vector Z_i of in class i, $\|WZ - B\|_F^2$ denotes the classification error, $B = [0, 0, L, b_N] \in R^{m \times N}$ are the class labels of input feature. $b_i = [0, 0, L1L, 0]^T \in R^m$ is a label vector. $W \in R^{m \times k}$ denotes the matrix of classifier parameters, and λ_1, λ_2, γ_1 and γ_2 are the scale adjustment parameters.

In our proposed model, the representation-constrained term $\|WZ - B\|_F^2$ and coefficients incoherence term $\|W\|_F^2$ are introduced in Eq. 1.

3.2 Optimization Process

Obviously, the function of Eq. 1 is not co-convex to (D; W; Z), when the other two variables are fixed, it is convex for each of D, W, and Z. So, we can optimize D, W and Z respectively to make the Eq. 1 be three sub-problems, i.e., update the Z when D and W are fixed, update D when W and Z are fixed, and update W when D and Z are fixed. Let us explain the details.

Updating Z: When D and W are constant value, it can be regarded as sparse coding problem for solving Z. When Z_i is updated, all $Z_j(j \neq i)$ are also fixed. Thus, for each Z_i, the objective function in Eq. 2 can be replaced by:

$$\langle Z \rangle = \arg\min\{\|A - DZ\|_F^2 + \lambda_1\|Z\|_1 + \lambda_2\|Z - m\|_F^2 + \gamma_1\|WZ - B\|_F^2 \tag{2}$$

By solving Eq. 2, we have:

$$Z_i = \{D^TD + (\lambda_1 + \lambda_2)I + \gamma_1 W^TW\}^{-1}(D^TA_i + \lambda_2 m_i + \gamma_1 W^T b_i) \tag{3}$$

Updating D: When Z and W are constant value, Eq. 1 can be regarded as solving $D = [D_1, D_2, L, D_K]$ sparse coding problem. When D_i is updated, all $D_j(j \neq i)$ are also fixed. Thus, Eq. 1 can be replaced by:

$$\langle D \rangle = \arg\min\left\{\|A - DZ\|_F^2\right\}, s.t.\|d_c\|_2 = 1, \forall c \in \{1, 2, \cdots, k\}. \tag{4}$$

The above problem in Eq. 4 can be solved effectively by the Lagrange dual method.
Updating W: When D and Z are fixed, Eq. 1 can be replaced by:

$$\langle W \rangle = \arg\min\left\{\gamma_1\|WZ - B\|_F^2 + \gamma_2\|W\|_F^2\right\} \tag{5}$$

Obviously, Eq. 5 can be solved using the least square method. Thus we can get the following solution:

$$W_i = b_i Z_i^T (Z_i Z_i^T + \frac{\gamma_2}{\gamma_1} I)^{-1} \qquad (6)$$

Therefore, according to the above equations, the optimized values of all parameters in Eq. 1 can be got.

4 Experimental Results

To evaluate the proposed model, we compare it with the state-of-the-art methods for face recognition with occlusion. Sparse representation-based approaches: sparse representation based face classification (SRC) [15], robust sparse coding (RSC) [16], correntropy-based sparse representation (CESR) [17] and extended sparse representation-based classification (ESRC) [19].

4.1 Results on the AR Database with Real-World Occlusion

We evaluate the performance of our proposed model in dealing with real occlusion using the AR face database [18], which consists of 4000 frontal-face images from 126 subjects (70 men and 56 women). Each subject has two separate sessions and 13 images for each session. These images are taken under different variations, including various facial expressions, illumination variations and occlusions (such as sunglasses and scarf).

In the first group, all the rest samples with occlusion from the 80 subjects in session 1 and session 2 are used as testing set, which is divided into three subsets in session 1 or session 2, respectively. (sunglasses subset and scarf subset). The final results with the existing methods are shown in Table 1. Based on the results, we can draw the following conclusions:

- In the same session (session 1 or session 2), the face recognition performances of these existing methods are much better on sunglasses subset than on scarf subset. That is because the sunglasses occlude roughly 20% of the image, while the scarf occlude roughly 40% of the image.

Table 1. Recognition rates for different methods on the AR database.

Method	Session1:		Session2:	
	Sunglass	Scarf	Sunglass	Scarf
SRC	40.83	25.33	22.92	13.33
RSC	71.67	59.58	52.92	35.83
CESR	86.24	83.75	65.42	57.50
ESRC	63.75	16.25	41.67	10.00
Ours	**89.68**	**86.48**	**70.16**	**64.29**

- The performances of some sparse representation-based face recognition approaches such as SRC, RSC and CESR, are bad to address occluded problem for face recognition. For example, the recognition rates of SRC, RSC and CESR are only 13.33%, 35.83% and 10.00% on scarf subset from session 2, respectively. Lack of sufficient training samples to represent the test sample is the main reason.
- Our proposed algorithm obtains significantly higher recognition rates than most of these compared methods, the recognition results is 89.68%, 86.48%, 70.16% and 64.29%, respectively. It indicates that our proposed model is more robust to occlusion variation than these existing methods.

4.2   Results on the CAS-PEAL Database with Real Occlusion

The CAS-PEAL [18] face database consists of 9594 images of 1040 subjects (595 males and 445 females), which are obtained in different variations, including pose, expression, accessory, lighting, time and distance. Each subject is captured under at least two kinds of these variations. Thus, here we take a subset with normal and different accessory variations, which contains 3038 images of 434 subjects and 7 images for each subject. So each subject has 1 neutral image, 3 images with glasses/sunglasses, and 3 images with hats. Finally, all the images are cropped to 120×100 size.

In each recognition process, we select 350 subjects of interest for training and testing, and the remaining 84 subjects are considered as external data for learning the occlusion variation dictionary. In training process, we choose only the neutral image of each of the 350 subjects. While in testing process, we consider three separate test subsets of the 350 subjects. The first test subset constitute with 3 images of each subject wearing glasses/ sunglasses (glass subset). The second test subset constitute with 3 images of each subject wearing hats (hat subset). The third test subset constitute with 6 images of the subject from glass subset and hat subset.

The final recognition rates for all the methods on CAS-PEAL database are given in Table 2. Based on the results, we can get the following conclusions:

Table 2. Recognition rates for different methods On the CAS-PEAL databas.

Method	Sunglass	Hat
SRC	79.05	42.24
RSC	89.62	80.10
CESR	89.33	29.43
ESRC	89.71	63.52
Ours	**92.68**	**87.56**

- The hats occlusion subset is more challenging than the glasses/sunglasses occlusion subset on the database.
- SRC-based face recognition approaches, such as ESRC, RSC and CESR improve the face recognition performance of ordinary SRC for the glasses/sunglasses occlusion, but their performance is not good to the hats occlusion. For example, the

recognition rate of CESR can reach up to 89.33% for the glasses/sunglasses occlusion, but it degrades seriously for the hats occlusion, only 29.43%.

- Our proposed algorithm achieves the best results for all subsets. That is because the representation-constrained and the representation coefficients are more discriminative, and the corresponding classification method is effective to reveal such information. It indicates that proposed model can well learn the occlusion variation, and is also effective to detect occlusion cases.

5 Conclusion

In this paper, we present a novel sparse representation-based classification model and apply the alternating direction method of multipliers to solve it. Different from traditional sparse representation which task is to minimize the reconstruction error only, in this proposed model, two terms, the representation-constrained term and the coefficient incoherence term are introduced to ensure that the learned dictionary has the powerful discriminative ability. Proposed model takes advantage of the structural characteristics of noise and provides a unified framework for integrating error detection and error support into one sparse model. Extensive experiments demonstrate that the proposed model is robust to occlusions.

Acknowledgments. This research was partly supported by National Science Foundation, China (No. 61702226, 61672263), the Natural Science Foundation of Jiangsu Province (Grant no. BK20170200), supported by "the Fundamental Research Funds for the Central Universities (JUSRP11854).

References

1. Tai, Y., Yang, J., Luo, L., Zhang, F.L., Qian, J.J.: Learning discriminative singular value decomposition representation for face recognition. Pattern Recognit. **50**(C), 1–16 (2016)
2. Zhang, G., Zou, W., Zhang, X., et al.: Singular value decomposition based virtual representation for face recognition. Multim. Tools Appl. **5**(11), 1–16 (2017)
3. Hu, C., Lu, X., Ye, M., et al.: Singular value decomposition and local near neighbors for face recognition under varying illumination. Pattern Recogn. **64**, 60–83 (2017)
4. Lei, Z., Pietikainen, M., Li, S.Z.: Learning discriminant face descriptor. IEEE Trans. Pattern Anal. Mach. Intell. **36**(2), 289–302 (2014)
5. Lei, Z., Yi, D., Li, S.Z.: Learning stacked image descriptor for face recognition. IEEE Trans. Circuits Syst. Video Technol. **26**(9), 1685–1696 (2016)
6. Zhang, T., Yang, Z., Jia, W., et al.: Fast and robust head detection with arbitrary pose and occlusion. Multimed. Tools Appl. **74**(21), 9365–9385 (2015)
7. Wang, D., Lu, H., Yang, M.H.: Kernel collaborative face recognition. Pattern Recogn. **48**(10), 3025–3037 (2015)
8. Wang, M., Hu, Z., Sun, Z., et al.: Kernel collaboration representation-based manifold regularized model for unconstrained face recognition. Signal Image Video Process. (C), **12** (5), 1–8 (2018)

9. Hua, J., Wang, H., Ren, M., et al.: Collaborative representation analysis methods for feature extraction. Neural Comput. Appl. **28**(S1), 1–7 (2016)

10. Yang, J., Luo, L., Qian, J., Tai, Y., Zhang, F., Xu, Y.: Nuclear norm based matrix regression with applications to face recognition with occlusion and illumination changes. IEEE Trans. Pattern Anal. Mach. Intell. **39**(1), 156–171 (2017)

11. Fan, Z., Ni, M., Zhu, Q., Sun, C.: L0-norm sparse representation based on modified genetic algorithm for face recognition. J. Vis. Commun. Image Represent. **28**, 15–20 (2015)

12. Han, B., Wu, D.: Image representation by compressive sensing for visual sensor networks. J. Vis. Commun. Image Represent. **21**, 325–333 (2010)

13. Jorge, S., Javier, R.: Exponential family fisher vector for image classification. Pattern Recognit. **59**, 26–32 (2015)

14. Cheng, H., Liu, Z., Yang, L., Chen, X.: Sparse representations and learning in visual recognition: theory and applications. Signal Process. **93**, 1408–1425 (2013)

15. Wright, J., Yang, A.Y., Ganesh, A., Ma, Y.: Robust face recognition via sparse representation. IEEE Trans. Pattern Mach. Intel. **31**, 210–227 (2009)

16. Xu, Y., Zhang, B., Zhong, Z.F.: Multiple representations and sparse representations for image classification. Pattern Recognit. **68**, 9–14 (2015)

17. Yang, J., Wright, J., Huang, T., Ma, Y.: Image super-resolution via sparse representation. IEEE Trans. Image Process. **19**, 2861–2873 (2010)

18. Zhang, Z., Xu, Y., Yang, X., Li, X.: A survey of sparse representations: algorithm and applications. IEEE Access **3**, 490–530 (2015)

19. Lai, J., Jiang, X.: Class-wise sparse and collaborative patch representation for face recognition. IEEE Trans. Image Process. **25**(7), 3261–3272 (2016)

20. Liu, B.D., Shen, B., Gui, L., Wang, Y.X., Li, X., Yan, F., et al.: Face recognition using class specific dictionary learning for sparse representation and collaborative representation. Neurocomputing **204**, 198–210 (2016)

21. Zeng, S., Gou, J., Deng, L.: An antinoise sparse representation method for robust face recognition via joint l 1, and l 2, regularization. Expert Syst. Appl. **82**, 1–9 (2017)

22. Wen, C., Chiu, S., Tseng, Y., Lu, C.: The mask detection technology for occluded face analysis in the surveillance system J. Forensic Sci. **3**, 1–9 (2005)

23. Yoon, S.M., Kee, S.C.: Detection of partially occluded face using support vector machines. In: Proceedings of IAPR Conference on Machine Vision Applications, pp. 546–549 (2002)

24. Kim, J., Sung, Y., Yoon, S.M., Park, B.G.: A new video surveillance system employing occluded face detection. In: Ali, M., Esposito, F. (eds.) IEA/AIE 2005, vol. 3533, pp. 65–68. Springer, Heidelberg (2005). https://doi.org/10.1007/11504894_10

25. Choi, I., Kim, D.: Facial fraud discrimination using detection and classification. In: Bebis, G., et al. (eds.) ISVC 2010. LNCS, vol. 6455, pp. 199–208. Springer, Heidelberg (2010). https://doi.org/10.1007/978-3-642-17277-9_21

26. Dong, W., Soh, Y.: Image-based fraud detection in automatic teller machine. Int. J. Comput. Sci. Network Secur. **11**, 13–18 (2006)

27. Kakumanu, P., Makrogiannis, S., Bourbakis, N.: A survey of skin-color modeling and detection methods. Pattern Recognit. **3**, 1106–1122 (2007)

28. Zhang, Y., Martinez, A.M.: A weighted probabilistic approach to face recognition from multiple images and video sequences. Image Vis. Comput. **6**, 626–638 (2006)

29. Kim, J., Choi, J., Yi, J., Turk, M.: Effective representation using ICA for face recognition robust to local distortion and partial occlusion. IEEE Trans. Pattern Anal. Mach. Intell. **12**, 1977–1981 (2005)

30. Tan, X., Chen, S., Zhou, H. Zhang, F.: Recognizing partially occluded, expression variant faces from single training image per person with SOM and soft k-NN ensemble. IEEE Trans. Neural Networks **4**, 875–886 (2005)

31. Fidler, S., Skocaj, D., Leonardis, A.: Combining reconstructive and discriminative subspace methods for robust classification and regression by subsampling. IEEE PAMI **3**, 337–350 (2006)
32. Liu, Q., Yan, W., Lu, H., Ma, S.: Occlusion robust face recognition with dynamic similarity features. In: Proceedings of the 18th International Conference on Pattern Recognition (ICPR 2006), vol. 3, pp. 544–547 (2006)
33. Oh, H.J., Lee, K.M., Lee, S.U.: Occlusion invariant face recognition using selective local non-negative matrix factorization basis images. Image Vis. Comput. **11**, 1515–1523 (2008)
34. Rama, A., Tarres, F., Goldmann, L., Sikora, T.: More robust face recognition by considering occlusion information. In: Proceedings of the Eighth IEEE International Conference on Automatic Face Gesture Recognition (FG 2008), pp. 1–6 (2008)
35. Jia, H., Martinez, A.: Support vector machines in face recognition with occlusions. In: Proceedings of the IEEE Conference on Computer Vision and Pattern Recognition (CVPR 2009), pp. 136–141 (2009)
36. Zhou, Z., Wagner, A., Mobahi, H., Wright, J., Ma, Y.: Face recognition with contiguous occlusion using Markov random fields. In: Proceedings of the IEEE 12th International Conference on Computer Vision (ICCV 2009), pp. 1050–1057 (2009)
37. Lin, J., Ming, J., Crookes, D.: Robust face recognition with partial occlusion, illumination variation and limited training data by optimal feature selection. IET Comput. Vis. **1**, 23–32 (2011)
38. Struc, V., Dobrisek, S., Pavesic, N.: Confidence weighted subspace projection techniques for robust face recognition in the presence of partial occlusions. In: Proceedings of the 20th International Conference on Pattern Recognition (ICPR 2010), pp. 1334–1338 (2010)
39. Huang, S.-M., Yang, J.-F.: Robust face recognition under different facial expressions, illumination variations and partial occlusions. In: Proceedings of the 17th International Conference on Advances in Multimedia Modeling (MMM 2011), vol. 2, pp. 326–336 (2011)
40. Yang, T., Pan, Q., Li, J., Cheng, Y.M.: Real-time head tracking system with an active camera. In: Proceedings of the 5th World Congress on Intelligent Control and Automation, pp. 1910–1914 (2006)
41. Chen, M.L., Kee, S.: Head tracking with shape modeling and detection. In: Proceedings of the Second Canadian Conference on Computer and Robot Vision (2006)
42. Huang, W.M., Luo, R.J.: Real time head tracking and face and eyes detection. In: Proceedings of IEEE TENCON, pp. 507–510 (2002)
43. Yao, Z.R., Li, H.B.: Tracking a detected face with dynamic programming. Image Vis. Comput. **6**, 573–580 (2006)
44. Finlayson, G.D., Hordley, S.D., Lu, C., Drew, M.S.: On the removal of shadows from images. IEEE PAMI **25**(10), 59–68 (2006)
45. Zou, W., Li, Y., Yuan, K., Xu, D.: Real-time elliptical head contour detection under arbitrary pose and wide distance range. J. Vis. Commun. Image R. **20**, 217–228 (2009)
46. Sun, Y., Wang, X., Tang, X.: Deep learning face representation from predicting 10,000 classes. Computer Vision and Pattern Recognition, pp. 1891–1898. IEEE (2014)
47. Wang, D., Otto, C., Jain, A.K.: Face search at scale: 80 million gallery. Comput. Sci. 1–14 (2015)
48. Bach, F., Mairal, J., Ponce, J.: Task-driven dictionary learning. IEEE Trans. Pattern Anal. Mach. Intell. **34**(4), 791–804 (2012)
49. Jiang, Z., Lin, Z., Davis, L.S.: Label consistent k-svd: learning a discriminative dictionary for recognition. IEEE Trans. Pattern Anal. Mach. Intell. **35**(11), 2651–2664 (2013)
50. Yang, M., Zhang, L., Feng, X., Zhang, D.: Fisher discrimination dictionary learning for sparse representation. In: Proceedings, vol. 24(4), pp. 543–550 (2011)

51. Yang, M., Zhang, L., Feng, X., Zhang, D.: Sparse representation based fisher discrimination dictionary learning for image classification. Int. J. Comput. Vis. **109**(3), 209–232 (2014)
52. Kong, S., Wang, D.: A dictionary learning approach for classification: separating the particularity and the commonality. In: Fitzgibbon, A., Lazebnik, S., Perona, P., Sato, Y., Schmid, C. (eds.) ECCV 2012. LNCS, vol. 7572, pp. 186–199. Springer, Heidelberg (2012). https://doi.org/10.1007/978-3-642-33718-5_14
53. Zhou, N., Shen, Y., Peng, J., Fan, J.: Learning inter-related visual dictionary for object recognition. In: IEEE Conference on Computer Vision and Pattern Recognition, vol. 157, pp. 3490–3497. IEEE Computer Society (2012)
54. Wen, Y.D., Zhang, K.P., Li, Z.F., et al.: A Discriminative Feature Learning Approach for Deep Face Recognition. **47**(9), pp. 499–515 (2016)

Author Index

Printed in the United States
By Bookmasters